2008 Edition

Conformity and Conflict

JAMES SPRADLEY
Late, Macalester College

DAVID W. McCURDY
Macalester College

2008 EDITION

CONFORMITY AND CONFLICT

Readings in Cultural Anthropology

PEARSON

Boston   New York   San Francisco
Mexico City   Montreal   Toronto   London   Madrid   Munich   Paris
Hong Kong   Singapore   Tokyo   Cape Town   Sydney

Series Editor: Dave Repetto
Series Editorial Assistant: Jack Cashman
Marketing Manager: Kelly May
Editorial Production Service: Omegatype Typography, Inc.
Composition Buyer: Linda Cox
Manufacturing Buyer: Debbie Rossi
Electronic Composition: Omegatype Typography, Inc.
Cover Administrator: Kristina Mose-Libon

For related titles and support materials, visit our online catalog at www.ablongman.com.

Between the time website information is gathered and then published, it is not unusual for some sites to have closed. Also, the transcription of URLs can result in typographical errors. The publisher would appreciate notification where these errors occur so that they may be corrected in subsequent editions.

A previous edition was published under *Conformity and Conflict*, Twelfth Edition, copyright © 2006, 2003, 2000, 1997, 1994 Pearson Education, Inc.

ISBN-13:   978-0-205-59328-6
ISBN-10:   0-205-59328-3

Printed in the United States of America

10   9   8   7   6   5   4   3   2   RRD-VA   11   10   09   08   07

Photo Credits: Page xvi, Sean Sprague/Stock Boston; Page 58, Jim Cornfield/Corbis; Page 102, Charles & Josette Lenars/Corbis; Page 142, Ferdinando Scianna/Magnum Photos; Page 178, Sheila Nardulli/Liaison Agency; Page 218, Ricardo Beliel/Brazil-Photos/Alamy; Page 260, Oswaldo Paez, AP Wide World; Page 294, Daily Union, John Petrovic/AP Wide World; Page 340, Kenneth Hamm/Photo Japan; Page 386, Lionel Delevigne/Stock Boston.

To Barbara Spradley and Carolyn McCurdy

List of Web Articles

Access classic ***Conformity and Conflict*** readings online
using the access code included with the book.

Contents

ONE

TWO

THREE

FOUR

FIVE

SIX

SEVEN

EIGHT

TEN

Access classic ***Conformity and Conflict*** readings online using the access code included with the book.

Preface

Cultural anthropology has a twofold mission: to understand other cultures and communicate that understanding. Thirty-five years ago, in preparing the first edition of this book, Jim Spradley and I sought to make communication easier and more enjoyable for teachers and students alike. We focused on the twin themes stated in the title—conformity (order) and conflict (change)—while organizing selections into sections based on traditional topics. We balanced the coverage of cultures between non-Western and Western (including North American) societies so students could make their own cultural comparisons and see the relation between anthropology and their own lives. We chose articles that reflected interesting topics in anthropology, but we also looked for selections that illustrated important concepts and theories, because we believed that anthropology provides a unique and powerful way to look at human experience. We searched extensively for scholarly articles written with insight, clarity, and where suitable material was absent, encouraged anthropologists to send us original material. Students and instructors of hundreds of colleges and universities responded enthusiastically to our efforts and a pattern was set that carried through eleven editions.

New original readings are commissioned for each new edition, which unfortunately means that we need to remove articles to make room. After thirty-five years, the book would probably be too heavy to carry otherwise. It is lamentable that the articles that are removed are often every bit as intriguing and relevant as when they were originally written. The 2008 Edition of *Conformity and Conflict*, through the magic of the Web, brings back some old favorites. While the printed book remains the same as the twelfth edition, some favorite articles from the tenth and eleventh editions have been posted on a special website, which you can reach by following instructions on the access card included with this book. You will find short capsule descriptions of each Web reading located on the website. We are glad to bring these readings back into the spotlight, and we hope you enjoy them.

I have also maintained the expanded special features that have appeared in past editions. Part introductions include discussion of many basic anthropological definitions for instructors who do not want to use a standard textbook but find it useful to provide students with a terminological foundation. Article introductions seek to tie selections to anthropological concepts and explanations in a coherent and systematic way.

Several student aids are retained in the 2008 Edition. Lists of key terms accompany each part introduction. Each article is followed by several review questions; the Web-only articles retain their review questions as well. There is a glossary and subject index at the back of the book.

A complimentary instructor's manual and test bank is available from the publisher. The manual contains a summary of each article along with a large selection of true-false and multiple-choice questions for articles and part introductions.

It has always been my aim to provide a book that meets the needs of students and instructors. To help with this goal, I encourage you to send your comments and ideas for improving *Conformity and Conflict* to me at dcmccurdy@comcast.net.

Many people have made suggestions that guided this revision of *Conformity and Conflict*. I am especially grateful to George and Sharon Gmelch, Union College; Sonia Patten and Dianna Shandy, Macalester College; and the reviewers for this edition: Margaret L. Brown, Washington University; Elizabeth L. H. Chettur, Boston University; Elizabeth Fathman, Washington University's University College; Alanson L. Hertzberg, Consumnes River College; Dorothy Hodgson, Rutgers University; Donna J. Myers, State University of West Virginia; Mary R. Vermilion, University of Illinois at Chicago; and Ellen Zimmerman, Framingham State College. I would also like to thank my editor, Dave Repetto, for his guidance and work on this volume.

WORLD MAP AND GEOGRAPHICAL PLACEMENT OF READINGS

The numbers on this map correspond to the reading numbers and indicate the places on which the articles focus. Screened maps also accompany the readings themselves, and boxed areas on those maps highlight the subject locations. Readings labeled as world on this global map do not include boxed areas.

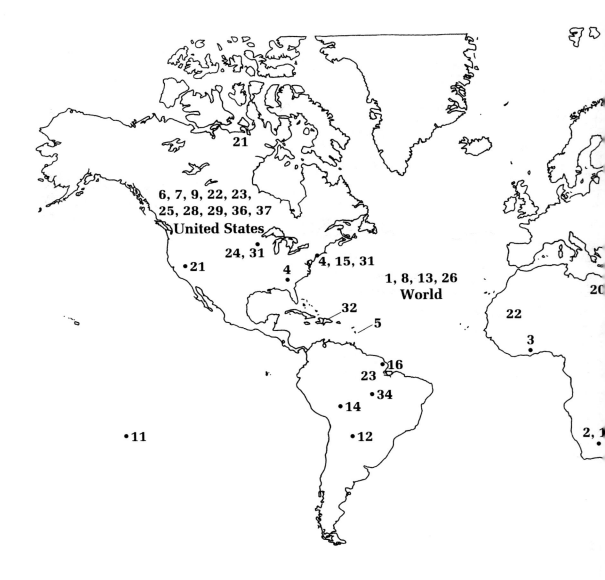

21

6, 7, 9, 22, 23,
25, 28, 29, 36, 37
United States

24, 31

•21

4

4, 15, 31

1, 8, 13, 26
World

32

5

16

23

34

•14

•12

•11

22

3

20

2, 1

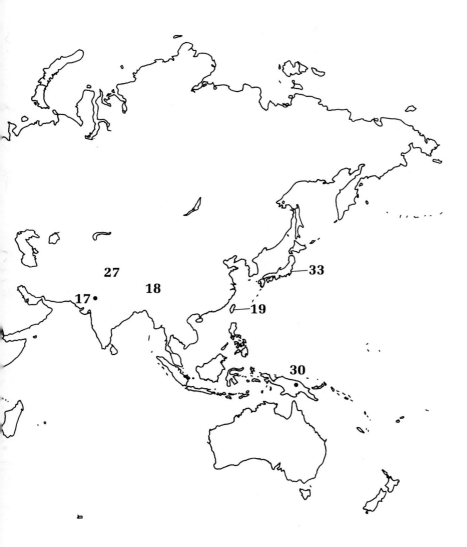

27

17 •

18

33

19

30

ONE

Culture and Ethnography

Culture, as its name suggests, lies at the heart of cultural anthropology. And the concept of **culture,** along with ethnography, sets anthropology apart from other social and behavioral sciences. Let us look more closely at these concepts.

To understand what anthropologists mean by *culture,* imagine yourself in a foreign setting, such as a market town in India, forgetting what you might already know about that country. You step off a bus onto a dusty street where you are immediately confronted by strange sights, sounds, and smells. Men dress in Western clothes, but of a different style. Some women drape themselves in long shawls that entirely cover their bodies. They peer at you through a small gap in this garment as they walk by. Buildings are one- or two-story affairs, open at the front so you can see inside. Near you some people sit on wicker chairs eating strange foods. Most unusual is how people talk. They utter vocalizations unlike any you have ever heard, and you wonder how they can possibly understand each other. But obviously they do, since their behavior seems organized and purposeful.

Scenes such as this confronted early explorers, missionaries, and anthropologists, and from their observations an obvious point emerged. People living in various parts of the world looked and behaved in dramatically different ways. And these differences correlated with groups. The people of India had customs different from those of the Papuans; the British did not act and dress like the Iroquois.

Two possible explanations for group differences came to mind. Some argued that group behavior was inherited. Dahomeans of the African Gold Coast, for example, were characterized as particularly "clever and adaptive" by one British colonial official, while, according to the same authority, another African group was "happy-go-lucky and improvident." Usually implied in such statements was the idea that group members were born that way. Such thinking persists to the present and in its most malignant extreme takes the form of racism.

READINGS IN THIS SECTION

But a second explanation also emerged. Perhaps, rather than a product of inheritance, the behavior characteristic of a group was learned. The way people dressed, what they ate, how they talked—all these could more easily be explained as acquisitions. Thus a baby born on the African Gold Coast would, if immediately transported to China and raised like other children there, grow up to dress, eat, and talk like a Chinese. Cultural anthropologists focus on the explanation of learned behavior.

The idea of learning, and a need to label the lifestyles associated with particular groups, led to the definition of culture. In 1871, British anthropologist Sir Edward Burnet Tylor argued that "Culture . . . is that complex whole which includes knowledge, belief, art, law, morals, custom, and any other capabilities and habits acquired by man as a member of society."[1] The definition we present here places more emphasis on the importance of knowledge than does Tylor's. We will say that *culture is the learned and shared knowledge that people use to generate behavior and interpret experience.*

Important to this definition is the idea that culture is a kind of knowledge, not behavior. It is in people's heads. It reflects the mental categories they learn from others as they grow up. It helps them *generate* behavior and *interpret* what they experience. At the moment of birth, we lack a culture. We don't yet have a system of beliefs, knowledge, and patterns of customary behavior. But from that moment until we die, each of us participates in a kind of universal schooling that teaches us our native culture. Laughing and smiling are genetic responses, but as infants we soon learn when to smile, when to laugh, and even how to laugh. We also inherit the potential to cry, but we must learn our cultural rules for when crying is appropriate.

As we learn our culture, we acquire a way to interpret experience. For example, Americans learn that dogs are like little people in furry suits. Dogs live in our houses, eat our food, share our beds. They hold a place in our hearts; their loss causes us to grieve. Villagers in India, on the other hand, often view dogs as pests that are useful only for hunting (in those few parts of the country where one still can hunt) and as watchdogs. Quiet days in Indian villages are often punctuated by the yelp of a dog that has been threatened or actually hurt by its master or a bystander.

Clearly, it is not the dogs that are different in these two societies. Rather, it is the meaning that dogs have for people that varies. And such meaning is cultural; it is learned as part of growing up in each group.

There are two basic kinds of culture, explicit and tacit. **Explicit culture** is cultural knowledge that people can talk about. As you grow up, for example, you learn that there are words for many things you encounter. There are items such as *clothes,* actions such as *playing,* emotional states such as *sadness,* ways to talk such as *yelling,* and people such as *mother.* Recognizing that culture may be explicit is important to the ethnographic process discussed below. If people

---

[1]Edward Burnet Tylor, *Primitive Culture* (New York: Harper Torchbooks, Harper & Row, 1958; originally published by John Murray, London, 1871), p. 1.

have words for cultural categories, anthropologists can use interviews or observations of people talking to uncover them. Because so much culture is explicit, words—both spoken and written—become essential to the discovery and understanding of a culture.

Tacit culture is cultural knowledge that people lack words for. For example, as we grow up we learn to recognize and use a limited number of sound categories such as /d/, /e/, and /f/. Although anthropological linguists have given sound categories a name *(phonemes)*, nonlinguists lack such a term. Instead, we learn our sound categories by hearing and replicating them and we use them unconsciously. No parent said, "Now let's work on our phonemes tonight, dear," to us when we were little.

Anthropologist Edward Hall pioneered the study of tacit culture. He noted, for example, that middle-class North Americans observe four speaking distances—intimate, personal, social, and public—without naming them. (Hall, not his informants, invented the terms above.) Hall also noticed that people from other societies observed different tacit speaking distances, so that a Latin American's closer (than North American) personal speaking distance made North Americans uncomfortable because it seemed intimate. Because it is unspoken, tacit culture can only be discovered through behavioral observation.

Ethnography is the process of discovering and describing a particular culture. It involves anthropologists in an intimate and personal activity as they attempt to learn how the members of a particular group see their worlds.

But which groups qualify as culture-bearing units? How does the anthropologist identify the existence of a culture to study? This was not a difficult question when anthropology was a new science. As Tylor's definition notes, culture was the whole way of life of a people. To find it, one sought out distinctive ethnic units, such as Bhil tribals in India or Apaches in the American Southwest. Anything one learned from such people would be part of their culture.

But discrete cultures of this sort are becoming more difficult to find. The world is increasingly divided into large national societies, each subdivided into a myriad of subgroups. Anthropologists are finding it increasingly attractive to study such subgroups, because they form the arena for most of life in complex society. And this is where the concept of the microculture enters the scene.

Microcultures are systems of cultural knowledge characteristic of subgroups within larger societies. Members of a microculture will usually share much of what they know with everyone in the greater society but will possess a special cultural knowledge that is unique to the subgroup. For example, a college fraternity has a microculture within the context of a university and a nation. Its members have special daily routines, jokes, and meanings for events. It is this shared knowledge that makes up their microculture and that can serve as the basis for ethnographic study. More and more, anthropologists are turning to the study of microcultures, using the same ethnographic techniques they employ when they investigate the broader culture of an ethnic or national group.

More than anything else, it is ethnography that is anthropology's unique contribution to social science. Most scientists, including many who view people in social context, approach their research as **detached observers.** As social scientists, they observe the human subjects of their study, categorize what they see, and generate theory to account for their findings. They work from the outside, creating a system of knowledge to account for other people's behavior. Although this is a legitimate and often useful way to conduct research, it is not the main task of ethnography.

Ethnographers seek out the insider's viewpoint. Because culture is the knowledge people use to generate behavior and interpret experience, the ethnographer seeks to understand group members' behavior from the inside, or cultural, perspective. Instead of looking for a **subject** to observe, ethnographers look for an **informant** to teach them the culture. Just as a child learns its native culture from parents and other people in its social environment, the ethnographer learns another culture by inferring folk categories from the observation of behavior and by asking informants what things mean.

Anthropologists employ many strategies during field research to understand another culture better. But all strategies and all research ultimately rest on the cooperation of informants. An informant is neither a subject in a scientific experiment nor a **respondent** who answers the investigator's questions. An informant is a teacher who has a special kind of pupil: a professional anthropologist. In this unique relationship a transformation occurs in the anthropologist's understanding of an alien culture. It is the informant who transforms the anthropologist from a tourist into an ethnographer. The informant may be a child who explains how to play hopscotch, a cocktail waitress who teaches the anthropologist to serve drinks and to encourage customers to leave tips, an elderly man who teaches the anthropologist to build an igloo, or a grandmother who explains the intricacies of Zapotec kinship. Almost any individual who has acquired a repertoire of cultural behavior can become an informant.

Ethnography is not as easy to do as we might think. For one thing, North Americans are not taught to be good listeners. We prefer to observe and draw our own conclusions. We like a sense of control in social contexts; passive listening is a sign of weakness in our culture. But listening and learning from others is at the heart of ethnography, and we must put aside our discomfort with the student role.

It is also not easy for informants to teach us about their cultures. Culture often lies below a conscious level. A major ethnographic task is to help informants remember their culture.

Naive realism may also impede ethnography. **Naive realism** is the belief that people everywhere see the world in the same way. It may, for example, lead the unwary ethnographer to assume that beauty is the same for all people everywhere or, to use our previous example, that dogs should mean the same thing in India as they do in the United States. If an ethnographer fails to control his or her own naive realism, inside cultural meanings will surely be overlooked.

Culture shock and ethnocentrism may also stand in the way of ethnographers. **Culture shock** is a state of anxiety that results from cross-cultural misunderstanding. Immersed alone in another society, the ethnographer understands few of the culturally defined rules for behavior and interpretation used by his or her hosts. The result is anxiety about proper action and an inability to interact appropriately in the new context.

Ethnocentrism can be just as much of a liability. **Ethnocentrism** is the belief and feeling that one's own culture is best. It reflects our tendency to judge other people's beliefs and behavior using values of our own native culture. Thus if we come from a society that abhors painful treatment of animals, we are likely to react with anger when an Indian villager hits a dog with a rock. Our feeling is ethnocentric.

It is impossible to rid ourselves entirely of the cultural values that make us ethnocentric when we do ethnography. But it is important to control our ethnocentric feeling in the field if we are to learn from informants. Informants resent negative judgment.

Finally, the role assigned to ethnographers by informants affects the quality of what can be learned. Ethnography is a personal enterprise, as all the articles in this section illustrate. Unlike survey research using questionnaires or short interviews, ethnography requires prolonged social contact. Informants will assign the ethnographer some kind of role and what that turns out to be will affect research.

The selections in Part One illustrate several points about culture and ethnography. The first piece, by the late James Spradley, takes a close look at the concept of culture and its role in ethnographic research. The second, by Richard Lee, illustrates how a simple act of giving can have a dramatically different cultural meaning in two societies, leading to cross-cultural misunderstanding. Laura Bohannan's article deals with the concept of naive realism and its role in cross-cultural misunderstanding. When she tells the classic story of *Hamlet* to African Tiv elders, the plot takes on an entirely different meaning as they use their own cultural knowledge in its interpretation. In the fourth selection, Claire Sterk describes how she conducted ethnographic field research under difficult circumstances. She sought to learn the culture of prostitutes working in New York City and Atlanta as part of a broader research interest in the spread and control of AIDS. The fifth article, by George Gmelch, which is revised and updated for this edition of *Conformity and Conflict*, explores how fieldwork in another culture can increase understanding of one's own.

Key Terms

I

Ethnography and Culture

James P. Spradley

Most Americans associate science with detached observation; we learn to observe whatever we wish to understand, introduce our own classification of what is going on, and explain what we see in our own terms. In this selection, James Spradley argues that cultural anthropologists work differently. Ethnography is the work of discovering and describing a particular culture; culture is the learned, shared knowledge that people use to generate behavior and interpret experience. To get at culture, ethnographers must learn the meanings of action and experience from the insider's or informant's point of view. Many of the examples used by Spradley also show the relevance of anthropology to the study of culture in the United States.

Ethnographic fieldwork is the hallmark of cultural anthropology. Whether in a jungle village in Peru or on the streets of New York, the anthropologist goes to where people live and "does fieldwork." This means participating in activities, asking questions, eating strange foods, learning a new language, watching ceremonies, taking fieldnotes, washing clothes, writing letters home, tracing out genealogies, observing play, interviewing informants, and hundreds of other things. This vast range of activities often obscures the nature of the most fundamental task of all fieldwork: doing ethnography.

Ethnography is the work of describing a culture. The central aim of ethnography is to understand another way of life from the native point of view. The goal of ethnography, as Malinowski put it, is "to grasp the native's point of view, his relation to life, to realize *his* vision of *his* world."[1] Fieldwork, then, involves the disciplined study of what the world is like to people who have learned to see, hear, speak, think, and act in ways that are different. Rather than *studying people*, ethnography means *learning from people*. Consider the following illustration.

George Hicks set out, in 1965, to learn about another way of life, that of the mountain people in an Appalachian valley.[2] His goal was to discover their culture, to learn to see the world from their perspective. With his family he moved into Little Laurel Valley, his daughter attended the local school, and his wife became one of the local Girl Scout leaders. Hicks soon discovered that stores and storekeepers were at the center of the valley's communication system, providing the most important social arena for the entire valley. He learned this by watching what other people did, by following their example, and slowly becoming part of the groups that congregated daily in the stores. He writes:

> At least once each day I would visit several stores in the valley, and sit in on the groups of gossiping men or, if the storekeeper happened to be alone, perhaps attempt to clear up puzzling points about kinship obligations. I found these hours, particularly those spent in the presence of the two or three excellent storytellers in the Little Laurel, thoroughly enjoyable. . . . At other times, I helped a number of local men gather corn or hay, build sheds, cut trees, pull and pack galax, and search for rich stands of huckleberries. When I needed aid in, for example, repairing frozen water pipes, it was readily and cheerfully provided.[3]

In order to discover the hidden principles of another way of life, the researcher must become a *student*. Storekeepers and storytellers and local farmers become *teachers*. Instead of studying the "climate," the "flora," and the "fauna" that made up the environment of this Appalachian valley, Hicks tried to discover how these mountain people defined and evaluated trees and galax and huckleberries. He did not attempt to describe social life in terms of what

---

[1]Bronislaw Malinowski, *Argonauts of the Western Pacific* (London: Routledge, 1922), p. 22.

[2]George Hicks, *Appalachian Valley* (New York: Holt, Rinehart, and Winston, 1976).

[3]Hicks, p. 3.

most Americans know about "marriage," "family," and "friendship"; instead he sought to discover how these mountain people identified relatives and friends. He tried to learn the obligations they felt toward kinsmen and discover how they felt about friends. Discovering the *insider's view* is a different species of knowledge from one that rests mainly on the outsider's view, even when the outsider is a trained social scientist.

Consider another example, this time from the perspective of a non-Western ethnographer. Imagine an Inuit woman setting out to learn the culture of Macalester College. What would she, so well schooled in the rich heritage of Inuit culture, have to do in order to understand the culture of Macalester College students, faculty, and staff? How would she discover the patterns that made up their lives? How would she avoid imposing Inuit ideas, categories, and values on everything she saw?

First, and perhaps most difficult, she would have to set aside her belief in *naive realism*, the almost universal belief that all people define the *real* world of objects, events, and living creatures in pretty much the same way. Human languages may differ from one society to the next, but behind the strange words and sentences, all people are talking about the same things. The naive realist assumes that love, snow, marriage, worship, animals, death, food, and hundreds of other things have essentially the same meaning to all human beings. Although few of us would admit to such ethnocentrism, the assumption may unconsciously influence our research. Ethnography starts with a conscious attitude of almost complete ignorance: "I don't know how the people at Macalester College understand their world. That remains to be discovered."

This Inuit woman would have to begin by learning the language spoken by students, faculty, and staff. She could stroll the campus paths, sit in classes, and attend special events, but only if she consciously tried to see things from the native point of view would she grasp their perspective. She would need to observe and listen to first-year students during their week-long orientation program. She would have to stand in line during registration, listen to students discuss the classes they hoped to get, and visit departments to watch faculty advising students on course selection. She would want to observe secretaries typing, janitors sweeping, and maintenance personnel plowing snow from walks. She would watch the more than 1,600 students crowd into the post office area to open their tiny mailboxes, and she would listen to their comments about junk mail and letters from home or no mail at all. She would attend faculty meetings to watch what went on, recording what professors and administrators said and how they behaved. She would sample various courses, attend "keggers" on weekends, read the *Mac Weekly*, and listen by the hour to students discussing things like their "relationships," the "football team," and "work study." She would want to learn the *meanings* of all these things. She would have to listen to the members of this college community, watch what they did, and participate in their activities to learn such meanings.

The essential core of ethnography is this concern with the meaning of actions and events to the people we seek to understand. Some of these meanings are directly expressed in language; many are taken for granted and communicated only indirectly through word and action. But in every society people make constant use of these complex meaning systems to organize their behavior, to understand themselves and others, and to make sense out of the world in which they live. These systems of meaning constitute their culture; ethnography always implies a theory of culture.

Culture

When ethnographers study other cultures, they must deal with three fundamental aspects of human experience: what people do, what people know, and the things people make and use. When each of these is learned and shared by members of some group, we speak of them as *cultural behavior, cultural knowledge,* and *cultural artifacts.* Whenever you do ethnographic fieldwork, you will want to distinguish among these three, although in most situations they are usually mixed together. Let's try to unravel them.

Recently I took a commuter train from a western suburb to downtown Chicago. It was late in the day, and when I boarded the train, only a handful of people were scattered about the car. Each was engaged in a common form of *cultural behavior: reading.* Across the aisle a man held the *Chicago Tribune* out in front of him, looking intently at the small print and every now and then turning the pages noisily. In front of him a young woman held a paperback book about twelve inches from her face. I could see her head shift slightly as her eyes moved from the bottom of one page to the top of the next. Near the front of the car a student was reading a large textbook and using a pen to underline words and sentences. Directly in front of me I noticed a man looking at the ticket he had purchased and reading it. It took me an instant to survey this scene, and then I settled back, looked out the window, and read a billboard advertisement for a plumbing service proclaiming it would open any plugged drains. All of us were engaged in the same kind of cultural behavior: reading.

This common activity depended on a great many *cultural artifacts,* the things people shape or make from natural resources. I could see artifacts like books and tickets and newspapers and billboards, all of which contained tiny black marks arranged into intricate patterns called "letters." And these tiny artifacts were arranged into larger patterns of words, sentences, and paragraphs. Those of us on that commuter train could read, in part, because of still other artifacts: the bark of trees made into paper; steel made into printing presses; dyes of various colors made into ink; glue used to hold book pages together; large wooden frames to hold billboards. If an ethnographer wanted to understand the full cultural meaning in our society, it would involve a careful study of these and many other cultural artifacts.

Although we can easily see behavior and artifacts, they represent only the thin surface of a deep lake. Beneath the surface, hidden from view, lies a vast reservoir of *cultural knowledge.* Think for a moment what the people on that train needed to know in order to read. First, they had to know the grammatical rules for at least one language. Then they had to learn what the little marks on paper represented. They also had to know the meaning of space and lines and pages. They had learned cultural rules like "move your eyes from left to right, from the top of the page to the bottom." They had to know that a sentence at the bottom of a page continues on the top of the next page. The man reading a newspaper had to know a great deal about columns and the spaces between columns and what headlines mean. All of us needed to know what kinds of messages were intended by whoever wrote what we read. If a person cannot distinguish the importance of a message on a billboard from one that comes in a letter from a spouse or child, problems would develop. I knew how to recognize when other people were reading. We all knew it was impolite to read aloud on a train. We all knew how to feel when reading things like jokes or calamitous news in the paper. Our culture has a large body of shared knowledge that people learn and use to engage in this behavior called *reading* and make proper use of the artifacts connected with it.

Although cultural knowledge is hidden from view, it is of fundamental importance because we all use it constantly to generate behavior and interpret our experience. Cultural knowledge is so important that I will frequently use the broader term *culture* when speaking about it. Indeed, I will define culture as *the acquired knowledge people use to interpret experience and generate behavior.* Let's consider another example to see how people use their culture to interpret experience and do things.

One afternoon in 1973 I came across the following news item in the *Minneapolis Tribune:*

Crowd Mistakes Rescue Attempt, Attacks Police

Nov. 23, 1973. Hartford, Connecticut. Three policemen giving a heart massage and oxygen to a heart attack victim Friday were attacked by a crowd of 75 to 100 persons who apparently did not realize what the policemen were doing.

Other policemen fended off the crowd of mostly Spanish-speaking residents until an ambulance arrived. Police said they tried to explain to the crowd what they were doing, but the crowd apparently thought they were beating the woman.

Despite the policemen's efforts the victim, Evangelica Echevacria, 59, died.

Here we see people using their culture. Members of two different groups observed the same event, but their *interpretations* were drastically different. The crowd used their cultural knowledge (a) to interpret the behavior of the policemen as cruel and (b) to act on the woman's behalf to put a stop to what they perceived as brutality. They had acquired the cultural principles for acting and interpreting things in this way through a particular shared experience.

The policemen, on the other hand, used their cultural knowledge (a) to interpret the woman's condition as heart failure and their own behavior as a lifesaving effort and (b) to give her cardiac massage and oxygen. They used artifacts like an oxygen mask and an ambulance. Furthermore, they interpreted the actions of the crowd in an entirely different manner from how the crowd saw their own behavior. The two groups of people each had elaborate cultural rules for interpreting their experience and for acting in emergency situations, and the conflict arose, at least in part, because these cultural rules were so different.

We can now diagram this definition of culture and see more clearly the relationships among knowledge, behavior, and artifacts (Figure 1). By identifying cultural knowledge as fundamental, we have merely shifted the emphasis from behavior and artifacts to their *meaning*. The ethnographer observes behavior but goes beyond it to inquire about the meaning of that behavior. The ethnographer sees artifacts and natural objects but goes beyond them to discover what meanings people assign to these objects. The ethnographer observes and records emotional states but goes beyond them to discover the meaning of fear, anxiety, anger, and other feelings.

As represented in Figure 1, cultural knowledge exists at two levels of consciousness. *Explicit culture* makes up part of what we know, a level of knowledge people can communicate about with relative ease. When George Hicks asked storekeepers and others in Little Laurel Valley about their relatives, he

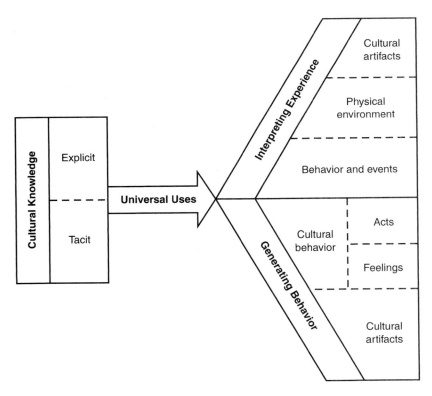

FIGURE 1

discovered that any adult over fifty could tell him the genealogical connections among large numbers of people. They knew how to trace kin relationships and the cultural rules for appropriate behavior among kins. All of us have acquired large areas of cultural knowledge such as this which we can talk about and make explicit.

At the same time, a large portion of our cultural knowledge remains *tacit,* outside our awareness. Edward Hall has done much to elucidate the nature of tacit cultural knowledge in his books *The Silent Language* and *The Hidden Dimension.*[4] The way each culture defines space often occurs at the level of tacit knowledge. Hall points out that all of us have acquired thousands of spatial cues about how close to stand to others, how to arrange furniture, when to touch others, and when to feel cramped inside a room. Without realizing that our tacit culture is operating, we begin to feel uneasy when someone from another culture stands too close, breathes on us when talking, touches us, or when we find furniture arranged in the center of the room rather than around the edges. Ethnography is the study of both explicit and tacit cultural knowledge. . . .

The concept of culture as acquired knowledge has much in common with symbolic interactionism, a theory that seeks to explain human behavior in terms of meanings. Symbolic interactionism has its roots in the work of sociologists like Cooley, Mead, and Thomas. Blumer has identified three premises on which this theory rests.

The first premise is that "human beings act toward things on the basis of the meanings that the things have for them."[5] The policemen and the crowd in our earlier example interacted on the basis of the meanings things had for them. The geographic location, the types of people, the police car, the policemen's movements, the sick woman's behavior, and the activities of the onlookers—all were *symbols* with special meanings. People did not act toward the things themselves, but to their meanings.

The second premise underlying symbolic interactionism is that the "meaning of such things is derived from, or arises out of, the social interaction that one has with one's fellows."[6] Culture, as a shared system of meanings, is learned, revised, maintained, and defined in the context of people interacting. The crowd came to share their definitions of police behavior through interacting with one another and through past associations with the police. The police officers acquired the cultural meanings they used through interacting with other officers and members of the community. The culture of each group was inextricably bound up with the social life of their particular communities.

The third premise of symbolic interactionism is that "meanings are handled in, and modified through, an interpretive process used by the person dealing with

[4]Edward T. Hall, *The Silent Language* (Garden City, NY: Doubleday, 1959); *The Hidden Dimension* (Garden City, NY: Doubleday, 1966).

[5] Herbert Blumer, *Symbolic Interactionism* (Englewood Cliffs, NJ: Prentice-Hall, 1969), p. 2.

[6]Blumer, p. 2.

the things he encounters."[7] Neither the crowd nor the policemen were automatons, driven by their culture to act in the way they did. Rather, they used their cultural knowledge to interpret and evaluate the situation. At any moment, a member of the crowd might have interpreted the behavior of the policemen in a slightly different way, leading to a different reaction.

We may see this interpretive aspect more clearly if we think of culture as a cognitive map. In the recurrent activities that make up everyday life, we refer to this map. It serves as a guide for acting and for interpreting our experience; it does not compel us to follow a particular course. Like this brief drama between the policemen, a dying woman, and the crowd, much of life is a series of unanticipated social occasions. Although our culture may not include a detailed map for such occasions, it does provide principles for interpreting and responding to them. Rather than a rigid map that people must follow, culture is best thought of as

> a set of principles for creating dramas, for writing script, and of course, for recruiting players and audiences. . . . Culture is not simply a cognitive map that people acquire, in whole or in part, more or less accurately, and then learn to read. People are not just map-readers; they are map-makers. People are cast out into imperfectly charted, continually revised sketch maps. Culture does not provide a cognitive map, but rather a set of principles for map making and navigation. Different cultures are like different schools of navigation to cope with different terrains and seas.[8]

If we take *meaning* seriously, as symbolic interactionists argue we must, it becomes necessary to study meaning carefully. We need a theory of meaning and a specific methodology designed for the investigation of it.

Review Questions

1. What is the definition of *culture?* How is this definition related to the way anthropologists do ethnographic fieldwork?

2. What is the relationship among cultural behavior, cultural artifacts, and cultural knowledge?

3. What is the difference between tacit and explicit culture? How can anthropologists discover these two kinds of culture?

4. What are some examples of naive realism in the way Americans think about people in other societies?

[7]Blumer, p. 2.

[8]Charles O. Frake, "Plying Frames Can Be Dangerous: Some Reflections on Methodology in Cognitive Anthropology," *Quarterly Newsletter of the Institute for Comparative Human Development* 3 (1977): 6–7.

2

Eating Christmas in the Kalahari

Richard Borshay Lee

What happens when an anthropologist living among the !Kung of Africa decides to be generous and to share a large animal with everyone at Christmastime? This compelling account of the misunderstanding and confusion that resulted takes the reader deeper into the nature of culture. Richard Lee carefully traces how the !Kung perceived his generosity and taught the anthropologist something about his own culture.

The !Kung Bushmen's knowledge of Christmas is thirdhand. The London Missionary Society brought the holiday to the southern Tswana tribes in the early nineteenth century. Later, native catechists spread the idea far and wide among the Bantu-speaking pastoralists, even in the remotest corners of the Kalahari Desert. The Bushmen's idea of the Christmas story, stripped to its essentials, is "praise the birth of white man's god-chief"; what keeps their interest in the

Originally published as "A Naturalist at Large: Eating Christmas in the Kalahari" by Richard Borshay Lee. Reprinted with permission from *Natural History,* December 1969, pp. 14–22, 60–64. Copyright © 1969 by Natural History Magazine, Inc.

holiday high is the Tswana-Herero custom of slaughtering an ox for his Bushmen neighbors as an annual goodwill gesture. Since the 1930s, part of the Bushmen's annual round of activities has included a December congregation at the cattle posts for trading, marriage brokering, and several days of trance dance feasting at which the local Tswana headman is host.

As a social anthropologist working with !Kung Bushmen, I found that the Christmas ox custom suited my purposes. I had come to the Kalahari to study the hunting and gathering subsistence economy of the !Kung, and to accomplish this it was essential not to provide them with food, share my own food, or interfere in any way with their food-gathering activities. While liberal handouts of tobacco and medical supplies were appreciated, they were scarcely adequate to erase the glaring disparity in wealth between the anthropologist, who maintained a two-month inventory of canned goods, and the Bushmen, who rarely had a day's supply of food on hand. My approach, while paying off in terms of data, left me open to frequent accusations of stinginess and hardheartedness. By their lights, I was a miser.

The Christmas ox was to be my way of saying thank you for the cooperation of the past year; and since it was to be our last Christmas in the field, I was determined to slaughter the largest, meatiest ox that money could buy, insuring that the feast and trance dance would be a success.

Through December I kept my eyes open at the wells as the cattle were brought down for watering. Several animals were offered, but none had quite the grossness that I had in mind. Then, ten days before the holiday, a Herero friend led an ox of astonishing size and mass up to our camp. It was solid black, stood five feet high at the shoulder, had a five-foot span of horns, and must have weighed 1,200 pounds on the hoof. Food consumption calculations are my specialty, and I quickly figured that bones and viscera aside, there was enough meat—at least four pounds—for every man, woman, and child of the 150 Bushmen in the vicinity of /ai/ai who were expected at the feast.

Having found the right animal at last, I paid the Herero £20 ($56) and asked him to keep the beast with his herd until Christmas day. The next morning word spread among the people that the big solid black one was the ox chosen by /ontah (my Bushman name; it means, roughly, "whitey") for the Christmas feast. That afternoon I received the first delegation. Ben!a, an outspoken sixty-year-old mother of five, came to the point slowly.

"Where were you planning to eat Christmas?"

"Right here at /ai/ai," I replied.

"Alone or with others?"

"I expect to invite all the people to eat Christmas with me."

"Eat what?"

"I have purchased Yehave's black ox, and I am going to slaughter and cook it."

"That's what we were told at the well but refused to believe it until we heard it from yourself."

"Well, it's the black one," I replied expansively, although wondering what she was driving at.

"Oh, no!" Ben!a groaned, turning to her group. "They were right." Turning back to me she asked, "Do you expect us to eat that bag of bones?"

"Bag of bones! It's the biggest ox at /ai/ai."

"Big, yes, but old. And thin. Everybody knows there's no meat on that old ox. What did you expect us to eat off it, the horns?"

Everybody chuckled at Ben!a's one-liner as they walked away, but all I could manage was a weak grin.

That evening it was the turn of the young men. They came to sit at our evening fire. /gaugo, about my age, spoke to me man-to-man.

"/ontah, you have always been square with us," he lied. "What has happened to change your heart? That sack of guts and bones of Yehave's will hardly feed one camp, let alone all the Bushmen around /ai/ai." And he proceeded to enumerate the seven camps in the /ai/ai vicinity, family by family. "Perhaps you have forgotten that we are not few, but many. Or are you too blind to tell the difference between a proper cow and an old wreck? That ox is thin to the point of death."

"Look, you guys," I retorted, "that is a beautiful animal, and I'm sure you will eat it with pleasure at Christmas."

"Of course we will eat it; it's food. But it won't fill us up to the point where we will have enough strength to dance. We will eat and go home to bed with stomachs rumbling."

That night as we turned in, I asked my wife, Nancy, "What did you think of the black ox?"

"It looked enormous to me. Why?"

"Well, about eight different people have told me I got gypped; that the ox is nothing but bones."

"What's the angle?" Nancy asked. "Did they have a better one to sell?"

"No, they just said that it was going to be a grim Christmas because there won't be enough meat to go around. Maybe I'll get an independent judge to look at the beast in the morning."

Bright and early, Halingisi, a Tswana cattle owner, appeared at our camp. But before I could ask him to give me his opinion on Yehave's black ox, he gave me the eye signal that indicated a confidential chat. We left the camp and sat down.

"/ontah, I'm surprised at you; you've lived here for three years and still haven't learned anything about cattle."

"But what else can a person do but choose the biggest, strongest animal one can find?" I retorted.

"Look, just because an animal is big doesn't mean that it has plenty of meat on it. The black one was a beauty when it was younger, but now it is thin to the point of death."

"Well, I've already bought it. What can I do at this stage?"

"Bought it already? I thought you were just considering it. Well, you'll have to kill it and serve it, I suppose. But don't expect much of a dance to follow."

My spirits dropped rapidly. I could believe that Ben!a and /gaugo just might be putting me on about the black ox, but Halingisi seemed to be an impartial critic. I went around that day feeling as though I had bought a lemon of a used car.

In the afternoon it was Tomazo's turn. Tomazo is a fine hunter, a top trance performer . . . and one of my most reliable informants. He approached the subject of the Christmas cow as part of my continuing Bushman education.

"My friend, the way it is with us Bushmen," he began, "is that we love meat. And even more than that, we love fat. When we hunt we always search for the fat ones, the ones dripping with layers of white fat: fat that turns into a clear, thick oil in the cooking pot, fat that slides down your gullet, fills your stomach and gives you a roaring diarrhea," he rhapsodized.

"So, feeling as we do," he continued, "it gives us pain to be served such a scrawny thing as Yehave's black ox. It is big, yes, and no doubt its giant bones are good for soup, but fat is what we really crave, and so we will eat Christmas this year with a heavy heart."

The prospect of a gloomy Christmas now had me worried, so I asked Tomazo what I could do about it.

"Look for a fat one, a young one . . . smaller, but fat. Fat enough to make us //gom (evacuate the bowels), then we will be happy."

My suspicions were aroused when Tomazo said that he happened to know a young, fat, barren cow that the owner was willing to part with. Was Tomazo working on commission, I wondered? But I dispelled this unworthy thought when we approached the Herero owner of the cow in question and found that he had decided not to sell.

The scrawny wreck of a Christmas ox now became the talk of the /ai/ai water hole and was the first news told to the outlying groups as they began to come in from the bush for the feast. What finally convinced me that real trouble might be brewing was the visit from u!au, an old conservative with a reputation for fierceness. His nickname meant spear and referred to an incident thirty years ago in which he had speared a man to death. He had an intense manner; fixing me with his eyes, he said in clipped tones:

"I have only just heard about the black ox today, or else I would have come here earlier. /ontah, do you honestly think you can serve meat like that to people and avoid a fight?" He paused, letting the implications sink in. "I don't mean fight you, /ontah; you are a white man. I mean a fight between Bushmen. There are many fierce ones here, and with such a small quantity of meat to distribute, how can you give everybody a fair share? Someone is sure to accuse another of taking too much or hogging all the choice pieces. Then you will see what happens when some go hungry while others eat."

The possibility of at least a serious argument struck me as all too real. I had witnessed the tension that surrounds the distribution of meat from a kudu or gemsbok kill, and had documented many arguments that sprang up from a real or imagined slight in meat distribution. The owners of a kill may spend up to two hours arranging and rearranging the piles of meat under the gaze of a circle of recipients before handing them out. And I knew that the Christmas feast at /ai/ai would be bringing together groups that had feuded in the past.

Convinced now of the gravity of the situation, I went in earnest to search for a second cow; but all my inquiries failed to turn one up.

The Christmas feast was evidently going to be a disaster, and the incessant complaints about the meagerness of the ox had already taken the fun out of it for me. Moreover, I was getting bored with the wisecracks, and after losing my temper a few times, I resolved to serve the beast anyway. If the meat fell short, the hell with it. In the Bushmen idiom, I announced to all who would listen:

"I am a poor man and blind. If I have chosen one that is too old and too thin, we will eat it anyway and see if there is enough meat there to quiet the rumbling of our stomachs."

On hearing this speech, Ben!a offered me a rare word of comfort. "It's thin," she said philosophically, "but the bones will make a good soup."

At dawn Christmas morning, instinct told me to turn over the butchering and cooking to a friend and take off with Nancy to spend Christmas alone in the bush. But curiosity kept me from retreating. I wanted to see what such a scrawny ox looked like on butchering, and if there *was* going to be a fight, I wanted to catch every word of it. Anthropologists are incurable that way.

The great beast was driven up to our dancing ground, and a shot in the forehead dropped it in its tracks. Then, freshly cut branches were heaped around the fallen carcass to receive the meat. Ten men volunteered to help with the cutting. I asked /gaugo to make the breast bone cut. This cut, which begins the butchering process for most large game, offers easy access for removal of the viscera. But it also allows the hunter to spot-check the amount of fat on an animal. A fat game animal carries a white layer up to an inch thick on the chest, while in a thin one, the knife will quickly cut to bone. All eyes fixed on his hand as /gaugo, dwarfed by the great carcass, knelt to the breast. The first cut opened a pool of solid white in the black skin. The second and third cut widened and deepened the creamy white. Still no bone. It was pure fat; it must have been two inches thick.

"Hey /gau," I burst out, "that ox is loaded with fat. What's this about the ox being too thin to bother eating? Are you out of your mind?"

"Fat?" /gau shot back. "You call that fat? This wreck is thin, sick, dead!" And he broke out laughing. So did everyone else. They rolled on the ground, paralyzed with laughter. Everybody laughed except me; I was thinking.

I ran back to the tent and burst in just as Nancy was getting up. "Hey, the black ox. It's fat as hell! They were kidding about it being too thin to eat. It was a joke or something. A put-on. Everyone is really delighted with it."

"Some joke," my wife replied. "It was so funny that you were ready to pack up and leave /ai/ai."

If it had indeed been a joke, it had been an extraordinarily convincing one, and tinged, I thought, with more than a touch of malice, as many jokes are.

Nevertheless, that it was a joke lifted my spirits considerably, and I returned to the butchering site where the shape of the ox was rapidly disappearing under the axes and knives of the butchers. The atmosphere had become festive. Grinning broadly, their arms covered with blood well past the elbow, men packed chunks of meat into the big cast-iron cooking pots, fifty pounds to the load, and muttered and chuckled all the while about the thinness and worthlessness of the animal and /ontah's poor judgment.

We danced and ate that ox two days and two nights; we cooked and distributed fourteen potfuls of meat and no one went home hungry and no fights broke out.

But the "joke" stayed in my mind. I had a growing feeling that something important had happened in my relationship with the Bushmen and that the clue lay in the meaning of the joke. Several days later, when most of the people had dispersed back to the bush camps, I raised the question with Hakekgose, a Tswana man who had grown up among the !Kung, married a !Kung girl, and who probably knew their culture better than any other non-Bushman.

"With us whites," I began, "Christmas is supposed to be the day of friendship and brotherly love. What I can't figure out is why the Bushmen went to such lengths to criticize and belittle the ox I had bought for the feast. The animal was perfectly good and their jokes and wisecracks practically ruined the holiday for me."

"So it really did bother you," said Hakekgose. "Well, that's the way they always talk. When I take my rifle and go hunting with them, if I miss, they laugh at me for the rest of the day. But even if I hit and bring one down, it's no better. To them, the kill is always too small or too old or too thin; and as we sit down on the kill site to cook and eat the liver, they keep grumbling, even with their mouths full of meat. They say things like, 'Oh, this is awful! What a worthless animal! Whatever made me think that this Tswana rascal could hunt!' "

"Is this the way outsiders are treated?" I asked.

"No, it is their custom; they talk that way to each other, too. Go and ask them."

/gaugo had been one of the most enthusiastic in making me feel bad about the merit of the Christmas ox. I sought him out first.

"Why did you tell me the black ox was worthless, when you could see that it was loaded with fat and meat?"

"It is our way," he said, smiling. "We always like to fool people about that. Say there is a Bushman who has been hunting. He must not come home and announce like a braggart, 'I have killed a big one in the bush!' He must first sit down in silence until I or someone else comes up to his fire and asks, 'What did you see today?' He replies quietly, 'Ah, I'm no good for hunting. I saw nothing at all [pause] just a little tiny one.' Then I smile to myself," /gaugo continued, "because I know he has killed something big.

"In the morning we make up a party of four or five people to cut up and carry the meat back to the camp. When we arrive at the kill we examine it and cry out, 'You mean to say you have dragged us all the way out here in order to make us cart home your pile of bones? Oh, if I had known it was this thin I wouldn't have come.' Another one pipes up, 'People, to think I gave up a nice day in the shade for this. At home we may be hungry, but at least we have nice cool water to drink.' If the horns are big, someone says, 'Did you think that somehow you were going to boil down the horns for soup?'

"To all this you must respond in kind. 'I agree,' you say, 'this one is not worth the effort; let's just cook the liver for strength and leave the rest for the hyenas. It is not too late to hunt today and even a duiker or a steenbok would be better than this mess.'

"Then you set to work nevertheless; butcher the animal, carry the meat back to the camp and everyone eats," /gaugo concluded.

Things were beginning to make sense. Next, I went to Tomazo. He corroborated /gaugo's story of the obligatory insults over a kill and added a few details of his own.

"But," I asked, "why insult a man after he has gone to all that trouble to track and kill an animal and when he is going to share the meat with you so that your children will have something to eat?"

"Arrogance," was his cryptic answer.

"Arrogance?"

"Yes, when a young man kills much meat he comes to think of himself as a chief or a big man, and he thinks of the rest of us as his servants or inferiors. We can't accept this. We refuse one who boasts, for someday his pride will make him kill somebody. So we always speak of his meat as worthless. This way we cool his heart and make him gentle."

"But why didn't you tell me this before?" I asked Tomazo with some heat.

"Because you never asked me," said Tomazo, echoing the refrain that has come to haunt every field ethnographer.

The pieces now fell into place. I had known for a long time that in situations of social conflict with Bushmen I held all the cards. I was the only source of tobacco in a thousand square miles, and I was not incapable of cutting an individual off for noncooperation. Though my boycott never lasted longer than a few days, it was an indication of my strength. People resented my presence at the water hole, yet simultaneously dreaded my leaving. In short I was a perfect target for the charge of arrogance and for the Bushman tactic of enforcing humility.

I had been taught an object lesson by the Bushmen; it had come from an unexpected corner and had hurt me in a vulnerable area. For the big black ox was to be the one totally generous, unstinting act of my year at /ai/ai and I was quite unprepared for the reaction I received.

As I read it, their message was this: There are no totally generous acts. All "acts" have an element of calculation. One black ox slaughtered at Christmas does not wipe out a year of careful manipulation of gifts given to serve your own ends. After all, to kill an animal and share the meat with people is really no more than the Bushmen do for each other every day and with far less fanfare.

In the end, I had to admire how the Bushmen had played out the farce—collectively straight-faced to the end. Curiously, the episode reminded me of the

Good Soldier Schweik and his marvelous encounters with authority. Like Schweik, the Bushmen had retained a thoroughgoing skepticism of good intentions. Was it this independence of spirit, I wondered, that had kept them culturally viable in the face of generations of contact with more powerful societies, both black and white? The thought that the Bushmen were alive and well in the Kalahari was strangely comforting. Perhaps, armed with that independence and with their superb knowledge of their environment, they might yet survive the future.

Review Questions

1. What was the basis of the misunderstanding experienced by Lee when he gave an ox for the Christmas feast held by the !Kung?

2. Construct a model of cross-cultural misunderstanding, using the information presented by Lee in this article.

3. Why do you think the !Kung ridicule and denigrate people who have been successful hunters or who have provided them with a Christmas ox? Why do Americans expect people to be grateful to receive gifts?

3

Shakespeare in the Bush

Laura Bohannan

All of us use the cultural knowledge we acquire as members of our own society to organize our perception and behavior. Most of us are also naive realists: we tend to believe our culture mirrors a reality shared by everyone. But cultures are different, and other people rarely behave or interpret experience according to our cultural plan. In this article, Laura Bohannan describes her attempt to tell the classic story of Hamlet *to Tiv elders in West Africa. At each turn in the story, the Tiv interpret the events and motives in Hamlet using their own cultural knowledge. The result is a very different version of the classic play.*

Reprinted with permission by the author from *Natural History* magazine, August/September 1966. Copyright © 1966 by Laura Bohannan.

Just before I left Oxford for the Tiv in West Africa, conversation turned to the season at Stratford. "You Americans," said a friend, "often have difficulty with Shakespeare. He was, after all, a very English poet, and one can easily misinterpret the universal by misunderstanding the particular."

I protested that human nature is pretty much the same the whole world over; at least the general plot and motivation of the greater tragedies would always be clear—everywhere—although some details of custom might have to be explained and difficulties of translation might produce other slight changes. To end an argument we could not conclude, my friend gave me a copy of *Hamlet* to study in the African bush: it would, he hoped, lift my mind above its primitive surroundings, and possibly I might, by prolonged meditation, achieve the grace of correct interpretation.

It was my second field trip to that African tribe, and I thought myself ready to live in one of its remote sections—an area difficult to cross even on foot. I eventually settled on the hillock of a very knowledgeable old man, the head of a homestead of some hundred and forty people, all of whom were either his close relatives or their wives and children. Like the other elders of the vicinity, the old man spent most of his time performing ceremonies seldom seen these days in the more accessible parts of the tribe. I was delighted. Soon there would be three months of enforced isolation and leisure, between the harvest that takes place just before the rising of the swamps and the clearing of new farms when the water goes down. Then, I thought, they would have even more time to perform ceremonies and explain them to me.

I was quite mistaken. Most of the ceremonies demanded the presence of elders from several homesteads. As the swamps rose, the old men found it too difficult to walk from one homestead to the next, and the ceremonies gradually ceased. As the swamps rose even higher, all activities but one came to an end. The women brewed beer from maize and millet. Men, women, and children sat on their hillocks and drank it.

People began to drink at dawn. By midmorning the whole homestead was singing, dancing, and drumming. When it rained, people had to sit inside their huts: there they drank and sang or they drank and told stories. In any case, by noon or before, I either had to join the party or retire to my own hut and my books. "One does not discuss serious matters when there is beer. Come, drink with us." Since I lacked their capacity for the thick native beer, I spent more and more time with *Hamlet*. Before the end of the second month, grace descended on me. I was quite sure that *Hamlet* had only one possible interpretation, and that one universally obvious.

Early every morning, in the hope of having some serious talk before the beer party, I used to call on the old man at his reception hut—a circle of posts supporting a thatched roof above a low mud wall to keep out wind and rain. One day I crawled through the low doorway and found most of the men of the homestead sitting huddled in their ragged cloths on stools, low plank beds, and reclining chairs, warming themselves against the chill of the rain around a smoky fire. In the center were three pots of beer. The party had started.

The old man greeted me cordially. "Sit down and drink." I accepted a large calabash full of beer, poured some into a small drinking gourd, and tossed it down. Then I poured some more into the same gourd for the man second in seniority to my host before I handed my calabash over to a young man for further distribution. Important people shouldn't ladle beer themselves.

"It is better like this," the old man said, looking at me approvingly and plucking at the thatch that had caught in my hair. "You should sit and drink with us more often. Your servants tell me that when you are not with us, you sit inside your hut looking at a paper."

The old man was acquainted with four kinds of "papers": tax receipts, bride price receipts, court fee receipts, and letters. The messenger who brought him letters from the chief used them mainly as a badge of office, for he always knew what was in them and told the old man. Personal letters for the few who had relatives in the government or mission stations were kept until someone went to a large market where there was a letter writer and reader. Since my arrival, letters were brought to me to be read. A few men also brought me bride price receipts, privately, with requests to change the figures to a higher sum. I found moral arguments were of no avail, since in-laws are fair game, and the technical hazards of forgery difficult to explain to an illiterate people. I did not wish them to think me silly enough to look at any such papers for days on end, and I hastily explained that my "paper" was one of the "things of long ago" of my country.

"Ah," said the old men. "Tell us."

I protested that I was not a storyteller. Storytelling is a skilled art among them; their standards are high, and the audiences critical—and vocal in their criticism. I protested in vain. This morning they wanted to hear a story while they drank. They threatened to tell me no more stories until I told them one of mine. Finally, the old man promised that no one would criticize my style "for we know you are struggling with our language." "But," put in one of the elders, "you must explain what we do not understand, as we do when we tell you our stories." Realizing that here was my chance to prove *Hamlet* universally intelligible, I agreed.

The old man handed me some more beer to help me on with my storytelling. Men filled their long wooden pipes and knocked coals from the fire to place in the pipe bowls; then, puffing contentedly, they sat back to listen. I began in the proper style, "Not yesterday, not yesterday, but long ago, a thing occurred. One night three men were keeping watch outside the homestead of the great chief, when suddenly they saw the former chief approach them."

"Why was he no longer their chief?"

"He was dead," I explained. "That is why they were troubled and afraid when they saw him."

"Impossible," began one of the elders, handing his pipe on to his neighbor, who interrupted, "Of course it wasn't the dead chief. It was an omen sent by a witch. Go on."

Slightly shaken, I continued. "One of these three was a man who knew things"—the closest translation for scholar, but unfortunately it also meant witch. The second elder looked triumphantly at the first. "So he spoke to the dead chief, saying, 'Tell us what we must do so you may rest in your grave,' but the dead chief did not answer. He vanished, and they could see him no more. Then the man who knew things—his name was Horatio—said this event was the affair of the dead chief's son, Hamlet."

There was a general shaking of heads around the circle. "Had the dead chief no living brothers? Or was this son the chief?" "No," I replied. "That is, he had one living brother who became the chief when the elder brother died."

The old men muttered: such omens were matters for chiefs and elders, not for youngsters; no good could come of being behind a chief's back; clearly Horatio was not a man who knew things.

"Yes, he was," I insisted, shooing a chicken away from my beer. "In our country the son is next to the father. The dead chief's younger brother had become the great chief. He had also married his elder brother's widow only about a month after the funeral."

"He did well," the old man beamed and announced to the others, "I told you that if we knew more about Europeans, we would find they really were very like us. In our country also," he added to me, "the younger brother marries the elder brother's widow and becomes the father of his children. Now, if your uncle, who married your widowed mother, is your father's full brother, then he will be a real father to you. Did Hamlet's father and uncle have one mother?"

His question barely penetrated my mind; I was too upset and thrown too far off balance by having one of the most important elements of *Hamlet* knocked straight out of the picture. Rather uncertainly I said that I thought they had the same mother, but I wasn't sure—the story didn't say. The old man told me severely that these genealogical details made all the difference and that when I got home I must ask the elders about it. He shouted out the door to one of his younger wives to bring his goatskin bag.

Determined to save what I could of the mother motif, I took a deep breath and began again. "The son Hamlet was very sad because his mother had married again so quickly. There was no need for her to do so, and it is our custom for a widow not to go to her next husband until she has mourned for two years."

"Two years is too long," objected the wife, who had appeared with the old man's battered goatskin bag. "Who will hoe your farms for you while you have no husband?"

"Hamlet," I retorted without thinking, "was old enough to hoe his mother's farms himself. There was no need for her to remarry." No one looked convinced. I gave up. "His mother and the great chief told Hamlet not to be sad, for the great chief himself would be a father to Hamlet. Furthermore, Hamlet would be the next chief: therefore he must stay to learn the things of a chief. Hamlet agreed to remain, and all the rest went off to drink beer."

While I paused, perplexed at how to render Hamlet's disgusted soliloquy to an audience convinced that Claudius and Gertrude had behaved in the best possible manner, one of the younger men asked me who had married the other wives of the dead chief.

"He had no other wives," I told him.

"But a chief must have many wives! How else can he brew beer and prepare food for all his guests?"

I said firmly that in our country even chiefs had only one wife, that they had servants to do their work, and that they paid them from tax money.

It was better, they returned, for a chief to have many wives and sons who would help him hoe his farms and feed his people; then everyone loved the chief who gave much and took nothing—taxes were a bad thing.

I agreed with the last comment, but for the rest fell back on their favorite way of fobbing off my questions: "That is the way it is done, so that is how we do it."

I decided to skip the soliloquy. Even if Claudius was here thought quite right to marry his brother's widow, there remained the poison motif, and I knew they would disapprove of fratricide. More hopefully I resumed, "That night Hamlet kept watch with the three who had seen his dead father. The dead chief again appeared, and although the others were afraid, Hamlet followed his dead father off to one side. When they were alone, Hamlet's dead father spoke."

"Omens can't talk!" The old man was emphatic.

"Hamlet's dead father wasn't an omen. Seeing him might have been an omen, but he was not." My audience looked as confused as I sounded. "It *was* Hamlet's dead father. It was a thing we call a 'ghost.'" I had to use the English word, for unlike many of the neighboring tribes, these people didn't believe in the survival after death of any individuating part of the personality.

"What is a 'ghost'? An omen?"

"No, a 'ghost' is someone who is dead but who walks around and can talk, and people can hear him and see him but not touch him."

They objected. "One can touch zombis."

"No, no! It was not a dead body the witches had animated to sacrifice and eat. No one else made Hamlet's dead father walk. He did it himself."

"Dead men can't walk," protested my audience as one man.

I was quite willing to compromise. "A 'ghost' is a dead man's shadow."

But again they objected. "Dead men cast no shadows."

"They do in my country," I snapped.

The old man quelled the babble of disbelief that rose immediately and told me with that insincere, but courteous, agreement one extends to the fancies of the young, ignorant, and superstitious, "No doubt in your country the dead can also walk without being zombis." From the depths of his bag he produced a withered fragment of kola nut, bit off one end to show it wasn't poisoned, and handed me the rest as a peace offering.

"Anyhow," I resumed, "Hamlet's dead father said that his own brother, the one who became chief, had poisoned him. He wanted Hamlet to avenge him. Hamlet believed this in his heart, for he did not like his father's brother." I took another swallow of beer. "In the country of the great chief, living in the same homestead, for it was a very large one, was an important elder who was often with the chief to advise and help him. His name was Polonius. Hamlet was courting his daughter, but her father and her brother . . . [I cast hastily about for some tribal analogy] warned her not to let Hamlet visit her when she was alone on her farm, for he would be a great chief and so could not marry her."

"Why not?" asked the wife, who had settled down on the edge of the old man's chair. He frowned at her for asking stupid questions and growled, "They lived in the same homestead."

"That was not the reason," I informed them. "Polonius was a stranger who lived in the homestead because he helped the chief, not because he was a relative."

"Then why couldn't Hamlet marry her?"

"He could have," I explained, "but Polonius didn't think he would. After all, Hamlet was a man of great importance who ought to marry a chief's daughter, for in his country a man could have only one wife. Polonius was afraid that if Hamlet made love to his daughter, then no one else would give a high price for her."

"That might be true," remarked one of the shrewder elders, "but a chief's son would give his mistress's father enough presents and patronage to more than make up the difference. Polonius sounds like a fool to me."

"Many people think he was," I agreed. "Meanwhile Polonius sent his son Laertes off to Paris to learn the things of that country, for it was the homestead of a very great chief indeed. Because he was afraid that Laertes might waste a lot of money on beer and women and gambling, or get into trouble by fighting, he sent one of his servants to Paris secretly, to spy out what Laertes was doing. One day Hamlet came upon Polonius's daughter Ophelia. He behaved so oddly he frightened her. Indeed"—I was fumbling for words to express the dubious quality of Hamlet's madness—"the chief and many others had also noticed that when Hamlet talked one could understand the words but not what they meant. Many people thought that he had become mad." My audience suddenly became much more attentive. "The great chief wanted to know what was wrong with Hamlet, so he sent for two of Hamlet's age mates [school friends would have taken long explanation] to talk to Hamlet and find out what troubled his heart. Hamlet, seeing that they had been bribed by the chief to betray him, told them nothing. Polonius, however, insisted that Hamlet was mad because he had been forbidden to see Ophelia, whom he loved."

"Why," inquired a bewildered voice, "should anyone bewitch Hamlet on that account?"

"Bewitch him?"

"Yes, only witchcraft can make anyone mad, unless, of course, one sees the beings that lurk in the forest."

I stopped being a storyteller, took out my notebook and demanded to be told more about these two causes of madness. Even while they spoke and I jotted notes, I tried to calculate the effect of this new factor on the plot. Hamlet had not been exposed to the beings that lurk in the forest. Only his relatives in the male line could bewitch him. Barring relatives not mentioned by Shakespeare, it had to be Claudius who was attempting to harm him. And, of course, it was.

For the moment I staved off questions by saying that the great chief also refused to believe that Hamlet was mad for the love of Ophelia and nothing else. "He was sure that something much more important was troubling Hamlet's heart."

"Now Hamlet's age mates," I continued, "had brought with them a famous storyteller. Hamlet decided to have this man tell the chief and all his homestead a story about the man who had poisoned his brother because he desired his brother's wife and wished to be chief himself. Hamlet was sure the great chief could not hear the story without making a sign if he was indeed guilty, and then he would discover whether his dead father had told him the truth."

The old man interrupted, with deep cunning. "Why should a father lie to his son?" he asked.

I hedged: "Hamlet wasn't sure that it really was his dead father." It was impossible to say anything, in that language, about devil-inspired visions.

"You mean," he said, "it actually was an omen, and he knew witches sometimes send false ones. Hamlet was a fool not to go to one skilled in reading omens and divining the truth in the first place. A man-who-sees-the-truth could have told him how his father died, if he really had been poisoned, and if there was witchcraft in it; then Hamlet could have called the elders to settle the matter."

The shrewd elder ventured to disagree. "Because his father's brother was a great chief, one-who-sees-the-truth might therefore have been afraid to tell it. I think it was for that reason that a friend of Hamlet's father—a witch and an elder—sent an omen so his friend's son would know. Was the omen true?"

"Yes," I said, abandoning ghosts and the devil; a witch-sent omen it would have to be. "It was true, for when the storyteller was telling his tale before all the homestead, the great chief rose in fear. Afraid that Hamlet knew his secret, he planned to have him killed."

The stage set of the next bit presented some difficulties of translation. I began cautiously. "The great chief told Hamlet's mother to find out from her son what he knew. But because a woman's children are always first in her heart, he had the important elder Polonius hide behind a cloth that hung against the wall of Hamlet's mother's sleeping hut. Hamlet started to scold his mother for what she had done."

There was a shocked murmur from everyone. A man should never scold his mother.

"She called out in fear, and Polonius moved behind the cloth. Shouting 'A rat!' Hamlet took his machete and slashed through the cloth." I paused for a dramatic effect. "He had killed Polonius!"

The old men looked at each other in supreme disgust. "That Polonius truly was a fool and a man who knew nothing! What child would not know enough to shout, 'It's me!'" With a pang, I remembered that these people are ardent hunters, always armed with bow, arrow, and machete; at the first rustle in the grass an arrow is aimed and ready, and the hunter shouts "Game!" If no human voice answers immediately, the arrow speeds on its way. Like a good hunter Hamlet had shouted, "A rat!"

I rushed in to save Polonius's reputation. "Polonius did speak. Hamlet heard him. But he thought it was the chief and wished to kill him to avenge his father. He had meant to kill him earlier that evening. . . ." I broke down, unable to describe to these pagans, who had no belief in individual afterlife, the difference between dying at one's prayers and dying "unhousell'd, disappointed, unaneled."

This time I had shocked my audience seriously. "For a man to raise his hands against his father's brother and the one who has become his father—that is a terrible thing. The elders ought to let such a man be bewitched."

I nibbled at my kola nut in some perplexity, then pointed out that after all the man had killed Hamlet's father.

"No," pronounced the old man, speaking less to me than to the young men sitting behind the elders. "If your father's brother has killed your father, you must appeal to your father's age mates; *they* may avenge him. No man may use violence against his senior relatives." Another thought struck him. "But if his father's brother had indeed been wicked enough to bewitch Hamlet and make him mad, that would be a good story indeed, for it would be his fault that Hamlet, being mad, no longer had any sense and thus was ready to kill his father's brother."

There was a murmur of applause. *Hamlet* was again a good story to them, but it no longer seemed quite the same story to me. As I thought over the coming complications of plot and motive, I lost courage and decided to skim over dangerous ground quickly.

"The great chief," I went on, "was not sorry that Hamlet had killed Polonius. It gave him a reason to send Hamlet away, with his two treacherous age mates, with letters to a chief of a far country, saying that Hamlet should be killed. But Hamlet changed the writing on their papers, so that the chief killed his age mates instead." I encountered a reproachful glare from one of the men whom I had told undetectable forgery was not merely immoral but beyond human skill. I looked the other way.

"Before Hamlet could return, Laertes came back for his father's funeral. The great chief told him Hamlet had killed Polonius. Laertes swore to kill Hamlet because of this, and because his sister Ophelia, hearing her father had been killed by the man she loved, went mad and drowned in the river."

"Have you already forgotten what we told you?" The old man was reproachful. "One cannot take vengeance on a madman; Hamlet killed Polonius in his madness. As for the girl, she not only went mad, she was drowned. Only witches can make people drown. Water itself can't hurt anything. It is merely something one drinks and bathes in."

I began to get cross. "If you don't like the story, I'll stop."

The old man made soothing noises and himself poured me some more beer. "You tell the story well, and we are listening. But it is clear that the elders of your country have never told you what the story really means. No, don't interrupt! We believe you when you say your marriage customs are different, or your clothes and weapons. But people are the same everywhere; therefore, there are always witches and it is we, the elders, who know how witches work. We told you it was the great chief who wished to kill Hamlet, and now your own words have proved us right. Who were Ophelia's male relatives?"

"There were only her father and her brother." Hamlet was clearly out of my hands.

"There must have been many more; this also you must ask of your elders when you get back to your country. From what you tell us, since Polonius was dead, it must have been Laertes who killed Ophelia, although I do not see the reason for it."

We had emptied one pot of beer, and the old men argued the point with slightly tipsy interest. Finally one of them demanded of me, "What did the servant of Polonius say on his return?"

With difficulty I recollected Reynaldo and his mission. "I don't think he did return before Polonius was killed."

"Listen," said the elder, "and I will tell you how it was and how your story will go, then you may tell me if I am right. Polonius knew his son would get into trouble, and so he did. He had many fines to pay for fighting, and debts from gambling. But he had only two ways of getting money quickly. One was to marry off his sister at once, but it is difficult to find a man who will marry a woman desired by the son of a chief. For if the chief's heir commits adultery with your wife, what can you do? Only a fool calls a case against a man who will someday be his judge. Therefore Laertes had to take the second way: he killed his sister by witchcraft, drowning her so he could secretly sell her body to the witches."

I raised an objection. "They found her body and buried it. Indeed Laertes jumped into the grave to see his sister once more—so, you see, the body was truly there. Hamlet, who had just come back, jumped in after him."

"What did I tell you?" The elder appealed to the others. "Laertes was up to no good with his sister's body. Hamlet prevented him, because the chief's heir, like a chief, does not wish any other man to grow rich and powerful. Laertes would be angry, because he would have killed his sister without benefit to himself. In our country he would try to kill Hamlet for that reason. Is this not what happened?"

"More or less," I admitted. "When the great chief found Hamlet was still alive, he encouraged Laertes to try to kill Hamlet and arranged a fight with machetes between them. In the fight both the young men were wounded to death. Hamlet's mother drank the poisoned beer that the chief meant for Hamlet in case he won the fight. When he saw his mother die of poison, Hamlet, dying, managed to kill his father's brother with his machete."

"You see, I was right!" exclaimed the elder.

"That was a very good story," added the old man, "and you told it with very few mistakes. There was just one more error, at the very end. The poison Hamlet's mother drank was obviously meant for the survivor of the fight, whichever it was. If Laertes had won, the great chief would have poisoned him, for no one would know that he arranged Hamlet's death. Then, too, he need not fear Laertes's witchcraft; it takes a strong heart to kill one's only sister by witchcraft.

"Sometime," concluded the old man, gathering his ragged toga about him, "you must tell us some more stories of your country. We, who are elders, will instruct you in their true meaning, so that when you return to your own land your elders will see that you have not been sitting in the bush, but among those who know things and who have taught you wisdom."

Review Questions

1. In what ways does Bohannan's attempt to tell the story of Hamlet to the Tiv illustrate the concept of naive realism?

2. Using Bohannan's experience of telling the story of *Hamlet* to the Tiv and the response of the Tiv elders to her words, illustrate cross-cultural misunderstanding.

3. What are the most important parts of *Hamlet* that the Tiv found it necessary to reinterpret?

4

Fieldwork on Prostitution in the Era of AIDS

Claire E. Sterk

Many Americans associate social research with questionnaires, structured interviews, word association tests, and psychological experiments. They expect investigators to control the research setting and ask for specific information, such as age, income, place of residence, and opinions about work or national events. But ethnographic fieldwork is different. Cultural anthropologists may administer formal research instruments such as questionnaires, but largely their goal is to discover culture, to view the actions and knowledge of a group through the eyes of its members. In this sense, ethnographers are more like students; cultural informants are more like teachers. To implement ethnographic research, anthropologists must often become part of the worlds they seek to understand. They arrive as strangers, seek entrance into a group, meet and develop relationships of trust with informants,

From *Tricking and Tripping* by Claire E. Sterk (Putnam Valley, NY: Social Change Press, 2000), pp. 14–20. Reprinted by permission.

and wrestle with the ethical dilemmas that naturally occur when someone wants to delve into the lives of others.

These are the challenges discussed in this selection by Claire Sterk. Working inside the United States, as many anthropologists do these days, she engaged in a long-term study of prostitutes in New York City and Atlanta. Her research required her to discover the places where her informants worked and hung out, introduce herself, develop rapport, and conduct open-ended interviews that permitted informants to teach her about their lives. During this process, she learned not to depend too much on contacts (gatekeepers) she met initially, that it was helpful to know something about respondents but to avoid an "expert" role, to refrain from expressing her own opinions about the culture and lives of her subjects, and to manage a variety of ethical questions. She ends by listing six themes that emerged from her ethnographic study.

> Prostitution is a way of life. IT IS THE LIFE.
> We make money for pimps who promise us
> > love and more,
> but if we don't produce, they shove us out the door.
>
> We turn tricks who have sex-for-pay.
> They don't care how many times we serve
> > every day.
>
> The Life is rough. The Life is tough.
> We are put down, beaten up, and left for dead.
> It hurts body and soul and messes with
> > a person's head.
>
> Many of us get high. Don't you understand it is
> > a way of getting by?
>
> The Life is rough. The Life is tough.
> We are easy to blame because we are lame.
> > —Piper, 1987[1]

One night in March of 1987 business was slow. I was hanging out on a stroll with a group of street prostitutes. After a few hours in a nearby diner/coffee shop, we were kicked out. The waitress felt bad, but she needed our table for some new customers. Four of us decided to sit in my car until the rain stopped. While three of us chatted about life, Piper wrote this poem. As soon as she read it to us, the conversation shifted to more serious topics—pimps, customers, cops, the many hassles of being a prostitute, to name a few. We decided that if I ever finished a book about prostitution, the book would start with her poem.

This book is about the women who work in the lower echelons of the prostitution world. They worked in the streets and other public settings as well as

---

[1]The names of the women who were interviewed for this study, as well as those of their pimps and customers, have been replaced by pseudonyms to protect their privacy.

crack houses. Some of these women viewed themselves primarily as prostitutes, and a number of them used drugs to cope with the pressures of the life. Others identified themselves more as drug users, and their main reason for having sex for money or other goods was to support their own drug use and often the habit of their male partner. A small group of women interviewed for this book had left prostitution, and most of them were still struggling to integrate their past experiences as prostitutes in their current lives.

The stories told by the women who participated in this project revealed how pimps, customers, and others such as police officers and social and health service providers treated them as "fallen" women. However, their accounts also showed their strengths and the many strategies they developed to challenge these others. Circumstances, including their drug use, often forced them to sell sex, but they all resisted the notion that they might be selling themselves. Because they engaged in an illegal profession, these women had little status: their working conditions were poor, and their work was physically and mentally exhausting. Nevertheless, many women described the ways in which they gained a sense of control over their lives. For instance, they learned how to manipulate pimps, how to control the types of services and length of time bought by their customers, and how to select customers. While none of these schemes explicitly enhanced their working conditions, they did make the women feel stronger and better about themselves.

In this [article], I present prostitution from the point of view of the women themselves. To understand their current lives, it was necessary to learn how they got started in the life, the various processes involved in their continued prostitution careers, the link between prostitution and drug use, the women's interactions with their pimps and customers, and the impact of the AIDS epidemic and increasing violence on their experiences. I also examined the implications for women. Although my goal was to present the women's thoughts, feelings, and actions in their own words, the final text is a sociological monograph compiled by me as the researcher. . . .

The Sample

. . . The research was conducted during the last ten years in the New York City and Atlanta metropolitan areas. One main data source was participant observation on streets, in hotels and other settings known for prostitution activity, and in drug-use settings, especially those that allowed sex-for-drug exchanges. Another data source was in-depth, life-history interviews with 180 women ranging in age from 18 to 59 years, with an average age of 34. One in two women was African-American and one in three white; the remaining women were Latina. Three in four had completed high school, and among them almost two-thirds had one or more years of additional educational training. Thirty women had graduated from college.

Forty women worked as street prostitutes and did not use drugs. On average, they had been prostitutes for 11 years. Forty women began using drugs an average of three years after they began working as prostitutes, and the average time they had worked as prostitutes was nine years. Forty women used drugs an average of five years before they became prostitutes, and on the average they had worked as prostitutes for eight years. Another forty women began smoking crack and exchanging sex for crack almost simultaneously, with an average of four years in the life. Twenty women who were interviewed were ex-prostitutes.

Comments on Methodology

When I tell people about my research, the most frequent question I am asked is how I gained access to the women rather than what I learned from the research. For many, prostitution is an unusual topic of conversation, and many people have expressed surprise that I, as a woman, conducted the research. During my research some customers indeed thought I was a working woman, a fact that almost always amuses those who hear about my work. However, few people want to hear stories about the women's struggles and sadness. Sometimes they ask questions about the reasons why women become prostitutes. Most of the time, they are surprised when I tell them that the prostitutes as well as their customers represent all layers of society. Before presenting the findings, it seems important to discuss the research process, including gaining access to the women, developing relationships, interviewing, and then leaving the field.

Locating Prostitutes and Gaining Entree

One of the first challenges I faced was to identify locations where street prostitution took place. Many of these women worked on strolls, streets where prostitution activity is concentrated, or in hotels known for prostitution activity. Others, such as the crack prostitutes, worked in less public settings such as a crack house that might be someone's apartment.

I often learned of well-known public places from professional experts, such as law enforcement officials and health care providers at emergency rooms and sexually transmitted disease clinics. I gained other insights from lay experts, including taxi drivers, bartenders, and community representatives such as members of neighborhood associations. The contacts universally mentioned some strolls as the places where many women worked, where the local police focused attention, or where residents had organized protests against prostitution in their neighborhoods.

As I began visiting various locales, I continued to learn about new settings. In one sense, I was developing ethnographic maps of street prostitution. After several visits to a specific area, I also was able to expand these maps by adding information about the general atmosphere on the stroll, general characteristics of the various people present, the ways in which the women and customers connected, and the overall flow of action. In addition, my visits allowed the regular actors to notice me.

I soon learned that being an unknown woman in an area known for prostitution may cause many people to notice you, even stare at you, but it fails to yield many verbal interactions. Most of the time when I tried to make eye contact with one of the women, she quickly averted her eyes. Pimps, on the other hand, would stare at me straight on and I ended up being the one to look away. Customers would stop, blow their horn, or wave me over, frequently yelling obscenities when I ignored them. I realized that gaining entree into the prostitution world was not going to be as easy as I imagined it. Although I lacked such training in any of my qualitative methods classes, I decided to move slowly and not force any interaction. The most I said during the initial weeks in a new area was limited to "How are you" or "Hi." This strategy paid off during my first visits to one of the strolls in Brooklyn, New York. After several appearances, one of the women walked up to me and sarcastically asked if I was looking for something. She caught me off guard, and all the answers I had practiced did not seem to make sense. I mumbled something about just wanting to walk around. She did not like my answer, but she did like my accent. We ended up talking about the latter and she was especially excited when I told her I came from Amsterdam. One of her friends had gone to Europe with her boyfriend, who was in the military. She understood from her that prostitution and drugs were legal in the Netherlands. While explaining to her that some of her friend's impressions were incorrect, I was able to show off some of my knowledge about prostitution. I mentioned that I was interested in prostitution and wanted to write a book about it.

Despite the fascination with my background and intentions, the prostitute immediately put me through a Streetwalker 101 test, and apparently I passed. She told me to make sure to come back. By the time I left, I not only had my first conversation but also my first connection to the scene. Variations of this entry process occurred on the other strolls. The main lesson I learned in these early efforts was the importance of having some knowledge of the lives of the people I wanted to study, while at the same time refraining from presenting myself as an expert.

Qualitative researchers often refer to their initial connections as gatekeepers and key respondents. Throughout my fieldwork I learned that some key respondents are important in providing initial access, but they become less central as the research evolves. For example, one of the women who introduced me to her lover, who was also her pimp, was arrested and disappeared for months. Another entered drug treatment soon after she facilitated my access. Other key respondents provided access to only a segment of the players on a scene. For example, if a woman worked for a pimp, [she] was unlikely . . . to introduce me to women working for another pimp. On one stroll my initial contact was with a pimp whom nobody liked. By associating with him, I almost lost the opportunity to meet other pimps. Some key respondents were less connected than promised—for example, some of the women who worked the street to support their drug habit. Often their connections were more frequently with drug users and less so with prostitutes.

Key respondents tend to be individuals central to the local scene, such as, in this case, pimps and the more senior prostitutes. Their function as gate-keepers often is to protect the scene and to screen outsiders. Many times I had to prove that I was not an undercover police officer or a woman with ambitions to become a streetwalker. While I thought I had gained entree, I quickly learned that many insiders subsequently wondered about my motives and approached me with suspicion and distrust.

Another lesson involved the need to proceed cautiously with self-nominated key respondents. For example, one of the women presented herself as knowing everyone on the stroll. While she did know everyone, she was not a central figure. On the contrary, the other prostitutes viewed her as a failed streetwalker whose drug use caused her to act unprofessionally. By associating with me, she hoped to regain some of her status. For me, however, it meant limited access to the other women because I affiliated myself with a woman who was marginal to the scene. On another occasion, my main key respondent was a man who claimed to own three crack houses in the neighborhood. However, he had a negative reputation, and people accused him of cheating on others. My initial alliance with him delayed, and almost blocked, my access to others in the neighborhood. He intentionally tried to keep me from others on the scene, not because he would gain something from that transaction but because it made him feel powerful. When I told him I was going to hang out with some of the other people, he threatened me until one of the other dealers stepped in and told him to stay away. The two of them argued back and forth, and finally I was free to go. Fortunately, the dealer who had spoken up for me was much more central and positively associated with the local scene. Finally, I am unsure if I would have had success in gaining entrance to the scene had I not been a woman.

Developing Relationships and Trust

The processes involved in developing relationships in research situations amplify those involved in developing relationships in general. Both parties need to get to know each other, become aware and accepting of each other's roles, and engage in a reciprocal relationship. Being supportive and providing practical assistance were the most visible and direct ways for me as the researcher to develop a relationship. Throughout the years, I have given countless rides, provided child care on numerous occasions, bought groceries, and listened for hours to stories that were unrelated to my initial research questions. Gradually, my role allowed me to become part of these women's lives and to build rapport with many of them.

Over time, many women also realized that I was uninterested in being a prostitute and that I genuinely was interested in learning as much as possible about their lives. Many felt flattered that someone wanted to learn from them and that they had knowledge to offer. Allowing women to tell their stories and engaging in a dialogue with them probably were the single most important techniques that allowed me to develop relationships with them. Had I only wanted to focus on the questions I had in mind, developing such relationships might have been more difficult.

At times, I was able to get to know a woman only after her pimp endorsed our contact. One of my scariest experiences occurred before I knew to work through the pimps, and one such man had some of his friends follow me on my way home one night. I will never know what plans they had in mind for me because I fortunately was able to escape with only a few bruises. Over a year later, the woman acknowledged that her pimp had gotten upset and told her he was going to teach me a lesson.

On other occasions, I first needed to be screened by owners and managers of crack houses before the research could continue. Interestingly, screenings always were done by a man even if the person who vouched for me was a man himself. While the women also were cautious, the ways in which they checked me out tended to be much more subtle. For example, one of them would tell me a story, indicating that it was a secret about another person on the stroll. Although I failed to realize this at the time, my field notes revealed that frequently after such a conversation, others would ask me questions about related topics. One woman later acknowledged that putting out such stories was a test to see if I would keep information confidential.

Learning more about the women and gaining a better understanding of their lives also raised many ethical questions. No textbook told me how to handle situations in which a pimp abused a woman, a customer forced a woman to engage in unwanted sex acts, a customer requested unprotected sex from a woman who knew she was HIV infected, or a boyfriend had unrealistic expectations regarding a woman's earnings to support his drug habit. I failed to know the proper response when asked to engage in illegal activities such as holding drugs or money a woman had stolen from a customer. In general, my response was to explain that I was there as a researcher. During those occasions when pressures became too severe, I decided to leave a scene. For example, I never returned to certain crack houses because pimps there continued to ask me to consider working for them.

Over time, I was fortunate to develop relationships with people who "watched my back." One pimp in particular intervened if he perceived other pimps, customers, or passersby harassing me. He also was the one who gave me my street name: Whitie (indicating my racial background) or Ms. Whitie for those who disrespected me. While this was my first street name, I subsequently had others. Being given a street name was a symbolic gesture of acceptance. Gradually, I developed an identity that allowed me to be both an insider and an outsider. While hanging out on the strolls and other gathering places, including crack houses, I had to deal with some of the same uncomfortable conditions as the prostitutes, such as cold or warm weather, lack of access to a rest room, refusals from owners for me to patronize a restaurant, and of course, harassment by customers and the police.

I participated in many informal conversations. Unless pushed to do so, I seldom divulged my opinions. I was more open with my feelings about situations and showed empathy. I learned quickly that providing an opinion can backfire. I agreed that one of the women was struggling a lot and stated that I felt sorry for her. While I meant to indicate my genuine concern for her, she heard that I felt sorry for her because she was a failure. When she finally, after several weeks, talked with me again, I was able to explain to her that I was not judging her, but rather felt concerned for her. She remained cynical and many times asked me for favors to make up for my mistake. It took me months before I felt comfortable telling her that I felt I had done enough and that it was time to let go. However, if she was not ready, she needed to know that I would no longer go along. This was one of many occasions when I learned that although I wanted to facilitate my work as a researcher, that I wanted people to like and trust me, I also needed to set boundaries.

Rainy and slow nights often provided good opportunities for me to participate in conversations with groups of women. Popular topics included how to work safely, what to do about condom use, how to make more money. I often served as a health educator and a supplier of condoms, gels, vaginal douches, and other feminine products. Many women were very worried about the AIDS epidemic. However, they also were worried about how to use a condom when a customer refused to do so. They worried particularly about condom use when they needed money badly and, consequently, did not want to propose that the customer use one for fear of rejection. While some women became experts at "making" their customers use a condom—for example, by hiding it in their mouth prior to beginning oral sex—others would carry condoms to please me but never pull one out. If a woman was HIV positive and I knew she failed to use a condom, I faced the ethical dilemma of challenging her or staying out of it.

Developing trusting relationships with crack prostitutes was more difficult. Crack houses were not the right environment for informal conversations. Typically, the atmosphere was tense and everyone was suspicious of each other. The best times to talk with these women were when we bought groceries together, when I helped them clean their homes, or when we shared a meal. Often the women were very different when they were not high than they were when they were high or craving crack. In my conversations with them, I learned that while I might have observed their actions the night before, they themselves might not remember them. Once I realized this, I would be very careful to omit any detail unless I knew that the woman herself did remember the event.

In-Depth Interviews

All interviews were conducted in a private setting, including women's residences, my car or my office, a restaurant of the women's choice, or any other setting the women selected. I did not begin conducting official interviews until I developed relationships with the women. Acquiring written informed consent prior to the interview was problematic. It made me feel awkward. Here I was asking the women to sign a form after they had begun to trust me. However, often I felt more upset about this technicality than the women themselves. As soon as they realized that the form was something the university required, they seemed to understand. Often they laughed about the official statements, and some asked if I was sure the form was to protect them and not the school. None of the women refused to sign the consent form, although some refused to sign it right away and asked to be interviewed later.

In some instances the consent procedures caused the women to expect a formal interview. Some of them were disappointed when they saw I only had a few structured questions about demographic characteristics, followed by a long list of open-ended questions. When this disappointment occurred, I reminded the women that I wanted to learn from them and that the best way to do so was by engaging in a dialogue rather than interrogating them. Only by letting the women identify their salient issues and the topics they wanted to address was I able to gain an insider's perspective. By being a careful listener and probing for additional information and explanation, I as the interviewer, together with the women, was able to uncover the complexities of their lives. In addition, the nature of the interview allowed me to ask questions about contradictions in a woman's story. For example, sometimes a woman would say that she always used a condom. However, later on in the conversation she would indicate that if she needed drugs she would never use one. By asking her to elaborate on this, I was able to begin developing insights into condom use by type of partner, type of sex acts, and social context.

The interviewer becomes much more a part of the interview when the conversations are in-depth than when a structured questionnaire is used. Because I was so integral to the process, the way the women viewed me may have biased their answers. On the one hand, this bias might be reduced because of the extent to which both parties already knew each other; on the other, a woman might fail to give her true opinion and reveal her actions if she knew that these went against the interviewer's opinion. I suspected that some women played down the ways in which their pimps manipulated them once they knew that I was not too fond of these men. However, some might have taken more time to explain the relationship with their pimp in order to "correct" my image.

My background, so different from that of these women, most likely affected the nature of the interviews. I occupied a higher socioeconomic status. I had a place to live and a job. In contrast to the nonwhite women, I came from a different racial background. While I don't know to what extent these differences played a role, I acknowledge that they must have had some effect on this research.

Leaving the Field

Leaving the field was not something that occurred after completion of the fieldwork, but an event that took place daily. Although I sometimes stayed on the strolls all night or hung out for several days, I always had a home to return to. I had a house with electricity, a warm shower, a comfortable bed, and a kitchen. My house sat on a street where I had no fear of being shot on my way there and where I did not find condoms or syringes on my doorstep.

During several stages of the study, I had access to a car, which I used to give the women rides or to run errands together. However, I will never forget the cold night when everyone on the street was freezing, and I left to go home. I turned up the heat in my car, and tears streamed down my cheeks. I appreciated the heat, but I felt more guilty about that luxury than ever before. I truly felt like an outsider, or maybe even more appropriate, a betrayer.

Throughout the years of fieldwork, there were a number of times when I left the scene temporarily. For example, when so many people were dying from AIDS, I was unable to ignore the devastating impact of this disease. I needed an emotional break.

Physically removing myself from the scene was common when I experienced difficulty remaining objective. Once I became too involved in a woman's life and almost adopted her and her family. Another time I felt a true hatred for a crack house owner and was unable to adhere to the rules of courteous interactions. Still another time, I got angry with a woman whose steady partner was HIV positive when she failed to ask him to use a condom when they had sex.

I also took temporary breaks from a particular scene by shifting settings and neighborhoods. For example, I would invest most of my time in women from a particular crack house for several weeks. Then I would shift to spending more time on one of the strolls, while making shorter and less frequent visits to the crack house. By shifting scenes, I was able to tell people why I was leaving and to remind all of us of my researcher role.

While I focused on leaving the field, I became interested in women who had left the life. It seemed important to have an understanding of their past and current circumstances. I knew some of them from the days when they were working, but identifying others was a challenge. There was no gathering place for ex-prostitutes. Informal networking, advertisements in local newspapers, and local clinics and community settings allowed me to reach twenty of these women. Conducting interviews with them later in the data collection process prepared me to ask specific questions. I realized that I had learned enough about the life to know what to ask. Interviewing ex-prostitutes also prepared me for moving from the fieldwork to writing.

It is hard to determine exactly when I left the field. It seems like a process that never ends. Although I was more physically removed from the scene, I continued to be involved while analyzing the data and writing this book. I also created opportunities to go back, for example, by asking women to give me feedback on parts of the manuscript or at times when I experienced writer's block and my car seemed to automatically steer itself to one of the strolls. I also have developed other research projects in some of the same communities. For example, both a project on intergenerational drug use and a gender-specific intervention project to help women remain HIV negative have brought me back to the same population. Some of the women have become key respondents in these new projects, while others now are members of a research team. For example, Beth, one of the women who has left prostitution, works as an outreach worker on another project.

Six Themes in the Ethnography of Prostitution

The main intention of my work is to provide the reader with a perspective on street prostitution from the point of view of the women themselves. There are six fundamental aspects of the women's lives as prostitutes that must be considered. The first concerns the women's own explanations for their involvement in prostitution and their descriptions of the various circumstances that led them to become prostitutes. Their stories include justifications such as traumatic past experiences, especially sexual abuse, the lack of love they experienced as children, pressures by friends and pimps, the need for drugs, and most prominently, the economic forces that pushed them into the life. A number of women describe these justifications as excuses, as reflective explanations they have developed after becoming a prostitute.

The women describe the nature of their initial experiences, which often involved alienation from those outside the life. They also show the differences in the processes between women who work as prostitutes and use drugs and women who do not use drugs.

Although all these women work either on the street or in drug-use settings, their lives do differ. My second theme is a typology that captures these differences, looking at the women's prostitution versus drug-use identities. The typology distinguishes among (a) streetwalkers, women who work strolls and who do not use drugs; (b) hooked prostitutes, women who identify themselves mainly as prostitutes but who upon their entrance into the life also began using drugs; (c) prostituting addicts, women who view themselves mainly as drug users and who became prostitutes to support their drug habit; and (d) crack prostitutes, women who trade sex for crack.

This typology explains the differences in the women's strategies for soliciting customers, their screening of customers, pricing of sex acts, and bargaining for services. For example, the street-walkers have the most bargaining power, while such power appears to be lacking among the crack prostitutes.

Few prostitutes work in a vacuum. The third theme is the role of pimps, a label that most women dislike and for which they prefer to substitute "old man" or "boyfriend." Among the pimps, one finds entrepreneur lovers, men who mainly employ street-walkers and hooked prostitutes and sometimes prostituting addicts. Entrepreneur lovers engage in the life for business reasons. They treat the women as their employees or their property and view them primarily as an economic commodity. The more successful a woman is in earning them money, the more difficult it is for that woman to leave her entrepreneur pimp.

Most prostituting addicts and some hooked prostitutes work for a lover pimp, a man who is their steady partner but who also lives off their earnings. Typically, such pimps employ only one woman. The dynamics in the relationship between a prostitute and her lover pimp become more complex when both partners use drugs. Drugs often become the glue of the relationship.

For many crack prostitutes, their crack addiction serves as a pimp. Few plan to exchange sex for crack when they first begin using; often several weeks or months pass before a woman who barters sex for crack realizes that she is a prostitute.

Historically, society has blamed prostitutes for introducing sexually transmitted diseases into the general population. Similarly, it makes them scapegoats for the spread of HIV/AIDS. Yet their pimps and customers are not held accountable. The fourth theme in the anthropological study of prostitution is the impact of the AIDS epidemic on the women's lives. Although most are knowledgeable about HIV risk behaviors and the ways to reduce their risk, many misconceptions exist. The women describe the complexities of condom use, especially with steady partners but also with paying customers. Many women have mixed feelings about HIV testing, wondering how to cope with a positive test result while no cure is available. A few of the women already knew their HIV-infected status, and the discussion touches on their dilemmas as well.

The fifth theme is the violence and abuse that make common appearances in the women's lives. An ethnography of prostitution must allow the women to describe violence in their neighborhoods as well as violence in prostitution and drug-use settings. The most common violence they encounter is from customers. These men often assume that because they pay for sex they buy a woman. Apparently, casual customers pose more of a danger than those who are regulars. The types of abuse the women encounter are emotional, physical, and sexual. In addition to customers, pimps and boyfriends abuse the women. Finally, the women discuss harassment by law enforcement officers.

When I talked with the women, it often seemed that there were no opportunities to escape from the life. Yet the sixth and final theme must be the escape from prostitution. Women who have left prostitution can describe the process of their exit from prostitution. As ex-prostitutes they struggle with the stigma of their past, the challenges of developing a new identity, and the impact of their past on current intimate relationships. Those who were also drug users often view themselves as ex-prostitutes and recovering addicts, a perspective that seems to create a role conflict. Overall, most ex-prostitutes find that their past follows them like a bad hangover.

Review Questions

1. Based on reading this selection, how is ethnographic research different from other social science approaches to research?

2. What can ethnographic research reveal that other forms of research cannot? What can the use of questionnaires and observational experiments reveal about people that ethnographic research might miss?

3. What were some of the techniques used by Sterk to enter the field, conduct her research, and leave the field? What problems did she face?

4. What advice does Sterk have for aspiring ethnographers?

5. What are some of the ethical issues faced by anthropologists when they conduct ethnographic research?

5

Lessons from the Field

George Gmelch

Ethnographic fieldwork is a valued tradition in anthropology. Most anthropologists believe that the experience of living and working in another culture is essential to successful research. They also realize, however, that there is more to the experience than discovering and describing the culture of others. Like a rite of passage, fieldwork is an intense personal experience, one that yields deeper insight into one's own culture and personal life. It is this reflexive power of fieldwork that George Gmelch discusses in this revised and updated version of "Lessons from the Field." He bases his analysis on the experiences of undergraduate students he has sent to do fieldwork in Barbados since 1978. He argues that, after a stressful beginning, students gain valuable new insight into their own views on materialism, gender, race, social class, the United States, and the value of education as well as Barbadian culture.

Sara, Eric, and Kristen heave their backpacks and suitcases—all the gear they'll need for the next ten weeks—into the back of the institute's battered Toyota pickup. Sara, a tense grin on her face, gets up front with me; the others climb in the back and try to make themselves comfortable on the luggage.

Leaving Bellairs Research Institute on the west coast of Barbados, we drive north past the island's posh resorts. Their names—Cobblers Cove, Coral Reef Club, Coconut Creek, and Glitter Bay—evoke images of tropical paradise. The scene changes abruptly once we leave the coast and move from tourism to agriculture. Here, amid the green and quiet of rolling sugar cane fields, there are no more white faces. Graceful cabbage palms flank a large plantation house, one of the island's former "great houses." On the edge of its cane fields is a tenantry, a cluster of small board houses whose inhabitants are the descendants of the slaves who once worked on the plantation.

Two monkeys emerge from a gully and cross the road. I tell Sara that they came to Barbados aboard slave ships 300 years ago, but she is absorbed in her own thoughts and doesn't seem to hear me. I've taken enough students to the field to have an idea of what's on her mind. What will her village be like? (The one we just passed through looked unusually poor.) Will the family she is going to live with like her? Will she like them? Will she be up to the challenge? Many people are walking along the road; clusters of men sit outside a rum shop shouting loudly while slamming dominoes on a wobbly plywood table.

Earlier in the day, Eric told me that many of the ten students in the field program thought they had made a mistake coming to Barbados. If they had chosen to go on the term abroad to Greece or England or even Japan, they mused, they would be together on a campus, among friends. They wouldn't have to live in a village. They wouldn't have to go out and meet people and try to make friends with all these strangers. To do it all alone now seemed more of a challenge than many wanted.

We continue driving toward the northeastern corner of the island to the village of Pie Corner, where Sara will live. Several miles out we can see huge swells rolling in off the Atlantic, beating against the cliffs. This is the unsheltered side of the island. The village only has a few hundred people but six churches. Marcus Hinds and his family all come out to the truck to welcome Sara. Mrs. Hinds gives her a big hug, as though she were a returning relative, and daughter Yvette takes her into the yard to show her the pigs and chickens, and then on a tour of the small house. The bedroom is smaller than Sara imagined, barely larger than the bed. She puzzles over where to put all her stuff, while I explain to the Hinds, again, the nature of the program. Sara, I tell them, will be spending most of her time in the village talking to people and participating as much as possible in the life of the community, everything from attending church to cutting sugar cane. My description doesn't fit their conception of what a university education is all about. The everyday lives of people in their community are probably not something they think worthy of a university student's attention.

Back in the truck, Eric and Kristen ask me anxiously how their villages compare to Sara's. Kristen begins to bite her nails.

For twenty years I have been taking students to the field with my colleague and wife, Sharon Gmelch, and we have acquired a great deal of knowledge about what students have learned from the foreign cultures in which they live. But it wasn't until serving on a committee that was evaluating my college's international study programs, that I ever thought much about what my students learned about their own culture by living in another. The belief that you have to live abroad before you can truly understand your own culture has gained wide acceptance on college campuses today. But what exactly is it students learn?

I questioned other anthropologists who also took students to the field and they too were unclear about its lessons. A search through the literature didn't help. All the research on the educational outcomes of foreign study had been on students who study at universities abroad, not in more immersive, anthropology field schools.

My curiosity aroused, I decided to examine the experiences of our students in Barbados. Through a questionnaire, interviews, and analysis of their field notes and journals, I looked at their adjustment to Bajan village life and what they learned about themselves and their culture by living on a Caribbean island.

Rural Life

Living in a Barbadian village brings many lessons in the differences between rural and urban. About 90 percent of our students come from suburbs or cities and have never lived in the countryside before. For them, a significant part of their experience in Barbados is living with people who are close to the land. Their host families, like most villagers, grow crops and raise animals. Each morning, before dawn, the students wake to the sounds of animals in the yard. They quickly begin to learn about the behavior of chickens, pigs, sheep, and cows. They witness animals giving birth and being slaughtered. They see the satisfaction families get from consuming food they have produced themselves.

Even inside their village homes the students live close to "nature." They may share their bedrooms with green lizards, mice, cockroaches, and sometimes a whistling frog. They become aware of how different are the sounds of the countryside, and they are struck by the darkness of the sky and the brightness of the stars at night with no city lights to diminish their intensity. A student from Long Island said it was "like living in a planetarium."

The social world of the village is quite unlike the communities they come from. In doing a household survey, they discover that people know virtually everyone in the village. And they often know them in more than one context, not just as neighbors but perhaps also as members of the same church, and as teammates on the village cricket or soccer team. Relationships are not single-stranded as they often are in suburban America.

Most students have never known a place of such intimacy, where relationships are also embedded with so many different meanings and a shared history. In their journals, some students reflect upon and compare the warmth, friendliness, and frequent sharing of food and other resources that occurs in the village with the impersonality, individualism, and detachment of suburban life at home. But they also learn the drawbacks to living in a small community: there is no anonymity. People are nosy and unduly interested in the affairs of their neighbors. The students discover that they too may be the object of local gossip. Several female students learned from village friends that there were stories afoot that they were either mistresses to their host fathers or sleeping with their host brothers. The gossip hurt, for the students—like any anthropologist—had worked hard to gain acceptance and worried about the damage such rumors might do to their reputations.

One of the biggest adjustments students must make to village life is the absence of the diversions and entertainment that they are accustomed to at home. Early in their stay there seems little to do apart from their research. At times they are bored, lonely, and desperate to escape the village, but they are not allowed to leave except on designated days. (All students initially hate this restriction, but by the end of the term they understand the rationale behind it.) This isolation forces students to satisfy their needs for recreation and companionship within their communities. They do so by hanging out with the villagers, a practice which strengthens friendships and results in a good deal of informal education about Bajan life and culture.

Pace of Life

Students discover that the pace of life is slower than home. Much slower. As her host mother explained to Sara, "There are only two speeds in Barbados: slow and dead stop." Languor is an accommodation to the hot, tropical climate. But also, compared to Americans, Bajans are in less of a hurry to get things done. At the shop or post office in town customers wait to be served until the clerk finishes chatting with others. Bajans think little of being late for appointments. Accustomed to the punctuality and hectic pace of North American life, our students are often impatient and frustrated. But as they socialize more with village friends, their compulsive haste begins to dissipate. They sense a different time, one that is unhurried and attuned to the place. They begin to see things they didn't notice before, the bit of earth they're sitting on, the cane fields, the blue sky, and the palm trees. As the term passes, students come to value this unhurried way of life, and by the time they leave the island most are determined to maintain a more tranquil, relaxed lifestyle when they return home.

Race

In Barbados our students become members of a racial minority for the first time in their lives. During their first few weeks in the field they become acutely aware of their own race, of their being white while everyone around them is dark.

Students are often called "white girl" or "white boy" by people in the village until they get to know one another. Village children have sometimes asked to touch a student's skin, marveling at the blue veins that show through it. They sometimes ask students with freckles if they have a skin disease. Others want to feel straight hair. Characteristically, one student during the second week wrote:

> I have never been in a situation before where I was a minority purely due to the color of my skin, and treated differently because of it. When I approach people I am very conscious of having white skin. Before I never thought of myself as having color.

The students are surprised that Barbadians speak so openly about racial difference, something that is not done at home in the United States. A few students become hypersensitive to race during the early weeks of their stay. When leaving their villages, they travel on a crowded bus on which they are the only whites. Often they are stared at. (As the bus heads into the countryside, the passengers may worry that the student has missed his or her stop or has taken the wrong bus.) Students notice that as the bus fills up, the seat next to them is often the last to be taken.

Concerns about race—even the very awareness of race—diminish rapidly, however, as the students make friends and become integrated into their villages. In fact, by the end of the term most said they were "rarely" aware of being white. Several students described incidents in which they had become so unaware of skin color that they were shocked when someone made a remark or did something to remind them of their being different. Kristen was startled when, after shaking her hand, an old woman from her village remarked that she had never touched the hand of a white person before. Several students reported being surprised when they walked by a mirror and got a glimpse of their white skin. One student wrote that although she knew she wasn't black, she no longer felt white.

What is the outcome of all this? Do students now have an understanding of what it means to be a minority, and does this translate into their having more empathy at home? I think so. All the students from the previous Barbados programs whom I questioned about the impact of their experiences mentioned a heightened empathy for African Americans, and some included other minorities as well. Several said that when they first returned home, they wanted to go up to any black person they saw and have a conversation. "But I kept having to remind myself," reported Megan when I saw her on campus later, "that most blacks in America are not West Indians and they wouldn't understand where I am coming from."

Gender

Female students quickly learn that gender relations are quite different in Barbados. Often, the most difficult adjustment for women students is learning how to deal with the frequent and aggressive advances of Bajan men. At the end of her first week in the field, Jenny described a plight common to the students:

> When I walk through the village, the guys who hang out at the rum shop yell comments. I have never heard men say some of the things they tell me here. My friend Andrew tells me that most of the comments are actually compliments. Yet I still feel weird . . . I am merely an object that they would like to conquer. I hate that feeling, so I am trying to get to know these guys. I figure that if they know me as a person and a friend, they will stop with the demeaning comments. Maybe it's a cultural thing they do to all women.

Indeed, many Bajan men feel it is their right as males to accost women in public with hissing, appreciative remarks, and offers of sex. This sexual bantering is tolerated by Bajan women who generally ignore the men's comments. Most women consider it harmless, if annoying; some think it flattering. Students like Jenny, however, are not sure what to make of it. They do not know whether it is being directed at them because local men think white girls are "loose" or whether Bajan men behave in this fashion toward all women. Anxious to be accepted and not wanting to be rude or culturally insensitive, most female students tolerate the remarks the best they can, while searching for a strategy to politely discourage them. Most find that as people get to know them by name, the verbal harassment subsides.

But they still must get accustomed to other sexual behavior. For example, when invited to their first neighborhood parties most are shocked at the sexually explicit dancing, in which movements imitate intercourse. One female student wrote, after having been to several *fetes* or parties:

> I was watching everyone dance when I realized that even the way we dance says a lot about culture. We are so conservative at home. Inhibited. In the U.S. one's body is a personal, private thing, and when it is invaded we get angry. We might give a boyfriend some degree of control over our bodies, but no one else. Bajans aren't nearly as possessive about their bodies. Men and women can freely move from one dance partner to the next without asking, and then grind the other person—it's like having sex with your clothes on.

Students discover that even more than in the United States, women are regarded by men as both subordinates and sexual objects. Masculinity is largely based on men's sexual conquest of women and on their ability to give them pleasure. Being sexually active, a good sex partner, and becoming a father all enhance young men's status among their male peers. As time passes, the students see male dominance in other areas of Barbadian life as well: women earn less than men, are more likely to be unemployed, and are less likely to attain political office, all despite their doing better and going further in school. They conclude that though U.S. society is sexist, Barbados is far more so.

Materialism and Consumption

Many students arrive at a new awareness of wealth and materialism. One of the strongest initial perceptions the students have of their villages is that the people are poor: most of their houses are tiny, their diets are restricted, and they have few of the amenities and comforts the students are accustomed to. Even little things may remind them of the difference in wealth, as Betsy recounted after her first week in the field:

> At home [Vermont] when I go into a convenience store and buy a soda, I don't think twice about handing the clerk a 20 dollar bill. But here when you hand a man in the rum shop a 20 dollar bill [equals $10 US], they often ask if you have something smaller. It makes me self conscious of how wealthy I appear, and of how little money the rum shop man makes in a day.

The initial response of the students to the poverty they perceive around them is to feel embarrassed and even guilty that they have and consume so much. However, as the students get to know families better, they no longer see poverty. Even the houses no longer seem so small. They discover that most people not only manage quite well on what they have but are also reasonably content. In fact, most students eventually come to believe that the villagers are more satisfied with their lives than are most Americans. Regardless of whether this is true, it's an important perception for students, whose ideas about happiness have been shaped by an ethos which measures success and satisfaction materially. About his host family, Dan said:

> I ate off the same plate and drank from the same cup every night. We only had an old fridge, an old stove, and an old TV, and a few dishes and pots and pans. But that was plenty. Mrs. H. never felt like she needed any more. And after awhile I never felt like I needed any more either.

Ellen recounted her reactions to a car that her host father had just purchased.

> He was thrilled, talking about how great this car was. When he pulled up in a used Toyota Corolla, I laughed to myself. It was the exact same car that I had just bought at home, the only car that a poor student could afford, and by American standards certainly nothing flashy. But to my host father it was top of the line, and he was ecstatic. To me it was a reminder that everything is relative . . .

Many said that when they returned home from Barbados they were surprised at the number of their possessions. Compared to Barbadians, their middle-class parents' lifestyle seemed incredibly extravagant and wasteful. When the students return to campus, they don't bring nearly as many things with them as they had before. Some go through their drawers and closets and give the things they don't really need to the Good Will or Salvation Army. Most said they would no longer take luxuries like hot showers for granted. Amy wrote:

> When I came back I saw how out of control the students here are. It's just crazy. They want so much, they talk about how much money they need to make, as if these things are necessities and you'll never be happy without them. Maybe I was like that too, but now I know I don't need those things; sure I'd like a great car, but I don't need it.

When alumni of the program were asked in a survey how they had been changed by their experience in Barbados, most believed they were less materialistic today. For example, Susan said, "I remember bringing some perfume to Barbados because I was used to wearing it every day. But when I got there I only wore it once, it just seemed unnecessary, and I haven't really worn perfume since. Even now, ten years later, I don't mind wearing the same clothes often. I just think Barbados taught me how to find comfort in simple things."

Social Class

American students, particularly compared to their European counterparts, have little understanding of social class. Even after several weeks in Barbados, most students are fairly oblivious to class and status distinctions in their villages. The U.S. suburbs that most grow up in are fairly homogenous in social composition and housing. Most homes fall in the same general price range. In contrast, the Barbadian villages the students live in exhibit a broad spectrum, ranging from large two-story masonry homes usually built by returning migrants to tiny board houses owned by farmers who eke out a living from a few acres. The students are slow to translate such differences in the material conditions of village households into class differences. Also, Barbadians' well-developed class consciousness, fostered by three centuries of British rule, is foreign to U.S. students steeped in a culture that stresses, at least in its rhetoric, egalitarianism.

Students gradually become aware of status distinctions from the comments that their host families make about other people. But they also learn about class and status by making mistakes, by violating norms concerning relationships between different categories of people. After Kristen walked home through the village carrying a bundle on her head, she learned that there are different standards of behavior for the more affluent families. "Mrs. C. told me never to do that again, that only poor people carry things on their heads, and that my doing it reflected badly on her family."

As in most field situations, the first villagers to offer the student friendship are sometimes marginal members of the community. This creates special problems because the students are usually guests in the homes of respectable and often high-status village families. Host parents become upset when they discover their student has been seeing a disreputable man or woman. Most serious is the occasional female student who goes out with a lower-class local man or "beach boy." She enters into this relationship oblivious to what the local reaction might be, and equally oblivious to how little privacy there is in a village where everyone knows everyone else's business. Amy said she wrongly assumed that people would look favorably upon her going out with a local guy because it would show that she wasn't prejudiced and that she found blacks just as desirable as whites. Johanna was befriended by some Rastafarians living nearby—orthodox Rastas who wore no clothes, lived off the land, and slept in caves in the hills above her village. When villagers discovered she had been seeing the Rastas, her home stay mother nearly evicted her and others gave her the cold shoulder. Johanna wrote in her field notes, "I have discovered the power of a societal norm: nice girls don't talk to Rastas. When girls who were formerly nice talk to Rastas, they cease to be known as nice. Exceptions none."

New Perspectives on Being American

In learning about Barbadian society, students inevitably compare Barbadian customs to the way things are done at home in the United States. The students are often assisted in such comparisons by villagers who are curious and ask questions. Most villagers already have opinions about the United States, mostly formed from watching American television and movies, from observing visiting tourists, and, for some, from their own travel. The students are surprised at how much Bajans, even those who are less educated, know about the United States. They discover, however, that the villagers' perspectives are often at odds with their own. Jay put it best: "They have a love/hate attitude towards the U.S. They think of the U.S. as a great place to shop, and that we have good movies and good fashion. But, they also think we are dumb, too talkative, too full of ourselves, too patriotic, and that our government is dangerous." Indeed, most students learn that Bajans like the open friendliness and sunny optimism of individual Americans, and they admire the economic opportunities and freedoms the society affords. But they also think middle-class Americans are pampered and overly materialistic. Bajans are puzzled about why such a wealthy nation has so many people living in poverty and in prisons, and why, unlike poor Caribbean islands, there is not good health care for everyone. They also don't think black people get a fair shake in the United States.

Early in the term, students often find themselves defending the United States from criticism and stereotypes. Jay described in his journal getting very annoyed when a guest at his host family's dinner table railed against the United

States and talked about the chemical adulteration of American chicken. He knew this to be true, but later he said, "I couldn't take it anymore and fought back. I felt like an idiot afterward, defending American chicken."

Over time, the students become less defensive, and more sympathetic to the criticisms, particularly to the notion of Americans as pampered and wastefully materialistic, and the feeling that the U.S. government is somewhat of an international bully. What makes our students question their own society after a few months in Barbados? Part of the answer is found in their growing appreciation of Bajan life and local people. They begin to see things from the perspective of their village friends. They begin to understand the degree to which American culture—especially its media, music, entertainment, and consumer goods—overwhelms local cultures. They see that many Bajans, for example, know more about the President of the United States than their own Governor General or Prime Minister, and that they know Tiger Woods and Kobe Bryant better than their own cricket stars. Some students become quite critical of the U.S. government, especially its often unilateral and self-interested policies, as when it refused to sign international treaties on global warming, on land mines, and on a World Criminal Court.

The students' exposure to North Americans vacationing in Barbados also influences their perceptions of themselves as Americans. When they go to the beach or town, they often encounter tourists and are reminded of villagers' criticisms. They are sometimes embarrassed by what they see and hear—Americans who are loud, demanding, and even condescending in their dealings with locals. Some tourists (though not just Americans) enter shops and walk the streets in skimpy beach attire never thinking that it may be offensive to local people. Students are appalled that tourists can come all the way to Barbados to vacation and hardly know anything about the place or its people. They are irritated that many tourists only view Barbados as a playground—a place to lounge on the beach, swim, snorkel, dive, sail, dance, and drink—and have little curiosity about its geography, history of colonization and slavery, or current underdevelopment. They are horrified when they themselves are mistaken for tourists, since they take pride in their knowledge of local culture. One outcome of this, say the alumni of the field programs, is that when they travel today they believe they are more curious and sensitive than other tourists. Some even try to pass themselves off as Canadian.

Education

Most students return home from Barbados with a more positive attitude toward education. I believe this stems both from their experiences in doing research and from seeing the high value that villagers place on formal education, which is their chief means of upward mobility. Students are accorded respect and adult status largely because they are working toward a university degree. Also, as the weeks pass, most students become deeply involved in their own research. They are surprised at how much satisfaction they get from doing something that they previously regarded as "work." Students from past terms have said they didn't see education as an end in itself, something to be enjoyed, until doing fieldwork in Barbados. Emily wrote about her attitude change after returning from the field:

> I feel isolated from many of my old friends on campus, and I no longer feel guilty missing social events. . . . I appreciate my education more and I do much more work for my own understanding and enjoyment rather than just for the exam or grades. I find myself on a daily basis growing agitated with those who don't appreciate what is being offered to them here. Several of my classmates blow off class and use other peoples' notes. A lot of what I feel is from seeing how important education was to my Bajan friends in Barbados compared to the lax attitude of my friends here.

Students spend much of their time in the field talking to people; a good part of each day is spent in conversations that they must direct onto the topics that they are investigating. To succeed at their studies, they learn to be inquisitive, to probe sensitively into the villager's knowledge of events and culture. They learn to concentrate, to listen to what they are being told, and to recall it later so that they can record it in field notes. They become proficient at maintaining lengthy conversations with adults and at asking pertinent questions. These are interpersonal and communication skills they bring back with them and make use of in many aspects of their own lives and in their future work.

Clearly, getting to know another culture is to look in the proverbial mirror and get a glimpse of oneself and of what it means to be American. As the world's economies intertwine and its societies move closer to becoming a "global village," it is more imperative than ever that we seek to understand other peoples and cultures. Without understanding there can be neither respect, mutual prosperity, nor lasting peace. "The tragedy about Americans," noted Mexican novelist Carlos Fuentes, "is that they understand others so little." Students who study abroad not only enrich themselves, but, in countless small ways, also help bridge the gulf between "them" and "us."

Review Questions

1. What are the main ways that fieldwork in Barbados changes students' perceptions of their own culture and personal lives?

2. How does the behavior of U.S. tourists in Barbados change students' perception of their own nation?

3. How does life in a Barbadian rural community affect students' views of U.S. materialism, gender, and social class?

4. How do you think fieldwork achieves the personal transformations described by Gmelch in the students he has sent to Barbados?

TWO

Language and Communication

Culture is a system of symbols that allows us to represent and communicate our experience. We are surrounded by symbols: the flag, a new automobile, a diamond ring, billboard pictures, and, of course, spoken words.

A **symbol** is anything that we can perceive with our senses that stands for something else. Almost anything we experience can come to have symbolic meaning. Every symbol has a referent that it calls to our attention. The term *lawn*, for example, refers to a field of grass plants. When we communicate with symbols, we call attention not only to the referent but also to numerous connotations of the symbol. In U.S. culture we associate lawns with places such as homes and golf courses; actions such as mowing, fertilizing, and raking; and activities such as backyard games and barbeques. Human beings have the capacity to assign meaning to anything they experience in an arbitrary fashion, which allows limitless possibilities for communication.

Symbols greatly simplify the task of communication. Once we learn that a word such as *barn*, for example, stands for a certain type of building, we can communicate about a whole range of specific buildings that fit into the category. And we can communicate about barns in their absence; we can even invent flying barns and dream about barns. Symbols make it possible to communicate the immense variety of human experience, whether past or present, tangible or intangible, good or bad.

Many channels are available to human beings for symbolic communication: sound, sight, touch, and smell. Language, our most highly developed communication system, uses the channel of sound (or, for some deaf people, sight). **Language** is a system of cultural knowledge used to generate and interpret speech. It is a feature of every culture and a distinctive characteristic of the human animal. **Speech** refers to the behavior that produces vocal sounds. Our distinction between language and speech is like the one made between culture and behavior. Language is part of culture, the system of knowledge that generates behavior. Speech is the behavior generated and interpreted by language.

Every language is composed of three subsystems for dealing with vocal symbols: phonology, grammar, and semantics. Let's look briefly at each of these.

Phonology consists of the categories and rules for forming vocal symbols. It is concerned not directly with meaning but with the formation and recognition of the vocal sounds to which we assign meaning. For example, if you utter the word *bat,* you have followed a special set of rules for producing and ordering sound categories characteristic of the English language.

A basic element defined by phonological rules for every language is the phoneme. **Phonemes** are the minimal categories of speech sounds that serve to keep utterances apart. For example, speakers of English know that the words *bat, cat, mat, hat, rat,* and *fat* are different utterances because they hear the sounds /b/, /c/, /m/, /h/, /r/, and /f/ as different categories of sounds. In English, each of these is a phoneme. Our language contains a limited number of phonemes from which we construct all our vocal symbols.

Phonemes are arbitrarily constructed, however. Each phoneme actually classifies slightly different sounds as though they were the same. Different languages may divide up the same range of speech sounds into different sound categories. For example, speakers of English treat the sound /t/ as a single phoneme. Hindi speakers take the same general range and divide it into four phonemes: /t/, /t^h/, /T/, and /T^h/. (The lowercase *t*'s are made with the tongue against the front teeth, while the uppercase *T*'s are made by touching the tongue to the roof of the mouth further back than would be normal for an English speaker. The *h* indicates a puff of air, called *aspiration,* associated with the *t* sound.) Americans are likely to miss important distinctions among Hindi words because they hear these four different phonemes as a single one. Hindi speakers, on the other hand, tend to hear more than one sound category as they listen to English speakers pronounce *t*'s. The situation is reversed for /w/ and /v/. We treat these as two phonemes, whereas Hindi speakers hear them as one. For them, the English words *wine* and *vine* sound the same.

Phonology also includes rules for ordering different sounds. Even when we try to talk nonsense, we usually create words that follow English phonological rules. It would be unlikely, for example, for us ever to begin a word with the phoneme /ng/—usually written in English as "ing." It must come at the end or in the middle of words.

Grammar is the second subsystem of language. **Grammar** refers to the categories and rules for combining vocal symbols. No grammar contains rules for combining every word or element of meaning in the language. If this were the case, grammar would be so unwieldy that no one could learn all the rules in a lifetime. Every grammar deals with *categories* of symbols, such as the ones we call *nouns* and *verbs.* Once you know the rules covering a particular category, you can use it in appropriate combinations.

Morphemes are the categories in any language that carry meaning. They are minimal units of meaning that cannot be subdivided. Morphemes occur in more complex patterns than you may think. The term *bats*, for example, is actually two morphemes, /bat/ meaning a flying mammal and /s/ meaning plural. Even more confusing, two different morphemes may have the same sound shape. /Bat/ can refer to a wooden club used in baseball as well as a flying mammal.

The third subsystem of every language is semantics. **Semantics** refers to the categories and rules for relating vocal symbols to their referents. Like the rules of grammar, semantic rules are simple instructions for combining things; they instruct us to combine words with what they refer to. A symbol can be said to *refer* because it focuses our attention and makes us take account of something. For example, /bat/ refers to a family of flying mammals, as we have already noted.

Language regularly occurs in a social context, and to understand its use fully it is important to recognize its relation to sociolinguistic rules. **Sociolinguistic rules** combine meaningful utterances with social situations into appropriate messages.

Although language is the most important human vehicle for communication, almost anything we can sense may represent a **nonlinguistic symbol** that conveys meaning. The way we sit, how we use our eyes, how we dress, the car we own, the number of bathrooms in our house—all these things carry symbolic meaning. We learn what they mean as we acquire culture. Indeed, a major reason we feel so uncomfortable when we enter a group from a strange culture is our inability to decode our host's symbolic world.

The articles in this part illustrate several important aspects of language and communication. The first, by David Thomson, describes the hypothesis generated in the 1930s by a young linguist named Benjamin Lee Whorf. Whorf argued that, instead of merely labeling reality, the words and grammatical structure of a language can actually determine the way its speakers perceive the world. Thomson reviews and evaluates this hypothesis and shows that, although language may not create reality, it can affect our perceptions, as illustrated by the use of words in U.S. advertising and political doublespeak. The second selection, by James Spradley and Brenda Mann, focuses on the sociolinguistic rules that organize communication. Using the example of a seemingly simple act, asking for a drink in a bar, they show how it represents one of a complex set of speech events that involve speech acts and components of speech acts. The result is a message that far exceeds the literal meaning of words alone. The third article, by Enid Schildkrout, looks at nonverbal symbols, notably those that humans send with body art. From tattoos to makeup, body art is used to convey life-change events, group membership, and a variety of other messages. The final selection, by Deborah Tannen, looks at another aspect of language—conversation styles. Focusing on the different speaking styles of men and women in the workplace, she describes and analyzes how conversation styles themselves carry meaning and unwittingly lead to misunderstanding.

Key Terms

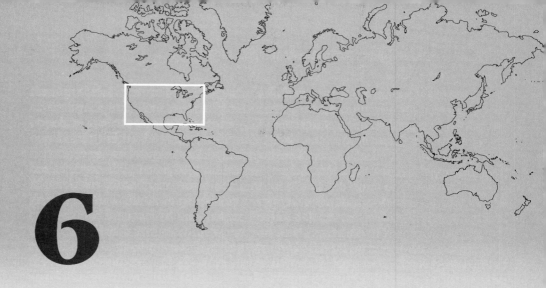

6

The Sapir-Whorf Hypothesis: Worlds Shaped by Words

David S. Thomson

For many people, language mirrors reality. Words are labels for what we sense; they record what is already there. This view, which is another manifestation of what we have called naive realism, *is clearly challenged by previous selections in this book. Members of different societies may not share cultural categories; words from one language often cannot be translated directly into another. In the 1930s, a young linguist named Benjamin Lee Whorf took the objection to the "words label reality" assertion one step further by arguing that words and grammatical structure actually shape reality. This piece by David Thomson describes Whorf's theory, shows how linguists have evaluated it, and applies it in modified form to the use of words, euphemisms, and doublespeak in the modern United States.*

The scene is the storage room at a chemical plant. The time is evening. A night watchman enters the room and notes that it is partially filled with gasoline drums. The drums are in a section of the room where a sign says "Empty Barrels." The watchman lights a cigarette and throws the still-hot match into one of the empty barrels.

The result: an explosion.

The immediate cause of the explosion, of course, was the gasoline fumes that remained in the barrels. But it could be argued that a second cause of the explosion was the English language. The barrels were empty of their original contents and so belonged under the empty sign. Yet they were not empty of everything—the fumes were still present. English has no word—no single term—that can convey such a situation. Containers in English are either empty or they are not; there is no word describing the ambiguous state of being empty and yet not empty. There is no term in the language for "empty but not quite" or "empty of original contents but with something left over." There being no word for such an in-between state, it did not occur to the watchman to think of the explosive fumes.

This incident is hypothetical, but the questions about language it raises are real. The example of the gasoline drums often was cited by Benjamin Lee Whorf to illustrate a revolutionary theory he had about language. Whorf was an unusual man who combined two careers, for he was both a successful insurance executive and a brilliant (and largely self-taught) linguistic scholar. Language, he claimed, may be shaped by the world, but it in turn shapes the world. He reasoned that people can think about only those things that their language can describe or express. Without the words or structures with which to articulate a concept, that concept will not occur. To turn the proposition around, if a language is rich in ways to express certain sorts of ideas, then the speakers of that language will habitually think along those linguistic paths. In short, the language that humans speak governs their view of reality; it determines their perception of the world. The picture of the universe shifts from tongue to tongue.

The originator of this startling notion came from an intellectually active New England family. Whorf's brother John became an artist of note and his brother Richard a consummately professional actor. Benjamin's early bent was not for drawing or acting but photography, especially the chemistry that was involved in developing pictures, and this interest may have influenced his choice of the Massachusetts Institute of Technology, where he majored in chemical engineering. After he was graduated from M.I.T. he became a specialist in fire prevention and in 1919 went to work for the Hartford Fire Insurance Company. His job was to inspect manufacturing plants, particularly chemical plants, that the Hartford insured to determine whether they were safe and thus good insurance risks. He quickly became highly skilled at his work. "In no time at all," wrote C. S. Kremer, then the Hartford's board chairman, "he became in my opinion as thorough and fast a fire prevention inspector as there ever has been."

Whorf was a particularly acute chemical engineer. On one occasion he was refused admittance to inspect a client's building because, a company official maintained, a secret process was in use here. "You are making such-and-such a product?" asked Whorf. "Yes," said the official. Whorf pulled out a pad and scribbled the formula of the supposedly secret process, adding coolly, "You couldn't do it any other way." Needless to say, he was allowed to inspect the building. Whorf rose in the Hartford hierarchy to the post of assistant secretary of the company in 1940. But then in 1941 his health, never strong, gave way, and he died at the early age of forty-four.

While Whorf was becoming a successful insurance executive, he was also doing his revolutionary work in linguistics. He started by studying Hebrew but then switched to Aztec and other related languages of Mexico. Later he deciphered Maya inscriptions, and tried to reconstruct the long-lost language of the ancient Maya people of Mexico and Central America. Finally he tackled the complexities of the still-living language of the Hopi Indians of Arizona. He published his findings in respected anthropological and linguistic journals, earning the praise and respect of scholars in the two fields—all without formal training in linguistic science. As his fame as a linguist spread, the Hartford obligingly afforded him vacations and leaves to travel to the Southwest in pursuit of the structure and lexicon of the Hopi. He also put in countless hours in the Watkinson Library in Connecticut, a rich repository of Mexican and Indian lore.

It was primarily his study of Hopi that impelled Whorf toward his revolutionary ideas. He was encouraged and aided by the great cultural anthropologist and linguist of Yale, Edward Sapir, and the idea that language influences a person's view of the world is generally known as the Sapir-Whorf hypothesis. Whorf formulated it a number of times, but perhaps his clearest statement comes from his 1940 essay "Science and Linguistics": "The background linguistic system (in other words, the grammar) of each language is not merely a reproducing instrument for voicing ideas but rather is itself the shaper of ideas. . . . We dissect nature along lines laid down by our native language. The categories and types that we isolate from the world of phenomena we do not find there because they stare every observer in the face; on the contrary, the world is presented in a kaleidoscopic flux of impressions which has to be organized by our minds—and this means largely by the linguistic systems in our minds."

These ideas developed from Whorf's study of the Hopi language. He discovered that it differs dramatically from languages of the Indo-European family such as English or French, particularly in its expression of the concept of time. English and its related languages have three major tenses—past, present, and future ("it was," "it is," "it will be")—plus the fancier compound tenses such as "it will have been." Having these tenses, Whorf argued, encourages Europeans and Americans to think of time as so many ducks in a row. Time past is made up of uniform units of time—days, weeks, months, years—and the future is similarly measured out. This division of time is essentially artificial, Whorf said, since people can only experience the present. Past and future are only abstractions, but Westerners think of them as real because their language virtually forces them to do so. This view of time has given rise to the fondness in Western cultures for diaries, records, annals, histories, clocks, calendars, wages paid by the hour or day, and elaborate timetables for the use of future time. Time is continually quantified. If Westerners set out to build a house they establish a deadline; the work will be completed at a specified time in the future, such as May 5 or October 15.

Hopis do not behave this way; when they start to weave a mat they are not concerned about when it will be completed. They work on it desultorily, then quit, then begin again; the finished product may take weeks. This casual progress is not laziness but a result of the Hopi's view of time—one symptom of the fact that their language does not have the past, present, and future tenses. Instead it possesses two modes of thought: the objective, that is, things that exist now, and the subjective, things that can be thought about and therefore belong to a state of becoming. Things do not become in terms of a future measured off in days, weeks, months. Each thing that is becoming has its own individual life rhythms, growing or declining or changing in much the same manner as a plant grows, according to its inner nature. The essence of Hopi life, therefore, Whorf said, is preparing in the present so that those things that are capable of becoming can in fact come to pass. Thus weaving a mat is preparing a mat to become a mat; it will reach that state when its nature so ordains—whenever that will be.

This view of the future is understandable, Whorf noted, in an agricultural people whose welfare depends on the proper preparing of earth and seeds and plants for the hoped-for harvest. It also helps explain why the Hopi have such elaborate festivals, rituals, dances, and magic ceremonies: All are intended to aid in the mental preparation that is so necessary if the crops, which the Hopi believe to be influenced by human thought, are to grow properly. This preparing involves "much visible activity," Whorf said, "introductory formalities, preparing of special food . . . intensive sustained muscular activity like running, racing, dancing, which is thought to increase the intensity of development of events (such as growth of crops), mimetic and other magic preparations based on esoteric theory involving perhaps occult instruments like prayer sticks, prayer feathers, and prayer meal, and finally the great cyclic ceremonies and dances, which have the significance of preparing rain and crops." Whorf went on to note that the very noun for *crop* is derived from the verb that means "to prepare." *Crop* therefore is in the Hopi language literally "the prepared." Further, the Hopi prayer pipe, which is smoked as an aid in concentrating good thoughts on the growing fields of corn and wheat, is named *na'twanpi*, "instrument of preparing."

The past to the Hopi, Whorf believed, is also different from the chronological time sense of the speakers of Indo-European languages. The past is not a uniform row of days or weeks to the Hopi. It is rather an undifferentiated stream in which many deeds were done that have accumulated and prepared the present and will continue to prepare the becoming that is ahead. Everything is connected, everything accumulates. The past is not a series of events, separated and completed, but is present in the present.

To Whorf these striking differences in the Hopi language and sense of time implied that the Hopi live almost literally in another world from the speakers of Indo-European languages. The Hopi language grew out of its speakers' peculiar circumstances: As a geographically isolated agricultural people in a land where rainfall was scanty, they did the same things and prayed the same prayers year after year and thus did not need to have past and future tenses. But the language, once it had developed, perpetuated their particular and seemingly very different world view.

Many linguists and anthropologists who have worked with American Indians of the Southwest have been convinced that Whorf's theories are by and large correct. Other linguists are not convinced, however, and through the years since Whorf's death they have attacked his proposals. The controversy is unlikely to be settled soon, if ever. One of the problems is the difficulty of setting up an experiment that would either prove or disprove the existence of correlations between linguistic structure and nonlinguistic behavior. It would be fruitless to go about asking people of various cultures their opinions as to whether the language they spoke had determined the manner in which they thought, had dictated their view of the world. Nobody would be able to answer such a question, for a people's language is so completely embedded in their consciousness that they would be unable to conceive of any other way of interpreting the world.

Despite the near impossibility of proving or disproving Whorf's theory, it will not go away but keeps coming back, intriguing each succeeding generation of linguists. It is certainly one of the most fascinating theories created by the modern mind. It is comparable in some ways to Einstein's theory of relativity. Just as Einstein said that how people saw the phenomena of the universe was relative to their point of observation, so Whorf said that a people's world view was relative to the language they spoke.

And demonstrations of Whorf's ideas are not entirely lacking. They come mainly from studies of color—one of the very few aspects of reality that can be specified by objective scientific methods and also is rather precisely specified by people's naming of colors. In this instance it is possible to compare one person's language, expressing that person's view of the world, with another's language for exactly the same characteristic of the world. The comparison can thus reveal different views that are linked to different descriptions of the same reality. English-speakers view purple as a single relatively uniform color; only if pressed and then only with difficulty will they make any attempt to divide it into such shades as lavender and mauve. But no English-speaker would lump orange with purple; to the users of English, those colors are completely separate, for no single word includes both of them. If other languages made different distinctions in the naming of color—if lavender and mauve were always separate, never encompassed by a word for purple, or if orange and purple were not distinguished but were called by a name that covered both—then it would seem that the users of those languages interpreted those colors differently.

Such differences in color-naming, it turns out, are fairly widespread. Linguist H. A. Gleason compared the color spectrum as described by English-speaking persons to the way it was labeled by speakers of Bassa, a language spoken in Liberia, and by speakers of Shona, spoken in Rhodesia. English-speaking people, when seeing sunlight refracted through a prism, identify by name at least six colors—purple, blue, green, yellow, orange, and red. The speakers of Shona, however, have only three names for the colors of the spectrum. They group orange, red, and purple under one name. They also lump blue and green-blue under one of their other color terms and use their third word to identify yellow and the yellower hues of green. The speakers of Bassa are similarly restricted by a lack of handy terms for color, for they have only two words for the hues of the spectrum.

Gleason's observations prompted psychologists to perform an experiment that also showed the influence words can have on the way colors are handled intellectually and remembered. It was an ingenious and complex experiment with many checks and double checks of the results, but in essence it boiled down to something like this: English-speaking subjects were shown a series of color samples—rather like the little "chips" provided by a paint store to help customers decide what color to paint the living room. The subjects were then asked to pick out the colors they had seen from a far larger array of colors. It turned out that they could more accurately pick out the right colors from the larger selection when the color involved had a handy, ordinary name like "green." The subjects had difficulty with the ambiguous, in-between colors such as off-purples and misty blues. In other words, a person can remember a color better if that person's language offers a handy label for it, but has trouble when the language does not offer such a familiar term. Again the human ability to differentiate reality seemed to be affected by the resources offered by language.

Richness of linguistic resource undoubtedly helps people to cope with subtle gradations in the things they deal with every day. The Hanunóo people of the Philippine Islands have different names for ninety-two varieties of rice. They can easily distinguish differences in rice that would be all but invisible to English-speaking people, who lump all such grains under the single word *rice.* Of course, English-speakers can make distinctions by resorting to adjectives and perhaps differentiate long-grain, brown rice from small-grain, yellow rice, but surely no European or American would, lacking the terms, have a sufficiently practiced eye to distinguish ninety-two varieties of rice. Language is essentially a code that people use both to think and to communicate. As psychologist Roger Brown sums up the rice question: "Among the Hanunóo, who have names for ninety-two varieties of rice, any one of those varieties is highly codable in the array of ninety-one other varieties. The Hanunóo have a word for it and so can transmit it efficiently and presumably can recognize it easily. Among speakers of English one kind of rice among ninety-one other kinds would have very low codability."

Brown goes on to suppose that the Hanunóo set down in New York would be baffled by the reality around them partly because they would then be the ones lacking the needed words. "If the Hanunóo were to visit the annual Automobile Show in New York City, they would find it difficult to encode distinctively any particular automobile in that array. But an American having such lexical resources as *Chevrolet, Ford, Plymouth, Buick, Corvette, hard-top, convertible, four-door, station wagon,* and the like could easily encode ninety-two varieties."

The very existence of so many different languages, each linked to a distinctive culture, is itself support of a sort for Whorf's hypothesis. At least since the time of the Tower of Babel, no single tongue has been shared by all the people of the world. Many attempts have been made to invent an international language, one so simply structured and easy to learn it would be used by everyone around the globe as a handy adjunct to their native speech. Yet even the most successful of these world languages, Esperanto, has found but limited acceptance.

There are international languages, however, to serve international cultures. The intellectual disciplines of music, dance, and mathematics might be considered specialized cultures; each is shared by people around the world, and each has an international language, used as naturally in Peking as in Paris. English is a world language in certain activities that straddle national boundaries, such as international air travel; it serves for communications between international flights and the ground in every country—a Lufthansa pilot approaching Athens talks with the airport control tower neither in German nor in Greek but in English.

The trouble with most attempts to lend credence to the Sapir-Whorf hypothesis is that, while they indicate connections between culture and language, they do not really prove that a language shaped its users' view of the world. Just because the speakers of Shona have only three main distinctions of color does not mean that their "world view" is all that different from that of the English-speaker who has more convenient color terms. Shona speakers obviously see all the colors in the rainbow that English-speakers see. Their eyes are physiologically the same. Their comparative poverty of words for those colors merely means that it is harder for them to talk about color. Their "code" is not so handy; the colors' codability is lower.

Critics also point out that Whorf may have mistaken what are called dead metaphors for real differences in the Hopi language. All languages are loaded with dead metaphors—figures of speech that have lost all figurative value and are now just familiar words. The word "goodbye" is a dead metaphor. Once it meant "God be with you," but in its contracted form it conjures up no thought or picture of God. If a Whorfian linguist who was a native speaker of Hopi turned the tables and analyzed English he might conclude that English-speakers were perpetually thinking of religion since this everyday word incorporates a reference to God—a ridiculous misreading of a term that has lost all of its original religious significance. In like fashion, perhaps Whorf was read-ing too much into the Hopi lexicon and grammar, seeing significances where there were none.

The argument about how far Whorf's ideas can be stretched has gone on for several decades and promises to go on for several more. Most psychologists believe that all people see pretty much the same reality; their languages merely have different words and structures to approximate in various idiosyncratic ways a picture of that reality. And yet the experts accept what might be called modified Whorfism—a belief in the power of language to affect, if not to direct, the perception of reality. If a language is rich in terms for certain things or ideas—possesses extensive codability for them—then the people speaking that language can conceive of, and talk about, those things or ideas more conve-niently. If different languages do not give their speakers entirely different world views, they certainly influence thinking to some degree.

Even within the Indo-European family of languages, some tongues have words for concepts that other tongues lack. German is especially rich in philo-sophical terms that have no exact counterparts in English, French, Italian—or any known language. One is *Weltschmerz,* which combines in itself meanings that it takes three English phrases to adequately convey—"weariness of life," "pessimistic outlook," and "romantic discontent." Another German word that has no direct translation is *Weltanschauung.* To approximate its meaning in English requires a number of different terms—"philosophy of life," "world out-look," "ideology"—for all of these elements are included in the German word. *Weltanschauung* is untranslatable into any single English term. It represents an idea for which only German has a word. Possessing the convenient term, Ger-man writers can develop this idea more easily than the users of other languages, and thus explore its ramifications further.

Even when a word from one language may seem to be easily translatable into another, it often is not really equivalent. The French term *distingué* would appear to translate easily enough into the English *distinguished.* But the French use their word in ways that no English-speaker would ever employ for *distin-guished.* A Frenchman might reprimand his son by saying that his impolite be-havior was not *distingué* or he might tell his wife that a scarf she has worn out to dinner is charmingly *distingué.* The word does not mean "distinguished" as English-speakers employ the term, but something more like "suitable," or "ap-propriate," or "in keeping with polite standards." It is simply not the same word in the two languages no matter how similar the spelling. It represents a differ-ent idea, connoting a subtle difference in mental style.

In some cases the existence of a word leads users of it down tortured log-ical paths toward dead ends. The common word *nothing* is one example. Since there is a word for the concept, points out philosopher George Pitcher, it tempts people to think that "nothing" is a real entity, that somehow it exists, a palpa-ble realm of not-being. It has in fact led a number of philosophers, including the twentieth-century French thinker Jean-Paul Sartre, to spend a great deal of effort speculating about the nature of "nothing." The difficulty of this philosophic dilemma is indicated by a typical Sartre sentence on the subject: "The Being by which Nothingness arrives in the world must nihilate. Nothingness in its Being, and even so it still runs the risk of establishing Nothingness as a transcendent in the very heart of immanence unless it nihilates Nothingness in its being in connection with its own being." Sartre could hardly have gotten himself tangled up in such agonized prose had French lacked a noun for *le neant*, nothing, and the value to human welfare of his attempt to explain is open to question.

The power of language to influence the world can be seen not only in comparisons of one tongue to another, but also within a single language. The way in which people use their native tongue—choosing one term over another to express the same idea or action, varying structures or phrases for different situations—has a strong effect on their attitudes toward those situations. Distasteful ideas can be made to seem acceptable or even desirable by careful choices of words, and language can make actions or beliefs that might otherwise be considered correct appear to be obsolescent or naive. Value judgments of many kinds can be attached to seemingly simple statements. Shakespeare may have believed that "a rose by any other name would smell as sweet," but he was wrong, as other theatrical promoters have proved repeatedly. A young English vaudevillian known as Archibald Leach was a minor comedian until he was given the more romantic name of Cary Grant. The new name did not make him a star, but it did create an atmosphere in which he could demonstrate his talent, suggesting the type of character he came to exemplify.

If the power of a stage name to characterize personality seems of relatively minor consequence in human affairs, consider the effect of a different sort of appellation: "boy." It was—and sometimes still is—the form of address employed by whites in the American South in speaking to black males of any age. This word, many authorities believe, served as an instrument of subjugation. It implied that the black was not a man but a child, someone not mature enough to be entrusted with responsibility for himself, let alone authority over others. His inferior position was thus made to seem natural and justified, and it could be enforced without compunction.

Characterizing people by tagging them with a word label is a world-wide practice. Many peoples use a single word to designate both themselves and the human race. "The Carib Indians, for example, have stated with no equivocation, 'We alone are people,'" reported anthropologist Jack Conrad. "Similarly, the ancient Egyptians used the word *romet* (men) only among themselves and in no case for strangers. The Lapps of Scandinavia reserve the term 'human being' for those of their own kind, while the Cherokee Indians call themselves *Ani-Yun-wiya*, which means 'principal people.' The Kiowa Indians of the Southwest are willing to accept other peoples as human, but the very name, *Kiowa*, meaning 'real people,' shows their true feeling." The effect of reserving a term indicating "human" to one group is far-reaching. It alters the perception of anyone from outside that group. He is not called "human," and need not be treated as human.

Like an animal, he can be entrapped, beaten, or even killed with more or less impunity. This use of a word to demote whole groups from the human class is often a wartime tactic—the enemy is referred to by a pejorative name to justify killing him.

While language can be twisted to make ordinarily good things seem bad, it can also be twisted in the opposite direction to make bad things seem good or run-of-the-mill things better than they really are. The technique depends on the employment of euphemisms, a term derived from the Greek for "words of good omen." A euphemism is roundabout language that is intended to conceal something embarrassing or unpleasant. Some classes of euphemism—little evasions that people use every day—are inoffensive enough. It is when such cloudy doubletalk invades the vital areas of politics and foreign affairs that it becomes perilous.

A large and commonly used—and relatively harmless—class of euphemism has to do with bodily functions. Many people shy away from frank talk about excretion or sex; in fact, many of the old, vivid terms—the four-letter words—are socially taboo. So people for centuries have skirted the edge of such matters, inventing a rich vocabulary of substitute terms. Americans offered turkey on Thanksgiving commonly say "white meat" or "dark meat" to announce their preference. These terms date back to the nineteenth century when it was considered indelicate to say "breast" or "leg." *Toilet,* itself a euphemism coined from the French *toilette* ("making oneself presentable to the outside world"), long ago became tainted and too graphic for the prudish. The list of euphemistic substitutes is almost endless, ranging from the commonplace *washroom, bathroom,* and *restroom* (whoever rests in a restroom?) to *john, head,* and *Chic Sale* in the United States, and in England the *loo. Loo* may be derived from a mistaken English pronunciation of the French *l'eau,* water. Or it may be a euphemism derived from a euphemism. The French, with Gallic delicacy, once commonly put the number 100 on bathroom doors in hotels. It is easy to see how an English person might have mistaken the number for the word *loo.* Meanwhile, ladies in restaurants have adopted "I'm going to powder my nose" or, in England, where it once cost a penny to use public toilets, "I'm going to spend a penny."

Another generally harmless use of euphemistic language is the practice, especially notable in the United States, of giving prestigious names to more-or-less ordinary trades. As H. L. Mencken pointed out in *The American Language,* his masterly examination of English as spoken in the United States, ratcatchers are fond of calling themselves "exterminating engineers" and hairdressers have long since showed a preference for "beautician." The *-ician* ending, in fact, has proved very popular, doubtless because it echoes "physician" and thus sounds both professional and scientific. In the late nineteenth century undertakers had already begun to call themselves "funeral directors," but starting in 1916 ennobled themselves even further by battening on the newer euphemistic coinage, "mortician." Meanwhile a tree trimmer became a "tree surgeon" (that love of medicine again) and a press agent became a "publicist" or, even more grandly, a "public relations counsel."

Americans (and the English, too) not only chose high-sounding euphemisms for their professions but also gave new and gaudy names to their places of business. Thus pawn shops became "loan offices," saloons became "cocktail rooms," pool halls became "billiard parlors," and barber shops "hairstyling salons."

Purists might say that such shading or blunting of the stark truth leads to moral decay, but it is difficult to see why anybody should be the worse for allowing women to excuse themselves by pleading that they must powder their noses. There are euphemisms, however, that are clearly anything but harmless. These are evasive, beclouding phraseologies that hide truths people must clearly perceive if they are to govern themselves intelligently and keep a check on those in positions of power. Slick phrases, slippery evasions—words deliberately designed to hide unpleasant truth rather than reveal it—can so becloud political processes and so easily hide mistaken policies that the entire health of a nation is imperiled.

The classic treatise on the political misuse of language in modern times is the 1946 essay "Politics and the English Language" by the British writer George Orwell. "In our time, political speech and writing are largely the defence of the indefencible," Orwell said. "Thus political language has to consist largely of euphemism, question-begging and sheer cloudy vagueness." He concluded, "Such phraseology is needed if one wants to name things without calling up mental pictures of them. . . . When there is a gap between one's real and one's declared aims, one turns as it were instinctively to long words and exhausted idioms, like a cuttlefish squirting out ink."

Orwell supplied numerous examples to buttress his charges. "Defenceless villages are bombarded from the air, the inhabitants driven out into the countryside, the cattle machine-gunned, the huts set on fire with incendiary bullets: this is called *pacification.*" He went on to observe that in Stalin's Russia people were "imprisoned for years without trial or shot in the back of the neck or sent to die of scurvy in Arctic lumber camps: this is called *elimination of unreliable elements.*"

Orwell, who died at the age of forty-six in 1950, did not live to collect even more deplorable distortions of language. The French clothed their brutal war in Algeria with a veil of euphemism; the North Koreans accused the South Koreans of "aggression" when the North invaded the South. The United States invented a whole lexicon of gobbledygook to disguise the horror of the war in Vietnam: "protective reaction strike" (the bombing of a Vietnamese village); "surgical bombing" (the same as protective reaction strike); "free-fire zone" (an area in which troops could shoot anything that moved, including helpless villagers); "new life hamlet" (a refugee camp for survivors of a surgical bombing).

Perhaps the most appalling use of this type of euphemism was the word employed by the Nazis for their program to exterminate all of Europe's Jews. The word is *Endlösung,* which means final solution. Behind that verbal façade the Nazis gassed, burned, shot, or worked to death some six million Jews from Germany, France, Poland, and other conquered parts of Europe. Hitler and

Gestapo chief Himmler often employed the euphemism among themselves, and it was always used in official records—but not necessarily to preserve secrecy for purposes of state security. Apparently the euphemism shielded the Nazis from themselves. Openly brutal and murderous as they were, they could not face up to the horrible reality of what they were doing, and they had to hide it in innocuous language.

Such distortion of language can do more than disguise truth. It can turn truth around, so that the idea conveyed is the opposite of actuality. After the USSR savagely crushed the Hungarian rebellion in 1956 the Soviet aggression was made to seem, in the twisted language used by other Communist dictatorships, an expression of friendship. The Peking radio commented after the rebellion was put down: "The Hungarian people can see that Soviet policy toward the people's democracies is truly one of equality, friendship, and mutual assistance, not of conquest, aggression, and plunder."

The possibility that such topsy-turvy language might ultimately make the world topsy-turvy—an ironic demonstration of the fundamental truth of Benjamin Lee Whorf's insights—was raised in a dramatic way by George Orwell. His novel *1984*, a chilling and convincing description of life in a totalitarian society, shows how language might destroy reality. In the imaginary nation of Oceania the official language is Newspeak, which is intended to facilitate "doublethink," the ability to accept simultaneously ideas contradicting each other. The Oceania state apparatus includes a Ministry of Truth, its headquarters building emblazoned with three slogans: "WAR IS PEACE"; "FREEDOM IS SLAVERY"; "IGNORANCE IS STRENGTH." There are also other ministries, Orwell explained: "The Ministry of Peace, which concerned itself with war; the Ministry of Love, which maintained law and order." Anyone who would use language this way, Orwell made clear, denies the meaning of his or her words. He or she has lost touch with reality and substituted for it an emptiness concealed in sounds that once had meaning.

There is another threat to language besides the intentional twisting of words by demagogues and others who would control people's thoughts. It is less obvious, but a danger nevertheless: simple imprecision, slovenliness, mindlessness in the use of the language. It seems a small matter that English-speakers increasingly confuse *uninterested* with *disinterested*, for example. But these words do not mean the same thing. *Disinterested* means impartial, not taking sides. *Uninterested* means lacking in interest, bored. A judge should be *disinterested* but never *uninterested*. Many such changes result from the inevitable evolution of language as it changes over the years, but the change can be a loss. The slow erosion of distinctions, visible in much writing, audible in many conversations, makes language imprecise and thus clumsy and ineffective as communication.

Among the symptoms of such erosion are stock phrases that people mindlessly repeat, substituting noise for thought. Everyone has heard speechmakers use such clichés as "having regard to," "play into the hands of," "in the interest of," "no axe to grind." Although this brief list is drawn from Orwell's essay of

1946 these exhausted clichés are still heard. Such verbal dead limbs do not distort thought but rather tend to obliterate it in a cloud of meaninglessness. "The slovenliness of our language makes it easier for us to have foolish thoughts," wrote Orwell. And ultimately, as has been pointed out by commentator Edwin Newman in his book *Strictly Speaking,* "Those for whom words have lost their value are likely to find that ideas have also lost their value."

Review Questions

1. According to Thomson, what is the Sapir-Whorf hypothesis? Give some examples.

2. According to Whorf, how can grammar affect people's perceptions? Give examples.

3. The Sapir-Whorf hypothesis has been tested in several ways. What are some of the tests of the hypothesis described by Thomson, and how have these modified the theory?

4. What are some of the ways in which language affects or modifies perception in modern America? Can you add examples from your own experience to those presented by Thomson?

7

How to Ask for a Drink

James P. Spradley and Brenda J. Mann

Most of us focus on verbal sounds, vocabulary, and grammar when we attempt to learn a new language. But mastery of these linguistic elements is only part of the task of verbal communication. Although we may not be consciously aware of it, talking often involves such tasks as enhancing our social status, manipulating how others see us, and acquiring social acceptance. To do this effectively we must skillfully identify and use what ethnographers of speaking call speech events *and* speech acts. *In this selection by James Spradley and Brenda Mann, we see that verbal communication in a male-oriented bar (and by extension, any verbal dialogue) is much more than a literal exchange of words. Using the example of two underage drinkers, the authors show that such* boys *must skillfully choose between different speech events such as* asking for a drink, asking about drinks, *and* hustling, *and speech acts, such as* muttering *and* asking, *to guide their talk and create the impression that they are men with the right to drink in this public setting. Finally, the authors point out that speech performance includes a set of components including a purpose, message content, channel, setting, tone, participants, and outcome.*

Brady's Bar is obviously a place to drink. Every night a crowd of college-age men and women visit the bar for this purpose. But even a casual observer could not miss the fact that Brady's is also a place to *talk*. Drinking and talking are inseparable. The lonely drinker who sits in silence is either drawn into conversation or leaves the bar. Everyone feels the anxious insecurity of such a person, seemingly alone in the crowd at Brady's. It is also believed that drinking affects the way people talk, lubricating the social interchange. If liquor flows each night in Brady's like a stream from behind the bar, talking, laughing, joking, and dozens of simultaneous conversations cascade like a torrent from every corner of the bar. Early in our research we became aware that our ethnography would have to include an investigation of this speech behavior.

The importance of drinking and talking has also been observed by anthropologists in other societies. Take, for example, the Subanun of the Philippine Islands, studied by Charles Frake. Deep in the tropical rain forests of Zamboanga Peninsula on the island of Mindanao, these people live in small family groups, practicing swidden agriculture. Social ties outside the family are maintained by networks to kin and neighbors rather than through some larger formal organization. Social encounters beyond the family occur on frequent festive occasions that always include "beer" drinking. Unlike Brady's Bar with separate glasses for each person, the Subanun place fermented mash in a single, large Chinese jar and drink from this common container by using a long bamboo straw. A drinking group gathers around the jar, water is poured over the mash, and each person in turn sucks beer from the bottom of the jar. As the water passes through the mash it is transformed into a potent alcoholic beverage. There are elaborate rules for these drinking sessions that govern such activities as competitive drinking, opposite-sexed partners drinking together under the cover of a blanket, and games where drinking is done in chugalug fashion. But the drinking is secondary to the talking on these occasions and what Frake has said about the Subanun might easily apply to Brady's Bar:

> The Subanun expression for drinking talk, . . . "talk from the straw," suggests an image of the drinking straw as a channel not only of the drink but also of drinking talk. The two activities, drinking and talking, are closely interrelated in that how one talks bears on how much one drinks and the converse is, quite obviously, also true . . . Especially for an adult male, one's role in the society at large, insofar as it is subject to manipulation, depends to a considerable extent on one's verbal performance during drinking encounters.[1]

[1]Charles O. Frake, "How to Ask for a Drink in Subanun," *American Anthropologist* 66, no. 6, (1964): 128–129.

[Here] we will examine the verbal performances of those who participate in the social life at Brady's. We focus on a single speech event, *asking for a drink* . . .

The Ethnography of Speaking

. . . What would a stranger have to know to act appropriately as a cocktail waitress and to interpret behavior from her perspective? An ethnography of speaking asks this question in reference to the way people talk. It goes beyond the usual linguistic study that analyzes speech in abstraction from its usage. Instead of describing linguistic rules that generate *meaningful* utterances, we sought to discover the sociolinguistic rules that generate *appropriate* utterances. This approach is extremely important because people at Brady's are not interested in merely saying things that make sense; they seek instead to say things that reveal to others their skill in verbal performances. Indeed, this often requires that a person utter nonsense, at least so it seems to the outsider.

In order to discover the rules for using speech, we began by recording what people said to one another, noting whenever possible the gestures, tone of voice, setting, and other features of the verbal interaction. Then we examined these samples of speech usage for recurrent patterns and went back to listen for more instances. At first we sought to identify the major speech events that were typical of the bar. A speech event refers to activities that are directly governed by rules for speaking. On any evening the waitress participates in many different speech events. For example, Denise enters the bar shortly after 6:30 in the evening and almost her first act is to exchange some form of *greeting* with the bartender, the day employees who are present, and any regulars she recognizes. At the bar she *asks for a drink,* saying to John, "I'd like a gin gimlet." This particular speech event takes many forms and is one that Denise will hear repeatedly from customers throughout the evening. She will also label this speech event *taking an order.* John refuses her request, fixes a Coke instead, and replies, "You know you can't have a drink now, you start work in thirty minutes."

The evening begins slowly so Denise stands at her station talking to a regular customer. They are participating in a speech event called a *conversation.* As more customers arrive, Denise will say, "Hi, Bill," "Good to see you, George. Where have you been lately?" "Hi, how are things at the 'U' these days?" and other things to *greet* people as they walk in. She will *give orders* to the bartender, *answer the phone,* make an *announcement* about last call, and possibly get into an *argument* with one table when she tries to get them to leave on time. Like the other girls, Denise has learned the cultural rules in this bar for identifying particular speech events and participating in the verbal exchanges they involve. She has acquired the rules for greeting people, for arguing, and for giving orders, rules that define the appropriate ways to speak in such events.

It wouldn't take long for a stranger to see that *asking for a drink* is probably the most frequent speech event that occurs in the bar. But, although it is an important activity, it appears to be a rather simple act. A stranger would only have to know the name of one drink, say Pabst Beer, and any simple English utterance that expresses a desire in order to appropriately ask for a drink. The waitress approaches the table, asks, "What would you like?" and a customer can simply say, "I'll have a Pabst." And once a person knows all the names for the other beverages it is possible to use this sentence to ask for any drink the bartenders can provide. A stranger might even go out of the bar thinking that asking for a drink is a rather trivial kind of speech behavior. That was certainly our impression during the first few weeks of fieldwork.

But as time went on we discovered that this speech event is performed in dozens of different ways. The people who come to Brady's have elaborated on a routine event, creating alternative ways for its execution. The well socialized individual knows the rules for selecting among these alternatives and for manipulating them to his own advantage. Asking for a drink thus becomes a kind of stage on which the customer can perform for the waitress and also the audience of other customers. A newcomer to the bar is frequently inept at these verbal performances, and one can observe regulars and employees smiling at one another or even laughing at some ill-timed and poorly performed effort at asking for a drink. Our goal was not to predict what people would say when they asked for a drink but to specify the alternative ways they could ask for a drink, the rules for selecting one or another alternative, and the social function of these ways of talking. We especially wanted to know how the waitress would interpret the alternatives she encountered in the course of her work. At the heart of the diverse ways to ask for a drink was a large set of speech acts, and it was largely through observing the way people manipulated these different acts that we discovered how to ask for a drink in Brady's Bar.

Speech Acts

In order to describe the way people *use* speech we begin with the speech act as the minimal unit for analysis. In every society people use language to accomplish purposes: to insult, to gather information, to persuade, to greet others, to curse, to communicate, etc. An act of speaking to accomplish such purposes can be a single word, a sentence, a paragraph, or even an entire book. A speech act refers to the way any utterance, whether short or long, is used and the rules for this use.

Our informants at Brady's Bar recognized many different categories of speech acts. They not only identified them for us but would frequently refer to one or another speech act during conversations in the bar. For example, at the end of a typically long evening the employees and a few real regulars are sitting around the bar talking about the events of the night. "Those guys in the upper section tonight were really obnoxious," recalls Sue. "They started off *giving me shit* about the way I took their orders and then all night long they kept *calling* my name. After last call they kept *hustling* me and when I finally came right out and said no, they really *slammed* me." The other waitress, Sandy, talks of the seven

Annies [slang for a nearby women's college] who were sitting at one of her tables: "They kept *asking* me to tell them what went into drinks and they were drinking Brandy Alexanders, Singapore Slings, Brandy Manhattans, and Peapickers. Then they kept *muttering* their orders all evening so I could hardly hear and *bickering* over the prices and *bitching* about the noise—it was really awful."

Giving shit, calling, hustling, slamming, asking, muttering, bickering, and *bitching* are all ways to talk; they are speech acts used at Brady's Bar. There are at least thirty-five such named speech acts that our informants recognized and these form a folk taxonomy shown in Figure 1.

Components of Speech Acts

The terms shown in this taxonomy refer to the *form* that messages take. But, in order to understand any speech act and the rules for its use, one must examine the various *components* of such acts. For instance, a waitress who hears a customer say, "Hey, sexy, what are you doing after work tonight?" also pays attention to the time and place of this utterance, who said it, the intention of the speaker, the tone of voice, and many other components. If said by a female customer, the waitresses would probably be shocked and offended. On the other hand, such an utterance by a *regular* male customer, especially early in the evening, might be interpreted as *teasing.* If said in a serious tone of voice by a male a few minutes before closing, the waitress would see this as *hustling.* Each of these components enters into the rules for using speech acts. Let's take a typical event to look briefly at the components that are the most important in asking for a drink.

It is Friday evening shortly before 10 P.M. In a few minutes the bouncer will assume his duties at the door. Some tables are empty in both sections but the waitresses expect a rush of customers before 10:30. Two males enter and go directly to vacant stools at the bar; Sandy stands idly at her station watching them. The bartender has his back turned when they sit down, but when he turns around one of the newcomers asks quickly and firmly: "Could I please have a Schlitz?" The other one immediately adds, "Make mine Miller's." Without a word the bartender, who has never seen these two customers before, gets the beers, opens the bottles, and sets them down on the bar with two glasses. He collects their money and returns some change before turning to check other customers' needs. Sandy, her tables taken care of, has watched the brief interaction and thinks to herself, "If those *boys* had sat in my section I would have carded them both and asked them to leave—they can't be a day over 17." About five minutes later when the bartender has his attention on other matters, the two customers quietly move to one of the tables in Sandy's section and finish their beers. Later, when Sandy checks their table, one of them orders again, "Could we please have another round?" Without a word she clears their empty bottles and brings another Schlitz and Miller's. Let us look more closely at the

WAYS TO TALK AT BRADY'S BAR	Slamming	
	Talking	
	Telling	
	Giving shit	
	Asking	
	Begging	
	Begging off	
	Gossiping	
	Joking	
	Teasing	
	Muttering	
	Ordering	
	Swearing	
	Sweet talking	
	Pressuring	
	Arguing	
	Bantering	
	Lying	
	Bitching	
	P.R.ing	
	Babbling	
	Harping	
	Crying over a beer	
	Hustling	
	Introducing	
	Flirting	
	Daring	
	Bickering	
	Apologizing	
	Calling	
	Greeting	
	Bullshitting	
	Hassling	
	Admitting	
	Giving orders	

FIGURE 1   Some Speech Acts Used in Brady's Bar

components of these speech acts the two young customers have used to ask for drinks.

1. *Purpose.* Because asking for a drink can be done with any number of different speech acts, customers tend to select ones that will achieve certain ends. In addition to a drink they may want to tell others something about themselves, demonstrate their prowess with females generally, set the stage for later interaction with the waitress, etc. In this case, the two customers want to gain admittance to the adult world of male drinking. Even more, they want to pass as *men,* circumventing entirely the stigma of merely being *boys.* They could probably borrow I.D. cards from college friends that would legitimize their presence. But such a tactic would also announce to everyone, through the public experience of being carded, that they had not yet gained *unquestioned* right to participation in this male world. They have learned that the skillful use of language can be an effective substitute for age and manliness.

2. *Message Content.* Schlitz and Miller's are both common drinks for young males. Had either of these customers asked for a daiquiri, a Marguerita on the rocks, or a Smith and Currants, it would have created suspicion. Not that male customers *never* drink these beverages—they do on rare occasions. But because these are female drinks it would have called attention to other characteristics of the customers. Instead of creating the impression that they were "ordinary men," such a request would have made others wonder whether they were *ordinary,* and even more important, whether they were really *men.* An order of scotch and soda, bourbon and seven, whiskey and water, or gin and tonic would not have cast doubt on their maleness but might have been a reason for others to question their age. Men often order such drinks but, in this case, asking for any one of these would obviously contrast with their youthful appearance. By ordering two usual drinks of young men—common beers like Schlitz and Miller's—they effectively created a protective screen around their true identities.

3. *Message Form.* "Could I please have a . . ." is the polite form of *asking* in Brady's Bar. The second customer also *asked* when he added, "Make mine . . ." But they could have *ordered* in a more direct statement. They might have *asked for information* with a question about the kinds of beers available. They could have *muttered* an order in an effort to avoid attention. Other forms were also available but asking politely helped ensure an impression of knowledgeable confidence. Other speech acts could easily bring suspicion in the same way that ordering an unusual drink might have done.

4. *Channel.* People at Brady's ask for drinks by using one of several different channels. A person who regularly drinks the same beverage and does so repeatedly on a single night may receive a drink on the house. By his drinking *behavior* he can thus be asking for a free drink. When a regular enters the bar, his very presence asks for a drink, and he can merely take a place at the bar or a table and the drink appears. Various gestures are another frequently used channel as when a regular walks in and holds up his index finger or nods his head. The waitress takes his order from memory and delivers it to the waiting customer. Asking for a drink by gesture instead of the verbal channel was not possible for the two young customers because of their status as persons off the street. When someone does use one of these other channels it serves as a public announcement of status in the bar.

5. *Setting.* The setting of a speech act refers to the time and place it is spoken. Even though Brady's is a small bar, the place where a person speaks can change the social significance of what is said. Individuals at the bar tend to take on some of the "sacred maleness" associated with that location. Drinking at the tables tends to convey less experience and, combined with an appearance of youth, can be sufficient reason for carding a customer. A person who enters, and walks confidently to the bar, communicates the unstated message that he is a man, a mature drinker, one whose presence at the bar is not to be questioned. By timing their entry prior to 10:00 P.M. they also circumvent the possibility of being carded by the bouncer. Once a drink is served at the bar, the same customers who would have been carded at a table, and probably excluded, can move with immunity to a table in either section. In order for a waitress to ask them for I.D.'s at that point would require that she violate the implicit rule that bartenders know better than waitresses, something few girls are eager to do in such a public manner. By timing the round ordered from a waitress to follow the drinks ordered from a bartender, the customer can ask for a drink and also accomplish other desired ends.

6. *Tone.* A customer who enters the bar is probably not always aware of the manner or tone he uses to ask for a drink. It may have been days since he asked for a drink in any bar and his tone of voice and general manner of speech may be conditioned by experiences earlier in the day. But, to the waitress who hears hundreds of people asking for drinks, the tone communicates a great deal. The person who asks questions about drinks or who hesitates, communicates more than the kind of drink desired. The customer who uses this occasion to hustle the waitress or tease her must carefully manipulate the tone of any utterance to avoid being seen as inept or crude. The two customers who asked for a Schlitz and Miller's exuded confidence in their manner of speaking. By eliminating any hesitancy from the speech act they effectively communicated to the bartender as well as to other customers that they were men who knew their way around in bars.

7. *Participants.* Speech acts are used between two people or between groups of people. In Brady's Bar, the participants in any communicative event can change the meaning and consequences in the same way that other components do. Asking the *bartender* instead of the *waitress* allows underage males to escape the emasculation of being carded by females. When a couple enters the bar and the girl is underage, a quick firm order for both by the male will mask the girl's discomfort and keep her from being carded. An underage *regular,* on the other hand, can order from either the bartender or waitress without worrying about being carded. . . . *Who* is talking to *whom* is one of the most significant variables in understanding the way people talk.

But asking for a drink is not merely a communication between a customer and employee. Nearby customers and employees participate in the exchanges as an attentive audience. Many speech acts cannot be understood at Brady's unless we consider the audience before whom a speaker performs. The two young men who ordered at the bar were not only seeking to get around the barrier of carding but also to communicate their claim to adult male status, especially to those at the center of this male-oriented social world.

8. *Outcome.* The regular participants in the social life at Brady's learn to use language successfully and thereby achieve a variety of ends. Not everyone who manipulates the various features of a speech act accomplish their intentions. Some customers *hustle* a waitress when asking for a drink but to no avail. Some seek to avoid being carded, only to find themselves required to show their I.D. or leave. Others make a claim to privileged intimacy or special status, only to find their performance inept and open to derision. But there are other outcomes that often lie outside the awareness of the actors. In this case the two customers successfully escaped the degradation of carding, demonstrated their manliness and adulthood to their audience, and paved the way for an evening of uninterrupted drinking at a table served by a cocktail waitress. But equally important, their skillful performance in asking for a drink set in motion the social processes that could eventually change their status in Brady's Bar from underage persons-off-the-street to regular customers. For having escaped the carding process once, they have established their right to drink at Brady's, and subsequent visits will reinforce this right. . . .

Review Questions

1. Based on your reading of "How to Ask for a Drink," what evidence indicates that there is more to verbal communication than the literal message conveyed by words?

2. What do Spradley and Mann mean by the phrase "ethnography of speaking"? How did they do ethnographic research on speaking in Brady's bar?

3. What do Spradley and Mann mean by the terms "speech event" and "speech act"? Give examples of each from the article.

4. Using this reading selection, name and give examples of the "components of speech acts" identified by Spradley and Mann.

5. Identify a social setting from your own experience where verbal (and nonverbal) communication occurs. Identify a kind of actor in this setting and list all the speech events and speech acts you can think of that involve such a person. Choose one speech act and analyze it by describing its components.

8

Body Art as Visual Language

Enid Schildkrout

Most people think language refers to speaking; talking stands out as a hall-mark of humanity. But virtually anything we can apprehend with our senses may act as a symbol that communicates meaning. Cars may suggest going places, traffic jams, social status, and personal identity. Smells can remind us of seasons, food, and people. In this article, Enid Schildkrout describes a special kind of nonverbal symbol, body art. Defined as any decorative addi-tion to or alteration of the human body, body art may be temporary or per-manent, dramatic or subdued, colorful or plain. It may appear in the form of tattoos, piercings, brands, painted designs, hairstyles, makeup, and many other varieties. However it is created and no matter where it is found, body art always transmits meanings, from ideals of beauty, important life transi-tions, and religious epics to social status and personal rebellion.

"Body Art as Visual Language" and excerpt from "Teacher's Corner: Bodyart" by Enid Schildkrout as appeared in *AnthroNotes*, Vol. 22, No. 2, Winter 2001, pp. 1–3, 4–6.

Body art is not just the latest fashion. In fact, if the impulse to create art is one of the defining signs of humanity, the body may well have been the first canvas. Alongside paintings on cave walls created by early humans over 30,000 years ago, we find handprints and ochre deposits suggesting body painting. Some of the earliest mummies known—like the "Ice Man" from the Italian-Austrian Alps, known as Otzi, and others from central Asia, the Andes, Egypt, and Europe—date back to 5,000 years. People were buried with ornaments that would have been worn through body piercings, and remains of others show intentionally elongated or flattened skulls. Head shaping was practiced 5,000 years ago in Chile and until the 18th century in France. Stone and ceramic figurines found in ancient graves depict people with every kind of body art known today. People have always marked their bodies with signs of individuality, social status, and cultural identity.

The Language of Body Art

There is no culture in which people do not, or did not, paint, pierce, tattoo, reshape, or simply adorn their bodies. Fashions change and forms of body art come and go, but people everywhere do something or other to "package" their appearance. No sane or civilized person goes out in the raw; everyone grooms, dresses, or adorns some part of their body to present to the world. Body art communicates a person's status in society; displays accomplishments; and encodes memories, desires, and life histories.

Body art is a visual language. To understand it one needs to know the vocabulary, including the shared symbols, myths, and social values that are written on the body. From tattoos to top hats, body art makes a statement about the person who wears it. But body art is often misunderstood and misinterpreted because its messages do not necessarily translate across cultures. Elaborately pictorial Japanese tattooing started among men in certain occupational groups and depicts the exploits of a gangster hero drawn from a Chinese epic. The tattoos have more meaning to those who know the stories underlying the images than they do to people unfamiliar with the tales. Traditional Polynesian tattooing is mainly geometric and denotes rank and political status but more recently has been used to define ethnic identity within Pacific island societies.

In an increasingly global world, designs, motifs, even techniques of body modification move across cultural boundaries, but in the process their original meanings are often lost. An animal crest worn as a tattoo, carved into a totem pole, or woven into a blanket may signify membership in a particular clan among Indians on the Northwest Coast of North America, but when worn by people outside these cultures, the designs may simply refer to the wearer's identification with an alternative way of life. Polynesian or Indonesian tattoo designs worn by Westerners are admired for the beauty of their graphic qualities, but their original cultural meanings are rarely understood. A tattoo from Borneo was once worn to light the path of a person's soul after death, but in New York or Berlin it becomes a sign of rebellion from "coat and tie" culture.

Because body art is such an obvious way of signaling cultural differences, people often use it to identify, exoticize, and ostracize others. Tattoos, scarification, or head shaping may be a sign of high status in one culture and low status in another, but to a total outsider these practices may appear to be simply "mutilation." From the earliest voyages of discovery to contemporary tourism, travelers of all sorts—explorers and missionaries, soldiers and sailors, traders and tourists—have brought back images of the people they meet. These depictions sometimes reveal as much about the people looking at the body art as about the people making and wearing it. Some early images of Europeans and Americans by non-Westerners emphasized elaborate clothing and facial hair. Alternatively, Western images of Africans, Polynesians, and Native Americans focused on the absence of clothes and the presence of tattoos, body paint, and patterns of scars. Representations of body art in engravings, paintings, photographs, and film are powerful visual metaphors that have been used both to record cultural differences and to proclaim one group's supposed superiority over another.

Body Art: Permanent and Ephemeral

Most people think that permanent modification of the skin, muscles, and bones is what body art is all about. But if one looks at body art as a form of communication, there is no logical reason to separate permanent forms of body art, like tattoos, scarification, piercing, or plastic surgery, from temporary forms, such as makeup, clothing, or hairstyles. Punks and sideshow artists may have what appears to be extreme body art, but everyone does it in one way or another. All of these modifications convey information about a person's identity.

Nonetheless, some forms of body art are undeniably more permanent than others. The decision to display a tattoo is obviously different from the decision to change the color of one's lipstick or dye one's hair. Tattooing, piercing, and scarification are more likely to be ways of signaling one's place in society, or an irreversible life passage like the change from childhood to adulthood. Temporary forms of body art, like clothing, ornaments, and painting, more often mark a moment or simply follow a fashion. But these dichotomies don't stand up to close scrutiny across cultures: tattoos and scarification marks are often done to celebrate an event and dying or cutting one's hair, while temporary, may signal a life-changing event, such as a wedding or a funeral.

Cultural Ideals of Beauty

Ideas of beauty vary from one culture to another. Some anthropologists and psychologists believe that babies in all cultures respond positively to certain kinds of faces. The beautiful body is often associated with the healthy body and nonthreatening facial expressions and gestures. But this does not mean that beauty is defined the same way in all cultures. People's ideas about the way a healthy person should look are not the same in all cultures: some see fat as an indication of health and wealth while others feel quite the opposite. People in some cultures admire and respect signs of aging, while others do all they can to hide gray hair and wrinkles.

Notwithstanding the fact that parents often make decisions for their children, like whether or not to pierce the ears of infants, in general I would maintain that to be considered art and not just a marking, body art has to have some measure of freedom and intentionality in its creation. The brands put on enslaved people, or the numbers tattooed on concentration camp victims, or the scars left from an unwanted injury are body markings, not body art. . . .

Body Art Techniques

Body Painting

Body painting, the most ephemeral and flexible of all body art, has the greatest potential for transforming a person into something else—a spirit, a work of art, another gender, even a map to a sacred place including the afterlife. It can be simply a way of emphasizing a person's visual appeal, a serious statement of allegiance, or a protective and empowering coating.

Natural clays and pigments made from a great variety of plants and minerals are often mixed with vegetable oils and animal fat to make body paint. These include red and yellow ochre (iron rich clay), red cam wood, cinnabar, gold dust, many roots, fruits and flowers, cedar bark, white kaolin, chalk, and temporary skin dyes made from indigo and henna leaves. People all over the world adorn the living and also treat the dead with body paint.

The colors of body paint often have symbolic significance, varying from culture to culture. Some clays and body paints are felt to have protective and auspicious properties, making them ideal for use in initiation rituals, for weddings, and for funerals—all occasions of transition from one life stage to another.

Historically, body paints and dyes have been important trade items. Indians of North America exchanged many valuable items for vermilion, which is mercuric sulphide (an artificial equivalent of the natural dye made from cinnabar). Mixed with red lead by European traders, it could cause or sometimes caused mercury poisoning in the wearer.

Makeup

Makeup consists of removable substances—paint, powders, and dyes—applied to enhance or transform appearance. Commonly part of regular grooming, makeup varies according to changing definitions of beauty. For vanity and social acceptance, or for medicinal or ritual purposes, people regularly transform every visible part of their body. They have tanned or whitened skin; changed the color of their lips, eyes, teeth, and hair; and added or removed "beauty" spots.

From the 10th to the 19th century, Japanese married women and courtesans blackened their teeth with a paste made from a mixture of tea and sake soaked in iron scraps; black teeth were considered beautiful and sexually appealing.

Makeup can accentuate the contrast between men and women, camouflage perceived imperfections, or signify a special occasion or ritual state. Makeup, like clothing and hairstyles, allows people to reinvent themselves in everyday life.

Rituals and ceremonies often require people to wear certain kinds of makeup, clothing, or hairstyles to indicate that a person is taking on a new identity (representing an ancestor or a spirit in a masquerade, for example) or transforming his or her social identity as in an initiation ceremony, wedding, graduation, or naming ceremony. Male Japanese actors in Kabuki theater represent women by using strictly codified paints and motifs, and the designs and motifs of Chinese theatrical makeup indicate the identity of a character.

Hair

Hair is one [of] the easiest and most obvious parts of the body subject to change, and combing and washing hair is part of everyday grooming in most cultures. Styles of combing, braiding, parting, and wrapping hair can signify status and gender, age and ritual status, or membership in a certain group.

Hair often has powerful symbolic significance. Covering the head can be a sign of piety and respect, whether in a place of worship or all the time. Orthodox Jewish women shave their heads but also cover them with wigs or scarves. Muslim women in many parts of the world cover their heads, and sometimes cover their faces too, with scarves or veils. Sikh men in India never cut their hair and cover their heads with turbans. And the Queen of England is rarely seen without a hat.

Cutting hair is a ritual act in some cultures and heads are often shaved during rituals that signify the passage from one life stage to another. Hair itself, once cut, can be used as a symbolic substance. Being part, and yet not part, of a person, living or dead, hair can take on the symbolic power of the person. Some Native Americans formerly attached hair from enemies to war shirts, while warriors in Borneo formerly attached hair from captured enemies to war shields.

Reversing the normal treatment of hair, whatever that is in a particular culture, can be a sign of rebellion or of special status. Adopting the uncombed hair of the Rastafarians can be a sign of rebellion among some people, while for Rastafarians it is a sign of membership in a particular religious group. In many cultures people in mourning deliberately do not comb or wash their hair for a period of time, thereby showing that they are temporarily not part of normal everyday life.

What we do with our hair is a way of expressing our identity, and it is easy to look around and see how hair color, cut, style, and its very presence or absence, tells others much about how we want to be seen.

Body Shaping

The shape of the human body changes throughout life, but in many cultures people have found ways to permanently or temporarily sculpt the body. To conform to culturally defined ideals of male and female beauty, people have bound the soft bones of babies' skulls or children's feet, stretched their necks with rings, removed ribs to achieve tiny waists, and most commonly today, sculpted the body through plastic surgery.

Becoming fat is a sign of health, wealth, and fertility in some societies, and fattening is sometimes part of a girl's coming of age ceremony. Tiny waists, small feet, and large or small breasts and buttocks have been prized or scorned as ideals of female beauty. Less common are ways of shaping men's bodies but developing muscles, shaping the head, or gaining weight are ways in which cultural ideals of male beauty and power have been expressed.

Head shaping is still done in parts of South America. For the Inca of South America and the Maya of Central America and Mexico, a specially shaped head once signified nobility. Because the skull bones of infants and children are not completely fused, the application of pressure with pads, boards, bindings, or massage results in a gently shaped head that can be a mark of high status or local identity.

While Western plastic surgery developed first as a way of correcting the injuries of war, particularly after WW II, today people use plastic surgery to smooth their skin, remove unwanted fat, and reshape parts of their bodies.

Scarification

Permanent patterns of scars on the skin, inscribed onto the body through scarification, can be signs of beauty and indicators of status. In some cultures, a smooth, unmarked skin represents an ideal of beauty, but people in many other cultures see smooth skin as a naked, unattractive surface. Scarification, also called cicatrization, alters skin texture by cutting the skin and controlling the body's healing process. The cuts are treated to prevent infection and to enhance the scars' visibility. Deep cuts leave visible incisions after the skin heals, while inserting substances like clay or ash in the cuts results in permanently raised wheals or bumps, known as keloids. Substances inserted into the wounds may result in changes in skin color, creating marks similar to tattoos. Cutting elaborate and extensive decorative patterns into the skin usually indicates a permanent change in a person's status. Because scarification is painful, the richly scarred person is often honored for endurance and courage. Branding is a form of scarification that creates a scar after the surface of the skin has been burned. Branding was done in some societies as a part of a rite of passage, but in western Europe and elsewhere branding, as well as some forms of tattoo, were widely used to mark captives, enslaved peoples, and criminals. Recently, some individuals and members of fraternities on U.S. college campuses have adopted branding as a radical form of decoration and self-identification.

Tattooing

Tattoo is the insertion of ink or some other pigment through the outer covering of the body, the epidermis, into the dermis, the second layer of skin. Tattooists use a sharp implement to puncture the skin and thus make an indelible mark, design, or picture on the body. The resulting patterns or figures vary according to the purpose of the tattoo and the materials available for its coloration.

Different groups and cultures have used a variety of techniques in this process. Traditional Polynesian tattooists punctured the skin by tapping a needle with a small hammer. The Japanese work by hand but with bundles of needles set in wooden handles. Since the late 19th century, the electric tattoo machine and related technological advances in equipment have revolutionized tattoo[ing] in the West, expanding the range of possible designs, the colors available, and the ease with which a tattoo can be applied to the body. Prisoners have used materials as disparate as guitar strings and reconstructed electric shavers to create tattoos. Tattoos are usually intended as permanent markings, and it is only recently through the use of expensive laser techniques that they can be removed.

While often decorative, tattoos send important cultural messages. The "text" on the skin can be read as a commitment to some group, an emblem of a rite of passage, or a personal or fashion statement. In fact, cosmetic tattooing of eyebrows and eyeliner is one of the fastest growing of all tattoo enterprises. Tattoos can also signify bravery and commitment to a long, painful process—as is the case with Japanese full body tattooing or Maori body and facial patterns. Though there have been numerous religious and social injunctions against tattooing, marking the body in this way has been one of the most persistent and universal forms of body art.

Piercing

Body piercing, which allows ornaments to be worn in the body, has been a widespread practice since ancient times. Piercing involves long-term insertion of an object through the skin in a way that permits healing around the opening. Most commonly pierced are the soft tissues of the face, but many peoples, past and present, have also pierced the genitals and the chest. Ear, nose, and lip ornaments, as well as pierced figurines, have been found in ancient burials of the Inca and Moche of Peru, the Aztecs and Maya of ancient Mexico, and in graves of central Asian, European, and Mediterranean peoples.

The act of piercing is often part of a ritual change of status. Bleeding that occurs during piercing is sometimes thought of as an offering to gods, spirits, or ancestors. Particular ornaments may be restricted to certain groups—men or women, rulers or priests—or may be inserted as part of a ceremony marking a change in status. Because ornaments can be made of precious and rare materials, they may signal privilege and wealth. . . .

Cultural Significance of Body Art

Body art takes on specific meanings in different cultures. It can serve as a link with ancestors, deities, or spirits. Besides being decorative, tattoos, paint, and scars can mediate the relationships between people and the supernatural world. The decorated body can serve as a shield to repel evil or as a means of attracting good fortune. Tattoos in central Borneo had the same designs as objects of everyday use and shielded people from dangerous spirits. Selk'nam men in Tierra del Fuego painted their bodies to transform themselves into spirits for initiation ceremonies. Australian Aborigines painted similar designs on cave walls and their bodies to indicate the location of sacred places revealed in dreams.

Transitions in status and identity, for example the transition between childhood and adulthood, are often seen as times of danger. Body art protects a vulnerable person, whether an initiate, a bride, or a deceased person, in this transitional phase. To ensure her good fortune, an Indian bride's hands and feet are covered in henna designs that also emphasize her beauty. For protection during initiation, a central African Chokwe girl's body is covered in white kaolin. In many societies, both the dead and those who mourn them are covered with paints and powders for decoration and protection.

Worldwide travel, large-scale migrations, and increasing access to global networks of communication mean that body art today is a kaleidoscopic mix of traditional practices and new inventions. Materials, designs, and practices move from one cultural context to another. Traditional body art practices are given new meanings as they move across cultural and social boundaries.

Body art is always changing, and in some form or another always engaging: it allows people to reinvent themselves—to rebel, to follow fashion, or to play and experiment with new identities. Like performance artists and actors, people in everyday life use body art to cross boundaries of gender, national identity, and cultural stereotypes.

Body art can be an expression of individuality, but it can also be an expression of group identity. Body art is about conformity and rebellion, freedom and authority. Its messages and meanings only make sense in the context of culture, but because it is such a personal art form, it continually challenges cultural assumptions about the ideal, the desirable, and the appropriately presented body.

Review Questions

1. What is the definition of body art? Are there marks on or alterations to the body that would not be classified as body art?

2. What is a symbol and why is body art classified as symbolic?

3. What forms can body art take?

4. What are some of the general meanings that examples of body art can have in different societies?

5. What effect has globalization had on the forms and meanings of body art?

9

Conversation Style: Talking on the Job

Deborah Tannen

In Schildkrout's article, we looked at the important role played by nonverbal symbols in human communication. Speaking distances, gestures, smiles, and a host of other tacit signs make up this silent language. In this piece excerpted from her book about conversation in the workplace, Deborah Tannen discusses a second tacit dimension of communication, conversation style. Looking at the different ways men and women approach or avoid asking for help on the job, she argues that gender differences in conversation style are responsible not only for miscommunication but also for misguided evaluations and moral judgments about the performance and character of co-workers.

People have different conversational styles, influenced by the part of the country they grew up in, their ethnic backgrounds and those of their parents, their age, class, and gender. But conversational style is invisible. Unaware that these and other aspects of our backgrounds influence our ways of talking, we think we are simply saying what we mean. Because we don't realize that others' styles are different, we are often frustrated in conversations. Rather than seeing the culprit as differing styles, we attribute troubles to others' intentions (she doesn't like me), abilities (he's stupid), or character (she's rude, he's inconsiderate), our own failure (what's wrong with me?), or the failure of a relationship (we just can't communicate). . . .

Although I am aware of the many influences on conversational style and have spent most of my career studying and writing about them . . . style differences influenced by gender receive particular attention [here]. This is not only because these are the differences people most want to hear about (although this is so and is a factor), but also because there is something fundamental about our categorization by gender. When you spot a person walking down the street toward you, you immediately and automatically identify that person as male or female. You will not necessarily try to determine which state they are from, what their class background is, or what country their grandparents came from. A secondary identification, in some places and times, may be about race. But, while we may envision a day when a director will be able to cast actors for a play without reference to race, can we imagine a time when actors can be cast without reference to their sex?

Few elements of our identities come as close to our sense of who we are as gender. If you mistake people's cultural background—you thought they were Greek, but they turn out to be Italian; you assumed they'd grown up in Texas, but it turns out they're from Kentucky; you say "Merry Christmas" and they say, "we don't celebrate Christmas; we're Muslim"—it catches you off guard and you rearrange the mental frame through which you view them. But if someone you thought was male turns out to be female—like the jazz musician Billy Tipton, whose own adopted sons never suspected that their father was a woman until the coroner broke the news to them after his (her) death—the required adjustment is staggering. Even infants discriminate between males and females and react differently depending on which they confront.

Perhaps it is because our sense of gender is so deeply rooted that people are inclined to hear descriptions of gender patterns as statements about gender *identity*—in other words, as absolute differences rather than a matter of degree and percentages, and as universal rather than culturally mediated. The patterns I describe are based on observations of particular speakers in a particular place and time: mostly (but not exclusively) middle-class Americans of European background working in offices at the present time. Other cultures evince very different patterns of talk associated with gender—and correspondingly different assumptions about the "natures" of women and men. I don't put a lot of store in talk about "natures" or what is "natural." People in every culture will tell you that the behaviors common in their own culture are "natural." I also don't put a lot of store in people's explanations that their way of talking is a natural response to their environment, as there is always an equally natural and opposite way of responding to the same environment. We all tend to regard the way things are as the way things have to be—as only natural.

The reason ways of talking, like other ways of conducting our daily lives, come to seem natural is that the behaviors that make up our lives are ritualized. Indeed, the "ritual" character of interaction is at the heart of this book. Having grown up in a particular culture, we learn to do things as the people we encounter do them, so the vast majority of our decisions about how to speak become automatic. You see someone you know, you ask "How are you?," chat, then take your leave, never pausing to ponder the many ways you could handle this interaction differently—and would, if you lived in a different culture. Just as an American automatically extends a hand for a handshake while a Japanese automatically bows, what the American and Japanese find it natural to say is a matter of convention learned over a lifetime.

No one understood the ritual nature of everyday life better than sociologist Erving Goffman, who also understood the fundamental role played by gender in organizing our daily rituals. In his article "The Arrangement Between the Sexes," Goffman pointed out that we tend to say "sex-linked" when what we mean is "sex-class-linked." When hearing that a behavior is "sex-linked," people often conclude that the behavior is to be found in every individual of that group, and that it is somehow inherent in their sex, as if it came hooked to a chromosome. Goffman suggests the term "genderism" (on the model, I assume, of "mannerism," not of "sexism") for "a sex-class linked individual behavioral practice." This is the spirit in which I intend references to gendered patterns of behavior: not to imply that there is anything inherently male or female about particular ways of talking, nor to claim that every individual man or woman adheres to the pattern, but rather to observe that a larger percentage of women or men *as a group* talk in a particular way, or individual women and men *are more likely* to talk one way or the other.

That individuals do not always fit the pattern associated with their gender does not mean that the pattern is not typical. Because more women or men speak in a particular way, that way of speaking becomes associated with women or men—or, rather, it is the other way around: More women or men learn to speak particular ways *because* those ways are associated with their own gender. And individual men or women who speak in ways associated with the other gender will pay a price for departing from cultural expectations.

If my concept of how gender displays itself in everyday life has been influenced by Goffman, the focus of my research—talk—and my method for studying it grow directly out of my own discipline, linguistics. My understanding of what goes on when people talk to each other is based on observing and listening as well as tape-recording, transcribing, and analyzing conversation. In response to my book *You Just Don't Understand*, I was contacted by people at many companies who asked whether I could help them apply the insights in that book to the problem of "the glass ceiling": Why weren't women advancing as quickly as the men who were hired at the same time? And more generally, they wanted to understand how to integrate women as well as others who were historically not "typical" employees into the increasingly diverse workforce. I realized that in order to offer insight, I needed to observe what was really going on in the workplace. . . .

Women and Men Talking on the Job

Amy was a manager with a problem: She had just read a final report written by Donald, and she felt it was woefully inadequate. She faced the unsavory task of telling him to do it over. When she met with Donald, she made sure to soften the blow by beginning with praise, telling him everything about his report that was good. Then she went on to explain what was lacking and what needed to be done to make it acceptable. She was pleased with the diplomatic way she had managed to deliver the bad news. Thanks to her thoughtfulness in starting with praise, Donald was able to listen to the criticism and seemed to understand what was needed. But when the revised report appeared on her desk, Amy was shocked. Donald had made only minor, superficial changes, and none of the necessary ones. The next meeting with him did not go well. He was incensed that she was now telling him his report was not acceptable and accused her of having misled him. "You told me before it was fine," he protested.

Amy thought she had been diplomatic; Donald thought she had been dishonest. The praise she intended to soften the message "This is unacceptable" sounded to him like the message itself: "This is fine." So what she regarded as the main point—the needed changes—came across to him as optional suggestions, because he had already registered her praise as the main point. She felt he hadn't listened to her. He thought she had changed her mind and was making him pay the price.

Work days are filled with conversations about getting the job done. Most of these conversations succeed, but too many end in impasses like this. It could be that Amy is a capricious boss whose wishes are whims, and it could be that Donald is a temperamental employee who can't hear criticism no matter how it is phrased. But I don't think either was the case in this instance. I believe this was one of innumerable misunderstandings caused by differences in conversational style. Amy delivered the criticism in a way that seemed to her self-evidently considerate, a way she would have preferred to receive criticism herself: taking into account the other person's feelings, making sure he knew that her ultimate negative assessment of his report didn't mean she had no appreciation of his abilities. She offered the praise as a sweetener to help the nasty-tasting news go down. But Donald didn't expect criticism to be delivered in that way, so he mistook the praise as her overall assessment rather than a preamble to it.

This conversation could have taken place between two women or two men. But I do not think it is a coincidence that it occurred between a man and a woman. . . . Conversational rituals common among men often involve using opposition such as banter, joking, teasing, and playful put-downs, and expending effort to avoid the one-down position in the interaction. Conversational rituals common among women are often ways of maintaining an appearance of equality, taking into account the effect of the exchange on the other person, and expending effort to downplay the speakers' authority so they can get the job done without flexing their muscles in an obvious way.

When everyone present is familiar with these conventions, they work well. But when ways of speaking are not recognized as conventions, they are taken literally, with negative results on both sides. Men whose oppositional strategies are interpreted literally may be seen as hostile when they are not, and their efforts to ensure that they avoid appearing one-down may be taken as arrogance. When women use conversational strategies designed to avoid appearing boastful and to take the other person's feelings into account, they may be seen as less confident and competent than they really are. As a result, both women and men often feel they are not getting sufficient credit for what they have done, are not being listened to, are not getting ahead as fast as they should.

When I talk about women's and men's characteristic ways of speaking, I always emphasize that both styles make sense and are equally valid in themselves, though the difference in styles may cause trouble in interaction. In a sense, when two people form a private relationship of love or friendship, the bubble of their interaction is a world unto itself, even though they both come with the prior experience of their families, their community, and a lifetime of conversations. But someone who takes a job is entering a world that is already functioning, with its own characteristic style already in place. Although there are many influences such as regional background, the type of industry involved, whether it is a family business or a large corporation, in general, workplaces that have previously had men in positions of power have already established male-style interaction as the norm. In that sense, women, and others whose styles are different, are not starting out equal, but are at a disadvantage. Though talking at work is quite similar to talking in private, it is a very different enterprise in many ways.

When Not Asking Directions
Is Dangerous to Your Health

If conversational-style differences lead to troublesome outcomes in work as well as private settings, there are some work settings where the outcomes of style are a matter of life and death. Healthcare professionals are often in such situations. So are airline pilots.

Of all the examples of women's and men's characteristic styles that I discussed in *You Just Don't Understand*, the one that (to my surprise) attracted the most attention was the question "Why don't men like to stop and ask for directions?" Again and again, in the responses of audiences, talk-show hosts, letter writers, journalists, and conversationalists, this question seemed to crystallize the frustration many people had experienced in their own lives. And my explanation seems to have rung true: that men are more likely to be aware that asking for directions, or for any kind of help, puts them in a one-down position.

With regard to asking directions, women and men are keenly aware of the advantages of their own style. Women frequently observe how much time they would save if their husbands simply stopped and asked someone instead of driving around trying in vain to find a destination themselves. But I have also been told by men that it makes sense not to ask directions because you learn a lot about a neighborhood, as well as about navigation, by driving around and finding your own way.

But some situations are more risky than others. A Hollywood talk-show producer told me that she had been flying with her father in his private airplane when he was running out of gas and uncertain about the precise location of the local landing strip he was heading for. Beginning to panic, the woman said, "Daddy! Why don't you radio the control tower and ask them where to land?" He answered, "I don't want them to think I'm lost." This story had a happy ending, else the woman would not have been alive to tell it to me.

Some time later, I repeated this anecdote to a man at a cocktail party—a man who had just told me that the bit about directions was his favorite part of my book, and who, it turned out, was also an amateur pilot. He then went on to tell me that he had had a similar experience. When learning to fly, he got lost on his first solo flight. He did not want to humiliate himself by tuning his radio to the FAA emergency frequency and asking for help, so he flew around looking for a place to land. He spotted an open area that looked like a landing field, headed for it—and found himself deplaning in what seemed like a deliberately hidden landing strip that was mercifully deserted at the time. Fearing he had stumbled upon an enterprise he was not supposed to be aware of, let alone poking around in, he climbed back into the plane, relieved that he had not gotten into trouble. He managed to find his way back to his home airport as well, before he ran out of gas. He maintained, however, that he was certain that more than a few small-plane crashes have occurred because other amateur pilots who did not want to admit they were lost were less lucky. In light of this, the amusing question of why men prefer not to stop and ask for directions stops being funny.

The moral of the story is not that men should immediately change and train themselves to ask directions when they're in doubt, any more than women should immediately stop asking directions and start honing their navigational skills by finding their way on their own. The moral is flexibility: Sticking to habit in the face of all challenges is not so smart if it ends up getting you killed. If we all understood our own styles and knew their limits and their alternatives, we'd be better off—especially at work, where the results of what we do have repercussions for co-workers and the company, as well as for our own futures.

To Ask or Not to Ask

An intern on duty at a hospital had a decision to make. A patient had been admitted with a condition he recognized, and he recalled the appropriate medication. But that medication was recommended for a number of conditions, in different dosages. He wasn't quite sure what dose was right for this condition. He had to make a quick decision: Would he interrupt the supervising resident during a meeting to check the dose, or would he make his best guess and go for it?

What was at stake? First and foremost, the welfare, and maybe even the life, of the patient. But something else was at stake too—the reputation, and eventually the career, of the intern. If he interrupted the resident to ask about the dosage, he was making a public statement about what he didn't know, as well as making himself something of a nuisance. In this case, he went with his guess, and there were no negative effects. But, as with small-plane crashes, one wonders how many medical errors have resulted from decisions to guess rather than ask.

It is clear that not asking questions can have disastrous consequences in medical settings, but asking questions can also have negative consequences. A physician wrote to me about a related experience that occurred during her medical training. She received a low grade from her supervising physician. It took her by surprise because she knew that she was one of the best interns in her group. She asked her supervisor for an explanation, and he replied that she didn't know as much as the others. She knew from her day-to-day dealings with her peers that she was one of the most knowledgeable, not the least. So she asked what evidence had led him to his conclusion. And he told her, "You ask more questions."

There is evidence that men are less likely to ask questions in a public situation, where asking will reveal their lack of knowledge. One such piece of evidence is a study done in a university classroom, where sociolinguist Kate Remlinger noticed that women students asked the professor more questions than men students did. As part of her study, Remlinger interviewed six students at length, three men and three women. All three men told her that they would not ask questions in class if there was something they did not understand. Instead, they said they would try to find the answer later by reading the textbook, asking a friend, or, as a last resort, asking the professor in private during office hours. As one young man put it, "If it's vague to me, I usually don't ask. I'd rather go home and look it up."

Of course, this does not mean that no men will ask questions when they are in doubt, nor that all women will; the differences, as always, are a matter of likelihood and degree. As always, cultural differences play a role too. It is not unusual for American professors to admit their own ignorance when they do not know the answer to a student's question, but there are many cultures in which professors would not, and students from those cultures may judge American professors by those standards. A student from the Middle East told a professor at a California university that she had just lost all respect for one of his colleagues. The reason: She had asked a question in class, and the offending professor had replied, "I don't know offhand, but I'll find out for you."

The physician who asked her supervisor why he gave her a negative evaluation may be unusual in having been told directly what behavior led to the misjudgment of her skill. But in talking to doctors and doctors-in-training around the country, I have learned that there is nothing exceptional about her experience, that it is common for interns and residents to conceal their ignorance by not asking questions, since those who do ask are judged less capable. Yet it seems that many women who are more likely than men to ask questions (just as women are more likely to stop and ask for directions when they're lost) are unaware that they may make a negative impression at the same time that they get information. Their antennae have not been attuned to making sure they don't appear one-down.

This pattern runs counter to two stereotypes about male and female styles: that men are more focused on information and that women are more sensitive. In regard to classroom behavior, it seems that the women who ask questions are more focused on information, whereas the men who refrain from doing so are more focused on interaction—the impression their asking will make on others. In this situation, it is the men who are more sensitive to the impression made on others by their behavior, although their concern is, ultimately, the effect on themselves rather than on others. And this sensitivity is likely to make them look better in the world of work. Realizing this puts the intern's decision in a troubling perspective. He had to choose between putting his career at risk and putting the patient's health at risk.

It is easy to see benefits of both styles: Someone willing to ask questions has ready access to a great deal of information—all that is known by the people she can ask. But just as men have told me that asking directions is useless since the person you ask may not know and may give you the wrong answer, some people feel they are more certain to get the right information if they read it in a book, and they are learning more by finding it themselves. On the other hand, energy may be wasted looking up information someone else has at hand, and I have heard complaints from people who feel they were sent on wild-goose chases by colleagues who didn't want to admit they really were not sure of what they pretended to know.

The reluctance to say "I don't know" can have serious consequences for an entire company—and did: On Friday, June 17, 1994, a computer problem prevented Fidelity Investments from calculating the value of 166 mutual funds. Rather than report that the values for these funds were not available, a manager decided to report to the National Association of Securities Dealers that the values of these funds had not changed from the day before. Unfortunately, June 17 turned out to be a bad day in the financial markets, so the values of Fidelity's funds that were published in newspapers around the country stood out as noticeably higher than those of other funds. Besides the cost and inconvenience to brokerage firms who had to re-compute their customers' accounts, and the injustice to investors who made decisions to buy or sell based on inaccurate information, the company was mightily embarrassed and forced to apologize publicly. Clearly this was an instance in which it would have been preferable to say, "We don't know."

Flexibility, again, is key. There are many situations in which it serves one well to be self-reliant and discreet about revealing doubt or ignorance, and others in which it is wise to admit what you don't know.

Review Questions

1. What does Tannen mean by *conversational style?*

2. What is the important style difference in the way men and women ask for directions or help, according to Tannen?

3. What is Tannen's hypothesis about why males avoid asking other people for directions?

4. In Tannen's perspective, what conclusions do men and women draw about each other when they display typically different approaches to asking directions?

THREE

Ecology and Subsistence

Ecology is the relationship of an organism to other elements within its environmental sphere. Every species, no matter how simple or complex, fits into a larger complex ecological system; each adapts to its ecological niche unless rapid environmental alterations outstrip the organism's ability and potential to adapt successfully. An important aim of ecological studies is to show how organisms fit within particular environments. Such studies also look at the effect environments have on the shape and behavior of life forms.

Every species has adapted biologically through genetically produced variation and natural selection. For example, the bipedal (two-footed) locomotion characteristic of humans is one possible adaptation to walking on the ground. It also permitted our ancestors to carry food, tools, weapons, and almost anything else they desired, enabling them to range out from a home base and bring things back for others to share.

Biological processes have led to another important human characteristic, the development of a large and complex brain. The human brain is capable of holding an enormous inventory of information. With it, we can classify the parts of our environment and retain instructions for complex ways to deal with the things in our world. Because we can communicate our knowledge symbolically through language, we are able to teach one another. Instead of a genetic code that directs behavior automatically, we operate with a learned cultural code. Culture gives us the ability to behave in a much wider variety of ways and to change rapidly in new situations. With culture, people have been able to live successfully in almost every part of the world.

Cultural ecology is the way people use their culture to adapt to particular environments. All people live in a **physical environment,** the world they can experience through their senses, but they will conceive of it in terms that seem most important to their adaptive needs and cultural perspective. We call this perspective the **cultural environment.**

All human societies must provide for the material needs of their members. People everywhere have to eat, clothe themselves, provide shelter against the elements, and take care of social requirements such as hospitality, gift giving, and proper dress.

Societies employ several different strategies to meet their material needs, strategies that affect their complexity and internal organization as well as relationships to the natural environment and to other human groups. Anthropologists often use these **subsistence strategies** to classify different groups into five types: hunter-gatherers, horticulturalists, pastoralists, agriculturalists, and industrialists. Let us look briefly at each of these.

People who rely on **hunting and gathering** depend on wild plants and animals for subsistence. Hunter-gatherers forage for food, moving to different parts of their territories as supplies of plants, animals, and water grow scarce. They live in small bands of from 10 to 50 people and are typically egalitarian, leading a life marked by sharing and cooperation. Because hunter-gatherer bands are so small, they tend to lack formal political, legal, and religious structure, although members have regular ways to make group decisions, settle disputes, and deal ritually with the questions of death, adversity, social value, and world identification.

Hunter-gatherers tend to see themselves as part of the environment, not masters of it. This view shapes a religious ritual aimed at the maintenance and restoration of environmental harmony. All people lived as hunter-gatherers until about 10,000 years ago, when the first human groups began to farm and dwell in more permanent settlements. Today few hunter-gatherers survive. Most have lost their habitats to more powerful groups bent on economic and political exploitation.

Horticulture represents the earliest farming strategy, one that continues on a diminishing basis among many groups today. Horticulturalists garden. They often use a technique called **slash-and-burn agriculture,** which requires them to clear and burn over wild land and, with the aid of a digging stick, sow seeds in the ashes. When fields lose their fertility after a few years, they are abandoned and new land is cleared. Although horticulturalists farm, they often continue to forage for wild foods and still feel closely related to the natural environment.

Horticulture requires a substantial amount of undeveloped land, so overall population densities must remain fairly low. But the strategy permits higher population densities than hunting and gathering, so horticulturalists tend to live in larger permanent settlements numbering from 50 to 250 individuals. (Some horticultural societies have produced chiefdomships with much larger administrative and religious town centers.) Although they are still small by our standards, horticultural communities are large enough to require more complex organizational strategies. They often display more elaborate kinship systems based on descent, political structures that include headmen or chiefs, political alliances, religions characterized by belief in a variety of supernatural beings, and the beginnings of social inequality. Many of today's so-called tribal peoples are horticulturalists.

Pastoralism is a subsistence strategy based on the herding of domesticated animals such as cattle, goats, sheep, and camels. Although herding strategies vary from one environment to another, pastoralists share some general attributes. They move on a regular basis during the year to take advantage of fresh sources of water and fodder for their animals. They usually congregate in large encampments for part of the year when food and water are plentiful, then divide into smaller groups when these resources become scarce. Pastoralists often display a strong sense of group identity and pride, a fierce independence, and skill at war and raiding. Despite attempts by modern governments to place them in permanent settlements, many pastoral groups in Africa and Asia continue their nomadic lifestyle.

Agriculture is still a common subsistence strategy in many parts of the world. Agriculture refers to a kind of farming based on the intensive cultivation of permanent land holdings. Agriculturalists usually use plows and organic fertilizers and may irrigate their fields in dry conditions.

Agrarian societies are marked by a high degree of social complexity. They are often organized as nation-states with armies and bureaucracies, social stratification, markets, extended families and kin groups, and some occupational specialization. Religion takes on a formal structure and is organized as a separate institution.

The term **industrialism** labels the final kind of subsistence strategy. Ours is an industrial society, as is much of the Western, and more recently, the Asian world. Industrial nations are highly complex; they display an extensive variety of subgroups and social statuses. Industrial societies tend to be dominated by market economies in which goods and services are exchanged on the basis of price, supply, and demand. There is a high degree of economic specialization, and mass marketing may lead to a depersonalization of human relations. Religious, legal, political, and economic systems find expression as separate institutions in a way that might look disjointed to hunter-gatherers or others from smaller, more integrated societies.

The study of cultural ecology involves more than an understanding of people's basic subsistence strategies. Each society exists in a distinctive environment. Although a group may share many subsistence methods with other societies, there are always special environmental needs that shape productive techniques. Andean farmers, for example, have developed approximately 3,000 varieties of potatoes to meet the demands of growing conditions at different elevations in their mountain habitat. Bhil farmers in India have learned to create fields by damming up small streams in their rugged Aravalli hill villages. Otherwise, they would find it difficult to cultivate there at all. American farmers learned to "contour-plow" parallel to slopes in response to water erosion and now increasingly use plowless (no-till) farming to prevent the wind from carrying away precious topsoil.

No matter how successful their microenvironmental adjustments are, most groups in the world now face more serious adaptive challenges. One difficulty is the exploitation of their lands by outsiders, who are often unconstrained by adaptive necessity. A second is the need to overexploit the environment to meet market demand. (See Part Four for articles on market pressures.) In either case, many local peoples find that their traditional subsistence techniques no longer work. They have lost control of their own environmental adjustment and must struggle to adapt to outsiders and what is left of their habitat.

Finally, just as humans adapt culturally to their environments, altering them in the process, environments may biologically adapt to humans. For example, intensive agriculture in the United States provides greater food sources for deer. In response, the number of deer has risen by as much as 400 percent. Animals domesticated by humans, such as cows, pigs, chickens, sheep, goats, dogs, and cats, have also experienced both genetic modification and increased numbers from their association with people. Less obviously, microbes have evolved to take advantage of the growing human presence. Some subsist on human wastes; others, including many that cause epidemic diseases, have evolved to subsist on people themselves.

The !Kung, described by Richard Lee in the first selection, provide an excellent example of a traditional foraging lifestyle. The update to this article by Richard Lee and Megan Biesele show that the same bands of people who once lived on wild foods in the Kalahari now find themselves confined to small government-mandated settlements. Cattle herders tend their animals on the desert lands once occupied by the !Kung. The second article, by Jared Diamond, describes the fate of Easter Islanders who overexploited their small island ecosystem. The example serves as a warning to people everywhere as populations grow and resources diminish. The third selection, by Richard Reed, is a sobering reminder of what can happen to a horticultural people who once subsisted in harmony with their tropical forest habitat, but who now find themselves being displaced by colonists. These outsiders have stripped the forest bare. Nevertheless, the horticultural model is emerging as the most economical solution for sustained use of the forest in today's world.

Key Terms

agriculture   *p. 105*
cultural ecology   *p. 103*
cultural environment   *p. 103*
ecology   *p. 103*
horticulture   *p. 104*
hunting and gathering   *p. 104*

industrialism   *p. 105*
pastoralism   *p. 105*
physical environment   *p. 103*
slash-and-burn agriculture   *p. 104*
subsistence strategies   *p. 104*

10

The Hunters: Scarce Resources in the Kalahari

Richard Borshay Lee

Until about 10,000 years ago, everyone in the world survived by hunting and gathering wild foods. They lived in intimate association with their natural environments and employed a complex variety of strategies to forage for food and other necessities of life. Agriculture displaced foraging as the main subsistence technique over the next few thousand years, but some hunter-gatherers lived on in the more remote parts of the world. This study by Richard Lee was done in the early 1960s and describes the important features of one of the last foraging groups, the Ju/'hoansi-!Kung living in the Kalahari Desert. It argues against the idea, held by many anthropologists at that time, that hunter-gatherers live a precarious, hand-to-mouth existence. Instead, Lee found that the !Kung, depending more on vegetable foods than meat, actually spent little time collecting food and managed to live long and fruitful lives in their difficult desert home. The update by Lee and Megan Biesele that appears at the end of the article details the events that have led the !Kung to settle down permanently to life as small-scale farmers and cattle raisers.

The current anthropological view of hunter-gatherer subsistence rests on two questionable assumptions. First is the notion that these people are primarily dependent on the hunting of game animals, and second is the assumption that their way of life is generally a precarious and arduous struggle for existence.

Recent data on living hunter-gatherers show a radically different picture. We have learned that in many societies, plant and marine resources are far more important than are game animals in the diet. More important, it is becoming clear that, with few conspicuous exceptions, the hunter-gatherer subsistence base is at least routine and reliable and at best surprisingly abundant. Anthropologists have consistently tended to underestimate the viability of even those "marginal isolates" of hunting peoples that have been available to ethnographers.

The purpose of this paper is to analyze the food-getting activities of one such "marginal" people, the !Kung Bushmen of the Kalahari Desert. Three related questions are posed: How do the Bushmen make a living? How easy or difficult is it for them to do this? What kinds of evidence are necessary to measure and evaluate the precariousness or security of a way of life? And after the relevant data are presented, two further questions are asked: What makes this security of life possible? To what extent are the Bushmen typical of hunter-gatherers in general?

Bushman Subsistence

The !Kung Bushmen of Botswana are an apt case for analysis. They inhabit the semi-arid northwest region of the Kalahari Desert. With only six to nine inches of rainfall per year, this is, by any account, a marginal environment for human habitation. In fact, it is precisely the unattractiveness of their homeland that has kept the !Kung isolated from extensive contact with their agricultural and pastoral neighbors.

Fieldwork was carried out in the Dobe area, a line of eight permanent waterholes near the South-West Africa border and 125 miles south of the Okavango River. The population of the Dobe area consists of 466 Bushmen, including 379 permanent residents living in independent camps or associated with Bantu cattle posts, as well as 87 seasonal visitors. The Bushmen share the area with some 340 Bantu pastoralists largely of the Herero and Tswana tribes. The ethnographic present refers to the period of fieldwork: October 1963 to January 1965.

The Bushmen living in independent camps lack firearms, livestock, and agriculture. Apart from occasional visits to the Herero for milk, these !Kung are entirely dependent upon hunting and gathering for their subsistence. Politically they are under the nominal authority of the Tswana headman, although they pay no taxes and receive very few government services. European presence amounts to one overnight government patrol every six to eight weeks. Although Dobe-area !Kung have had some contact with outsiders since the 1880s, the majority of them continue to hunt and gather because there is no viable alternative locally available to them.

Each of the fourteen independent camps is associated with one of the permanent waterholes. During the dry season (May–October) the entire population is clustered around these wells. Table 1 shows the numbers at each well at the end of the 1964 dry season. Two wells had no camp residents and one large well supported five camps. The number of camps at each well and the size of each camp changed frequently during the course of the year. The "camp" is an open aggregate of cooperating persons which changes in size and composition from day to day. Therefore, I have avoided the term "band" in describing the !Kung Bushman living groups.

Each waterhole has a hinterland lying within a six-mile radius that is regularly exploited for vegetable and animal foods. These areas are not territories in the zoological sense, since they are not defended against outsiders. Rather, they constitute the resources that lie within a convenient walking distance of a waterhole. The camp is a self-sufficient subsistence unit. The members move out each day to hunt and gather, and return in the evening to pool the collected foods in such a way that every person present receives an equitable share. Trade in foodstuffs between camps is minimal; personnel do move freely from camp to camp, however. The net effect is of a population constantly in motion. On the

TABLE 1   Numbers and Distribution of Resident Bushmen and Bantu by Waterhole*

Name of Waterhole	No. of Camps	Population of Camps	Other Bushmen	Total Bushmen	Bantu
Dobe	2	37	—	37	—
!angwa	1	16	23	39	84
Bate	2	30	12	42	21
!ubi	1	19	—	19	65
!gose	3	52	9	61	18
/ai/ai	5	94	13	107	67
!xabe	—	—	8	8	12
Mahopa	—	—	23	23	73
Total	14	248	88	336	340

*Figures do not include 130 Bushmen outside area on the date of census.

average, an individual spends a third of his time living only with close relatives, a third visiting other camps, and a third entertaining visitors from other camps.

Because of the strong emphasis on sharing, and the frequency of movement, surplus accumulation of storable plant foods and dried meat is kept to a minimum. There is rarely more than two or three days' supply of food on hand in a camp at any time. The result of this lack of surplus is that a constant subsistence effort must be maintained throughout the year. Unlike agriculturalists, who work hard during the planting and harvesting seasons and undergo "seasonal unemployment" for several months, the Bushmen hunter-gatherers collect food every third or fourth day throughout the year.

Vegetable foods comprise from 60 to 80 percent of the total diet by weight, and collecting involves two or three days of work per woman per week. The men also collect plants and small animals, but their major contribution to the diet is the hunting of medium and large game. The men are conscientious but not particularly successful hunters; although men's and women's work input is roughly equivalent in terms of man-day of effort, the women provide two to three times as much food by weight as the men.

Table 2 summarizes the seasonal activity cycle observed among the Dobe-area !Kung in 1964. For the greater part of the year, food is locally abundant and easily collected. It is only during the end of the dry season in September and October, when desirable foods have been eaten out in the immediate vicinity of the waterholes, that the people have to plan longer hikes of 10 to 15 miles and carry their own water to those areas where the mongongo nut is still available. The important point is that food is a constant, but distance required to reach food is a variable; it is short in the summer, fall, and early winter, and reaches its maximum in the spring.

This analysis attempts to provide quantitative measures of subsistence status, including data on the following topics: abundance and variety of resources, diet selectivity, range size and population density, the composition of the work force, the ratio of work to leisure time, and the caloric and protein levels in the diet. The value of quantitative data is that they can be used comparatively and also may be useful in archeological reconstruction. In addition, one can avoid the pitfalls of subjective and qualitative impressions; for example, statements about food "anxiety" have proven to be difficult to generalize across cultures.

Abundance and Variety of Resources

It is impossible to define "abundance" of resources absolutely. However, one index of *relative* abundance is whether or not a population exhausts all the food available from a given area. By this criterion, the habitat of the Dobe-area Bushmen is abundant in naturally occurring foods. By far the most important food is the mongongo (mangetti) nut (*Ricinodendron rautanenii* Schinz). Although tens of thousands of pounds of these nuts are harvested and eaten each year, thousands more rot on the ground each year for want of picking.

TABLE 2   The Bushman Annual Round

	Jan.	Feb.	Mar.	April	May	June	July	Aug.	Sept.	Oct.	Nov.	Dec.
Season	*Summer Rains*			*Autumn Dry*		*Winter Dry*			*Spring Dry*			*First Rains*
Availability of water	Temporary summer pools everywhere			Large summer pools			Permanent waterholes only					Summer pools developing
Group moves	Widely dispersed at summer pools			At large summer pools			All population restricted to permanent waterholes					Moving out to summer pools
Men's subsistence activities	1. Hunting with bow, arrows, and dogs (year-round) 2. Running down immatures 3. Some gathering (year-round)					Trapping small game in snares				Running down newborn animals		
Women's subsistence activities	1. Gathering of mongongo nuts (year-round) 2. Fruits, berries, melons					Roots, bulbs, resins				Roots, leafy greens		
Ritual activities	Dancing, trance performances, and ritual curing (year-round)				Boys' initiation*							†
Relative subsistence hardship			Water-food distance minimal			Increasing distance from water to food				Water-food distance minimal		

*Held once every five years; none in 1963–64.

†New Year's: Bushmen join the celebrations of their missionized Bantu neighbors.

The mongongo nut, because of its abundance and reliability, alone accounts for 50 percent of the vegetable diet by weight. In this respect it resembles a cultivated staple crop such as maize or rice. Nutritionally it is even more remarkable, for it contains five times the calories and ten times the protein per cooked unit of the cereal crops. The average daily per capita consumption of 300 nuts yields about 1,260 calories and 56 grams of protein. This modest portion, weighing only about 7.5 ounces, contains the caloric equivalent of 2.5 pounds of cooked rice and the protein equivalent of 14 ounces of lean beef.

Furthermore, the mongongo nut is drought resistant, and it will still be abundant in the dry years when cultivated crops may fail. The extremely hard outer shell protects the inner kernel from rot and allows the nuts to be harvested for up to twelve months after they have fallen to the ground. A diet based on mongongo nuts is in fact more reliable than one based on cultivated foods, and it is not surprising, therefore, that when a Bushman was asked why he hadn't taken to agriculture, he replied: "Why should we plant, when there are so many mongongo nuts in the world?"

Apart from the mongongo, the Bushmen have available eighty-four other species of edible food plants, including twenty-nine species of fruits, berries, and melons and thirty species of roots and bulbs. The existence of this variety allows for a wide range of alternatives in subsistence strategy. During the summer months the Bushmen have no problem other than to choose among the tastiest and most easily collected foods. Many species, which are quite edible but less attractive, are bypassed, so that gathering never exhausts *all* the available plant foods of an area. During the dry season the diet becomes much more eclectic and the many species of roots, bulbs, and edible resins make an important contribution. It is this broad base that provides an essential margin of safety during the end of the dry season, when the mongongo nut forests are difficult to reach. In addition, it is likely that these rarely utilized species provide important nutritional and mineral trace elements that may be lacking in the more popular foods.

Diet Selectivity

If the Bushmen were living close to the "starvation" level, then one would expect them to exploit every available source of nutrition. That their life is well above this level is indicated by the data in Table 3. Here all the edible plant species are arranged in classes according to the frequency with which they were observed to be eaten. It should be noted that although there are some eighty-five species available, about 90 percent of the vegetable diet by weight is drawn from only twenty-three species. In other words, 75 percent of the listed species provide only 10 percent of the food value.

In their meat-eating habits, the Bushmen show a similar selectivity. Of the 223 local species of animals known and named by the Bushmen, 54 species are classified as edible, and of these only 17 species were hunted on a regular basis. Only a handful of the dozens of edible species of small mammals, birds, reptiles,

TABLE 3 !Kung Bushman Plant Foods

Food Class	Part Eaten								Totals (percentages)		
	Fruit and Nut	Bean and Root	Fruit and Stalk	Root, Bulb	Fruit, Berry, Melon	Resin	Leaves	Seed, Bean	Total Number of Species in Class	Estimated Contribution by Weight to Vegetable Diet	Estimated Contribution of Each Species
I. Primary Eaten daily throughout year (mongongo nut)	1	—	—	—	—	—	—	—	1	c.50	c.50*
II. Major Eaten daily in season	1	1	1	1	4	—	—	—	8	c.25	c.3†
III. Minor Eaten several times per week in season	—	—	—	7	3	2	2	—	14	c.15	c.1
IV. Supplementary Eaten when classes I-III locally unavailable	—	—	—	9	12	10	1	—	32	c.7	c.0.2
V. Rare Eaten several times per year	—	—	—	9	4	—	—	—	13	c.3	c.0.1‡
VI. Problematic Edible but not observed to be eaten	—	—	—	4	6	4	1	2	17	nil	nil
Total Species	2	1	1	30	29	16	4	2	85	100	—

*1 species constitutes 50 percent of the vegetable diet by weight.

†23 species constitute 90 percent of the vegetable diet by weight.

‡62 species constitute the remaining 10 percent of the diet.

and insects that occur locally are regarded as food. Such animals as rodents, snakes, lizards, termites, and grasshoppers, which in the literature are included in the Bushman diet, are despised by the Bushmen of the Dobe area.

Range Size and Population Density

The necessity to travel long distances, the high frequency of moves, and the maintenance of populations at low densities are also features commonly associated with the hunting and gathering way of life. Density estimates for hunters in western North America and Australia have ranged from 3 persons/square mile to as low as 1 person/100 square miles. In 1963–65, the resident and visiting Bushmen were observed to utilize an area of about 1,000 square miles during the course of the annual round for an effective population density of 41 persons/100 square miles. Within this area, however, the amount of ground covered by members of an individual camp was surprisingly small. A day's round-trip of twelve miles serves to define a "core" area six miles in radius surrounding each water point. By fanning out in all directions from their well, the members of a camp can gain access to the food resources of well over 100 square miles of territory within a two-hour hike. Except for a few weeks each year, areas lying beyond this six-mile radius are rarely utilized, even though they are no less rich in plants and game than are the core areas.

Although the Bushmen move their camps frequently (five or six times a year), they do not move them very far. A rainy season camp in the nut forests is rarely more than ten or twelve miles from the home waterhole, and often new campsites are occupied only a few hundred yards away from the previous one. By these criteria, the Bushmen do not lead a free-ranging nomadic way of life. For example, they do not undertake long marches of 30 to 100 miles to get food, since this task can be readily fulfilled within a day's walk of home base. When such long marches do occur they are invariably for visiting, trading, and marriage arrangements, and should not be confused with the normal routine of subsistence.

Demographic Factors

Another indicator of the harshness of a way of life is the age at which people die. Ever since Hobbes characterized life in the state of nature as "nasty, brutish and short," the assumption has been that hunting and gathering is so rigorous that members of such societies are rapidly worn out and meet an early death. Silberbauer, for example, says of the Gwi Bushmen of the central Kalahari that "life expectancy . . . is difficult to calculate, but I do not believe that many live beyond 45." And Coon has said of hunters in general:

> The practice of abandoning the hopelessly ill and aged has been observed in many parts of the world. It is always done by people living in poor environments where it is necessary to move about frequently to obtain food, where food is scarce, and transportation difficult. . . . Among peoples who are forced to live in this way the

oldest generation, the generation of individuals who have passed their physical peak, is reduced in numbers and influence. There is no body of elders to hand on tradition and control the affairs of younger men and women, and no formal system of age grading.

The !Kung Bushmen of the Dobe area flatly contradict this view. In a total population of 466, no fewer than 46 individuals (17 men and 29 women) were determined to be over sixty years of age, a proportion that compares favorably to the percentage of elderly in industrialized populations.

The aged hold a respected position in Bushmen society and are the effective leaders of the camps. Senilicide is extremely rare. Long after their productive years have passed, the old people are fed and cared for by their children and grandchildren. The blind, the senile, and the crippled are respected for the special ritual and technical skills they possess. For instance, the four elders at !gose waterhole were totally or partially blind, but this handicap did not prevent their active participation in decision making and ritual curing.

Another significant feature of the composition of the work force is the late assumption of adult responsibility by the adolescents. Young people are not expected to provide food regularly until they are married. Girls typically marry between the ages of fifteen and twenty, and boys about five years later, so that it is not unusual to find healthy, active teenagers visiting from camp to camp while their older relatives provide food for them.

As a result, the people in the twenty to sixty age group support a surprisingly large percentage of nonproductive young and old people. About 40 percent of the population in camps contributes little to the food supplies. This allocation of work to young and middle-aged adults allows for a relatively carefree childhood and adolescence and a relatively unstrenuous old age.

Leisure and Work

Another important index of ease or difficulty of subsistence is the amount of time devoted to the food quest. Hunting has usually been regarded by social scientists as a way of life in which merely keeping alive is so formidable a task that members of such societies lack the leisure time necessary to "build culture." The !Kung Bushmen would appear to conform to the rule, for as Lorna Marshall says:

> It is vividly apparent that among the !Kung Bushmen, ethos, or "the spirit which actuates manners and customs," is survival. Their time and energies are almost wholly given to this task, for life in their environment requires that they spend their days mainly in procuring food.

It is certainly true that getting food is the most important single activity in Bushman life. However, this statement would apply equally well to small-scale agricultural and pastoral societies too. How much time is *actually* devoted to the food quest is fortunately an empirical question. And an analysis of the work effort of the Dobe Bushmen shows some unexpected results. From July 6 to August 2, 1964, I recorded all the daily activities of the Bushmen living at the Dobe waterhole. Because of the coming and going of visitors, the camp population fluctuated in size day by day, from a low of 23 to a high of 40, with a mean of 31.8 persons. Each day some of the adult members of the camp went out to hunt and/or gather while others stayed home or went visiting. The daily recording of all personnel on hand made it possible to calculate the number of man-days of work as a percentage of total number of man-days of consumption.

Although the Bushmen do not organize their activities on the basis of a seven-day week, I have divided the data this way to make them more intelligible. The workweek was calculated to show how many days out of seven each adult spent in subsistence activities (Table 4, Column 7). Week II has been eliminated from the totals since the investigator contributed food. In week I, the people spent an average of 2.3 days in subsistence activities, in week II, 1.9 days, and in week IV, 3.2 days. In all, the adults of the Dobe camp worked about two and a half days a week. Since the average working day was about six hours long, the fact emerges that !Kung Bushmen of Dobe, despite their harsh environment, devote from twelve to nineteen hours a week to getting food. Even the hardest-working individual in the camp, a man named ≠oma who went out hunting on sixteen of the twenty-eight days, spent a maximum of thirty-two hours a week in the food quest.

Because the Bushmen do not amass a surplus of foods, there are no seasons of exceptionally intensive activities such as planting and harvesting, and no seasons of unemployment. The level of work observed is an accurate reflection of the effort required to meet the immediate caloric needs of the group. This

TABLE 4   Summary of Dobe Work Diary

Week	(1) Mean Group Size	(2) Adult-Days	(3) Child-Days	(4) Total Man-Days of Consumption	(5) Man-Days of Work	(6) Meat (lbs.)	(7) Average Workweek /Adult	(8) Index of Subsistence Effort
I (July 6–12)	25.6 (23–29)	114	65	179	37	104	2.3	.21
II (July 13–19)	28.3 (23–27)	125	73	198	22	80	1.2	.11
III (July 20–26)	34.3 (29–40)	156	84	240	42	177	1.9	.18
IV (July 27–Aug. 2)	35.6 (32–40)	167	82	249	77	129	3.2	.31
4-wk. total	30.9	562	304	866	178	490	2.2	.21
Adjusted total*	31.8	437	231	668	156	410	2.5	.23

*See text

Key: Column 1: Mean group size = $\dfrac{\text{total man-days of consumption}}{7}$.

Column 7: Workweek = the number of workdays per adult per week.

Column 8: Index of subsistence effort = $\dfrac{\text{man-days of work}}{\text{man-days of consumption}}$ (e.g., in Week I, the value of "S" = 21, i.e., 21 days of work/100 days of consumption or 1 workday produces food for 5 consumption days).

work diary covers the midwinter dry season, a period when food is neither at its most plentiful nor at its scarcest levels, and the diary documents the transition from better to worse conditions (see Table 5). During the fourth week the gatherers were making overnight trips to camps in the mongongo nut forests seven to ten miles distant from the waterhole. These longer trips account for the rise in the level of work, from twelve or thirteen to nineteen hours per week.

If food getting occupies such a small proportion of a Bushman's waking hours, then how *do* people allocate their time? A woman gathers on one day enough food to feed her family for three days, and spends the rest of her time resting in camp, doing embroidery, visiting other camps, or entertaining visitors from other camps. For each day at home, kitchen routines, such as cooking, nut cracking, collecting firewood, and fetching water, occupy one to three hours of her time. This rhythm of steady work and steady leisure is maintained throughout the year.

The hunters tend to work more frequently than the women, but their schedule is uneven. It is not unusual for a man to hunt avidly for a week and then do nothing at all for two or three weeks. Since hunting is an unpredictable business and subject to magical control, hunters sometimes experience a run of bad luck and stop hunting for a month or longer. During these periods, visiting, entertaining, and especially dancing are the primary activities of men. (Unlike the Hadza, gambling is only a minor leisure activity.)

The trance dance is the focus of Bushman ritual life; over 50 percent of the men have trained as trance-performers and regularly enter trance during the course of the all-night dances. At some camps, trance dances occur as frequently as two or three times a week, and those who have entered trances the night before rarely go out hunting the following day. . . . In a camp with five or more hunters, there are usually two or three who are actively hunting and several others who are inactive. The net effect is to phase the hunting and non-hunting so that a fairly steady supply of meat is brought into camp.

Caloric Returns

Is the modest work effort of the Bushmen sufficient to provide the calories necessary to maintain the health of the population? Or have the !Kung, in common with some agricultural peoples, adjusted to a permanently substandard nutritional level?

During my fieldwork I did not encounter any cases of kwashiorkor, the most common nutritional disease in the children of African agricultural societies. However, without medical examinations, it is impossible to exclude the possibility that subclinical signs of malnutrition existed.

Another measure of nutritional adequacy is the average consumption of calories and proteins per person per day. The estimate for the Bushmen is based on observations of the weights of foods of known composition that were brought into Dobe camp on each day of the study period. The per-capita figure is obtained by dividing the total weight of foodstuffs by the total number of persons in the camp. These results are set out in detail elsewhere and can only be summarized

TABLE 5   Caloric and Protein Levels in the !Kung Bushman Diet, July–August, 1964

| | Per-Capita Consumption | | | | |
Class of Food	Percentage Contribution to Diet by Weight	Weight in Grams	Protein in Grams	Calories per Person per Day	Percentage Caloric Contribution of Meat and Vegetables
Meat	37	230	34.5	690	33
Mongongo nuts	33	210	56.7	1,260	67
Other vegetable foods	30	190	1.9	190	
Total all sources	100	630	93.1	2,140	100

here. During the study period 410 pounds of meat were brought in by the hunters of the Dobe camp, for a daily share of nine ounces of meat per person. About 700 pounds of vegetables were gathered and consumed during the same period. Table 5 sets out the calories and proteins available per capita in the !Kung Bushman diet from meat, mongongo nuts, and other vegetable sources.

This output of 2,140 calories and 93.1 grams of protein per person per day may be compared with the Recommended Daily Allowances (RDA) for persons of the small size and stature but vigorous activity regime of the !Kung Bushmen. The RDA for Bushmen can be estimated at 1,975 calories and 60 grams of protein per person per day. Thus it is apparent that food output exceeds energy requirements by 165 calories and 33 grams of protein. One can tentatively conclude that even a modest subsistence effort of two or three days' work per week is enough to provide an adequate diet for the !Kung Bushmen.

The Security of Bushman Life

I have attempted to evaluate the subsistence base of one contemporary hunter-gatherer society living in a marginal environment. The !Kung Bushmen have available to them some relatively abundant high-quality foods, and they do not have to walk very far or work very hard to get them. Furthermore, this modest work effort provides sufficient calories to support not only active adults, but also a large number of middle-aged and elderly people. The Bushmen do not have to press their youngsters into the service of the food quest, nor do they have to dispose of the oldsters after they have ceased to be productive.

The evidence presented assumes an added significance because this security of life was observed during the third year of one of the most severe droughts in South Africa's history. Most of the 576,000 people of Botswana are pastoralists and agriculturalists. After the crops had failed three years in succession and over 100,000 head of cattle had died on the range for lack of water, the World Food Program of the United Nations instituted a famine relief program which has grown to include 180,000 people, over 30 percent of the population. This program did not touch the Dobe area in the isolated northwest corner of the country, and the Herero and Tswana women there were able to feed their families only by joining the Bushman women to forage for wild foods. Thus the natural plant resources of the Dobe area were carrying a higher proportion of population than would be the case in years when the Bantu harvested crops. Yet this added pressure on the land did not seem to adversely affect the Bushmen.

In one sense it was unfortunate that the period of my fieldwork happened to coincide with the drought, since I was unable to witness a "typical" annual subsistence cycle. However, in another sense, the coincidence was a lucky one, for the drought put the Bushmen and their subsistence system to the acid test and, in terms of adaptation to scarce resources, they passed with flying colors. One can postulate that their subsistence base would be even more substantial during years of higher rainfall.

What are the crucial factors that make this way of life possible? I suggest that the primary factor is the Bushmen's strong emphasis on vegetable food sources. Although hunting involves a great deal of effort and prestige, plant foods provide from 60 to 80 percent of the annual diet by weight. Meat has come to be regarded as a special treat; when available, it is welcomed as a break from the routine of vegetable foods, but it is never depended upon as a staple. No one ever goes hungry when hunting fails.

The reason for this emphasis is not hard to find. Vegetable foods are abundant, sedentary, and predictable. They grow in the same place year after year, and the gatherer is guaranteed a day's return of food for a day's expenditure of energy. Game animals, by contrast, are scarce, mobile, unpredictable, and difficult to catch. A hunter has no guarantee of success and may in fact go for days or weeks without killing a large mammal. During the study period, there were eleven men in the Dobe camp, of whom four did no hunting at all. The seven active men spent a total of 78 man-days hunting, and this work input yielded eighteen animals killed, or one kill for every four man-days of hunting. The probability of any one hunter making a kill on a given day was 0.23. By contrast, the probability of a woman finding plant food on a given day was 1.00. In other words, hunting and gathering are not equally felicitous subsistence alternatives.

Consider the productivity per man-hour of the two kinds of subsistence activities. One man-hour of hunting produces about 100 edible calories, and of gathering, 240 calories. Gathering is thus seen to be 2.4 times more productive than hunting. In short, hunting is a *high-risk, low-return* subsistence activity, while gathering is a *low-risk, high-return* subsistence activity.

It is not at all contradictory that the hunting complex holds a central place in the Bushmen ethos and that meat is valued more highly than vegetable foods. Analogously, steak is valued more highly than potatoes in the food preferences of our own society. In both situations the meat is more "costly" than the vegetable food. In the Bushman case, the cost of food can be measured in terms of time and energy expended. By this standard, 1,000 calories of meat "costs" ten man-hours, while the "cost" of 1,000 calories of vegetable foods is only four man-hours. Further, it is to be expected that the less predictable, more expensive food source would have a greater accretion of myth and ritual built up around it than would the routine staples of life, which rarely if ever fail.

Conclusions

Three points ought to be stressed. First, life in the state of nature is not necessarily nasty, brutish, and short. The Dobe-area Bushmen live well today on wild plants and meat, in spite of the fact that they are confined to the least productive portion of the range in which Bushman peoples were formerly found. It is likely that an even more substantial subsistence would have been characteristic of these hunters and gatherers in the past, when they had the pick of African habitats to choose from.

Second, the basis of Bushman diet is derived from sources other than meat. This emphasis makes good ecological sense to the !Kung Bushmen and appears to be a common feature among hunters and gatherers in general. Since a 30 to 40 percent input of meat is such a consistent target for modern hunters in a variety of habitats, is it not reasonable to postulate a similar percentage for prehistoric hunters? Certainly the absence of plant remains on archeological sites is by itself not sufficient evidence for the absence of gathering. Recently abandoned Bushman campsites show a similar absence of vegetable remains, although this paper has clearly shown that plant foods comprise over 60 percent of the actual diet.

Finally, one gets the impression that hunting societies have been chosen by ethnologists to illustrate a dominant theme, such as the extreme importance of environment in the molding of certain cultures. Such a theme can best be exemplified by cases in which the technology is simple and/or the environment is harsh. This emphasis on the dramatic may have been pedagogically useful, but unfortunately it has led to the assumption that a precarious hunting subsistence base was characteristic of all cultures in the Pleistocene. This view of both modern and ancient hunters ought to be reconsidered. Specifically I am suggesting a shift in focus away from the dramatic and unusual cases, and toward a consideration of hunting and gathering as a persistent and well-adapted way of life.

Epilogue: The Ju/'hoansi in 1994[1]

In 1963 perhaps three-quarters of the Dobe Ju/'hoansi were living in camps based primarily on hunting and gathering while the rest were attached to Black cattle posts. Back then there had been no trading stores, schools, or clinics, no government feeding programs, boreholes, or airstrips, and no resident civil servants (apart from the tribally-appointed headman, his clerk, and constable). By

---

[1]Excerpted from Richard B. Lee and Megan Biesele, "A Local Culture in the Global System: The Ju/'hoansi-!Kung Today," *General Anthropology* 1(1) (Fall 1994): pp. 1, 3–5.

1994 all these institutions and facilities were in place and the Dobe people were well into their third decade of rapid social change; they had been transformed in a generation from a society of foragers, some of whom herded and worked for others, to a society of small-holders who eked out a living by herding, farming, and craft production, along with some hunting and gathering.

Ju villages today look like others in Botswana. The beehive-shaped grass huts are gone, replaced by semi-permanent mud-walled houses behind makeshift stockades to keep out cattle. Villages ceased to be circular and tight-knit. Twenty-five people who lived in a space twenty by twenty meters now spread themselves out in a line village several hundred meters long. Instead of looking across the central open space at each other, the houses face the kraal where cattle and goats are kept, inscribing spatially a symbolic shift from reliance on each other to reliance on property in the form of herds.

Hunting and gathering, which provided Dobe Ju with over 85 percent of their subsistence as recently as 1964, now supplies perhaps 30 percent of their food. The rest is made up of milk and meat from domestic stock, store-bought mealie (corn) meal, and vast quantities of heavily-sugared tea whitened with powdered milk. Game meat and foraged foods and occasional produce from gardens makes up the rest of the diet. However, for most of the 1980s government and foreign drought relief provided the bulk of the diet. . . .

In the long run, Dobe-area Ju/'hoansi face serious difficulties. Since 1975, wealthy Tswana have formed borehole syndicates to stake out ranches in remote areas. With 99-year leases, which can be bought and sold, ownership is tantamount to private tenure. By the late 1980s borehole drilling was approaching the Dobe area. If the Dobe Ju do not form borehole syndicates soon, with overseas help, their traditional foraging areas may be permanently cut off from them by commercial ranching.

Review Questions

1. How does Lee assess the day-to-day quality of !Kung life when they lived as foragers? How does this view compare with that held by many anthropologists in the early 1960s?

2. What evidence does Lee give to support his view about the !Kung?

3. According to Lee, !Kung children are not expected to work until after they are married; old people are supported and respected. How does this arrangement differ from behavior in our own society, and what might explain the difference?

4. What was a key to successful subsistence for the !Kung and other hunter-gatherers, according to Lee?

5. In what ways has life changed for the !Kung since 1964? What has caused these changes?

11

Adaptive Failure:
Easter's End

Jared Diamond

Customs can often be explained as human responses to material necessity. But people may not always adapt successfully, as Jared Diamond shows in this discussion of the rise and fall of Easter Island civilization. Basing his conclusions on recent archaeological excavations, he notes that in A.D. 400, when the Polynesian ancestors of today's Easter Island population arrived on the island, they found a heavily forested and fertile land. Within a few hundred years, the islanders numbered between 7,000 to 20,000 and lived in a politically complex, prosperous society. By the 1400s, however, the forest was destroyed, making it impossible for people to build ocean-going canoes or continue the manufacture of stone heads, for which the island later became famous. Bird and sea mammal populations, once a major source of food, had also been decimated. Political chaos ensued and islanders turned to cannibalism as a dietary supplement. Diamond concludes that Easter Island civilization declined because environmental destruction occurred slowly and because social concerns took precedence over conservation. In this sense, the island's fate serves as a warning about humanity's future in a highly stressed world environment.

Among the most riveting mysteries of human history are those posed by vanished civilizations. Everyone who has seen the abandoned buildings of the Khmer, the Maya, or the Anasazi is immediately moved to ask the same question: Why did the societies that erected those structures disappear?

Their vanishing touches us as the disappearance of other animals, even the dinosaurs, never can. No matter how exotic those lost civilizations seem, their framers were humans like us. Who is to say we won't succumb to the same fate? Perhaps someday New York's skyscrapers will stand derelict and overgrown with vegetation, like the temples at Angkor Wat and Tikal.

Among all such vanished civilizations, that of the former Polynesian society on Easter Island remains unsurpassed in mystery and isolation. The mystery stems especially from the island's gigantic stone statues and its impoverished landscape, but it is enhanced by our associations with the specific people involved: Polynesians represent for us the ultimate in exotic romance, the background for many a child's, and an adult's, vision of paradise. My own interest in Easter was kindled over 30 years ago when I read Thor Heyerdahl's fabulous accounts of his *Kon-Tiki* voyage.

But my interest has been revived recently by a much more exciting account, one not of heroic voyages but of painstaking research and analysis. My friend David Steadman, a paleontologist, has been working with a number of other researchers who are carrying out the first systematic excavations on Easter intended to identify the animals and plants that once lived there. Their work is contributing to a new interpretation of the island's history that makes it a tale not only of wonder but of warning as well.

Easter Island, with an area of only 64 square miles, is the world's most isolated scrap of habitable land. It lies in the Pacific Ocean more than 2,000 miles west of the nearest continent (South America), 1,400 miles from even the nearest habitable island (Pitcairn). Its subtropical location and latitude—at 27 degrees south, it is approximately as far below the equator as Houston is north of it—help give it a rather mild climate, while its volcanic origins make its soil fertile. In theory, this combination of blessings should have made Easter a miniature paradise, remote from problems that beset the rest of the world.

The island derives its name from its "discovery" by the Dutch explorer Jacob Roggeveen, on Easter (April 5) in 1722. Roggeveen's first impression was not of a paradise but of a wasteland: "We originally, from a further distance, have considered the said Easter Island as sandy; the reason for that is this, that we counted as sand the withered grass, hay, or other scorched and burnt vegetation, because its wasted appearance could give no other impression than of a singular poverty and barrenness."

The island Roggeveen saw was a grassland without a single tree or bush over ten feet high. Modern botanists have identified only 47 species of higher plants native to Easter, most of them grasses, sedges, and ferns. The list includes just two species of small trees and two of woody shrubs. With such flora, the islanders Roggeveen encountered had no source of real firewood to warm themselves during Easter's cool, wet, windy winters. Their native animals included nothing larger than insects, not even a single species of native bat, land bird, land snail, or lizard. For domestic animals, they had only chickens.

European visitors throughout the eighteenth and early nineteenth centuries estimated Easter's human population at about 2,000, a modest number considering the island's fertility. As Captain James Cook recognized during his brief visit in 1774, the islanders were Polynesians (a Tahitian man accompanying Cook was able to converse with them). Yet despite the Polynesians' well-deserved fame as a great seafaring people, the Easter Islanders who came out to Roggeveen's and Cook's ships did so by swimming or paddling canoes that Roggeveen described as "bad and frail." Their craft, he wrote, were "put together with manifold small planks and light inner timbers, which they cleverly stitched together with very fine twisted threads. . . . But as they lack the knowledge and particularly the materials for caulking and making tight the great number of seams of the canoes, these are accordingly very leaky, for which reason they are compelled to spend half the time in bailing." The canoes, only ten feet long, held at most two people, and only three or four canoes were observed on the entire island.

With such flimsy craft, Polynesians could never have colonized Easter from even the nearest island, nor could they have traveled far offshore to fish. The islanders Roggeveen met were totally isolated, unaware that other people existed. Investigators in all the years since his visit have discovered no trace of the islanders' having any outside contacts: not a single Easter Island rock or product has turned up elsewhere, nor has anything been found on the island that could have been brought by anyone other than the original settlers or the Europeans. Yet the people living on Easter claimed memories of visiting the uninhabited Sala y Gomez reef 260 miles away, far beyond the range of the leaky canoes seen by Roggeveen. How did the islanders' ancestors reach that reef from Easter, or reach Easter from anywhere else?

Easter Island's most famous feature is its huge stone statues, more than 200 of which once stood on massive stone platforms lining the coast. At least 700 more, in all stages of completion, were abandoned in quarries or on ancient roads between the quarries and the coast, as if the carvers and moving crews had thrown down their tools and walked off the job. Most of the erected statues were carved in a single quarry and then somehow transported as far as six miles—despite heights as great as 33 feet and weights up to 82 tons. The abandoned statues, meanwhile, were as much as 65 feet tall and weighed up to 270 tons. The stone platforms were equally gigantic: up to 500 feet long and 10 feet high, with facing slabs weighing up to 10 tons.

Roggeveen himself quickly recognized the problem the statues posed: "The stone images at first caused us to be struck with astonishment," he wrote, "because we could not comprehend how it was possible that these people, who are devoid of heavy thick timber for making any machines, as well as strong ropes, nevertheless had been able to erect such images." Roggeveen might have added that the islanders had no wheels, no draft animals, and no source of power except their own muscles. How did they transport the giant statues for miles, even before erecting them? To deepen the mystery, the statues were still standing in

1770, but by 1864 all of them had been pulled down, by the islanders themselves. Why then did they carve them in the first place? And why did they stop?

The statues imply a society very different from the one Roggeveen saw in 1722. Their sheer number and size suggest a population much larger than 2,000 people. What became of everyone? Furthermore, that society must have been highly organized. Easter's resources were scattered across the island: the best stone for the statues was quarried at Rano Raraku near Easter's northeast end; red stone, used for large crowns adorning some of the statues, was quarried at Puna Pau, inland in the southwest; stone carving tools came mostly from Aroi in the northwest. Meanwhile, the best farmland lay in the south and east, and the best fishing grounds on the north and west coasts. Extracting and redistributing all those goods required complex political organization. What happened to that organization, and how could it ever have arisen in such a barren landscape?

Easter Island's mysteries have spawned volumes of speculation for more than two and a half centuries. Many Europeans were incredulous that Polynesians—commonly characterized as "mere savages"—could have created the statues or the beautifully constructed stone platforms. In the 1950s, Heyerdahl argued that Polynesia must have been settled by advanced societies of American Indians, who in turn must have received civilization across the Atlantic from more advanced societies of the Old World. Heyerdahl's raft voyages aimed to prove the feasibility of such prehistoric transoceanic contacts. In the 1960s the Swiss writer Erich von Däniken, an ardent believer in Earth visits by extraterrestrial astronauts, went further, claiming that Easter's statues were the work of intelligent beings who owned ultramodern tools, became stranded on Easter, and were finally rescued.

Heyerdahl and von Däniken both brushed aside overwhelming evidence that the Easter Islanders were typical Polynesians derived from Asia rather than from the Americas and that their culture (including their statues) grew out of Polynesian culture. Their language was Polynesian, as Cook had already concluded. Specifically, they spoke an eastern Polynesian dialect related to Hawaiian and Marquesan, a dialect isolated since about A.D. 400, as estimated from slight differences in vocabulary. Their fishhooks and stone adzes resembled early Marquesan models. Last year DNA extracted from 12 Easter Island skeletons was also shown to be Polynesian. The islanders grew bananas, taro, sweet potatoes, sugarcane, and paper mulberry—typical Polynesian crops, mostly of Southeast Asian origin. Their sole domestic animal, the chicken, was also typically Polynesian and ultimately Asian, as were the rats that arrived as stowaways in the canoes of the first settlers.

What happened to those settlers? The fanciful theories of the past must give way to evidence gathered by hardworking practitioners in three fields: archeology, pollen analysis, and paleontology.

Modern archeological excavations on Easter have continued since Heyerdahl's 1955 expedition. The earliest radiocarbon dates associated with human activities are around A.D. 400 to 700, in reasonable agreement with the approximate settlement date of 400 estimated by linguists. The period of statue construction peaked around 1200 to 1500, with few if any statues erected thereafter. Densities of archeological sites suggest a large population; an estimate of 7,000 people is widely quoted by archeologists, but other estimates range up to 20,000, which does not seem implausible for an island of Easter's area and fertility.

Archeologists have also enlisted surviving islanders in experiments aimed at figuring out how the statues might have been carved and erected. Twenty people, using only stone chisels, could have carved even the largest completed statue within a year. Given enough timber and fiber for making ropes, teams of at most a few hundred people could have loaded the statues onto wooden sleds, dragged them over lubricated wooden tracks or rollers, and used logs as levers to maneuver them into a standing position. Rope could have been made from the fiber of a small native tree, related to the linden, called the hauhau. However, that tree is now extremely scarce on Easter, and hauling one statue would have required hundreds of yards of rope. Did Easter's now barren landscape once support the necessary trees?

That question can be answered by the technique of pollen analysis, which involves boring out a column of sediment from a swamp or pond, with the most recent deposits at the top and relatively more ancient deposits at the bottom. The absolute age of each layer can be dated by radiocarbon methods. Then begins the hard work: examining tens of thousands of pollen grains under a microscope, counting them, and identifying the plant species that produced each one by comparing the grains with modern pollen from known plant species. For Easter Island, the bleary-eyed scientists who performed that task were John Flenley, now at Massey University in New Zealand, and Sarah King of the University of Hull in England.

Flenley and King's heroic efforts were rewarded by the striking new picture that emerged of Easter's prehistoric landscape. For at least 30,000 years before human arrival and during the early years of Polynesian settlement, Easter was not a wasteland at all. Instead, a subtropical forest of trees and woody bushes towered over a ground layer of shrubs, herbs, ferns, and grasses. In the forest grew tree daisies, the rope-yielding hauhau tree, and the toromiro tree, which furnishes a dense, mesquite-like firewood. The most common tree in the forest was a species of palm now absent on Easter but formerly so abundant that the bottom strata of the sediment column were packed with its pollen. The Easter Island palm was closely related to the still-surviving Chilean wine palm, which grows up to 82 feet tall and 6 feet in diameter. The tall, unbranched trunks of the Easter Island palm would have been ideal for transporting and erecting statues and constructing large canoes. The palm would also have been a valuable food source, since its Chilean relative yields edible nuts as well as sap from which Chileans make sugar, syrup, honey, and wine.

What did the first settlers of Easter Island eat when they were not glutting themselves on the local equivalent of maple syrup? Recent excavations by David Steadman, of the New York State Museum at Albany, have yielded a picture of Easter's original animal world as surprising as Flenley and King's picture of its plant world. Steadman's expectations for Easter were conditioned by his experiences elsewhere in Polynesia, where fish are overwhelmingly the main food at archeological sites, typically accounting for more than 90 percent of the bones in ancient Polynesian garbage heaps. Easter, though, is too cool for the coral reefs beloved by fish, and its cliffgirded coastline permits shallow-water fishing in only a few places. Less than a quarter of the bones in its early garbage heaps (from the period 900 to 1300) belonged to fish; instead, nearly one-third of all bones came from porpoises.

Nowhere else in Polynesia do porpoises account for even 1 percent of discarded food bones. But most other Polynesian islands offered animal food in the form of birds and mammals, such as New Zealand's now extinct giant moas and Hawaii's now extinct flightless geese. Most other islanders also had domestic pigs and dogs. On Easter, porpoises would have been the largest animal available—other than humans. The porpoise species identified at Easter, the common dolphin, weighs up to 165 pounds. It generally lives out at sea, so it could not have been hunted by line fishing or spearfishing from shore. Instead, it must have been harpooned far offshore, in big seaworthy canoes built from the extinct palm tree.

In addition to porpoise meat, Steadman found, the early Polynesian settlers were feasting on seabirds. For those birds, Easter's remoteness and lack of predators made it an ideal haven as a breeding site, at least until humans arrived. Among the prodigious numbers of seabirds that bred on Easter were albatross, boobies, frigate birds, fulmars, petrels, prions, shearwaters, storm petrels, terns, and tropic birds. With at least 25 nesting species, Easter was the richest seabird breeding site in Polynesia and probably in the whole Pacific.

Land birds as well went into early Easter Island cooking pots. Steadman identified bones of at least six species, including barn owls, herons, parrots, and rail. Bird stew would have been seasoned with meat from large numbers of rats, which the Polynesian colonists inadvertently brought with them; Easter Island is the sole known Polynesian island where rat bones outnumber fish bones at archeological sites. (In case you're squeamish and consider rats inedible, I still recall recipes for creamed laboratory rat that my British biologist friends used to supplement their diet during their years of wartime food rationing.)

Porpoises, seabirds, land birds, and rats did not complete the list of meat sources formerly available on Easter. A few bones hint at the possibility of breeding seal colonies as well. All these delicacies were cooked in ovens fired by wood from the island's forests.

Such evidence lets us imagine the island onto which Easter's first Polynesian colonists stepped ashore some 1,600 years ago, after a long canoe voyage from eastern Polynesia. They found themselves in a pristine paradise. What then happened to it? The pollen grains and the bones yield a grim answer.

Pollen records show that destruction of Easter's forests was well under way by the year 800, just a few centuries after the start of human settlement. Then charcoal from wood fires came to fill the sediment cores, while pollen of palms and other trees and woody shrubs decreased or disappeared, and pollen of the grasses that replaced the forest became more abundant. Not long after 1400 the palm finally became extinct, not only as a result of being chopped down but also because the now ubiquitous rats prevented its regeneration: of the dozens of preserved palm nuts discovered in caves on Easter, all had been chewed by rats and could no longer germinate. While the hauhau tree did not become extinct in Polynesian times, its numbers declined drastically until there weren't enough left to make ropes from. By the time Heyerdahl visited Easter, only a single, nearly dead toromiro tree remained on the island, and even that lone survivor has now disappeared. (Fortunately, the toromiro still grows in botanical gardens elsewhere.)

The fifteenth century marked the end not only for Easter's palm but for the forest itself. Its doom had been approaching as people cleared land to plant gardens; as they felled trees to build canoes, to transport and erect statues, and to burn; as rats devoured seeds; and probably as the native birds died out that had pollinated the trees' flowers and dispersed their fruit. The overall picture is among the most extreme examples of forest destruction anywhere in the world: the whole forest gone, and most of its tree species extinct.

The destruction of the island's animals was as extreme as that of the forest: without exception, every species of native land bird became extinct. Even shellfish were overexploited, until people had to settle for small sea snails instead of larger cowries. Porpoise bones disappeared abruptly from garbage heaps around 1500; no one could harpoon porpoises anymore, since the trees used for constructing the big seagoing canoes no longer existed. The colonies of more than half of the seabird species breeding on Easter or on its offshore islets were wiped out.

In place of these meat supplies, the Easter Islanders intensified their production of chickens, which had been only an occasional food item. They also turned to the largest remaining meat source available: humans, whose bones became common in late Easter Island garbage heaps. Oral traditions of the islanders are rife with cannibalism; the most inflammatory taunt that could be snarled at an enemy was "The flesh of your mother sticks between my teeth." With no wood available to cook these new goodies, the islanders resorted to sugarcane scraps, grass, and sedges to fuel their fires.

All these strands of evidence can be wound into a coherent narrative of a society's decline and fall. The first Polynesian colonists found themselves on an island with fertile soil, abundant food, bountiful building materials, ample lebensraum, and all the prerequisites for comfortable living. They prospered and multiplied.

After a few centuries, they began erecting stone statues on platforms, like the ones their Polynesian forebears had carved. With passing years, the statues and platforms became larger and larger, and the statues began sporting ten-ton red crowns—probably in an escalating spiral of one-upmanship, as rival clans tried to surpass each other with shows of wealth and power. (In the same way, successive Egyptian pharaohs built ever-larger pyramids. Today Hollywood movie moguls near my home in Los Angeles are displaying their wealth and power by building ever more ostentatious mansions. Tycoon Marvin Davis topped previous moguls with plans for a 50,000-square-foot house, so now Aaron Spelling has topped Davis with a 56,000-square-foot house. All that those buildings lack to make the message explicit are ten-ton red crowns.) On Easter, as in modern America, society was held together by a complex political system to redistribute locally available resources and to integrate the economies of different areas.

Eventually Easter's growing population was cutting the forest more rapidly than the forest was regenerating. The people used the land for gardens and the wood for fuel, canoes, and houses—and, of course, for lugging statues. As forest disappeared, the islanders ran out of timber and rope to transport and erect their statues. Life became more uncomfortable—springs and streams dried up, and wood was no longer available for fires.

People also found it harder to fill their stomachs, as land birds, large sea snails, and many seabirds disappeared. Because timber for building seagoing canoes vanished, fish catches declined and porpoises disappeared from the table. Crop yields also declined, since deforestation allowed the soil to be eroded by rain and wind, dried by the sun, and its nutrients to be leeched from it. Intensified chicken production and cannibalism replaced only part of all those lost foods. Preserved statuettes with sunken cheeks and visible ribs suggest that people were starving.

With the disappearance of food surpluses, Easter Island could no longer feed the chiefs, bureaucrats, and priests who had kept a complex society running. Surviving islanders described to early European visitors how local chaos replaced centralized government and a warrior class took over from the hereditary chiefs. The stone points of spears and daggers, made by the warriors during their heyday in the 1600s and 1700s, still litter the ground of Easter today. By around 1700, the population began to crash toward between one-quarter and one-tenth of its former number. People took to living in caves for protection against their enemies. Around 1770 rival clans started to topple each other's statues, breaking the heads off. By 1864 the last statue had been thrown down and desecrated.

As we try to imagine the decline of Easter's civilization, we ask ourselves, "Why didn't they look around, realize what they were doing, and stop before it was too late? What were they thinking when they cut down the last palm tree?"

I suspect, though, that the disaster happened not with a bang but with a whimper. After all, there are those hundreds of abandoned statues to consider. The forest the islanders depended on for rollers and rope didn't simply disappear one day—it vanished slowly, over decades. Perhaps war interrupted the moving teams; perhaps by the time the carvers had finished their work, the last rope snapped. In the meantime, any islander who tried to warn about the dangers of progressive deforestation would have been overridden by vested interests of carvers, bureaucrats, and chiefs, whose jobs depended on continued deforestation. Our Pacific Northwest loggers are only the latest in a long line of loggers to cry, "Jobs over trees!" The changes in forest cover from year to year would have been hard to detect: yes, this year we cleared those woods over there, but trees are starting to grow back again on this abandoned garden site here. Only older people, recollecting their childhoods decades earlier, could have recognized a difference. Their children could no more have comprehended their parents' tales than my eight-year-old sons today can comprehend my wife's and my tales of what Los Angeles was like 30 years ago.

Gradually trees became fewer, smaller, and less important. By the time the last fruit-bearing adult palm tree was cut, palms had long since ceased to be of economic significance. That left only smaller and smaller palm saplings to clear each year, along with other bushes and treelets. No one would have noticed the felling of the last small palm.

By now the meaning of Easter Island for us should be chillingly obvious. Easter Island is Earth writ small. Today, again, a rising population confronts shrinking resources. We too have no emigration valve, because all human societies are linked by international transport, and we can no more escape into space than the Easter Islanders could flee into the ocean. If we continue to follow our present course, we shall have exhausted the world's major fisheries, tropical rain forests, fossil fuels, and much of our soil by the time my sons reach my current age.

Every day newspapers report details of famished countries—Afghanistan, Liberia, Rwanda, Sierra Leone, Somalia, the former Yugoslavia, Zaire—where soldiers have appropriated the wealth or where central government is yielding to local gangs of thugs. With the risk of nuclear war receding, the threat of our ending with a bang no longer has a chance of galvanizing us to halt our course. Our risk now is of winding down, slowly, in a whimper. Corrective action is blocked by vested interests, by well-intentioned political and business leaders, and by their electorates, all of whom are perfectly correct in not noticing big changes from year to year. Instead, each year there are just somewhat more people, and somewhat fewer resources, on Earth.

It would be easy to close our eyes or to give up in despair. If mere thousands of Easter Islanders with only stone tools and their own muscle power sufficed to destroy their society, how can billions of people with metal tools and machine power fail to do worse? But there is one crucial difference. The Easter Islanders had no books and no histories of other doomed societies. Unlike the Easter Islanders, we have histories of the past—information that can save us. My main hope for my sons' generation is that we may now choose to learn from the fates of societies like Easter's.

Review Questions

1. What was the ecology of Easter Island when Polynesians first arrived on the island about A.D. 400, according to Jared Diamond?

2. What were the main sources of food eaten by Easter Islanders in the early years of island habitation?

3. What changes occurred in the Easter Island environment due to human exploitation? How did these changes affect the life and social organization of the islanders?

4. How does Diamond explain the inability of Easter Islanders to see the effect they were having on their island's habitat?

5. How does the Easter Island case apply to what is happening in the world today?

12

Forest Development
the Indian Way

Richard K. Reed

To most industrialized peoples, the practice of slash-and-burn agriculture seems wasteful. Horticulturalists use axes and machetes to fell forests, burn the debris, and then plant in the ashes. Within a few short years, the fields are abandoned and the farmer moves on. For people used to thinking of agriculture as intensively planted permanent fields, slash-and-burn agriculture seems destructive. In this article, Richard Reed challenges this simplistic notion. Describing the production practices of the Guaraní Indians living in the tropical forests of Paraguay, and detailing the destruction of their original way of life by the infiltration of colonos *(non-Indian colonists), he shows that Indian slash-and-burn agriculture combined with commercial harvesting of natural products offers a more sustainable and economically sound means for all people to prosper in these fragile forests.*

When I arrived in Itanaramí that very first time, it felt like I had left the modern world behind. This small Guaraní Indian village was hidden deep in the Paraguayan forests, surrounded by hundreds of miles of wilderness. I took a jeep to the end of a rutted dirt road and followed winding footpaths for two days into the heart of one of South America's great natural areas. Trees shaded the trail I took over the low hills, and clear streams offered cool refreshment in the valleys. Entering the community, the path opened into a small clearing and Veraju's small thatch roof jutted up through the tangle of the family's overgrown garden. His family was busy in the house yard, preparing manioc from the garden and game from the hunt. The rest of the settlement was similarly embedded in the forest, each home set in a small clearing along the narrow footpath. Houses seemed isolated from the world, protected from modernity by the high trees and verdant foliage of this vast forest.

I soon discovered that the isolation was illusory. Their house lots were strewn with machetes from Costa Rica and clothes were sewn from Brazilian polyester cloth. Even the most isolated households bought salt and soap and fish hooks from traders.

Guaraní made their living by gardening and hunting, but they also obtained cash by gathering and selling goods from the forest, especially the leaves of the wild yerba-maté plant (*Ilex Paraguayensis*), which is brewed in a caffeinated infusion throughout southern South America. And the commercial work was not new. A little research showed that the Guaraní had sold the leaf to Brazilian, Argentine, and Bolivian merchants since at least 1590. They had developed a way to mine the forest for its wealth without destroying the resources on which they depend.

The Threatened Forests

But the Guaraní's environment was threatened even then. The world's great tropical regions had become prime targets for a new kind of economic development. Ranchers and farmers, from Brazil to Indonesia, flocked to the jungle frontiers armed with chainsaws and bulldozers. They built roads, clear-cut timber, and denuded the land of foliage, often burning the trees and brush as they went.

The scope of this human invasion staggers the mind. In recent times, development destroys hundreds of square miles of virgin tropical forest each day. In the Amazon alone, an area half the size of Louisiana is cleared every year. We are discovering that not only are the forests finite, but they are rapidly disappearing. At this rate, authorities predict that the forests will be gone by the year 2050!

The future of this development is as finite as the resources it depends on. The march of progress, which seems so powerful and necessary, will soon destroy the very resources it requires. We can either choose to abandon our current development strategies or we will be forced to change.

As a result, the modern world is searching for models of development that promote growth within the world's finite resources. This *sustainable development* differs from conventional strategies in several important respects. First, it recognizes that resources are finite and protects those resources even as we benefit from them. Second, sustainable development emphasizes the relationship between economic, ecological, and social systems, striving to protect the integrity of all three. Third, sustainable development promotes social stability by distributing the benefits and raising the standard of living of all people.

As the modern world searches for technological solutions to its increasingly obvious problems, I discovered that the Guaraní offered a proven model for sustainable tropical forest development. More than simply providing their subsistence, they had developed a *commercial* system that gave them access to the world marketplace without destroying the forests they depended on.

We may ask what accounts for this successful adaptation. What subsistence strategies permit them to live within the ecological limits of the forest? Can such people provide a model for successful tropical forest management? If so, perhaps indigenous peoples will be as important to our future as the oxygen-giving forests they live in. Let's look at the factors that allowed the Guaraní of eastern Paraguay to prosper in the forest and the lessons we may learn from them.

The Guaraní

Before the encroachment of outsiders, the Guaraní Indians were well adapted to their forest environment. Like most horticulturalists, they lived in small, widely scattered communities. Because their population densities were low, and because they practiced a mixture of slash-and-burn agriculture and foraging, they placed a light demand on forest resources. Small size also meant a more personal social organization and an emphasis on cooperation and sharing. Although of greater size and complexity than hunter-gatherer bands, Guaraní villages contained many of the cultural values found in these nomadic societies.

Since that first visit twenty years ago, I have continued to conduct ethnographic fieldwork in the small group of Guaraní villages that include Itanaramí. The residents of these communities are among the last of the Guaraní Indians still living in the forests of southern South America. They are the remnants of an ethnic group that 400 years ago dominated southern Brazil and Paraguay from the Atlantic Ocean to the Andes. The Guaraní have suffered as disease, slavers, and colonists have invaded their forests. Today, only 30,500 Guaraní remain in isolated settlements where the tropical forest survives—and even these are threatened.

The forests of Itanaramí have high canopies that shelter both animal and human populations. When I first arrived in the region, the expanse of trees was broken only by streams and rivers that drain westward to the broad, marshy valley of the Paraná River. Viewed from the ground, the density of the forest growth was matched only by the diversity of plant species.

Itanaramí itself is built along a small stream that gives the settlement its name. To my uninformed eye, it was difficult to recognize the existence of a village at all when I first arrived there. Homesteads—which consisted of a clearing, a thatched hut, and a field—were scattered in the forest, often out of sight of one another. A closer look revealed that pathways through the forest connected houses to each other and to a slightly larger homestead, that of the *tamoi* (literally grandfather), the group's religious leader. As in many small societies, households were tied together by kinship, which wove a tapestry of relations that organized social affairs and linked Itanaramí to other Guaraní communities.

I discovered that Guaraní culture emphasized sharing and cooperation. Sisters often shared work and childcare. Brothers usually hunted together. Food was distributed among members of the extended family, including cousins, aunts, and uncles. Families distributed abundance with compatriots who had less—and expected the same treatment in return. People emphasized the general welfare, not personal wealth.

The *tamoi*, although in no sense a leader with formal authority, commanded considerable respect in the community. He settled disputes, chastised errant juniors, and led the entire community in evening religious ceremonies where all drank *kanguijy* (fermented corn), danced, and chanted to the gods.

The people of Itanaramí not only lived in the forest, they saw themselves as of it. The forest was basic to indigenous cosmology. The people referred to themselves as *ka'aguygua,* or "people of the forest." Villagers often named their children after the numerous forest songbirds, symbolizing their close personal ties to the environment.

Sustainable Production

Guaraní had lived in their present locale for centuries and had dwelled throughout the tropical forests of lowland South America for thousands of years. During all this time, they had exploited flora, fauna, and soils of the forests without doing permanent harm. The secret of their success was their production strategy. The Indians mixed agriculture with gathering, hunting, and fishing in a way that permitted the environment to recover. They even collected forest products for sale to outsiders, again without causing environmental damage.

Guaraní farming was well suited to forest maintenance. Using a form of shifting agriculture called slash-and-burn farming, the Indians permitted the forest to recover from the damage of field clearing. The way Veraju, the tamoi of Itanaramí, and his wife, Kitu, farmed provides a typical example. When the family needed to prepare a new field, it was Veraju who did the heavy work. He cut the trees and undergrowth to make a half-acre clearing near his house. Then he, Kitu, and some of their five children burned the fallen trees and brush, creating an ash that provided a powerful fertilizer for the thin forest soils. When the field was prepared, Kitu used a digging stick fashioned from a sapling to poke small holes in the ground, and planted the staple Guaraní crops, beans and manioc root (from which tapioca is made). Interspersed with the basic staples, they added the slower-growing banana, sugar cane, and orange trees to round out their diet. When the crops matured, it was Kitu and her daughters who harvested them.

The secret to successful slash-and-burn agriculture is field "shifting" or rotation. Crops flourish the first year and are plentiful the next, but the sun and rain soon take their toll on the exposed soil. The thin loam layer, so typical of tropical forests, degenerates rapidly to sand and clay. Grasses, weeds, and insect pests, rare in the deep forest, eventually discover the vulnerable crops. By the third year, the poor soils are thick with weeds and grow only a sparse corn crop and few small manioc roots. Rather than replant a fourth time, Veraju and Kitu would clear a new field nearby where soils are naturally more fertile and the forest can be burned for additional ash fertilizer. Although fallow, their old field was not abandoned. They continued to return periodically for fruit and to root out the remaining manioc.

The surrounding forest quickly reclaims the old field; roots penetrate the opening from the forest edge and animals wander through it dropping seeds in their path. As the forest returns, the decaying matter once again strengthens the depleted soil. After several years the plot will be distinguished only as one of the citrus groves that are scattered throughout the unbroken forest. In this way, the forest produces a sustained yield without degrading the natural ecosystem.

The forest recovers sufficiently fast for the same plot to be cleared and re-planted within ten or fifteen years. This "swidden" system results in the cyclic use of a large area of forest, with a part under cultivation and a much larger portion lying fallow in various stages of recomposition.

If farming formed the only subsistence base, the Guaraní would have had to clear much larger gardens. But they also turned to other forest resources—game, fish, and forest products—to meet their needs. Guaraní men often formed small groups to hunt large animals such as deer, tapir, and peccary with guns purchased from outsiders or with the more traditional bows and arrows they make themselves. A successful hunt provides enough meat to share liberally with friends. Men also trapped smaller mammals, such as armadillo and paca (a large rodent). They fashioned snares and deadfall traps from saplings, tree trunks, and cactus fiber twine. These were set near homesteads, along streams, and at the edges of gardens. Traps not only provided meat, but also killed animals that would otherwise eat the crops.

Fish also supplied protein for the Guaraní diet and reduced dependence on agricultural produce. Many rivers and streams flow near Itanaramí on flat bottomland. These watercourses meander in broad loops that may be cut off as the river or stream changes course during a flood. Meanders, called oxbows, make ideal fishing spots. In addition to hook and line, men captured the fish by using a poison extracted from the bark of the *timbo* vine. Floated over the surface of the water, the poison stuns the fish and allows them to be caught by hand.

The forest also supplied a variety of useful products for the Guaraní. They made houses from tree trunks and bamboo stalks; rhododendron vines secured thatched roofs. Villagers collected wild honey and fruit to add sweetness to their diets. If the manioc in the fields were insufficient, wild tubers provided a basic staple. Even several species of insect larva and ants were collected as tasty and nutritious supplements to the daily meal. Finally, the Indians knew about a wide variety of medicinal plants. They processed roots, leaves, flowers, and seeds to release powerful alkaloids, making teas and poultices for the sick and injured.

But the Guaraní were not isolated from commercial goods. Almost five hundred years ago, White traders entered the forests of the Guaraní and gave

Indians access to world markets. The Guaraní continued to produce for most of their needs, but items such as machetes, hooks, soap, and salt were more easily bought than manufactured or collected. As they did with farming and hunting, Guaraní turned to the forest to meet such economic needs. They regularly collected two forest products, yerba-maté and leaves from wild orange trees, which have an oil used in flavorings and perfumes, to raise the necessary funds.

It is important to note the special Guaraní knowledge and values associated with subsistence activities. Because they lived in the forest for such a long time, and because they would have nowhere to turn if their own resources disappeared, they relied on a special and complex knowledge of how the forest works and how it can be used.

For example, Guaraní, such as Veraju, distinguished among a variety of "ecozones," each with a unique combination of soil, flora, and fauna. They recognized obvious differences between the high forests on the hills, the deep swamps of river basins, and the grassy savannahs of the high plains. But they made more subtle distinctions within these larger regions. For example, they called the low scrub along rivers *ca'ati*. Flooded each year during the rainy season, this region supported bamboo groves that harbored small animals for trapping and provided material for house construction. The forests immediately above the flood plain look like an extension of the ca'ati, but to the Guaraní they differed in important ways. This ecozone supported varieties of bamboo that were useless in house construction but that attracted larger animals, such as peccary, which they hunted. In all, the Guaraní distinguished among nine resource zones, each with distinctive soils, flora, fauna, and uses. These subtle distinctions among ecozones enabled the Guaraní to use the forest to its best benefit. By shifting their subsistence efforts from one zone to another, just as they shifted their fields from one spot to the next, the Guaraní assured that the forest environment, with its rich variety of life, would always be able to renew itself.

The Impact of Unsustainable Development

In the last few years, intensive commercial development has come to the region in which Itanaramí lies. Paraguay's deforestation rates are among the highest in the world, raising the specter of complete ecological destruction. White *colonos* (settlers), armed with chain saws and earthmovers, attack the trees. They vandalize the land without awareness of the carefully integrated ecozones. As the trees fall, the forest products, such as yerba maté, are destroyed. So are the mammals and fish, the bamboo and the rhododendron vines, the honey and the fruits, and the fallow fields. As these resources disappear, so does the economy of the once self-sufficient Guaraní. Without their traditional mode of subsistence, it has become impossible to maintain their kin-organized society, the influence of the tamoi, and the willingness to share. Indian communities are destroyed by poverty and disease, and the members who remain join the legions of poor laborers who form the lowest class of the national society. In short, the Guaraní lose their ability to survive as an independent ethnic group.

Recent intensive development began near Itanaramí with a road that colonists cut through the jungle to the village. Through this gash in the forest moved logging trucks, bulldozers, farm equipment, and buses. Accompanying the machinery of development were farmers, ranchers, and speculators, hoping to make a quick profit from the verdant land. They descended from their vehicles onto the muddy streets of a newly built frontier town. They cleared land for general stores and bars, which were soon filled with merchandise and warm beer. By day, the air in the town was fouled by truck noise and exhaust fumes; by night it was infused with the glare of electric lights and the noise of blaring tape players.

Soon the settlers began to fell the forest creating fields for cotton, soybeans, and pasture. Survey teams cleared boundaries and drew maps. Lumber gangs camped in the forests, clear-cutting vast tracts of trees. Valuable timber was hauled off to new lumber mills; everything else was piled and burned. Massive bulldozers created expanses of sunlight in the previously unbroken forest. Within months, grass, cotton, and soybeans sprouted in the exposed soils. Where once the land had been home for game, it now provided for cattle. Herds often clogged the roads, competing with trucks hauling cotton to market and busses loaded with new colonists. Settlers fenced in the fields and cut lanes through the remaining forest to mark off portions that would be private property (off-limits to Indians).

The road and fields reached Itanaramí in 1994. A cement bridge was built over the stream and chainsaws, logging trucks, and bulldozers assaulted the forests the Guaraní once used for gardens, farming, and hunting. The footpath that once carried Guaraní to the tamoi's house now carries their timber to market in Brazil. The families are left with barren house lots.

Moreover, by destroying the forest resources surrounding the Guaraní villages of the region, colonos set in motion a process that destroyed the native culture and society. Guaraní communities became islands surrounded by a sea of pastures and farm fields. Although the Indians held onto their gardens, they lost the forest resources needed to sustain their original mode of subsistence, which depended on hunting, fishing, and gathering in the forest as well as farming. These economic changes forced alterations in the Indian community.

First, without the forest to provide game, fish, and other products, the Guaraní became dependent on farming alone for their survival. Without wild foods, they had to plant more corn and beans. Without the forest production of yerba maté leaves to collect for sale, they were also forced to plant cash crops such as cotton and tobacco. These changes forced them to clear gardens that were over twice the size of their previous plots.

While the loss of the forest for hunting and gathering increased their dependence on agriculture, the fences and land titles of the new settlers reduced the land available to the Indians for cultivation. Families soon cleared the last of the remaining high forests that they controlled. Even the once forested stream banks were denuded.

After they had cleared their communities' high forest, Indian farmers were forced to replant fields without allowing sufficient fallow time for soils to rejuvenate. Crops suffered from lack of nutrients and yields declined despite additional effort devoted to clearing and weeding. Commercial crops, poorly suited to the forest soils, did even worse. As production suffered, the Indians cleared and farmed even larger areas. The resulting spiral of poor harvests and enlarged farms outstripped the soil's capacity to produce and the Guaraní's ability to care for the crops. Food in the Indian communities grew scarce. The diet was increasingly restricted to nonnutritious manioc as a dietary staple because it was the only plant that could survive in the exhausted soils.

The Guaraní felt the ecological decline in other ways. The loss of game and poor crop yields exacerbated health problems. Settlers brought new diseases such as colds and flu into the forest. The Guaraní have little inherited resistance to these illnesses and poor nutrition reduced their defenses even further. Disease not only sapped the adults' energy for farming and childcare, it increased death rates at all ages. Tuberculosis, which well-fed Guaraní had rarely contracted, became the major killer in the community.

The environmental destruction took a psychological toll as well. Guaraní began to fall into depression, get drunk on cheap cane liquor, and, all too often, commit suicide. A number of suicides were noted among the Guaraní in Brazil in the 1990s and subsequent research in Paraguay showed that indigenous peoples were killing themselves at almost fifty times the national average. The epidemic hit 15- to 24-year-olds the hardest. These young people saw little future for themselves, their families, and their people.

Deforestation also disrupted social institutions. Without their subsistence base, many Guaraní needed additional cash to buy food and goods. Indian men were forced to seek work as farmhands, planting pastures and picking cotton on land where they once hunted. Women stayed at home to tend children and till the deteriorating soils of the family farms.

The search for wage labor eventually forced whole Guaraní families to move. Many jobs were available on the new farms that had replaced the forest. Entire families left home for hovels they constructed on the land of their employers. From independent farmers and gatherers, they became tenants of *patrones* (landowners). Patrones prohibited the Guaraní farmhands from planting gardens of their own, so the displaced Indians were forced to buy all their food, usually from the patrones themselves. Worse, patrones set their own inflated prices on the food and goods sold to Indians. Dependence on the patrones displaced the mutual interdependence of traditional Guaraní social organization.

As individuals and families left the Guaraní villages in search of work on surrounding farms and ranches, tamoi leaders lost influence. It became impossible to gather disparate relatives and friends for religious ritual. The distances were too great for the elders' nieces and nephews to seek out counsel and medicines. Moreover, the diseases and problems suffered by the Guaraní were increasingly caused by people and powers outside the forest. The tamoi could neither control nor explain the changing world.

Finally, as the forest disappeared, so did its power to symbolize Guaraní entity. No longer did young Indians see themselves as "people of the forest." Increasingly, they called themselves *indios*, the pejorative slur used by their non-Indian neighbors.

Today, many of the Guaraní of eastern Paraguay remain in small but impoverished communities in the midst of a frontier society based on soybean farming and cattle ranching. The households that previously were isolated individual plots are now concentrated in one small area without forest for farming or privacy. The traditional tamoi continue to be the center of the social and religious life of the community, but no longer exert influence over village decisions, which are increasingly dominated by affairs external to the local community.

Development and Ecology

Some people might argue that the Guaraní need to learn from their new neighbors, that they need to change their traditional ways and adopt the economy and culture of the more modern, prosperous society. The problems the Guaraní suffer, they claim, are a result of their traditional economy and culture. Change might be painful for today's Indians, but will provide unequaled opportunity for their descendents.

Unfortunately, this argument ignores the fact that recent development is destroying the resources on which the new farming and ranching depend. The long-run implications of forest clearing are disastrous, not simply for the Guaraní and other Indians, but for settlers and developers as well. The tropical forest ecosystem is extremely fragile. When the vegetable cover is destroyed, the soil quickly disappears. Erosion clogs rivers with silt and the soils left behind are baked to a hardpan on which few plants can survive. Rainwater previously captured by foliage and soil is quickly lost to runoff, drying the winds that feed the regional rain systems. Although first harvests in frontier areas seem bountiful, long-term farming and ranching are unprofitable as the soils, deprived of moisture and the rejuvenating forces of the original forest, are reduced to a "red desert."

Returning to Itanaramí today, one notices that many of the fields first cleared by ranchers in 1996 have already been abandoned. And even worse, leaving the cleared land fallow does not restore it. Once destroyed, the forest plants cannot reclaim the huge expanses of hardpan left by unsustainable development.

Nor have developers been interested in husbanding the land. The colonos who clear the forests are concerned with short-term profit. Entrepreneurs and peasant farmers maximize immediate returns on their labor and investment, unaware of the environmental costs that subsidize their earnings. When the trees and soils of one area are exhausted, the farmers, ranchers, and loggers move farther into the virgin forest in search of new resources. The process creates a wave of development that leaves destruction in its wake. Unlike the Guaraní who have developed sustainable systems, developers do not stay and contend with the environmental destruction caused by their activities.

Indigenous Models
for Sustainable Development

Rather than the Guaraní learning to adapt to our models of development, perhaps we need to take a lesson from indigenous peoples. If we hope to survive in the rain forest, we must learn from the people who have not only survived, but prospered commercially in this fragile environment. International agencies and national governments have begun to recognize that our development strategies are doomed to failure. Although deforestation continues unchecked in many regions of the Amazon Basin, forest conservation programs are using the experience of indigenous people to promote sustainable development in the forest.

Such is the case in Paraguay where a program is being implemented to preserve the remaining tropical forests. Groups like the Guaraní of Itanaramí, so recently threatened by encroaching development, are providing a model for newcomers to earn a profit from the natural resources, while protecting the existing environment. The natural forests of some of the Guaraní are the last remaining undisturbed subtropical forest in eastern Paraguay. With the help of Nature Conservancy, an area of 280 square miles has been set aside as a biosphere reserve. Although small, the program is attempting to protect a much larger buffer zone around the reserve by promoting rational land use by colonists. Aided by anthropologists who have made detailed studies of Indian commercial harvesting, planners are integrating the Indians' own models of agro-forestry into new production strategies for colonos. Guaraní techniques of commercial extraction have been of special interest, particularly the harvest of yerba maté, as it will economically outperform destructive farming in the long run. Teams of planners are teaching newcomers to tend and harvest their own tree crops. Far from being backward and inefficient, the mixed horticultural subsistence strategies of indigenous forest groups have turned out to be the most practical way to manage the fragile tropical forest environment.

Review Questions

1. Anthropologists claim that subsistence strategies affect a society's social organization and ideology. Evaluate this assertion in light of reading about the way the Guaraní live in their rain forest environment.

2. Why is horticulture more environmentally sensible than intensive agricultural and pastoral exploitation of the Amazonian rain forest?

3. Guaraní Indians are largely subsistence farmers and foragers. How do they use their forest environment without destroying it?

4. How have *colonos* disrupted the lives of Guaraní villagers? What does this tell us about the relationship between subsistence and social structure?

5. How can the Guaraní use their rain forest habitat to make money, and what does their experience suggest as a way to integrate forest exploitation into a market economy without environmental destruction?

FOUR

Economic Systems

People everywhere experience wants that can be satisfied only by the acquisition and use of material goods and the services of others. To meet such wants, humans rely on an aspect of their cultural inventory, the **economic system,** which we will define as the provision of goods and services to meet biological and social wants.

The meaning of the term *want* can be confusing. It can refer to what humans *need* for their survival. We must eat, drink, maintain a constant body temperature, defend ourselves, and deal with injury and illness. The economic system meets these needs by providing food, water, clothing, shelter, weapons, medicines, and the cooperative services of others.

But material goods serve more than just our survival needs: they meet our culturally defined *wants* as well. We need clothes to stay warm, but we want garments of a particular style, cut, and fabric to signal our status, rank, or anything else we wish to communicate socially. We need food to sustain life, but we want particular foods prepared in special ways to fill our aesthetic and social desires. Services and goods may also be exchanged to strengthen ties between people or groups. Birthday presents may not always meet physical needs, but they clearly function to strengthen the ties between the parties to the exchange.

Part of the economic system is concerned with **production,** which means rendering material items useful and available for human consumption. Production systems must designate ways to allocate resources. The **allocation of resources** refers to the cultural rules people use to assign rights to the ownership and use of resources. Production systems must also include technologies. Americans usually associate technology with the tools and machines used for manufacturing, rather than with the knowledge for doing it. But many anthropologists link the concept directly to culture. Here we will define **technology** as the cultural knowledge for making and using tools and extracting and refining raw materials.

Production systems also include a **division of labor,** which refers to the rules that govern the assignment of jobs to people. In hunting and gathering societies, labor is most often divided along the lines of gender, and sometimes age. In these societies, almost everyone knows how to produce, use, and collect the necessary material goods. In industrial society, however, jobs are highly specialized, and labor is divided, at least ideally, on the basis of skill and experience. Rarely do we know how to do someone else's job in our complex society.

The **unit of production,** meaning the persons or groups responsible for producing goods, follows a pattern similar to the way labor is divided in various societies. Among hunter-gatherers, there is little specialization; individuals, families, groups of friends, or sometimes bands form the units of production. But in our own complex society, we are surrounded by groups specially organized to manufacture, transport, and sell goods.

Another part of the economic system is **distribution.** There are three basic modes of distribution: market exchange, reciprocal exchange, and redistribution.

We are most conscious of market exchange because it lies at the heart of our capitalist system. **Market exchange** is the transfer of goods and services based on price, supply, and demand. Every time we enter a store and pay for something, we engage in market exchange. The price of an item may change with the supply. For example, a discount store may lower the price of a television set because it has too many of the appliances on hand. Prices may go up, however, if everyone wants the sets when there are few to sell. Money is often used in market systems; it enables people to exchange a large variety of items easily. Barter involves the trading of goods, not money, but it, too, is a form of market exchange because the number of items exchanged may also vary with supply and demand. Market exchange appears in human history when societies become larger and more complex. It is well suited for exchange between the strangers who make up these larger groups.

Although we are not so aware of it, we also engage in reciprocal exchange. **Reciprocal exchange** involves the transfer of goods and services between two people or groups based on role obligations. Birthday and holiday gift giving is a fine example of reciprocity. On these occasions we exchange goods not because we necessarily need or want them, but because we are expected to do so as part of our status and role. Parents should give gifts to their children, for example; children should reciprocate. If we fail in our reciprocal obligations, we signal an unwillingness to continue the relationship. Small, simply organized societies, such as the !Kung described earlier, base their exchange systems on reciprocity. Complex ones like ours, although largely organized around the market or redistribution, still manifest reciprocity between kin and close friends.

Finally, there is **redistribution,** the transfer of goods and services between a central collecting source and a group of individuals. Like reciprocity, redistribution is based on role obligation. Taxes typify this sort of exchange in the United States. We must pay our taxes because we are citizens, not because we are buying something. We receive goods and services back—education, transportation, roads, defense—but not necessarily in proportion to the amount we contribute. Redistribution may be the predominant mode of exchange in socialist societies.

Anthropologists also frequently talk about two kinds of economies. In the past, many of the world's societies had **subsistence economies** organized around the need to meet material necessities and social obligations. Subsistence economies are typically associated with smaller groups. They occur at a local level. Such economies depend most on the non-market-exchange mechanisms: reciprocity and redistribution. Their members are occupational generalists. Most people can do most jobs, although there may be distinctions on the basis of gender and age. The !Kung described by Richard Lee in Parts One and Three of this book had subsistence economies as do most horticulturalists.

Market economies differ from subsistence economies in their size and motive for production. Although reciprocity and redistribution exist in market economies, market exchange drives production and consumption. Market economies are larger (indeed, there is a growing world market economy that includes almost everyone) and are characterized by high economic specialization, as well as impersonality. The American economy is market-driven as are most national systems. If they have not been already, most subsistence economies will, in the near future, be absorbed into national market systems.

The selections in this part illustrate several of the concepts discussed. In the first article, Lee Cronk looks at gift giving, a classic example of reciprocity. He finds that gifts can cement relationships, confer prestige, and obligate subordinates. In the second selection, Jack Weatherford deals with the impact of the world market on the social organization and economy of the indigenous peoples of Peru, Bolivia, and Colombia who grow coca and prepare the drug for market. In the third article, Philippe Bourgois writes about why Latino African Americans work in the inner-city shadow economy of New York drug selling. Limited to service jobs in New York's formal economy, which they often find degrading, they prefer to perform the unpleasant work of selling drugs in the "informal" economy.

Key Terms

allocation of resources   *p. 143*
distribution   *p. 144*
division of labor   *p. 143*
economic system   *p. 143*
market economies   *p. 145*
market exchange   *p. 144*

production   *p. 143*
reciprocal exchange   *p. 144*
redistribution   *p. 144*
subsistence economies   *p. 145*
technology   *p. 143*
unit of production   *p. 144*

13

Reciprocity and the Power of Giving

Lee Cronk

As we saw in the introduction to Part Four, reciprocity constitutes an important exchange system in every society. At the heart of reciprocal exchange is the idea of giving. In this article, Lee Cronk explores the functions of giving using a variety of examples from societies around the world. Giving may be benevolent. It may be used to strengthen existing relationships or to form new ones. Gifts may also be used aggressively to "fight" people, to "flatten" them with generosity. Givers often gain position and prestige in this way. Gifts may also be used to place others in debt so that one can control them and require their loyalty. Cronk shows that, in every society, from !Kung hxaro *exchange to American foreign aid, there are "strings attached" to giving that affect how people and groups relate to each other.*

"Strings Attached" by Lee Cronk. This article is reprinted by permission of *The Sciences* and is from the May/June 1989 issue.

During a trek through the Rockies in the 1830s, Captain Benjamin Louis E. de Bonneville received a gift of a fine young horse from a Nez Percé chief. According to Washington Irving's account of the incident, the American explorer was aware that "a parting pledge was necessary on his own part, to prove that this friendship was reciprocated." Accordingly, he "placed a handsome rifle in the hands of the venerable chief; whose benevolent heart was evidently touched and gratified by this outward and visible sign of amity."

Even the earliest white settlers in New England understood that presents from natives required reciprocity, and by 1764, "Indian gift" was so common a phrase that the Massachusetts colonial historian Thomas Hutchinson identified it as "a proverbial expression, signifying a present for which an equivalent return is expected." Then, over time, the custom's meaning was lost. Indeed, the phrase now is used derisively, to refer to one who demands the return of a gift. How this cross-cultural misunderstanding occurred is unclear, but the poet Lewis Hyde, in his book *The Gift*, has imagined a scenario that probably approaches the truth.

Say that an Englishman newly arrived in America is welcomed to an Indian lodge with the present of a pipe. Thinking the pipe a wonderful artifact, he takes it home and sets it on his mantelpiece. When he later learns that the Indians expect to have the pipe back, as a gesture of goodwill, he is shocked by what he views as their short-lived generosity. The newcomer did not realize that, to the natives, the point of the gift was not to provide an interesting trinket but to inaugurate a friendly relationship that would be maintained through a series of mutual exchanges. Thus, his failure to reciprocate appeared not only rude and thoughtless but downright hostile. "White man keeping" was as offensive to native Americans as "Indian giving" was to settlers.

In fact, the Indians' tradition of gift giving is much more common than our own. Like our European ancestors, we think that presents ought to be offered freely, without strings attached. But through most of the world, the strings themselves are the main consideration. In some societies, gift giving is a tie between friends, a way of maintaining good relationships, whereas in others it has developed into an elaborate, expensive, and antagonistic ritual designed to humiliate rivals by showering them with wealth and obligating them to give more in return.

In truth, the dichotomy between the two traditions of gift giving is less behavioral than rhetorical: our generosity is not as unconditional as we would like to believe. Like European colonists, most modern Westerners are blind to the purpose of reciprocal gift giving, not only in non-Western societies but also, to some extent, in our own. Public declarations to the contrary, we, too, use gifts to nurture long-term relationships of mutual obligation, as well as to embarrass our rivals and to foster feelings of indebtedness. And this ethic touches all aspects of contemporary life, from the behavior of scientists in research networks to superpower diplomacy. Failing to acknowledge this fact, especially as we give money, machines, and technical advice to peoples around the world, we run the risk of being misinterpreted and, worse, of causing harm.

Much of what we know about the ethics of gift giving comes from the attempts of anthropologists to give things to the people they are studying. Richard Lee, of the University of Toronto, learned a difficult lesson from the !Kung hunter-gatherers, of the Kalahari desert, when, as a token of goodwill, he gave them an ox to slaughter at Christmas. Expecting gratitude, he was shocked when the !Kung complained about having to make do with such a scrawny "bag of bones." Only later did Lee learn, with relief, that the !Kung belittle all gifts. In their eyes, no act is completely generous, or free of calculation; ridiculing gifts is their way of diminishing the expected return and of enforcing humility on those who would use gifts to raise their own status within the group.

Rada Dyson-Hudson, of Cornell University, had a similar experience among the Turkana, a pastoral people of northwestern Kenya. To compensate her informants for their help, Dyson-Hudson gave away pots, maize meal, tobacco, and other items. The Turkana reaction was less than heartwarming. A typical response to a gift of a pot, for example, might be, "Where is the maize meal to go in this pot?" or, "Don't you have a bigger one to give me?" To the Turkana, these are legitimate and expected questions.

The Mukogodo, another group of Kenyan natives, responded in a similar way to gifts Beth Leech and I presented to them during our fieldwork in 1986. Clothing was never nice enough, containers never big enough, tobacco and candies never plentiful enough. Every gift horse was examined carefully, in the mouth and elsewhere. Like the !Kung, the Mukogodo believe that all gifts have an element of calculation, and they were right to think that ours were no exception. We needed their help, and their efforts to diminish our expectations and lessen their obligations to repay were as fair as our attempts to get on their good side.

The idea that gifts carry obligations is instilled early in life. When we gave Mukogodo children candies after visiting their villages, their mothers reminded them of the tie: "Remember these white people? They are the ones who gave you candy." They also reinforced the notion that gifts are meant to circulate, by asking their children to part with their precious candies, already in their mouths. Most of the youngsters reluctantly surrendered their sweets, only to have them immediately returned. A mother might take, at most, a symbolic nibble from her child's candy, just to drive home the lesson.

The way food, utensils, and other goods are received in many societies is only the first stage of the behavior surrounding gift giving. Although repayment is expected, it is crucial that it be deferred. To reciprocate at once indicates a desire to end the relationship, to cut the strings; delayed repayment makes the strings longer and stronger. This is especially clear on the Truk Islands, of Micronesia, where a special word—*niffag*—is used to designate objects moving through the island's exchange network. From the Trukese viewpoint, to return niffag on the same day it is received alters its nature from that of a gift to that of a sale, in which all that matters is material gain.

After deciding the proper time for response, a recipient must consider how to make repayment, and that is dictated largely by the motive behind the gift. Some exchange customs are designed solely to preserve a relationship. The !Kung have a system, called *hxaro*, in which little attention is paid to whether the items exchanged are equivalent. Richard Lee's informant !Xoma explained to him that "Hxaro is when I take a thing of value and give it to you. Later, much later, when you find some good thing, you give it back to me. When I find something good I will give it to you, and so we will pass the years together." When Lee tried to determine the exact exchange values of various items (Is a spear worth three strings of beads, two strings, or one?), !Xoma explained that any return would be all right: "You see, we don't trade with things, we trade with people!"

One of the most elaborate systems of reciprocal gift giving, known as *kula*, exists in a ring of islands off New Guinea. Kula gifts are limited largely to shell necklaces, called *soulava*, and armbands, called *mwali*. A necklace given at one time is answered months or years later with an armband, the necklaces usually circulating clockwise, and the armbands counterclockwise, through the archipelago. Kula shells vary in quality and value, and men gain fame and prestige by having their names associated with noteworthy necklaces or armbands. The shells also gain value from their association with famous and successful kula partners.

Although the act of giving gifts seems intrinsically benevolent, a gift's power to embarrass the recipient and to force repayment has, in some societies, made it attractive as a weapon. Such antagonistic generosity reached its most elaborate expression, during the late nineteenth century, among the Kwakiutl, of British Columbia.

The Kwakiutl were acutely conscious of status, and every tribal division, clan, and individual had a specific rank. Disputes about status were resolved by means of enormous ceremonies (which outsiders usually refer to by the Chinook Indian term *potlatch*), at which rivals competed for the honor and prestige of giving away the greatest amount of property. Although nearly everything of value was fair game—blankets, canoes, food, pots, and, until the mid-nineteenth century, even slaves—the most highly prized items were decorated sheets of beaten copper, shaped like shields and etched with designs in the distinctive style of the Northwest Coast Indians.

As with the kula necklaces and armbands, the value of a copper sheet was determined by its history—by where it had been and who had owned it—and a single sheet could be worth thousands of blankets, a fact often reflected in its name. One was called "Drawing All Property from the House," and another, "About Whose Possession All Are Quarreling." After the Kwakiutl began to acquire trade goods from the Hudson's Bay Company's Fort Rupert post, in 1849, the potlatches underwent a period of extreme inflation, and by the 1920s, when items of exchange included sewing machines and pool tables, tens of thousands of Hudson's Bay blankets might be given away during a single ceremony.

In the 1880s, after the Canadian government began to suppress warfare between tribes, potlatching also became a substitute for battle. As a Kwakiutl man once said to the anthropologist Franz Boas, "The time of fighting is past. . . . We do not fight now with weapons: we fight with property." The usual Kwakiutl word for potlatch was *p!Esa*, meaning to flatten (as when one flattens a rival under a pile of blankets), and the prospect of being given a large gift engendered real fear. Still, the Kwakiutl seemed to prefer the new "war of wealth" to the old "war of blood."

Gift giving has served as a substitute for war in other societies, as well. Among the Siuai, of the Solomon Islands, guests at feasts are referred to as attackers, while hosts are defenders, and invitations to feasts are given on short notice in the manner of "surprise attacks." And like the Kwakiutl of British Columbia, the Mount Hagen tribes of New Guinea use a system of gift giving called *moka* as a way of gaining prestige and shaming rivals. The goal is to become a tribal leader, a "big-man." One moka gift in the 1970s consisted of several hundred pigs, thousands of dollars in cash, some cows and wild birds, a truck, and a motorbike. The donor, quite pleased with himself, said to the recipient, "I have won. I have knocked you down by giving so much."

Although we tend not to recognize it as such, the ethic of reciprocal gift giving manifests itself throughout our own society, as well. We, too, often expect something, even if only gratitude and a sense of indebtedness, in exchange for gifts, and we use gifts to establish friendships and to manipulate our positions in society. As in non-Western societies, gift giving in America sometimes takes a benevolent and helpful form; at other times, the power of gifts to create obligations is used in a hostile way.

The Duke University anthropologist Carol Stack found a robust tradition of benevolent exchange in an Illinois ghetto known as the Flats, where poor blacks engage in a practice called swapping. Among residents of the Flats, wealth comes in spurts; hard times are frequent and unpredictable. Swapping, of clothes, food, furniture, and the like, is a way of guaranteeing security, of making sure that someone will be there to help out when one is in need and that one will get a share of any windfalls that come along.

Such networks of exchange are not limited to the poor, nor do they always involve objects. Just as the exchange of clothes creates a gift community in the Flats, so the swapping of knowledge may create one among scientists. Warren Hagstrom, a sociologist at the University of Wisconsin, in Madison, has pointed out that papers submitted to scientific journals often are called contributions, and, because no payment is received for them, they truly are gifts. In contrast, articles written for profit—such as this one—often are held in low esteem: scientific status can be achieved only through *giving* gifts of knowledge.

Recognition also can be traded upon, with scientists building up their gift-giving networks by paying careful attention to citations and acknowledgments. Like participants in kula exchange, they try to associate themselves with renowned and prestigious articles, books, and institutions. A desire for recognition, however, cannot be openly acknowledged as a motivation for research, and it is a rare scientist who is able to discuss such desires candidly. Hagstrom was able to find just one mathematician (whom he described as "something of a social isolate") to confirm that "junior mathematicians want recognition from big shots and, consequently, work in areas prized by them."

Hagstrom also points out that the inability of scientists to acknowledge a desire for recognition does not mean that such recognition is not expected by those who offer gifts of knowledge, any more than a kula trader believes it is all right if his trading partner does not answer his gift of a necklace with an armband. While failure to reciprocate in New Guinean society might once have meant warfare, among scientists it may cause factionalism and the creation of rivalries.

Whether in the Flats of Illinois or in the halls of academia, swapping is, for the most part, benign. But manipulative gift giving exists in modern societies, too—particularly in paternalistic government practices. The technique is to offer a present that cannot be repaid, coupled with a claim of beneficence and omniscience. The Johns Hopkins University anthropologist Grace Goodell documented one example in Iran's Khūzestān Province, which, because it contains most of the country's oil fields and is next door to Iraq, is a strategically sensitive area. Goodell focused on the World Bank–funded Dez irrigation project, a showpiece of the shah's ambitious "white revolution" development plan. The scheme involved the irrigation of tens of thousands of acres and the forced relocation of people from their villages to new, model towns. According to Goodell, the purpose behind dismantling local institutions was to enhance central government control of the region. Before development, each Khūzestāni village had been a miniature city-state, managing its own internal affairs and determining its own relations with outsiders. In the new settlements, decisions were made by government bureaucrats, not townsmen, whose autonomy was crushed under the weight of a large and strategically placed gift.

On a global scale, both the benevolent and aggressive dimensions of gift giving are at work in superpower diplomacy. Just as the Kwakiutl were left only with blankets with which to fight after warfare was banned, the United States and the Soviet Union now find, with war out of the question, that they are left only with gifts—called concessions—with which to do battle. Offers of military cutbacks are easy ways to score points in the public arena of international opinion and to shame rivals, and failure either to accept such offers or to respond with even more extreme proposals may be seen as cowardice or as bellicosity. Mikhail Gorbachev is a virtuoso, a master potlatcher, in this new kind of competition, and, predictably, Americans often see his offers of disarmament and openness as gifts with long strings attached. One reason U.S. officials were buoyed last December [1988], when, for the first time since the Second World War, the Soviet Union accepted American assistance, in the aftermath of the Armenian earthquake, is that it seemed to signal a wish for reciprocity rather than dominance—an unspoken understanding of the power of gifts to bind people together.

Japan, faced with a similar desire to expand its influence, also has begun to exploit gift giving in its international relations. In 1989, it will spend more than ten billion dollars on foreign aid, putting it ahead of the United States for the second consecutive year as the world's greatest donor nation. Although this move was publicly welcomed in the United States as the sharing of a burden, fears, too, were expressed that the resultant blow to American prestige might cause a further slip in our international status. Third World leaders also have complained that too much Japanese aid is targeted at countries in which Japan has an economic stake and that too much is restricted to the purchase of Japanese goods—that Japan's generosity has less to do with addressing the problems of underdeveloped countries than with exploiting those problems to its own advantage.

The danger in all of this is that wealthy nations may be competing for the prestige that comes from giving gifts at the expense of Third World nations. With assistance sometimes being given with more regard to the donors' status than to the recipients' welfare, it is no surprise that, in recent years, development aid often has been more effective in creating relationships of dependency, as in the case of Iran's Khūzestān irrigation scheme, than in producing real development. Nor that, given the fine line between donation and domination, offers of help are sometimes met with resistance, apprehension and, in extreme cases, such as the Iranian revolution, even violence.

The Indians understood a gift's ambivalent power to unify, antagonize, or subjugate. We, too, would do well to remember that a present can be a surprisingly potent thing, as dangerous in the hands of the ignorant as it is useful in the hands of the wise.

Review Questions

1. What does Cronk mean by *reciprocity*? What is the social outcome of reciprocal gift giving?

2. According to Cronk, what are some examples of benevolent gift giving?

3. How can giving be used to intimidate other people or groups? Give some examples cited by Cronk and think of some from your own experience.

4. How does Cronk classify gift-giving strategies such as government foreign aid? Can you think of other examples of the use of exchange as a political device?

14

Cocaine and the Economic Deterioration of Bolivia

Jack Weatherford

The demands of the world market have eroded local subsistence economies for centuries. Lands once farmed by individual families to meet their own needs now grow sugarcane, cotton, grain, or vegetables for market. Deprived of their access to land, householders must work as day laborers or migrate to cities to find jobs. Villages are denuded of the men, who have gone else-where for work, leaving women to farm and manage the family. The rhythm and structure of daily village life are altered dramatically. In this article, Jack Weatherford describes the impact of a new world market for cocaine on the structure and lives of rural Bolivians. Fed by an insatiable demand in Europe and the United States, the Bolivian cocaine trade has drawn males from the countryside, disrupted communications, destroyed families, unbalanced the local diet, and upset traditional social organization.

"They say you Americans can do anything. So, why can't you make your own cocaine and let our children come home from the coca plantations in the Chapare?" The Indian woman asked the question with confused resignation. In the silence that followed, I could hear only the rats scurrying around in the thatched roof. We continued shelling corn in the dark. The large house around us had once been home to an extended clan but was now nearly empty.

There was no answer to give her. Yet it was becoming increasingly obvious that the traditional Andean system of production and distribution built over thousands of years was now crumbling. Accompanying the destruction of the economic system was a marked distortion of the social and cultural patterns of the Quechua Indians. Since early in Inca history, the village of Pocona where I was working had been a trading village connecting the highlands, which produced potatoes, with the lowlands, which produced coca, a mildly narcotic plant used by the Incas. Over the past decade, however, new market demands from Europe and the United States have warped this system. Now the commodity is cocaine rather than the coca leaves, and the trade route bypasses the village of Pocona.

Bolivian subsistence patterns range from hunting and gathering in the jungle to intensive farming in the highlands, and since Inca times many parts of the country have depended heavily on mining. In the 1980s all of these patterns have been disrupted by the Western fad for one particular drug. Adoption of cocaine as the "drug of choice" by the urban elite of Europe and America has opened up new jungle lands and brought new Indian groups into Western economic systems. At the same time, the cocaine trade has cut off many communities such as Pocona from their traditional role in the national economy. Denied participation in the legal economy, they have been driven back into a world of barter and renewed isolation.

The vagaries of Western consumerism produce extensive and profound effects on Third World countries. It makes little difference whether the demand is for legitimate products such as coffee, tungsten, rubber, and furs marketed through legal corporations, or for illegal commodities such as opium, marijuana, cocaine, and heroin handled through criminal corporations. The same economic principles that govern the open, legal market also govern the clandestine, illegal markets, and the effects of both are frequently brutal.

Before coming to this Bolivian village, I assumed that if Americans and Europeans wanted to waste their money on cocaine, it was probably good that some of the poor countries such as Bolivia profit from it. In Cochabamba, the city in the heart of the cocaine-producing area, I had seen the benefits of this trade among the *narco chic* who lived in a new suburb of houses styled to look like Swiss chalets, Spanish haciendas, and English country homes. All these homes were surrounded by large wrought-iron fences, walls with broken glass set in the tops, and with large dogs that barked loudly and frequently. Such homes cost up to a hundred thousand dollars, an astronomical sum for Bolivia. I had also seen the narco elite of Cochabamba wearing gold chains and the latest Miami fashions and driving Nissans, Audis, Ford Broncos, an occasional BMW, or even a Mercedes through the muddy streets of the city. Some of their children attended the expensive English-speaking school; much of Cochabamba's meager nightlife catered to the elite. But as affluent as they may be in Bolivia, this elite would probably not earn as much as working-class families in such cities as Detroit, Frankfurt, or Tokyo.

Traveling outside of Cochabamba for six hours on the back of a truck, fording the same river three times, and following a rugged path for the last twenty-five kilometers, I reached Pocona and saw a different face of the cocaine trade. Located in a valley a mile and a half above sea level, Pocona is much too high to grow the coca bush. Coca grows best below six thousand feet, in the lush area called the Chapare where the eastern Andes meet the western edge of the Amazon basin and rain forest.

Like the woman with whom I was shelling corn, most of the people of Pocona are older, and community life is dominated by women together with their children who are still too young to leave. This particular woman had already lost both of her sons to the Chapare. She did not know it at the time, but within a few months, she was to lose her husband to the same work as well. With so few men, the women are left alone to plant, work, and harvest the fields of potatoes, corn, and fava beans, but with most of the work force missing, the productivity of Pocona has declined substantially.

In what was once a moderately fertile valley, hunger is now a part of life. The daily diet consists almost exclusively of bread, potato soup, boiled potatoes, corn, and tea. The majority of their daily calories comes from the potatoes and from the sugar that they put in their tea. They have virtually no meat or dairy products and very few fresh vegetables. These products are now sent to the Chapare to feed the workers in the coca fields, and the people of Pocona cannot compete against them. The crops that the people of Pocona produce are now difficult to sell because truck drivers find it much more profitable to take goods in and out of the Chapare rather than face the long and unprofitable trip to reach such remote villages as Pocona.

Despite all the hardships caused by so many people being away from the village, one might assume that more cash should be flowing into Pocona from the Chapare, where young men easily earn three dollars a day—three times the average daily wage of porters or laborers in Cochabamba. But this assumption was contradicted by the evidence of Pocona. As one widowed Indian mother of four explained, the first time her sixteen-year-old son came home, he brought bags of food, presents, and money for her and the younger children. She was very glad that he was working in the Chapare. On the second visit home he brought only a plastic bag of white powder for himself, and instead of bringing food, he took away as much as he could carry on the two-day trip back into the Chapare.

The third time, he told his mother that he could not find enough work in the Chapare. As a way to earn more money he made his mother bake as much bread as she could, and he took Mariana, his ten-year-old sister, with him to sell the bread to the workers in the Chapare. According to the mother, he beat the little girl and abused her repeatedly. Moreover, the money she made disappeared. On one of Mariana's trips home to get more bread, the mother had no more wheat or corn flour to supply her son. So, she sent Mariana away to Cochabamba to work as a maid. The enraged son found where Mariana was working and went to the home to demand that she be returned to him. When the family refused, he tried but failed to have her wages paid to him rather than to his mother. Mariana was separated from her family and community, but at least she was not going to be one more of the prostitutes in the Chapare, and for her mother that was more important.

The standard of living in Pocona was never very high, but with the advent of the cocaine boom in Bolivia, the standard has declined. Ten years ago, Pocona's gasoline-powered generator furnished the homes with a few hours of electric light each night. The electricity also allowed a few families to purchase radios, and occasionally someone brought in a movie projector to show a film in a large adobe building on the main square. For the past two years, the people of Pocona have not been able to buy gasoline for their generator. This has left the village not only without electricity but without entertainment and radio or film contact with the outside world. A few boys have bought portable radios with their earnings from the Chapare, but their families were unable to replace the batteries. Nights in Pocona are now both dark and silent.

In recent years the national economy of Bolivia has been virtually destroyed, and peasants in communities such as Pocona are reverting to barter as the only means of exchange. The value of the peso may rise or fall by as much as 30 percent in a day; the peasants cannot take a chance on trading their crops for money that may be worth nothing in a week. Cocaine alone has not been responsible for the destruction of the Bolivian economy, but it has been a major contributor. It is not mere coincidence that the world's largest producer of coca is also the country with the world's worst inflation.

During part of 1986, inflation in Bolivia varied at a rate between 2,000 and 13,000 percent, if calculated on a yearly basis. Prices in the cities changed by the hour, and on some days the dollar would rise at the rate of more than 1 percent per hour. A piece of bread cost 150,000 pesos, and an American dollar bought between two and three million pesos on the black market. Large items such as airplane tickets were calculated in the billions of pesos, and on one occasion I helped a man carry a large box of money to pay for such a ticket. It took two professional counters half an hour to count the bills. Workers were paid in stacks of bills that were often half a meter high. Because Bolivia is too undeveloped to print its money, the importation of its own bills printed in West Germany and Brazil was one of the leading imports in the mid-1980s.

Ironically, by no longer being able to participate fully in the money economy, the villagers of Pocona who have chewed coca leaves for centuries now find it difficult to afford the leaves. The narcotics industry pays such a high price that the people of Pocona can afford only the rejected trash from the cocaine industry. Whether chewed or made into a tea, the coca produces a mild lift somewhat like a cup of coffee but without the jagged comedown that follows a coffee high. Coca also reduces hunger, thirst, headaches, stomach pains, and the type of altitude sickness known as *sorroche.*

Were this all, coca use might be viewed as merely a bad habit somewhat like drinking coffee, smoking cigarettes, or overindulging in chocolates, but unlike these practices coca actually has a number of marked health benefits. The coca leaf is very high in calcium. In a population with widespread lactose intolerance and in a country without a national system of milk distribution, this calcium source is very important. The calcium also severely reduces cavities in a population with virtually no dental services outside the city. Coca also contains large amounts of vitamins A, C, and D, which are often lacking in the starchy diets of the mountain peasants.

Without coca, and with an excess of corn that they cannot get to market, the people of Pocona now make more *chicha,* a form of home-fermented corn beer that tastes somewhat like the silage that American dairymen feed their cows. It is ironic that as an affluent generation of Americans are decreasing their consumption of alcohol in favor of drugs such as cocaine, the people of Pocona are drinking more alcohol to replace their traditional coca. *Chicha,* like most beers, is more nutritious than other kinds of distilled spirits but lacks the health benefits of the coca leaves. It also produces intoxication, something that no amount of coca leaves can do. Coca chewing is such a slow process and produces such a mild effect that a user would have to chew a bushel of leaves to equal the impact of one mixed drink or one snort of cocaine.

In many ways, the problems and complaints of Pocona echo those of any Third World country with a cash crop, particularly those caught in the boom-and-bust cycle characteristic of capitalist systems. Whether it is the sisal boom of the Yucatán, the banana boom of Central America, the rubber boom of Brazil, or the cocaine boom in Bolivia, the same pattern develops. Rural villages are depleted of their work forces. Family and traditional cultural patterns disintegrate. And the people are no longer able to afford certain local products that suddenly become valued in the West. This is what happened to Pocona.

Frequently, the part of a country that produces the boom crop benefits greatly, while other areas suffer greatly. If this were true in Bolivia, benefits accruing in the coca-producing area of the Chapare would outweigh the adjustment problems of such villages as Pocona. As it turns out, however, the Chapare has been even more adversely affected.

Most of the young men who go to the Chapare do not actually work in the coca fields. The coca bush originated in this area and does not require extensive care. One hectare can easily produce eight hundred kilograms of coca leaves in a year, but not much labor is needed to pick them. After harvesting, the leaves are dried in the sun for three to four days. Most of these tasks can easily be done by the farmer and his family. Wherever one goes in the Chapare one sees coca leaves spread out on large drying cloths. Old people or young children walk up and down these cloths, turning the drying leaves with their whisk brooms.

The need for labor, especially the labor of strong young men, comes in the first stage of cocaine production, in the reduction of large piles of leaves into a small quantity of *pasta*, or coca paste from which the active ingredient, cocaine, can then be refined. Three hundred to five hundred kilograms of leaves must be used to make one kilogram of pure cocaine. The leaves are made into *pasta* by soaking them in vats of kerosene and by applying salt, acetone, and sulfuric acid. To make the chemical reaction occur, someone must trample on the leaves for several days—a process very much like tromping on grapes to make wine, only longer. Because the corrosive mixture dissolves shoes or boots, the young men walk barefooted. These men are called *pisacocas* and usually work in the cool of the night, pounding the green slime with their feet. Each night the chemicals eat away more skin and very quickly open ulcers erupt. Some young men in the Chapare now have feet that are so diseased that they are incapable of standing, much less walking. So, instead, they use their hands to mix the *pasta*, but their hands are eaten away even faster than their feet. Thousands and possibly tens of thousands of young Bolivian men now look like lepers with permanently disfigured hands and feet. It is unlikely that any could return to Pocona and make a decent farmer.

Because this work is painful, the *pisacocas* smoke addictive cigarettes coated with *pasta*. This alleviates their pain and allows them to continue walking the coca throughout the night. The *pasta* is contaminated with chemical residues, and smoking it warps their minds as quickly as the acids eat their hands and feet. Like Mariana's brother, the users become irrational, easily angered, and frequently violent.

Once the boys are no longer able to mix coca because of their mental or their physical condition, they usually become unemployed. If their wounds heal, they may be able to work as loaders or haulers, carrying the cocaine or transporting the controlled chemicals used to process it. By and large, however, women and very small children, called *hormigas* (ants), are better at this work. Some of the young men then return home to their villages; others wander to Cochabamba, where they might live on the streets or try to earn money buying and selling dollars on the black market.

The cocaine manufacturers not only supply their workers with food and drugs, they keep them sexually supplied with young girls who serve as prostitutes as well. Bolivian health officials estimate that nearly half of the people living in the Chapare today have venereal disease. As the boys and girls working there return to their villages, they take these diseases with them. Increasing numbers of children born to infected mothers now have bodies covered in syphilitic sores. In 1985, a worse disease hit with the first case of AIDS. Soon after the victim died, a second victim was diagnosed.

In an effort to control its own drug problem, the United States is putting pressure on Bolivia to eradicate coca production in the Andean countries. The army invaded the Chapare during January of 1986, but after nearly three weeks of being surrounded by the workers in the narcotics industry and cut off from their supply bases, the army surrendered. In a nation the size of Texas and California combined, but with a population approximately the size of the city of Chicago, it is difficult for the government to control its own territory. Neither the Incas nor the Spanish conquistadores were ever able to conquer and administer the jungles of Bolivia, where there are still nomadic bands of Indians who have retreated deep into the jungle to escape Western encroachment. The army of the poorest government in South America is no better able to control this country than its predecessors. The government runs the cities, but the countryside and the jungles operate under their own laws.

One of the most significant effects of the coca trade and of the campaigns to eradicate it has come on the most remote Indians of the jungle area. As the campaign against drugs has pushed production into more inaccessible places and as the world demand has promoted greater cultivation of coca, the coca growers are moving into previously unexplored areas. A coca plantation has been opened along the Chimore river less than an hour's walk from one of the few surviving bands of Yuqui Indians. The Yuquis, famous for their eight-foot-long bows and their six-foot arrows, are now hovering on the brink of extinction. In the past year, the three bands of a few hundred Yuquis have lost eleven members in skirmishes with outsiders. In turn, they killed several outsiders this year and even shot the missionary who is their main champion against outside invaders.

According to the reports of missionaries, other Indian bands have been enlisted as workers in cocaine production and trafficking, making virtual slaves out of them. A Bolivian medical doctor explained to me that the Indians are fed the cocaine in their food as a way of keeping them working and preventing their escape. Through cocaine, the drug traffickers may be able to conquer and control these last remnants of the great Indian nations of the Americas. If so, they will accomplish what many have failed to do in the five-hundred-year campaign of Europeans to conquer the free Indians.

The fate of the Indians driven out of their homelands is shown in the case of Juan, a thirteen-year-old Indian boy from the Chimore river where the Yuquis live. I found him one night in a soup kitchen for street children operated in the corner of a potato warehouse by the Maryknoll priests. Juan wore a bright orange undershirt that proclaimed in bold letters Fairfax District Public Schools. I sat with him at the table coated in potato dust while he ate his soup with his fellow street children, some of whom were as young as four years old. He told me what he could remember of his life on the Chimore; he did not know to which tribe he was born or what language he had spoken with his mother. It was difficult for Juan to talk about his Indian past in a country where it is a grave insult to be called an Indian. Rather than talk about the Chimore or the Chapare, he wanted to ask me questions because I was the first American he had ever met. Was I stronger than everyone else, because he had heard that Americans were the strongest people in the world? Did we really have wolves and bears in North America, and was I afraid of them? Had I been to the Chapare? Did I use cocaine?

In between his questions, I found out that Juan had come to Cochabamba several years ago with his mother. The two had fled the Chapare, but he did not know why. Once in the city they lived on the streets for a few years until his mother died, and he had been living alone ever since. He had become a *polilla* (moth), as they call such street boys. To earn money he washed cars and sold cigarettes laced with *pasta*. When he tired of talking about himself and asking about the animals of North America, he and his two friends made plans to go out to one of the nearby *pasta* villages the next day.

Both the Chapare (which supplied the land for growing coca) and highland villages such as Pocona (which supplied the labor) were suffering from the cocaine boom. Where, then, is the profit? The only other sites in Bolivia are the newly developed manufacturing towns where cocaine is refined. Whereas in the past most of this refining took place in Colombia, both the manufacturers and the traffickers find it easier and cheaper to have the work done in Bolivia, closer to the source of coca leaves and closer to much cheaper sources of labor. The strength of the Colombian government and its closeness to the United States also make the drug trafficking more difficult there than in Bolivia, with its weak, unstable government in La Paz.

Toco is one of the villages that has turned into a processing point for cocaine. Located at about the same altitude as Pocona but only a half-day by truck from the Chapare, Toco cannot grow coca, but the village is close enough to the source to become a major producer of the *pasta*. Traffickers bring in the large shipments of coca leaves and work them in backyard "kitchens." Not only does Toco still have its young men at home and still have food and electricity, but it has work for a few hundred young men from other villages.

Unlike Pocona, for which there are only a few trucks each week, trucks flow in and out of Toco every day. Emblazoned with names such as Rambo, El Padrino (The Godfather), and Charles Bronson rather than the traditional truck names of San José, Virgen de Copacabana, or Flor de Urkupina, these are the newest and finest trucks found in Bolivia. Going in with a Bolivian physician and another anthropologist from the United States, I easily got a ride, along with a dozen Indians, on a truck which was hauling old car batteries splattered with what appeared to be vomit.

A few kilometers outside of Toco we were stopped by a large crowd of Indian peasants. Several dozen women sat around on the ground and in the road spinning yarn and knitting. Most of the women had babies tied to their shoulders in the brightly colored *awayu* cloth, which the women use to carry everything from potatoes to lambs. Men stood around with farm tools, which they now used to block the roads. The men brandished their machetes and rakes at us, accusing us all of being smugglers and *pisacocas*. Like the Indians on the truck with us, the three of us stood silent and expressionless in the melee.

The hostile peasants were staging an ad hoc strike against the coca trade. They had just had their own fields of potatoes washed away in a flash flood. Now without food and without money to replant, they were demanding that someone help them or they would disrupt all traffic to and from Toco. Shouting at us, several of them climbed on board the truck. Moving among the nervous passengers, they checked for a shipment of coca leaves, kerosene, acid, or anything else that might be a part of the coca trade. Having found nothing, they reluctantly let us pass with stern warnings not to return with cocaine or *pasta*. A few weeks after our encounter with the strikers, their strike ended and most of the men went off to look for work in the Chapare and in Toco; without a crop, the cocaine traffic was their only hope of food for the year.

On our arrival in Toco we found out that the batteries loaded with us in the back of the truck had been hollowed out and filled with acid to be used in making *pasta*. *Chicha* vomit had been smeared around to discourage anyone from checking them. After removal of the acid, the same batteries were then filled with plastic bags of cocaine to be smuggled out of Toco and into the town of Cliza and on to Cochabamba and the outside world.

Toco is an expanding village with new cement-block buildings going up on the edge of town and a variety of large plumbing pipes, tanks, and drains being installed. It also has a large number of motorcycles and cars. By Bolivian standards it is a rich village, but it is still poorer than the average village in Mexico or Brazil. Soon after our arrival in Toco, we were followed by a handful of men wanting to sell us *pasta*, and within a few minutes the few had grown to nearly fifty young men anxious to assist us. Most of them were on foot, but some of them circled us in motorcycles, and many of them were armed with guns and machetes. They became suspicious and then openly hostile when we convinced them that we did not want to buy *pasta*. To escape them we took refuge in the home of an Indian family and waited for the mob to disperse.

When we tried to leave the village a few hours later, we were trapped by a truckload of young men who did not release us until they had checked with everyone we had met with in the village. They wondered why we were there if not to buy *pasta*. We were rescued by the doctor who accompanied us; she happened to be the niece of a popular Quechua writer. Evoking the memory of her uncle who had done so much for the Quechua people, she convinced the villagers of Toco that we were Bolivian doctors who worked with her in Cochabamba, and that we were not foreigners coming to buy *pasta* or to spy on them. An old veteran who claimed that he had served in the Chaco War with her uncle vouched for us, but in return for having saved us he then wanted us to buy *pasta* from him.

The wealth generated by the coca trade from Bolivia is easy to see. It is in the European cars cruising the streets of Cochabamba and Santa Cruz, and in the nice houses in the suburbs. It is in the motorcycles and jeeps in Toco, Cliza, and Trinidad. The poverty is difficult to see because it is in the remote villages like Pocona, among the impoverished miners in the village of Porco, and intertwined in the lives of peasants throughout the highland districts of Potosí and

Oruro. But it is in communities such as Pocona that 70 percent of the population of Bolivia lives. For every modern home built with cocaine money in Cochabamba, a tin mine lies abandoned in Potosí that lost many of its miners when the world price for tin fell and they had to go to the Chapare for food. For every new car in Santa Cruz or every new motorcycle in Toco, a whole village is going hungry in the mountains.

The money for coca does not go to the Bolivians. It goes to the criminal organizations that smuggle the drugs out of the country and into the United States and Europe. A gram of pure cocaine on the streets of Cochabamba costs five dollars; the same gram on the streets of New York, Paris, or Berlin costs over a hundred dollars. The price increase occurs outside Bolivia.

The financial differential is evident in the case of the American housewife and mother sentenced to the Cochabamba prison after being caught with six and a half kilograms of cocaine at the airport. Like all the other women in the prison, she now earns money washing laundry by hand at a cold-water tap in the middle of the prison yard. She receives the equivalent of twenty cents for each pair of pants she washes, dries, and irons. In Bolivian prisons, the prisoner has to furnish his or her own food, clothes, medical attention, and even furniture.

She was paid five thousand dollars to smuggle the cocaine out of Bolivia to the Caribbean. Presumably someone else was then to be paid even more to smuggle it into the United States or Europe. The money that the American housewife received to smuggle the cocaine out of the country would pay the salary of eighty *pisacocas* for a month. It would also pay the monthly wages of two hundred fifty Bolivian schoolteachers, who earn the equivalent of twenty U.S. dollars per month in pay. Even though her price seemed high by Bolivian standards, it is a small part of the final money generated by the drugs. When cut and sold on the streets of the United States, her shipment of cocaine would probably bring in five to seven million dollars. Of that amount, however, only about five hundred dollars goes to the Bolivian farmer.

The peasant in the Chapare growing the coca earns three times as much for a field of coca as he would for a field of papayas. But he is only the first in a long line of people and transactions that brings the final product of cocaine to the streets of the West. At the end of the line, cocaine sells for four to five times its weight in gold.

The United States government made all aid programs and loans to Bolivia dependent on the country's efforts to destroy coca. This produces programs in which Bolivian troops go into the most accessible areas and uproot a few fields of aging or diseased coca plants. Visiting drug-enforcement agents from the United States together with American congressmen applaud, make their reports on the escalating war against drugs, and then retire to a city hotel where they drink hot cups of coca tea and cocktails.

These programs hurt primarily the poor farmer who tries to make a slightly better living by growing coca rather than papayas. The raids on the fields and cocaine factories usually lead to the imprisonment of ulcerated *pisococas* and women and children *hormigas* from villages throughout Bolivia.

Local authorities present the burned fields and full prisons to Washington visitors as proof that the Bolivian government has taken a hard stance against drug trafficking.

International crime figures with bank accounts in New York and Zurich get the money. Bolivia ends up with hunger in its villages, young men with their hands and feet permanently maimed, higher rates of venereal disease, chronic food shortages, less kerosene, higher school dropout rates, increased drug addiction, and a worthless peso.

Review Questions

1. List and describe the major effects of the cocaine trade on rural Bolivian life.

2. Why have the production of coca and the manufacture of cocaine created a health hazard in Bolivia?

3. Why has the cocaine trade benefited the Bolivian economy so little?

4. How has the cocaine trade disrupted village social organization in Bolivia?

15

Office Work and the Crack Alternative

Philippe Bourgois

Market economies are standard features of most countries in today's world. Almost everywhere, there is a formal market economy identified by visible, legal, organized economic structures and activities, which economists attempt to measure and governments can tax and regulate. Banks, factories, corporations, retail outlets—these and other publicly organized economic units are usually part of the formal economy.

But underneath the formal economy lies an informal system often called the shadow *or* underground *economy. The shadow economy is usually small-scale, personal, and at times illegal. Governments find it difficult to tax and regulate the shadow economy. Yet it is the shadow economy that provides a living for hundreds of millions of largely poor men and women around the world today.*

In this article, Philippe Bourgois focuses on part of the shadow economy in the United States, the illegal sale of crack by Puerto Rican immigrants

165

in New York City. He argues that the loss of manufacturing jobs in New York is a key to understanding the rise of drug dealing in Spanish Harlem. Manufacturing jobs once provided dignified and stable employment for poorly educated, unskilled Puerto Rican men and women. As factories closed during the 1960s, '70s, and '80s, the unemployed could find work only in service industries such as security corporations, law firms, and insurance companies. Because they were uneducated and culturally different, they could hold only minimum wage jobs in such worlds, as they are usually controlled by educated, largely Anglo people who openly look down on them. In the end, they could achieve higher status and often higher income in their own ethnic community by dealing drugs. The result has been a destructive spiral into addiction, murder, and prison. Bourgois concludes the article with an addendum noting that high employment in the late 1990s provided more work opportunities for Puerto Ricans in the formal economy and that crack dealing has largely given way to the less visible sale of marijuana and heroin.

For a total of approximately three and a half years during the late 1980s and early 1990s, I lived with my wife and young son in an irregularly heated, rat-filled tenement in East Harlem, New York. This two-hundred-square-block neighborhood—better known locally as *El Barrio* or Spanish Harlem—is visibly impoverished yet it is located in the heart of New York, the richest city in the Western Hemisphere. It is literally a stone's throw from multimillion-dollar condominiums. Although one in three families survived on some form of public assistance in 1990, the majority of El Barrio's 110,600 Puerto Rican and African-American residents fall into the ranks of the working poor.[1] They eke out an uneasy subsistence in entry-level service and manufacturing jobs in one of the most expensive cities in the world.

The public sector (e.g., the police, social welfare agencies, the Sanitation Department) has broken down in El Barrio and does not function effectively. This has caused the legally employed residents of the neighborhood to lose control of their streets and public spaces to the drug economy. My tenement's block was not atypical and within a few hundred yards' radius I could obtain heroin, crack, powder cocaine, hypodermic needles, methadone, Valium, angel dust, marijuana, mescaline, bootleg alcohol, and tobacco. Within two hundred feet of my stoop there were three competing crack houses selling vials at two, three, and five dollars. Several doctors operated "pill mills" on the blocks around me,

---

[1]According to the 1990 Census, in East Harlem 48.3 percent of males and 35.2 percent of females over sixteen were officially reported as employed—compared to a citywide average of 64.3 percent for men and 49 percent for women. Another 10.4 percent of the men and 5.7 percent of the women in East Harlem were actively looking for legal work. . . . In El Barrio as a whole, 60 percent of all households reported legally earned incomes. Twenty-six percent received Public Assistance, 6.3 percent received Supplemental Security Income, and 5 percent received Medicaid benefits.

writing prescriptions for opiates and barbiturates upon demand. In the projects within view of my living-room window, the Housing Authority police arrested a fifty-five-year-old mother and her twenty-two-year-old daughter while they were "bagging" twenty-two pounds of cocaine into ten-dollar quarter-gram "Jumbo" vials of adulterated product worth over a million dollars on the streets. The police found twenty-five thousand dollars in cash in small-denomination bills in this same apartment.[2] In other words, there are millions of dollars' worth of business going on directly in front of the youths growing up in East Harlem tenements and housing projects. Why should these young men and women take the subway downtown to work minimum-wage jobs—or even double minimum-wage jobs—in downtown offices when they can usually earn more, at least in the short run, by selling drugs on the street corner in front of their apartment or schoolyard?

This dynamic underground economy is predicated on violence and substance abuse. It has spawned what I call a "street culture" of resistance and self-destruction. The central concern of my study is the relationship of street culture to the worlds of work accessible to street dealers—that is, the legal and illegal labor markets that employ them and give meaning to their lives. I hope to show the local-level implications of the global-level restructuring of the U.S. economy away from factory production and toward services. In the process, I have recorded the words and experiences of some unrepentant victims who are part of a network of some twenty-five street-level crack dealers operating on and around my block. To summarize, I am arguing that the transformation from manufacturing to service employment—especially in the professional office work setting—is much more culturally disruptive than the already revealing statistics on reductions in income, employment, unionization, and worker's benefits would indicate. Low-level service sector employment engenders a humiliating ideological—or cultural—confrontation between a powerful corps of white office executives and their assistants versus a younger generation of poorly educated, alienated, "colored" workers. It also often takes the form of a sharply polarized confrontation over gender roles.

Shattered Working-Class Dreams

All the crack dealers and addicts whom I have interviewed had worked at one or more legal jobs in their early youth. In fact, most entered the labor market at a younger age than the typical American. Before they were twelve years old they were bagging groceries at the supermarket for tips, stocking beers off-the-books in local *bodegas,* or shining shoes. For example, Primo, the night manager at a video game arcade that sells five-dollar vials of crack on the block where I lived, pursued a traditional working-class dream in his early

---

[2]Both of these police actions were reported in the local print and television media, but I am withholding the cities to protect the anonymity of my street address.

adolescence. With the support of his extended kin who were all immersed in a working-class "common sense," he dropped out of junior high school to work in a local garment factory:

> I was like fourteen or fifteen playing hooky and pressing dresses and whatever they were making on the steamer. They was cheap, cheap clothes.
>
> My mother's sister was working there first and then her son, my cousin Willie—the one who's in jail now—was the one they hired first, because his mother agreed: "If you don't want to go to school, you gotta work."
>
> So I started hanging out with him. I wasn't planning on working in the factory. I was supposed to be in school; but it just sort of happened.

Ironically, young Primo actually became the agent who physically moved the factory out of the inner city. In the process, he became merely one more of the 445,900 manufacturing workers in New York City who lost their jobs as factory employment dropped 50 percent from 1963 to 1983 . . .

Almost all the crack dealers had similar tales of former factory jobs. For poor adolescents, the decision to drop out of school and become a marginal factory worker is attractive. It provides the employed youth with access to the childhood "necessities"—sneakers, basketballs, store-bought snacks—that sixteen-year-olds who stay in school cannot afford. In the descriptions of their first forays into legal factory-based employment, one hears clearly the extent to which they, and their families, subscribed to mainstream working-class ideologies about the dignity of engaging in "hard work" rather than education.

Had these enterprising, early-adolescent workers from El Barrio not been confined to the weakest sector of manufacturing in a period of rapid job loss, their teenage working-class dreams might have stabilized. Instead, upon reaching their mid-twenties, they discovered themselves to be unemployable high school dropouts. This painful realization of social marginalization expresses itself across a generational divide. The parents and grandparents of the dealers continue to maintain working-class values of honesty and hard work which conflict violently with the reality of their children's immersion in street culture. They are constantly accused of slothfulness by their mothers and even by friends who have managed to maintain legal jobs. They do not have a regional perspective on the dearth of adequate entry-level jobs available to "functional illiterates" in New York, and they begin to suspect that they might indeed be "*vago bons*" [lazy bums] who do not *want* to work hard and cannot help themselves. Confused, they take refuge in an alternative search for career, meaning, and ecstasy in substance abuse.

Formerly, when most entry-level jobs were found in factories, the contradiction between an oppositional street culture and traditional working-class, masculine, shop-floor culture was less pronounced—especially when the work site was protected by a union. Factories are inevitably rife with confrontational hierarchies. Nevertheless, on the shop-floor, surrounded by older union workers, high school dropouts who are well versed in the latest and toughest street culture styles function effectively. In the factory, being tough and violently macho has high cultural value; a certain degree of opposition to the foreman and the "bossman" is expected and is considered appropriate.

In contrast, this same oppositional street-identity is nonfunctional in the professional office worker service sector that has burgeoned in New York's high-finance-driven economy. It does not allow for the humble, obedient, social interaction—often across gender lines—that professional office workers routinely impose on their subordinates. A qualitative change has occurred, therefore, in the tenor of social interaction in office-based employment. Workers in a mail room or behind a photocopy machine cannot publicly maintain their cultural autonomy. Most concretely, they have no union; more subtly, there are few fellow workers surrounding them to insulate them and to provide them with a culturally based sense of class solidarity.[3] Instead they are besieged by supervisors and bosses from an alien, hostile, and obviously dominant culture who ridicule street culture. Workers like Primo appear inarticulate to their professional supervisors when they try to imitate the language of power in the workplace and instead stumble pathetically over the enunciation of unfamiliar words. They cannot decipher the hastily scribbled instructions—rife with mysterious abbreviations—that are left for them by harried office managers. The "common sense" of white-collar work is foreign to them; they do not, for example, understand the logic for filing triplicate copies of memos or for post-dating invoices. When they attempt to improvise or show initiative they fail miserably and instead appear inefficient, or even hostile, for failing to follow "clearly specified" instructions.

Their "social skills" are even more inadequate than their limited professional capacities. They do not know how to look at their fellow co-service workers, let alone their supervisors, without intimidating them. They cannot walk down the hallway to the water fountain without unconsciously swaying their shoulders aggressively as if patrolling their home turf. Gender barriers are an even more culturally charged realm. They are repeatedly reprimanded for harassing female coworkers.

The cultural clash between white "yuppie" power and inner-city "scrambling jive" in the service sector is much more than a superficial question of style. It is about access to power. Service workers who are incapable of obeying the rules of interpersonal interaction dictated by professional office culture will never be upwardly mobile. Their supervisors will think they are dumb or have a "bad attitude." Once again, a gender dynamic exacerbates the confusion and sense of insult experienced by young, male inner-city employees because most supervisors in the lowest reaches of the service sector are women. Street culture does not allow males to be subordinate across gender lines.

---

[3]Significantly, there are subsectors of the service industry that are relatively unionized—such as hospital and custodial work—where there is a limited autonomous space for street culture and working-class resistance.

"Gettin' Dissed"

On the street, the trauma of experiencing a threat to one's personal dignity has been frozen linguistically in the commonly used phrase "to diss," which is short for "to disrespect." Significantly, one generation ago ethnographers working in rural Puerto Rico specifically noted the importance of the traditional Puerto Rican concept of *respeto* in mediating labor relations:

> The good owner "respects" (*respeta*) the laborer. . . . It is probably to the interest of the landowner to make concessions to his best workers, to deal with them on a respect basis, and to enmesh them in a network of mutual obligations.[4]

Puerto Rican street-dealers do not find respect in the entry-level service sector jobs that have increased two-fold in New York's economy since the 1950s. On the contrary, they "get dissed" in the new jobs that are available to them. Primo, for example, remembers the humiliation of his former work experiences as an "office boy," and he speaks of them in a race- and gender-charged idiom:

> I had a prejudiced boss. She was a fucking "ho'," Gloria. She was white. Her name was Christian. No, not Christian, Kirschman. I don't know if she was Jewish or not. When she was talking to people she would say, "He's illiterate."
>
> So what I did one day was, I just looked up the word, "illiterate," in the dictionary and I saw that she's saying to her associates that I'm stupid or something! Well, I am illiterate anyway.

The most profound dimension of Primo's humiliation was being obliged to look up in the dictionary the word used to insult him. In contrast, in the underground economy, he is sheltered from this kind of threat:

> Rocky [the crack house franchise owner] he would never disrespect me that way. He wouldn't tell me that because he's illiterate too. Plus I've got more education than him. I got a GED. . . .

Primo excels in the street's underground economy. His very persona inspires fear and respect. In contrast, in order to succeed in his former office job, Primo would have had to self-consciously alter his street identity and mimic the professional cultural style that office managers require of their subordinates and colleagues. Primo refused to accept his boss's insults and he was unable to imitate her interactional styles. He was doomed, consequently, to a marginal position behind a photocopy machine or at the mail meter. Behavior considered appropriate in street culture is considered dysfunctional in office settings.

---

[4]Eric Wolf, "San Jose: Subcultures of a 'Traditional' Coffee Municipality," in Julian Stewart (ed.), *The People of Puerto Rico* (Chicago: University of Chicago Press, 1956), p. 235.

In other words, job requirements in the service sector are largely cultural style and this conjugates powerfully with racism.

> I wouldn't have mind that she said I was illiterate. What bothered me was that when she called on the telephone, she wouldn't want me to answer even if my supervisor who was the receptionist was not there. [Note how Primo is so low in the office hierarchy that his immediate supervisor is a receptionist.]
>
> When she hears my voice it sounds like she's going to get a heart attack. She'd go, "Why are you answering the phones?"
>
> That bitch just didn't like my Puerto Rican accent.

Primo's manner of resisting this insult to his cultural dignity exacerbated his marginal position in the labor hierarchy:

> And then, when I did pick up the phone, I used to just sound *Porta'rrrican* on purpose.

In contrast to the old factory sweatshop positions, these just-above-minimum-wage office jobs require intense interpersonal contact with the middle and upper-middle classes. Close contact across class lines and the absence of a working-class autonomous space for eight hours a day in the office can be a claustrophobic experience for an otherwise ambitious, energetic, young, inner-city worker.

Caesar, who worked for Primo as lookout and bodyguard at the crack house, interpreted this requirement to obey white, middle-class norms as an affront to his dignity that specifically challenged his definition of masculinity:

> I had a few jobs like that [referring to Primo's "telephone diss"] where you gotta take a lot of shit from bitches and be a wimp.
>
> I didn't like it but I kept on working, because "Fuck it!" you don't want to fuck up the relationship. So you just be a punk [shrugging his shoulders dejectedly].

One alternative for surviving at a workplace that does not tolerate a street-based cultural identity is to become bicultural: to play politely by "the white woman's" rules downtown only to come home and revert to street culture within the safety of one's tenement or housing project at night. Tens of thousands of East Harlem residents manage this tightrope, but it often engenders accusations of betrayal and internalized racism on the part of neighbors and childhood friends who do not have—or do not want—these bicultural skills.

This is the case, for example, of Ray, a rival crack dealer whose tough street demeanor conflates with his black skin to "disqualify" him from legal office work. He quit a "nickel-and-dime messenger job downtown" in order to sell crack full time in his project stairway shortly after a white woman fled from him shrieking down the hallway of a high-rise office building. Ray and the terrified woman had ridden the elevator together, and, coincidentally, Ray had stepped off on the same floor as her to make a delivery. Worse yet, Ray had been trying to act like a "debonair male" and suspected the contradiction between his inadequate appearance and his chivalric intentions was responsible for the woman's terror:

> You know how you let a woman go off the elevator first? Well that's what I did to her but I may have looked a little shabby on the ends. Sometime my hair not combed. You know. So I could look a little sloppy to her maybe when I let her off first.

What Ray did not quite admit until I probed further is that he too had been intimidated by the lone white woman. He had been so disoriented by her taboo, unsupervised proximity that he had forgotten to press the elevator button when he originally stepped on after her:

> She went in the elevator first but then she just waits there to see what floor I press. She's playing like she don't know what floor she wants to go to because she wants to wait for me to press my floor. And I'm standing there and I forgot to press the button. I'm thinking about something else—I don't know what was the matter with me. And she's thinking like, "He's not pressing the button; I guess he's following me!"

As a crack dealer, Ray no longer has to confront this kind of confusing humiliation. Instead, he can righteously condemn his "successful" neighbors who work downtown for being ashamed of who they were born to be:

> When you see someone go downtown and get a good job, if they be Puerto Rican, you see them fix up their hair and put some contact lens in their eyes. Then they fit in. And they do it! I seen it.
> They turn-overs. They people who want to be white. Man, if you call them in Spanish, it wind up a problem.
> When they get nice jobs like that, all of a sudden, you know, they start talking proper.

Self-Destructive Resistance

During the 1980s, the real value of the minimum wage for legally employed workers declined by one-third. At the same time, social services were cut. The federal government, for example, decreased the proportion of its contribution to New York City's budget by over 50 percent . . . The breakdown of the inner city's public sector is no longer an economic threat to the expansion of New York's economy because the native-born labor force it shelters is increasingly irrelevant.
New immigrants arrive every day, and they are fully prepared to work hard for low wages under unsavory conditions. Like the parents and grandparents

of Primo and Caesar, many of New York's newest immigrants are from isolated rural communities or squalid shanty towns where meat is eaten only once a week and there is no running water or electricity. Half a century ago Primo's mother fled precisely the same living conditions these new immigrants are only just struggling to escape. Her reminiscences about childhood in her natal village reveal the time warp of improved material conditions, cultural dislocation, and crushed working-class dreams that is propelling her second-generation son into a destructive street culture:

> I loved that life in Puerto Rico, because it was a healthy, healthy, healthy life.
>
> We always ate because my father always had work, and in those days the custom was to have a garden in your patio to grow food and everything that you ate.
>
> We only ate meat on Sundays because everything was cultivated on the same little parcel of land. We didn't have a refrigerator, so we ate *bacalao* [salted codfish], which can stay outside and a meat that they call *carne de vieja* [shredded beef], and sardines from a can. But thanks to God, we never felt hunger. My mother made a lot of cornflour.
>
> Some people have done better by coming here, but many people haven't. Even people from my barrio, who came trying to find a better life [*buen ambiente*] just found disaster. Married couples right from my neighborhood came only to have the husband run off with another woman.
>
> In those days in Puerto Rico, when we were in poverty, life was better. Everyone will tell you life was healthier and you could trust people. Now you can't trust anybody.
>
> What I like best was that we kept all our traditions . . . our feasts. In my village, everyone was either an Uncle or an Aunt. And when you walked by someone older, you had to ask for their blessing. It was respect. There was a lot of respect in those days [original quote in Spanish].

The Jewish and Italian-American white workers that Primo's mother replaced a generation ago when she came to New York City in hope of building a better future for her children were largely absorbed into an expanding economy that allowed them to be upwardly mobile. New York's economy always suffered periodic fluctuations, such as during the Great Depression, but those difficult periods were always temporary. The overall trend was one of economic growth. Primo's generation has not been so lucky. The contemporary economy does not particularly need them, and ethnic discrimination and cultural barriers overwhelm them whenever they attempt to work legally and seek service-sector jobs. Worse yet, an extraordinarily dynamic underground drug economy beckons them.

Rather than bemoaning the structural adjustment which is destroying their capacity to survive on legal wages, streetbound Puerto Rican youths celebrate their "decision" to bank on the underground economy and to cultivate their street identities. Caesar and Primo repeatedly assert their pride in their street careers. For example, one Saturday night after they finished their midnight shift at the crack house, I accompanied them on their way to purchase "*El*

Sapo Verde" [The Green Toad], a twenty-dollar bag of powder cocaine sold by a new company three blocks away. While waiting for Primo and Caesar to be "served" by the coke seller a few yards away, I engaged three undocumented Mexican men drinking beer on a neighboring stoop in a conversation about finding work in New York. One of the new immigrants was already earning five hundred dollars a week fixing deep-fat-fry machines. He had a straightforward racist explanation for why Caesar—who was standing next to me—was "unemployed":

> OK, OK, I'll explain it to you in one word: Because the Puerto Ricans are brutes! [Pointing at Caesar] Brutes! Do you understand?
>
> Puerto Ricans like to make easy money. They like to leech off of other people. But not us Mexicans! No way! We like to work for our money. We don't steal. We came here to work and that's all [original quote in Spanish].

Instead of physically assaulting the employed immigrant for insulting him, Caesar embraced the racist tirade, ironically turning it into the basis for a new, generational-based, "American-born," urban cultural pride. In fact, in his response, he ridicules what he interprets to be the hillbilly naiveté of the Mexicans who still believe in the "American Dream." He spoke slowly in street-English as if to mark sarcastically the contrast between his "savvy" Nuyorican (New York-born Puerto Rican) identity versus the limited English proficiency of his detractor:

> That's right, m'a man! We is real vermin lunatics that sell drugs. We don't want no part of society. "Fight the Power!"[5]
>
> What do we wanna be working for? We rather live off the system. Gain weight, lay women.
>
> When we was younger, we used to break our asses too [gesturing towards the Mexican men who were straining to understand his English]. I had all kinds of stupid jobs too . . . advertising agencies . . . computers.
>
> But not no more! Now we're in a rebellious stage. We rather evade taxes, make quick money, and just survive. But we're not satisfied with that either. Ha!

Conclusion: Ethnography and Oppression

The underground economy and the social relations thriving off of it are best understood as modes of resistance to subordination in the service sector of the new U.S. economy. This resistance, however, results in individual self destruction and wider community devastation through substance abuse and violence. This complex and contradictory dynamic whereby resistance leads to self-destruction in the inner city is difficult to convey to readers in a clear and re-

---

[5]"Fight the Power" is a rap song composed in 1990 by the African-American group, Public Enemy.

sponsible manner. Mainstream society's "common sense" understanding of social stratification around ethnicity and class assumes the existence of racial hierarchies and blames individual victims for their failures. This makes it difficult to present ethnographic data from inner-city streets without falling prey to a "pornography of violence" or a racist voyeurism.

The public is not persuaded by a structural economic understanding of Caesar and Primo's "self-destruction." Even the victims themselves psychologize their unsatisfactory lives. Similarly, politicians and, more broadly, public policy ignore the fundamental structural economic facts of marginalization in America. Instead the first priority of federal and local social "welfare" agencies is to change the psychological—or at best the "cultural"—orientations of misguided individuals . . . U.S. politicians furiously debate family values while multinational corporations establish global free-trade zones and unionized factory employment in the U.S. continues to disappear as overseas sweatshops multiply. Social science researchers, meanwhile, have remained silent for the most part. They politely ignore the urgent social problems engulfing the urban United States. The few marginal academic publications that do address issues of poverty and racism are easily ignored by the media and mainstream society. . . .

Epilogue

In the six years since this article was first published, four major dynamics have altered the tenor of daily life on the streets of East Harlem and have deeply affected the lives of the crack dealers and their families depicted in these pages: (1) the U.S. economy entered the most prolonged period of sustained growth in its recorded history, (2) the size of the Mexican immigrant population in New York City and especially in East Harlem increased dramatically, (3) the War on Drugs escalated into a quasi-official public policy of criminalizing and incarcerating the poor and the socially marginal, and (4) drug fashion trends among inner-city youth rendered marijuana even more popular and crack and heroin even less popular among Latinos and African Americans.

Crack, cocaine, and heroin are still all sold on the block where I lived, but they are sold less visibly by a smaller number of people. It is still easy to purchase narcotics throughout East Harlem, but much of the drug dealing has moved indoors, out of sight, dealers no longer shouting out the brand names of their drugs. Most importantly, heroin and crack continue to be spurned by Latino and African-American youth who have seen the ravages those drugs committed on the older generations in their community. Nevertheless, in the U.S. inner city there remains an aging hardcore cohort of addicts. In most large cities crack is most visibly ensconced in predominantly African-American neighborhoods on the poorest blocks, often surrounding large public housing projects. In New York City, Puerto Rican households also continue to be at the epicenter of this ongoing, but now more self-contained, stationary cyclone of crack consumption.

In contrast to crack, heroin consumption has increased. Throughout most of the United States, heroin is cheaper and purer than in the early 1990s, belying any claims that the War on Drugs is winnable. Heroin's new appeal, however, is primarily among younger whites outside the ghetto for whom crack was never a drug of choice. It is not a drug of choice among Latino and African-American youth.

To summarize, both heroin and crack continue to be part of a multi-billion-dollar business that ravages inner-city families with special virulence. The younger generations of East Harlem residents, however, are more involved as sellers rather than consumers. Those Latino and African-American youth who do use crack or heroin generally try to hide the fact from their friends.

More important than changing drug-consumption fashions or the posturing of politicians over drug war campaigns has been the dramatic long-term improvement in the U.S. economy resulting in record low rates of unemployment. Somewhat to my surprise, some of the crack dealers and their families have benefited from this sustained economic growth. Slightly less than half have been allowed to enter the lower echelons of the legal labor market. For example, during the summer of 2000: one dealer was a unionized doorman, another was a home health care attendant, another was a plumber's assistant, three others were construction workers for small-time unlicensed contractors, and one was a cashier in a discount tourist souvenir store. Three or four of the dealers were still selling drugs, but most of them tended to be selling marijuana instead of crack or heroin. Three other dealers were in prison with long-term sentences and ironically were probably employed at well below minimum wage in the United States' burgeoning prison-based manufacturing sector. In short, the dramatic improvement in the U.S. economy has forced employers and unions to integrate more formally marginalized Puerto Ricans and African Americans into the labor market than was the case in the late 1980s and early 1990s when the research for this [article] was conducted. Nevertheless, even at the height of the growth in the U.S. economy in the year 2000, a large sector of street youth found themselves excluded. These marginals have become almost completely superfluous to the legal economy; they remain enmeshed in a still-lucrative drug economy, a burgeoning prison system, and a quagmire of chronic substance abuse. From a long-term political and economic perspective, the future does not bode well for inner-city poor of New York. In the year 2000, the United States had the largest disparity between rich and poor of any industrialized nation in the world—and this gap was not decreasing.

Review Questions

1. What kinds of jobs in the formal economy could Puerto Ricans living in East Harlem hold forty years ago? How did these jobs enable the men to preserve respect as it was defined in their culture?

2. What kinds of jobs are currently available to Puerto Rican men in New York's service economy? How do these jobs challenge the men's self-respect?

3. What structural changes in New York's formal economy have changed over the past forty years? How have these changes affected the lives of young men living in Spanish Harlem?

4. Why do Puerto Rican men take pride in their street identities?

5. Why does Bourgois claim that the Puerto Rican men's resistance to work in the legal economy leads to "self-destruction" and "wider community devastation"?

FIVE

Kinship and Family

Social life is essential to human existence. We remain in the company of other people from the day we are born to the time of our death. People teach us to speak. They show us how to relate to our surroundings. They give us the help and the support we need to achieve personal security and mental well-being. Alone, we are relatively frail, defenseless primates; in groups we are astonishingly adaptive and powerful. Yet despite these advantages, well-organized human societies are difficult to achieve. Some species manage to produce social organization genetically. But people are not like bees or ants. We lack the genetically coded directions for behavior that make these insects successful social animals. Although we seem to inherit a general need for social approval, we also harbor individual interests and ambitions that can block or destroy close social ties. To overcome these divisive tendencies, human groups organize around several principles designed to foster cooperation and group loyalty. Kinship is among the strongest of these.

We may define **kinship** as the complex system of culturally defined social relationships based on marriage (the principle of **affinity**) and birth (the principle of **consanguinity**). The study of kinship involves consideration of such principles as descent, kinship status and roles, family and other kinship groups, marriage, and residence. In fact, kinship has been such an important organizing factor in many of the societies studied by anthropologists that it is one of the most elaborate areas of the discipline. What are some of the important concepts?

First is descent. **Descent** is based on the notion of a common heritage. It is a cultural rule tying together people on the basis of reputed common ancestry. Descent functions to guide inheritance, group loyalty, and, above all, the formation of families and extended kinship groups.

There are three main rules of descent. One is **patrilineal descent,** which links relatives through males only. In patrilineal systems, females are part of their father's line, but their children descend from the husbands. **Matrilineal descent** links relatives through females only. Males belong to their mother's line; the children of males descend from the wives. **Bilateral descent** links a person to kin through both males and females simultaneously. Americans are said to have bilateral descent, whereas most of the people in India, Japan, and China are patrilineal. Such groups as the Apache and Trobriand Islanders are matrilineal.

Descent often defines groups called, not surprisingly, **descent groups.** One of these is the **lineage,** a localized group that is based on unilineal (patrilineal or matrilineal) descent and that usually has some corporate powers. In the Marshall Islands, for example, the matriline holds rights to land, which, in turn, it allots to its members. Lineages in India sometimes hold rights to land but are a more important arena for other kinds of decisions such as marriage. Lineage mates must be consulted about the advisability, timing, and arrangements for weddings. (See Article 17.)

Clans are composed of lineages. Clan members believe they are all descended from a common ancestor, but because clans are larger, members cannot trace their genealogical relationships to everyone in the group. In some societies, clans may be linked together in even larger groups called **phratries.** Because phratries are usually large, the feeling of common descent they offer is weaker.

Ramages, or cognatic kin groups, are based on bilateral descent. They often resemble lineages in size and function but provide more recruiting flexibility. An individual can choose membership from among several ramages where he or she has relatives.

Another important kinship group is the family. This unit is more difficult to define than we may think, because people have found so many different ways to organize "familylike" groups. Here we will follow anthropologist George P. Murdock's approach and define the **family** as a kin group consisting of at least one married couple sharing the same residence with their children and performing sexual, reproductive, economic, and educational functions. A **nuclear family** consists of a single married couple and their children. An **extended family** consists of two or more married couples and their children. Extended families have a quality all their own and are often found in societies where family performance and honor are paramount to the reputation of individual family members. Extended families are most commonly based on patrilineal descent. Women marry into such families and must establish themselves among the line members and other women who live there.

Marriage, the socially approved union of a man and a woman, is a second major principle of kinship. (Readers should note growing pressure to include same-sex marriages in this definition.) The regulation of marriage takes elaborate forms from one society to the next. Marriage may be **exogamous,** meaning marriage outside any particular named group, or **endogamous,** indicating the opposite. Bhil tribals of India, for example, are clan and village exogamous (they should marry outside these groups), but tribal endogamous (they should marry other Bhils).

Marriage may also be **monogamous,** where it is preferred that only one woman should be married to one man at a time, or **polygamous,** meaning that one person may be married to more than one person simultaneously. There are two kinds of polygamy, **polygyny,** the marriage of one man with more than one woman simultaneously, and **polyandry,** the marriage of one woman with more than one man.

Many anthropologists view marriage as a system of alliances between families and descent lines. Viewed in these terms, rules such as endogamy and exogamy can be explained as devices to link or internally strengthen various kinship groups. The **incest taboo,** a legal rule that prohibits sexual intercourse or marriage between particular classes of kin, is often explained as a way to extend alliances between kin groups.

Finally, the regulation of marriage falls to the parents and close relatives of eligible young people in many societies. These elders concern themselves with more than wedding preparations; they must also see to it that young people marry appropriately, which means they consider the reputation of prospective spouses and their families' economic strength and social rank.

The selections in Part Five illustrate several aspects of kinship systems. In the first article, Nancy Scheper-Hughes looks at the relationship that poor Brazilian mothers have with their infants. Because babies die so often, mothers must delay forming attachments to them until their children show that they can survive. The second article, by David McCurdy, looks at the way kinship organizes life for the inhabitants of a Rajasthani Bhil village. Arranging a marriage requires use and consideration of clans, lineages, families, and weddings. Despite its origin in peasant society, the Indian kinship system is proving useful as people try to cope with a modernizing society. The third article, by Clifford Geertz, describes the only society known in the world in which people do not marry. Despite this, the matrilineal Na of China take lovers, have children, and build extended families consisting of women, their brothers, and their children. Finally, Margery Wolf looks at the structure of the Taiwanese extended family from the point of view of the women who constitute it. It is only by establishing her own uterine family that a woman can gain power within the patrilineal group.

Key Terms

affinity   *p. 179*
bilateral descent   *p. 180*
clan   *p. 180*
consanguinity   *p. 179*
descent   *p. 179*
descent groups   *p. 180*
endogamy   *p. 180*
exogamy   *p. 180*
extended family   *p. 180*
family   *p. 180*
incest taboo   *p. 181*
kinship   *p. 179*

lineage   *p. 180*
marriage   *p. 180*
matrilineal descent   *p. 180*
monogamy   *p. 180*
nuclear family   *p. 180*
patrilineal descent   *p. 179*
phratry   *p. 180*
polyandry   *p. 181*
polygamy   *p. 180*
polygyny   *p. 181*
ramage   *p. 180*

16

Mother's Love: Death without Weeping

Nancy Scheper-Hughes

Kinship systems are based on marriage and birth. Both, anthropologists as-
sume, create ties that can link kin into close, cooperative, enduring struc-
tures. What happens to such ties, however, in the face of severe hardship
imposed by grinding poverty and urban migration? Can we continue to as-
sume, for example, that there will be a close bond between mother and child?
This is the question pursued by Nancy Scheper-Hughes in the following ar-
ticle about the mother–infant relationship among poor women in a Brazil-
ian shantytown. The author became interested in the question following a
"baby die-off" in the town of Bom Jesus in 1965. She noticed that mothers
seemed to take these events casually. After twenty-five years of research in the
Alto do Cruzeiro shantytown there, she has come to see such indifference as
a cultural response to high rates of infant death due to poverty and malnu-
trition. Mothers, and surrounding social institutions such as the Catholic
church, expect babies to die easily. Mothers concentrate their support on ba-
bies who are "fighters" and let themselves grow attached to their children only

when they are reasonably sure that the offspring will survive. The article also provides an excellent illustration of what happens to kinship systems in the face of poverty and social dislocation. Such conditions may easily result in the formation of woman-headed families and in a lack of the extended kinship networks so often found in more stable, rural societies.

> I have seen death without weeping
> The destiny of the Northeast is death
> Cattle they kill
> To the people they do something worse
> —Anonymous Brazilian singer (1965)

"Why do the church bells ring so often?" I asked Nailza de Arruda soon after I moved into a corner of her tiny mud-walled hut near the top of the shantytown called the Alto do Cruzeiro (Crucifix Hill). I was then a Peace Corps volunteer and a community development/health worker. It was the dry and blazing hot summer of 1965, the months following the military coup in Brazil, and save for the rusty, clanging bells of N.S. das Dores Church, an eerie quiet had settled over the market town that I call Bom Jesus da Mata. Beneath the quiet, however, there was chaos and panic. "It's nothing," replied Nailza, "just another little angel gone to heaven."

Nailza had sent more than her share of little angels to heaven, and sometimes at night I could hear her engaged in a muffled but passionate discourse with one of them, two-year-old Joana. Joana's photograph, taken as she lay propped up in her tiny cardboard coffin, her eyes open, hung on a wall next to one of Nailza and Ze Antonio taken on the day they eloped.

Nailza could barely remember the other infants and babies who came and went in close succession. Most had died unnamed and were hastily baptized in their coffins. Few lived more than a month or two. Only Joana, properly baptized in church at the close of her first year and placed under the protection of a powerful saint, Joan of Arc, had been expected to live. And Nailza had dangerously allowed herself to love the little girl.

In addressing the dead child, Nailza's voice would range from tearful imploring to angry recrimination: "Why did you leave me? Was your patron saint so greedy that she could not allow me one child on this earth?" Ze Antonio advised me to ignore Nailza's odd behavior, which he understood as a kind of madness that, like the birth and death of children, came and went. Indeed, the premature birth of a stillborn son some months later "cured" Nailza of her "inappropriate" grief, and the day came when she removed Joana's photo and carefully packed it away.

More than fifteen years elapsed before I returned to the Alto do Cruzeiro, and it was anthropology that provided the vehicle of my return. Since 1982 I have returned several times in order to pursue a problem that first attracted my attention in the 1960s. My involvement with the people of the Alto do Cruzeiro now spans a quarter of a century and three generations of parenting in a community where mothers and daughters are often simultaneously pregnant.

The Alto do Cruzeiro is one of three shantytowns surrounding the large market town of Bom Jesus in the sugar plantation zone of Pernambuco in Northeast Brazil, one of the many zones of neglect that have emerged in the shadow of the now tarnished economic miracle of Brazil. For the women and children of the Alto do Cruzeiro the only miracle is that some of them have managed to stay alive at all.

The Northeast is a region of vast proportions (approximately twice the size of Texas) and of equally vast social and developmental problems. The nine states that make up the region are the poorest in the country and are representative of the Third World within a dynamic and rapidly industrializing nation. Despite waves of migrations from the interior to the teeming shantytowns of coastal cities, the majority still live in rural areas on farms and ranches, sugar plantations and mills.

Life expectancy in the Northeast is only forty years, largely because of the appallingly high rate of infant and child mortality. Approximately one million children in Brazil under the age of five die each year. The children of the Northeast, especially those born in shantytowns on the periphery of urban life, are at a very high risk of death. In these areas, children are born without the traditional protection of breast-feeding, subsistence gardens, stable marriages, and multiple adult caretakers that exists in the interior. In the hillside shantytowns that spring up around cities or, in this case, interior market towns, marriages are brittle, single parenting is the norm, and women are frequently forced into the shadow economy of domestic work in the homes of the rich or into unprotected and oftentimes "scab" wage labor on the surrounding sugar plantations, where they clear land for planting and weed for a pittance, sometimes less than a dollar a day. The women of the Alto may not bring their babies with them into the homes of the wealthy, where the often-sick infants are considered sources of contamination, and they cannot carry the little ones to the riverbanks where they wash clothes because the river is heavily infested with schistosomes and other deadly parasites. Nor can they carry their young children to the plantations, which are often several miles away. At wages of a dollar a day, the women of the Alto cannot hire baby sitters. Older children who are not in school will sometimes serve as somewhat indifferent caretakers. But any child not in school is also expected to find wage work. In most cases, babies are simply left at home alone, the door securely fastened. And so many also die alone and unattended.

Bom Jesus da Mata, centrally located in the plantation zone of Pernambuco, is within commuting distance of several sugar plantations and mills. Consequently, Bom Jesus has been a magnet for rural workers forced off their small subsistence plots by large landowners wanting to use every available piece of land for sugar cultivation. Initially, the rural migrants to Bom Jesus were squatters who were given tacit approval by the mayor to put up temporary straw huts on each of the three hills overlooking the town. The Alto do Cruzeiro is the oldest, the largest, and the poorest of the shantytowns. Over the past three decades many of the original migrants have become permanent residents, and the primitive and temporary straw huts have been replaced by small homes (usually of two rooms) made of wattle and daub, sometimes covered with plaster. The more affluent residents use bricks and tiles. In most Alto homes, dangerous kerosene lamps have been replaced by light bulbs. The once tattered rural garb, often fashioned from used sugar sacking, has likewise been replaced by store-bought clothes, often castoffs from a wealthy *patrão* (boss). The trappings are modern, but the hunger, sickness, and death that they conceal are traditional, deeply rooted in a history of feudalism, exploitation, and institutionalized dependency.

My research agenda never wavered. The questions I addressed first crystallized during a veritable "die-off" of Alto babies during a severe drought in 1965. The food and water shortages and the political and economic chaos occasioned by the military coup were reflected in the handwritten entries of births and deaths in the dusty, yellowed pages of the ledger books kept at the public registry office in Bom Jesus. More than 350 babies died in the Alto during 1965 alone—this from a shantytown population of little more than 5,000. But that wasn't what surprised me. There were reasons enough for the deaths in the miserable conditions of shantytown life. What puzzled me was the seeming indifference of Alto women to the death of their infants, and their willingness to attribute to their own tiny offspring an aversion to life that made their death seem wholly natural, indeed all but anticipated.

Although I found that it was possible, and hardly difficult, to rescue infants and toddlers from death by diarrhea and dehydration with a simple sugar, salt, and water solution (even bottled Coca-Cola worked fine), it was more difficult to enlist a mother herself in the rescue of a child she perceived as ill-fated for life or better off dead, or to convince her to take back into her threatened and besieged home a baby she had already come to think of as an angel rather than as a son or daughter.

I learned that the high expectancy of death, and the ability to face child death with stoicism and equanimity, produced patterns of nurturing that differentiated between those infants thought of as thrivers and survivors and those thought of as born already "wanting to die." The survivors were nurtured, while stigmatized, doomed infants were left to die, as mothers say, *a mingua*, "of neglect." Mothers stepped back and allowed nature to take its course. This pattern, which I call mortal selective neglect, is called passive infanticide by anthropologist Marvin Harris. The Alto situation, although culturally specific in the form that it takes, is not unique to Third World shantytown communities and may have its correlates in our own impoverished urban communities in some cases of "failure to thrive" infants.

I use as an example the story of Zezinho, the thirteen-month-old toddler of one of my neighbors, Lourdes. I became involved with Zezinho when I was called in to help Lourdes in the delivery of another child, this one a fair and robust little tyke with a lusty cry. I noted that while Lourdes showed great interest in the newborn, she totally ignored Zezinho who, wasted and severely malnourished, was curled up in a fetal position on a piece of urine- and feces-soaked cardboard placed under his mother's hammock. Eyes open and vacant, mouth slack, the little boy seemed doomed.

When I carried Zezinho up to the community day-care center at the top of the hill, the Alto women who took turns caring for one another's children (in order to free themselves for part-time work in the cane fields or washing clothes) laughed at my efforts to save Ze, agreeing with Lourdes that here was a baby without a ghost of a chance. Leave him alone, they cautioned. It makes no sense to fight with death. But I did do battle with Ze, and after several weeks of force-feeding (malnourished babies lose their interest in food), Ze began to succumb to my ministrations. He acquired some flesh across his taut chest bones, learned to sit up, and even tried to smile. When he seemed well enough, I returned him to Lourdes in her miserable scrap-material lean-to, but not without guilt about what I had done. I wondered whether returning Ze was at all fair to Lourdes and to his little brother. But I was busy and washed my hands of the matter. And Lourdes did seem more interested in Ze now that he was looking more human.

When I returned in 1982, there was Lourdes among the women who formed my sample of Alto mothers—still struggling to put together some semblance of life for a now grown Ze and her five other surviving children. Much was made of my reunion with Ze in 1982, and everyone enjoyed retelling the story of Ze's rescue and of how his mother had given him up for dead. Ze would laugh the loudest when told how I had had to force-feed him like a fiesta turkey. There was no hint of guilt on the part of Lourdes and no resentment on the part of Ze. In fact, when questioned in private as to who was the best friend he ever had in life, Ze took a long drag on his cigarette and answered without a trace of irony, "Why my mother, of course!" "But of course," I replied.

Part of learning how to mother in the Alto do Cruzeiro is learning when to let go of a child who shows that it "wants" to die or that it has no "knack" or no "taste" for life. Another part is learning when it is safe to let oneself love a child. Frequent child death remains a powerful shaper of maternal thinking and practice. In the absence of firm expectation that a child will survive, mother love as we conceptualize it (whether in popular terms or in the psychobiological notion of maternal bonding) is attenuated and delayed with consequences for infant survival. In an environment already precarious to young life, the emotional detachment of mothers toward some of their babies contributes even further to the spiral of high mortality–high fertility in a kind of macabre lock-step dance of death.

The average woman of the Alto experiences 9.5 pregnancies, 3.5 child deaths, and 1.5 stillbirths. Seventy percent of all child deaths in the Alto occur in the first six months of life, and 82 percent by the end of the first year. Of all deaths in the community each year, about 45 percent are of children under the age of five.

Women of the Alto distinguish between child deaths understood as natural (caused by diarrhea and communicable diseases) and those resulting from sorcery, the evil eye, or other magical or supernatural afflictions. They also recognize a large category of infant deaths seen as fated and inevitable. These hopeless cases are classified by mothers under the folk terminology "child sickness" or "child attack." Women say that there are at least fourteen different types of hopeless child sickness, but most can be subsumed under two categories—chronic and acute. The chronic cases refer to infants who are born small and wasted. They are deathly pale, mothers say, as well as weak and passive. They demonstrate no vital force, no liveliness. They do not suck vigorously; they hardly cry. Such babies can be this way at birth or they can be born sound but soon show no resistance, no "fight" against the common crises of infancy: diarrhea, respiratory infections, tropical fevers.

The acute cases are those doomed infants who die suddenly and violently. They are taken by stealth overnight, often following convulsions that bring on head banging, shaking, grimacing, and shrieking. Women say it is horrible to look at such a baby. If the infant begins to foam at the mouth or gnash its teeth or go rigid with its eyes turned back inside its head, there is absolutely no hope. The infant is "put aside"—left alone—often on the floor in a back room, and allowed to die. These symptoms (which accompany high fevers, dehydration, third-stage malnutrition, and encephalitis) are equated by Alto women with madness, epilepsy, and worst of all, rabies, which is greatly feared and highly stigmatized.

Most of the infants presented to me as suffering from chronic child sickness were tiny, wasted famine victims, while those labeled as victims of acute child attack seemed to be infants suffering from the deliriums of high fever or the convulsions that can accompany electrolyte imbalance in dehydrated babies.

Local midwives and traditional healers, praying women, as they are called, advise Alto women on when to allow a baby to die. One midwife explained: "If I can see that a baby was born unfortuitously, I tell the mother that she need not wash the infant or give it a cleansing tea. I tell her just to dust the infant with baby powder and wait for it to die." Allowing nature to take its course is not seen as sinful by these often very devout Catholic women. Rather, it is understood as cooperating with God's plan.

Often I have been asked how consciously women of the Alto behave in this regard. I would have to say that consciousness is always shifting between allowed and disallowed levels of awareness. For example, I was awakened early one morning in 1987 by two neighborhood children who had been sent to fetch me to a hastily organized wake for a two-month-old infant whose mother I had unsuccessfully urged to breast-feed. The infant was being sustained on sugar water, which the mother referred to as *soro* (serum), using a medical term for the infant's starvation regime in light of his chronic diarrhea. I had cautioned the mother that an infant could not live on *soro* forever.

The two girls urged me to console the young mother by telling her that it was "too bad" that her infant was so weak that Jesus had to take him. They were coaching me in proper Alto etiquette. I agreed, of course, but asked, "And what do *you* think?" Xoxa, the eleven-year-old, looked down at her dusty flip-flops and blurted out, "Oh, Dona Nanci, that baby never got enough to eat, but you must never say that!" And so the death of hungry babies remains one of the best kept secrets of life in Bom Jesus da Mata.

Most victims are waked quickly and with a minimum of ceremony. No tears are shed, and the neighborhood children form a tiny procession, carrying the baby to the town graveyard where it will join a multitude of others. Although a few fresh flowers may be scattered over the tiny grave, no stone or wooden cross will mark the place, and the same spot will be reused within a few months' time. The mother will never visit the grave, which soon becomes an anonymous one.

What, then, can be said of these women? What emotions, what sentiments motivate them? How are they able to do what, in fact, must be done? What does mother love mean in this inhospitable context? Are grief, mourning, and melancholia present, although deeply repressed? If so, where shall we look for them? And if not, how are we to understand the moral visions and moral sensibilities that guide their actions?

I have been criticized more than once for presenting an unflattering portrait of poor Brazilian women, women who are, after all, themselves the victims of severe social and institutional neglect. I have described these women as allowing some of their children to die, as if this were an unnatural and inhuman act rather than, as I would assert, the way any one of us might act, reasonably and rationally, under similarly desperate conditions. Perhaps I have not emphasized enough the real pathogens in this environment of high risk: poverty, deprivation, sexism, chronic hunger, and economic exploitation. If mother love is, as many psychologists and some feminists believe, a seemingly natural and universal maternal script, what does it mean to women for whom scarcity, loss, sickness, and deprivation have made that love frantic and robbed them of their grief, seeming to turn their hearts to stone?

Throughout much of human history—as in a great deal of the impoverished Third World today—women have had to give birth and to nurture children under ecological conditions and social arrangements hostile to child survival, as well as to their own well-being. Under circumstances of high childhood mortality, patterns of selective neglect and passive infanticide may be seen as active survival strategies.

They also seem to be fairly common practices historically and across cultures. In societies characterized by high childhood mortality and by a correspondingly high (replacement) fertility, cultural practices of infant and child care tend to be organized primarily around survival goals. But what this means is a pragmatic recognition that not all of one's children can be expected to live. The nervousness about child survival in areas of northeast Brazil, northern India, or Bangladesh, where a 30 percent or 40 percent mortality rate in the first years of life is common, can lead to forms of delayed attachment and a casual or benign neglect that serves to weed out the worst bets so as to enhance the life chances of healthier siblings, including those yet to be born. Practices similar to those that I am describing have been recorded for parts of Africa, India, and Central America.

Life in the Alto do Cruzeiro resembles nothing so much as a battlefield or an emergency room in an overcrowded inner-city public hospital. Consequently, morality is guided by a kind of "lifeboat ethics," the morality of triage. The seemingly studied indifference toward the suffering of some of their infants, conveyed in such sayings as "little critters have no feelings," is understandable in light of these women's obligation to carry on with their reproductive and nurturing lives.

In their slowness to anthropomorphize and personalize their infants, everything is mobilized so as to prevent maternal overattachment and, therefore, grief at death. The bereaved mother is told not to cry, that her tears will dampen the wings of her little angel so that she cannot fly up to her heavenly home. Grief at the death of an angel is not only inappropriate, it is a symptom of madness and of a profound lack of faith.

Infant death becomes routine in an environment in which death is anticipated and bets are hedged. While the routinization of death in the context of shantytown life is not hard to understand, and quite possible to empathize with, its routinization in the formal institutions of public life in Bom Jesus is not as easy to accept uncritically. Here the social production of indifference takes on a different, even a malevolent, cast.

In a society where triplicates of every form are required for the most banal events (registering a car, for example), the registration of infant and child death is informal, incomplete, and rapid. It requires no documentation, takes less than five minutes, and demands no witnesses other than office clerks. No questions are asked concerning the circumstances of the death, and the cause of death is left blank, unquestioned and unexamined. A neighbor, grandmother, older sibling, or common-law husband may register the death. Since most infants die at home, there is no question of a medical record.

From the registry office, the parent proceeds to the town hall, where the mayor will give him or her a voucher for a free baby coffin. The full-time municipal coffinmaker cannot tell you exactly how many baby coffins are dispatched each week. It varies, he says, with the seasons. There are more needed during the drought months and during the big festivals of Carnaval and Christmas and São Joao's Day because people are too busy, he supposes, to take their babies to the clinic. Record keeping is sloppy.

Similarly, there is a failure on the part of city-employed doctors working at two free clinics to recognize the malnutrition of babies who are weighed, measured, and immunized without comment and as if they were not, in fact, anemic, stunted, fussy, and irritated starvation babies. At best the mothers are told to pick up free vitamins or a health "tonic" at the municipal chambers. At worst, clinic personnel will give tranquilizers and sleeping pills to quiet the hungry cries of "sick-to-death" Alto babies.

The church, too, contributes to the routinization of, and indifference toward, child death. Traditionally, the local Catholic church taught patience and resignation to domestic tragedies that were said to reveal the imponderable workings of God's will. If an infant died suddenly, it was because a particular saint had claimed the child. The infant would be an angel in the service of his or her heavenly patron. It would be wrong, a sign of a lack of faith, to weep for a child with such good fortune. The infant funeral was, in the past, an event celebrated with joy. Today, however, under the new regime of "liberation theology," the bells of N.S. das Dores parish church no longer peal for the death of Alto babies, and no priest accompanies the procession of angels to the cemetery where their bodies are disposed of casually and without ceremony. Children bury children in Bom Jesus da Mata. In this most Catholic of communities, the coffin is handed to the disabled and irritable municipal gravedigger, who often chides the children for one reason or another. It may be that the coffin is larger than expected and the gravedigger can find no appropriate space. The children do not wait for the gravedigger to complete his task. No prayers are recited and no sign of the cross made as the tiny coffin goes into its shallow grave.

When I asked the local priest, Padre Marcos, about the lack of church ceremony surrounding infant and childhood death today in Bom Jesus, he replied: "In the old days, child death was richly celebrated. But those were the baroque customs of a conservative church that wallowed in death and misery. The new church is a church of hope and joy. We no longer celebrate the death of child angels. We try to tell mothers that Jesus doesn't want all the dead babies they send him." Similarly, the new church has changed its baptismal customs, now often refusing to baptize dying babies brought to the back door of a church or rectory. The mothers are scolded by the church attendants and told to go home and take care of their sick babies. Baptism, they are told, is for the living; it is not to be confused with the sacrament of extreme unction, which is the anointing of the dying. And so it appears to the women of the Alto that even the church has turned away from them, denying the traditional comfort of folk Catholicism.

The contemporary Catholic church is caught in the clutches of a double bind. The new theology of liberation imagines a kingdom of God on earth based on justice and equality, a world without hunger, sickness, or childhood mortality. At the same time, the church has not changed its official position on sexuality and reproduction, including its sanctions against birth control, abortion, and sterilization. The padre of Bom Jesus da Mata recognizes this contradiction intuitively, although he shies away from discussions on the topic, saying that he prefers to leave questions of family planning to the discretion and the "good consciences" of his impoverished parishioners. But this, of course, sidesteps the extent to which those good consciences have been shaped by traditional church teachings in Bom Jesus, especially by his recent predecessors. Hence, we can begin to see that the seeming indifference of Alto mothers toward the death of some of their infants is but a pale reflection of the official indifference of church and state to the plight of poor women and children.

Nonetheless, the women of Bom Jesus are survivors. One woman, Biu, told me her life history, returning again and again to the themes of child death, her first husband's suicide, abandonment by her father and later by her second husband, and all the other losses and disappointments she had suffered in her long forty-five years. She concluded with great force, reflecting on the days of Carnaval '88 that were fast approaching:

> No, Dona Nanci, I won't cry, and I won't waste my life thinking about it from morning to night. . . . Can I argue with God for the state that I'm in? No! And so I'll dance and I'll jump and I'll play Carnaval! And yes, I'll laugh and people will wonder at a *pobre* like me who can have such a good time.

And no one did blame Biu for dancing in the streets during the four days of Carnaval—not even on Ash Wednesday, the day following Carnaval '88 when we all assembled hurriedly to assist in the burial of Mercea, Biu's beloved *casula*, her last-born daughter who had died at home of pneumonia during the festivities. The rest of the family barely had time to change out of their costumes. Severino, the child's uncle and godfather, sprinkled holy water over the little angle while he prayed: "Mercea, I don't know whether you were called, taken, or thrown out of this world. But look down at us from your heavenly home with tenderness, with pity, and with mercy." So be it.

Review Questions

1. What did Scheper-Hughes notice about mothers' reactions during the baby die-off of 1965 in Bom Jesus, Brazil?

2. How do poor Brazilian mothers react to their infants' illnesses and death? How do other institutions, such as the church, clinic, and civil authorities respond? Give examples.

3. How does Scheper-Hughes explain the apparent indifference of mothers to the death of their infants?

4. What does the indifference of mothers to the deaths of their children say about basic human nature, especially the mother–child bond?

17

Family and Kinship in Village India

David W. McCurdy

Anyone who reads older ethnographic accounts of different cultures will inevitably run across terms such as clan, lineage, avunculocal, levirate, extended family, polyandry, cross-cousin, *and* Crow *terminology. All these terms and many more were created by anthropologists to describe categories, groups, social arrangements, and roles associated with the complex kinship systems that characterized so many of the groups they studied. The importance of kinship for one of these societies, that found in an Indian village, is the topic of this article by David McCurdy. He argues that kinship forms the core social groups and associations in rural India in a system well adapted to family-centered land-holding and small-scale farming. He concludes by pointing out that Indians have used their close family ties to adapt to life in the emerging cash-labor-oriented modernizing world.*

On a hot afternoon in May, 1962, I sat talking with three Bhil men in the village of Ratakote, located in southern Rajasthan, India.[1] We spoke about the results of recent national elections, their worry over a cattle disease that was afflicting the village herds, and predictions about when the monsoon rains would start. But our longest discussion concerned kin—the terms used to refer to them, the responsibilities they had toward one another, and the importance of marrying them off properly. It was toward the end of this conversation that one of the men, Kanji, said, "Now sāb (Bhili for sāhīb), you are finally asking about a good thing. This is what we want you to tell people about us when you go back to America."

As I thought about it later, I was struck by how different this social outlook was from mine. I doubt that I or any of my friends in the United States would say something like this. Americans do have kin. We have parents, although our parents may not always live together, and we often know other relatives, some of whom are likely to play important parts in our lives. We grow up in families and we often create new ones if we have children. But we also live in a social network of other people whom we meet at work or encounter in various "outside" social settings, and these people can be of equal or even greater importance to us than kin. Our social worlds include such non-kin structures as companies and other work organizations, schools, neighborhoods, churches and other religious groups, and voluntary associations, including recreational groups and social clubs. We are not likely to worry much about our obligations to relatives with the notable exceptions of our children and grandchildren (middle-class American parents are notoriously child-centered), and more grudgingly, our aging parents. We are not supposed to "live off" relatives or lean too heavily on them.

Not so in Ratakote. Ratakote's society, like many agrarian villages around the world, is kinship-centered. Villagers anchor themselves in their families. They spend great energy on creating and maintaining their kinship system. This actually is not so surprising. Elaborate kinship systems work well in agrarian societies where families tend to be corporate units and where peoples' social horizons are often limited to the distance they can walk in a day. For the same reasons, families in the United States were also stronger in the past when more of them owned farms and neighborhood businesses.

What may come as a surprise, however, is how resilient and strong Indian kinship systems such as Ratakote's have been in the face of recent economic changes, especially the growth of wage labor. Let us look more closely at the Bhil kinship system, especially at arranged marriage, to illustrate these ideas.

Arranging a Marriage

If there is anything that my American students have trouble understanding about India, it is arranged marriage. They can not imagine sitting passively by

---

[1]Ratakote is a Bhil tribal village located 21 miles southwest of Udaipur, Rajasthan, in the Aravalli hills. I did ethnographic research in the village from 1961 to 1963, and again in 1985, 1991, and 1994 for shorter periods of time.

while their parents advertise their charms and evaluate emerging nuptial candidates. The thought of living—to say nothing of having sex with—a total stranger seems out of the question to them. In our country, personal independence takes precedence over loyalty to family.

Not so in India. There, arranged marriage is the norm, and most young people, as well as their elders, accept and support the custom. (They often find it sexually exciting, too.) There are many reasons why this is so, but one stands out for discussion here. Marriage constructs alliances between families, lineages, and clans. The resulting kinship network is a pivotal structure in Indian society. It confers social strength and security. People's personal reputations depend on the quality and number of their allied kin. There is little question in their minds about who should arrange marriages. The decision is too important to leave up to inexperienced and impressionable young people.

As an aside I should note that young Indians play a greater part in the process than they used to. Middle-class boys often visit the families of prospective brides, where they manage to briefly "interview" them. They also tap into their kinship network to find out personal information about prospects. Young women also seek out information about prospective grooms. Bhils are no exception. They often conspire to meet those to whom they have been betrothed, usually at a fair or other public event where their contact is likely to go unnoticed. If they don't like each other, they will begin to pressure their parents to back out of the arrangement.

The importance of arranging a marriage was brought home to me several times during fieldwork in Ratakote, but one instance stands out most clearly. When I arrived in the village for a short stay in 1985, Kanji had just concluded marriage arrangements for his daughter, Rupani.[2] What he told me about the process underscored the important role kinship plays in the life of the village.

Kanji started by saying that he and his wife first discussed Rupani's marriage the previous year when the girl first menstruated. She seemed too young for such a union then so they had waited nine months before committing to the marriage process. Even then, Rupani was still only 15 years old. Kanji explained that everyone preferred early marriage for their children because young people were likely to become sexually active as they grew older and might fall in love and elope, preempting the arrangement process altogether. Now they figured that the time had come, and they began a series of steps to find a suitable spouse that would eventually involve most of their kin.

The first step was to consult the members of Kanji's *lineage*. Lineage is an anthropological term, not one used by Bhils. But Bhils share membership in local groups of relatives that meet the anthropological definition. Lineages (in this case patrilineages) include closely related men who are all descended from a known ancestor. Kanji's lineage consists of his two married brothers, three married sons of his deceased father's brother (his father is also dead), and his own married son when the latter is home. All are the descendants of his grandfather who had migrated to Ratakote many years earlier. He had talked with all

---

[2]Kanji and Rupani are not real people. Their experiences are a composite of several life histories.

of them informally about the possibility of his daughter's marriage before this. Now he called them together for formal approval.

The approval of lineage mates is necessary because they are essential to the marriage process. Each one of them will help spread the word to other villages that Rupani is available for marriage. They will loan money to Kanji for wedding expenses, and when it comes time for the wedding ceremony, they will provide much of the labor needed to prepare food and arrange required activities. Each family belonging to the lineage will host a special meal for the bride (the groom is similarly entertained in his village) during the wedding period, and one or two will help her make offerings to their lineal ancestors. The groom will also experience this ritual.

The lineage also has functions not directly related to marriage. It has the right to redistribute the land of deceased childless, male members, and it provides its members with political support. It sees to memorial feasts for deceased members. Its members may cooperatively plow and sow fields together and combine their animals for herding.

With lineage approval in hand, Kanji announced Rupani's eligibility in other villages. (Bhils are village exogamous, meaning they prefer to marry spouses from other communities.) Kanji and his lineage mates went about this by paying visits to feminal relatives in other villages. These are kin of the women, now living in Ratakote, who have married into his family. They also include the daughters of his family line who have married and gone to live in other villages, along with their husbands and husbands' kin.

Once the word has been spread, news of prospective candidates begins to filter in. It may arrive with feminal kin from other villages when they visit Ratakote. Or it may come from neighbors who are acting as go-betweens in Ratakote for kin who live in other villages and who seek partners for their children. Either way, a process of evaluation starts. Does the family of the suggested boy or girl have a good reputation? Are they hospitable to their in-laws? Do they meet their obligations to others? What is the reputation of the boy or girl they are offering in marriage? Is he or she tall or short, light or dark, robust or frail, cheerful or complaining, hardworking or lazy? What about their level of education? Does the family have sufficient land and animals? Have they treated other sons- and daughters-in-law well?

The most fundamental question to ask, however, is whether the prospective spouse is from the right clan. In anthropology, the term *clan* refers to an aggregate of people who all believe they are descended from a common ancestor. In Ratakote this group is called an *arak*. Araks are named and the names are used as surnames when Bhils identify themselves. Kanji comes from the pargi arak and is thus known as Kanji Pargi. There is Lalu Bodar, Naraji Katara, Dita Hiravat, Nathu Airi—all men named for one of the 36 araks found in Ratakote. Women also belong to their father's clan, but unlike many American women who adopt their husband's surname at marriage, they keep their arak name all their lives.

Araks are based on a rule of patrilineal descent. This means that their members trace ancestry through males only. (Matrilineal descent traces the line through females only, and bilateral descent, which is found in U.S. society, includes both sexes.) Patrilineal descent not only defines arak membership, it governs inheritance. (Sons inherit equally from their fathers in Ratakote; daughters do not inherit despite a national law giving them that right.) It says that the children of divorced parents stay with the father's family. It bolsters the authority of men over their wives and children. It supports the rule of patrilocality. It even defines the village view of conception. Men plant the "seeds" that grow into children; women provide the fields in which the seeds germinate and grow.

The arak symbolizes patrilineal descent. It is not an organized group, although the members of an arak worship the same mother goddess no matter where they live. Instead it is an identity, an indicator that tells people who their lineal blood relatives are. There are pargis in hundreds of other Bhil villages. Most are strangers to Kanji but if he meets pargis elsewhere, he knows they share a common blood heritage with him.

It is this sense of common heritage that affects marriage. Bhils, like most Indians, believe that clan (arak) mates are close relatives even though they may be strangers. Marriage with them is forbidden. To make sure incest is impossible, it is also forbidden to marry anyone from your mother's arak or your father's mother's arak, to say nothing of anyone else you know you are related to.

This point was driven home to me on another occasion when a neighbor of Kanji's, Kamalaji Kharadi, who was sitting smoking with several other men, asked me which arak I belonged to. Instead of letting it go at "McCurdy," I said that I didn't have an arak. I explained that Americans didn't have a kinship group similar to this, and that was why I had to ask questions about kinship.

My listeners didn't believe me. After all, I must have a father and you get your arak automatically from him. It is a matter of birth and all people are born. They looked at each other as if to say, "We wonder why he won't tell us what his arak is?", then tried again to get me to answer. My second denial led them to ask, "OK, then what is your wife's arak?" (If you can't get at it one way, then try another.) I answered that she didn't have an arak either. This caused a mild sensation. "Then how do you know if you have not married your own relative?", they asked, secretly, I think, delighted by the scandalous prospect.

The third step that occurred during the arrangement of Rupani's marriage came after the family had settled on a prospective groom. This step is the betrothal, and it took place when the groom's father and some of his lineage mates and neighbors paid a formal visit to Kanji's house. When they arrive, Kanji must offer his guests a formal meal, usually slaughtering a goat and distilling some liquor for the occasion. The bride, her face covered by her sari, will be brought out for a brief viewing, as well. But most of the time will be spent making arrangements—when will the actual wedding take place?; who will check the couple's horoscopes for fit?; how much will the bride price (also called bride wealth by many anthropologists) be?

Bride price (*dapa*) deserves special comment. It is usually a standard sum of money (about 700 rupees in 1985), although it may also include silver ornaments or other valuables. The dapa is given by the groom's father and his line to the parents of the bride. Bhils view this exchange as a compensation for the loss of the bride's services to her family. It also pays for a shift in her loyalty.

The exchange points up an important strain on families in patrilineal societies, the transfer of a woman from her natal family and line to those of her husband. This transfer includes not only her person, but her loyalty, labor, and children. Although she always will belong to her father's arak, she is now part of her husband's family, not his.

This problem is especially troublesome in India because of the close ties formed there by a girl and her parents. Parents know their daughter will leave when she marries, and they know that in her husband's house and village, she will be at a disadvantage. She will be alone, and out of respect for his parents her husband may not favor her wishes, at least in public. Because of this, they tend to give her extra freedom and support. In addition, they recognize the strain she will be under when she first goes to live with her new husband and his family. To ease her transition, they permit her to visit her parents frequently for a year or two. They also may try to marry her into a village where other women from Ratakote have married, so that she has some kin or at least supporters.

After her marriage, a woman's parents and especially her brothers find it hard not to care about her welfare. Their potential interest presents a built-in structural conflict that could strain relations between the two families if nothing were done about it.

A solution to this problem is to make the marriage into an exchange, and bride price is one result. Bride price also helps to dramatize the change in loyalty and obligation accompanying the bride's entrance into her new family.

Bhils have also devised a number of wedding rituals to dramatize the bride's shift in family membership. The bride must cry to symbolize that she is leaving her home. The groom ritually storms the bride's house at the beginning of the final ceremony. He does so like a conquering hero, drawing his sword to strike a ceremonial arch placed over the entrance while simultaneously stepping on a small fire (he wears a slipper to protect his foot), ritually violating the household's sacred hearth. At the end of the wedding, the groom, with some friends, engages in a mock battle with the bride's brothers and other young men, and symbolically abducts her. The meaning of this ritual is a dramatic equivalent of a father "giving away the bride" at American weddings.

One additional way of managing possible tension between in-laws is the application of respect behavior. The parents of the bride must always treat those of the groom and their relatives with respect. They must not joke in their presence, and they must use respectful language and defer to the groom's parents in normal conversation. In keeping with the strong patrilineal system, a groom may not accept important gifts from his wife's family except on ritual occasions, such as weddings, when exchange is expected. A groom may help support his own father, but he should not do so with his in-laws. That is up to their sons.

Bride price exchange also sets in motion a life-long process of mutual hospitality between the two families. Once the marriage has taken place, the families will become part of each other's feminal kin. They will exchange gifts on some ritual occasions, open their houses to each other, and, of course, help one another make future marriages.

The Future of Indian Kinship

On our last trip to India in 1994, my wife and I learned that Rupani had delivered three children since her wedding. Kanji had visited them a few months before we arrived, and he said that Rupani was happy and that he had wonderful grandchildren. But he also mentioned that her husband now spent most of his time in the nearby city of Udaipur working in construction there. He sent money home, but his absence left Rupani to run the house and raise the children by herself, although she did so with the assistance of his parents and lineage mates.

Rupani's case is not unusual. Every morning 70 or 80 men board one of the 20 or so busses that travel the road, now paved, that runs through Ratakote to the city. There they wait to be recruited by contractors for day labor at a low wage. If they are successful, gain special skills, or make good connections, they may get more permanent, better-paying jobs and live for weeks at a time in the city.

The reason they have to take this kind of work is simple. Ratakote has more than doubled in population since 1962. (The village had a population of 1,184 in 1963. By 1994 an estimate put the number at about 2,600.) There is not enough land for everyone to farm nor can the land produce enough to feed the growing population, even in abundant years. Work in the city is the answer, especially for householders whose land is not irrigated like Kanji's.

Cash labor has a potential to break down the kinship system that Bhils value so highly. It frees men and women from economic dependence on the family (since they make their own money working for someone else). It takes up time, too, making it difficult for them to attend the leisurely eleven-day weddings of relatives or meet other obligations to kin that require their presence. With cash labor, one's reputation is likely to hinge less on family than on work. For some, work means moving the family altogether. Devaji Katara, one of Kanji's neighbors, has a son who has moved with his wife and children to the Central Indian city of Indore. He has a good factory job there, and the move has kept them together. By doing so, however, he and they are largely removed from the kinship loop.

Despite these structural changes, kinship in Ratakote and for India as a whole remains exceptionally strong. Even though they may live farther away, Bhil sons and daughters still visit their families regularly. They send money home, and they try to attend weddings. They talk about their kin, too, and surprisingly, they continue the long process of arranging marriage for their children.

Perhaps one reason for kinship's vitality is the use to which kinship is put by many Indians. The people of Ratakote and other Indians have never given up teaching their children to respect their elders and subordinate their interests to those of the family. Family loyalty is still a paramount value. They use this loyalty to help each other economically. Family members hire each other in business. They take one another in during hard times. They offer hospitality to each other. Unlike Americans who feel guilty about accepting one-sided help from relatives, Indians look to the future. Giving aid now may pay off with a job or a favor later. Even if it doesn't, it is the proper thing to do.

Instead of breaking up the kinship network, work that takes men and families away from the village has simply stretched it out. An Indian student I know has found relatives in every American city he has visited. He knows of kin in Europe and southeast Asia too. Anywhere he goes he is likely to have relatives to stay with and to help him. When he settles down he will be expected to return the favor. Another Indian acquaintance, who went to graduate school in the United States and who continues to work here, has sent his father thousands of dollars to help with the building of a house. This act, which would surprise many Americans, seems perfectly normal to him.

Kanji is not disturbed by the economic changes that are overtaking the quiet agricultural pace of Ratakote. I last left him standing in front of his house with a grandson in his arms. His son, who had left the village in 1982 to be a "wiper" on a truck, returned to run the farm. He will be able to meet the family's obligation to lineage and feminal kin. For Kanji, traditional rules of inheritance have pulled a son and, for the moment at least, a grandson, back into the bosom of the family where they belong.

Review Questions

1. What are the main ways that kinship organizes Bhil society in Ratakote, according to McCurdy?

2. What is meant by the terms *clan, lineage, family, patrilineal descent, patrilocal residence, alliance,* and *feminal kin group?* Give examples of each.

3. Why do Bhil parents feel that marriage is too important a matter to be left up to their children?

4. What attributes do Bhil parents look for in a prospective bride or groom? How do young people try to influence the marriage partner their parents choose for them?

5. Although the U.S. kinship system seems limited by comparison to India's, many argue that it is more important than most of us think. Can you think of ways this might be true?

18

Life without Fathers or Husbands

Clifford Geertz

Cross-cultural comparison is a basic feature of the anthropological enterprise and a source of evidence for many explanations put forward by authors reprinted in this book. For example, some anthropologists argue that hunter/gathers lack warfare. By comparing ethnographies of hunter/gatherer groups and looking for the absence or presence of warlike activity, the assertion can be tested and, if necessary, modified.

This article provides comparative evidence for another general assertion about human behavior and social organization. A long-held view in anthropology is that marriage, the socially approved union between two people, is a feature of all societies. Marriage, anthropologists assert, leads to the formation of a basic domestic unit, the nuclear family, creates systems of descent that confer group identity, allies kinship groups with one another, and provides for the legitimate birth and nurturing of children.

From "The Visit," *The New York Review of Books,* October 18, 2001, pp. 27–30. Copyright © 2001 by NYREV, Inc. Reprinted by permission.

But is this universally true? This article, by Clifford Geertz, reviews the work of Chinese anthropologist, Cia Hua.[1] Based on extended fieldwork among a Chinese tribal group, the Na, Hua describes a matrilineal society that lacks marriage entirely. Women and their children live with brothers and other close matrilineal kin in the same household. Men make appointments to "visit" women in their houses (several ways are described here), arriving late at night and leaving just before dawn. Men and women are likely to sleep with many members of the opposite sex during their lifetimes and do not form permanent relationships. Despite this unusual arrangement, Na society has successfully survived for centuries, until now that is. Under intense pressure from the Chinese government to marry in the "approved" way, the system is breaking down.

> Love and marriage, love and marriage
> Go together like a horse and carriage
> Dad was told by mother
> You can't have one without the other
>   —"Love and Marriage," Sammy
>   Cahn and Jimmy van Heusen[2]

Not everywhere.

Among the Na, a tribal people hidden away in the Yongning hills of Yunnan province in southern China and the subject of the French-trained Chinese anthropologist Cai Hua's provocative new monograph, there is no marriage, in fact or word. Mothers exist, as do children, but there are no dads. Sexual intercourse takes place between casual, opportunistic lovers, who develop no broader, more enduring relations to one another. The man "visits," usually furtively, the woman at her home in the middle of the night as impulse and opportunity appear, which they do with great regularity. Almost everyone of either sex has multiple partners, serially or simultaneously; simultaneously usually two or three, serially as many as a hundred or two. There are no nuclear families, no in-laws, no stepchildren. Brothers and sisters, usually several of each, reside together, along with perhaps a half-dozen of their nearer maternal relatives, from birth to death under one roof—making a living, keeping a household, and raising the sisters' children.

---

[1]This article represents a review of Cia Hua, *A Society without Fathers or Husbands: The Na of China*, translated from the French by Asti Hustvedt (New York: Zone Books, 2001). All quotes included in the article are taken from this book.

[2]"Love and Marriage" by Sammy Cahn and Jimmy van Heusen. Copyright © 1955 (renewed) by Cahn Music Co. and Barton Music Corp. All rights reserved; used by permission of Warner Brothers Publications U.S. Inc.

The incest taboo is of such intensity that not only may one not sleep with opposite sex members of one's own household, one cannot even allude to sexual matters in their presence. One may not curse where they can hear, or sit with them in the same row at the movies, lest an emotional scene appear on the screen. As paternity is socially unrecognized, and for the most part uncertain, fathers may happen, now and again, to sleep with daughters. A man is free to sleep with his mother's brother's daughter, who is not considered any kind of relative, not even a "cousin." There is no word for bastard, none for promiscuity, none for infidelity; none, for that matter, for incest, so unthinkable is it. Jealousy is infra dig:

> "You know, Luzo [who is nineteen] has not had a lot of [lovers], but he has made many visits [his friend said]. This is because he only goes to the homes of beauties. In particular, he goes to visit Seno, a pretty girl in our village. Do you want to go [visit her] at her house?" he asked me.
>
> "No! If I go there, Luzo will be jealous," I answered.
>
> "How could I be jealous!" [Luzo] responded. "You can ask whomever you want. You will see that . . . we don't know how to be jealous."
>
> "He's right!" his friend interjected. And to explain himself he added: "Girls [are available] to everyone. Whoever wants to can visit them. There is nothing to be jealous about."

Obviously, this is an interesting place for an anthropologist—especially for an anthropologist brought up on that King Charles's head of his profession, "kinship theory."

There are two major variants of such theory, "descent theory" and "alliance theory," and the Na, Hua says, fit neither of them. In the first, associated with the name of the British anthropologist A. R. Radcliffe-Brown and his followers, the "nuclear," "basic," or "elementary" family—a man, his wife, and their children—"founded as it is on natural requirements," is universal, and "forms the hard core around which any social organization revolves." The relationship between parents and children, "filiation," is critical, and out of it are developed various "jural," that is, normative, rules of descent which group certain sets of relatives together against others: lineages, clans, kindreds, and the like. "Families can be compared to threads which it is the task of nature to warp in order that the social fabric can develop."

In the alliance model, deriving in the main from the French anthropologist, and Hua's mentor, Claude Lévi-Strauss, "the institutionalized exchange of women" between families "by the alliance of marriage [is taken] to be the central point of kinship." The universality of the incest taboo, "a natural phenomenon," necessitates marriage and the creation of the "transversal [that is, affinal or 'in-law'] networks of alliances [that] engender all social organization."

Since the Na have no matrimonial relationship they falsify both theories. They neither form elementary families out of which a filiative social fabric can be spun, nor, though they have a variety of the incest taboo (an odd variety, in that with its father-daughter twist it does not exclude all primary relatives), do they form twined and expandable affinal networks, or indeed any networks of "in-laws" at all. "From now on," Hua proclaims at the end of his book, "marriage can no longer be considered the only possible institutionalized mode of sexual behavior." The Na "visit" demonstrates that

> Marriage, affinity, alliance of marriage, family, [usually considered] essential to anthropology, . . . seem absent from this culture. The Na case attests to the fact that marriage and the family (as well as the Oedipus complex) can no longer be considered universal, neither logically nor historically.

This is a little grand, for there are other "institutionalized modes of sexual behavior"—concubinage, prostitution, wife-borrowing—just about everywhere, and whether the Oedipus complex is universal or not, or even whether it exists at all, is not dependent upon marital arrangements. But clearly, "the visit" is an unusual, perhaps though one never knows what is coming next out of Papua, the Amazon, or Central Asia—a unique institution sustaining a most unusual "kinship system," its existence often regarded as impossible. It is a system in which the facts of reproduction (though recognized—the Na know where babies come from) are incidental and all ties are (conceived to be) "blood ties"— the entire house can be called consanguineous.

The Na "visit," for all its fluidity, opportunism, and apparent freedom from moral or religious anxiety, is as well outlined a social institution, as deeply embedded in a wider social structure, as marriage is elsewhere. (The Na are Tibetan-style Buddhists, nearly a third of the adult men being monks, whose sexual practices, a handful of Lhasa-bound celibates aside, are the same as those of laymen.) This is clear from the exact and explicit terminology that marks it out:

> Society calls a man and a woman who set up this kind of sexual relationship *nana sésé hing,* which means people in a relationship of furtive meetings; the man and the woman discreetly call each other *açia* ["discreetly" because of the "incest" taboo against public references to sexuality where opposite sex consanguines may hear them]. The term *açia* is made up of the diminutive prefix *a* and the root *çia.* The Na add *a* to names and proper nouns to indicate intimacy, affection, friendship, and respect; *çia,* when used as a noun, means lover. The same word is used for both sexes, and as a verb it means literally to lie down and figuratively to mate, to sleep and to tempt. *Açia* means lover.
>
> A Na saying depicts those who are *açia* very well: . . . It is not enough to say that we are *çia* for it to be so, sleeping together once makes (us) *çia.*

The enactment of such a relationship shows the same detailed cultural patterning: it is not a matter of brute and unfettered physical desire, but of a modeled, almost balletic self-control. The rendezvous takes place in the bedroom of the woman around midnight. (A bit earlier in the winter, Hua says, a bit later in the summer.) The man comes in near-perfect quietness, does what he does (Hua is wholly silent about what that might be and about how the cries of love are muffled), and leaves at cockcrow, creeping as stealthily back to his own house. As men and women enjoy "complete equality" and are "in daily contact, in town, in the workplace, and elsewhere," either can make the first advance and either may accept or refuse:

> A girl might say to a boy, "Come stay at my house tonight." The boy might then respond, "Your mother is not easygoing." And then the girl might say, "She won't scold you. Come secretly in the middle of the night." If the boy accepts, he says, "Okay." If the boy refuses, he says, "I don't want to come. I'm not going to come over to sleep." In this case, no matter what the girl says, nothing will change his mind.
>
> When the man takes the initiative . . . he often uses the expression "I'll come to your house tonight, okay?," to which the woman responds with a smile or by saying, "Okay." Some come straight out and ask "Do you want to be my *açia*?" If a woman refuses . . . , she can use a ready-made formula: "No, it is not possible. I already have one for tonight." In that case, the man will not insist.

There are other, more oblique ways of making one's wishes known. One can snatch away some personal object—a scarf, a pack of cigarettes—from the desired partner. If he or she does not protest, the tryst is on. One can shout from a distance, "Hey, hey, do you want to trade something?" If you get a "hey, hey" back, you exchange belts and fix an appointment. These days, Chinese movies—shown virtually every night, though they are imperfectly understood by the Tibeto-Burmese-speaking Na—are a particularly favored setting for putting things in motion:

> The young men and women purchase tickets and wait in front of the theater, getting to know each other. . . . One man can offer several women a ticket, just as one woman can offer a ticket to more than one man. Once a ticket is handed over, the man and woman move away from each other and only get back together inside the theater. During the film, the viewers talk loudly, often drowning out the sound from the speakers. If they have had a good time during the movie and reached an agreement, they leave discreetly to spend an amorous night together.

The "amorous night" itself may be a one-time thing. Or it may be repeated at shorter or longer intervals over the course of months or years. It may be begun, broken off for awhile, then begun again. It may be stopped altogether at any time by either party, usually without prior notice or much in the way of explanation. It does not, in short, involve any sort of exclusive and permanent "horse and carriage" commitment. But it, too, is, for all its fluidity and seeming negligence, carefully patterned—framed and hemmed in by an elaborate collection of cultural routines, a love-nest ethic.

When the *amant* arrives at the *amante*'s house, usually after having climbed over a fence or two and thrown a bone to the guard dog, he will give some sort of signal of his presence—toss pebbles on the roof, crouch at the woman's bedroom window (Hua says that every man in a village complex—four or five hundred people—knows the location of every woman's bedroom), or, if he is confident of being received or has been there often, simply knock on the front door. "In a household where there are women of the age to receive visitors [there may be several such on one night, and even a woman may have, in turn, more than one visitor], every evening after nightfall, the men of the house will not open the front door."

Usually, the woman who is waiting will herself open the door and the two will creep wordlessly off to her bedroom. If the wrong woman opens the door—a sister or a cousin, or perhaps even one of those "not easygoing" mothers—this causes little embarrassment: the man simply proceeds to the right woman's bedroom. During the encounter, the lovers must whisper "so that nothing will reach the ears of the woman's relatives, above all the men (especially uncles and great-uncles)."

No one can force anyone else in these matters. The woman can always, and at any time, refuse the man's entreaties and send him packing. A woman may never, in any case, visit a man; so if she is scorned she is just out of luck. A legend accounts for this virtually unique exception to rigorous symmetry of the system:

> When humanity originated, no one knew how to regulate visits. Abaodgu, the god in charge of setting all the rules, proposed the following test: he ordered that a man be shut up in a house and that a woman be sent to join him. To reach the man, the woman had to pass through nine doors. At dawn, she had reached the seventh door. Then Abaodgu tested the man, who succeeded in passing through three doors. . . . Abaodgu [concluded] that women were too passionate [to do] the visiting. . . . The men [would have to] visit the women.

Hua goes on to trace out, methodically and in remorseless detail, the variations, the social ramifications, and the ethnographical specifics of all this, worried, not without reason, that if he does not make his arguments over and over again and [retell] every last fact he has gathered in four periods of fieldwork (1985, 1986, 1988–1989, 1992) his account will not be believed.

He describes two other, special and infrequent "modalities" of sexual encounter—"the conspicuous visit" and "cohabitation." In the conspicuous visit, which always follows upon a series of furtive visits, the effort to conceal the relationship is abandoned ("vomited up," as the idiom has it), mainly because the principals have grown older, perhaps tired of the pretense and folderol, and everyone knows about them anyway.

In cohabitation, an even rarer variant, a household that is short of women by means of which to produce children or of men to labor for it in its fields will adopt a man or woman from a household with a surplus to maintain its reproductive or economic viability, the adopted one becoming a sort of permanent conspicuous visitor (more or less: these arrangements often break up too).

Among chiefly families, called *zhifu,* a Chinese word for "regional governor," successive relationships are established over several generations, leading to a peculiar household alternation of chiefship and a greater restriction on who may mate with whom. . . .

After centuries of resistance to efforts to bring it into line with what is around it—that is, Han propriety—[the Na] cosmos is now apparently at last dissolving. The pressures on the Na to shape up and mate morally like normal human beings have been persistent and unremitting. As early as 1656, the Manchurian Qing, troubled by succession problems among "barbarian" tribes, decreed that the chiefs of such tribes, including the Na, must marry in the standard way and produce standard sons, grandsons, and cousins to follow them legitimately into office.

The extent to which this rule was enforced varied over time with the strengths and interests of the various dynasties. But the intrusion of Han practices—virilocality (by which married couples live near the husband's parents), patrifiliation (making kinship through fathers central), polygynous marriage (i.e., involving several wives), written genealogies, and "ancestor worship" (the Na cast the ashes of their dead unceremoniously across the hillsides)—into the higher reaches of Na society provided an alternative cultural model, a model that the Na, for the most part, contrived to keep at bay. Members of chiefly families, and some of the wealthy commoners and resident immigrants, began to marry to preserve their estates and to secure a place in the larger Chinese society. But most of the population proceeded as before, despite being continuously reviled as "primitive," "depraved," "backward," "licentious," "unclean," and ridden with sexual disease. (The last was, and is, more or less true. "More than 50 percent of Na adults have syphilis . . . a significant percentage of the women are sterile . . . people are deformed. . . . The . . . population is stagnating.")

This cultural guerrilla war, with edicts from the center and evasions from the periphery, continued fitfully for nearly three hundred years, until the arrival of the Communists in the 1950s rendered matters more immediate.[3] The Party considered the tradition of the visit "a 'backward and primitive custom' . . . contraven[ing] the matrimonial legislation of the People's Republic of China . . . [and disrupting] productiveness at work because the men think of nothing but running off to visit someone." The Party's first move against the tradition was a regulation designed to encourage nuclear family formation by distributing land to men who would set up and maintain such a family. When this failed to have any effect at all ("the government could not understand how it was possible that Na men did not want to have their own land"), it moved on, during the Great Leap Forward, to a full press effort to "encourage monogamy" through a licensing system, an effort "guided" by the recommendation of two groups of ethnologists, who insisted that, "with planning," Na men and women

---

[3]The Communists of course came to power in 1949, but the Na area remained essentially Kuomintang country until 1956, when the Party installed its own local government, placing Han commissars in the region and effectively ending the traditional chiefship system.

could be led toward setting up families as economic units and raising their children together. Though this was a bit more successful—in Hua's "sample" seven couples officially married—it too soon ran out of steam in the face of Na indifference to the sanctions involved.

The small carrot and the little stick having failed to produce results, the Party proceeded in the period of the Cultural Revolution (1966–1969) to get real about the problem. Dedicated to the national project of "sweeping out the four ancients" (customs, habits, morality, culture), the People's Commune of Yongning pronounced it "shameful not to know who one's genitor is" and imposed marriage by simple decree on any villager involved in a conspicuous visit relationship. But this too failed. As soon as the cadres departed, the couples broke up.

Finally, in 1974, the provincial governor of Yunnan, declaring that "the reformation of this ancient matrimonial system comes under the framework of the class struggle in the ideological domain and therefore constitutes a revolution in the domain of the superstructure" (one can almost hear the collective Na, *Huh?*), made it the law that: (1) everyone under fifty in a relationship "that has lasted for a long time" must officially marry forthwith at commune headquarters; (2) every woman who has children must publically state who their genitor is, cart him off to headquarters, and marry him; (3) those who divorce without official sanction will have their annual grain ration suspended; (4) any child born out of wedlock will also not get a ration and must be supported by his genitor until age eighteen; and, (5) visiting, furtive or conspicuous, was forbidden.

This, supported by nightly meetings of the local military brigade and some collusive informing, seemed finally to work—after a fashion, and for a while:

> [The] District government sent a Jeep filled with marriage licenses to the People's Commune of Yongning. Ten and twenty at a time, couples were rounded up in the villages . . . and a leader would take their fingerprints on the marriage form and hand them each a marriage license. . . . [When] the day [for the ceremony] came, horse-drawn carriages were sent into the villages to provide transportation for the "newlyweds" to [Party] headquarters. . . . They each received a cup of tea, a cigarette, and several pieces of candy, and then everybody participated in a traditional dance. The government called this "the new way of getting married."

It was new enough, but for the Na it was ruinous. "No other ethnic group in China underwent as deep a disruption as the Na did during the Cultural Revolution," Hua writes in a rare show of feeling. "To understand the trouble this reform caused in Na society, it is enough to imagine a reform in our society, but with the reverse logic":

> During that period [one of Hua's informants said], the tension was so high that our thoughts never strayed from this subject. No one dared to make a furtive visit. Before, we were like roosters. We took any woman we could catch. We went to a

woman's house at least once a night. But, with that campaign, we got scared. We did not want to get married and move into someone else's house, and as a result, we no longer dared to visit anyone. Because of this, we took a rest for a few years.

After the accession of Deng Xiaoping in 1981, the more draconian of these measures—the denial of rations, the exposure of genitors—were softened or suspended, and emphasis shifted toward "educational," that is, assimilationist approaches. In particular, the expansion of the state school system, where "all the textbooks are impregnated with Han ideas and values," is leading to rapid and thorough Sinicization of the Na. Today—or, anyway, in 1992—the school, assisted by movies and other "modern" imports, is accomplishing what political pressure could not: the withering away of "Na-ism":

> When students graduate from middle school, they must complete a form that includes a column requesting information on their civil status. Unable to fill in the blank asking for the name of their father, they suddenly become aware they do not have a father, while their classmates from other ethnic backgrounds do. Some of the Na students, usually the most brilliant ones, find a quiet spot where they can cry in private. . . . The message [of the school] is clear. . . . There is only one culture that is legitimate, and that is Han culture.

In China, as elsewhere, it is not licentiousness that powers most fear. Nor even immorality. It is difference.

Review Questions

1. Based on the evidence described in Geertz's article, what is the basic domestic unit in Na society and what are its main social and economic functions?

2. The Na are a matrilineal society. Do you think that the absence of marriage described for them in this article could also occur in a patrilineal society? What is it about matrilineal society that is more likely to make such an arrangement possible?

3. Despite an appearance of unbounded "free love" described for Na male/female relationships, Na culture does systematize such activity. What are the culturally defined ways that Na men and women meet and set up assignations? Are there taboos and other restrictions on their sexual activity defined by their culture?

4. How does Na society manage the basic functional needs that marriage is claimed to meet in most other societies?

5. What is the Chinese government's response to the lack of marriage among the Na. How have they tried to change the practice?

19

Uterine Families and the Women's Community

Margery Wolf

The size and organization of extended families vary from one society to the next, but extended families often share some important attributes. They are most often based on a rule of patrilineal descent. For men, the patrilineal family extends in an unbroken line of ancestors and descendants. Membership is permanent; loyalty assured. For women, the patrilineal family is temporary. Born into one family and married into another, women discover that their happiness and interests depend on bearing children to create their own uterine family. This and the importance of a local women's group are the subjects of this article by Margery Wolf in her discussion of Taiwanese family life.

Reprinted from *Women and the Family in Rural Taiwan* by Margery Wolf with the permission of the publishers, Stanford University Press, www.sup.org. Copyright © 1972 by the Board of Trustees of the Leland Stanford Junior University. All rights reserved.

Few women in China experience the continuity that is typical of the lives of the menfolk. A woman can and, if she is ever to have any economic security, must provide the links in the male chain of descent, but she will never appear in anyone's genealogy as that all-important name connecting the past to the future. If she dies before she is married, her tablet will not appear on her father's altar; although she was a temporary member of his household, she was not a member of his family. A man is born into his family and remains a member of it throughout his life and even after his death. He is identified with the family from birth, and every action concerning him, up to and including his death, is in the context of that group. Whatever other uncertainties may trouble his life, his place in the line of ancestors provides a permanent setting. There is no such secure setting for a woman. She will abruptly leave the household into which she is born, either as an infant or as an adult bride, and enter another whose members treat her with suspicion or even hostility.

A man defines his family as a large group that includes the dead, and not-yet-born, and the living members of his household. But how does a woman define her family? This is not a question that China specialists often consider, but from their treatment of the family in general, it would seem that a woman's family is identical with that of the senior male in the household in which she lives. Although I have never asked, I imagine a Taiwanese man would define a woman's family in very much those same terms. Women, I think, would give quite a different answer. They do not have an unchanging place, assigned at birth, in any group, and their view of the family reflects this.

When she is a child, a woman's family is defined for her by her mother and to some extent by her grandmother. No matter how fond of his daughter the father may be, she is only a temporary member of his household and useless to his family—he cannot even marry her to one of his sons as he could an adopted daughter. Her irrelevance to her father's family in turn affects the daughter's attitude toward it. It is of no particular interest to her, and the need to maintain its continuity has little meaning for her beyond the fact that this continuity matters a great deal to some of the people she loves. As a child she probably accepts to some degree her grandmother's orientation toward the family: the household, that is, those people who live together and eat together, including perhaps one or more of her father's married brothers and their children. But the group that has the most meaning for her and with which she will have the most lasting ties is the smaller, more cohesive unit centering on her mother, that is, the uterine family—her mother and her mother's children. Father is important to the group, just as grandmother is important to some of the children, but he is not quite a member of it, and for some uterine families he may even be "the enemy." As the girl grows up and her grandmother dies and a brother or two marries, she discovers that her mother's definition of the family is becoming less exclusive and may even include such outsiders as her brother's new wife. Without knowing precisely when it happened, she finds that her brother's interests and goals have shifted in a direction she cannot follow. Her mother does not push her aside, but when the mother speaks of the future, she speaks in terms of her son's future. Although the mother sees her uterine family as adding new members and another generation, her daughter sees it as dissolving, leaving her with strong particular relationships, but with no group to which she has permanent loyalties and obligations.

When a young woman marries, her formal ties with the household of her father are severed. In one of the rituals of the wedding ceremony the bride's father or brothers symbolically inform her by means of spilt water that she, like the water, may never return, and when her wedding sedan chair passes over the threshold of her father's house, the doors are slammed shut behind her. If she is ill-treated by her husband's family, her father's family may intervene, but unless her parents are willing to bring her home and support her for the rest of her life (and most parents are not), there is little they can do beyond shaming the other family. This is usually enough.

As long as her mother is alive, the daughter will continue her contacts with her father's household by as many visits as her new situation allows. If she lives nearby she may visit every few days, and no matter where she lives she must at least be allowed to return at New Year. After her mother dies her visits may become perfunctory, but her relations with at least one member of her uterine family, the group that centered on her mother, remain strong. Her brother plays an important ritual role throughout her life. She may gradually lose contact with her sisters as she and they become more involved with their own children, but her relations with her brother continue. When her sons marry, he is the guest of honor at the wedding feasts, and when her daughters marry he must give a small banquet in their honor. If her sons wish to divide their father's estate, it is their mother's brother who is called on to supervise. And when she dies, the coffin cannot be closed until her brother determines to his own satisfaction that she died a natural death and that her husband's family did everything possible to prevent it.

With the ritual slam of her father's door on her wedding day, a young woman finds herself quite literally without a family. She enters the household of her husband—a man who in an earlier time, say fifty years ago, she would never have met and who even today, in modern rural Taiwan, she is unlikely to know very well. She is an outsider, and for Chinese an outsider is always an object of deep suspicion. Her husband and her father-in-law do not see her as a member of their family. But they do see her as essential to it; they have gone to great expense to bring her into their household for the purpose of bearing a new generation for their family. Her mother-in-law, who was mainly responsible for negotiating the terms of her entry, may harbor some resentment over the hard bargaining, but she is nonetheless eager to see another generation added to *her* uterine family. A mother-in-law often has the same kind of ambivalence toward her daughter-in-law as she has toward her husband—the younger woman seems a member of her family at times and merely a member of the household at others. The new bride may find that her husband's sister is hostile or at best condescending, both attitudes reflecting the daughter's distress at an outsider who seems to be making her way right into the heart of the family.

Chinese children are taught by proverb, by example, and by experience that the family is the source of their security, and relatives the only people who can be depended on. Ostracism from the family is one of the harshest sanctions that can be imposed on erring youth. One of the reasons mainlanders as individuals are considered so untrustworthy on Taiwan is the fact that they are not subject to the controls of (and therefore have no fear of ostracism from) their families. If a timid new bride is considered an object of suspicion and potentially dangerous because she is a stranger, think how uneasy her own first few months must be surrounded by strangers. Her irrelevance to her father's family may result in her having little reverence for descent lines, but she has warm memories of the security of the family her mother created. If she is ever to return to this certainty and sense of belonging, a woman must create her own uterine family by bearing children, a goal that happily corresponds to the goals of the family into which she has married. She may gradually create a tolerable niche for herself in the household of her mother-in-law, but her family will not be formed until she herself forms it of her own children and grandchildren. In most cases, by the time she adds grandchildren, the uterine family and the household will almost completely overlap, and there will be another daughter-in-law struggling with loneliness and beginning a new uterine family.

The ambiguity of a man's position in relation to the uterine families accounts for much of the hostility between mother-in-law and daughter-in-law. There is no question in the mind of the older woman but that her son is her family. The daughter-in-law might be content with this situation once her sons are old enough to represent her interests in the household and in areas strictly under men's control, but until then, she is dependent on her husband. If she were to be completely absorbed into her mother-in-law's family—a rare occurrence unless she is a *simpua*—there would be little or no conflict; but under most circumstances she must rely on her husband, her mother-in-law's son, as her spokesman, and here is where the trouble begins. Since it is usually events within the household that she wishes to affect, and the household more or less overlaps with her mother-in-law's uterine family, even a minor foray by the younger woman suggests to the older one an all-out attack on everything she has worked so hard to build in the years of her own loneliness and insecurity. The birth of grandchildren further complicates their relations, for the one sees them as new members for her family and the other as desperately needed recruits to her own small circle of security.

In summary, my thesis contends . . . that because we have heretofore focused on men when examining the Chinese family—a reasonable approach to a patrilineal system—we have missed not only some of the system's subtleties but also its near-fatal weaknesses. With a male focus we see the Chinese family as a line of descent, bulging to encompass all the members of a man's household and spreading out through his descendants. With a female focus, however, we see the Chinese family not as a continuous line stretching between the vague horizons of past and future, but as a contemporary group that comes into existence out of one woman's need and is held together insofar as she has the strength to do so, or, for that matter, the need to do so. After her death the uterine family survives only in the mind of her son and is symbolized by the special attention he gives her earthly remains and her ancestral tablet. The rites themselves are demanded by the ideology of the patriliny, but the meaning they hold for most sons is formed in the uterine family. The uterine family has no ideology, no formal structure, and no public existence. It is built out of sentiments and loyalties that die with its members, but it is no less real for all that. The descent lines of men are born and nourished in the uterine families of women, and it is here that a male ideology that excludes women makes its accommodations with reality.

Women in rural Taiwan do not live their lives in the walled courtyards of their husband's households. If they did, they might be as powerless as their stereotype. It is in their relations in the outside world (and for women in rural Taiwan that world consists almost entirely of the village) that women develop sufficient backing to maintain some independence under their powerful mothers-in-law and even occasionally to bring the men's world to terms. A successful venture into the men's world is no small feat when one recalls that the men of a village were born there and are often related to one another, whereas the women are unlikely to have either the ties of childhood or the ties of kinship to unite them. All the same, the needs, shared interests, and common problems of women are reflected in every village in a loosely knit society that can when needed be called on to exercise considerable influence.

Women carry on as many of their activities as possible outside the house. They wash clothes on the riverbank, clean and pare vegetables at a communal pump, mend under a tree that is a known meetingplace, and stop to rest on a bench or group of stones with other women. There is a continual moving back and forth between kitchens, and conversations are carried on from open doorways through the long, hot afternoons of summer. The shy young girl who enters the village as a bride is examined as frankly and suspiciously by the women as an animal that is up for sale. If she is deferential to her elders, does not criticize or compare her new world unfavorably with the one she has left, the older residents will gradually accept her presence on the edge of their conversations and stop changing the topic to general subjects when she brings the family laundry to scrub on the rocks near them. As the young bride meets other girls in her position, she makes allies for the future, but she must also develop relationships with the older women. She learns to use considerable discretion in making and receiving confidences, for a girl who gossips freely about the affairs of her husband's household may find herself labeled a troublemaker. On the other hand, a girl who is too reticent may find herself always on the outside of the group, or worse yet, accused of snobbery. I described in *The House of Lim* the plight of Lim Chui-ieng, who had little village backing in her troubles with her husband and his family as the result of her arrogance toward the women's community. In Peihotien the young wife of the storekeeper's son suffered a similar lack of support. Warned by her husband's parents not to be too "easy" with the other villagers lest they try to buy things on credit, she obeyed to the point of being considered unfriendly by the women of the village. When she began to have serious troubles with her husband and eventually his family, there was no one in the village she could turn to for solace, advice, and, most important, peacemaking.

Once a young bride has established herself as a member of the women's community, she has also established for herself a certain amount of protection. If the members of her husband's family step beyond the limits of propriety in their treatment of her—such as refusing to allow her to return to her natal home for her brother's wedding or beating her without serious justification—she can complain to a woman friend, preferably older, while they are washing vegetables at the communal pump. The story will quickly spread to the other women, and one of them will take it on herself to check the facts with another member of the girl's household. For a few days the matter will be thoroughly discussed whenever a few women gather. In a young wife's first few years in the community, she can expect to have her mother-in-law's side of any disagreement given fuller weight than her own—her mother-in-law has, after all, been a part of the community a lot longer. However, the discussion itself will serve to curb many offenses. Even if the older woman knows that public opinion is falling to her side, she will still be somewhat more judicious about refusing her daughter-in-law's next request. Still, the daughter-in-law who hopes to make use of the village forum to depose her mother-in-law or at least gain herself special privilege will discover just how important the prerogatives of age and length of residence are. Although the women can serve as a powerful protective force for their defenseless younger members, they are also a very conservative force in the village.

Taiwanese women can and do make use of their collective power to lose face for their menfolk in order to influence decisions that are ostensibly not theirs to make. Although young women may have little or no influence over their husbands and would not dare express an unsolicited opinion (and perhaps not even a solicited one) to their fathers-in-law, older women who have raised their sons properly retain considerable influence over their sons' actions, even in activities exclusive to men. Further, older women who have displayed years of good judgment are regularly consulted by their husbands about major as well as minor economic and social projects. But even men who think themselves free to ignore the opinions of their women are never free of their own concept, face. It is much easier to lose face than to have face. We once asked a male friend in Peihotien just what "having face" amounted to. He replied, "When no one is talking about a family, you can say it has face." This is precisely where women wield their power. When a man behaves in a way that they consider wrong, they talk about him—not only among themselves, but to their sons and husbands. No one "tells him how to mind his own business," but it becomes abundantly clear that he is losing face and by continuing in this manner may bring shame to the family of his ancestors and descendants. Few men will risk that.

The rules that a Taiwanese man must learn and obey to be a successful member of his society are well developed, clear, and relatively easy to stay within. A Taiwanese woman must also learn the rules, but if she is to be a successful woman, she must learn not to stay within them, but to *appear* to stay within them; to manipulate them, but not to appear to be manipulating them; to teach them to her children, but not to depend on her children for her protection. A truly successful Taiwanese woman is a rugged individualist who has learned to depend largely on herself while appearing to lean on her father, her husband, and her son. The contrast between the terrified young bride and the loud, confident, often lewd old woman who has outlived her mother-in-law and her husband reflects the tests met and passed by not strictly following the rules and by making purposeful use of those who must. The Chinese male's conception of women as "narrow-hearted" and socially inept may well be his vague recognition of this facet of women's power and technique.

The women's subculture in rural Taiwan is, I believe, below the level of consciousness. Mothers do not tell their about-to-be-married daughters how to establish themselves in village society so that they may have some protection from an oppressive family situation, nor do they warn them to gather their children into an exclusive circle under their own control. But girls grow up in village society and see their mothers and sisters-in-law settling their differences to keep them from a public airing or presenting them for the women's community to judge. Their mothers have created around them the meaningful unit in their father's households, and when they are desperately lonely and unhappy in the households of their husbands, what they long for is what they have lost. . . . [Some] areas in the subculture of women . . . mesh perfectly into the main culture of the society. The two cultures are not symbiotic because they are not sufficiently independent of one another, but neither do they share identical goals or necessarily use the same means to reach the goals they do share. Outside the village the women's subculture seems not to exist. The uterine family also has no public existence, and appears almost as a response to the traditional family organized in terms of a male ideology.

Review Questions

1. According to Wolf, what is a uterine family, and what relatives are likely to be members?

2. Why is the uterine family important to Chinese women who live in their husband's patrilineal extended families?

3. What is the relationship between a woman's uterine family and her power within her husband's family?

4. Why might the existence of the uterine family contribute to the division of extended families into smaller constituent parts?

5. How do you think a Chinese woman's desire to have a uterine family affects attempts to limit the Chinese population?

SIX

Identity, Roles, and Groups

For most of us, social interaction is unconscious and automatic. We associate with other people from the time we are born. Of course we experience moments when we feel socially awkward and out of place, but generally we learn to act toward others with confidence. Yet our unconscious ease masks an enormously complex process. When we enter a social situation, how do we know what to do? What should we say? How are we supposed to act? Are we dressed appropriately? Are we talking to the right person? Without knowing it, we have learned a complex set of cultural categories for social interaction that enables us to estimate the social situation, identify the people in it, act appropriately, and recognize larger groups of people.

Status and roles are basic to social intercourse. **Status** refers to the categories of different kinds of people who interact. The old saying, "You can't tell the players without a program," goes for our daily associations as well. Instead of a program, however, we identify the actors by a range of signs, from the way they dress to the claims they make about themselves. Most statuses are named, so we may be heard to say things like, "That's President Gavin," or "She's a lawyer," when we explain social situations to others. This identification of actors is a prerequisite for appropriate social interaction.

Roles are the rules for action associated with particular statuses. We use them to interpret and generate social behavior. For example, a professor plays a role in the classroom. Although often not conscious of this role, the professor will stand, use the blackboard, look at notes, and speak with a slightly more formal air than usual. The professor does not wear blue jeans and a T-shirt, chew gum, sit cross-legged on the podium, or sing. These actions might be appropriate for this person when assuming the identity of "friend" at a party, but they are out of place in the classroom.

People also always relate to each other in **social situations,** the settings in which social interaction takes place. Social situations consist of a combination of times, places, objects, and events. For example, if we see a stranger carrying a television set across campus at four o'clock in the afternoon, we will probably ignore the activity. Most likely someone is simply moving. But if we see the same person carrying the set at four in the morning, we may suspect a theft. Only the time has changed, but it is a significant marker of the social situation. Similarly, we expect classrooms to be associated with lectures, and stethoscopes to be part of medical exams. Such places and objects mark the social situations of which they are part.

People also belong to groups. **Social groups** are organized collections of individuals. They are often named—the Republican Party, American Motorcyclist Association, General Motors—although some, such as friends who meet for drinks after work on Fridays, may be anonymous and less formal. Social groups have several attributes. The people who belong to them normally recognize their common membership and share the goals of the group. The group should share an "inside" culture and its members should interact with each other. Groups are also organized internally in some way. Tasks are often divided among members. Finally, groups usually link to one another. For example, when a couple marries, their union connects the families of the bride and groom. There are some collections of people that we might think of as groups that do not fit this definition. "Middle-class" people, for example, are an aggregate, not a social group, because they are not an interacting organized collective. No one says, "I am meeting tonight with my middle-class men's association."

As societies around the world grow larger, it becomes more difficult to identify groups. People may do most of their socializing in **social networks,** the individuals with whom they regularly interact. Networks are not groups; they are only defined in relation to a particular individual. Nonetheless they are important because they may involve a substantial part of an individual's social interaction. A "social messiness" also afflicts interaction worldwide. People freely travel and enter new social situations where culture is not fully shared. Individuals can interact in dozens of different social situations each day.

Groups form around several principles. Every society has kinship groups, the topic of the previous section of this book. Ethnic groups organize around a shared cultural background. Some groups, such as the American Association of Retired Persons, are based on age. Others, like the National Organization for Women, are based on gender. The Macalester/Groveland Community Association is a territorial group. Many groups, such as the Gold Wing Road Riders Association (a national motorcycle group), Ford Motor Company (an economic group), and Mothers Against Drunk Driving (an interest group) organize around common goals and interests. Many groups are built around several of these design principles at once.

Finally groups can also be organized around social hierarchy. Some degree of **inequality** is part of most human interaction. One spouse may dominate another; a child may receive more attention than his or her siblings; the boss's friends may be promoted faster than other employees. But inequality becomes most noticeable when it systematically affects whole classes of people. In its most obvious form, inequality emerges as **social stratification,** which is characterized by regularly experienced unequal access to valued economic resources and prestige.

Anthropologists recognize at least two kinds of social stratification: class and caste. **Class** stratification restricts individuals' access to valued resources and prestige within a partially flexible system. Although it is often a difficult process, individuals may change rank in a class system if they manage to acquire the necessary prerequisites.

Many sociologists and anthropologists believe that there is an American class system and use terms such as *lower class, working class, middle class,* and *upper class* to designate the unequal positions within it. Americans born into poverty lack access to goods and prestige in this system but can change class standing if they acquire wealth and symbols of higher standing on a continuing basis. Upward mobility is difficult to achieve, however, and few people at the bottom of the system manage to change rank significantly. Indeed, many social scientists feel there is now a permanent underclass in the United States.

Caste defines a second kind of social stratification, one based on permanent membership. People are born into castes and cannot change membership, no matter what they do. In India, for example, caste is a pervasive feature of social organization. South Asians are born into castes and remain members for life; intercaste marriage is forbidden. In the past, castes formed the building blocks of rural Indian society. They were governed by strict rules of deference and served to allocate access to jobs, land, wealth, and power. Cash labor and new industrial jobs have eroded the economic aspect of the system today, but caste persists as a form of rank throughout most of the Indian subcontinent.

Several anthropologists and sociologists have argued that American racial groups are the equivalent of Indian castes. Black and white Americans keep their racial identity for life; nothing can change one's race. Racial identity clearly affects chances for the acquisition of prestige and economic success.

Caste identity, whether Indian or American, tends to preserve and create cultural difference. There is noticeable cultural variation among members of castes in most Indian villages, just as cultural variation occurs among black and white people in the United States.

Using the idea of social stratification, anthropologists have constructed a rough classification of societies into three types: egalitarian, rank, and stratified. **Egalitarian societies** lack formal social stratification. They may display inequality in personal relations based on age, gender, or personal ability, but no category of persons within the same sex or age group has special privilege. Hunter-gatherer societies are most likely to be egalitarian.

Rank societies contain unequal access to prestige, but not to valued economic resources. In such societies there may be chiefs or other persons with authority and prestige, and they may gain access to rank by birth, but their positions give them no substantial economic advantage. Horticultural societies, including some chiefdomships, fit this category.

Stratified societies organize around formal modes of social stratification, as their name suggests. Members of stratified societies are likely to form classes or castes, and inequality affects access to both prestige and economic resources. Most complex societies, including agrarian and industrialized states, fit into this type.

Inequality may also be based on other human attributes, such as age and gender. In many societies, including our own, age and gender affect access to prestige, power, and resources. It is common for men to publicly outrank women along these dimensions, particularly in societies threatened by war or other adversity that requires male intervention.

The articles in this part explore the nature of status, role, and inequality. The first, by Elizabeth Fernea and Robert Fernea, describes the importance of the veil as a symbol defining the role and rank of women in the Middle East. The second selection, by Ernestine Friedl, explores the reasons behind differences in power experienced by women in hunting and gathering societies. Friedl concludes that women's power is governed by access to control over public resources. The Third article, by Meredith Small, describes a study of menstrual taboos among the West African Dogon conducted by anthropologist Beverly Strassmann. Small relates that Strassmann sees the nightly banishment of menstruating Dogon women to a special hut as a way to reveal their state of fertility. Men use the signs to determine paternity and prevent cuckoldry. The fourth article, by Jeffrey Fish, looks at the way Americans define race. Seen by most Americans as a biologically determined subspecies of human beings, but actually a culturally defined taxonomy based on the classification of one's parents, race in the United States is entirely different from racial categories in Brazil.

Key Terms

caste *p. 221*	social groups *p. 220*
class *p. 221*	social networks *p. 220*
egalitarian societies *p. 221*	social situation *p. 219*
inequality *p. 220*	social stratification *p. 220*
rank societies *p. 221*	status *p. 219*
role *p. 219*	stratified societies *p. 221*

20

Symbolizing Roles: Behind the Veil

Elizabeth W. Fernea and Robert A. Fernea

Most societies have some things that serve as key symbols. The flag of the United States, for example, stands not only for the nation, but for a variety of important values that guide American behavior and perception. In this article, Elizabeth Fernea and Robert Fernea trace the meaning of another key symbol: the veil worn by women in the Middle East. Instead of reference to a national group, the veil codes many of the values surrounding the role of women. Often viewed by Westerners as a symbol of female restriction and inequality, for the women who wear it the veil signals honor, personal protection, the sanctity and privacy of the family, wealth and high status, and city life.

Blue jeans have come to mean America all over the world; three-piece wool suits signal businessmen; and in the 1980s pink or green hair said "punk." What do we notice, however, in societies other than our own? Ishi, the last of a "lost" tribe of North American Indians who stumbled into twentieth-century California in 1911, is reported to have said that the truly interesting objects in the white culture were pockets and matches. Rifa'ah Tahtawi, one of the first young Egyptians to be sent to Europe to study in 1826, wrote an account of French society in which he noted that Parisians used many unusual objects of dress, among them something called a belt. Women wore belts, he said, apparently to keep their bosoms erect, and to show off the slimness of their waists and the fullness of their hips. Europeans are still fascinated by the Stetson hats worn by American cowboys; an elderly Dutch woman of our acquaintance recently carried six enormous Stetsons back to the Hague as presents for the male members of her family.

Like languages (Inca, French) or food (tacos, hamburgers), clothing has special meaning for people who wear it that strangers may not understand. But some objects become charged with meaning to other cultures. The veil is one article of clothing used in Middle Eastern societies that stirs strong emotions in the West. "The feminine veil has become a symbol: that of the slavery of one portion of humanity," wrote French ethnologist Germaine Tillion in 1966. A hundred years earlier, Sir Richard Burton, British traveler, explorer, and translator of the *Arabian Nights,* recorded a different view. "Europeans inveigh against this article [the face veil] . . . for its hideousness and jealous concealment of charms made to be admired," he wrote in 1855. "It is, on the contrary, the most coquettish article of women's attire . . . it conceals coarse skins, fleshy noses, wide mouths and vanishing chins, whilst it sets off to best advantage what in these lands is most lustrous and liquid—the eye. Who has not remarked this at a masquerade ball?"

In the present generation, the veil has become a focus of attention for Western writers, both popular and academic, who take a measure of Burton's irony and Tillion's anger to equate modernization of the Middle East with the discarding of the veil and to look at its return in Iran and in a number of Arab countries as a sure sign of retrogression. "Iran's 16 million women have come a long way since their floor-length cotton veil officially was abolished in 1935," an article noted in the 1970s, just before the Shah was toppled. Today [1986], with Ayatollah Khomeini in power, those 16 million Iranian women have put their veils back on again, as if to say that the long way they have come is not in the direction of the West.

The thousands of words written about the appearance and disappearance of the veil and of *purdah* (the seclusion of women) do little to help us understand the Middle East or the cultures that grew out of the same Judeo-Christian roots as our own. The veil and the all-enveloping garments that inevitably accompany it (the *milayah* in Egypt, the *abbayah* in Iraq, the *chadoor* in Iran, the *yashmak* in Turkey, the *burga'* in Afghanistan, and the *djellabah* and the *haik* in North Africa) are only the outward manifestations of cultural practices and meanings that are rooted deep in the history of Mediterranean and Southwest Asian society and are now finding expression once again. Today, with the resurgence of Islam, the veil has become a statement of difference between the Middle East and the Western world, a boundary no easier to cross now than it was during the Crusades or during the nineteenth century, when Western colonial powers ruled the area.

In English, the word *veil* has many definitions, and some of them are religious, just as in the Middle East. In addition to a face cover, the term also means "a piece of material worn over the head and shoulders, a part of a nun's head dress." The Arabic word for veiling and secluding comes from the root word *hajaba*, meaning "barrier." A *hijab* is an amulet worn to keep away the evil eye; it also means a diaphragm used to prevent conception. The gatekeeper or doorkeeper who guards the entrance to a government minister's office is a *hijab*, and in a casual conversation a person might say, "I want to be more informal with my friend so-and-so, but she always puts a *hijab* [barrier] between us."

In Islam, the Koranic verse that sanctions a barrier between men and women is called the Sura of the *hijab* (curtain): "Prophet, enjoin your wives, your daughters and the wives of true believers to draw their garments close round them. That is more proper, so that they may be recognized and not molested. Allah is forgiving and merciful." Notice, however, that veils of the first true believers did not conceal but rather announced the religious status of the women who wore them, drawing attention to the fact that they were Muslims and therefore to be treated with respect. The special Islamic dress worn by increasing numbers of modern Muslim women has much the same effect; it also says, "Treat me with respect."

Certainly some form of seclusion and of veiling was practiced before the time of Muhammad, at least among the urban elites and ruling families, but it was his followers, the first converts to Islam, who used veiling to signal religious faith. According to historic traditions, the *hijab* was established after the wives of the Prophet Muhammad were insulted by people coming to the mosque in search of the Prophet. Muhammad's wives, they said, had been mistaken for slaves. The custom of the *hijab* was thus established, and in the words of historian Nabia Abbott, "Muhammad's women found themselves, on the one hand, deprived of personal liberty, and on the other hand, raised to a position of honor and dignity." It is true, nonetheless, that the forms and uses of veiling and seclusion have varied greatly in practice over the last thousand years since the time of the Prophet, and millions of Muslim women have never been veiled at all. It is a luxury poorer families cannot afford, since any form of arduous activity, such as working in the fields, makes its use impossible. Thus it is likely that the use of the veil was envied by those who could not afford it, for it signaled a style of life that was generally admired. Burton, commenting on the Muslims portrayed in the *Arabian Nights,* says, "The women, who delight in restrictions which tend to their honour, accepted it willingly and still affect it, they do not desire a liberty or rather a license which they have learned to regard as inconsistent with their time-honored notions of feminine decorum and delicacy. They would think very meanly of a husband who permitted them to be exposed, like hetairae, to the public gaze."

The veil bears many messages about its wearers and their society, and many men and women in Middle Eastern communities today would quickly denounce nineteenth-century Orientalists like Sir Richard Burton and deny its importance. Nouha al Hejelan, wife of the Saudi Arabian ambassador to London, told Sally Quinn of *The Washington Post,* "If I wanted to take it all off [the *ab-bayah* and veil], I would have long ago. It wouldn't mean as much to me as it does to you." Basima Bezirgan, a contemporary Iraqi feminist, says, "Compared to the real issues that are involved between men and women in the Middle East today, the veil itself is unimportant." A Moroccan linguist, who buys her clothes in Paris, laughs when asked about the veil. "My mother wears a *djellabah* and a veil. I have never worn them. But so what? I still cannot get divorced as easily as a man, and I am still a member of my family group and responsible to them for everything I do. What is the veil? A piece of cloth." However, early Middle Eastern feminists felt differently. Huda Sharawi, an early Egyptian activist who formed the first Women's Union, removed her veil in public in 1923, a dramatic gesture to demonstrate her dislike of society's attitude toward women and her defiance of the system.

"The seclusion of women has many purposes," states Egyptian anthropologist Nadia Abu Zahra. "It expresses men's status, power, wealth, and manliness. It also helps preserve men's image of virility and masculinity, but men do not admit this; on the contrary they claim that one of the purposes of the veil is to guard women's honor." The veil and *purdah* are symbols of restriction, in men's behavior as well as women's. A respectable woman wearing conservative Islamic dress today on a public street is signaling, "Hands off! Don't touch me or you'll be sorry." Cowboy Jim Sayre of Deadwood, South Dakota, says, "If you deform a cowboy's hat, he'll likely deform you." A man who approaches a veiled woman is asking for similar trouble; not only the woman but also her family is shamed, and serious problems may result. "It is clear," says Egyptian anthropologist Ahmed Abou Zeid, "that honor and shame which are usually attributed to a certain individual or a certain kinship group have in fact a bearing on the total social structure, since most acts involving honor or shame are likely to affect the existing social equilibrium."

Veiling and seclusion almost always can be related to the maintenance of social status. The extreme example of the way the rich could use this practice was found among the wealthy sultans of pre-revolutionary Turkey. Stories of their women, kept in harems and guarded by eunuchs, formed the basis for much of the Western folklore concerning the nature of male-female relationships in Middle Eastern society. The forbidden nature of seclusion inflamed the Western imagination, but the Westerners who created erotic fantasies in films and novels would not have been able to enter the sultans' palaces any more than they could have penetrated their harems! It was eroticism plus opulence and luxury, the signs of wealth, that captured the imagination of the Westerners—and still does, as witnessed by the popularity of "Dallas" and "Dynasty."

The meaning associated with veiling or a lack of veiling changes according to locality. Most village women in the Egyptian delta have not veiled, nor have the Berber women of North Africa, but no one criticizes them for this. "In the village, no one veils, because everyone is considered a member of the same large family," explained Aisha Bint Muhammad, a working-class wife of Marrakesh. "But in the city, veiling is *sunnah*, required by our religion." Veiling has generally been found in towns and cities, among all classes, where families feel that it is necessary to distinguish themselves from strangers. Some women who must work without the veil in factories and hotels may put such garments on when they go out on holidays or even walk on the streets after work.

Veiling and *purdah* not only indicate status and wealth; they also have some religious sanction and protect women from the world outside the home. *Purdah* delineates private space and distinguishes between the public and private sectors of society, as does the traditional architecture of the area. Older Middle Eastern houses do not have picture windows facing on the street, nor do they have walks leading invitingly to front doors. Family life is hidden away from strangers; behind blank walls may lie courtyards and gardens, refuges from the heat, cold, and bustle of the outside world, the world of nonkin that is not to be trusted. Outsiders are pointedly excluded.

Even within the household, among her close relatives, a traditional Muslim woman may veil before those kinsmen whom she could legally marry. If her maternal or paternal cousins, her brothers-in-law, or her sons-in-law come to call, she covers her head, or perhaps her whole face. To do otherwise, to neglect such acts of respect and modesty, would be considered shameless.

The veil does more than protect its wearers from known and unknown intruders; it can also conceal identity. Behind the anonymity of the veil, women can go about a city unrecognized and uncriticized. Nadia Abu Zahra reports anecdotes of men donning women's veils in order to visit their lovers undetected; women may do the same. The veil is such an effective disguise that Nouri Al-Sa'id, the late prime minister of Iraq, attempted to escape death from revolutionary forces in 1958 by wearing the *abbayah* and veil of a woman; only his shoes gave him away. When houses of prostitution were closed in Baghdad in the early 1950s, the prostitutes donned the same clothing to cruise the streets. Flashing open their outer garments was an advertisement to potential customers.

Political dissidents in many countries have used the veil for their own ends. The women who marched, veiled, through Cairo during the Nationalist demonstrations against the British after World War I were counting on the strength of Western respect for the veil to protect them against British gunfire. At first they were right. Algerian women also used the protection of the veil to carry bombs through French army checkpoints during the Algerian revolution. But when the French discovered the ruse, Algerian women discarded the veil and dressed like Europeans to move about freely.

The multiple meanings and uses of *purdah* and the veil do not fully explain how such practices came to be so deeply embedded in Mediterranean society. However, their origins lie in the asymmetrical relationship between men and women and the resulting attitudes about men's and women's roles. Women, according to Fatma Mernissi, a Moroccan sociologist, are seen by men in Islamic societies as in need of protection because they are unable to control their sexuality and hence are a danger to the social order. In other words, they need to be restrained and controlled so that men do not give way to the impassioned desire they inspire, and society can thus function in an orderly way.

The notion that women present a danger to the social order is scarcely limited to Muslim society. Anthropologist Julian Pitt-Rivers has pointed out that the supervision and seclusion of women was also found in Christian Europe, even though veiling was not usually practiced there. "The idea that women not subjected to male authority are a danger is a fundamental one in the writings of the moralists from the Archpriest of Talavera to Padre Haro, and it is echoed in the modern Andalusian *pueblo*. It is bound up with the fear of ungoverned female sexuality which had been an integral element of European folklore ever since prudent Odysseus lashed himself to the mast to escape the sirens."

Pitt-Rivers is writing about northern Mediterranean communities, which, like those of the Middle Eastern societies, have been greatly concerned with family honor and shame rather than with individual guilt. The honor of the Middle Eastern extended family, its ancestors and its descendants, is the highest social value. The misdeeds of the grandparents are indeed visited on their grandchildren, but so also grandparents may be disgraced by grandchildren. Men and women always remain members of their natal families. Marriage is a legal contract, but a fragile one that is often broken; the ties between brother and sister, mother and child, father and child are lifelong and enduring. The larger natal family is the group to which the individual man or woman belongs and to which the individual owes responsibility in exchange for the social and economic security that the family group provides. It is the group that is socially honored—or dishonored—by the behavior of the individual.

Both male honor and female honor are involved in the honor of the family, but each is expressed differently. The honor of a man, *sharaf*, is a public matter, involving bravery, hospitality, and piety. It may be lost, but it may also be regained. The honor of a woman, *'ard*, is a private matter involving only one thing, her sexual chastity. Once believed to be lost, it cannot be regained. If the loss of female honor remains only privately known, a rebuke may be all that takes place. But if the loss of female honor becomes public knowledge, the other members of the family may feel bound to cleanse the family name. In extreme cases, the cleansing may require the death of the offending female member. Although such killings are now criminal offenses in the Middle East, suspended sentences are often given, and the newspapers in Cairo and Baghdad frequently carry sad stories of runaway sisters "gone bad" in the city, and the revenge taken upon them in the name of family honor by their brothers or cousins.

This emphasis on female chastity, many say, originated in the patrilineal society's concern with the paternity of the child and the inheritance that follows the male line. How could the husband know that the child in his wife's womb was his son? He could not know unless his wife was a virgin at marriage. Marriages were arranged by parents, and keeping daughters secluded from men was the best way of seeing that a girl remained a virgin until her wedding night.

Middle Eastern women also look upon seclusion as practical protection. In the Iraqi village where we lived from 1956 to 1958, one of us (Elizabeth) wore the *abbayah* and found that it provided a great deal of protection from prying eyes, dust, heat, and flies. Parisian women visiting Istanbul in the sixteenth century were so impressed by the ability of the all-enveloping garment to keep dresses clean of mud and manure and to keep women from being attacked by importuning men that they tried to introduce it into French fashion. Many women have told us that they felt self-conscious, vulnerable, and even naked when they first walked on a public street without the veil and *abbayah*—as if they were making a display of themselves.

The veil, as it has returned in the last decade in a movement away from wearing Western dress, has been called a form of "portable seclusion," allowing women to maintain a modest appearance that indicates respectability and religious piety in the midst of modern Middle Eastern urban life. This new style of dress always includes long skirts, long sleeves, and a head covering (scarf or turban). Some outfits are belted, some are loose, and some include face veils and shapeless robes, as well as gloves so that no skin whatsoever is exposed to the public eye. However, these clothes are seldom black, like the older garments. The women wearing such clothes in Egypt may work in shops or offices or go to college; they are members of the growing middle class.

This new fashion has been described by some scholars as an attempt by men to reassert their Muslim identity and to reestablish their position as heads of families, even though both spouses often must work outside the home. According to this analysis, the presence of the veil is a sign that the males of the household are in control of their women and are more able to assume the responsibilities disturbed or usurped by foreign colonial powers, responsibilities which continue to be threatened by Western politics and materialism. Other scholars argue that it is not men who are choosing the garb today but women themselves, using modest dress as a way of communicating to the rest of the world that though they may work outside their homes, they are nonetheless pious Muslims and respectable women.

The veil is the outward sign of a complex reality. Observers are often deceived by the absence of that sign and fail to see that in Middle Eastern societies (and in many parts of Europe) where the garb no longer exists, basic attitudes are unchanged. Women who have taken off the veil continue to play the old roles within the family, and their chastity remains crucial. A woman's behavior is still the key to the honor and the reputation of her family, no matter what she wears.

In Middle Eastern societies, feminine and masculine continue to be strong poles of identification. This is in marked contrast to Western society, where for more than a generation greater equality between men and women has been reflected in the blurring of distinctions between male and female clothing. Western feminists continue to state that biology is not the basis of behavior and therefore should not be the basis for understanding men's and women's roles. But almost all Middle Eastern reformers, whether upper or middle class, intellectuals or clerics, argue from the assumption of a fundamental, God-given difference, social and psychological as well as physical, between men and women. There are important disagreements among these reformers today about what should be done, however.

Those Muslim reformers still strongly influenced by Western models call for equal access to divorce, child custody, and inheritance; equal opportunities for education and employment; abolition of female circumcision and "crimes of honor"; an end to polygamy; and a law regulating the age of marriage. But of growing importance are reformers of social practice who call for a return to the example set by the Prophet Muhammad and his early followers; they wish to begin by eliminating what they feel to be the licentious practices introduced by Western influence, such as sexual laxity and the consumption of alcohol. To them, change in the laws affecting women should be in strict accord with their view of Islamic law, and women should begin by expressing their modesty and piety by wearing the new forms of veiling in public life. Seclusion may be impossible in modern urban societies, but conservative dress, the new form of veiling, is an option for women that sets the faithful Muslim apart from the corrupt world of the nonbeliever as it was believed to do in the time of the Prophet.

A female English film director, after several months in Morocco, said in an interview, "This business about the veil is nonsense. We all have our veils, between ourselves and other people. The question is what the veils are used for, and by whom." Today the use of the veil continues to trigger Western reaction, for as Islamic dress, it is not only a statement about the honor of the family or the boundary between family and stranger. Just as the changes in the nun's dress in the United States tell us something about the woman who wears it and the society of which she is a part, the various forms of veiling today communicate attitudes and beliefs about politics and religious morality as well as the roles of men and women in the Middle East.

Review Questions

1. What is the meaning to Westerners of the veil worn by Middle Eastern women? How does this view reflect Western values?

2. List the symbolic meanings of the veil to Middle Eastern women. How do these meanings relate to the Muslim concept of *purdah* and to other important Middle Eastern values?

3. There has been a resurgence of the veil in several Middle Eastern societies over the past few years. How can you explain this change?

4. Using this article as a model, analyze the meaning of some American articles of clothing. How do these relate to core values in the United States?

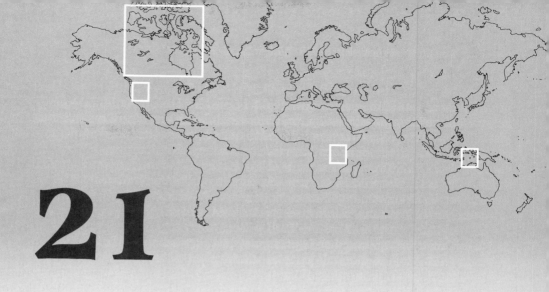

21

Society and Sex Roles

Ernestine Friedl

Many anthropologists claim that males hold formal authority over females in every society. Although the degree of masculine authority may vary from one group to the next, males always have more power. For some researchers, this unequal male–female relationship is the result of biological inheritance. As with other primates, they argue, male humans are naturally more aggressive, females more docile. Ernestine Friedl challenges this explanation in this selection. Comparing a variety of hunting and gathering groups, she concludes that relations between men and women are shaped by a culturally defined division of labor based on sex, not by inherited predisposition. Given access to resources that circulate publicly, women can attain equal or dominant status in any society, including our own.

"Society and Sex Roles" by Ernestine Friedl as appeared in *Human Nature* magazine, April 1978. Reprinted by permission of the author.

"Women must respond quickly to the demands of their husbands," says anthropologist Napoleon Chagnon, describing the horticultural Yanomamö Indians of Venezuela. When a man returns from a hunting trip, "the woman, no matter what she is doing, hurries home and quietly but rapidly prepares a meal for her husband. Should the wife be slow in doing this, the husband is within his rights to beat her. Most reprimands . . . take the form of blows with the hand or with a piece of firewood. . . . Some of them chop their wives with the sharp edge of a machete or axe, or shoot them with a barbed arrow in some nonvital area, such as the buttocks or leg."

Among the Semai agriculturalists of central Malaya, when one person refuses the request of another, the offended party suffers *punan*, a mixture of emotional pain and frustration. "Enduring *punan* is commonest when a girl has refused the victim her sexual favors," reports Robert Dentan. "The jilted man's 'heart becomes sad.' He loses his energy and his appetite. Much of the time he sleeps, dreaming of his lost love. In this state he is in fact very likely to injure himself 'accidentally.'" The Semai are afraid of violence; a man would never strike a woman.

The social relationship between men and women has emerged as one of the principal disputes occupying the attention of scholars and the public in recent years. Although the discord is sharpest in the United States, the controversy has spread throughout the world. Numerous national and international conferences, including one in Mexico sponsored by the United Nations, have drawn together delegates from all walks of life to discuss such questions as the social and political rights of each sex and even the basic nature of males and females.

Whatever their position, partisans often invoke examples from other cultures to support their ideas about the proper role of each sex. Because women are clearly subservient to men in many societies, like the Yanomamö, some experts conclude that the natural pattern is for men to dominate. But among the Semai no one has the right to command others, and in West Africa women are often chiefs. The place of women in these societies supports the argument of those who believe that sex roles are not fixed, that if there is a natural order, it allows for many different arrangements.

The argument will never be settled as long as the opposing sides toss examples from the world's cultures at each other like intellectual stones. But the effect of biological differences on male and female behavior can be clarified by looking at known examples of the earliest forms of human society and examining the relationship between technology, social organization, environment, and sex roles. The problem is to determine the conditions in which different degrees of male dominance are found, to try to discover the social and cultural arrangements that give rise to equality or inequality between the sexes, and to attempt to apply this knowledge to our understanding of the changes taking place in modern industrial society.

As Western history and the anthropological record have told us, equality between the sexes is rare; in most known societies females are subordinate. Male dominance is so widespread that it is virtually a human universal; societies in which women are consistently dominant do not exist and have never existed.

Evidence of a society in which women control all strategic resources like food and water, and in which women's activities are the most prestigious, has never been found. The Iroquois of North America and the Lovedu of Africa came closest. Among the Iroquois, women raised food, controlled its distribution, and helped to choose male political leaders. Lovedu women ruled as queens, exchanged valuable cattle, led ceremonies, and controlled their own sex lives. But among both the Iroquois and Lovedu, men owned the land and held other positions of power and prestige. Women were equal to men; they did not have ultimate authority over them. Neither culture was a true matriarchy.

Patriarchies are prevalent, and they appear to be strongest in societies in which men control significant goods that are exchanged with people outside the family. Regardless of who produces food, the person who gives it to others creates the obligations and alliances that are at the center of all political relations. The greater the male monopoly on the distribution of scarce items, the stronger their control of women seems to be. This is most obvious in relatively simple hunter-gatherer societies.

Hunter-gatherers, or foragers, subsist on wild plants, small land animals, and small river or sea creatures gathered by hand; large land animals and sea mammals hunted with spears, bows and arrows, and blow guns; and fish caught with hooks and nets. The three hundred thousand hunter-gatherers alive in the world today include the Eskimos, the Australian aborigines, and the Pygmies of Central Africa.

Foraging has endured for two million years and was replaced by farming and animal husbandry only ten thousand years ago; it covers more than 99 percent of human history. Our foraging ancestry is not far behind us and provides a clue to our understanding of the human condition.

Hunter-gatherers are people whose ways of life are technologically simple and socially and politically egalitarian. They live in small groups of 50 to 200 and have neither kings, nor priests, nor social classes. These conditions permit anthropologists to observe the essential bases for inequalities between the sexes without the distortions induced by the complexities of contemporary industrial society.

The source of male power among hunter-gatherers lies in their control of a scarce, hard to acquire, but necessary nutrient—animal protein. When men in a hunter-gatherer society return to camp with game, they divide the meat in some customary way. Among the !Kung San of Africa, certain parts of the animal are given to the owner of the arrow that killed the beast, to the first hunter to sight the game, to the one who threw the first spear, and to all men in the hunting party. After the meat has been divided, each hunter distributes his share to his blood relatives and his in-laws, who in turn share it with others. If an animal is large enough, every member of the band will receive some meat.

Vegetable foods, in contrast, are not distributed beyond the immediate household. Women give food to their children, to their husbands, to other members of the household, and rarely, to the occasional visitor. No one outside the family regularly eats any of the wild fruits and vegetables that are gathered by the women.

The meat distributed by the men is a public gift. Its source is widely known, and the donor expects a reciprocal gift when other men return from a successful hunt. He gains honor as a supplier of a scarce item and simultaneously obligates others to him.

These obligations constitute a form of power or control over others, both men and women. The opinions of hunters play an important part in decisions to move the village; good hunters attract the most desirable women; people in other groups join camps with good hunters; and hunters, because they already participate in an internal system of exchange, control exchange with other groups for flint, salt, and steel axes. The male monopoly on hunting unites men in a system of exchange and gives them power; gathering vegetable food does not give women equal power even among foragers who live in the tropics, where the food collected by women provides more than half the hunter-gatherer diet.

If dominance arises from a monopoly on big-game hunting, why has the male monopoly remained unchallenged? Some women are strong enough to participate in the hunt and their endurance is certainly equal to that of men. Dobe San women of the Kalahari Desert in Africa walk an average of 10 miles a day carrying from 15 to 33 pounds of food plus a baby.

Women do not hunt, I believe, because of four interrelated factors: variability in the supply of game; the different skills required for hunting and gathering; the incompatibility between carrying burdens and hunting; and the small size of seminomadic foraging populations.

Because the meat supply is unstable, foragers must make frequent expeditions to provide the band with gathered food. Environmental factors such as seasonal and annual variation in rainfall often affect the size of the wildlife population. Hunters cannot always find game, and when they do encounter animals, they are not always successful in killing their prey. In northern latitudes, where meat is the primary food, periods of starvation are known in every generation. The irregularity of the game supply leads hunter-gatherers in areas where plant foods are available to depend on these predictable foods a good part of the time. Someone must gather the fruits, nuts, and roots and carry them back to camp to feed unsuccessful hunters, children, the elderly, and anyone who might not have gone foraging that day.

Foraging falls to the women because hunting and gathering cannot be combined on the same expedition. Although gatherers sometimes notice signs of game as they work, the skills required to track game are not the same as those required to find edible roots or plants. Hunters scan the horizon and the land for traces of large game; gatherers keep their eyes to the ground, studying the distribution of plants and the texture of the soil for hidden roots and animal holes. Even if a woman who was collecting plants came across the track of an antelope, she could not follow it; it is impossible to carry a load and hunt at the same time. Running with a heavy load is difficult, and should the animal be sighted, the hunter would be off balance and could neither shoot an arrow nor throw a spear accurately.

Pregnancy and child care would also present difficulties for a hunter. An unborn child affects a woman's body balance, as does a child in her arms, on her back, or slung at her side. Until they are two years old, many hunter-gatherer children are carried at all times, and until they are four, they are carried some of the time.

An observer might wonder why young women do not hunt until they become pregnant, or why mature women and men do not hunt and gather on alternate days, with some women staying in camp to act as wet nurses for the young. Apart from the effects hunting might have on a mother's milk production, there are two reasons. First, young girls begin to bear children as soon as they are physically mature and strong enough to hunt, and second, hunter-gatherer bands are so small that there are unlikely to be enough lactating women to serve as wet nurses. No hunter-gatherer group could afford to maintain a specialized female hunting force.

Because game is not always available, because hunting and gathering are specialized skills, because women carrying heavy loads cannot hunt, and because women in hunter-gatherer societies are usually either pregnant or caring for young children, for most of the last two million years of human history men have hunted and women have gathered.

If male dominance depends on controlling the supply of meat, then the degree of male dominance in a society should vary with the amount of meat available and the amount supplied by the men. Some regions, like the East African grasslands and the North American woodlands, abounded with species of large mammals; other zones, like tropical forests and semideserts, are thinly populated with prey. Many elements affect the supply of game, but theoretically, the less meat provided exclusively by the men, the more egalitarian the society.

All known hunter-gatherer societies fit into four basic types: those in which men and women work together in communal hunts and as teams gathering edible plants, as did the Washo Indians of North America; those in which men and women each collect their own plant foods although the men supply some meat to the group, as do the Hadza of Tanzania; those in which male hunters and female gatherers work apart but return to camp each evening to share their acquisitions, as do the Tiwi of North Australia; and those in which the men provide all the food by hunting large game, as do the Eskimo. In each case the extent of male dominance increases directly with the proportion of meat supplied by individual men and small hunting parties.

Among the most egalitarian of hunter-gatherer societies are the Washo Indians, who inhabited the valleys of the Sierra Nevada in what is now southern California and Nevada. In the spring they moved north to Lake Tahoe for the large fish runs of sucker and native trout. Everyone—men, women, and children—participated in the fishing. Women spent the summer gathering edible berries and seeds while the men continued to fish. In the fall some men hunted deer, but the most important source of animal protein was the jackrabbit, which was captured in communal hunts. Men and women together drove the rabbits into nets tied end to end. To provide food for the winter, husbands and wives worked as teams in the late fall to collect pine nuts.

Since everyone participated in most food-gathering activities, there were no individual distributors of food and relatively little difference in male and female rights. Men and women were not segregated from each other in daily activities; both were free to take lovers after marriage; both had the right to separate whenever they chose; menstruating women were not isolated from the rest of the group; and one of the two major Washo rituals celebrated hunting while the other celebrated gathering. Men were accorded more prestige if they had killed a deer, and men directed decisions about the seasonal movement of the group. But if no male leader stepped forward, women were permitted to lead. The distinctive feature of groups such as the Washo is the relative equality of the sexes.

The sexes are also relatively equal among the Hadza of Tanzania, but this near-equality arises because men and women tend to work alone to feed themselves. They exchange little food. The Hadza lead a leisurely life in the seemingly barren environment of the East African Rift Gorge, which is, in fact, rich in edible berries, roots, and small game. As a result of this abundance, from the time they are ten years old, Hadza men and women gather much of their own food. Women take their young children with them into the bush, eating as they forage, and collect only enough food for a light family meal in the evening. The men eat berries and roots as they hunt for small game, and should they bring down a rabbit or a hyrax, they eat the meat on the spot. Meat is carried back to the camp and shared with the rest of the group only on those rare occasions when a poisoned arrow brings down a large animal—an impala, a zebra, an eland, or a giraffe.

Because Hadza men distribute little meat, their status is only slightly higher than that of the women. People flock to the camp of a good hunter and the camp might take on his name because of his popularity, but he is in no sense a leader of the group. A Hadza man and a woman have an equal right to divorce, and each can repudiate a marriage simply by living apart for a few weeks. Couples tend to live in the same camp as the wife's mother, but they sometimes make long visits to the camp of the husband's mother. Although a man may take more than one wife, most Hadza males cannot afford to indulge in this luxury. In order to maintain a marriage, a man must supply both his wife and his mother-in-law with some meat and trade goods, such as beads and cloth, and the Hadza economy gives few men the wealth to provide for more than one wife and mother-in-law. Washo equality is based on cooperation; Hadza equality is based on independence.

In contrast to both these groups, among the Tiwi of Melville and Bathurst Islands off the northern coast of Australia, male hunters dominate female gatherers. The Tiwi are representative of the most common form of foraging society, in which the men supply large quantities of meat, although less than half the food consumed by the group. Each morning Tiwi women, most with babies on their backs, scatter in different directions in search of vegetables, grubs, worms, and small game such as bandicoots, lizards, and opossums. To track the game, they use hunting dogs. On most days women return to camp with some meat and with baskets full of *korka,* the nut of a native palm, which is soaked and mashed to make a porridge-like dish. The Tiwi men do not hunt small game and do not hunt every day, but when they do they often return with kangaroo, large lizards, fish, and game birds.

The porridge is cooked separately by each household and rarely shared outside the family, but the meat is prepared by a volunteer cook, who can be male or female. After the cook takes one of the parts of the animal traditionally reserved for him or her, the animal's "boss," the one who caught it, distributes the rest to all near kin and then to all others residing with the band. Although the small game supplied by the women is distributed in the same way as the big game supplied by the men, Tiwi men are dominant because the game they kill provides most of the meat.

The power of Tiwi men is clearest in their betrothal practices. Among the Tiwi, a woman must always be married. To ensure this, female infants are betrothed at birth and widows are remarried at the gravesides of their late husbands. Men form alliances by exchanging daughters, sisters, and mothers in marriage, and some collect as many as twenty-five wives. Tiwi men value the quantity and quality of the food many wives can collect and the many children they can produce.

The dominance of the men is offset somewhat by the influence of adult women in selecting their next husbands. Many women are active strategists in the political careers of their male relatives, but to the exasperation of some sons attempting to promote their own futures, widowed mothers sometimes insist on selecting their own partners. Women also influence the marriages of their daughters and granddaughters, especially when the selected husband dies before the bestowed child moves to his camp.

Among the Eskimo, representative of the rarest type of forager society, inequality between the sexes is matched by inequality in supplying the group with food. Inland Eskimo men hunt caribou throughout the year to provision the entire society, and maritime Eskimo men depend on whaling, fishing, and some hunting to feed their extended families. The women process the carcasses, cut and sew skins to make clothing, cook, and care for the young; but they collect no food of their own and depend on the men to supply all the raw materials for their work. Since men provide all the meat, they also control the trade in hides, whale oil, seal oil, and other items that move between the maritime and inland Eskimos.

Eskimo women are treated almost exclusively as objects to be used, abused, and traded by men. After puberty all Eskimo girls are fair game for any interested male. A man shows his intentions by grabbing the belt of a woman, and if she protests, he cuts off her trousers and forces himself upon her. These encounters are considered unimportant by the rest of the group. Men offer their wives' sexual services to establish alliances with trading partners and members of hunting and whaling parties.

Despite the consistent pattern of some degree of male dominance among foragers, most of these societies are egalitarian compared with agricultural and industrial societies. No forager has any significant opportunity for political leadership. Foragers, as a rule, do not like to give or take orders, and assume leadership only with reluctance. Shamans (those who are thought to be possessed by spirits) may be either male or female. Public rituals conducted by women in order to celebrate the first menstruation of girls are common, and the symbolism in these rituals is similar to that in the ceremonies that follow a boy's first kill.

In any society, status goes to those who control the distribution of valued goods and services outside the family. Equality arises when both sexes work side by side in food production, as do the Washo, and the products are simply distributed among the workers. In such circumstances, no person or sex has greater access to valued items than do others. But when women make no contribution to the food supply, as in the case of the Eskimo, they are completely subordinate.

When we attempt to apply these generalizations to contemporary industrial society, we can predict that as long as women spend their discretionary income from jobs on domestic needs, they will gain little social recognition and power. To be an effective source of power, money must be exchanged in ways that require returns and create obligations. In other words, it must be invested.

Jobs that do not give women control over valued resources will do little to advance their general status. Only as managers, executives, and professionals are women in a position to trade goods and services, to do others favors, and therefore to obligate others to them. Only as controllers of valued resources can women achieve prestige, power, and equality.

Within the household, women who bring in income from jobs are able to function on a more nearly equal basis with their husbands. Women who contribute services to their husbands and children without pay, as do some middle-class Western housewives, are especially vulnerable to dominance. Like Eskimo women, as long as their services are limited to domestic distribution they have little power relative to their husbands and none with respect to the outside world.

As for the limits imposed on women by their procreative functions in hunter-gatherer societies, childbearing and child care are organized around work as much as work is organized around reproduction. Some foraging groups space their children three to four years apart and have an average of only four to six children, far fewer than many women in other cultures. Hunter-gatherers nurse their infants for extended periods, sometimes for as long as four years. This custom suppresses ovulation and limits the size of their families. Sometimes, although rarely, they practice infanticide. By limiting reproduction, a woman who is gathering food has only one child to carry.

Different societies can and do adjust the frequency of birth and the care of children to accommodate whatever productive activities women customarily engage in. In horticultural societies, where women work long hours in gardens that may be far from home, infants get food to supplement their mothers' milk, older children take care of younger children, and pregnancies are widely spaced. Throughout the world, if a society requires a woman's labor, it finds ways to care for her children.

In the United States, as in some other industrial societies, the accelerated entry of women with preschool children into the labor force has resulted in the development of a variety of child-care arrangements. Individual women have called on friends, relatives, and neighbors. Public and private child-care centers are growing. We should realize that the declining birth rate, the increasing acceptance of childless or single-child families, and de-emphasis on motherhood are adaptations to a sexual division of labor reminiscent of the system of production found in hunter-gatherer societies.

In many countries where women no longer devote most of their productive years to childbearing, they are beginning to demand a change in the social relationship of the sexes. As women gain access to positions that control the exchange of resources, male dominance may become archaic, and industrial societies may one day become as egalitarian as the Washo.

Review Questions

1. According to Friedl, what factor accounts for the different degrees of dominance and power between males and females found in hunter-gatherer societies?

2. What are the four types of hunter-gatherer societies considered by Friedl in this article, and what is it about the structure of each that relates to the distribution of power and dominance between males and females?

3. Some anthropologists believe that male dominance is inherited. Comment on this assertion in light of Friedl's article.

4. Why does Friedl believe that women will gain equality with men in industrial society?

22

A Woman's Curse?

Meredith F. Small

Many societies around the world treat menstruating women as taboo. Seen as unclean, such women may be evicted from the kitchen, admonished not to touch men's belongings, excluded from sacred places, and even required to sleep in a separate menstrual hut. It is this last requirement that attracted Beverly Strassmann to study the West African Dogon. Among the Dogon, menstruating women crowd each night into a small, cramped menstrual hut built outside village walls. Although they dislike doing so, they believe, as do Dogon men, that their condition is a danger to the gods. Disaster may befall their village if they fail to conform.

Strassmann looked for another explanation, however. Based on years of observation in several Dogon villages, she concluded that the custom serves as an overt sign of a woman's condition that can be used by men to infer the paternity of children. If a woman goes to the menstrual hut, she is clearly not pregnant or lactating. If she is absent and not lactating, chances are she is pregnant. The hut signals information about a woman that would otherwise be hidden.

In this article, Meredith Small describes Strassmann's study and shows that Strassmann has also collected data that says something about the impact of menstruation for women in this country. Dogon women menstruate about 110 times during their fertile lives; Western women do so approximately 350 times. Dogon women menstruate less because they are pregnant more often and because they nurse their babies for at least 20 months. Menstruation rarely, if ever, occurs under these conditions. Western women do neither and use birth control pills to bring on menstruation month after month. The high menstruation rate, Small concludes, may be the cause of higher cancer rates. She concludes with the admonition that in the West, we should work with the body, not against it.

The passage from girlhood to womanhood is marked by a flow of blood from the uterus. Without elaborate ceremony, often without discussion, girls know that when they begin to menstruate, their world is changed forever. For the next thirty years or so, they will spend much energy having babies, or trying not to, reminded at each menstruation that either way, the biology of reproduction has a major impact on their lives.

Anthropologists have underscored the universal importance of menstruation by documenting how the event is interwoven into the ideology as well as the daily activities of cultures around the world. The customs attached to menstruation take peculiarly negative forms: the so-called menstrual taboos. Those taboos may prohibit a woman from having sex with her husband or from cooking for him. They may bar her from visiting sacred places or taking part in sacred activities. They may forbid her to touch certain items used by men, such as hunting gear or weapons, or to eat certain foods or to wash at certain times. They may also require that a woman paint her face red or wear a red hip cord, or that she segregate herself in a special hut while she is menstruating. In short, the taboos set menstruating women apart from the rest of their society, marking them as impure and polluting.

Anthropologists have studied menstrual taboos for decades, focusing on the negative symbolism of the rituals as a cultural phenomenon. Perhaps, suggested one investigator, taking a Freudian perspective, such taboos reflect the anxiety that men feel about castration, an anxiety that would be prompted by women's genital bleeding. Others have suggested that the taboos serve to prevent menstrual odor from interfering with hunting, or that they protect men from microorganisms that might otherwise be transferred during sexual intercourse with a menstruating woman. Until recently, few investigators had considered the possibility that the taboos—and the very fact of menstruation—might instead exist because they conferred an evolutionary advantage.

In the mid-1980s the anthropologist Beverly I. Strassmann of the University of Michigan in Ann Arbor began to study the ways men and women have evolved to accomplish (and regulate) reproduction. Unlike traditional anthropologists, who focus on how culture affects human behavior, Strassmann was convinced that the important role played by biology was being neglected.

Menstruation, she suspected, would be a key for observing and understanding the interplay of biology and culture in human reproductive behavior.

To address the issue, Strassmann decided to seek a culture in which making babies was an ongoing part of adult life. For that she had to get away from industrialized countries, with their bias toward contraception and low birthrates. In a "natural-fertility population," she reasoned, she could more clearly see the connection between the physiology of women and the strategies men and women use to exploit that physiology for their own reproductive ends.

Strassmann ended up in a remote corner of West Africa, living in close quarters with the Dogon, a traditional society whose indigenous religion of ancestor worship requires that menstruating women spend their nights at a small hut. For more than two years Strassmann kept track of the women staying at the hut, and she confirmed the menstruations by testing urine samples for the appropriate hormonal changes. In so doing, she amassed the first long-term data describing how a traditional society appropriates a physiological event—menstruation—and refracts that event through a prism of behaviors and beliefs.

What she found explicitly challenges the conclusions of earlier investigators about the cultural function of menstrual taboos. For the Dogon men, she discovered, enforcing visits to the menstrual hut serves to channel parental resources into the upbringing of their own children. But more, Strassmann, who also had training as a reproductive physiologist, proposed a new theory of why menstruation itself evolved as it did—and again, the answer is essentially a story of conserving resources. Finally, her observations pose provocative questions about women's health in industrialized societies, raising serious doubts about the tactics favored by Western medicine for developing contraceptive technology.

Menstruation is the visible stage of the ovarian cycle, orchestrated primarily by hormones secreted by the ovaries: progesterone and a family of hormones called estrogens. At the beginning of each cycle (by convention, the first day of a woman's period) the levels of the estrogens begin to rise. After about five days, as their concentrations increase, they cause the blood- and nutrient-rich inner lining of the uterus, called the endometrium, to thicken and acquire a densely branching network of blood vessels. At about the middle of the cycle, ovulation takes place, and an egg makes its way from one of the two ovaries down one of the paired fallopian tubes to the uterus. The follicle from which the egg was released in the ovary now begins to secrete progesterone as well as estrogens, and the progesterone causes the endometrium to swell and become even richer with blood vessels—in short, fully ready for a pregnancy, should conception take place and the fertilized egg become implanted.

If conception does take place, the levels of estrogens and progesterone continue to rise throughout the pregnancy. That keeps the endometrium thick enough to support the quickening life inside the uterus. When the baby is born and the new mother begins nursing, the estrogens and progesterone fall to their initial levels, and lactation hormones keep them suppressed. The uterus thus lies quiescent until frequent lactation ends, which triggers the return to ovulation.

If conception does not take place after ovulation, all the ovarian hormones also drop to their initial levels, and menstruation—the shedding of part of the uterine lining—begins. The lining is divided into three layers: a basal layer that is constantly maintained, and two superficial layers, which shed and regrow with each menstrual cycle. All mammals undergo cyclical changes in the state of the endometrium. In most mammals the sloughed-off layers are resorbed into the body if fertilization does not take place. But in some higher primates, including humans, some of the shed endometrium is not resorbed. The shed lining, along with some blood, flows from the body through the vaginal opening, a process that in humans typically lasts from three to five days.

Of course, physiological facts alone do not explain why so many human groups have infused a bodily function with symbolic meaning. And so in 1986 Strassmann found herself driving through the Sahel region of West Africa at the peak of the hot season, heading for a sandstone cliff called the Bandiagara Escarpment, in Mali. There, permanent Dogon villages of mud or stone houses dotted the rocky plateau. The menstrual huts were obvious: round, low-roofed buildings set apart from the rectangular dwellings of the rest of the village.

The Dogon are a society of millet and onion farmers who endorse polygyny, and they maintain their traditional culture despite the occasional visits of outsiders. In a few Dogon villages, in fact, tourists are fairly common, and ethnographers had frequently studied the Dogon language, religion and social structure before Strassmann's arrival. But her visit was the first time someone from the outside wanted to delve into an intimate issue in such detail.

It took Strassmann a series of hikes among villages, and long talks with male elders under the thatched-roof shelters where they typically gather, to find the appropriate sites for her research. She gained permission for her study in fourteen villages, eventually choosing two. That exceptional welcome, she thinks, emphasized the universality of her interests. "I'm working on all the things that really matter to [the Dogon]—fertility, economics—so they never questioned my motives or wondered why I would be interested in these things," she says. "It seemed obvious to them." She set up shop for the next two and a half years in a stone house in the village, with no running water or electricity. Eating the daily fare of the Dogon, millet porridge, she and a research assistant began to integrate themselves into village life, learning the language, getting to know people and tracking visits to the menstrual huts.

Following the movements of menstruating women was surprisingly easy. The menstrual huts are situated outside the walled compounds of the village, but in full view of the men's thatched-roof shelters. As the men relax under their shelters, they can readily see who leaves the huts in the morning and returns to them in the evening. And as nonmenstruating women pass the huts on their way to and from the fields or to other compounds, they too can see who is spending the night there. Strassmann found that when she left her house in the evening to take data, any of the villagers could accurately predict whom she would find in the menstrual huts.

The huts themselves are cramped, dark buildings—hardly places where a woman might go to escape the drudgery of work or to avoid an argument with her husband or a co-wife. The huts sometimes become so crowded that some occupants are forced outside—making the women even more conspicuous. Although babies and toddlers can go with their mothers to the huts, the women consigned there are not allowed to spend time with the rest of their families. They must cook with special pots, not their usual household possessions. Yet they are still expected to do their usual jobs, such as working in the fields.

Why, Strassmann wondered, would anyone put up with such conditions?

The answer, for the Dogon, is that a menstruating woman is a threat to the sanctity of religious altars, where men pray and make sacrifices for the protection of their fields, their families and their village. If menstruating women come near the altars, which are situated both indoors and outdoors, the Dogon believe that their aura of pollution will ruin the altars and bring calamities upon the village. The belief is so ingrained that the women themselves have internalized it, feeling its burden of responsibility and potential guilt. Thus violations of the taboo are rare, because a menstruating woman who breaks the rules knows that she is personally responsible if calamities occur.

Nevertheless, Strassmann still thought a more functional explanation for menstrual taboos might also exist, one closely related to reproduction. As she was well aware, even before her studies among the Dogon, people around the world have a fairly sophisticated view of how reproduction works. In general, people everywhere know full well that menstruation signals the absence of a pregnancy and the possibility of another one. More precisely, Strassmann could frame her hypothesis by reasoning as follows: Across cultures, men and women recognize that a lack of menstrual cycling in a woman implies she is either pregnant, lactating or menopausal. Moreover, at least among natural-fertility cultures that do not practice birth control, continual cycles during peak reproductive years imply to people in those cultures that a woman is sterile. Thus, even though people might not be able to pinpoint ovulation, they can easily identify whether a woman will soon be ready to conceive on the basis of whether she is menstruating. And that leads straight to Strassmann's insightful hypothesis about the role of menstrual taboos: information about menstruation can be a means of tracking paternity.

"There are two important pieces of information for assessing paternity," Strassmann notes: timing of intercourse and timing of menstruation. "By forcing women to signal menstruation, men are trying to gain equal access to one part of that critical information." Such information, she explains, is crucial to Dogon men, because they invest so many resources in their own offspring. Descent is marked through the male line; land and the food that comes from the land is passed down from fathers to sons. Information about paternity is thus crucial to a man's entire lineage. And because each man has as many as four wives, he cannot possibly track them all. So forcing women to signal their menstrual periods, or lack thereof, helps men avoid cuckoldry.

To test her hypothesis, Strassmann tracked residence in the menstrual huts for 736 consecutive days, collecting data on 477 complete cycles. She noted who was at each hut and how long each woman stayed. She also collected urine from ninety-three women over a ten-week period, to check the correlation between residence in the menstrual hut and the fact of menstruation.

The combination of ethnographic records and urinalyses showed that the Dogon women mostly play by the rules. In 86 percent of the hormonally detected menstruations, women went to the hut. Moreover, none of the tested women went to the hut when they were not menstruating. In the remaining 14 percent of the tested menstruations, women stayed home from the hut, in violation of the taboo, but some were near menopause and so not at high risk for pregnancy. More important, none of the women who violated the taboo did it twice in a row. Even they were largely willing to comply.

Thus, Strassmann concluded, the huts do indeed convey a fairly reliable signal, to men and to everyone else, about the status of a woman's fertility. When she leaves the hut, she is considered ready to conceive. When she stops going to the hut, she is evidently pregnant or menopausal. And women of prime reproductive age who visit the hut on a regular basis are clearly infertile.

It also became clear to Strassmann that the Dogon do indeed use that information to make paternity decisions. In several cases a man was forced to marry a pregnant woman, simply because everyone knew that the man had been the woman's first sexual partner after her last visit to the menstrual hut. Strassmann followed one case in which a child was being brought up by a man because he was the mother's first sexual partner after a hut visit, even though the woman soon married a different man. (The woman already knew she was pregnant by the first man at the time of her marriage, and she did not visit the menstrual hut before she married. Thus the truth was obvious to everyone, and the real father took the child.)

In general, women are cooperative players in the game because without a man, a woman has no way to support herself or her children. But women follow the taboo reluctantly. They complain about going to the hut. And if their husbands convert from the traditional religion of the Dogon to a religion that does not impose menstrual taboos, such as Islam or Christianity, the women quickly cease visiting the hut. Not that such a religious conversion quells a man's interest in his wife's fidelity: far from it. But the rules change. Perhaps the sanctions of the new religion against infidelity help keep women faithful, so the men can relax their guard. Or perhaps the men are willing to trade the reproductive advantages of the menstrual taboo for the economic benefits gained by converting to the new religion. Whatever the case, Strassmann found an almost perfect correlation between a husband's religion and his wives' attendance at the hut. In sum, the taboo is established by men, backed by supernatural forces, and internalized and accepted by women until the men release them from the belief.

But beyond the cultural machinations of men and women that Strassmann expected to find, her data show something even more fundamental—and surprising—about female biology. On average, she calculates, a woman in a natural-fertility population such as the Dogon has only about 110 menstrual periods in her lifetime. The rest of the time she will be prepubescent, pregnant, lactating or menopausal. Women in industrialized cultures, by contrast, have more than three times as many cycles: 350 to 400, on average, in a lifetime. They reach menarche (their first menstruation) earlier—at age twelve and a half, compared with the onset age of sixteen in natural-fertility cultures. They have fewer babies, and they lactate hardly at all. All those factors lead women in the industrialized world to a lifetime of nearly continuous menstrual cycling.

The big contrast in cycling profiles during the reproductive years can be traced specifically to lactation. Women in more traditional societies spend most of their reproductive years in lactation amenorrhea, the state in which the hormonal changes required for nursing suppress ovulation and inhibit menstruation. And it is not just that the Dogon bear more children (eight to nine on average); they also nurse each child on demand rather than in scheduled bouts, all through the night as well as the day, and intensely enough that ovulation simply stops for about twenty months per child. Women in industrialized societies typically do not breast-feed as intensely (or at all), and rarely breast-feed each child for as long as the Dogon women do. (The average for American women is four months.)

The Dogon experience with menstruation may be far more typical of the human condition over most of evolutionary history than is the standard menstrual experience in industrialized nations. If so, Strassmann's findings alter some of the most closely held beliefs about female biology. Contrary to what the Western medical establishment might think, it is not particularly "normal" to menstruate each month. The female body, according to Strassmann, is biologically designed to spend much more time in lactation amenorrhea than in menstrual cycling. That in itself suggests that oral contraceptives, which alter hormone levels to suppress ovulation and produce a bleeding, could be forcing a continual state of cycling for which the body is ill-prepared. Women might be better protected against reproductive cancers if their contraceptives mimicked lactation amenorrhea and depressed the female reproductive hormones, rather than forcing the continual ebb and flow of menstrual cycles.

Strassmann's data also call into question a recently popularized idea about menstruation: that regular menstrual cycles might be immunologically beneficial for women. In 1993 the controversial writer Margie Profet, whose ideas about evolutionary and reproductive biology have received vast media attention, proposed in *The Quarterly Review of Biology* that menstruation could have such an adaptive value. She noted that viruses and bacteria regularly enter the female body on the backs of sperm, and she hypothesized that the best way to get them out is to flush them out. Here, then, was a positive, adaptive role for something unpleasant, an evolutionary reason for suffering cramps each month. Menstruation, according to Profet, had evolved to rid the body of pathogens. The "antipathogen" theory was an exciting hypothesis, and it helped win Profet a MacArthur Foundation award. But Strassmann's work soon showed that Profet's ideas could not be supported because of one simple fact: under less-industrialized conditions, women menstruate relatively rarely.

Instead, Strassmann notes, if there is an adaptive value to menstruation, it is ultimately a strategy to conserve the body's resources. She estimates that maintaining the endometrial lining during the second half of the ovarian cycle takes substantial metabolic energy. Once the endometrium is built up and ready to receive a fertilized egg, the tissue requires a sevenfold metabolic increase to remain rich in blood and ready to support a pregnancy. Hence, if no pregnancy is forthcoming, it makes a lot of sense for the body to let part of the endometrium slough off and then regenerate itself, instead of maintaining that rather costly but unneeded tissue. Such energy conservation is common among vertebrates: male rhesus monkeys have shrunken testes during their non-breeding season, Burmese pythons shrink their guts when they are not digesting, and hibernating animals put their metabolisms on hold.

Strassmann also suggests that periodically ridding oneself of the endometrium could make a difference to a woman's long-term survival. Because female reproductive hormones affect the brain and other tissues, the metabolism of the entire body is involved during cycling. Strassmann estimates that by keeping hormonal low through half the cycle, a woman can save about six days' worth of energy for every four nonconceptive cycles. Such caloric conservation might have proved useful to early hominids who lived by hunting and gathering, and even today it might be helpful for women living in less affluent circumstances than the ones common in the industrialized West.

But perhaps the most provocative implications of Strassmann's work have to do with women's health. In 1994 a group of physicians and anthropologists published a paper, also in *The Quarlerly Review of Biology,* suggesting that the reproductive histories and lifestyles of women in industrialized cultures are at odds with women's naturally evolved biology, and that the differences lead to greater risks of reproductive cancers. For example, the investigators estimated that women in affluent cultures may have a hundredfold greater risk of breast cancer than do women who subsist by hunting and gathering. The increased risk is probably caused not only by low levels of exercise and a high-fat diet, but also by a relatively high number of menstrual cycles over a lifetime. Repeated exposure to the hormones of the ovarian cycle—because of early menarche, late menopause, lack of pregnancy and little or no breast-feeding—is implicated in other reproductive cancers as well.

Those of us in industrialized cultures have been running an experiment on ourselves. The body evolved over millions of years to move across the landscape looking for food, to live in small kin-based groups, to make babies at intervals of four years or so and to invest heavily in each child by nursing intensely for years. How many women now follow those traditional patterns? We move little, we rely on others to get our food, and we rarely reproduce or lactate. Those culturally initiated shifts in lifestyles may pose biological risks.

Our task is not to overcome that biology, but to work with it. Now that we have a better idea of how the female body was designed, it may be time to re-work our lifestyles and change some of our expectations. It may be time to borrow from our distant past or from our contemporaries in distant cultures, and treat our bodies more as nature intended.

Review Questions

1. What is the menstrual taboo according to Meredith Small? How is it expressed in many countries of the world?

2. What causes menstruation? How does Small explain its biological function?

3. Small describes a study of the Dogon by Beverly Strassmann. What is Strassmann's theory about the function of the incest taboo in Dogon society? What evidence supports her conclusions?

4. How is the lifetime rate of menstruation among Dogon women different from rates among Western women? What explains the difference?

5. How does a high rate of lifetime menstruation affect Western women's health? How can the Dogon experience inform the way Western women treat their bodies according to Small?

23

Mixed Blood

Jeffrey M. Fish

Many Americans believe that people can be divided into races. For them, races are biologically defined groups. Anthropologists, on the other hand, have long argued that U.S. racial groups are American cultural constructions; they represent the way Americans classify people rather than a genetically determined reality. In this article, Jeffrey Fish demonstrates the cultural basis of race by comparing how races are defined in the United States and Brazil. In America, a person's race is determined not by how he or she looks, but by his or her heritage. A person will be classified as black, for example, if one of his or her parents is classified that way no matter what the person looks like. In Brazil, on the other hand, people are classified into a series of tipos *on the basis of how they look. The same couple may have children classified into three or four different* tipos *based on a number of physical markers such as skin color and nose shape. As a result, Fish's daughter, who has brown skin and whose mother is Brazilian, can change her race from black in the United States to* moreno *(brunette), a category just behind* branca *(blond) in Brazil, by simply taking a plane there.*

Last year my daughter, who had been living in Rio de Janeiro, and her Brazilian boyfriend paid a visit to my cross-cultural psychology class. They had agreed to be interviewed about Brazilian culture. At one point in the interview I asked her, "Are you black?" She said, "Yes." I then asked him the question, and he said "No."

"How can that be?" I asked. "He's darker than she is."

Psychologists have begun talking about race again. They think that it may be useful in explaining the biological bases of behavior. For example, following publication of *The Bell Curve*, there has been renewed debate about whether black–white group differences in scores on IQ tests reflect racial differences in intelligence. (Because this article is about race, it will mainly use racial terms, like black and white, rather than cultural terms, like African-American and European-American.)

The problem with debates like the one over race and IQ is that psychologists on both sides of the controversy make a totally unwarranted assumption: that there is a biological entity called "race." If there were such an entity, then it would at least be possible that differences in behavior between "races" might be biologically based.

Before considering the controversy, however, it is reasonable to step back and ask ourselves "What is race?" If, as happens to be the case, race is not a biologically meaningful concept, then looking for biologically based racial differences in behavior is simply a waste of time.

The question "What is race?" can be divided into two more limited ones. The answers to both questions have long been known by anthropologists, but seem not to have reached other social or behavioral scientists, let alone the public at large. And both answers differ strikingly from what we Americans think of as race.

The first question is "How can we understand the variation in physical appearance among human beings?" It is interesting to discover that Americans (including researchers, who should know better) view only a part of the variation as "racial," while other equally evident variability is not so viewed.

The second question is "How can we understand the kinds of racial classifications applied to differences in physical appearance among human beings?" Surprisingly, different cultures label these physical differences in different ways. Far from describing biological entities, American racial categories are merely one of numerous, very culture-specific schemes for reducing uncertainty about how people should respond to other people. The fact that Americans believe that Asians, blacks, Hispanics, and whites constitute biological entities called races is a matter of cultural interest rather than scientific substance. It tells us something about American culture—but nothing at all about the human species.

The short answer to the question "What is race?" is: There is no such thing. Race is a myth. And our racial classification scheme is loaded with pure fantasy.

Let's start with human physical variation. Human beings are a species, which means that people from anywhere on the planet can mate with others from anywhere else and produce fertile offspring. (Horses and donkeys are two different species because, even though they can mate with each other, their offspring—mules—are sterile.)

Our species evolved in Africa from earlier forms and eventually spread out around the planet. Over time, human populations that were geographically separated from one another came to differ in physical appearance. They came by these differences through three major pathways: mutation, natural selection, and genetic drift. Since genetic mutations occur randomly, different mutations occur and accumulate over time in geographically separated populations. Also, as we have known since Darwin, different geographical environments select for different physical traits that confer a survival advantage. But the largest proportion of variability among populations may well result from purely random factors; this random change in the frequencies of already existing genes is known as genetic drift.

If an earthquake or disease kills off a large segment of a population, those who survive to reproduce are likely to differ from the original population in many ways. Similarly, if a group divides and a subgroup moves away, the two groups will, by chance, differ in the frequency of various genes. Even the mere fact of physical separation will, over time, lead two equivalent populations to differ in the frequency of genes. These randomly acquired population differences will accumulate over successive generations along with any others due to mutation or natural selection.

A number of differences in physical appearance among populations around the globe appear to have adaptive value. For example, people in the tropics of Africa and South America came to have dark skins, presumably, through natural selection, as protection against the sun. In cold areas, like northern Europe or northern North America, which are dark for long periods of time, and where people covered their bodies for warmth, people came to have light skins—light skins make maximum use of sunlight to produce vitamin D.

The indigenous peoples of the New World arrived about 15,000 years ago, during the last ice age, following game across the Bering Strait. (The sea level was low enough to create a land bridge because so much water was in the form of ice.) Thus, the dark-skinned Indians of the South American tropics are descended from light-skinned ancestors, similar in appearance to the Eskimo. In other words, even though skin color is the most salient feature thought by Americans to be an indicator of race—and race is assumed to have great time depth—it is subject to relatively rapid evolutionary change.

Meanwhile, the extra ("epicanthic") fold of eyelid skin, which Americans also view as racial, and which evolved in Asian populations to protect the eye against the cold, continues to exist among South American native peoples because its presence (unlike a light skin) offers no reproductive disadvantage. Hence, skin color and eyelid form, which Americans think of as traits of different races, occur together or separately in different populations.

Like skin color, there are other physical differences that also appear to have evolved through natural selection—but which Americans do not think of as racial. Take, for example, body shape. Some populations in very cold climates, like the Eskimo, developed rounded bodies. This is because the more spherical an object is, the less surface area it has to radiate heat. In contrast, some populations in very hot climates, like the Masai, developed lanky bodies. Like the tubular pipes of an old-fashioned radiator, the high ratio of surface area to volume allows people to radiate a lot of heat.

In terms of American's way of thinking about race, lanky people and rounded people are simply two kinds of whites or blacks. But it is equally reasonable to view light-skinned people and dark-skinned people as two kinds of "lankys" or "roundeds." In other words, our categories for racial classification of people arbitrarily include certain dimensions (light versus dark skin) and exclude others (rounded versus elongated bodies).

There is no biological basis for classifying race according to skin color instead of body form—or according to any other variable, for that matter. All that exists is variability in what people look like—and the arbitrary and culturally specific ways different societies classify that variability. There is nothing left over that can be called race. This is why race is a myth.

Skin color and body form do not vary together: Not all dark-skinned people are lanky; similarly, light-skinned people may be lanky or rounded. The same can be said of the facial features Americans think of as racial—eye color, nose width (actually, the ratio of width to length), lip thickness ("evertedness"), hair form, and hair color. They do not vary together either. If they did, then a "totally white" person would have very light skin color, straight blond hair, blue eyes, a narrow nose, and thin lips; a "totally black" person would have very dark skin color, black tight curly hair, dark brown eyes, a broad nose, and thick lips; those in between would have—to a correlated degree—wavy light brown hair, light brown eyes, and intermediate nose and lip forms.

While people of mixed European and African ancestry who look like this do exist, they are the exception rather than the rule. Anyone who wants to can make up a chart of facial features (choose a location with a diverse population, say, the New York City subway) and verify that there are people with all possible admixtures of facial features. One might see someone with tight curly blond hair, light skin, blue eyes, broad nose, and thick lips—whose features are half "black" and half "white." That is, each of the person's facial features occupies one end or the other of a supposedly racial continuum, with no intermediary forms (like wavy light brown hair). Such people are living proof that supposedly racial features do not vary together.

Since the human species has spent most of its existence in Africa, different populations in Africa have been separated from each other longer than East Asians or Northern Europeans have been separated from each other or from Africans. As a result, there is remarkable physical variation among the peoples of Africa, which goes unrecognized by Americans who view them all as belonging to the same race.

In contrast to the very tall Masai, the diminutive stature of the very short Pygmies may have evolved as an advantage in moving rapidly through tangled forest vegetation. The Bushmen of the Kalahari desert have very large ("steatopygous") buttocks, presumably to store body fat in one place for times of food scarcity, while leaving the rest of the body uninsulated to radiate heat. They also have "peppercorn" hair. Hair in separated tufts, like tight curly hair, leaves space to radiate the heat that rises through the body to the scalp; straight hair lies flat and holds in body heat, like a cap. By viewing Africans as constituting a single race, Americans ignore their greater physical variability, while assigning racial significance to lesser differences between them.

Although it is true that most inhabitants of northern Europe, east Asia, and central Africa look like Americans' conceptions of one or another of the three purported races, most inhabitants of south Asia, southwest Asia, north Africa, and the Pacific islands do not. Thus, the 19th century view of the human species as comprised of Caucasoid, Mongoloid, and Negroid races, still held by many Americans, is based on a partial and unrepresentative view of human variability. In other words, what is now known about human physical variation does not correspond to what Americans think of as race.

In contrast to the question of the actual physical variation among human beings, there is the question of how people classify that variation. Scientists classify things in scientific taxonomies—chemists' periodic table of the elements, biologists' classification of life forms into kingdoms, phyla, and so forth.

In every culture, people also classify things along culture-specific dimensions of meaning. For example, paper clips and staples are understood by Americans as paper fasteners, and nails are not, even though, in terms of their physical properties, all three consist of differently shaped pieces of metal wire. The physical variation in pieces of metal wire can be seen as analogous to human physical variation; and the categories of cultural meaning, like paper fasteners versus wood fasteners, can be seen as analogous to races. Anthropologists refer to these kinds of classifications as folk taxonomies.

Consider the avocado—is it a fruit or a vegetable? Americans insist it is a vegetable. We eat it in salads with oil and vinegar. Brazilians, on the other hand, would say it is a fruit. They eat it for dessert with lemon juice and sugar.

How can we explain this difference in classification?

The avocado is an edible plant, and the American and Brazilian folk taxonomies, while containing cognate terms, classify some edible plants differently. The avocado does not change. It is the same biological entity, but its folk classification changes, depending on who's doing the classifying.

Human beings are also biological entities. Just as we can ask if an avocado is a fruit or a vegetable, we can ask if a person is white or black. And when we ask race questions, the answers we get come from folk taxonomies, not scientific ones. Terms like "white" or "black" applied to people—or "vegetable" or "fruit" applied to avocados—do not give us biological information about people or avocados. Rather, they exemplify how cultural groups (Brazilians or Americans) classify people and avocados.

Americans believe in "blood," a folk term for the quality presumed to be carried by members of so-called races. And the way offspring—regardless of their physical appearance—always inherit the less prestigious racial category of mixed parentage is called "hypo-descent" by anthropologists. A sentence thoroughly intelligible to most Americans might be, "Since Mary's father is white and her mother is black, Mary is black because she has black 'blood.'" American researchers who think they are studying racial differences in behavior would, like other Americans, classify Mary as black—although she has just as much white "blood."

According to hypo-descent, the various purported racial categories are arranged in a hierarchy along a single dimension, from the most prestigious ("white"), through intermediary forms ("Asian"), to the least prestigious ("black"). And when a couple come from two different categories, all their children (the "descent" in "hypo-descent") are classified as belonging to the less prestigious category (thus, the "hypo"). Hence, all the offspring of one "white" parent and one "black" parent—regardless of the children's physical appearance—are called "black" in the United States.

The American folk concept of "blood" does not behave like genes. Genes are units which cannot be subdivided. When several genes jointly determine a trait, chance decides which ones come from each parent. For example, if eight genes determine a trait, a child gets four from each parent. If a mother and a father each have the hypothetical genes BBBBWWWW, then a child could be born with any combination of B and W genes, from BBBBBBBB to WWWWWWWW. In contrast, the folk concept "blood" behaves like a uniform and continuous entity. It can be divided in two indefinitely—for example, quadroons and octoroons are said to be people who have one-quarter and one-eighth black "blood," respectively. Oddly, because of hypo-descent, Americans consider people with one-eighth black "blood" to be black rather than white, despite their having seven-eighths white "blood."

Hypo-descent, or "blood," is not informative about the physical appearance of people. For example, when two parents called black in the United States have a number of children, the children are likely to vary in physical appearance. In the case of skin color, they might vary from lighter than the lighter parent to darker than the darker parent. However, they would all receive the same racial classification—black—regardless of their skin color.

All that hypo-descent tells you is that, when someone is classified as something other than white (e.g., Asian), at least one of his or her parents is classified in the same way, and that neither parent has a less prestigious classification (e.g., black). That is, hypo-descent is informative about ancestry—specifically, parental classification—rather than physical appearance.

There are many strange consequences of our folk taxonomy. For example, someone who inherited no genes that produce "African"-appearing physical features would still be considered black if he or she has a parent classified as black. The category "passing for white" includes many such people. Americans have the curious belief that people who look white but have a parent classified as black are "really" black in some biological sense, and are being deceptive if they present themselves as white. Such examples make it clear that race is a social rather than a physical classification.

From infancy, human beings learn to recognize very subtle differences in the faces of those around them. Black babies see a wider variety of black faces than white faces, and white babies see a wider variety of white faces than black faces. Because they are exposed only to a limited range of human variation, adult members of each "race" come to see their own group as containing much wider variation than others. Thus, because of this perceptual learning, blacks see greater physical variation among themselves than among whites, while whites see the opposite. In this case, however, there is a clear answer to the question of which group contains greater physical variability. Blacks are correct.

Why is this the case?

Take a moment. Think of yourself as an amateur anthropologist and try to step out of American culture, however briefly.

It is often difficult to get white people to accept what at first appears to contradict the evidence they can see clearly with their own eyes—but which is really the result of a history of perceptual learning. However, the reason that blacks view themselves as more varied is not that their vision is more accurate. Rather, it is that blacks too have a long—but different—history of perceptual learning from that of whites (and also that they have been observers of a larger range of human variation).

The fact of greater physical variation among blacks than whites in America goes back to the principle of hypo-descent, which classifies all people with one black parent and one white parent as black. If they were all considered white, then there would be more physical variation among whites. Someone with one-eighth white "blood" and seven-eighths black "blood" would be considered white; anyone with any white ancestry would be considered white. In other words, what appears to be a difference in biological variability is really a difference in cultural classification.

Perhaps the clearest way to understand that the American folk taxonomy of race is merely one of many—arbitrary and unscientific like all the others—is to contrast it with a very different one, that of Brazil. The Portuguese word that in the Brazilian folk taxonomy corresponds to the American "race" is "*tipo.*" *Tipo*, a cognate of the English word "type," is a descriptive term that serves as a kind of shorthand for a series of physical features. Because people's physical features vary separately from one another, there are an awful lot of tipos in Brazil.

Since tipos are descriptive terms, they vary regionally in Brazil—in part reflecting regional differences in the development of colloquial Portuguese, but in part because the physical variation they describe is different in different regions. The Brazilian situation is so complex I will limit my delineation of tipos to some of the main ones used in the city of Salvador, Bahia, to describe people whose physical appearance is understood to be made up of African and European features. (I will use the female terms throughout; in nearly all cases the male term simply changes the last letter from *a* to *o*.)

Proceeding along a dimension from the "whitest" to the "blackest" tipos, a *loura* is whiter-than-white, with straight blond hair, blue or green eyes, light skin color, narrow nose, and thin lips. Brazilians who come to the United States think that a *loura* means a "blond" and are surprised to find that the American term refers to hair color only. A *branca* has light skin color, eyes of any color, hair of any color or form except tight curly, a nose that is not broad, and lips that are not thick. *Branca* translates as "white," though Brazilians of this tipo who come to the United States—especially those from elite families—are often dismayed to find that they are not considered white here, and, even worse, are viewed as Hispanic despite the fact that they speak Portuguese.

A *morena* has brown or black hair that is wavy or curly but not tight curly, tan skin, a nose that is not narrow, and lips that are not thin. Brazilians who come to the United States think that a *morena* is a "brunette," and are surprised to find that brunettes are considered white but *morenas* are not. Americans have difficulty classifying *morenas,* many of whom are of Latin American origin: Are they black or Hispanic? (One might also observe that *morenas* have trouble with Americans, for not just accepting their appearance as a given, but asking instead "Where do you come from?" "What language did you speak at home?" "What was your maiden name?" or even, more crudely, "What *are* you?")

A *mulata* looks like a *morena,* except with tight curly hair and a slightly darker range of hair colors and skin colors. A *preta* looks like a *mulata,* except with dark brown skin, broad nose, and thick lips. To Americans, *mulatas* and *pretas* are both black, and if forced to distinguish between them would refer to them as light-skinned blacks and dark-skinned blacks, respectively.

If Brazilians were forced to divide the range of tipos, from *loura* to *preta,* into "kinds of whites" and "kinds of blacks" (a distinction they do not ordinarily make), they would draw the line between *morenas* and *mulatas;* whereas Americans, if offered only visual information, would draw the line between *brancas* and *morenas.*

The proliferation of tipos, and the difference in the white–black dividing line, do not, however, exhaust the differences between Brazilian and American folk taxonomies. There are tipos in the Afro-European domain that are considered to be neither black nor white—an idea that is difficult for Americans visiting Brazil to comprehend. A person with tight curly blond (or red) hair, light skin, blue (or green) eyes, broad nose, and thick lips, is a *sarará.* The opposite features—straight black hair, dark skin, brown eyes, narrow nose, and thin lips—are those of a *cabo verde.* *Sarará* and *cabo verde* are both tipos that are considered by Brazilians in Salvador, Bahia, to be neither black nor white.

When I interviewed my American daughter and her Brazilian boyfriend, she said she was black because her mother is black (even though I am white). That is, from her American perspective, she has "black blood"—though she is a *morena* in Brazil. Her boyfriend said that he was not black because, viewing himself in terms of Brazilian tipos, he is a *mulato* (not a *preto*).

There are many differences between the Brazilian and American folk tax-onomies of race. The American system tells you about how people's parents are classified but not what they look like. The Brazilian system tells you what they look like but not about their parents. When two parents of intermediate ap-pearance have many children in the United States, the children are all of one race; in Brazil they are of many tipos.

Americans believe that race is an immutable biological given, but people (like my daughter and her boyfriend) can change their race by getting on a plane and going from the United States to Brazil—just as, if they take an avo-cado with them, it changes from a vegetable into a fruit. In both cases, what changes is not the physical appearance of the person or avocado, but the way they are classified.

I have focused on the Brazilian system to make clear how profoundly folk taxonomies of race vary from one place to another. But the Brazilian system is just one of many. Haiti's folk taxonomy, for example, includes elements of both ancestry and physical appearance, and even includes the amazing term (for for-eigners of African appearance) *un blanc noir*—literally, "a black white." In the classic study *Patterns of Race in the Americas,* anthropologist Marvin Harris gives a good introduction to the ways in which the conquests by differing Eu-ropean powers of differing New World peoples and ecologies combined with differing patterns of slavery to produce a variety of folk taxonomies. Folk tax-onomies of race can be found in many—though by no means all—cultures in other parts of the world as well.

The American concept of race does not correspond to the ways in which human physical appearance varies. Further, the American view of race ("hypo-descent") is just one among many folk taxonomies, [none] of which correspond to the facts of human physical variation. This is why race is a myth and why races as con-ceived by Americans (and others) do not exist. It is also why differences in be-havior between "races" cannot be explained by biological differences between them.

When examining the origins of IQ scores (or other behavior), psycholo-gists sometimes use the term "heritability"—a statistical concept that is not based on observations of genes or chromosomes. It is important to understand that questions about heritability of IQ have nothing to do with racial differences in IQ. "Heritability" refers only to the relative ranking of individuals *within* a population, under given environmental conditions, and not to differences *be-tween* populations. Thus, among the population of American whites, it may be that those with high IQs tend to have higher-IQ children than do those with low IQs. Similarly, among American blacks, it may be that those with high IQs also tend to have higher-IQ children.

In both cases, it is possible that the link between the IQs of parents and chil-dren may exist for reasons that are not entirely environmental. This heritability of IQ *within* the two populations, even if it exists, would in no way contradict the average social advantages of American whites as a group compared to the average social disadvantages of American blacks as a group. Such differences in social environments can easily account for any differences in the average test scores *between* the two groups. Thus, the heritability of IQ *within* each group is irrelevant to understanding differences *between* the groups.

Beyond this, though, studies of differences in behavior between "populations" of whites and blacks, which seek to find biological causes rather than only social ones, make a serious logical error. They assume that blacks and whites are populations in some biological sense, as sub-units of the human species. (Most likely, the researchers make this assumption because they are American and approach race in terms of the American folk taxonomy.)

In fact, though, the groups are sorted by a purely social rule for statistical purposes. This can easily be demonstrated by asking researchers how they know that the white subjects are really white and the black subjects are really black. There is no biological answer to this question, because race as a biological category does not exist. All that researchers can say is, "The tester classified them based on their physical appearance," or "Their school records listed their race," or otherwise give a social rather than biological answer.

So when American researchers study racial differences in behavior, in search of biological rather than social causes for differences between socially defined groups, they are wasting their time. Computers are wonderful machines, but we have learned about "garbage in/garbage out." Applying complex computations to bad data yields worthless results. In the same way, the most elegant experimental designs and statistical analyses, applied flawlessly to biologically meaningless racial categories, can only produce a very expensive waste of time.

As immigrants of varied physical appearance come to the United States from countries with racial folk taxonomies different from our own, they are often perplexed and dismayed to find that the ways they classify themselves and others are irrelevant to the American reality. Brazilians, Haitians, and others may find themselves labeled by strange, apparently inappropriate, even pejorative terms, and grouped together with people who are different from and unreceptive to them. This can cause psychological complications (a Brazilian immigrant—who views himself as white—being treated by an American therapist who assumes that he is not).

Immigration has increased, especially from geographical regions whose people do not resemble American images of blacks, whites, or Asians. Intermarriage is also increasing, as the stigma associated with it diminishes. These two trends are augmenting the physical diversity among those who marry each other—and, as a result, among their children. The American folk taxonomy of race (purportedly comprised of stable biological entities) is beginning to change to accommodate this new reality. After all, what race is someone whose four grandparents are black, white, Asian, and Hispanic?

Currently, the most rapidly growing census category is "Other," as increasing numbers of people fail to fit available options. Changes in the census categories every 10 years reflect the government's attempts to grapple with the changing self-identifications of Americans—even as statisticians try to maintain the same categories over time in order to make demographic comparisons. Perhaps they will invent one or more "multiracial" categories, to accommodate the wide range of people whose existence defies current classification. Perhaps they will drop the term "race" altogether. Already some institutions are including an option to "check as many as apply," when asking individuals to classify themselves on a list of racial and ethnic terms.

Thinking in terms of physical appearance and folk taxonomies helps to clarify the emotionally charged but confused topics of race. Understanding that different cultures have different folk taxonomies suggests that we respond to the question "What race is that person?" not by "Black" or "White," but by "Where?" and "When?"

Review Questions

1. What is Jeffrey Fish's main point about the way Americans define race?

2. What is the difference between the way race is defined in the United States and in Brazil? List the Brazilian folk taxonomy of *tipos* and how to translate *tipos* into U.S. racial categories.

3. What evidence challenges the view that races are biologically defined types? What evidence would have to exist to prove that the human species is genetically divided into races?

4. Why does Fish feel it is important to understand that race as Americans define it does not represent a biological reality?

SEVEN

Law and Politics

Ideally, culture provides the blueprint for a smoothly oiled social machine whose parts work together under all circumstances. But human society is not like a rigidly constructed machine. It is made of individuals who have their own special needs and desires. Personal interest, competition for scarce resources, and simple accident can cause nonconformity and disputes, resulting in serious disorganization.

One way we manage social disruption is through the socialization of children. As we acquire our culture, we learn the appropriate ways to look at experience, to define our existence, and to feel about life. Each system of cultural knowledge contains implicit values of what is desirable, and we come to share these values with other people. Slowly, with the acquisition of culture, most people find they *want* to do what they *must* do; the requirements of an orderly social life become personal goals.

Enculturation, however, is rarely enough. Disputes among individuals regularly occur in all societies, and how such disagreements are handled defines what anthropologists mean by the legal system. Some disputes are **infralegal;** they never reach a point where they are settled by individuals with special authority. Neighbors, for example, would engage in an infralegal dispute if they argued over who should pay for the damage caused by water that runs off one's land into the other's basement. So long as they don't take the matter to court or resort to violence, the dispute will remain infralegal. This dispute may become **extra-legal,** however, if it occurs outside the law and escalates into violence. Had the neighbors come to blows over the waterlogged basement, the dispute would have become extralegal. Feuds and wars are the best examples of this kind of dispute.

Legal disputes, on the other hand, involve socially approved mechanisms for their settlement. **Law** is the cultural knowledge that people use to settle disputes by means of agents who have the recognized authority to do so. Thus if the argument between neighbors cited previously ended up in court before a judge or referee, it would have become legal.

Although Americans often think of courts as synonymous with the legal system, societies have evolved a variety of structures for settling disputes. For example, some disputes may be settled by **self-redress,** meaning that wronged individuals are given the right to settle matters themselves. **Contests** requiring physical or mental combat between disputants may also be used to settle disputes. A trusted third party, or **go-between,** may be asked to negotiate with each side until a settlement is achieved. In some societies, supernatural power or beings may be used. In parts of India, for example, disputants are asked to take an oath in the name of a powerful deity or (at least in the past) to submit to a supernaturally controlled, painful, or physically dangerous test called an **ordeal.** Disputes may also be taken to a **moot,** an informal community meeting where conflict may be aired. At the moot, talk continues until a settlement is reached. Finally, disputes are often taken to **courts,** which are formally organized and include officials with authority to make and enforce decisions.

Political systems are closely related to legal ones and often involve some of the same offices and actors. The **political system** contains the process for making and carrying out public policy according to cultural categories and rules; **policy** refers to guidelines for action. The **public** are the people affected by the policy. Every society must make decisions that affect all or most of its members. The Mbuti Pygmies of the Ituri Forest described by anthropologist Colin Turnbull, for example, occasionally decide to conduct a communal hunt. Hunters set their nets together and wait for the appearance of forest game. Men, women, and children must work together as beaters to drive the animals toward the nets. When the Mbuti decide to hold a hunt, they make a political decision.

The political process requires that people make and abide by a particular policy, often in the face of competing plans. To do so a policy must have **support,** which is anything that contributes to its adoption and enforcement. Anthropologists recognize two main kinds of support: legitimacy and coercion. **Legitimacy** refers to people's positive evaluation of public officials and public policy. A college faculty, for example, may decide to institute the quarter system because a majority feel that quarters rather than semesters represent the "right length" for courses. Theirs is a positive evaluation of the policy. Some faculty members will oppose the change but will abide by the decision because they value the authority of faculty governance. For them the decision, although unfortunate, is legitimate.

Coercion, on the other hand, is support derived from the threat or use of force or the promise of short-term gain. Had the faculty members adopted the quarter system because they had been threatened with termination by the administration, they would have acted under coercion.

There are also other important aspects of the political process. Some members of a society may be given **authority,** the right to make and enforce public policy. In our country, elected officials are given authority to make certain decisions and exercise particular powers. However, formal political offices with authority do not occur in every society. Most hunting and gathering societies lack such positions, as do many horticulturalists. **Leadership,** which is the ability to influence others to act, must be exercised informally in these societies.

In the first article, Anne Sutherland describes what happens when the substantive laws of two culturally different groups collide in court. A young Gypsy man is convicted of using another family member's social security number although he has no intention to defraud anyone. The second article, by Barbara Joans, describes how an academic anthropologist was able to use her broad training as an expert witness in three court cases. The article illustrates the unique legal contribution anthropology can make in our increasingly multicultural society. The third selection, by Marvin Harris, traces the development of political leadership. He argues that small groups characterized by reciprocal exchange have no recognizable political officers and that many horticultural societies with redistributive economic exchange may develop "big men" who lead by example but still have no formal authority.

Key Terms

authority   *p. 262*
coercion   *p. 262*
contest   *p. 262*
court   *p. 262*
extralegal   *p. 261*
go-between   *p. 262*
infralegal   *p. 261*
law   *p. 261*
leadership   *p. 262*

legitimacy   *p. 262*
moot   *p. 262*
ordeal   *p. 262*
policy   *p. 262*
political system   *p. 262*
public   *p. 262*
self-redress   *p. 262*
support   *p. 262*

24

Cross-Cultural Law: The Case of the Gypsy Offender

Anne Sutherland

Every society recognizes a list of legal statutes, which anthropologists call substantive law, that define right from wrong. In the United States, for example, it is against the law for an individual to marry more than one person at a time. But what is proper in one country may be a crime in another. Unlike the United States, for example, in Iran it is legal for a person to be married simultaneously to more than one person. So what happens when members of one society live within and under the legal jurisdiction of another? This is the question explored by Anne Sutherland in this article on the legal plight of a young Gypsy man who is arrested for using the social security number of a relative on a car loan application. Despite the claim that using different identities of family members is a common Gypsy practice designed to hide their identities, and that he had no intention to defraud anyone by doing so, the young man receives a six-month jail term.

It is often the case that a law made for one set of purposes has another, unintended impact on a particular group. A recent law making the use of a false social security number a federal felony is intended to help prosecution of major drug crime syndicates, but it has a special impact on Gypsies in the United States. Gypsies, traditionally a nomadic people, frequently borrow each others' "American" names and social security numbers, viewing them as a kind of corporate property of their kin group or *vitsa*. They also often lack birth certificates and must obtain midwife or baptismal certificates to use for identification purposes when they try to obtain credit, enter school, or apply for welfare.

In this article, I shall examine the case of a nineteen-year-old Gypsy man who was convicted under the new social security law and served six months in jail. Arguments for the defense in the case followed three lines of reasoning: 1) that this law unfairly singled out Gypsies for punishment; 2) that there was no intent to commit a crime; and 3) that in using the social security numbers of relatives, Gypsies were following a time-honored tradition to remain anonymous and separate from non-Gypsy society.

Facts of the Case

In the fall of 1991 in St. Paul, Minnesota, a nineteen-year-old Gypsy man was convicted of the crime of using his five-year-old nephew's social security number to obtain credit to purchase a car. When the purchase was questioned by the car dealership, he returned the car and was arrested on a felony charge of using a false social security number. After he was arrested, police searched the apartment where he was staying. They found lists of names, addresses and social security numbers, leading them to suspect an organized crime ring.

In *The United States of America v. S.N.*,[1] it was "alleged that the defendant, S.N., while in the process of obtaining a new Ford Mustang from a car dealership, used a social security number that was not his own with intent to deceive." Under the statute 42 U.S.C. 408 (g)(2), a person who, with intent to deceive, falsely represents his or her number to obtain something of value or for any other purpose, is a felon.

In Mr. S.N.'s case there is no specific allegation that he intended to deprive another person permanently of property because the focus of the charging statute is false representation of numbers. The underlying purpose which motivates a person to falsely represent his or her number may be an essentially innocent purpose, but the statute, at least as it has been interpreted, does not appear to impose a burden of proof as to wrongful purpose.

The statute punishes the means (false number) which a person may employ to achieve any number of ends and it punishes those means as a felony.

---

[1]*United States v. Sonny Nicholas*, U.S. District Court, State of Minnesota, CR 4-91-137 (1991). Quotes from Philip Leavenworth, memorandum in support of a motion to declare 42 U.S.C.408(g)(2) unconstitutional.

The lawyer for the defense argued that the statute's failure to address the nature of the purpose to which false credentials are used is a serious flaw in the law and may punish those who would use the number for petty misconduct as felons. He also argued that there is a potential for discriminatory impact on Gypsies who use false credentials to conceal themselves from mainstream society. A Gypsy household may obtain a telephone by providing a false social security number and even if they pay the telephone bill without fail for years, they are felons under this law. S.N. not only made the payments for his car, but he returned it when the number was questioned. He is still a felon under this law.

The defense lawyer argued that the law is objectionable for two reasons. First, the law's disproportionate impact on the Gypsies is objectionable under the equal protection guaranteed in the Fifth Amendment of the U.S. Constitution. He argued that the law denies Gypsies equal protection of the law by irrationally and disproportionately punishing at the felony level certain traditional Gypsy actions which cause no positive injury to anyone. As evidence he used material from my book, *Gypsies: The Hidden Americans,* for testimony that Gypsies routinely use false social security numbers to acquire credit but do pay their bills and are available for repossession in case of default of payment. They get phone service, buy houses and cars and other household items on credit and have a record of payment that is probably better than the general population (*United States v. S.N., 1991*). They do this primarily to remain unknown by mainstream society rather than to cause loss or injury to any person.

Second, as the defense lawyer pointed out, there is a Supreme Court decision that requires the government to prove felonious intent when it seeks to punish a person for wrongful acquisition of another's property. S.N. maintained that he used a false social security number because of a Gypsy tradition to remain anonymous and because his own number had been used by other Gypsies. The government argued that there was a "ring" of Gypsies in the area where S.N. was living. At S.N.'s residence a number of false credentials and social security numbers were found which had been used to obtain cars illegally. Some of these cars are still missing. In other words, there was evidence that false identity had been used recently in the area to steal. In this case, however, S.N. had not stolen anything and was not being accused of stealing, but only of using a false social security number.

Because of the evidence of a ring of car thieves in the area, the prosecution hoped to use the threat of prosecution against S.N., the only Gypsy they had been able to arrest, to plea bargain for information regarding the other people involved in the alleged ring. These other people had disappeared immediately as soon as S.N. was arrested.

One of the problems in the case was that both the prosecution and even the defense had difficulty obtaining complete and accurate information on S.N. For example, they had difficulty determining his "real" name, a moot point for the Gypsies since they have a practice of using many "American" names although they only have one "Gypsy" name (*nav romano*). The Gypsy name of *o Spiro le Stevanosko* (or Spiro the son of Stevan) uses the noun declension characteristic of the Sanskrit-rooted Rom language and is not immediately translatable into English since it does not employ a surname. Spiro's identity can be pinned down by finding out what *vitsa* (a cognatic descent group) he belongs to so that he will not be confused with any other Spiro le Stevanoskos. The Spiro of our example is a *Kashtare* which is part of a larger "nation" of Gypsies or *natsia* called *Kalderasha* (coppersmith). For his "American" names he may take any of a number used by his relatives such as Spiro Costello, John Costello, John Marks, John Miller, Spiro John or Spiro Miller. His nickname is Rattlesnake Pete.

The Anthropologist as Cultural Broker

S.N.'s defense attorney contacted me after finding that he was less confused about S.N. after reading my book about Gypsies. He sought my help in determining whether S.N. was a Gypsy, what his name was, and any other cultural information (such as the use of social security numbers by Gypsies) that would help him with his case.

Consequently, one cold autumn day I drove to the federal holding prison, one and a half hours from the city, and met S.N. He was a thin young man, perpetually fearful of pollution from contact with non-Gypsies and suffering from the effects of several months of what for him was solitary confinement since he had not seen any of his people since being incarcerated. The telephone was his only link with people to whom he could relate, people from his own culture who spoke his language. His main contact was with a non-Gypsy woman who lived with one of his relatives. She was his link with the world he had known and the only "American" household he had been in before prison. Since my primary task was to determine if he was a Gypsy, first I talked to him about his relatives in Los Angeles and his *vitsa* (Yowane) and tried to establish what section of the *vitsa* I personally knew. This exchange of information about *vitsa* and Gypsies of mutual acquaintance is a normal one between Gypsies. The purpose was to establish a link between us.

Then I asked him about why he was in Minnesota. He talked about a seasonal expedition he and his brothers and cousins make to Minnesota to buy and sell cars and fix fenders before winter sets in. He claimed not to know where his brothers and cousins had gone or how he got into his present predicament.

For S.N., the most immediately effective action I could take was to see that he got the food he needed to stay "clean" in jail. When I met him he had lost fifteen pounds and was suffering demonstrable distress and nervousness. He was upset at being cut off from his culture and people for the first time in his life. In addition, he was distressed at being incarcerated and fearful for his safety. More importantly, he was worried he would become defiled or *marime*. A major concern of his was that if he ate food prepared by non-Gypsies who did not follow rules of cleanliness considered essential in the Gypsy culture, he would become *marime*, a condition of ritual impurity that would result in his being shunned by his relatives and other Gypsies. To protect himself, he avoided eating prison food in the hopes that when he was released from prison he would be able to return to his family without a period of physical exile, also called *marime* (or "rejected" as the Gypsies translate it into English). I arranged for his lawyer to provide him with money to buy food from the concession because it is packaged and untouched by non-Gypsies and therefore considered clean by Gypsy standards. He bought milk in cartons, candy bars and soft drinks and other packaged foods that, though they may lack in nutrition, at least were not defiling and kept him from starvation.

A further complicating factor for S.N. was that he spoke English as a second language. He had only a rudimentary ability to read, thus straining his grasp of his defense. And his only contact with relatives was by telephone since neither he nor they could write with any ease. Even though his limited English made it difficult for him to follow his own trial, the court did not provide a translator.

The Trial

The trial was held in Federal Court and centered around the constitutionality of a law that unfairly targets a particular ethnic group and the question of intent to commit a crime. My testimony was intended to establish that Gypsies may use false identification for a number of cultural reasons which may have no connection to any intent to commit a crime. For a traditionally nomadic group with pariah status in the wider society and a pattern of secretiveness and autonomy, concealing identity is a long-established pattern.

This pattern is widespread in all Gypsy groups in Eastern Europe, Western Europe, Russia, Latin America and the United States. It is a mechanism they have developed over centuries to protect themselves from a wider society that has persecuted them or driven them away. The recent case of the German government paying large sums to Romania to take back Gypsy refugees is only the latest in a historically established tradition of discrimination against Gypsies. The persecution of Gypsies in the Holocaust, in medieval Europe and in the early part of the 20th century in the United States has been well documented. Current events in Eastern Europe have shown a resurgence of extreme prejudice against Gypsies. Interviews in recent *New York Times* articles have pointed to a hatred of Gypsies so deep that there is talk of extermination.[2] Because of the history of violence against them, Gypsies have developed elaborate mechanisms of secrecy and have hidden their identity in order to survive. It will not be easy to get them to change this pattern that has stood them in good stead for so many centuries.

The purpose of my testimony was to establish that S.N. *was* a Gypsy and that Gypsies often use false identification without intent to defraud. They do

---

[2]See *New York Times*, November 17 and 28, 1993, for recent accounts of extreme prejudice against Gypsies.

so because as members of a *vitsa,* or cognatic descent group, identification is corporate in nature. Members of the group have corporate access to property owned by other members of the group. That property includes forms of identification.

An additional problem in the S.N. case was the question of identification from photographs. Here we encountered the age-old problem that members of one culture and race have trouble identifying individuals from another culture and race. In simple terms, to many non-Gypsies, all Gypsies look alike. Part of the case involved clearing up erroneous identification of S.N. in photos provided by the prosecution.

I was also asked to testify on my own personal experience with discrimination against Gypsies by the Minneapolis Police Department. One instance of discrimination I related to the court occurred during a talk I gave to some twenty police officers to help them understand Gypsy culture. When I had spoken about the strong sense of family and community among the Gypsies and how much they value their children, a police officer suggested that since the main problem law enforcement officers have is how to detain the Gypsies long enough to prosecute them, removing Gypsy children from their homes on any pretext would be an effective way to keep the parents in town.

Prejudice against Gypsies often goes unrecognized even by culturally and racially sensitive people. The assistant district attorney prosecuting S.N. offered me an article that he used to understand the Gypsies, entitled "Gypsies, the People and their Criminal Propensity,"[3] which quotes extensively from my work, including the fact that Gypsies have several names and that the same or similar non-Gypsy names are used over and over. The article concentrates on "criminal" behavior and never mentions the possibility that there are Gypsies who may not engage in criminal activities. In one section, quotations from my book on the ways Gypsies deal with the welfare bureaucracy were placed under the title, "Welfare Fraud," although by far most of the practices I described were legal. These concluding words in Part II are representative of the tone of the article:

> Officers should not be misled into thinking these people are not organized. They are indeed organized and operate under established rules of behavior, including those that govern marriage, living quarters, child rearing, the division of money and participation in criminal acts.

The implication of such statements is inflammatory. Gypsies have a culture, history, language and social structure, but that fact is distorted to imply that their social organization is partly for the purpose of facilitating criminal behavior. Their culture is viewed as a criminal culture. Gypsies have been fighting this view for hundreds of years. It is the view that they still combat in their relations

---

[3]Terry Getsay, *Kansas State FOP Journal,* Parts I, II, and III (1982): 18–30.

with law enforcement and the criminal justice system. It is the view that was promoted by the prosecution in this case.

In spite of the best efforts of S.N.'s attorney and my testimony that use of a false social security number did not necessarily indicate intent to commit a crime, he was convicted of illegally using a social security number and served about six months in jail.

Conclusions: Anthropology and Cultural Differences in the Courtroom

Anthropologists are often called in as expert witnesses in cases involving cultural difference. Most Native American legal cases, such as the *Mashpee* case reported by James Clifford,[4] center around Indian status, treaties and land rights. In St. Paul, a number of Hmong legal cases highlighted the conflict between traditional marriage (specifically, the age at which children may marry) and the legal status of minors in American law. With the Gypsies, there is yet another set of cultural issues in their contact with American law.

First is the question of the cultural conflict between a historically nomadic group and the state bureaucracy of settled people. Identification—a serious legal issue in a bureaucratic society composed of people with fixed abodes and a written language—has virtually no meaning for the nomadic Gypsies who consider descent and extended family ties the defining factor for identification.

Second is the conflict between Gypsy religious rules regarding ritual pollution and prison regulations. The Gypsies avoid situations, such as a job or jail, that require them to be in prolonged contact with non-Gypsies. Jail presents special problems because the Gypsies can become *marime*, that is, defiled by unclean food and living conditions. The psychological trauma that results from isolation from their community is compounded if they then emerge from jail and have to undergo a further isolation from relatives because of becoming *marime* in jail.

Finally, this case illustrates a cultural clash between the Rom Gypsy value on corporate kinship and the American value on individual rights. The rights and status of an individual Rom Gypsy is directly linked to his or her membership in the *vitsa*. Furthermore, the status of all members of the *vitsa* is affected by the behavior of each individual *vitsa* member. Since they are so intricately linked, reciprocity between *vitsi* members is expected. Members of a *vitsa* and family share economic resources, stay in each other's homes, help each other in work and preparation of rituals, loan each other cars, information, identification, and money. They also share the shame of immoral or incorrect behavior by one member and the stigma (*marime*) attached to going to jail. For the Gypsies, the American ideal of each individual having only one name, one social

---

[4]"Identity in Mashpee," in *The Predicament of Culture* (Cambridge: Harvard University Press, 1988), pp. 277–346.

security number, or a reputation based entirely on their own behavior is contrary to their experience and culture.

The analysis of an event such as a trial, especially an event that brings to the fore cultural difference, can be instructive for both cultures. In this article I have tried to present fundamental differences in the practices of American culture and U.S. law and the practices of Roma law and Gypsy culture. Understanding difference does not necessarily resolve conflict, but it can lead to a more humanitarian application of the law to different cultures. The United States, a country based on immigration and diversity, is in no position to ignore the cultural foundations of different ethnic groups, nor are different cultures in the United States exempt from a law because it is contrary to custom. However, the more aware the legal system is of cultural histories and custom, the greater its capacity for justice.

S.N. chose to pursue his case through the U.S. legal system. He made this choice partly because of the influence and advice of a brother who was married to an American lawyer. The rest of his family strongly opposed this decision, preferring to do it the way they always have, by fleeing or lying to avoid contact with the legal system. While he was in jail, the Gypsies in his community held a *Kris* (formal meeting) to explain his decision to work through the American courts rather than the traditional Gypsy way and to raise money for his defense. The outcome of that trial was that on his release S.N., as well as his brother and brother's wife, who was his lawyer, were "rejected" (*marime*) and totally ostracized by his family. At the same time, the conditions of his probation stipulated that S.N. could not associate with his family, and he was released early into the custody of his brother and his brother's wife. Ironically, in the end, both U.S. and Roma law were in agreement on the consequences of his "crime" but for opposite reasons. The American legal system viewed S.N.'s family as "criminal associates"; his family, on the other hand, viewed S.N. and his brother as *marime* for rejecting Gypsy culture. Nevertheless, the strength of Gypsy culture has always been its ability to keep its closely knit ties, and today S.N. and his brother are back in the bosom of the family.

As the world changes into the next millennium, more people than ever before in human history are on the move as migrants, immigrants, guest workers, refugees and even as tourists. At this time in history, many people are living in places that do not share their cultural and legal traditions. Studies of society and legal systems must search for ways to deal with this cultural encounter. Gypsies have probably the longest recorded history of continuous movement and adaptation to other societies and cultures. Their treatment is a barometer of justice and civilization.

Review Questions

1. What aspect of the "crime" committed by a young Gypsy man is due to cross-cultural difference, according to Sutherland?

2. How did the police interpret the lists of social security numbers and other evidence found in the young man's apartment? How did their interpretation of this evidence differ from the Gypsy's?

3. How does this case illustrate the role cultural anthropologists can play in everyday American life?

4. Can you think of other cases where immigrants or culturally different people run afoul of American substantive law?

25

Notes from an Expert Witness

Barbara Joans

North Americans increasingly live in a multicultural society that can easily generate disputes based on cross-cultural misunderstanding. As a result, anthropologists who had never thought of working outside the teaching profession have been called on to testify in cases that involve expert knowledge about a culture. (The author of the previous article was an authority on Gypsy culture, for example.) But some anthropologists have found that their broad training in anthropology's four fields and their preparation in ethnographic research methods enables them to serve as expert witnesses in cases that don't require prior knowledge of a particular culture. Instead, they come to the task with anthropological tools that permit them to develop appropriate testimony. This is what happened to the author of this article, Barbara Joans. She describes three cases where she served as an expert witness: a dispute between a welfare agency and Bannock-Shoshoni women, a civil case between a Plains Indian family and a funeral home over the mistaken cremation of a relative, and a child custody case pitting the anthropologist against a court-appointed psychologist. Joans relates how she was able to use her training in anthropological linguistics, ethnographic interviewing, ethnohistorical research, and the ability to spot cultural difference and ethnocentrism to discover evidence and prepare court briefs. Her experience illustrates the unique legal role anthropologists can play in an increasingly multicultural society.

In December 1978, a lawyer from the Idaho Legal Aid Society contacted me for help. He was representing six Bannock-Shoshoni women who were accused of withholding financial information while receiving supplemental security income (SSI). By that point in my life, I had settled on a career as an academic. My goal was to teach anthropology in a college or university, and that was what I was doing at Idaho State University in Pocatello when the lawyer approached me. I had not thought too much about the practical application of cultural anthropology although I knew that some anthropologists had always applied their academic knowledge. For example, several had advised the U.S. Government about societies the military would encounter during World War II and others were (and still are) involved in the design of overseas development programs following the War. Instead, the lure of the discipline for me had been its power to understand cultural groups in their own terms. Like most new graduate anthropologists in those days, my goal was to teach students how to acquire this cross-cultural perspective.

Although my career as an academic anthropologist is still primary—I teach college students and am the director of a museum—my perspective on the usefulness of anthropology changed when I accepted the lawyer's invitation. I was to become an expert witness and discover that my training as a cultural anthropologist, as well as in anthropology's other fields (anthropological linguistics, archaeology, and biological anthropology), was a practical asset in court. This, it turned out, was especially true because so many disputes that reach court involve cross-cultural misunderstandings that lead to conflict. Since that time I have served as an expert witness in several cases where anthropological training and perspective proved useful. Let me discuss three of them: the original case mentioned above about alleged income fraud in Pocatello, a dispute among American Indians over the disposal of the dead, and a child custody case in California.

Problems in Pocatello

One thousand Bannock-Shoshoni Indians live on the Fort Hall Indian reservation located about 10 miles from the southeast Idaho city of Pocatello. Life on the reservations is hard. Although the land is mostly desert, residents scrape out a meager living by farming. Some also make pottery and jewelry, which they sell to nearby townspeople. A few of the Indians rent part of their land to local Anglos for a small annual income.

It was this rent income that got six Bannock-Shoshoni women, all over sixty years old, in trouble with the Pocatello Social Services. The women were eligible for supplemental security income (SSI), which was distributed by the agency. SSI rules stated that recipients had to declare all their income each year to ensure their eligibility. The agency claimed that the women had failed to declare their land rent money in 1978 and therefore had to return their SSI income, which amounted to about $2,000 for each of them. The women, who had no way to pay this amount, claimed they didn't know they had to include the rent income in the annual statement, and the dispute ended up in court.

The issue before the court seemed clear. Had the Indian women understood what was expected of them? Finding a way to answer this question became my main task and language seemed to be the key. Although not a fully trained linguist, I did have "four-fields" training in anthropology as a graduate student. One of those fields is anthropological-linguistics, so I felt capable of using language as the criterion for cultural understanding in the Pocatello case. Because all the verbal exchanges between the Bannock-Shoshoni women and the SSI staff members had taken place in English (the rules regarding SSI were explained in English to the women at a community lunch meeting on the reservation), and the women normally spoke Bannock or Shoshoni as their everyday language, I chose the women's comprehension of English as an index of their general cultural understanding. If the Indian women had sufficiently understood the English used to explain SSI requirements to them, then the Pocatello Social Service people would have a justified claim. If the women's understanding of English was incomplete, the defense could make a good case for misunderstanding.

Even without any evidence I could have made the argument in court that because English was not the defendants' native language, they had been unable to understand the SSI rules. The prosecution would have countered, however, that the women could easily be observed carrying on conversations in English, which meant they could understand the rules, but flaunted them. I clearly needed a way to determine the women's *level* of English comprehension, not just their ability to speak it to some extent. To do this, I created a three-part system to test the English language sophistication of the Indian women.

Level one consisted of everyday common speech. For example, I asked questions in English such as "Are you hungry? Are you cold? How are you feeling?" From their answers, it was clear that all the women could understand English at this level.

Level two was more complex. Could they joke in English and understand the double-entendres, the mixed meanings, and the puns associated with jokes. Because they often joked about the behavior of Pocatello officials in their own language, I presented them with jokes in English about the same individuals. At this level, only one woman was able to follow my conversation and "get" what was funny about what I was saying.

Level three involved an understanding of the rules and regulations governing Indian lives and the ability to articulate rules in English. Even the woman who was able to joke about Pocatello officials in English could not articulate the government rules using that language. Although she could describe *reservation* rules using English, she could not use it successfully to explain the regulations presented to them in English by non-Indian Pocatello officials.

In short, all six Bannock Shoshoni women could speak and understand an everyday brand of English. One of them could even handle the nuances of joking in English. It was this ability that had lead Pocatello officials to *assume* the women could comprehend SSI rules written and stated in English. But my research revealed and my testimony would state that none of them understood governmental English. The "crime," I concluded, was clearly a case of cross-cultural misunderstanding based on lack of language competence and the women's failure to declare their rent income was, therefore, unintended.

I presented this evidence and my conclusions in court, and was gratified when the women were cleared of any misconduct. More than that, the case managed to effect some permanent change in the dealings between Pocatello officials and the Bannock-Shoshoni. From then on, both Bannock and Shoshoni languages had to be used in conjunction with English at all agency-related meetings. To prevent future misunderstandings, interpreters now had to be present at all times. For the first time in Idaho, variant cultural language patterns and cultural understandings were accepted in court as determinants of behavior. The Indian women had their day in court and had won. They also gained control over their economic resources.

The Unfortunate Cremation

The second case involved a civil suit. Several years ago I was hired to be an expert witness in a dispute between a Northwestern Plains Indian family and a funeral home. Once again, the dispute revolved around lack of communication and cultural differences. In this case the primary issue was the way the body of an American Indian should be treated. Several family members of a fairly typical Plains Indian group living in Northwestern United States faced a difficult situation. A deceased family member who had lived far away from home for over fifty years died and was, by mistake, wrongfully cremated. The family was furious. The employees at the funeral home where the cremation took place were remorseful. They had followed instructions to cremate the body given to them based on hospital records and these turned out to be wrong.

When members of the deceased family found out what had happened, they claimed that according to their religion, cremation was an abomination. Citing their Indian beliefs, the family feared that the dead man would never be able to find his homeland again and so would never rest in peace. They sued the funeral home for substantial damages.

The funeral service personnel were apologetic and contrite but the deed had been done. They could not take it back. From their perspective there had been a mistake, but one that was innocent and that did not warrant the large financial penalty sought by the family. Indeed, if the family won the award they were asking, it would bankrupt the business.

There was a second complication. It was not possible to verify with certainty that the ashes residing at the funeral home were entirely those of the deceased, because they may have been mixed with those of several other people. Given this situation, the deceased's family also claimed they should be compensated because no proper Plains Indian rituals and end-of-life ceremonies could ever be performed.

I was retained as an expert witness to evaluate several matters. Were the plaintiff's assertions about cremation commensurate with their traditional Indian beliefs? Did the fact that the deceased had left home many years before and was out of touch with family members matter in Indian society? Could funeral rites and disposal of the remains be accomplished under Indian custom if someone was cremated?

Most of my inquiry involved the methods of ethnohistory. To find out if cremation was ever used as an acceptable end-of-life ceremony, I collected information about both traditional and modern American Indian views concerning the care of the dead. Library research, rather than participant observation and linguistic analysis, was the main mode of inquiry. In the course of my research, I discovered three important facts: Under certain though admittedly unusual circumstances, cremation had occurred in Indian society. I also learned that there are many ways that Indians conduct funeral ceremonies and that these can be done even in the absence of *any* physical remains. Finally, I discovered that under traditional circumstances, Indian family members would not go fifty years without seeing important relatives. The deceased, himself, had defied Indian cultural norms.

This led me to ask some important questions. Since so much time had elapsed between family visits, was the grief expressed by family members genuine? Second, given the fact that family members (as it turned out) had not known where the deceased had been living, had his cremation genuinely offended the family's sense of tribal tradition or were they simply seeking revenge? And was the suit simply a way to make money? Finally, although the family was indeed injured, was their litigation also a way to deflect the pain and guilt associated with a lifetime of family avoidance and neglect toward the deceased?

In the end, my report resulted in an out-of-court settlement. Research indicated that fifty years was a long time for family members to stay out of touch. It also indicated that historically, tribal warriors who died far from home in battle were often cremated and that Plains Indians had held proper memorial services over their ashes. The differing parties read the report, the anthropological brief, considered the analysis, and decided to settle out of court. They used the anthropological brief as a guideline for resolving their differences and deciding on a fair settlement for all involved. The family received a sizable settlement and the funeral establishment was able to stay in business.

Coming to this settlement was not easy for the Indian family. They had to acknowledge that for their Indian Nation, fifty years was a long time to go between visits, especially since they had not been in touch with, nor tried to contact the deceased during that time. They also had to recognize that they had deliberately disregarded tribal history and traditions.

To reach this point in negotiations, family members had to experience and accept a number of attitudinal changes. First was to recognize that there were alternative forms of ceremonial burial and to acknowledge that ash, even mixed and impure ash remains, could be used in ceremonial ways. They also had to accept that they could still orchestrate memorial services and participate in traditional Plains Indian rituals in spite of the fact that the bodily remains were in the form of ash. With attitudinal change, they could recognize that cremation was not totally foreign to their traditions. Finally, family members had to recognize that they were and still are a people who have a wide variety of acceptable customs and that they still hold within themselves the ability to create new customs, new patterns, and use cultural adaptability to perform a fitting final ceremony for their deceased relative.

Child Custody: Anthropology versus Psychology

The third case, which involved a child custody dispute, illustrates a different issue: whether or not an anthropological brief that looks at differences in cultural values and expectations can be considered expert testimony along with expert opinion prepared by a psychologist. Unlike the cases described above, which involved American Indians and thus more obvious cross-cultural contrast and a clearer legitimate need for anthropological opinion, the welfare of a child within mainstream U.S. culture is a different matter and psychologists have regularly played the central role in such matters. Psychology is a long-established human science in the United States and psychological explanations appeal to culturally individualistic North Americans. Child psychologists have produced decades of research on child socialization and its impact on young, growing personalities. Anthropologists, on the other hand, are concerned more with the shared cultural rules of child training and the broader social contexts in which children are raised, a point of view that I was to present in a California courtroom in the context of a bitterly contested child custody case.

In 1994, I was hired by the child's father's counsel to act as an expert witness in family court. Both father and mother were battling for custody of their two-year-old daughter. The father wanted shared custody; the mother wanted complete custody. The mother, just divorced from the child's father and again pregnant, was planning both her second marriage and her departure from the United States. Her new family would be living abroad. The father was fighting not only for joint custody, but for the ability to continue being part of his child's life.

As is the issue in many child custody disputes, the case hinged on the adequacy of child care and parental effectiveness. The father, through a previous court order, had had temporary custody. Now he was asking for shared custody. In keeping with her new life, the mother wanted sole custody of the infant. This would enable her to move abroad.

The court-appointed psychologist conducted visits to the homes of both parents, and on the basis of his observations judged the mother to be the better parent. The mother's home was, at the time of his visit, child-free, because she did not have immediate custody and there were no other children living with her. She was offering, however, what would become a nuclear family arrangement complete with stay-at-home mother, new husband, and about-to-be-born half-sibling. Her uncluttered child-free home was described, in the psychologist's report, as elegant and spacious.

My anthropological approach was different. I also based my expert opinion on home visits, but in the anthropological tradition, on visits that lasted many hours for many days in both parental settings. On the basis of my observations, I judged the father to be an excellent parent. He lived close to his own parents and siblings. He hired a full-time nanny who daily brought the child to her cousin's home for play. The grandparents played an important custodial role. In short, it was like the extended families observed by anthropologists in many societies, fully operational and amazingly functional. The child was thriving.

But these observations were unimportant to the psychiatrist. He observed that the father's home was cluttered and furnished with aging, scratched furniture. The fact that the furniture was old, comfortable, and extremely child-friendly impressed him as a sign of careless housekeeping and sloppy home management rather than child-comfortable and user-friendly. On the other hand, he perceived the mother's then-childless home as a model of good taste; a clean and orderly environment ideal for child raising. And ethnicity and class probably played roles in his view as well. The mother, with an upper middle class home and Anglo-heritage appeared to him to provide a better environment than the one offered by the father, with his working-class Italian ancestry. The psychiatrist concluded on these bases that the mother would be the best parent for her little daughter.

Psychologists, like other social scientists, are neither neutral nor value-free. They, like the rest of the social science professional community, carry their socialization as Americans within. As a result, they rarely challenge U.S. evaluations of class-based behavior and values, or family structure. This is reflected in their evaluations of who will make the most suitable parents in custody cases. Major among these stereotypes, and clearly within the psychologist's court report, was the belief that the *nuclear family* is superior to other kinds of arrangements and that the mother–child bond is always the primary one.

As an anthropologist I also view the maternal bond as crucial, but not the only one of significance. In my evaluation of the father's home, I was struck by the significance of the child's social relationships. These were forged within a wholesome and happy multi-generational *extended family*. The family not only shared ritual events, such as birthdays, anniversaries, and national holidays together, they participated together in important, small, everyday proceedings as well. For example, all the cousins had milk and dessert daily at a big, wooden, scratched, and worn kitchen table. In contrast, the mother, pregnant with her husband-to-be's child, could at best offer her daughter space in a carefully manicured house as part of a blended family where she might eventually become the family stepchild. Taken to another country, it would be probable that the little girl would never see her father or extended kin again. Visiting her abroad would present a nearly insurmountable barrier for a working-class family.

Anthropologists go into situations with a cross-cultural focus, one that is broadened by exposure to countless descriptions of different cultural contexts. They know that many societies are organized around extended families, and that children can thrive under these conditions. They also know that neatness and cleanliness in the North American sense does not necessarily guarantee successful child-raising in the context of U.S. nuclear families.

Participant observation requires that we look at the total environment, both physical and social, and the specific family circumstances to make judgments about child welfare. By approaching people with this inclusive perspective, it is often possible to get answers to questions that at first we had not thought to ask. In the child custody case, I observed the broader picture of the child's living situation, one that included the human as well as the economic content, and discovered a smooth, well-functioning extended family that had been thriving for generations. I presented my findings in a carefully written document to the court.

I should make an aside here. The North American values on "middle-classness" extended to the way I had and still have to appear in court. I learned that if I did not dress and carry myself in the "proper way" in court, my testimonial impact would disappear. (For a dramatization of this point, see the popular film *My Cousin Vinny*.) For those of us used to living within the confines of academia, the rules for survival in courtroom change. Before going to trial, like a good anthropologist, I visited several courtrooms to see just what was considered appropriate attire for professional women. Working in the academy, it is easy to lose touch with what corporate or legal America wears. My first comment to the female lawyer who hired me on my last case was "take me to your wardrobe!"

Turning myself into a respectable, fully professional-looking expert witness took many weeks of work and patience. It also used up all the money I received from the retainer in the child custody case. Unlike academic apparel, clothes for professional women are frightfully expensive. But the makeover is considerably more extensive than mere adornment. It involves a completely different presentation of self. In order to be taken seriously by the court, lawyers, and the judge, I had to look the professional part. This required learning to re-walk in high heels, freshly shaved legs, wearing a brassiere, and talking without using my hands. To accomplish the latter, I practiced talking while sitting on my hands for three weeks. The final transformation came when I cut my long, admittedly wild and unruly, hair—a personal trademark.

As I walked into court, I looked exactly like every other professional woman in the courtroom. I was sleek and well-groomed, the very model of competence and respectability. I learned I could hold this pose for only about two hours. Fortunately, that was just about the right amount of time.

Unfortunately, professional dress and my credentials as an anthropologist were not enough. My anthropological brief, written as a court document, summarized my findings and examined how and why my analysis differed from the psychologist's. The brief also contained questions to be asked and answered in court, thus allowing me to reveal my own analysis of the situation. I was able to provide the court with a fresh perspective on the diversity of U.S. patterns of family life. I was also able to confirm that the nuclear family represents only one type of American family and frequently not the most common one.

Regrettably, the judge, while allowing my testimony, did not allow my brief to be entered into the court records. He permitted my research bibliography and *vita* to be submitted as evidence of competency, but refused the anthropological brief under the grounds that it would violate an initial court agreement that stipulated there would be only one social science professional (i.e., the court-appointed psychologist) permitted to submit a written evaluation. My inability to have my cultural analysis accepted as a written brief clearly weakened the father's case.

The judge took all the papers minus my brief home to consider his verdict, relying only on his recollection of what I had said in court. From the beginning, the admissibility of an anthropological perspective was suspect in his eyes. He had cross-examined me and my credentials for over an hour before he permitted my testimony. But in the end, he considered the psychologist the "real" expert on child welfare.

Even though the judge permitted my testimony, it is clear to me that anthropology has a long way to go before courts treat our field with the same kind of respect afforded psychology. Yet, in spite of the defeat, anthropology did establish a foothold in a professional courtroom setting. This foothold had previously belonged, at least in California, mainly to psychologists. Anthropological analysis was finally seen as appropriate to use in child custody issues. The community of lawyers, once the judge ruled that I could speak, apparently looked favorably on the entrance of another professional into their domain. Unfortunately, being unable to have my anthropological brief accepted as case appropriate analysis lost, for my client, the critical writings that might have won a more favorable decision. We lost the decision.

These days, over half of the anthropologists who are granted PhDs find careers entirely outside the academic setting. They work for environmental consulting firms, advertising agencies, government bureaus, and manufacturing companies among others. But it is also clear that in today's multicultural world, anthropological expertise has become increasingly useful and important in the settlement of disputes and that even full-time academics such as myself can play a significant role in the legal arena.

Review Questions

1. What kind of evidence did Barbara Joans collect to defend a group of Bannock-Shoshoni women against welfare fraud? What long-term effect did her testimony have on the way the Pocatello Social Services communicates with Indian clients?

2. How was Joans able to generate an out-of-court settlement in the dispute between a Plains Indian family and a funeral home? What aspect of her anthropological training was especially useful in this case?

3. What was "anthropological" about the brief Joans prepared in the California child custody case? Why did she lose?

26

Life without Chiefs

Marvin Harris

It may come as a surprise to most Americans, but there were, and in a few cases still are, societies in the world that lack formal political structure. Instead of presidents, mayors, senators, and directors of homeland security, there are headmen, big men, and chiefs who lead by their ability to persuade and impress without the authority to make *people act. In this article, Marvin Harris traces the evolution of political leadership, associating* headmen *with small hunting and gathering societies marked by reciprocal exchange, and* big men *with slightly larger horticultural societies that employ redistributive exchange. Chiefs also occupied the center of redistribution systems but their societies were larger and chiefs could inherit their positions. He concludes that human biological inheritance was shaped by a hunter-gatherer existence; there is nothing inherited about the political formalism and social inequality that characterize large state societies.*

Can humans exist without some people ruling and others being ruled? To look at the modern world, you wouldn't think so. Democratic states may have done away with emperors and kings, but they have hardly dispensed with gross inequalities in wealth, rank, and power.

However, humanity hasn't always lived this way. For about 98 percent of our existence as a species (and for four million years before then), our ancestors lived in small, largely nomadic hunting-and-gathering bands containing about 30 to 50 people apiece. It was in this social context that human nature evolved. It has been only about ten thousand years since people began to settle down into villages, some of which eventually grew into cities. And it has been only in the last two thousand years that the majority of people in the world have not lived in hunting-and-gathering societies. This brief period of time is not nearly sufficient for noticeable evolution to have taken place. Thus, the few remaining foraging societies are the closest analogues we have to the "natural" state of humanity.

To judge from surviving examples of hunting-and-gathering bands and villages, our kind got along quite well for the greater part of prehistory without so much as a paramount chief. In fact, for tens of thousands of years, life went on without kings, queens, prime ministers, presidents, parliaments, congresses, cabinets, governors, and mayors—not to mention the police officers, sheriffs, marshals, generals, lawyers, bailiffs, judges, district attorneys, court clerks, patrol cars, paddy wagons, jails, and penitentiaries that help keep them in power. How in the world did our ancestors ever manage to leave home without them?

Small populations provide part of the answer. With 50 people per band or 150 per village, everybody knew everybody else intimately. People gave with the expectation of taking and took with the expectation of giving. Because chance played a great role in the capture of animals, collection of wild foodstuffs, and success of rudimentary forms of agriculture, the individuals who had the luck of the catch on one day needed a handout on the next. So the best way for them to provide for their inevitable rainy day was to be generous. As expressed by anthropologist Richard Gould, "The greater the amount of risk, the greater the extent of sharing." Reciprocity is a small society's bank.

In reciprocal exchange, people do not specify how much or exactly what they expect to get back or when they expect to get it. That would besmirch the quality of that transaction and make it similar to mere barter or to buying and selling. The distinction lingers on in societies dominated by other forms of exchange, even capitalist ones. For we do carry out a give-and-take among close kin and friends that is informal, uncalculating, and imbued with a spirit of generosity. Teenagers do not pay cash for their meals at home or for the use of the family car, wives do not bill their husbands for cooking a meal, and friends give each other birthday gifts and Christmas presents. But much of this is marred by the expectation that our generosity will be acknowledged with expression of thanks.

Where reciprocity really prevails in daily life, etiquette requires that generosity be taken for granted. As Robert Dentan discovered during his fieldwork among the Semai of Central Malaysia, no one ever says "thank you" for the meat received from another hunter. Having struggled all day to lug the carcass of a pig home through the jungle heat, the hunter allows his prize to be cut up into exactly equal portions, which he then gives away to the entire group. Dentan explains that to express gratitude for the portion received indicates that you are the kind of ungenerous person who calculates how much you give and take: "In this context, saying 'thank you' is very rude, for it suggests, first, that one has calculated the amount of a gift and, second, that one did not expect the donor to be so generous." To call attention to one's generosity is to indicate that others are in debt to you and that you expect them to repay you. It is repugnant to egalitarian peoples even to suggest that they have been treated generously.

Canadian anthropologist Richard Lee tells how, through a revealing incident, he learned about this aspect of reciprocity. To please the !Kung, the "bushmen" of the Kalahari desert, he decided to buy a large ox and have it slaughtered as a present. After days of searching Bantu agricultural villages for the largest and fattest ox in the region, he acquired what appeared to be a perfect specimen. But his friends took him aside and assured him that he had been duped into buying an absolutely worthless animal. "Of course, we will eat it," they said, "but it won't fill us up—we will eat and go home to bed with stomachs rumbling." Yet, when Lee's ox was slaughtered, it turned out to be covered with a thick layer of fat. Later, his friends explained why they had said his gift was valueless, even though they knew better than he what lay under the animal's skin.

"Yes, when a young man kills much meat he comes to think of himself as a chief or a big man, and he thinks of the rest of us as his servants or inferiors. We can't accept this. We refuse one who boasts, for someday his pride will make him kill somebody. So we always speak of his meat as worthless. This way we cool his heart and make him gentle."

Lee watched small groups of men and women returning home every evening with the animals and wild fruits and plants that they had killed or collected. They shared everything equally, even with campmates who had stayed behind and spent the day sleeping or taking care of their tools and weapons.

"Not only do families pool that day's production, but the entire camp—residents and visitors alike—shares equally in the total quantity of food available," Lee observed. "The evening meal of any one family is made up of portions of food from each of the other families resident. There is a constant flow of nuts, berries, roots, and melons from one family fire-place to another, until each person has received an equitable portion. The following morning a different combination of foragers moves out of camp, and when they return late in the day, the distribution of foodstuffs is repeated."

In small, prestate societies, it was in everybody's best interest to maintain each other's freedom of access to the natural habitat. Suppose a !Kung with a lust for power were to get up and tell his campmates, "From now on, all this land and everything on it belongs to me. I'll let you use it but only with my permission and on the condition that I get first choice of anything you capture, collect, or grow." His campmates, thinking that he had certainly gone crazy, would pack up their few belongings, take a long walk, make a new camp, and resume their usual life of egalitarian reciprocity. The man who would be king would be left by himself to exercise a useless sovereignty.

The Headman: Leadership, Not Power

To the extent that political leadership exists at all among band-and-village societies, it is exercised by individuals called headmen. These headmen, however, lack the power to compel others to obey their orders. How can a leader be powerless and still lead?

The political power of genuine rulers depends on their ability to expel or exterminate disobedient individuals and groups. When a headman gives a command, however, he has no certain physical means of punishing those who disobey. So, if he wants to stay in "office," he gives few commands. Among the Eskimo, for instance, a group will follow an outstanding hunter and defer to his opinion with respect to choice of hunting spots. But in all other matters, the leader's opinion carries no more weight than any other man's. Similarly, among the !Kung, each band has its recognized leaders, most of whom are males. These men speak out more than others and are listened to with a bit more deference. But they have no formal authority and can only persuade, never command. When Lee asked the !Kung whether they had headmen—meaning powerful chiefs—they told him, "Of course we have headmen! In fact, we are all headmen. Each one of us is headman over himself."

Headmanship can be a frustrating and irksome job. Among Indian groups such as the Mehinacu of Brazil's Zingu National Park, headmen behave something like zealous scoutmasters on overnight cookouts. The first one up in the morning, the headman tries to rouse his companions by standing in the middle of the village plaza and shouting to them. If something needs to be done, it is the headman who starts doing it, and it is the headman who works harder than anyone else. He sets an example not only for hard work but also for generosity: After a fishing or hunting expedition, he gives away more of his catch than anyone else does. In trading with other groups, he must be careful not to keep the best items for himself.

In the evening, the headman stands in the center of the plaza and exhorts his people to be good. He calls upon them to control their sexual appetites, work hard in their gardens, and take frequent baths in the river. He tells them not to sleep during the day or bear grudges against each other.

Coping with Freeloaders

During the reign of reciprocal exchange and egalitarian headmen, no individual, family, or group smaller than the band or village itself could control access to natural resources. Rivers, lakes, beaches, oceans, plants and animals, the soil and subsoil were all communal property.

Among the !Kung, a core of people born in a particular territory say that they "own" the water holes and hunting rights, but this has no effect on the people who happen to be visiting and living with them at any given time. Since !Kung from neighboring bands are related through marriage, they often visit each other for months at a time and have free use of whatever resources they need without having to ask permission. Though people from distant bands must make a request to use another band's territory, the "owners" seldom refuse them.

The absence of private possession in land and other vital resources means that a form of communism probably existed among prehistoric hunting and collecting bands and small villages. Perhaps I should emphasize that this did not rule out the existence of private property. People in simple band-and-village societies own personal effects such as weapons, clothing, containers, ornaments, and tools. But why should anyone want to steal such objects? People who have a bush camp and move about a lot have no use for extra possessions. And since the group is small enough that everybody knows everybody else, stolen items cannot be used anonymously. If you want something, better to ask for it openly, since by the rules of reciprocity such requests cannot be denied.

I don't want to create the impression that life within egalitarian band-and-village societies unfolded entirely without disputes over possessions. As in every social group, nonconformists and malcontents tried to use the system for their own advantage. Inevitably there were freeloaders, individuals who consistently took more than they gave and lay back in their hammocks while others did the work. Despite the absence of a criminal justice system, such behavior eventually was punished. A widespread belief among band-and-village peoples attributes death and misfortune to the malevolent conspiracy of sorcerers. The task of identifying these evildoers falls to a group's shamans, who remain responsive to public opinion during their divinatory trances. Well-liked individuals who enjoy strong support from their families need not fear the shaman. But quarrelsome, stingy people who do not give as well as take had better watch out.

From Headman to Big Man

Reciprocity was not the only form of exchange practiced by egalitarian band-and-village peoples. Our kind long ago found other ways to give and take.

Among them the form of exchange known as redistribution played a crucial role in creating distinctions of rank during the evolution of chiefdoms and states.

Redistribution occurs when people turn over food and other valuables to a prestigious figure such as a headman, to be pooled, divided into separate portions, and given out again. The primordial form of redistribution was probably keyed to seasonal hunts and harvests, when more food than usual became available.

True to their calling, headmen-redistributors not only work harder than their followers but also give more generously and reserve smaller and less desirable portions for themselves than for anyone else. Initially, therefore, redistribution strictly reinforced the political and economic equality associated with reciprocal exchange. The redistributors were compensated purely with admiration and in proportion to their success in giving bigger feasts, in personally contributing more than anybody else, and in asking little or nothing for their effort, all of which initially seemed an innocent extension of the basic principle of reciprocity.

But how little our ancestors understood what they were getting themselves into! For if it is a good thing to have a headman give feasts, why not have several headmen give feasts? Or, better yet, why not let success in organizing and giving feasts be the measure of one's legitimacy as a headman? Soon, where conditions permit, there are several would-be headmen vying with each other to hold the most lavish feasts and redistribute the most food and other valuables. In this fashion there evolved the nemesis that Richard Lee's !Kung informants had warned about: the youth who wants to be a "big man."

A classic anthropological study of big men was carried out by Douglas Oliver among the Siuai, a village people who live on the South Pacific island of Bougainville, in the Solomon Islands. In the Siuai language, big men were known as *mumis*. Every Siuai boy's highest ambition was to become a *mumi*. He began by getting married, working hard, and restricting his own consumption of meats and coconuts. His wife and parents, impressed with the seriousness of his intentions, vowed to help him prepare for his first feast. Soon his circle of supporters widened and he began to construct a clubhouse in which his male followers could lounge about and guests could be entertained and fed. He gave a feast at the consecration of the clubhouse; if this was a success, the circle of people willing to work for him grew larger still, and he began to hear himself spoken of as a mumi. Larger and larger feasts meant that the mumi's demands on his supporters became more irksome. Although they grumbled about how hard they had to work, they remained loyal as long as their mumi continued to maintain and increase his renown as a "great provider."

Finally the time came for the new mumi to challenge the older ones. He did this at a *muminai* feast, where both sides kept a tally of all the pigs, coconut pies, and sago-almond puddings given away by the host mumi and his followers to the guest mumi and his followers. If the guests could not reciprocate with a feast as lavish as that of the challengers, their mumi suffered a great social humiliation, and his fall from mumihood was immediate.

At the end of a successful feast, the greatest of mumis still faced a lifetime of personal toil and dependence on the moods and inclinations of his followers. Mumihood did not confer the power to coerce others into doing one's bidding, nor did it elevate one's standard of living above anyone else's. In fact, because giving things away was the essence of mumihood, great mumis consumed less meat and other delicacies than ordinary men. Among the Kaoka, another Solomon Islands group, there is the saying, "The giver of the feast takes the bones and the stale cakes; the meat and the fat go to the others." At one great feast attended by 1,100 people, the host mumi, whose name was Soni, gave away thirty-two pigs and a large quantity of sago-almond puddings. Soni himself and some of his closest followers went hungry. "We shall eat Soni's renown," they said.

From Big Man to Chief

The slide (or ascent?) toward social stratification gained momentum wherever extra food produced by the inspired diligence of redistributors could be stored while awaiting muminai feasts, potlatches, and other occasions of redistribution. The more concentrated and abundant the harvest and the less perishable the crop, the greater its potential for endowing the big man with power. Though others would possess some stored-up foods of their own, the redistributor's stores would be the largest. In times of scarcity, people would come to him, expecting to be fed; in return, he could call upon those who had special skills to make cloth, pots, canoes, or a fine house for his own use. Eventually, the redistributor no longer needed to work in the fields to gain and surpass bigman status. Management of the harvest surpluses, a portion of which continued to be given to him for use in communal feasts and other communal projects (such as trading expeditions and warfare), was sufficient to validate his status. And, increasingly, people viewed this status as an office, a sacred trust, passed on from one generation to the next according to the rules of hereditary succession. His dominion was no longer a small, autonomous village but a large political community. The big man had become a chief.

Returning to the South Pacific and the Trobriand Islands, one can catch a glimpse of how these pieces of encroaching stratification fell into place. The Trobrianders had hereditary chiefs who held sway over more than a dozen villages containing several thousand people. Only chiefs could wear certain shell ornaments as the insignia of high rank, and it was forbidden for commoners to stand or sit in a position that put a chief's head at a lower elevation. British anthropologist Bronislaw Malinowski tells of seeing all the people present in the village of Bwoytalu drop from their verandas "as if blown down by a hurricane" at the sound of a drawn-out cry warning that an important chief was approaching.

Yams were the Trobrianders' staff of life; the chiefs validated their status by storing and redistributing copious quantities of them acquired through donations from their brothers-in-law at harvest time. Similar "gifts" were received by husbands who were commoners, but chiefs were polygymous and, having as many as a dozen wives, received many more yams than anyone else. Chiefs placed their yam supply on display racks specifically built for this purpose next to their houses. Commoners did the same, but a chief's yam racks towered over all the others.

This same pattern recurs, with minor variations, on several continents. Striking parallels were seen, for example, twelve thousand miles away from the Trobrianders, among chiefdoms that flourished throughout the southeastern region of the United States—specifically among the Cherokee, former inhabitants of Tennessee, as described by the eighteenth-century naturalist William Bartram.

At the center of the principal Cherokee settlements stood a large circular house where a council of chiefs discussed issues involving their villages and where redistributive feasts were held. The council of chiefs had a paramount who was the principal figure in the Cherokee redistributive network. At the harvest time a large crib, identified as the "chief's granary," was erected in each field. "To this," explained Bartram, "each family carries and deposits a certain quantity according to his ability or inclination, or none at all if he so chooses." The chief's granaries functioned as a public treasury in case of crop failure, a source of food for strangers or travelers, and as military store. Although every citizen enjoyed free access to the store, commoners had to acknowledge that it really belonged to the supreme chief, who had "an exclusive right and ability . . . to distribute comfort and blessings to the necessitous."

Supported by voluntary donations, chiefs could now enjoy lifestyles that set them increasingly apart from their followers. They could build bigger and finer houses for themselves, eat and dress more sumptuously, and enjoy the sexual favors and personal services of several wives. Despite these harbingers, people in chiefdoms voluntarily invested unprecedented amounts of labor on behalf of communal projects. They dug moats, threw up defensive earthen embankments, and erected great log palisades around their villages. They heaped up small mountains of rubble and soil to form platforms and mounds on top of which they built temples and big houses for their chief. Working in teams and using nothing but levers and rollers, they moved rocks weighing fifty tons or more and set them in precise lines and perfect circles, forming sacred precincts for communal rituals marking the change of seasons.

If this seems remarkable, remember that donated labor created the megalithic alignments of Stonehenge and Carnac, put up the great statues on Easter Island, shaped the huge stone heads of the Olmec in Vera Cruz, dotted Polynesia with ritual precincts set on great stone platforms, and filled the Ohio, Tennessee, and Mississippi valleys with hundreds of large mounds. Not until it was too late did people realize that their beautiful chiefs were about to keep the meat and fat for themselves while giving nothing but bones and stale cakes to their followers.

In the End

As we know, chiefdoms would eventually evolve into states, states into empires. From peaceful origins, humans created and mounted a wild beast that ate continents. Now that beast has taken us to the brink of global annihilation.

Will nature's experiment with mind and culture end in nuclear war? No one knows the answer. But I believe it is essential that we understand our past before we can create the best possible future. Once we are clear about the roots of human nature, for example, we can refute, once and for all, the notion that it is a biological imperative for our kind to form hierarchical groups. An observer viewing human life shortly after cultural takeoff would easily have concluded that our species was destined to be irredeemably egalitarian except for distinctions of sex and age. That someday the world would be divided into aristocrats and commoners, masters and slaves, billionaires and homeless beggars would have seemed wholly contrary to human nature as evidenced in the affairs of every human society then on Earth.

Of course, we can no more reverse the course of thousands of years of cultural evolution than our egalitarian ancestors could have designed and built the space shuttle. Yet, in striving for the preservation of mind and culture on Earth, it is vital that we recognize the significance of cultural takeoff and the great difference between biological and cultural evolution. We must rid ourselves of the notion that we are an innately aggressive species for whom war is inevitable. We must reject as unscientific claims that there are superior and inferior races and that the hierarchical divisions within and between societies are the consequences of natural selection rather than of a long process of cultural evolution. We must struggle to gain control over cultural selection through objective studies of the human condition and the recurrent process of history. Not only a more just society, but our very survival as a species may depend on it.

Review Questions

1. What is the difference among headmen, big men, and chiefs according to Harris?

2. What does Harris see as the connection between forms of leadership and modes of economic exchange? How does this connection work?

3. Harris makes a distinction between biological evolution and cultural evolution. What is the distinction and how does he apply it to types of leadership?

EIGHT

Religion, Magic, and Worldview

People seem most content when they are confident about themselves and the order of things around them. Uncertainty breeds debilitating anxiety; insecurity saps people's sense of purpose and their willingness to participate in social activity. Most of the time cultural institutions serve as a lens through which to view and interpret the world and respond realistically to its demands. But from time to time the unexpected or contradictory intervenes to shake people's assurance. A farmer may wonder about his skill when a properly planted and tended crop fails to grow. A wife may feel bewildered when the man she has treated with tenderness and justice for many years runs off with another woman. Death, natural disaster, and countless other forms of adversity strike without warning, eating away at the foundations of confidence. At these crucial points in life, many people use religion to help account for the vagaries of their experience.

Religion is the cultural knowledge of the supernatural that people use to cope with the ultimate problems of human existence.[1] In this definition, the term **supernatural** refers to a realm beyond normal experience. Belief in gods, spirits, ghosts, and magical power often defines the supernatural, but the matter is complicated by cultural variation and the lack of a clear distinction in many societies between the natural and the supernatural world. **Ultimate problems,** on the other hand, emerge from universal features of human life and include life's meaning, death, evil, and transcendent values. People everywhere wonder why they are alive, why they must die, and why evil strikes some individuals and not others. In every society, people's personal desires and goals may conflict with the values of the larger group. Religion often provides a set of **transcendent values** that override differences and unify the group.

[1]This definition draws on the work of Milton Yinger, *Religion, Society, and the Individual: An Introduction to the Sociology of Religion* (New York: Macmillan, 1957).

An aspect of religion that is more difficult to comprehend is its link to emotion. Ultimate problems "are more appropriately seen as deep-seated emotional needs," not as conscious, rational constructs, according to sociologist Milton Yinger.[2] Anthropologists may describe and analyze religious ritual and belief but find it harder to get at religion's deeper meanings and personal feelings.

Anthropologists have identified two kinds of supernatural power: personified and impersonal. **Personified supernatural force** resides in supernatural beings, in the deities, ghosts, ancestors, and other beings found in the divine world. For the Bhils of India, a *bhut*, or ghost, has the power to cause skin lesions and wasting diseases. *Bhagwan*, the equivalent of the Christian deity, controls the universe. Both possess and use personified supernatural force.

Impersonal supernatural force is a more difficult concept to grasp. Often called **mana,** the term used in Polynesian and Melanesian belief, it represents a kind of free-floating force lodged in many things and places. The concept is akin to the Western term *luck* and works like an electrical charge that can be introduced into things or discharged from them. Melanesians, for example, might attribute the spectacular growth of yams to some rocks lying in the fields. The rocks possess mana, which is increasing fertility. If yams fail to grow in subsequent years, they may feel that the stones have lost their power.

Supernatural force, both personified and impersonal, may be used by people in many societies. **Magic** refers to the strategies people use to control supernatural power. Magicians have clear ends in mind when they perform magic, and use a set of well-defined procedures to control and manipulate supernatural forces. For example, a Trobriand Island religious specialist will ensure a sunny day for a political event by repeating powerful sayings thought to affect the weather.

Sorcery uses magic to cause harm. For example, some Bhil *bhopas*, who regularly use magic for positive purposes, may also be hired to work revenge. They will recite powerful *mantras* (ritual sayings) over effigies to cause harm to their victims.

Witchcraft is closely related to sorcery because both use supernatural force to cause evil. But many anthropologists use the term to designate envious individuals who are born with or acquire evil power and who knowingly or unknowingly project it to hurt others. The Azande of Africa believe that most unfortunate events are due to witchcraft, and most Azande witches claim they were unaware of their power and apologize for its use.

Most religions possess ways to influence supernatural power or, if spirits are nearby, to communicate with it directly. For example, people may say **prayers** to petition supernatural beings. They may also give gifts in the form of **sacrifices** and offerings. Direct communication takes different forms. **Spirit possession** occurs when a supernatural being enters and controls the behavior of a human being. With the spirit in possession, others may talk directly with someone from the divine world. **Divination** is a second way to communicate with the supernatural. It usually requires material objects or animals to provide

---

[2]Yinger, p. 9.

answers to human-directed questions. The Bhils of India, for example, predict the abundance of summer rainfall by watching where a small bird specially caught for the purpose lands when it is released. If it settles on something green, rainfall will be plentiful; if it rests on something brown, the year will be dry.

Almost all religions involve people with special knowledge who either control supernatural power outright or facilitate others in their attempt to influence it. **Shamans** are religious specialists who directly control supernatural power. They may have personal relationships with spiritual beings or know powerful secret medicines and sayings. They are usually associated with curing. **Priests** are religious specialists who mediate between people and supernatural beings. They don't control divine power; instead, they lead congregations in ceremonies and help others petition the gods.

Worldview refers to a system of concepts and often unstated assumptions about life. It usually contains a **cosmology** about the way things are and a **mythology** about how things have come to be. Worldview presents answers to the ultimate questions: life, death, evil, and conflicting values.

Finally, anthropologists also study and report on the formation of new religions, especially those that occur as a result of deprivation and stress. These **revitalization movements,** as Anthony F. C. Wallace called them in 1956, are "deliberate, organized, conscious efforts by members of a society to construct a more satisfying culture."[3] Revitalization movements are usually related to rapid change that renders a traditional way of life ineffective. For example, when one cultural group becomes dominated by another, rapid change and loss of authority may make its original meaning system seem thin, ineffective, and contradictory. The resulting state of deprivation often causes members to rebuild their culture along what they consider to be more satisfying lines.

Wallace argued that revitalization movements go through five stages:

1. *A Steady State.* This is a normal state of society in which people, through their culture, are able to manage the chronic stresses of daily life.

2. *Period of Increased Individual Stress.* Individuals in a society experience new stress caused by such events as culture contact, defeat in war, political domination, or climatic change.

3. *Period of Cultural Distortion.* Stress levels continue to rise as normal stress-reducing techniques fail to work. Social organization begins to break down, causing additional stress, and various cultural elements become distorted and disjointed.

4. *Period of Revitalization.* This period is marked by its own stages. First, a prophet or leader comes forward with a new vision of the culture that requires change. Called a *mazeway reformulation*, this vision is intended to

---

[3]Anthony F. C. Wallace, "Revitalization Movements: Some Theoretical Considerations for Their Comparative Study," *American Anthropologist* 58, no. 2 (1956): 264–281.

produce a more integrated, satisfying, and adaptive culture. This is followed by the *communication* of the revitalization plan and, if it proves attractive, the plan's *organization* for wider dissemination, its *adoption* by many people, its *cultural transformation* of the society, and its *routinization* in daily life.

5. *A New Steady State.* If no additional stresses occur, the society should attain a new steady state at the end of the process.

Although not all revitalization movements are religious—the Marxist doctrine and communist revolution in Russia exemplify a political revitalization movement—most of the world's major religions probably started as revitalization movements and many smaller sects and movements fit the revitalization pattern today.

The first article, by Stanley Freed and Ruth Freed, describes how Sita, a low-caste Indian woman, is chronically possessed by the ghost of a friend who committed suicide. Stressed by the prospect of sexual relations with a new and strange husband, lack of support in her conjugal household, and the deaths of many friends and family members, ghost possession, argue the Freeds, reduces Sita's anxiety and gives her needed family support. The second article, by George Gmelch, is the latest revision of his earlier classic piece on the use of magic by American baseball players. He looks in detail at the rituals, taboos, and fetishes employed by the athletes. In the third article, Jill Dubisch illustrates the meaning and impact of ritual and pilgrimage. Using the "Run For the Wall", a motorcycle pilgrimage that involves travel from Los Angeles to the Vietnam Memorial in Washington, D.C., as an example, she shows how this difficult motorcycle ride evokes strong emotions and personal transformation among its participants. The final article, by Stephen Leavitt, analyzes a revitalization movement, the cargo cults and beliefs of New Guinea peoples. Noting that cargo movements originated as a response to changes and loss of power engendered by colonial control, he shows that cargo beliefs also connect people to their recently dead ancestors.

Key Terms

27

Taraka's Ghost

Stanley A. Freed and Ruth S. Freed

Most people meet life's challenges by using an array of normal, and often effective, cultural responses. U.S. traffic is dangerous, for example, but we use driving skills we have learned to survive with confidence on the road. But some circumstances fall beyond our everyday abilities. We exercise and eat properly, but still may unexpectedly become ill. We work diligently and skillfully at our jobs, yet fail to be promoted. Many anthropologists see a relationship between religion and the anxieties that are caused by stressful and seemingly unmanageable aspects of life. In this article, Stanley Freed and Ruth Freed describe such an association. They report that a low-caste girl, Sita, is possessed by Taraka, the ghost of a childhood friend who committed suicide. Sita is stressed by the need to have sex with a new husband, the lack of support that meets a bride in her husband's household, and the deaths of three friends and several brothers and sisters. Ghost possession reduces her anxiety and gains her the support of her natal and conjugal families.

When we saw our first ghost possession in a North Indian village, on a hot September day in the late 1950s, we were struck by the villagers' matter-of-fact response to what seemed an extraordinary event. We were seated with a group of low-caste villagers who were softly chatting in front of a mud hut. Sita, a newly married fifteen-year-old girl, was sitting on the ground, and, conforming to the proper behavior of a bride, she was inconspicuous and silent. Still wearing her bridal finery, her face veiled below the eyes, she worked her sewing machine, of which she was proud.

A man of her caste, who had recently lost his job, commented that sewing on a machine was man's work (at that time, it was mainly the province of the village tailor). The remark implied that Sita was doing something inappropriate, an insinuation to which, as a new bride, she could not respond. Moreover, the criticism struck at Sita's pride and joy, her sewing machine, which was part of her dowry. To her it was a talisman, protecting her and providing her with higher status than other brides of her caste, for she was the first to possess one.

Sita's mother-in-law, who had witnessed earlier ghost possessions of the girl, realized that the criticism had distressed Sita, and anticipating that Sita would again be possessed, the older woman abruptly began to discuss the ghost attacks that plagued the teenager. We couldn't imagine why the conversation had taken such a turn until Sita began to shiver, a symptom preceding possession. Despite the heat, she complained of feeling cold, so some women covered her with quilts. She moaned, breathed with difficulty, and then collapsed in a semiconscious state.

The spectators accepted that a ghost had possessed her and tried a variety of standard curing techniques. These ranged from engaging the ghost in conversation, identifying it, and trying to satisfy its wishes or demands so that it would leave voluntarily, to attempting to drive it away with verbal abuse and, if necessary, physically painful or unpleasant measures (applied to the victim but aimed at the ghost). First, the women propped Sita up in a sitting position and wafted smoke from some smoldering cow dung under her nose. She jerked violently, so they had to restrain her. Then they shouted at the ghost: "Who are you? Are you going?" The ghost, speaking through Sita, promised to leave, and the women released the girl. But they were not deluded. They suspected that the ghost would not leave permanently and that a cure would be difficult. "Ghosts don't keep their promises," they confided to us.

Sita again fell unconscious, a sign that the ghost had returned. To revive her, the women dropped stinging hookah water in her eyes and pulled her braids. Sita returned to semiconsciousness and emitted a high-pitched wail, which announced the ghost's presence and readiness to talk. There followed a conversation between the ghost (speaking through Sita) and Sita's in-laws and a few other women, in the course of which the ghost identified herself as Sita's cousin Taraka, who had committed suicide by drowning in a well. Taraka's ghost declared that she would not leave Sita. The spectators again attempted to drive out the ghost, but Sita finally relapsed into unconsciousness.

For a fortnight thereafter, Sita experienced a series of possessions, so her father-in-law called various exorcists. They used generally similar techniques, calling on their familiars—supernatural beings who served them—to assist with the cure. Among these familiars were Hanuman, the monkey god; Kalkaji, goddess of the cremation grounds, with whom ghosts are closely linked; Jahar or Guga Pir, a Hindu-Muslim saint, who cut off his maternal cousins' heads in battle and later buried himself alive; and the ghost of a conjurer from Dacca. Each curer began a session by calling on his familiars, thus reassuring Sita and her relatives as to his curing powers.

When Sita's possessions persisted, her father was notified. He brought two exorcists to collaborate in an all-night session to drive off the ghost. They first induced possession in Sita by the power of suggestion and by the hypnotic effects of chanting mantras (hymns) believed to have supernatural power and using a fire to focus her concentration. Then they tried to exorcise Taraka's ghost by verbal abuse, hitting Sita, squeezing rock salt between her fingers (which was painful), pulling her braids, and throwing bits of her hair into the fire. During the session, Sita alternated between seeing a ghost, falling into a semiconscious state while a ghost spoke through her, unconsciousness, and intermittent returns to consciousness. Sita was not cured, however, and soon thereafter left for an extended visit with her parents, who lived in another village.

During the rest of our stay in India, we came to learn more about the villagers' beliefs in ghosts and the particular circumstances that led to Sita's afflictions. In rural North India, almost all Hindus believe that the soul goes through a cycle of rebirths. Following a person's death, it becomes a ghost, lingering for thirteen days in the village cremation grounds. Villagers who adhere to the doctrines of the Arya Samaj, a reform sect of Hinduism, believe in only one God, Bhagwan, and expect his judgment after cremation. The majority of villagers, who follow a more traditional version of Hinduism with multiple supernatural beings, believe that the soul travels to the Land of the Dead, ruled by Yama, Lord of the Dead. There Yama and his scribe review the soul's past actions before deciding on its future.

The important element in what happens to the soul at death is its karma, the sum of its good and bad actions from all its past lives. After being judged, the soul may be reborn or, if the sum of its actions is unusually good, released from the cycle of rebirths to join with many other souls and the Universal Absolute, a neuter deity known also as the Ultimate Reality, the joining of all souls in one.

Many Hindus believe in an additional possibility: a soul may become a ghost that lingers, possibly for decades, haunting the places where it lived and died. These are the souls of people who die tortured, from disease, accident, suicide, or murder; who violate village norms of behavior; who die before the years allotted to them by Yama; or who never attain the satisfactions of adult life. The ghosts of persons who are murdered or commit suicide are the most malevolent and tarry longest.

Ghosts are feared because they are believed to attack the living to seize their souls. Many villagers, but not all, believe that being seized by a ghost can cause illness or death. Ghost possession is the most vivid form of attack, in which a ghost enters and speaks through its victim, who has fallen into semiconsciousness. After recovering, the victim does not remember what took place. Because people in a state of possession may attempt to commit suicide by drowning in a well or by jumping in front of a train, they are usually watched by relatives and neighbors.

There is often a relationship between a ghost and its victim. For example, we learned that Taraka was not only a cousin but also a very close friend of Sita's. Sita had lived with Taraka's family for six months. Engaged to a man of another village, Taraka had an illicit affair with a boy of her own village. Because she became pregnant, the loss of her premarital chastity could not be long concealed.

The virtue of daughters is crucial to family honor in North India, and a daughter's sexual misbehavior, if it becomes generally known, may force a father to get rid of her by inducing suicide or even by murder. Taraka's parents learned of her pregnancy and quickly arranged her wedding to her fiancé. They handed over only a small dowry, in case Taraka's in-laws, realizing she was pregnant, returned her.

When Taraka went to her husband's family to begin her marital life, her husband's parents immediately discovered that she was pregnant. Renouncing all rights to her, they returned her to her father. Despite Taraka's pleas, her father was unforgiving and told her to commit suicide. Shortly thereafter, when Taraka, Sita, and some other girls were playing, Taraka decided to leave the group and asked Sita to accompany her. Sita refused. Taraka ran from the group, went to a nearby well, jumped in, and drowned. Sita blamed herself for the suicide.

Taraka was one of Sita's three close childhood friends, all of whom she lost during the three years before her own marriage. Prior to Taraka's indiscretions and suicide, a schoolmate had been murdered by her father. She was raped by a schoolteacher, and even though the girl was the victim and the identity of the assailant was known, her father was furious and blamed her. He flew into a rage, raped and murdered her, and threw her into a well (villagers regard such crimes as family business and rarely interfere). Another of Sita's schoolmates died of typhoid and malaria, shortly after beginning sexual relations with her husband.

The episode of the untrustworthy schoolteacher worried Sita's mother, who took her daughter out of school. The abrupt end of her education was a shock to Sita, who wanted to be a schoolteacher herself. Instead, Sita and her mother went to visit her mother's brother in her mother's natal village. This was when Sita's life became entwined with Taraka's, for Taraka was this man's daughter.

In Sita's mind, the deaths of her friends were linked with mating, marriage, childbirth, and disappointed dreams of further education. This link was reinforced by other painful memories. As her parents' first-born child, Sita had lived through the deaths of four infant brothers and five infant sisters, who had died because they could not digest their mother's milk. Mother, daughter, and other villagers believed that a ghost had taken these infants' souls. (Two brothers born subsequently had survived.) With the memory of the deaths of her friends and infant siblings, the fifteen-year-old Sita went to her husband to consummate her marriage, on her second visit to her in-laws.

On the first night, Sita told her sister-in-law that she was afraid to sleep with her husband and implored her to stay with her instead. The sister-in-law did so, but when Sita awoke in the night, she found her husband sleeping beside her. They did not have sexual relations that night. The following day, Sita went to the well for water and either jumped or accidentally slipped and fell in. Fortunately, two men who were nearby threw her a rope and pulled her out. As a result of this incident, the young couple did not have sexual relations that night either, and the next day Sita returned to her parents' home.

The marriage was finally consummated on Sita's next visit to her husband, some months later. During the fourth night of sexual relations, however, Sita was possessed by Taraka's ghost, who said that Sita's husband was her husband. The statement indicated that Taraka's ghost had been with Sita at the time of Sita's wedding, which meant that both women were married to Sita's husband.

At best, a North Indian rural woman must make an extraordinary social and psychological adjustment when she marries. At an early age, she moves from her natal family, where she is loved, cherished, and indulged, to her marital family, where she is chaperoned and required to restrict her movements. She leaves her natal village to settle in the unfamiliar surroundings of her husband's village. She must adjust to her husband and his often large family, especially his parents, sisters, and brothers' wives. And in this rural society, where marriages are arranged by parents, the bride may not have even seen her husband before the wedding day (although nowadays at least some families arrange for the young couple to meet at the time of the engagement).

A married woman and her kin are regarded as social inferiors to her husband's kin. A new bride is expected to shoulder harder and more onerous household chores and farm work than the daughters in her husband's family (they too, when they marry and go to live with their husbands, will go through a similar experience). A new bride also is generally uninformed about the relation between menarche and childbirth and is apprehensive about beginning sexual relations with her husband. The social and psychological vulnerability of a bride makes her a prime candidate for attacks by ghosts. In Sita's case, with three friends who had all died before their allotted time and without issue, the ghosts were waiting in the wings. All three possessed Sita at one time or another, but Taraka's ghost was her main tormentor.

The transition from beloved and only surviving daughter to daughter-in-law was particularly stressful for Sita. Moreover, having been raised in a one caste village, she had faced little caste discrimination, but her husband's village was multicaste, and her caste was near the bottom of the hierarchy. Her fear of mating and bearing infants whose souls might be seized by ghosts was a source of stress, as were various physical ailments. These cultural, psychological, and physical stresses were preconditions for her possessions. Research by neuroscientists during the past two decades may shed light on the underlying physiological mechanism of ghost possession. Under the stress of mental or physical pain, the body produces morphinelike substances called endorphins, which relieve the pain and may trigger mental states called alternate, altered, or dissociative. Ghost possession is one such dissociative mental state.

Stress is not confined to brides or women in North India nor is ghost possession. On a return visit to the village in 1978, we recorded the cases of three young men who were troubled by ghosts. Although some of the details of the cases were different, they all involved the stresses of modern life, especially school examinations and job hunting. Education and employment are signs of economic responsibility that a girl's parents often require before entrusting their daughter to a young husband. For example, one of the young men, a 22-year-old member of the Potter caste, was desperate for a job because his wife's parents would not let their daughter come to live with him unless he found one.

The young man was possessed, according to his mother and sister, by the ghost of his mother's first husband's first wife. The belief that the ghost of a first wife will haunt her husband's next wife and children was a strong motif in village culture. In this case, the husband had subsequently passed away too, and his next wife had remarried and the children were of this marriage; but the principle was similar. Known as the Lady, this ghost had possessed the young man's older brother twenty years before under similar circumstances and was now intermittently possessing the younger man.

The young man was treated by two village exorcists. One was a high-caste Brahman. The other was the man whose remark had disturbed Sita twenty years before: unemployed at the time and subsequently saddened by the deaths of many of his infants and by his wife's long illness, he believed that the great god Shiva visited his home. Following this experience, he became an exorcist.

During our 1978 stay, we also interviewed Sita, who recounted her medical history. Now a poised, intelligent, 35-year-old woman, she recalled her early possessions, which had lasted three years until the birth of her first child. Then the possessions had become fits, which she described as follows:

> They start from the head. I feel giddy and drowsy. Then I can't see anything and everything goes dark. My legs, hands, and veins stiffen, then a pain goes to my stomach. I don't know what happens, but I have a pain in my heart, my eyes shut, and my tongue comes out. I shriek so loud that the whole village, even the Brahmans, know that I am having a fit. I have a weak heart. Whenever there is a fight in the family or elsewhere, or if I see a dead body, I have fits.

In 1978 Sita's fits were still taking place. Well acquainted with modern medicine—she went to modern hospitals for what she recognized as biological problems—she nonetheless blamed her twenty years of possessions and fits on Taraka's ghost. According to Sita, Taraka's ghost had possessed Taraka's mother, and she herself had then been infected through contact with Taraka's mother. She continued to consult indigenous curers, mainly exorcists, who drove off the ghost or gave her amulets to control it.

In the intervening years, Sita told us, her mother had given birth to three more infants who had died. The older of Sita's surviving brothers had died at age fourteen, and her grieving mother had died soon after. Sita's remaining brother became a schoolteacher with Sita's assistance, and she accompanied him and his wife on their honeymoon.

Sita's father was still alive, retired from military service. As a small child, Sita had idolized him—a soldier who traveled to other countries but came home every year for two months. The relationship persisted through the years. When she visited him every summer, free from the stress and anxiety of life in her marital family, she never had fits.

Sita detailed her pregnancies, illnesses, and operations in the years since we first met her. Pregnant nine times, she had six children born alive (one of whom died at age three), two miscarriages, and one induced abortion, prior to being sterilized in 1972. Sita's family had a history of an inability to digest milk, and her first child, a daughter, did not take Sita's milk. Sita's father arranged for Sita and her daughter to be hospitalized while the infant was fed glucose. Because of her father's influence, Sita thereafter went to hospitals for physical problems that she considered serious. She had an operation for kidney stones. She suffered from menstrual complaints and side effects from being sterilized. A constant worrier, she was badly disturbed when one of her brothers-in-law was diagnosed as having tuberculosis, for she feared that she might have it.

Nevertheless, with regard to her appearance, the maintenance of her household, and care of her children, she managed very well and, except for her fits, was in control of her life. The treatment for ghost possession and fits by exorcists and the various amulets they gave her for protection from Taraka's ghost relieved her anxiety and helped to reduce stress. They also brought her other advantages, especially support from her natal and marital families, a reduction in her workload, and permission to visit her retired father every summer. When we last saw her, Sita was the leader of the women of her family, confidently planning the education and future of her children.

Review Questions

1. What aspects of her life make Sita a prime candidate for ghost possession in Indian society?

2. What happens to the souls of dead people according to Hindu village belief? What accounts for the presence of ghosts?

3. How did ghost possession help Sita adjust to her life as a married woman?

28

Baseball Magic

George Gmelch

Americans pride themselves on their scientific approach to life and problem solving. But as George Gmelch demonstrates in this article, U.S. baseball players, much like people in many parts of the world, also turn to supernatural forces to ensure success. Following the pioneering analysis of Trobriand magic by Bronislaw Malinowski, Gmelch shows that, like Trobriand Islanders, baseball players use magic, including ritual, taboos, and fetishes, to manage the anxiety generated by unpredictable events that challenge human control.

On each pitching day for the first three months of a winning season, Dennis Grossini, a pitcher on a Detroit Tiger farm team, arose from bed at exactly 10:00 A.M. At 1:00 P.M. he went to the nearest restaurant for two glasses of iced tea and a tuna fish sandwich. When he got to the ballpark at 3:00 P.M., he put on the sweatshirt and jock he wore during his last winning game; one hour before the game he chewed a wad of Beech-Nut chewing tobacco. After each pitch during the game he touched the letters on his uniform and straightened his cap after each ball. Before the start of each inning he replaced the pitcher's rosin bag next to the spot where it was the inning before. And after every inning in which he gave up a run, he washed his hands.

When I asked which part of his ritual was most important, he said, "You can't really tell what's most important so it all becomes important. I'd be afraid to change anything. As long as I'm winning, I do everything the same."

Trobriand Islanders, according to anthropologist Bronislaw Malinowski, felt the same way about their fishing magic. Trobrianders fished in two different settings: in the *inner lagoon* where fish were plentiful and there was little danger, and on the *open sea* where fishing was dangerous and yields varied widely. Malinowski found that magic was not used in lagoon fishing, where men could rely solely on their knowledge and skill. But when fishing on the open sea, Trobrianders used a great deal of magical ritual to ensure safety and increase their catch.

Baseball, America's national pastime, is an arena in which players behave remarkably like Malinowski's Trobriand fishermen. To professional ballplayers, baseball is more than a game, it is an occupation. Because their livelihoods depend on how well they perform, many use magic in an attempt to control the chance that is built into baseball. There are three essential activities of the game: pitching, hitting, and fielding. In the first two, chance can play a surprisingly important role. The pitcher is the player least able to control the outcome of his efforts. He may feel great and have good stuff warming up in the bullpen and then get in the game and get clobbered. He may make a bad pitch and see the batter miss it for a strike or see it hit hard but right into the hands of a fielder for an out. Conversely, his best pitch may be blooped for a base hit. He may limit the opposing team to just a few hits yet lose the game, and he may give up many hits and win. And the good and bad luck don't always average out over the course of a season. For instance, this past season Jeriome Robertson gave up 1.4 more runs per game than his teammate Tim Redding but had a better win–loss record. Robertson went 15–9, while Redding was only 10–14. Both pitched for the same team—the Houston Astros—which meant they had the same fielders behind them. Regardless of how well a pitcher performs, the outcome of the game also depends upon the proficiency of his teammates, the ineptitude of the opposition, and luck.

Hitting, which many observers call the single most difficult task in the world of sports, is also full of uncertainty. Unless it's a home run, no matter how hard the batter hits the ball, fate determines whether it will go into a waiting glove or find a gap between the fielders. The uncertainty is compounded by the low success rate of hitting: the average hitter gets only one hit in every four trips to the plate, while the very best hitters average only one hit in every three trips. Fielding, which we will return to later, is the one part of baseball where chance does not play much of a role.

How does the risk and uncertainty in pitching and hitting affect players? How do they try to control the outcomes of their performance? These are questions that I first became interested in many years ago both as a ballplayer and as an anthropology student. I had devoted much of my youth to baseball, and played professionally as a first baseman in the Detroit Tiger organization in the 1960s. It was shortly after the end of one baseball season that I took an anthropology course called "Magic, Religion, and Witchcraft." As I listened to my professor describe the magical rituals of the Trobriand Islanders, it occurred to me that what these so-called "primitive" people did wasn't all that different from what my teammates and I did for luck and confidence at the ballpark.

Routines and Rituals

The most common way players attempt to reduce chance and their feelings of uncertainty is to develop a daily routine—a course of action which is regularly followed. Talking about the routines of ballplayers, Pittsburgh Pirates' coach Rich Donnelly said:

> They're like trained animals. They come out here [ballpark] and everything has to be the same, they don't like anything that knocks them off their routine. Just look at the dugout and you'll see every guy sitting in the same spot every night. It's amazing, everybody in the same spot. And don't you dare take someone's seat. If a guy comes up from the minors and sits here, they'll say, "Hey, Jim sits here, find another seat." You watch the pitcher warm up and he'll do the same thing every time. . . . You got a routine and you adhere to it and you don't want anybody knocking you off it.

Routines are comforting; they bring order into a world in which players have little control. And sometimes practical elements in routines produce tangible benefits, such as helping the player concentrate. But some of what players do goes beyond mere routine. These actions become what anthropologists define as *ritual*—prescribed behaviors in which there is no empirical connection between the means (e.g., tapping home plate three times) and the desired end (e.g., getting a base hit). Because there is no real connection between the two, rituals are not rational. Sometimes they are quite irrational. Similar to rituals are the nonrational beliefs that form the basis of taboos and fetishes, which players also use to bring luck to their side. But first let's take a close look at rituals.

Baseball rituals are infinitely varied. Most are personal, performed by individuals rather than by a team or group. Most are done in an unemotional manner, in much the same way players apply pine tar to their bats to improve the grip or dab eye black on their upper cheeks to reduce the sun's glare. A ballplayer may ritualize any activity that he considers important or somehow linked to good performance. Recall the variety of things that Dennis Grossini does, from specific times for waking and eating to foods and dress. Jason Bere of the White Sox listens to the same song on his Walkman before he pitches. Atlanta Brave Denny Neagle goes to a movie on days he is scheduled to start. Baltimore Oriole Glenn Davis used to chew the same gum every day during hitting streaks, saving it under his cap. Astros Infielder Julio Gotay always played with a cheese sandwich in his back pocket (he had a big appetite, so there might also have been a measure of practicality here). Wade Boggs of the Red Sox ate chicken before every game during his career, and that was just one of many elements in his pre- and postgame routine, which also included leaving his house for the ballpark at precisely the same time each day (1:47 for a 7:05 game).

Many hitters go through a series of preparatory rituals before stepping into the batter's box. These include tugging on their caps, touching their uniform letters or medallions, crossing themselves, and swinging, tapping, or bouncing the bat on the plate a prescribed number of times. Consider Cubs shortstop Nomar Garciaparra. After each pitch he steps out of the batters box, kicks the dirt with each toe, adjusts his right batting glove, adjusts his left batting glove, and touches his helmet before getting back into the box. Mike Hargrove, former Cleveland Indian first baseman, had so many time-consuming elements in his batting ritual that he was nicknamed "the human rain delay." Both players believe their batting rituals helped them regain their concentration after each pitch. But others wondered if the two had become prisoners of their superstitions. Another ritual associated with hitting is tagging a base when leaving and returning to the dugout between innings. Some players don't "feel right" unless they tag a specific base on each trip between dugout and field. One of my teammates added some complexity to his ritual by tagging third base on his way to the dugout only after the third, sixth, and ninth innings.

Players who have too many or particularly bizarre rituals risk being labeled as flakes, and not just by teammates but by fans and the media as well. For example, Mets pitcher Turk Wendell's eccentric rituals, which include wearing a necklace of teeth from animals he has killed, made him a cover story subject in the *New York Times Sunday Magazine*.

Baseball fans observe a lot of this ritual behavior, such as pitchers smoothing the dirt on the mound before each new batter, never realizing its importance to the player. The one ritual many fans do recognize, largely because it's a favorite of TV cameramen, is the "rally cap"—players in the dugout folding their caps and wearing them bill up in hopes of sparking a rally.

Most rituals grow out of exceptionally good performances. When a player does well, he seldom attributes his success to skill alone; he knows that his skills don't change much from day to day. So, then, what was different about today that can explain his three hits? He may attribute his success, in part, to an object, a food he ate, not having shaved, a new shirt he bought that day, or just about any behavior out of the ordinary. By repeating those behaviors, the player seeks to gain control over his performance, to bring more good luck. Outfielder John White explained how one of his rituals started:

> I was jogging out to centerfield after the national anthem when I picked up a scrap of paper. I got some good hits that night and I guess I decided that the paper had something to do with it. The next night I picked up a gum wrapper and had another good night at the plate. . . . I've been picking up paper every night since.

When outfielder Ron Wright played for the Calgary Cannons he shaved his arms once a week. It all began two years before when after an injury he shaved his arm so it could be taped, and then hit three homers. Now he not only has one of the smoothest swings in the minor leagues, but two of the smoothest forearms. Wade Boggs' routine of eating chicken before every game began when he was a rookie in 1982 and noticed a correlation between multiple-hit games and poultry plates (his wife has 40 chicken recipes). One of Montreal Expo farmhand Mike Saccocio's rituals also concerned food: "I got three hits one night after eating at Long John Silver's. After that when we'd pull into town, my first question would be, "Do you have a Long John Silver's?" Unlike Boggs, Saccocio abandoned his ritual and looked for a new one when he stopped hitting well.

When in a slump, most players make a deliberate effort to change their routines and rituals in an attempt to shake off their bad luck. One player tried taking different routes to the ballpark, another tried sitting in a different place in the dugout, another shaved his head, and several reported changing what they ate before the game. Years ago, some of my teammates rubbed their hands along the handles of the bats protruding from the bat bin in hopes of picking up some power or luck from the bats of others. I had one manager who would rattle the bat bin when the team was not hitting well, as if the bats were in a stupor and could be aroused by a good shaking.

Taboo

Taboos (the word comes from a Polynesian term meaning prohibition) are the opposite of rituals. These are things you shouldn't do. Breaking a taboo, players believe, leads to undesirable consequences or bad luck. Most players observe at least a few taboos, such as never stepping on the white foul lines. A few, like Nomar Garciaparra, leap over the entire basepath. One teammate of mine would never watch a movie on a game day, despite the fact that we played nearly every day from April to September. Another teammate refused to read anything before a game because he believed it weakened his batting eye.

Many taboos take place off the field, out of public view. On the day a pitcher is scheduled to start, he is likely to avoid activities he believes will sap his strength and detract from his effectiveness. Some pitchers avoid eating certain foods, others will not shave on the day of a game, refusing to shave again as long as they are winning. Early in one season Oakland's Dave Stewart had six consecutive victories and a beard by the time he lost.

Taboos usually grow out of exceptionally poor performances, which players, in search of a reason, attribute to a particular behavior. During my first season of pro ball I ate pancakes before a game in which I struck out three times. A few weeks later I had another terrible game, again after eating pancakes. The result was a pancake taboo: I never again ate pancakes during the season. Pitcher Jason Bere has a taboo that makes more sense in dietary terms: after eating a meatball sandwich and not pitching well, he swore off them for the rest of the season.

While most taboos are idiosyncratic, there are a few that all ballplayers hold and that do not develop out of individual experience or misfortune. These form part of the culture of baseball, and are sometimes learned as early as Little League. Mentioning a no-hitter while one is in progress is a well-known example.

Fetishes

Fetishes are charms, material objects believed to embody supernatural power that can aid or protect the owner. Good-luck charms are standard equipment for some ballplayers. These include a wide assortment of objects from coins, chains, and crucifixes to a favorite baseball hat. The fetishized object may be a new possession or something a player found that coincided with the start of a streak and which he holds responsible for his good fortune. While playing in the Pacific Coast League, Alan Foster forgot his baseball shoes on a road trip and borrowed a pair from a teammate. That night he pitched a no-hitter, which he attributed to the shoes. Afterwards he bought them from his teammate and they became a fetish. Expo farmhand Mark LaRosa's rock has a different origin and use:

> I found it on the field in Elmira after I had gotten bombed. It's unusual, perfectly round, and it caught my attention. I keep it to remind me of how important it is to concentrate. When I am going well I look at the rock and remember to keep my focus. The rock reminds me of what can happen when I lose my concentration.

For one season Marge Schott, former owner of the Cincinnati Reds, insisted that her field manager rub her St. Bernard "Schotzie" for good luck before each game. When the Reds were on the road, Schott would sometimes send a bag of the dog's hair to the field manager's hotel room. Religious medallions, which many Latino players wear around their necks and sometimes touch before going to the plate or mound, are also fetishes, though tied to their Roman Catholicism. Also relating to their religion, some players make the sign of the cross or bless themselves before every at bat (a few like Pudge Rodriguez do so before every pitch), and a few point to the heavens after hitting a home run.

Some players regard certain uniform numbers as lucky. When Ricky Henderson came to the Blue Jays in 1993, he paid teammate Turner Ward $25,000 for the right to wear number 24. Don Sutton got off cheaper. When he joined the Dodgers he convinced teammate Bruce Boche to give up number 20 in exchange for a new set of golf clubs. Oddly enough, there is no consensus about the effect of wearing number 13. Some players shun it, while a few request it. When Jason Giambi arrived with the Oakland A's his favorite number 7 was already taken, so he settled for 16 (the two numbers add up to 7). When he signed with the Yankees, number 7 (Mickey Mantle's old number) was retired and 16 was taken, so he settled for 25 (again, the numbers add up to 7).

Number preferences emerge in different ways. A young player may request the number of a former star, sometimes hoping that it will bring him the same success. Or he may request a number he associates with good luck. Colorado

Rockies' Larry Walker's fixation with the number 3 has become well known to baseball fans. Besides wearing 33, he takes three practice swings before stepping into the box, he showers from the third nozzle, sets his alarm for three minutes past the hour and he was married on November 3 at 3:33 P.M.[1] Fans in ballparks all across America rise from their seats for the seventh-inning stretch before the home club comes to bat because the number 7 is lucky, although the specific origin of this tradition has been lost.

Clothing, both the choice and the order in which it is put on, combine elements of both ritual and fetish. Some players put on the part of their uniform in a particular order. Expos farmhand Jim Austin always puts on his left sleeve, left pants leg, and left shoe before the right. Most players, however, single out one or two lucky articles or quirks of dress for ritual elaboration. After hitting two home runs in a game, for example, ex-Giant infielder Jim Davenport discovered that he had missed a buttonhole while dressing for the game. For the remainder of his career he left the same button undone. Phillies' Len Dykstra would discard his batting gloves if he failed to get a hit in a single at-bat. In a hitless game, he might go through four pair of gloves. For outfielder Brian Hunter the focus is shoes: "I have a pair of high tops and a pair of low tops. Whichever shoes don't get a hit that game, I switch to the other pair." At the time of our interview, he was struggling at the plate and switching shoes almost every day. For Birmingham Baron pitcher Bo Kennedy the arrangement of the different pairs of baseball shoes in his locker is critical:

> I tell the clubbies [clubhouse boys] when you hang stuff in my locker don't touch my shoes. If you bump them move them back. I want the Ponys in front, the turfs to the right, and I want them nice and neat with each pair touching each other. . . . Everyone on the team knows not to mess with my shoes when I pitch.

During hitting or winning streaks players may wear the same clothes day after day. Once I changed sweatshirts midway through the game for seven consecutive nights to keep a hitting streak going. Clothing rituals, however, can become impractical. Catcher Matt Allen was wearing a long sleeve turtle neck shirt on a cool evening in the New York-Penn League when he had a three-hit game. "I kept wearing the shirt and had a good week," he explained. "Then the weather got hot as hell, 85 degrees and muggy, but I would not take that shirt off. I wore it for another ten days—catching—and people thought I was crazy." Former Phillies, Expos, Twins, and Angels manager Gene Mauch never washed his underwear or uniform after a win. Perhaps taking a ritual to the extreme, Leo Durocher, managing the Brooklyn Dodgers to a pennant in 1941, spent three and a half weeks in the same gray slacks, blue coat, and knitted blue tie. Losing can produce the opposite effect, such as the Oakland A's players who went out and bought new street clothes in an attempt to break a 14-game losing streak.

[1]Lee Allen, "The Superstitions of Baseball Players," *New York Folklore Quarterly* 20, no. 20 (1964): 98–109.

Baseball's superstitions, like most everything else, change over time. Many of the rituals and beliefs of early baseball are no longer observed. In the 1920s–30s sportswriters reported that a player who tripped en route to the field would often retrace his steps and carefully walk over the stumbling block for "insurance." A century ago players spent time on and off the field intently looking for items that would bring them luck. To find a hairpin on the street, for example, assured a batter of hitting safely in that day's game. A few managers were known to strategically place a hairpin on the ground where a slumping player would be sure to find it. Today few women wear hairpins—a good reason the belief has died out. In the same era, Philadelphia Athletics manager Connie Mack hoped to ward off bad luck by employing a hunchback as a mascot. Hall of Famer Ty Cobb took on a young black boy as a good luck charm, even taking him on the road during the 1908 season. It was a not uncommon then for players to rub the head of a black child for good luck.

To catch sight of a white horse or a wagon-load of barrels were also good omens. In 1904 the manager of the New York Giants, John McGraw, hired a driver with a team of white horses to drive past the Polo Grounds around the time his players were arriving at the ballpark. He knew that if his players saw white horses, they would have more confidence and that could only help them during the game. Belief in the power of white horses survived in a few backwaters until the 1960s. A gray-haired manager of a team I played for in Drummondville, Quebec, would drive around the countryside before important games and during the playoffs looking for a white horse. When he was successful, he would announce it to everyone in the clubhouse.

One belief that appears to have died out recently is a taboo about crossed bats. Some of my Latino teammates in the 1960s took it seriously. I can still recall one Dominican player becoming agitated when another player tossed a bat from the batting cage and it landed on top of his bat. He believed that the top bat might steal hits from the lower one. In his view, bats contained a finite number of hits. It was once commonly believed that when the hits in a bat were used up no amount of good hitting would produce any more. Hall of Famer Honus Wagner believed each bat contained only 100 hits. Regardless of the quality of the bat, he would discard it after its 100th hit. This belief would have little relevance today, in the era of light bats with thin handles—so thin that the typical modern bat is lucky to survive a dozen hits without being broken. Other superstitions about bats do survive, however. Position players on the Class A Asheville Tourists would not let pitchers touch or swing their bats, not even to warm up. Poor-hitting players, as most pitchers are, were said to pollute or weaken the bats.

Uncertainty and Magic

The best evidence that players turn to rituals, taboos, and fetishes to control chance and uncertainty is found in their uneven application. They are associated mainly with pitching and hitting—the activities with the highest degree of chance—and not fielding. I met only one player who had any ritual in connection with fielding, and he was an error-prone shortstop. Unlike hitting and pitching, a fielder has almost complete control over the outcome of his performance. Once a ball has been hit in his direction, no one can intervene and ruin his chances of catching it for an out (except in the unlikely event of two fielders colliding). Compared with the pitcher or the hitter, the fielder has little to worry about. He knows that in better than 9.7 times out of 10 he will execute his task flawlessly. With odds like that there is little need for ritual.

Clearly, the rituals of American ballplayers are not unlike those of the Trobriand Islanders studied by Malinowski many years ago.[2] In professional baseball, fielding is the equivalent of the inner lagoon while hitting and pitching are like the open sea.

While Malinowski helps us understand how ballplayers respond to chance and uncertainty, behavioral psychologist B. F. Skinner sheds light on why personal rituals get established in the first place.[3] With a few grains of seed Skinner could get pigeons to do anything he wanted. He merely waited for the desired behavior (e.g., pecking) and then rewarded it with some food. Skinner then decided to see what would happen if pigeons were rewarded with food pellets regularly, every fifteen seconds, regardless of what they did. He found that the birds associate the arrival of the food with a particular action, such as tucking their head under a wing or walking in clockwise circles. About ten seconds after the arrival of the last pellet, a bird would begin doing whatever it associated with getting the food and keep doing it until the next pellet arrived. In short, the pigeons behaved as if their actions made the food appear. They learned to associate particular behaviors with the reward of being given seed.

Ballplayers also associate a reward—successful performance—with prior behavior. If a player touches his crucifix and then gets a hit, he may decide the gesture was responsible for his good fortune and touch his crucifix the next time he comes to the plate. Unlike pigeons, however, most ballplayers are quicker to change their rituals once they no longer seem to work. Skinner found that once a pigeon associated one of its actions with the arrival of food or water, only sporadic rewards were necessary to keep the ritual going. One pigeon, believing that hopping from side to side brought pellets into its feeding cup, hopped ten thousand times without a pellet before finally giving up. But, then, didn't Wade Boggs eat chicken before every game, through slumps and good times, for seventeen years?

Obviously the rituals and superstitions of baseball do not make a pitch travel faster or a batted ball find the gaps between the fielders, nor do the Trobriand rituals calm the seas or bring fish. What both do, however, is give their practitioners a sense of control, and with that, added confidence. And we all

---

[2]Bronislaw Malinowski, *Magic, Science and Religion and Other Essays* (Glencoe, IL: Free Press, 1948).

[3]B. F. Skinner, *Behavior of Organisms: An Experimental Analysis* (New York: Appleton Century, 1938).

know how important that is. If you really believe eating chicken or hopping over the foul lines will make you a better hitter, it probably will.

Review Questions

1. According to Gmelch, what is magic, and why to people practice it?

2. What parts of baseball are most likely to lead to magical practice? Why?

3. What is meant by the terms *taboo* and *fetish?* Illustrate these concepts using examples from this article.

4. How are Malinowski's and Skinner's theories of magic alike and different? What is each designed to explain?

5. Can you think of other areas of U.S. life where magic is practiced? Do the same theories used in this article account for these examples, too?

29

Run for the Wall: An American Pilgrimage

Jill Dubisch

Pilgrimages involve ritually structured travel that physically removes people from their everyday lives as they journey to places that evoke important, often life changing, emotions. As a ritual, pilgrimages are structured around repetitive acts that symbolize past events, places, stories, and meanings. They involve a ritual of separation, a liminal period, and a final reincorporation into normal life for those who embark on them. We often associate pilgrimages with religion, but they may also occur in more secular contexts with much the same effect. This is the case for a pilgrimage called the Run for the Wall, described by Jill Dubisch in this article. The "run" is a pilgrimage undertaken by motorcyclists who travel for ten days each spring from Los Angles to Washington, D.C., to commemorate soldiers lost during the Vietnam War. Started years ago by Vietnam veterans, it has grown to include other riders over the years as well. After they leave Los Angles, riders cross the United

States, stopping in towns along the way and occasionally participating in commemorations dedicated to the memory of veterans. Additional riders may join the run along the way, while others may drop out. Those who make it to Washington visit "the wall," their name for the Vietnam War Memorial bearing the names of all those who died in the war. Finally, they participate in "rolling thunder," a parade of thousands of motorcyclists ending at the U.S. Capitol, as a way to honor and "remember" soldiers who were captured, missing, and killed in the Vietnam War. Dubisch describes the ritual nature of the pilgrimage and details its emotional effect and transformative power for motorcyclists who participate.

They roared off the I-40 exit west of Flagstaff, Arizona, a motley crew of leather-clad, long-haired bikers on their Harleys. *Here they are*, we thought, as my partner Ray and I scrambled to pull our Honda Gold Wing motorcycle in behind them. Excitement washed over us, mingled with a large dose of anxiety. Could we really become part of this rough-looking crowd, we wondered, these wild looking riders with their black leather jackets, chains, headscarves, long hair, and beards? After all, these were *real* bikers—not the sort of riders we were used to from our mostly middle-aged Honda Gold Wing motorcycle club. And yet this was the group with whom we planned to spend the next ten days, accompanying them on a cross-country journey from Flagstaff to the Vietnam Veterans Memorial in Washington, D.C., an annual pilgrimage known as the Run for the Wall.

As we parked nervously at the end of the line of bikes on the shoulder of the road, waiting for our police escort for the parade into downtown Flagstaff, little did we know what awaited us in the days ahead. For on this journey across America, both we and the mostly Vietnam veterans with whom we rode would develop emotional bonds that extended well beyond the Run, and we would experience a transformation that would change our lives. Such a transformation was not to be won easily, however, for the journey, a gruelling ten-day motorcycle ride, was fraught not only with all the dangers of the road that any motorcycle journey entails, but also with the emotional dangers involved in reawakening memories of a difficult period in our history—the era of the Vietnam War and the political protest and social disruption that were the consequences of that war. What's more, in the course of this journey, our very view of the country in which we lived would change, as we were fed and lodged and greeted with smiles, tears, and ceremonies—and occasionally with hostility or fear—in small communities all across America. The couple that finally returned home three weeks later on their motorcycle were not the same people who left Flagstaff that day in early May of 1996. The ride turned out to be a pilgrimage, a ritual passage that personally transformed both us and those with whom we road.

But who were these people who streamed off the highway and into our lives that day? Why did they term their journey a pilgrimage and why were they making such a pilgrimage so many years after the Vietnam War had ended? And why did they make this journey on motorcycles? Why would those who are not veterans choose to accompany them? And why would communities along the journey's route turn out to feed and celebrate the veterans and to wish them "welcome home"? In order to answer these questions, it is necessary to address not only the issue of the still-unhealed "wounds" of the Vietnam War and to examine the nature of pilgrimage, but also more generally to consider the nature of ritual and its role in American life.

The Run for the Wall: An American Ritual

The Run for the Wall begins every year in mid-May as several hundred motorcycle riders gather at a motel in southern California in preparation for their journey across the United States from California to Washington, D.C. Although many of the riders might be mistaken for outlaw bikers, with their beards, headscarves, boots, and black leather jackets, in fact, most are Vietnam veterans, and the journey they are about to undertake is no mere outing or biker joy ride. Rather, they are at the beginning of a serious, and often emotional and painful endeavor, a journey with a mission, a pilgrimage, whose final destination is the most powerful of American secular shrines, the Vietnam Veterans Memorial—the Wall.

The Run first took place in 1989, when a group of Vietnam veterans decided to ride their motorcycles across the country to the recently inaugurated Vietnam Veterans Memorial. Their intention was, as one of those original riders explained to me, "to say goodbye" to their fallen comrades whose names were on the Wall, and they saw the journey as a one-time event. However, the enthusiastic welcome the group received in the communities where they stopped in the course of their ride, and the ceremonies and hospitality with which they were greeted, as one rider told me, made them realize "we had to do it again." And so the Run for the Wall has taken place every year, and grown every year, so much that recently it has added a more southern route to the original Midwestern route with which the Run began.

During this ten-day journey across the United States, the riders travel several hundred miles a day on their motorcycles. Some go "all the way" to D.C., while others travel shorter distances with the group, replaced by others who join along the route, so that at times the group may have from 200 to 300 riders, forming a line stretching several miles down the highway. During the journey, the riders are greeted with ceremonies performed by local organizations such as veterans' groups and local motorcycle organizations. They visit VFW and American legion halls, Vietnam memorials, local parks and community halls. They are honored and fed and put up for the night at local camping grounds. Few of them pay for a single meal along the way, and camping is always free.

But many of these veterans are making another journey as well—a journey into the past and their own painful memories, to a time of personal danger and fear and grief, and of national dissention and conflict that split a generation—

to that painful period of American history, the Vietnam War, a war that (as the 2004 presidential campaign showed) remains controversial to this day. And when the group arrives at its final destination, the Vietnam Veterans Memorial, an arrival always timed for the Friday of Memorial Day weekend, the memories become intensely painful, as the riders confront the names of dead comrades—and the non-veterans the names of dead relatives and friends—and relive once more all the traumatic memories of the war.

And yet the aim of this journey is not simply to confront the past, or to evoke its pain. Rather, the participants describe the aims of their pilgrimage as twofold: as a means of healing the individual wounds of the war and as a ride on behalf of all veterans, but especially those "left behind," the prisoners of war (POWs) and those missing in action (MIAs). Nor are these causes the concern of veterans alone. On this ritual journey, veterans are accompanied by family, friends, and other supporters, and also, since that day in 1996 when we first joined the Run, by two social scientists.

The Anthropology of Pilgrimage

When I joined the Run for the Wall it was not the first time I had been involved with a pilgrimage, however. For a number of years I had done anthropological fieldwork at the shrine of the Madonna of the Annunciation on the Greek island of Tinos, one of that country's most famous pilgrimage sites and the destination of thousands of Orthodox Christian pilgrims every year.[1] Although my work on Tinos was deeply involving and often emotional, I was an outsider, not a Greek Orthodox Christian, and from a different culture, and I did not myself participate in pilgrimage. Thus when I joined the Run for the Wall, it was the first time I had really been a pilgrim myself, and had taken part in a journey with a personal, as well as professional, significance.

"Pilgrimage" is a word that usually conjures up visions of sacred journeys connected with the great world religions—the Muslim pilgrimage to Mecca, Catholic pilgrimage to Lourdes or Santiago, or perhaps a journey of Hindus to the sacred waters of the Ganges in India. But pilgrimage is by no means limited to such religious traditions, and in fact it can take a variety of forms. Pilgrimage can range from large-scale journeys such as those that devout Muslims make to Mecca, to small individual journeys such as the Irish make to a healing well, or Americans to a family reunion. It can be mandated and structured by religious traditions or religious authorities, or undertaken as a purely individual quest. It can be motivated by spiritual needs or by the desire for solutions to such pragmatic physical problems as illness or the inability to bear a child. It is, in short, a highly flexible, variable, and multi-faceted ritual activity.

This notion of a journey, whether it is actual physical travel or metaphoric, is part of what gives pilgrimages their common structure and their widespread

[1]See Jill Dubisch, *In a Different Place* (Princeton, NJ: Princeton University Press, 1995).

appeal. The journey is a powerful symbol and is connected with the idea that one needs to go to a "different place"—to the wilderness, to a sacred locale, to the site of powerful events and away from the place of one's ordinary life—in order to achieve transformation, to touch the sacred, or to receive important messages from the other world. Thus while pilgrimage is a journey, it is not just any kind of journey. It is not taken out of pleasure or simple practical necessity (though it may also include these elements). Rather it is a journey with a purpose, a mission, a ritual act that carries the pilgrim to a place with special meaning or power. Nor need such journeys be strictly religious in nature. The Run for the Wall and journeys to Elvis Presley's home at Graceland or to Ground Zero at the World Trade Center in New York City, for example, do not fit within established religious traditions, yet they are seen by many of their participants as pilgrimages.

Pilgrimage destinations themselves draw people for a variety of reasons. Certain places are special, often by virtue of things that have happened there, whether a human event, such as the Battle of Gettysburg, or the appearance or act of a divine being, such as an apparition of the Virgin Mary at Lourdes in France. In other cases, the origins of the pilgrimage site may be lost in time, and the site simply known for its miraculous powers, as is the case with the healing wells of Ireland. And some pilgrimage sites attract people through the physical powers of place, as with mountains in Chinese pilgrimage, or the red rock "vortexes" of Sedona, Arizona. But journeys are also metaphorical. The idea of life as a moral and spiritual journey is deeply ingrained in the Christian religion. (And it is no coincidence that in the 1960s a psychedelic experience, in which one journeyed in mind but not in body, was termed a "trip"!)

The Anthropology of Ritual

I have spoken of pilgrimage as a "ritual," but what, exactly, are rituals, and why are they important? And what sort of ritual is pilgrimage?

Robbie Davis-Floyd, in her book *Birth as an American Rite of Passage*, defines ritual as "a patterned, repetitive, and symbolic enactment of a cultural belief or value."[2] According to Davis-Floyd, the primary purpose of ritual is "transformation," and for this reason rituals are often performed to mark important occasions, times, or transitions. From the perspective of those performing the rituals, there are a variety of purposes in carrying out ritual activities: to maintain order in the world, to connect with gods or ancestors, to protect, to express group or individual identity, or because the rituals are mandated by the religious system of the society. Rituals can bring about changes, as when rites of passage such as baptism or marriage transform individuals by moving them from one social status or stage of life to another. Rituals also mark off ordinary life from times when special activities are permitted or required.

[2]Robbie Davis-Floyd, *Birth as an American Rite of Passage* (Berkeley, CA: University of California Press, 1992), p. 8.

The carnival period preceding Lent in Catholic cultures both allows creativity and license absent in ordinary life and at the same time signals the beginning of the period of abstinence to follow, a period that itself parallels and dramatizes the sufferings of Christ before the crucifixion and resurrection. Similarly, a pilgrimage is an activity and time set apart, and pilgrimage may take place at times of special significance, such as holy days or national days of commemoration. Thus the Run for the Wall is timed so that its arrival at the Vietnam Veterans Memorial takes place on Memorial Day weekend, a period of remembering the war dead and of patriotic activities.

This brings up another important feature of rituals. As the famous scholar of religion, Mircea Eliade pointed out, rituals often reenact the important myths of society, showing us why they are the way they are. Thus Christian Easter rituals enact the crucifixion and resurrection, while the Jewish Passover meal, the Seder, recounts the Jews' flight from Egypt. Nor need such rituals be religious in nature. The Fourth of July in the United States, for example, commemorates the signing of the Declaration of Independence and serves as an occasion to proclaim American values of freedom, patriotism, and community. Rituals may also seek to rewrite or reshape the past. In the Run for the Wall, as I will show, veterans seek, among other things, to transform the meaning of being a Vietnam veteran from shame to pride, and to give veterans a chance for the homecoming reception most never had when they returned from Vietnam. ("Welcome home, brother" is the ritual greeting extended to these veterans by other veterans on the Run and by those who greet them along the way.)

Symbolism plays an important role in rituals. Victor Turner, an anthropologist who devoted much of his work to the study of ritual, saw symbols as having two poles: the ideological and the sensory. On the one hand, rituals engage our senses of sound, touch, sight, taste and smell (the sensory pole). On the other hand, they also convey important messages about social values (the ideological pole). Although contemporary anthropologists would see these two dimensions as intertwined, with each embedded in the other (rather than as opposite poles), they would agree that it is the combination of the ideological and the sensory that makes rituals so powerful and moving, for they engage more than just our intellects. For this reason, people sometimes find themselves moved by the rituals of other groups or cultures, even when they themselves do not share the values of those performing the ritual.

Although rituals are often perceived as being "traditional," passed on in the same form from generation to generation, the fact is that rituals are an ongoing human activity and must be re-created every time they are performed. Hence rituals are subject to both intentional and unintentional change. Moreover, new rituals are created regularly, and old ones modified. The Run for the Wall has now become a yearly "tradition," the ritual activities carried out in the course of its journey modified and added to every year by both the participants and by those who host them along the way.

It is clear that rituals are a rich source of data for the anthropologist and important windows on the culture in which they occur. For this reason, I like

Renato Rosaldo's description of rituals as "busy intersections," places where "a number of distinct social processes interact."[3] It is just such a "busy intersection" that we find in the annual motorcycle pilgrimage known as the Run for the Wall.

Pilgrimage as Ritual

One reason that the journey—as both symbol and as an actual activity—is so powerful is that it has the potential to create what anthropologists call a "liminal" state. Liminality is an important feature of those rituals we call "rites of passage," in which individuals or groups move from one stage or condition to another. Victor Turner and his wife, Edith Turner, saw pilgrimage as one type of rite of passage. When one is on a pilgrimage, the liminal period is marked by the physical separation created by the journey itself. Ordinary duties are left behind, and time and space take on different meanings. This may induce an altered state of consciousness that renders the pilgrim more receptive to both the messages of the journey and the healing or other transformations that pilgrimage can effect. Thus once the pilgrimage is over, the pilgrim often has experienced an inner transformation, such as healing of physical or psychological ills, atonement for sin, or spiritual renewal. Transformation of social status or identity may also take place. Vietnam veterans who participate in the Run for the Wall may return home with newly created identities *as* veterans (an identity they may have previously played down or denied), and they may also find that they have finally begun to heal the long-buried wounds of Vietnam.

To see how these various features of pilgrimage and ritual are represented on the Run for the Wall, let us look at some of the events that take place in the course of this ten-day journey. But before that, it is necessary to address two important elements of American culture that come together to define this pilgrimage: the Vietnam War and motorcycle riding.

The Vietnam War

The Run for the Wall's focus on the POW/MIA issue carries the message that the Vietnam War in some sense is not really over (a message also made clear in the 2004 presidential campaign and the frequent comparisons of the Iraq war to Vietnam). Despite the fact that the Vietnam war officially ended thirty years ago, unresolved conflicts over the meaning of the war, and the fact that it is a war that the United States did not "win," have made the memories of the war difficult and contentious, not only for veterans but for Americans generally. In addition, many veterans are still struggling to come to terms with their own roles in the war, as their faith in themselves—and in the values of their culture—

[3]*Culture and Truth* (New York: Beacon 1989), p. 17.

was shaken by the experience. When these veterans returned home, their belief that they would be honored for having fought and risked their lives in defense of their country by those they thought they were defending was undermined by the indifference, and sometimes outright hostility, with which a number of homecoming veterans were received.

Because of such a reception, many veterans were reluctant to speak of their experiences in Vietnam or to connect or identify themselves with other veterans. They saw their postcombat symptoms as signs of their own craziness, and not the consequences of a shared experience. Although veterans who ended up in therapy groups in veterans' hospitals had some opportunity to talk about their experiences, many, if not most, Vietnam veterans bore their emotional burdens alone.

Many of these returning veterans thus sought to put Vietnam behind them and to "get on with their lives." It was only later that some of them, at least, began to feel the delayed traumatic effects of their wartime experience and found their carefully constructed postwar lives crumbling. It is from the need to address both the long-term and delayed consequences of the war, both for themselves and others, that many of the participants came to be involved in the Run for the Wall.

But why motorcycles?

Motorcycles in American Culture

Motorcycles have long held an attraction for veterans, from the returning veterans of World War II (some of whom formed the first Hell's Angels club) to current veterans of the Iraq war. For many of those who ride them, motorcycles symbolize important American values of freedom, self-reliance, patriotism, and individualism. Assertion of these values, and particularly patriotism, is evident among at least some groups of bikers—and certainly on the Run for the Wall—in the form of American flags, eagles, and other similar emblems decorating the motorcycles, the jackets, and the tee shirts of the bikers.

Many bikers also see themselves as a breed apart, "rebels" against the norms and restrictions of conventional society (even if only for the weekends they can "escape" on their motorcycles). The sense of marginality that some veterans felt on their return to civilian life, and the difficulty they may experience in adapting to that life, thus fit with the marginality of at least some segments of motorcycle culture, especially that of the "outlaw" bikers and similar groups. Motorcycle riding can also have important therapeutic effects, providing a space in which veterans feel that they can "clear their heads" and find some peace from the memories and emotional traumas that continue to haunt them.

There is a sense of solidarity and "brotherhood" that exists among bikers that is also important in the Run for the Wall. This sense of brotherhood echoes the camaraderie of warriors in combat; indeed, participating in the Run for the Wall is for some like going into battle again—this time for the POW/MIA cause and for the healing of fellow veterans. This is echoed in the military formation of the riders, rolling two by two in a long column down the highway, and in the element of danger present in any motorcycle ride, as well as in the roar of the motorcycles themselves.

By riding motorcycles, the participants in the Run for the Wall also set themselves apart from those making a cross-country journey by ordinary means. The parade of motorcycles (at points numbering several hundred bikes) riding side by side in formation down the highway presents an impressive sight, which is part of the strategy employed by the Run in its political agenda—calling attention to the POW/MIA issue. At the same time, riding motorcycles represents a more conventional element of pilgrimage—the role that hardship and suffering often play in the pilgrim's journey. Such suffering emphasizes the importance of the journey and leads to a feeling of accomplishment among those who have succeeded in reaching their destination. This sense of accomplishment is reflected in the honoring of those who have gone "all the way," that is, made the entire journey from California to Washington, D.C. The physical sensations of motorcycle riding—the noise, the motion, the riding in formation with several hundred other motorcycles, the hazards of the road—also combine to create a psychological receptivity to the ritual messages imparted along the journey's route.

But what are these messages, and how are they imparted in the course of the Run's many rituals? In order to answer this question, let us look at several of the ritual stops made during the Run for the Wall's long cross-country journey.

The Navajo Reservation and the Brotherhood of Warriors

Since its inception, the Run for the Wall, while maintaining the same basic itinerary (from California to Washington in ten days, arriving the Friday of Memorial Day weekend), has also regularly altered, added, and sometimes eliminated the various stops and ceremonies that punctuate the journey. In 1998, a new stop was added to the Run for the Wall, as the organizers of the Run responded to an invitation from the Navajo Reservation to ride to the still in progress Navajo Vietnam Veterans Memorial at Window Rock on the Run's third day out.

That particular year, the Run had endured snow on its way through the mountains of Northern Arizona and temperatures hovering around forty degrees Fahrenheit as we crossed the high desert along Interstate 40 toward Gallup (with a wind chill close to zero for those riding on motorcycles). As we turned off the interstate toward the Navajo Nation administrative center of Window Rock, we were met by a contingent of Navajo police who escorted us along the narrow two-lane road that led through the reservation. All along the route, groups of Navajo stood next to cars and pick-up trucks, waving and applauding as we rode by. As we pulled into the parking lot beneath the dramatic red rock formation that gives the town of Window Rock its name, we saw crowds of Navajo gathered around the lot and on the rocks above. We rolled to a stop and the crowd burst into enthusiastic applause. In response, the bikers gunned their engines in a collective roar. From the podium at one end of the parking lot, a Navajo leader said, "Look around you, white men—you're surrounded by Indians. We'll take your bikes. You can have our horses." His comment acknowledged both the differences that separated the Navajo from the mostly Anglo group of bikers and the shared military history that connected them. In the ceremonies that followed, Navajo leaders gave the Run a Navajo Nation flag to carry to the Wall, a Navajo folk singer performed a song he wrote in memory of a brother who died in Vietnam, Navajo children took our pictures while balancing precariously on the rocks above, and there was a demonstration by the last living World War II "code talkers" (Navajo who had participated in a secret military operation that used the Navajo language as a code). Then, as the desert light dimmed around the mystical formation of Window Rock, Navajo and non-Navajo warriors saluted while a bugler played "Taps."

At Window Rock what might be seen as an opposition (Anglo/Native American) is transformed into a common culture of the brotherhood of warriors. The horse and the motorcycle are both warrior's symbols, a dead warrior is memorialized (reminding all those present of the common sacrifices made by Navajo and non-Navajo), Navajo are connected to the riders and to the riders' destination—the Vietnam Memorial—through the presentation of the flag that the riders will carry to D.C., tying the Navajo not only to the pilgrims but also to the powerful symbols of the nation's capital and thus to the nation itself. The cold, grueling ride that preceded these ceremonies for the Run for the Wall participants placed us all in an altered and receptive state that made this ceremony at Window Rock one of the most emotionally powerful events of our pilgrimage.

The Power of Places: Evoking the Memory and Emotion of the Past at Angel Fire, New Mexico

On its fourth day out, the Run stops at the Vietnam Memorial at Angel Fire, New Mexico, high in the mountains near Taos. Although to most people it is best known as a ski area, to those who have participated in the Run for the Wall it will always be one of the most beautiful and powerful places associated with their pilgrimage. Here, high on a knoll and surrounded by a wind-swept alpine valley and snow-topped mountain peaks, stands a beautiful chapel, shaped like a white wing rising against the New Mexico sky. Next to the chapel is a memorial and museum of the Vietnam War, with photographs and exhibits. In the chapel itself, photographs of New Mexican men who died in Vietnam, looking terribly young in their military uniforms, stretches across the wall above a tier of seats descending to the lower part of the chapel and the simple cross that is the building's only ornament. There are often flowers or other offerings at the base of the cross, and on each tier of seats sits a box of tissues, mute testimony to the powerful emotions this stark and simple memorial evokes.

The memorial and chapel were built by Dr. Victor Westphal who lost his son in Vietnam, and who is now himself buried on the memorial's grounds. (Until 2004, Dr. Westphal was there to greet the Run every year, the latter years in a wheelchair.) The first year we were on the Run, there was a service held in the chapel for a veteran who had died the year before and who had been one of the original organizers of the Run. His wife spoke eloquently of what the Run's support had meant to her in her own mourning. Her words had particular resonance with this group of Vietnam veterans, many of whom still grieve for the loss of comrades in a war that was over decades ago. Then a young woman with an incredibly pure voice sang "Amazing Grace." There was not one of those wild tough bikers who had so intimidated us at the beginning of our journey who was not at that point in tears.

Many veterans have spoken to us about the significance of Angel Fire in their own spiritual and psychic journey toward healing. For those who felt they had gotten past the traumas of Vietnam and moved on with their lives, for those who had come on the Run thinking they were "just going for a ride" with fellow biker vets, Angel Fire awakened memories and reopened wounds that had never completely healed. At this point, many began to realize they had much left from the past that they had not confronted, that had continued to affect their lives and the lives of those around them. For these individuals, Angel Fire was not simply a stop on their pilgrimage; rather, it was the beginning of their *real* pilgrimage.

Part of the power of Angel Fire lies in its setting—the remoteness, the beauty, the steep, winding and somewhat hazardous mountain roads that must be traversed to get there. This creates a receptivity to the emotions of the past that are evoked by the memorial. Nor is it only those on the Run who journey here for pilgrimage. Ceremonies are held here on other days as well: on Veterans' Day and on Father's Day, in honor of the men killed in Vietnam whose children never had a chance to know them. And in between such events, more solitary pilgrimages are made by those drawn by the power of the site.

Limon, Colorado: Remembering the Missing and the Dead

Limon, Colorado is the Run's stop on its fifth night. It is a long day, riding from Cimarron, New Mexico, the previous night's stop, making several ceremonial stops along the way (including, one year, at the Colorado Vietnam memorial in Pueblo), ending up at this small town in eastern Colorado on the edge of the Great Plains. After checking into motels or the local KOA campground (where camping, as everywhere on the Run's journey, is free), many riders mount up again for the half hour ride east to the town of Hugo, where they will be served a wonderful feast prepared by the local women. Afterwards, everyone regroups at the KOA for the evening's ceremony, conducted by members of Task Force Omega, a group of families of POWs and MIAs. Here every year, as dusk falls, the names of the Colorado Missing in Action are read in a candlelight ritual that varies from year to year. On the 1999 Run, a "V" of candelabra was set up in a space near the tents, and we formed into couples, each couple assigned a month and given a list of names of those who had gone missing in Vietnam in that month. As each month was called, the woman read the names on her list. As each name was read in the gathering darkness, the man called out, "Still on patrol, sir!" Afterwards we all joined hands in a "healing circle."

The Run for the Wall's journey is punctuated with rituals such as these, rituals created by Run for the Wall participants and by the individuals and groups that host them along the way. Most of these rituals, in one way or another, commemorate the missing and the dead of the Vietnam War. In the ritual at Limon, it is specifically the missing who are memorialized, providing a ritual for those who have been left in limbo—both the missing themselves and those they have left behind, who have had no space provided for mourning those they have lost. The audience participation in the ritual joins all of us with those who are missing, and with those who mourn. The light of candles, the growing darkness, the open spaces of the looming plains ahead and the mountains behind us create a powerful ritual atmosphere, as do the voices of the dead responding to the calling of their names. They are still here, they remind us, still connected, and we should not forget. ("Missing but not forgotten," we responded in unison another year, as the names of the missing were read at this same ceremony.)

At the Wall: Confronting the Sacred Space

The Vietnam Veterans Memorial, with its two black granite wings engraved with the names of the over 58,000 American soldiers who died in Vietnam, is a particularly powerful symbol in that it memorializes both the individual and the collective dead. For many veterans, it is the Wall, and not individual grave sites, where the spirits of their dead comrades reside. And for many veterans, it is such an emotional and powerful place that they can scarcely bear to think about it, let alone visit. On my first journey with the Run, one veteran, also riding with the group for the first time, told me how terrified he was as we drew closer to our destination. He did manage to complete the journey, but, like many others, he was overcome with grief once he reached the memorial. For many, it is only because they have the support of the other pilgrims on this journey that they are able to make this pilgrimage and to confront its destination at the end.

There are no collective rituals at the Wall. Each of the pilgrims from the Run carries out his (or her) own symbolic acts, whether that be leaving important objects (wreaths, military objects, photographs, letters, and flowers), making rubbings of names, praying, or simply sitting in sorrow and contemplating the many names carved on the black granite surface. Although individual in their expression of grief and remembrance, these are rituals that would be recognized by pilgrims everywhere. Indeed, it is such activities—both the acts themselves and the many physical markers they leave behind—that often mark powerful and popular pilgrimage sites.

For many who are involved with the Run, the Wall has almost mystical powers. People speak of "Wall magic," the force that draws people to the Wall and to each other for healing. To touch a name on the Wall, I was told, is to call forth the soul of the person who died. And some veterans who keep vigil at the Wall the night after the Run arrives (the "Night Patrol") report hearing a cacophony of voices coming from the black granite surface, as if all the dead were trying to speak to them at once. Thus the Wall serves as a place of connection between worlds, between the living and the dead, as well as a place for remembering and for healing.

The Return

There are no special rituals marking the homeward journey of the Run for the Wall participants. Riders return home singly or with groups of friends, make a quick and direct journey or stop to visit friends and family, as they wish. But they return as different people, for the Run for the Wall, like many pilgrimages, is, among other things, a rite of passage and a ritual of transformation. Some have found at least a measure of peace and healing through their journey, through the support of other veterans and of those who host them along the way, and through their confrontation with the Wall and all that it represents. Others have "come out of the woods," out of the shame and guilt and sense of isolation that being a veteran has entailed, and have begun to acknowledge, and even to be proud of, their status as veterans. All have been given an opportunity—and space and support—to mourn the dead for whom the veteran's grief is often still intense and surprisingly fresh. And in a sense, many have been given the opportunity to ritually reenact the Vietnam War by riding for a cause (the POW/MIA issue) with fellow veterans, on an intense, difficult, and sometimes dangerous mission, arriving—this time in triumph—in the nation's capitol. Here, instead of the indifference and even hostility that met them when they returned from Vietnam, they are greeted with warmth and enthusiasm. Thus through ritual, they, in some sense, at least, "rewrite" their own history, as well as that of the war, and become heroes, at last, in what is for many "the parade they never had."

Conclusion: The Journey that Has No End

Pilgrimage, an ancient ritual, continues to flourish today in a range of forms. To understand its continuing popularity, we must also look to the many reasons why people undertake such ritual journeys. One of the answers to this may lie in the creative potential of pilgrimage itself, for, as the Run for the Wall illustrates, it is a ritual readily adapted to a variety of situations and to a range of human needs. Indeed, pilgrimage may be a perfect ritual for a contemporary global world, as it both lends itself to our individual purposes and desires and connects us to the larger world.

Like most rituals, the Run for the Wall, also offers itself to many meanings and interpretations. That two individuals who opposed the Vietnam War, and who find some of the kinds of patriotic sentiments celebrated on the Run distasteful, can nonetheless find their participation in the Run for the Wall one of the most moving and powerful experiences of their lives, is testimony to this. It became clearer to me through my own participation the ways in which a pilgrimage, like other rituals, can be many, even contradictory, things at once: a political movement and a personal journey of healing, a celebration of the warrior and a memorial to the tragedy of war, an experience of liminality by the marginal and a mode of integration and the overcoming of marginality, a journey away and a coming home.

As I write this article, the United States is once again engaged in foreign wars, in Iraq and in Afghanistan, and these wars are increasingly reflected in the Run for the Wall and its rituals. (Even prior to these wars, the Run had already attracted some Gulf War veterans, and had begun to broaden its mission to include the veterans, and the missing and the dead, of all American wars.) In 2003, Lori Piestewa, the first Native American woman to die in combat, was memorialized at Run for the Wall ceremonies in Gallup, New Mexico. In the 2004 Run, we were joined by both returning Iraq veterans and those about to be deployed, and prayers were offered daily for the safety of all those serving. Remembering their own treatment when they returned from war, several veterans reminded participants to be sure that today's returning veterans were better received and cared for. As the Vietnam veterans on the Run can testify, the wounds of war are deep and long lasting. For these reasons, then, the Run for the Wall is a ritual journey whose end is nowhere in sight.

Review Questions

1. What does Dubisch mean by the term *ritual?* What are the basic parts of rituals?

2. What is a pilgrimage, according to Dubisch? What are the common features of a pilgrimage?

3. What kind of people started the Run for the Wall? Why? What effect does Dubisch say the run has on its participants?

4. Dubisch argues that the Run for the Wall has a strong emotional and transformative impact on those who participate. What appears to generate such intense feelings?

30

Cargo Beliefs and Religious Experience

Stephen C. Leavitt

Revitalization movements usually respond to a feeling of loss and power-
lessness caused by rapid change and colonial domination, and several have
given rise to great world religions. One of the most unusual examples of re-
vitalization movements, however, has occurred in New Guinea. These are
cargo cults (cargo is pidgin for Western goods) that attempt, through ritual,
to generate cargo wealth thought to be under the control of ancestral spirits.
In this article, Stephen Leavitt reviews the history and social functions of
cargo cults. But he goes a step further by showing how cargo cults meet the
needs of individuals, especially the need for support from one's immediate
ancestors.

In August 1984 I began two years' research among the Bumbita Arapesh in the East Sepik Province of Papua New Guinea. I had planned to study religious experience in a secret men's cult. Soon after I arrived, though, I was told that the men's cult was gone forever: only two months earlier several Bumbita acting in the name of Jesus had revealed the cult secrets to women and children, making it impossible for the men to return to cult activities. Nevertheless, I had come at an opportune time, some said, for Jesus himself was due to arrive and usher in a new age in November.

The Bumbita and their neighbors were in the midst of what was locally known as a "revival," a period of widespread Evangelical Christianity. Missionaries had been in the area since the 1950s when the South Sea Evangelical Mission had established a station in Bumbita territory. However, they had had only limited success in converting local people; many people had been baptized at some point, but most had also left the church again after their enthusiasm had died down. All agreed, though, that 1984 was different. The revelation of cult secrets meant that there was no turning back to the old religion.

As time passed, I learned that some of the Bumbita Christian ideas were quite different from our own. Most Bumbita did find in Christianity a promise of a transformed world of happiness, and they believed that when Jesus came, there would no longer be illness, hunger, or death. But many also hoped for the arrival of vast material wealth. In their view, Jesus would bring with him huge quantities of rice, tinned meat, clothing, housing materials, and other goods. These are the kinds of goods that Europeans had brought with them into the area. As many Bumbita see it, all of this material wealth must have a magical or spiritual origin—it must be their own ancestors who really own the wealth, and somehow the Europeans figured out how to acquire some of it. Through Jesus' return, the ancestors would now be passing all their wealth onto their living descendants and rightful heirs.

These ideas were familiar to me because they were similar to those found in "cargo cults," the well-known religious movements that had been going on for generations in Papua New Guinea. Cargo cults are religious movements that involve attempts, usually through ritual, to attain vast amounts of material wealth thought to be under the control of ancestral spirits. In the early days of European colonization of the Pacific, when supplies of cargo were routinely unloaded from ships, the display of wealth made a strong impression on the local peoples. Although their own societies had complex ritual and social systems, and although they had developed intricate seafaring technologies, the Pacific islanders were truly amazed at what the Europeans possessed. It was not long before religious movements appeared, seeking to explain this seemingly miraculous access to wealth. Cult leaders would tell people that the Europeans must be following special rituals, that if they too could follow them carefully, the ancestors would return with the cargo. The rituals often involved imitating strange behaviors observed in Europeans, such as forming rigid lines and marching in unison or singing hymns for hours on end in church services. Frequently, cargo movements incorporated Christian ideas learned from missionaries, even though the missions opposed this kind of reinterpretation of the Christian message.

In some instances, the rituals became very elaborate. People built imitation communication centers and airstrips with bamboo control towers in hopes that cargo-laden planes would then land. In one well-known cult, now called the "Johnson cult," leaders even collected money from their followers to send to the United States in hopes of buying President Lyndon Johnson.

The largest movement to touch the Bumbita area occurred in 1971, when the cult leader Yaliwan claimed that the removal of two cement geological survey markers from the top of a well-known mountain would release cargo from the mountain. Yaliwan's organization collected membership fees from people over a wide area. The idea was that if one was an official member, one would be sure to get a share of the cargo when it came. On the appointed day villagers in even distant areas stayed in their houses, in fear of a terrible cataclysm. The markers were unearthed and carried down the mountainside, but the ancestors' failure to arrive did not stop the movement. In fact, Yaliwan was subsequently elected to represent his district in the national parliament.

The recurring cargo movements posed serious problems for colonial administrators because, although the cults were most active, people would neglect their gardens and other work in hopes that a new world would soon be upon them. There was also a concern that people would be duped into giving hard-earned money to cult leaders. In fact, money-collecting for cargo cult activity was made illegal by the colonial government, and when Papua New Guinea gained independence in 1975, those laws remained on the books. Today, although the term "cargo cult" has a bad name in Papua New Guinea, people continue to have strong beliefs in the ancestral control of cargo, and these beliefs continue to find expression in Christian religious movements like the Bumbita revival in 1984.

The seemingly bizarre beliefs typical of cargo cults have intrigued anthropologists interested in religious movements and the impact of colonial rule. Researchers saw similarities between these cults and religious movements in other parts of the world. The emphasis on ritual, the reliance on visions of charismatic leaders, and the hopes for a complete world transformation are common features of cults organized in response to colonial domination. In the nineteenth century, for example, Native American religious movements such as the Ghost Dance sought to create a new world through the performance of key rituals. These movements had arisen in response to crises over the loss of cultural traditions and the disappearance of the buffalo. Anthropologists saw the cargo cult as another example of the way people try to regenerate meaning in a time of cultural crisis.

But the emphasis on ancestral control of cargo was distinctive, and to explain this feature anthropologists looked to the pre-existing cultural understandings of Pacific peoples. The traditional religions of Papua New Guinea emphasized the role of ancestral spirits in taking care of people. A family could produce a thriving crop of yams or sweet potatoes only with magical assistance from ancestral spirits. It therefore made sense to think that European food and other goods might also come from this supernatural source. In addition, traditional cultures in Papua New Guinea placed a great deal of emphasis on exchange and the giving of gifts as a basis for building relationships and achieving prestige. People cemented friendships, built alliances, and resolved disputes by mounting large-scale exchanges of food with others. They also competed with rivals by engaging in competitive exchanges.

The Europeans who arrived did not share the same view of how relationships are built. They had control over extremely attractive material goods, but they refused to enter into proper exchange relations with the local people. Instead, they instituted colonial control and acted as superiors. Some anthropologists have argued, then, that the Papua New Guinean preoccupation with cargo is a way of rebuilding a sense of independence and prestige in the face of colonial rule.

My own research suggests that these explanations make sense, but that they cannot be the whole answer. Contemporary Papua New Guineans know quite a bit about how commerce works and where material goods come from. Many earn money through jobs or cash-cropping, and they buy Western goods for themselves. European colonial control has been replaced by an independent government. Nevertheless, many people today—people who have gone through schools, worked in plantations or factories, and participated in failed cargo cults—continue to look for a way to get cargo from ancestors. Why do cargo ideas persist after so many years?

Cargo ideology has to be understood as part of a religious world view that gives meaning to the larger questions in life while it also addresses the most deeply personal concerns of individual believers. Colonial rule is gone and some money is now available, but Papua New Guineans must still deal with the fact that they are relatively insignificant players on the world stage, and they have relatively little wealth in comparison to people elsewhere. Cargo ideology takes these diffuse and irresolvable existential problems and translates them into an idiom that is deeply personal. Instead of having to think about their position in the world at large, people can focus on their relations with those close to them. The "ancestors" that people turn to for cargo are not distant and anonymous supernatural beings; they are in fact the spirits of fathers, mothers, and other close kin. This means that to really understand the central idea behind cargo— that ancestors will bring wealth and bestow it upon the living—one needs to think in terms of what it means personally for a given individual. Cargo ideas are about relations with deceased parents. Often, getting cargo means receiving a sign, a gift, from one's own parents or grandparents showing that they forgive, that they still care.

When Bumbita men and women try to understand cargo in terms of their relationships with their own parents, they are looking for a way to give real meaning to all the bewildering changes that have been going on around them. It is a way for them to recast their colonial experience in terms that they can understand and deal with. But there is a cost. The problem is that for most people, the bulk of the cargo has not—and never will—arrive. As the Bumbita see it, the ancestors are for some unknown reason still holding back. This means that their religious experience remains filled with feelings of longing and remorse. It can be a difficult emotional predicament.

To illustrate the personal side to religious experience, my work focuses on detailed narratives or stories collected from several individuals. The idea is to speak with a few people in depth, recording their narratives carefully, so that I can later follow their line of thinking in detail. This method has the virtue of showing the personal side to religious belief while at the same time allowing people's words to stand for themselves. A major drawback is that such individual stories cannot be viewed as "representative" of the society as a whole. Personal stories must necessarily remain personal. Nevertheless, I believe this approach offers a richer sense of themes that might well be a part of other people's experience as well.

To illustrate, let's look at the stories of two older men who, when they converted, adopted the Christian names "Matthew" and "John." Each was around sixty years old when I did my interviews (some 25 hours total). I visited them at their houses or asked them to visit me, and we usually talked, alone, for one to two hours in a sitting. I tried not to guide them too much, but I did make it known that I was interested in their religious beliefs.

Matthew, a widower, first converted to Christianity in 1967, and he remains one of the most vocal proponents of the Christian cause in the Bumbita area. Before converting he was trained as a sorcerer, and he admits that he practiced sorcery. Matthew is well known for his preoccupation with the local missionaries and with Europeans in general. Everywhere he goes he carries a large sack containing Christian literature, calendars of years past, photographs of his favorite missionaries, and even some letters from them sent from various countries. Every item in his bundle is tattered, stained, and frayed, showing signs of frequent handling. His house also has mementos of his relations with missionaries, including a child's plastic gramophone with a stack of 78 r.p.m. records of sermons translated by the mission into the Bumbita Arapesh language. Matthew has been active in every cargo movement that has touched the Bumbita area.

Interviews with Matthew showed that one attraction of cargo beliefs for him was to resolve feelings of guilt that he had toward his father who had died some years before. Throughout his adult life, Matthew had a troubled relationship with his father. He says that his father once tried to seduce his fiancée, when she was living in their hamlet. Matthew claims that when he found out, he even tried to kill his father with a spear. As punishment, the father was banished for life from the village. Matthew believes that his father later retaliated with sorcery by killing Matthew's wife (she died in childbirth). Although he and his father were reconciled later, Matthew still longs for some sign that his father had forgiven him—a sign that he had not received before his father died.

Matthew's story will show that he was searching for a sign of forgiveness from his dead father by cultivating relationships with European missionaries. Matthew's most startling belief was that among these missionaries was one who was really the ghost of his own father. It is, in fact, a common belief among the Bumbita that some Europeans are the spirits of dead relatives. But Matthew, more than most people, appeared to be longing to find his personal ghost and to get from him a gift of cargo that would signal his father's forgiveness. All of this came out in a story Matthew told me about his parting with a local missionary who was going home to Germany. Matthew had brought the missionary some yams and greens as a farewell gift. He describes the subsequent interaction:

> [I asked the missionary about his leaving, and] he said that he would stay. But then when I asked him [again], he didn't answer and I sat down. He went and got a funnel and filled it with salt for me, and then I asked him. I said, "I think you are my father. I think you have the face of my father, Turingi, and your wife is like my mother, Tinga'wen. I can see the resemblance." And there was no answer. He did not answer me because he was ashamed. He said, "Just take the salt and go. You shouldn't come and blabber too much." [laughs] And now you see here, I have written their names in my book.

Matthew is claiming here that his father has returned from the dead as a European missionary. He says he can tell by the quiet way the man reacted when he gave him food—he was ashamed, so he silently gives Matthew a gift of salt and tells him to be quiet about this.

In reality, the missionary most likely thought he was paying Matthew for the yams and greens, but Matthew has come to see it in another way, as a gesture of intimate communication. The missionary says nothing, and Matthew takes it as a tacit confession, as if to say, "Yes, I am your father, you have guessed it, but say nothing to anyone about it." The gift was for Matthew a silent symbolic statement about the goodwill in their relationship. Although the gift of salt was a trivial one, Matthew's reaction to it shows his longing for more extensive cargo: he wants to be given material wealth by Europeans because he believes this cargo is really a gift from his own dead kin signaling their love for him.

My interviews with a second man, John, also showed that dreams of cargo had a deep personal significance. Unlike Matthew, John was a highly respected leader in his day. He was now sixty years old and retired. John was a short man by Bumbita standards, and he retained a lively demeanor. John also felt that his father would be the ultimate source of the cargo. But although Matthew looked for father figures among the missionaries, John saw God himself as his father.

John looked for God to give his approval by giving him secret knowledge as a key to material wealth. In the Bumbita view, it is proper to expect a father-ancestor to offer secrets and magical help, and John is extending this idea to include the concept of cargo. As John saw it, with the cargo he could then become a great and powerful leader by distributing it to others, just as traditionally Bumbita leaders had built power by giving away pigs and yams. Like Matthew, John feels that receiving the cargo will be final proof of his father's good will and approval.

John said God communicated with him mostly through dreams. In Bumbita culture, dreams are regarded as real experiences, albeit in a spiritual realm. People use dreams as omens to guide them in their hunting or in their pursuit of love relationships. Here John related to me one dream he had had some two months before the interview in which I recorded it. The dream went as follows:

> I dreamt that I had gone inside a house. I went and I sat like this. Everything here, the books, the money, were heaped around. I was on the edge of it all. It was a big house. A huge house. A house of iron. It had rooms that went on and on and I was sitting at the fence in front. Now I don't know how to write things; reading, yes, I can read some, but [someone else] would have to write [for me]. . . . But my [dream] spirit, when I went into this house, I went and I myself wrote everything and I myself checked everything over. I wrote and straightened the books and put them aside. . . . Then I got up to come back and a voice said, "Now you have come."—it was like a sign, right? When you can see it all. [It said,] "Later, when you come back, you will sit at this spot. Yes, you will straighten up everything later. Now you have seen it and written everything down and straightened it up and you will go. Later when you come back, you will straighten it all up, later, not now." . . . I woke up and remembered this and then went to sleep again, and a voice said, "This man, . . . he will come and stay at this house and check everything and distribute it to the people here. . . . This man will become a king. The king for distributing everything, for checking everything."

In this dream, John identifies himself with the clerks in the warehouses, with those people he sees as controlling the material wealth. His view is that clerks are very powerful because they preside over the goods. He says that God made him a clerk to show him that he will in fact be like "a king" in the new age, doling out the fates of the people. His main activity in the dream is writing, a skill still associated with Europeans and a sore point for adults who see their children learning to write in school. In this dream John shows that he looks to God to make him a great leader by giving him the power to distribute cargo.

A second dream has some of the same messages, but here John's ideas about the dream show that, as with Matthew, the core emotional content has to do with his own father. The high position that John sees for himself in the new age must be given to him by God, and for John, that God is his actual father. In this account, I follow John's statements step by step to show how his thoughts lead him from a dream about cargo to his personal relationship with his own father. He begins,

> [One night] I took the Bible inside and made a fire and just lay down. I said, "God"—I prayed—"God, I want you to show me my present now, where is it? I want to see it. . . .
> I want you yourself to show me so I can see it . . . I want to see my present." All right, when I went to sleep, I went straight to it. Man, I went inside, they—a big house.

At this point, he stumbled over his words because he felt he had to hide part of the dream as he related it to me. He later revealed to me that it had not been "a big house" that he had seen in the dream, but actually a graveyard. The dead were presiding over the cargo in the graveyard. John said that he had originally hidden this fact from me because he had not wanted to be accused of being a "cargo cultist." He went on to say that he was not a cargo cultist but a "good man," that he had not sought out the details of the dream—God himself had given them to him. He wants me to take him seriously and not write him off as a cultist. What he is about to say is important to him. He continues:

> They had put up a cloth from Hong Kong. They had hung it up and it went down like this, at the door. When I went and lifted up this cloth and pulled it up—Sorry! Huge huge boxes, more and more of them, going up to the clouds. Many many boxes. . . . In just one box, there would be so much inside. With two or three there would be even more. I just gazed up at them like this. When I looked down, I saw mushrooms growing on the boxes, and I thought, "They were good here, but some of them, I think they have already rotted. Everything has rotted so there are mushrooms growing there." . . . I checked the ones that were on top and they were still good. You know, they went up and up and then at the top—I looked up, and I thought, "Hey, I hope a box doesn't come off and fall and break my head." So I lifted my leg onto one of the boxes and climbed on up and up and then I started and I was there lying in my bed. Then what did I do? I cried and cried over the present that God had shown me.

This dream conveys well the awe inspired by visions of cargo. The cargo here was under the control of the ancestors since, as he later confessed, the setting of the dream was really a graveyard and not a "house." As often happens in Bumbita dreams about the dead, an image of rot and decay appears in the dream, along with some anxiety, evident here in his fear that a case might fall on top of him. But unlike with most dreams about the dead, John interprets these images in a way that avoids unpleasantness. He points out that the decay indicates that God was saying that there would be so much cargo that much of it would rot with no one to use it, and he also succeeds in waking up before any boxes fall. John's euphoria over having had this dream points to the emotional power of the cargo itself. The cargo is a "present" that has deep meaning.

As his narrative continues, John then goes on immediately to link these cargo images to childhood memories of the amassed food of men from his father's generation. In Bumbita society, the ability to grow and display huge quantities of yams is the highest expression of male achievement. John continues,

> [Our ancestors] used to fill up the yams, in a huge bin. . . . We would dance and then go and give it to [our exchange partners]. So now I saw this image [of cargo in the dream], and it was just like what they used to do before, what [our fathers] did. It would go way up and up. Heaps and heaps of food, and given away. Now God has shown this to me. The present is hidden.

Here he links the heaps of food for exchange with the image of cargo from his dream. He talks of the mounds of food going "up and up," in what suggests a vision of a child's awe at the sight of such amounts of food. He links it with the awe he felt in the dream upon discovering the true extent of the wealth (the "present") controlled by the dead. Thus, the emotions he felt in his dream at the sight of the cargo were not unfamiliar—he remembers similar feelings from a time when senior men used to assemble food for exchange. In this way,

John reveals what is for him a symbolic link between the ancestors of his dream and the senior adult male figures from his youth.

John then returns immediately to the significance of his having been shown the "present." He says:

> The present that [God] has shown me, the present here, it will all happen. You will see it, I am happy with him too. All of the time that I walk around my thinking dwells on only this. I don't stray from it. I think only of this that God has shown me. I think of it like this. If a man is no good, if a man has sins, if he prays and asks God for something, then God won't answer his prayer. No way. Because this thing, the sin, is there. It closes off the path to God. . . . How is God going to tell you? . . . If you are a holy man, free, and you are with God, he will hear it and God will answer. You will see God.

By this point, John has gone from a dream's image of splendid cargo to a sense of awe at the power of older generations, and finally to the argument that seeing cargo proves he is right with God. All that remains is for him to make the transition to his own father. And indeed, immediately following the passage cited above, he continues:

> A good man will see [God] here. God, I know, the God of the Christians. My God is—if I am Christian, then my God is Christian. Now he has died, and now I have seen him. I know now. It is finished. [laughs] Sorry, if I talk on like this, then the happiness is going to well up now! He will come. My God . . . [overcome with emotion, he laughs to avoid crying. He pauses]
>
> SL: You said you have seen him, what does he look like, God?
>
> My God? A big man, a big man. Before he was short, but now that he has gone, he's a big man. Happiness. I am happy with him. True, if before, he weren't Christian, yes, he would have gone and been lost. . . . But he was already Christian when he died. So now he's there. He will look after me, he is with me. He was Christian already. Now he has shown me everything. Who is he? God the father.

As he becomes absorbed with what he is saying, his description of God's position on revealing secrets to sinners becomes almost a reverie in the memory of his own father, of a short man who now seems big to him, of someone who looks after him, and above all, of someone who has shown him an image of the mass of wealth that the ancestors control. John is overcome by the recognition that his father/God has decided to reserve a special place for him in the new age, that he, John, will be the new leader.

Thus John's Christianity, with its concern about cargo and its inspired hopes for reunion with the dead, also works its way back to a personal relationship with his own father. John's God is his father, and the cargo is his sign of reassurance. John has become convinced that by being a Christian he will acquire that cargo.

For the Bumbita, Christian doctrines preach that the ancestors have good will, that in the end, in the transformation that will come with the return of Christ, they will demonstrate that good will and they will deliver. In his final summation of his thoughts about his father, John expresses with some eloquence the personal significance of getting the cargo, of knowing about and seeing God. He says in a whisper, again fighting tears:

> Now [in my life] I am just the same as I was before. But in my dreams, yes, I get it all. Life will go on until Jesus comes. Then I will get it, I will know about him, I will see him. His thinking. His wishes. The eyes of my father. Me and him. The eyes of father God, I will know them.

Although each of these stories bears the stamp of two different personalities, they both reveal a perspective that is a well-known part of New Guinean ideas about cargo. At the heart of it is the hope that the world will be transformed by renewed relationships with spirits of the dead. What these narratives suggest is that when some Bumbita think about their futures, whether it be their own personal lives or their larger place on the world stage, they do so in terms of a familiar family scenario, with parental figures (spirits) sharing or withholding gifts. By thinking of the situation in this way, they can take the bewildering and difficult problems of coping with the colonial experience and translate them into a much more personal and familiar set of ideas about love and nurture. In the end, cargo is important because it is a visible sign that the spirits are there and that they do care.

The stories of Matthew and John show how beliefs about cargo in Papua New Guinea can take the shape they do from the role they play in giving meaning to individuals. Although it is dangerous to make broad generalizations from the accounts of two people, their stories do point to a personal side of cargo ideas that has not been emphasized in most anthropological explanations. To have a more complete understanding of religious experience, one has to pay close attention to what individual believers say about the significance of their beliefs for their own lives. In the case of cargo beliefs, we can see that there is more going on than one might at first think. It is not just that the Bumbita have come to some unusual conclusions about how to interpret the changes in their world—they are also making an active effort to integrate the changes into their deepest personal sense of who they are.

Review Questions

1. What are the main attributes of most cargo cults, according to Leavitt? Give some examples of the form cargo cults can take.

2. How have anthropologists tried to explain cargo cults?

3. Under what conditions do cargo cults occur, and what is their goal?

4. In what ways do cargo cults embrace the teaching of Christian missionaries?

5. Why does Leavitt think cargo cults persist? What is their religious function for individuals?

N I N E

Globalization

Several times a week, a small island freighter leaves Granada's Saint George's harbor loaded with fuel drums, crates of processed food, boxes containing manufactured goods, and an occasional motor scooter or car. When its hold is filled, 60 or 70 passengers, many of them women, troop across the gang plank and settle down among the freight or take a seat in a small cabin set aside for them on the upper aft deck. They are bound for their small island home, Carriacou, located about 35 miles by sea to the north. Most are returning from overseas work in New York, Britain, or mainland Europe, where they worked for a few years as maids and cleaners or at other service jobs. Carrying gifts of CD players, clothing, shoes, and other items manufactured outside their island, they will be greeted warmly by their relatives, whom they have alerted by phone or e-mail about the time of their arrival. Most returnees have already wired home money they saved from their off-island work and are beginning to think about using it to build a house or buy items that will make their lives easier and more secure.

The people returning to Carriacou illustrate a major trend that is sweeping the world: globalization. **Globalization** consists of powerful forces that reshape local conditions on an ever-intensifying scale.[1] Although places such as Carriacou may seem peripheral to globalization, the impact of international money, tourists, transportation, goods, and the movement of the island's peoples to other parts of the world have all affected the way people live there. And their experience is repeated in many other parts of the world.

Globalization may occur on several levels. In the most general and formal sense, we can talk about it as a world system. The **world system** is often defined in market terms and links nations and people together economically. More accurately, it is **transnational;** it consists of companies and patterns of exchange that transcend national borders and may evade control by individual

[1]This definition is taken from Emily Schultz and Robert Lavenda, *Cultural Anthropology: A Perspective on the Human Condition,* 6th ed. (New York: Oxford University Press, 2005), p. 363.

governments. An international company may have a headquarters located in Bermuda; manufacturing facilities in Atlanta, Mexico, and Shanghai; customer service representatives in Mumbai; and investors from thirty or forty different countries. Japanese cars and motorcycles sold in the United States reflect the transnational world system. So do the tuna caught by American trawlers in the Atlantic and shipped overnight to Japan to make sushi.

The world system affects local conditions by providing goods, stimulating production, and introducing ideas. As a result, local people can easily find themselves both motivated by and at the mercy of world markets. For example, the government of India, through its state and district development offices, encouraged tribals living in Southern Rajasthan to dedicate some of their cropland to sericulture (silk worm production). Local farmers borrowed money to build "cocoon houses," and to underwrite the cost of fertilizing mulberry bushes for the silk worms to eat. The World Bank advanced money for a small cocoon processing factory. The program was a success—farmers doubled their money each year; women earned wages in the processing plant—until, that is, the Chinese government arbitrarily lowered the price of the silk its farmers produced by half. Unable to compete, the Indian program failed, disrupting the lives of people who embraced it. Stories like this should not come as a surprise to American workers who have lost jobs to "outsourcing," and to factory workers in other countries who are now employed to take their place.

The international movement of people also illustrates globalization. **Refugees,** people who immigrate to other parts of the world because it is too dangerous for them to stay in their homeland, have moved to many countries. **Guest workers** (people granted permission to work in a country other than their own) are found in many parts of the world. Legal immigrants (and illegal immigrants) diversify populations in many nations. The result is that some societies are becoming **multicultural;** people with different cultural backgrounds live side by side. Just as companies can be transnational, so can immigrants, workers, and refugees. People who originate from the same cultural areas often communicate with one another, calling or e-mailing home, wiring money to each other, and forming a visiting network. **Tourism** is the world's largest industry and regularly brings people with different backgrounds into contact.

Finally, globalization is marked by cultural diffusion. **Cultural diffusion,** or cultural borrowing, represents the movement of cultural ideas and artifacts from one society to another. Coca Cola has diffused from the United States to many parts of the world; sushi has diffused from Japan to the United States and Europe. So have musical styles, forms of dress, words, and a variety of other cultural items.

In almost every case, societies that borrow aspects of another group's culture adapt them to their own ways of life. Borrowed items usually undergo **cultural hybridization;** they are a mixture of the borrowed and the local. A hamburger in China will probably not taste exactly like one cooked on the backyard grill of an American family. Curry in the United States tastes different from the "real thing" prepared in India. (Note that as the local size of immigrant populations rise, more genuine, meaning closer to its ethnic origins, food becomes available to the original residents as well.)

The articles in Part 9 illustrate several of these points. The first, by Dianna Shandy, is an updated version of an article included in the previous edition. It describes the ordeal faced by Nuer refugees as they attempt to gain admittance and establish a life in the United States. Fleeing the civil war that has wracked their home in southern Sudan, Nuer refugees must develop the skill and determination to pass through a series of bureaucratic hurdles to reach and adjust to life in the United States. Personal initiative, education, using U.S. NGOs, and the sharing of information about what works are keys to their success. The second selection, by Denise Brennan, looks at tourism, a less permanent way people move about the world. She focuses on the Dominican town of Sosúa and the young women who travel there to work in the sex trade. Sosúa is a destination for European men looking for inexpensive relations with attractive Caribbean women. The relationships it offers often disappoint sex workers who hope that intimate associations with Europeans will gain them a sponsor and visa for travel to Europe or money wired regularly by new boyfriends. In the third article, Ian Condry describes a form of pop culture, hip-hop, that has spread from the United States to Japan. Reviewing more general globalization theory, he shows how hip-hop has been hybridized in the Japanese context and how anthropologists, with their emphasis on local settings, can show what globalization means to people as they conduct their daily lives.

Key Terms

cultural diffusion   *p. 342*
cultural hybridization   *p. 342*
globalization   *p. 341*
guest workers   *p. 342*
multicultural   *p. 342*

refugees   *p. 342*
tourism   *p. 342*
transnational   *p. 341*
world system   *p. 341*

31

The Road to Refugee Resettlement

Dianna Shandy

In the early days of the discipline, anthropologists usually studied non-Western groups that they assumed were bounded and clearly definable. Such groups were named (often by outsiders) and were thought to have territories and a common language and culture. Although anthropologists recognized that many of the groups they studied had outside connections—that they freely borrowed culture, intermarried, and migrated—most still felt it was reasonable to talk about groups as if they were bounded units. However, the picture is changing, as this updated article by Dianna Shandy clearly shows. Today people are on the move. Some are migrants looking for economic opportunity; others are refugees. Here Shandy, using the case of the Nuer from southern Sudan, shows how refugees fleeing a perpetual civil war manage to gain relocation in the United States and how they have sought to adapt to the demands of life among Americans. A key to the process is the role played by the United Nations and social service agencies and the Nuer's own determination to better (in their terms) themselves.

A Nuer youth, Thok Ding *(not his real name)* lies prone alongside two other boys on the dusty, clay ground on the outskirts of a village in southern Sudan. A man crouches over him with a razor blade. Beginning with the right side, the man makes six parallel cuts from each side of the youth's forehead to the center to create scars called *gaar*. This ritual scarification, which has been outlawed in Nuer areas since the 1980s, still marks entry into manhood for many Nuer young men.

A few years later in Minneapolis, Minnesota, Thok sits in pained concentration in front of a computer screen in a driver's license examination office. Still weak in English, he struggles to recall the multiple choice response sequence he memorized to pass the exam, in this stressful, but less painful, American rite of passage into adulthood.

When I began ethnographic work among Nuer refugees living in Minnesota, Iowa, and several other regions of the United States in 1997, I immediately was struck by the incongruity of their lives. The Nuer are a famous people in anthropology. They were the subject of three books by the well-known late British social anthropologist, Sir E. E. Evans-Pritchard, who described their pastoralist mode of subsistence, complex segmented kinship system, and religion. Evans-Pritchard conducted research among the Nuer in the 1930s. He described the Nuer as a tall, independent, confident people whose existence revolved around the needs of their cattle, especially the requirement to move the animals from high to low ground and back again each year. During the dry season from September to April, the cattle were herded to lower ground where there was still water and grass. During the rainy season, the lowlands became a swampy lagoon and the herds had to be moved to the highlands where rain had restored the range. This transhumant lifestyle and the need to guard cattle against raiders from nearby tribes had shaped Nuer society. (The Nuer were also the subject of a well-known ethnographic film, "The Nuer," made by Robert Gardner and released in 1970, which showed them to be much as Evans-Pritchard had described them.)

So when I first met Nuer people in Minnesota in the mid-1990s, these Northeast African pastoralists seemed out of place. Tall (most men are well over six feet in height) and still displaying the (for men) prominent forehead scars received at their initiations, the Nuer had come to live in one of the coldest parts of the United States. Why had they left their ancestral home? What did their status as refugees mean and how did they get it? How had they managed to come to the United States? Why had they been located, as it turns out, in more than 30 different U.S. states? How would a people raised as cattle herders adapt to U.S. urban settings? Would they remain in the United States on a temporary or permanent basis? How would they maintain a relationship with the families they left behind? And finally in a broader sense, what does all this tell us about the interconnectedness of a globalizing world and about anthropology's role in it?

Becoming a Refugee

Until recently, most Americans called the people who settled here *immigrants*. No distinctions were made based on the reasons people had chosen to come here or the circumstances they had left behind. In general, their arrival was encouraged and welcome because the country was spacious and their skills and labor were needed.

Today, things are different. There are immigrants and *refugees*. In the past, refugees were a kind of immigrant. They were people who came here to escape from intolerable conditions in their homelands, such as pogroms, the threat of military conscription, civil wars, and famine. The fact that they were escaping from something, however, did not affect whether or not they could enter the United States. Most people, especially those from Europe, were welcome.

Over the last 50 years, however, refugees have come to occupy a formal status, both in the eyes of the United Nations and U.S. immigration officials. They are not just *internally displaced persons (IDPs)*, those who have left their homes but who are still in their own country. Officially, meaning how the United Nations and national governments define them, a refugee group is one that shares a "well-founded fear of persecution" based on any of five factors such as race, religion, nationality, membership in a particular social group, or political opinion, and who has left their home country. How the United Nations or national governments apply this definition when they seek to certify individuals as refugees varies. But the number of people that claim to fit this description and who seek asylum skyrocketed at the end of the Cold War in 1989 to an estimated 12 million in 2003.

Bureaucracies control who can be classified as a refugee. In 1950 the United Nations established a formal agency to help with the refugee "problem" headed by the United Nations High Commissioner for Refugees (UNHCR). The agency recognizes three options, or what it calls "durable solutions," to address the situation of refugees around the world: voluntary repatriation to the country of origin, integration into a country of asylum, or rarely, third country resettlement, meaning a move from one country of asylum to one that offers possibilities for a more permanent home. Initially housed in refugee camps, displaced people can apply for official refugee status with the hope of resettlement in another country, or that conditions will stabilize in their own country, allowing them to return home.

Many countries have agreed to take in a limited number of refugees as a way of settling them more permanently, and the United States is one of them. To do this, the United States sets a limit on the number of refugees it will accept each year and uses a bureaucratic process to screen prospective refugees it might be willing to take in. Over the past decade, the United States has re-settled an average of 87,000 refugees here each year, with a sharp dip in numbers in the wake of September 11, 2001. The process is complicated by the fact that the criteria for admission can change, different government officials interpret the criteria dissimilarly, and resettlement policy can shift from one year to the next. It is also complicated by cross-cultural misunderstanding. The U.S. bureaucracy works differently from the way governments operate in the refugee's country of origin. Languages are a major barrier. Categories of meaning are not shared. The screening process is intended to determine "real" refugees, or those who cannot be protected by their home governments, and "economic" migrants who leave their home voluntarily to seek a better life. In practice the distinction is often difficult to establish.

The Nuer living in Minnesota and other regions of the United States have managed to come through this process successfully. They have made it to camps that process refugees, discovered how to enter the bureaucratic process designed to certify them as refugees, learned how to tell a sufficiently convincing refugee story to gain certification and found a way to get on the list to be resettled in the United States.

Thok Ding's life illustrates this process. Thok was born in southern Sudan and lived in a small village. As in most Nuer households, Thok lived with his mother, father, siblings, and his father's extended family. Thok had family members who lived in a nearby town and attended school, but there was no school in his village. His first memory is of going to the forest to take care of his calves when he was seven or eight. He would leave home in the early morning with other boys his age, taking food with him to eat while he was grazing the cattle and protecting the calves from wild animals. Girls, on the other hand, would stay closer to home and were charged with milking the cows.

When he was in his early teens, he, along with other boys who were the same age, underwent the ritual scarification *gaar* ceremony ushering him into manhood. After undergoing this painful ritual, Thok said that now that he was a man, he could be "free." "You can do whatever you like. You can have a woman. You can have a home by yourself. You can live away from your parents."

Shortly after his initiation, the civil war that wracked the southern Sudan caught up with him. Fueled by events that extend back much further in time, civil war has engulfed the Sudan since just before it gained independence from joint English–Egyptian colonial rule until the present, with just a brief interlude of peace from the early 1970s until 1983. This ongoing strife in the Sudan frequently is attributed to social distinctions based on geography (north–south), ethnicity (Arab–African), and religion (Muslim–Christian). But, as the recent Darfur crisis has illustrated, these are fluid categories. From a southern perspective, northern Muslim Arabs entered their land in the 1800s looking for ivory and slaves. Northerners were favored under colonial rule, which gave them more power and increased tension with people, such as the Nuer, living in the south. Today, it is the Khartoum government, located in the north, that is engaged in war with southerners who seek self-government.

Nuer society has suffered cataclysmic shifts in the decades since Evans-Pritchard conducted his fieldwork, a fact well documented by anthropologist Sharon Hutchinson in her book *Nuer Dilemmas* published in 1996. For example, instead of merely regulating Nuer seasonal cattle drives, the change of seasons in the southern Sudan also dictates the rhythm of the civil war. The dry season makes it possible to move heavy artillery across the clay plains; during the wet season the same plains are impassible. The war and the displacement of Nuer and other southern Sudanese it has caused are the major cause of migration.

In the late 1980s, government troops attacked Thok's village, killing many people including his father. Although many of the survivors elected to stay and to keep herding cattle, with his father dead Thok felt it was wisest to leave Sudan after this tragedy. He traveled on foot for three days with his mother and siblings and their cattle to an Ethiopian refugee camp called Itang.

One feature of camp life was the presence of a Christian mission school, which provided Thok with his first taste of formal education, something that would prove useful later as he sought refugee status. He advanced quickly in school, skipping several grades. Seventh grade stands out for him as the real beginning of his education, however, because he passed a national exam. As a result, he was transferred to Gambela, another Ethiopian camp, to attend school, leaving his mother and siblings behind. Food scarcity made life in Gambela very difficult. Thok recalls that students were given only a small amount of corn each month. They would grind the grain into flour, cook the mixture with water, and eat it plain without a stew.

His education at Gambela progressed nicely, but was ended when war broke out in Ethiopia. Threatened by the dangers it posed, Thok rejoined his mother and siblings. Together they returned to Sudan where the United Nations had established a temporary camp to care for the Sudanese refugees who were streaming back across the border from Ethiopia. Thok weighed his options and decided to return to Ethiopia on his own. He went to the capital of Ethiopia, Addis Ababa, where he encountered some friends from school who shared information on how to get to refugee camps in Kenya.

He traveled to Kenya by bus, negotiating his way past border and police checkpoints along the way. He was arrested once by Kenyan police and had to spend the night in jail before they turned him over to the U.N. authorities that ran the nearby refugee camp. Once in the camp, he filled out a form that documented his background, and requested that he be considered for resettlement in another country. Because Thok had no relatives who had been resettled in other countries, he applied for resettlement anywhere that would accept refugees from the Sudan. These included Australia, Canada, and Sweden as well as the United States, the country that finally admitted him.

Two years elapsed from the time Thok arrived in the camp until he was sent to the United States. Life in the Kenyan camp was much more difficult than the one he had stayed at in Ethiopia. There was nothing to do, no river, no place to keep cattle, and no garden plots. Thok did, however, meet some friends he had made earlier in school, and together they cooked food and found ways to pass the long days in the camp. He and his friends also listened to the stories other Nuer told of their encounters with the refugee officials who interviewed people requesting resettlement. In a tragic commentary on how devastation can seem "normal," they learned that the biggest mistake people made was to invent dramatic stories to make themselves eligible for resettlement. For example, one Nuer man said, "People feel they need a reason, so they tell the person interviewing them that they killed someone and if they return to Sudan they will be put in jail. But the story didn't work because the interviewer thought the refugee must be a violent man." The Nuer men who worked as interpreters in the camps believed there was a better approach. "We told the community, we need to tell them the reality. Don't say you killed someone, just say you were caught in the crossfire." They had learned that the refugee officials were looking for certain kinds of experiences to determine who fit the criteria for refugee resettlement.

In addition to recounting a plausible story that indicates why they would be persecuted if they returned home, refugees must also pass a medical screening, and they must also sign a promissory note to repay the cost of their airfare to the United States once they have settled and found work. Thok passed through this process successfully, and with a ticket provided for him by the International Organization for Migration, flew to the United States. He was met at the airport by a representative from Lutheran Social Services, one of many U.S. voluntary agencies responsible for resettling refugees.

Adapting to America

Some immigrants to the United States rely on family or friends to help them find a home, job, and place in the country. But many refugees depend on voluntary agencies or "volags" to help with settlement. These agencies are under contract to the U.S. government and receive a stipend for each refugee that they place. Volags help refugees with such necessities as finding a place to live, getting a job, learning to ride the bus, and buying food. They also help them complete paperwork documenting the existence of family members who were left behind, since there may be a chance to bring them over later. Volags emphasize how important it is for refugees to find a job and become self-sufficient. Volags provide refugees with a small initial cash stipend to help them get established. But the money doesn't last long and refugees are encouraged to start working as soon as possible, often within the first week or two after arrival. An agency helped place Thok in Minnesota, found him an apartment, and assisted with a job search.

There were about thirty refugees from Sudan and Somalia on Thok's flight from Nairobi, Kenya, to New York's JFK International Airport. When Thok boarded the plane, he knew no one. By the time he arrived in New York many hours later, he felt like the eight Sudanese men he had traveled with were his new best friends. In a wrenching sort of dispersal, the eight men were all directed by airline staff to different gates at the airport to await the next leg of their journey to far-flung destinations, like San Diego, California; Nashville, Tennessee; Dallas, Texas; and Minneapolis, Minnesota.

A representative from Lutheran Social Services and a volunteer from a local church greeted Thok when he arrived on his own in Minneapolis. His few possessions fit in a small bag that he carried with him on the plane. The man from Lutheran Social Services gave him shampoo and a toothbrush and took him to Burger King. Thok found the food very strange and difficult to eat. Thok stayed the first night in the volunteer's home—a widower in his mid-sixties who regularly helped Lutheran Social Services in this way. Thok spoke some English, but he relied mostly on gestures to communicate with his host. The next day the volunteer took Thok to Lutheran Social Services to complete paperwork.

When they finished with the paperwork, the case manager who had met Thok at the airport took him to what was to be his apartment. Thok found the place to be very dirty, particularly the carpeting that had not been cleaned after the last tenants departed. There was a strong smell of cigarette smoke, cockroaches in the kitchen, and a very leaky faucet in the bathroom. Despite these problems, Thok would have his own place that would be affordable when he got a job. Later, the man Thok had stayed with the previous night brought over some furniture that had been donated by church members.

Over the coming week, Thok met with his case manager to discuss getting a job. Where refugees work and the kinds of jobs that they can get depend somewhat on the level of education and training they received prior to arrival in the United States. Upon arrival, most Nuer have little formal education and can, unfortunately, only find jobs that most people born in the United States do not want, such as unskilled factory worker, security guard, parking lot attendant, fast food server, and nursing home assistant. Or, if they do have a degree when they arrive, like many immigrants, they are "underemployed," or work in jobs below their level of credentials. Many of the Nuer who have settled in the upper Midwest have found work in meat packing plants. Thok first got a job filling beverage trays for airplanes at the airport after he arrived in the United States. His back and arms ached from the lifting he was required to do, and he did not like his boss.

Several weeks later, Thok spotted another Nuer man while he was shopping at Target. Thok did not know him personally, but after they started talking he discovered that he knew the village where the man was from in the Sudan. It was good to see someone from "home," and Thok invited him back to his apartment to cook a meal and eat together. This man had moved to Minnesota from Iowa and was able to tell Thok the names and even the phone numbers of some Nuer who were living in Des Moines. Thok knew some of these people from the refugee camps in Ethiopia, and the next day he bought a phone card to get in touch. Thok could hardly believe his ears when he heard his friend John Wal answer the phone. After a conversation that lasted until the phone card expired, Thok decided to board a bus and leave Minnesota to move to Iowa. John had talked about the sizable Nuer community living in Des Moines and the well-paying jobs offered by a meat packing company. Thok called his case manager and left a message saying that he was going. He packed his personal items, left the furniture in the apartment, and boarded a Greyhound bus.

In Des Moines, Thok moved in with John and another Nuer man. Thok worked in a packing plant for a while, but found it very difficult. At first his job was to kill pigs as they entered the processing line. He found it so hard to sleep at night after doing this over and over again all day that he asked to be transferred to some other part of the line. He still found the work exceedingly hard.

One motivation to find a job quickly is to make it possible to bring over his family members to join him, but Thok has not managed to do this yet. In addition to his mother and siblings, Thok would also like to bring over a wife. There are roughly three Nuer men for every Nuer woman in the United States, and most of the women are already married or engaged to be married. Thok and other Nuer men struggle with what they perceive as "the unreasonable levels of freedom" afforded to women in U.S. society. One way to marry a wife with more "traditional" Nuer values, or so men think, is to let their family facilitate a marriage in the Sudan or in Ethiopia and try to bring the wife over as a spouse or a refugee.

Staying in Touch

Refugee groups are deliberately "scattered" geographically across the United States when they are resettled. Policy makers believe that dispersal increases individuals' ability to adapt successfully to their new environment and that it decreases any disruptive impact on the host community that receives the refugees. However, even though refugees are "placed" in particular locales in the United States, they seldom stay put. Hmong, originally from the highlands of South East Asia, and now residents of Saint Paul, Minnesota, are a case in point and, like the Nuer, are well known for moving frequently after arrival in the United States. Nuer, who moved regularly as part of their lives in southern Sudan, continue a kind of nomadism in the United States and move frequently—from apartment to apartment, from city to city, and from state to state. As a result of having been resettled in more than thirty different states in America, Nuer have many residency options to consider and have a tendency to move where they have relatives, friends, or jobs.

Staying in contact is very important to many Nuer refugees. They are adept at devising strategies for remaining in contact with other Nuer dispersed across the United States and those whom they left behind in Africa. The process of incorporation into the United States as a refugee is also about maintaining ties to Africa. One aspect of Nuer life that sets them apart from the experiences of previous waves of immigrants to the United States is the means by which they keep in contact with those who remain at home in the Sudan, in refugee camps in neighboring African states, and around the world.

Immigrants have always retained some ties with the homes they left. But, in a 21st century context the possibilities for frequent, affordable, and rapid contact are greatly expanded. Anthropologists refer to these crosscutting social ties that span the borders of nation-states as *transnationalism*. For instance, Thok, who wants to marry, could phone his brother in Gambela, Ethiopia, to arrange the event. He can use Western Union to send money to his brother to buy cows to give to the prospective bride's father. In Nuer eyes, the groom does not even need to be present for the marriage to be legitimate, but this is not true in the eyes of immigration authorities. Even though the groom can do his part to sponsor the marriage from the United States, he still must travel to Ethiopia for the marriage to be recognized officially for immigration purposes. The bride can apply as a refugee herself but increases her chances of resettlement by also applying as a spouse joining her husband.

Sudan ranks third, after Palestine and Afghanistan, in a list of countries that has produced the most refugees. The number of displaced Sudanese exceeds three-quarters of a million people. Those in the diaspora maintain close ties with friends and family in the Sudan, in other African countries, and around the world. Therefore, a focus on the lives of Sudanese refugees in Africa is an important part of understanding Nuer refugees' lives in the United States. These transnational linkages influence Nuer peoples' decisions in the United States.

Conclusion

Refugees are a special category of immigrant to the United States. Often seen as victims of tragic circumstances, refugees are also amazingly adept at finding ways to survive these same circumstances. Refugees' lives depend on an international and national bureaucracy, and those who pass through the process represent a very small percentage of people who are displaced. Starting a life in a vastly different cultural environment than the one they were raised in presents a number of hardships. Refugees cope with these challenges by trying to maintain their original ethnic group identity. Transnational communication is one way to do this. So is moving to find people they know from their homelands.

Anthropologists, such as Evans-Pritchard, used to journey to faraway places to study distant "others." Nowadays it is often the objects of study that make the journey to the land of the anthropologists. Refugees such as the Nuer are among the latest newcomers to urban and suburban areas in the United States, and anthropologists can play a role in the adaptation process of Nuer in the United States. For example, some anthropologists work for voluntary agencies where what they learn about refugees through their ability to conduct ethnographic research helps to ease refugee adjustment to unfamiliar surroundings. Other anthropologists work at the federal and state levels to advise about the efficacy of the social programs designed to meet the needs of recently arrived populations and suggest changes if they are needed. Sometimes these roles take the form of advocacy.

But through it all, anthropologists still do fieldwork in much the same way. They learn the language of refugee populations, ask open-ended questions in interviews, conduct participant observation at such events as weddings, funerals, graduation ceremonies, and political meetings, and try to understand life from their informants' perspective.

Although he now knows an anthropologist, Thok Ding goes about his new life in the United States with the same independent determination that got him here in the first place. He will continue to move his residence if he thinks it will help him, increase his level of education, find better paying jobs, and eventually if all works out, marry a woman from the Sudan, bring his whole family to the United States and in the end, become a new American.

Review Questions

1. According to Shandy, what is the formal United Nations definition of a refugee?

2. What steps do displaced persons have to take to achieve resettlement as refugees?

3. How have Nuer refugees reorganized their lives to live successfully in the United States?

4. How have migrants to the United States changed the way anthropologists define groups they study and the focus of their research?

32

Men's Pleasure, Women's Labor: Tourism for Sex

Denise Brennan

Tourism is a major component of globalization and an increasingly impor-
tant source of income for many countries. Tourists travel for many reasons:
There are sights to see and tastes to appreciate in European winemaking cen-
ters and art museums, physical challenges to conquer on treks to Nepal's Hi-
malayas and rides down wild New Zealand rivers, and comfortable luxury to
be experienced in countless tropical beach and golfing resorts. However, one
attraction for travel that is rarely mentioned, but which is important in sev-
eral parts of the world, is the lure of sexual gratification. Such is the case in
the Dominican Republic town of Sosúa, the subject of this article by Denise
Brennan. Sosúa is a travel destination for male European tourists looking

Reprinted by permission of Waveland Press, Inc. from "Globalization, Women's Labor, and Men's
Pleasure: Sex Tourism in Sosúa, the Dominican Republic," in *Urban Life: Readings in the Anthro-*
pology of the City, 4th Edition. George Gmelch and Walter P. Zenner (Eds.) (Long Grove, IL: Waveland Press, Inc., 2002). All rights reserved.

*for inexpensive sex with island women. It is also the destination for Do-
minican women who are attracted to the possibilities—more money including money wires, sponsorship for emigration to Europe, a European visa—of
sex work with the European tourists. Tourists easily discover what Sosúa
has to offer by surfing the Internet, finding chat lines and advertisements
touting sex with "dirt cheap colored girls," and "something for everyone's
taste." Brennan's focus, however, is on the Dominican women themselves.
They flock to Sosúa for the possible release from poverty and hardship, but
rarely achieve these goals. Even when they attain more permanent relationships with clients, the associations rarely last. Describing the lives of three
women, Brennan concludes that the unequal association with foreign men
usually fails, and that the women do better if they rely on relationships with
Dominican men.*

Introduction

There is a new sex-tourist destination on the global sexual landscape: Sosúa,
the Dominican Republic. A beach town on the north coast, Sosúa has emerged
as a place of fantasy for white, European, male sex tourists desiring sex for
money with Afro-Caribbean women. But European men are not the only ones
who seek to fulfill fantasies in Sosúa. Dominican sex workers also arrive in
Sosúa with fantasies: fantasies of economic mobility, visas to Europe, and
maybe even romance. For them, Sosúa and its tourists represent an escape.
These women migrate from throughout the Dominican Republic with dreams
of European men "rescuing" them from a lifetime of foreclosed opportunities
and poverty. They hope to meet and marry European men who will sponsor
their (and their children's) migration to Europe. Yet, even though more and
more women and girls migrate to Sosúa every day, most leave Sosúa's sex trade
with little more than they had when they first arrived.

This article explores this paradoxical feature of sex tourism in Sosúa, and
examines why women continue to flock to Sosúa and how they make the most
of their time while there. Through the sex trade in this one tourist town, we see
how globalization affects sex workers and sex tourists differently. In this economy of desire, some dreams are realized, while others prove hollow. White,
middle-class and lower-middle class European visitors and residents are much
better positioned to secure what they want in Sosúa than poor, black Dominican sex workers and other Dominican migrants who are likely to be disillu-
sioned by Sosúa, tourism, and tourists. Globalization and accompanying
transnational processes that unfold—such as tourism and sex tourism—not
only open up opportunities but also reproduce unequal, dependent relations
along lines of gender, race, class, and nationality.

Dominican women who migrate to Sosúa and its sex trade are motivated
by the opportunity to meet, and possibly marry, a foreign tourist. Even if sex

workers do not marry clients, Sosúa holds out the promise of establishing a transnational relationship with the aid of new transnational technologies such as fax machines and international money wires. Without these transnational connections, Sosúa's sex trade would be no different than sex work in any other Dominican town. By migrating to Sosúa, these women are engaged in an economic strategy that is both very familiar and something altogether new. I argue that they try to use the sex trade as an *advancement* strategy, not just a *survival* strategy. In short, these marginalized single mothers try to take advantage of the global linkages that exploit them.

Though only a handful of women regularly receive money wires from ex-clients in Europe, and a rarer few actually move to Europe to live with their European sweethearts, success stories of women who are living out this fantasy circulate among the sex workers like Dominicanized versions of the movie *Pretty Woman*. Thus, Sosúa's myth of opportunity goes unchallenged and women, recruited through female social networks of family and close friends who have already migrated to Sosúa, keep on arriving, ready to find their Richard Gere. Yet what the women find there is a far cry from their fantasy images of fancy dinners, nightclubs, easy money, and visas off the island. One sex worker, Carmen,[1] insightfully sums up just how important fantasy is to constructing the image of Sosúa as a place of opportunity. For Carmen, Sosúa is not a place of endless opportunity, but a place of disappointment and unrealized dreams:

> Women come to Sosúa because of a *gran mentira* (big lie). They hear they can make money, and meet a gringo, and they come. . . . They come with their dreams, but then they find out it is all a lie.

Tourism and Sex Tourism in the Global Economy

Work choices available to poor women are determined not only by local factors, but by the Dominican Republic's place in the global economy. Dominican women's internal migration for sex work is a consequence of local economic and social transformations as well as larger, external forces, such as foreign investment in export-processing zones (factories) and tourism. Just as international investors see the Dominican Republic as a site of cheap labor, international tourists know it as a place to buy cheap sex.

The Internet

In sex tourism, first-world travelers/consumers seek exoticized, racialized "native" bodies in the developing world for cut-rate prices. These two components—race

[1] I have changed all the names of sex workers and the bars in which they work, as well as bar and restaurant owners.

and its associated stereotypes and expectations, and the economic disparities between the developed and developing worlds—characterize sex-tourist destinations throughout the world. So what are white men "desiring" when they decide to book a flight from Frankfurt, for example, to Puerto Plata (the nearest airport to Sosúa)? I turned to the Internet for answers. Any exploration of the relationship between globalization, women's work choices in the global economy, and women's migration for work must now investigate the role the Internet has in producing and disseminating racialized and sexualized stereotypes in the developing world. In particular, the Internet is quickly and radically transforming the sex trade in the developing world, since on-line travel services make it increasingly easy for potential sex tourists to research sex-tourist destinations and to plan trips. I looked at web sites which post writings from alleged sex tourists who share information about their sex trips. In the process, these web sites advertise not only their services, but also Dominican women as sexual commodities. One such web-site subscriber was impressed by the availability of "dirt cheap colored girls," while another boasted, "When you enter the discos, you will feel like you're in heaven! A tremendous number of cute girls and something for everyone's taste (if you like colored girls like me)!" There is little doubt that race is central to what these sex tourists desire in their travels.

International Tourism: Who Benefits?

International tourism, however, has not benefited local Dominicans—poor Dominicans—as much as many had hoped. Although development and foreign investment have brought first-world hotels and services to Sosúa, the local population still lives in third-world conditions. The most successful resorts in Sosúa are foreign owned, and even though they create employment opportunities for the local population, most of the new jobs are low-paying service jobs with little chance for mobility. Moreover, the multinational resorts that have moved into Sosúa have pushed small hotel and restaurant owners out of business. One restaurant owner, Luis, comments on the effects these large, all-inclusive hotels (tourists pay airfare, lodging, food, and even drinks ahead of time in their home countries) have on the Sosúa economy:

> These tourists hardly change even U.S. $100 to spend outside the hotel. Before the all-inclusive hotels, people would change between U.S. $1000–2000 and it would get distributed throughout the town: some for lodging, for food and entertainment. Now, not only do any of the local merchants [not] get any of the money, but it never even leaves the tourists' home countries—like Germany or Austria—where they pay for their vacation in advance.

Foreign ownership, repatriation of profits, and the monopolistic nature of these all-inclusive resorts make it difficult for the local population in tourist economies, such as in Sosúa, to profit significantly. With tourism as the largest industry in the global economy, it is not unusual for foreign firms to handle all four components of a tourist's stay: airlines, hotels, services, and tour operators. I interviewed the general manager (an Italian citizen) of a German hotel in Sosúa, for example, whose parent company is a German airline company. Eighty percent of the hotel's guests are German, all of whom paid for their travel "package" in Germany. Furthermore, this German company imported most of its management staff from Europe, as well as the furniture, fabrics, and other goods necessary to run the hotel. So much for opportunities for local Dominicans.

Migration Off the Island

Marginalized individuals in the global economy not only turn to tourism as an exit from poverty, but also to migration. Before examining Dominican women's use of the sex trade in Sosúa as a way to migrate overseas, we first must consider the history of migration between the Dominican Republic and New York in the past few decades. This migration circuit and the transnational cultural, political, and economic flows between these two spaces have led many Dominicans to look *fuera* (outside) for solutions to their economic problems rather than within Dominican borders.

Migration to Sosúa

This preoccupation with goods, capital, and opportunities that are "outside" helps explain why sex workers and other Dominican migrants imagine Sosúa as a place of opportunity. These women would go to New York if they could, but they do not have the social networks—immediate family members in New York—to sponsor them for visas. They therefore often view migrating internally to Sosúa as the closest they will ever get to the "outside." Both migration to New York and transnational relationships with foreign tourists are ways to access a middle-class lifestyle and its accompanying commodities. Without migration circuits to New York, these women have a greater chance to get overseas by marrying a tourist (no matter how slight a chance) than they do of obtaining a visa—legally—to the United States. In some ways, hanging out in the tourist bars in Sosúa is a better use of their time than waiting in line for a visa at the U.S. embassy in Santo Domingo.

Strategies for migration, including sex workers' attempts to build transnational ties, are a "response and resistance" to the Dominican Republic's integration into the global economy. This response is informed by ideologies that view New York, Germany, and other outside places as those where individuals are more likely to make economic gains than within the Dominican Republic. Sosúa, with its access to tourists and their vacation money, is the next best alternative to getting off the island. Carla, a first-time sex worker, explains why Sosúa draws women from throughout the country: "We come here because we dream of ticket" (airline ticket). But without a visa—which they can obtain through marriage—Dominican sex workers cannot use the airline ticket Carla describes. These single mothers must depend on their European clients-turned-boyfriends/husbands to sponsor them for visas off the island. These women are at once independent and dependent, strategic and exploited.

Choosing Sex Work in Sosúa over Other Labor Options

A question I routinely posed to sex workers—and which others have asked me, as a fieldworker/anthropologist working with women who sell sex—is why do these Dominican women decide to enter sex work? The majority of these women are mothers and first-time sex workers. With little formal education, few marketable skills, limited social networks, and minimal support from the fathers of their children, poor Dominican women have few opportunities to escape from poverty and periodic crises. Within this context, sex work appears as a potentially profitable alternative, especially in light of the low wages women earn within the insecure and low-paying informal sector. Working as a domestic, a hair stylist in a salon, or a waitress in a restaurant are typical ways sex workers participated in the paid labor market prior to migrating to Sosúa. Each job generally yields under 1000 pesos a month (U.S. $83), whereas sex workers charge 500 pesos for a sexual encounter with a foreign client. Felicia and Margarita, two friends who had migrated from the same town, found these kinds of jobs did not sufficiently provide for their families. They summed up the dilemma for women like themselves who leave school in their early teens, receive no other formal job training, and thus have few well-paying job options open to them:

> If you have a husband who pays for food and the house then you can work in jobs like hair styling. Otherwise it's not possible to work in jobs like this.

Maintaining the view that women's earnings are secondary or supplementary, these women nevertheless became the primary breadwinners once they separated from their husbands.

Since these women could have chosen to enter the sex trade in other Dominican towns, by choosing Sosúa sex workers actively choose to work with foreign rather than Dominican men. The selection of sex work over other work options, and the selection of Sosúa with its tourist clientele, demonstrate that sex work for these women is not just a survival strategy, but rather a strategy of advancement. This "choice" of the sex trade *in Sosúa* presents an important counter example to depictions of *all* sex workers (who are not coerced or forced into prostitution) in *all contexts* as powerless victims of male violence and exploitation.

Yet, without protection under the law, sex workers are vulnerable to clients' actions once they are out of public spaces and in private hotel rooms. These women risk battery, rape, and forced unprotected sex. Sex workers in Sosúa often discount the risks of violence and AIDS when faced with the potential payoffs of financial stability or a marriage proposal. And most recently, since so many women migrate to Sosúa from throughout the Dominican Republic, sex workers outnumber clients in the bars. Thus, in order to understand why women place themselves in a context of violence and uncertainty, we need to explore fully Sosúa's opportunity myth. How reliable are the payoffs and how high are the risks? Why might women achieve "success" through sex work in Sosúa? Can these poor, single mothers benefit from globalization and the transnational connections it engenders?

Sex Work: Short- and Long-Term Strategies

The payoff from working with foreign tourists can represent considerable long-term financial gains for the sex worker and her extended family—far more than from factory work, for example. Yet, not all women who arrive in Sosúa to pursue sex work desire to establish transnational ties. Some have long-term strategies, such as saving enough money to start a *colmado* (small grocery store) in their yard in their home communities. Others use sex work as a way to make ends meet in the immediate future, such as paying for children's school supplies or medical expenses. However, financial security, no matter how hard fought, often proves fleeting for the poorest segments of Dominican society. An exit from poverty might not be as permanent as the sex workers hope, even if they establish a relationship with a foreign tourist. Relationships go sour, and the extended family's only lifeline from poverty subsequently disintegrates. For every promise a tourist keeps, there are many more stories of disappointment. Even the success stories eventually cannot live up to the myths.

Sex work yields varying levels of rewards. For example, some women have savings accounts or build houses with their earnings, while others do not have enough money to pay the motorcycle taxi fare from their boarding houses to the tourist bars. How are some sex workers able to save, despite the obstacles, while most continue to live day to day? Success at sex work in Sosúa depends on both a planned-out strategy and a commitment to saving money, as well as luck. I cannot emphasize enough the role *chance* plays in sex workers' long-term ties with foreign clients. Whether clients stay in touch with the women is out of the women's control. One sex worker, Carmen, was thus skeptical that the Belgian client with whom she spent time during his three-week vacation in Sosúa actually would follow through on his promises to marry her and move her to Europe:

> I don't absolutely believe that he is going to marry me. You know, sure, when he was here he seemed to love me. But you know people leave and they forget.

In fact, months later, she still had not heard from him. I even helped Carmen write him a letter, which I mailed when I got back to the United States. It was returned to my address, unopened. Had she gotten the address wrong or did he give her a false address along with false proclamations of love and commitment?

Adding to the uncertainty and fragility of transnational relationships are other logistical obstacles to "success." Women must find ways to save money despite the drain on their resources from paying police bribes and living in an expensive tourist town where prices for food and rent are among the highest in the country. All of this combined with competition among sex workers for clients increase the likelihood of leaving Sosúa with little or no money saved. Furthermore, the majority of women arrive in Sosúa without knowing what they are getting into. They have heard of police roundups and know that they must vie with countless other women just like themselves to catch the attention of potential clients, but like most migrants, they are full of hope and dreams and believe that "it will be different for them." In gold-rush fashion, they arrive in Sosúa because they have heard of Sosúa's tourists and money, and they plan, without a specific strategy in mind, to cash in on the tourist boom. It only takes a few days in Sosúa to realize that the only way to quickly make big money is by establishing transnational relationships. New arrivals see veteran sex workers drop by the Codetel office (telephone and fax company) every day, hoping for faxes from clients in Europe or Canada. For those newcomers who want to receive money wires or marriage proposals from tourists overseas, they learn that they must establish similar ongoing transnational relationships.

Sex Workers' Stories

In order to explore how sex workers' time in Sosúa measures up to their fantasy images, I turn to the divergent experiences of three sex workers. Their stories underscore the difficulties of establishing a transnational relationship, as well as its fragility. Through sex workers' accounts of their relationships with foreign men, we get a sense of just how wildly unpredictable the course of these relationships can be.

Elena and Jürgen: Building and Breaking Transnational Ties

This story begins with Elena's release from jail. After being held for two days, twenty-two-year-old Elena went to the beach. When I saw her, back at her one-room wooden house, she was ecstatic. At the beach she had run into Jürgen, a German client who had just returned to Sosúa to see her. They had been sending faxes to one another since he left Sosúa after his last vacation, and he had mentioned in one of his faxes that he would be returning. He did not know where she lived, but figured he would find her that evening at the Anchor, Sosúa's largest tourist bar and a place where tourists go to drink, dance, and pick up sex workers. He brought her presents from Germany, including perfume and a matching gold necklace and bracelet. Elena was grinning ear to ear as she showed off her gifts, talking about Jürgen like a smitten schoolgirl:

I am cancelling everything for the weekend and am going to spend the entire time with him. We will go the beach and he will take me to nightclubs and to restaurants.

Elena began preparing for the weekend. Her two sisters who lived with her, ages fourteen and sixteen, would look after her six-year-old daughter, since Elena would stay with Jürgen in his tourist hotel. She chose the evening's outfit carefully, with plenty of help from her sisters, daughter, and a friend (a young sex worker) who lives with them since she has very little money. Elena provides for these four girls with her earnings from sex work. They all rotate between sharing the double bed and sleeping on the floor. Spending time with a tourist on his vacation means Elena would receive more gifts, maybe even some for her family, and would make good money. So they helped primp Elena, selecting billowy rayon pants that moved as she did, and a black lycra stretch shirt with long sheer sleeves that was cropped to reveal her slim stomach. She was meeting Jürgen at the Anchor, where I saw her later on, and she stood out in the crowd.

As soon as Jürgen's vacation ended, he went back to Germany with plans to return in a couple of months. Since he was self-employed in construction in Germany, he wanted to live part of the year in the Dominican Republic. Elena was very upset that Jürgen had left. She was incredibly shaken up and could not stop crying. I had heard sex workers often distinguish between relationships with tourists *por amor* (love) or *por residence* (residence/visas), but Elena's tears broke down that distinction. I realized then that Elena might be in love with Jürgen.

Unlike Carmen's relationship with her Belgian client, which ended with broken promises, Jürgen kept his word and wired money and kept in touch through faxes. Even more surprisingly, Jürgen returned to Sosúa only two months later. Within days of his arrival, he rented a two-bedroom apartment that had running water and an electrical generator (for daily blackouts). He also bought beds, living room furniture, and a large color TV. Elena was living out the fantasy of many sex workers in Sosúa: She was sharing a household with a European man who supported her and her dependents. Jürgen paid for food that Elena and her sisters prepared, and had cable TV installed. He also paid for Elena's daughter to attend a private school, and came home one day with school supplies for her. Occasionally, Jürgen took Elena, her daughter, and her sisters out to eat at one of the tourist restaurants that line the beach.

Elena had moved up in the world: Eating in tourist restaurants, sending a daughter to private school, and living in a middle-class apartment were all symbols of her increased social and economic mobility. As a female head of household who had been taking care of her daughter and sisters with her earnings from sex work, Elena quit sex work soon after meeting Jürgen and lived off of the money he gave her. Sex work, and the transnational relationship it had built, altered Elena's life as well as the lives of those who depended on her. But for how long?

As it turned out, Jürgen was not Elena's or the family's salvation. Soon after Elena and Jürgen moved in together, Elena found out she was pregnant.

Both she and Jürgen were very happy about having a baby. He had a teenage son living with his ex-wife in Germany and relished the idea of having another child. At first, he was helpful around the house and doted on Elena. But the novelty soon wore off and he returned to his routine of spending most days in the German-owned bar beneath their apartment. He also went out drinking at night, with German friends, hopping from bar to bar. He was drunk, or nearly so, day and night. Elena saw him less and less frequently and they fought often, usually over money.

Eventually he started staying out all night. On one occasion, a friend of Elena's (a sex worker) saw Jürgen at the Anchor talking with and later leaving with a Haitian sex worker. Elena knew he was cheating on her. But she did not want to raise this with Jürgen, explaining that men "do these things" and instead, she focused her anger on the fact that he was not giving her enough money to take care of the household. Ironically, Elena had more disposable income before she began to live with Jürgen. Back then, she would go out dancing and drinking with her friends—not looking for clients—but just to have fun. Now, without an income of her own, she was dependent upon Jürgen not only for household expenses but for her entertainment as well.

On more than one occasion I served as interpreter between the two during their attempts at "peace negotiations" after they had not spoken to one another for days. Since Elena does not speak any German or English, she asked me to help her understand why Jürgen was mad at her as well as to communicate her viewpoint to him. In preparation for one of these "negotiations," Elena briefed me on what she wanted me to explain to Jürgen:

> I want to know why he is not talking to me? And why is he not giving me any money? He is my *esposo* [husband in consensual union] and is supposed to give me money. I need to know if he is with me or with someone else. He pays for this house and paid for everything here. I need to know what is going on. You know I was fine living alone before, I'm able to do that. I took care of everything before, this is not a problem. But I need to know what is going to happen.

Since they were living together, and Jürgen was paying the bills, Elena considered them to be married. To Elena and her friends, Jürgen, as an *esposo*, was financially responsible for the household. But Jürgen saw things differently. He felt Elena thought he was "made of money" and was always asking him for more. He asked me to translate to her:

> I'm not a millionaire. I told Elena last week that I don't like her always asking for money. She did not listen. She asks me for money all day long. I don't want to be taken advantage of.

One day, without warning, Jürgen packed his bags and left for Germany for business. Elena knew this day would come, that Jürgen had to go to Germany to work. But she did not expect their relationship would be in such disarray, and that he would depart without leaving her money (although he did leave some food money with her younger sisters who turned it over to Elena). In Jürgen's absence, Elena took her daughter out of the private school, since the tuition soon became overdue, and she started working part-time at a small Dominican-owned restaurant. Once Jürgen returned to Sosúa from Germany a couple of months later, they split up for good. Elena moved out of their apartment back to the labyrinth of shanties on dirt paths off the main road. Her economic and social mobility was short-lived. She had not accumulated any savings or items she could pawn during her time with Jürgen. Jürgen never gave her enough money so that she could set some aside for savings. And all the things he bought for the apartment were his, not hers. When they vacated the apartment he took all of the furniture and the TV.

Her relationship with Jürgen dramatically changed Elena's life; she was, after all, having his child. But her social and economic status remained as marginal as ever. Even though she was living out many sex workers' fantasies of "marrying" a foreign tourist, she still lived like many poor Dominicans, struggling day to day without access to resources to build long-term economic security. When she and Jürgen fought, and he withheld money from her, she was less economically independent than she was as a sex worker, when she was certain to earn around 500 pesos a client. Although sex workers take on great risks—AIDS, abuse, and arrest—and occupy a marginal and stigmatized status in Dominican society, Elena's status as the "housewife" of a German resident was fragile and constantly threatened.

Jürgen now lives, Elena has heard, somewhere in Asia. Elena is back living in the same conditions as before she met Jürgen, except with one more child. She has not returned to sex work and makes significantly less money working in a restaurant. Her older married sisters (who also live in Sosúa) now help take care of their younger sisters, and Elena sends what money she can, though less than in her sex work days, to help out her parents.

Luisa's Money Wires

Luisa is an example of a sex worker whose transnational connections were those other sex workers envied, but her "success," like Elena's, ended without warning. She, quite remarkably, received U.S. $500 every two weeks from a client in Germany, who wanted her to leave sex work and start her own clothing store. She told him she had stopped working the tourist bars, and that she used the money to buy clothes for the store. Yet, when he found out that she was still working in the sex trade, had not opened a store, and was living with a Dominican boyfriend, he stopped wiring money.

At this juncture, Luisa was in over her head. She had not put any of the money in the bank in anticipation of the day when the money wires might dry up. She was renting a two-bedroom house that was twice the size and rent of friends' apartments. And, she sent money home to her mother in Santo Domingo, who was taking care of her twelve-year-old son. She also supported her Dominican boyfriend, who did not have a steady job. Other sex workers called him a *chulo* (pimp) since he lived off Luisa's earnings and money wires. They saw Luisa as foolish for bankrolling her boyfriend, especially since he was not the father of her son. She began hocking her chains and rings in one of Sosúa's half-dozen pawn shops. She eventually moved out of the house into a smaller apartment with her Dominican boyfriend, and returned to sex work.

As lucky as Luisa was to meet this German client at the Anchor, most of the women working the Anchor night after night never receive a single money wire transfer. Those who do generally receive smaller sums than Luisa did, on a much more infrequent and unpredictable basis. As Luisa's story demonstrates, a sex worker's luck can change overnight. There is no guarantee that money wires will continue once they begin. Luisa had no way of knowing that she would lose her "meal ticket," nor can she be certain that she will ever find another tourist to replace him. Furthermore, women cannot count on earning money in sex work indefinitely. Luisa is in her early thirties and knows that over the next few years it will be increasingly difficult to compete with the young women in the bars (some are as young as sixteen and seventeen, most are between nineteen and twenty-five). Yet, once sex workers make the decision to leave Sosúa and the sex trade, they face the same limited opportunities they confronted before they moved to Sosúa. They are still hampered by limited education, lack of marketable job skills, and not "knowing the right people." In fact, obstacles to economic and social mobility might have increased, especially if they are rumored to have AIDS. They might have to battle gossip in their home community and the stigma associated with sex work. After years of working in bars they might have a substance-abuse problem. And, they return to children who have grown up in their absence.

Carmen's Diversification Strategy

Carmen's story, compared to Elena's and Luisa's, is one of relative success, in which her relationships with Dominican clients figure prominently. In fact, supplementing uncertain income from foreign tourists by working with Dominican clients, as well as establishing long-term relationships with Dominican *amigos/clientes fijos* (friends/regular clients), supplies Carmen with a steady flow of income. Another sex worker, Ani, explains the function of *amigos:*

> You don't always have a client. You need *amigos* and *clientes fijos.* If you have a problem, like something breaks in your house, or your child is sick and you need money for the doctor or medicine, they can help.

For Carmen, working with Dominicans has proven much more reliable than establishing ties with foreign men. Carmen has saved enough money from four years in sex work to build a small house in Santo Domingo (the capital city five hours away where she will retire to take care of her mother and children). She has managed to save more money than most sex workers. I asked her why she thinks she was able to save money, while many of her friends do not have an extra centavo, and she answered:

> Because they give it to their men. Their husbands wait at home and drink while their women work. Not me. If I'm in the street with all the risks of disease and the police, I'm keeping the money or giving it to my kids. I'm not giving it to a man, no way. If women don't give the money to their men, they (the men) beat them.

She is careful not to let the men in her life know how much money she has saved in the bank (unlike Luisa), or the sources of the money. She has a steady relationship in particular with Jorge, who is her economic safety net, especially in times of crises. She describes their relationship:

> He is very young [she scrunched her nose up in disapproval of this point]. He lives with his mother in Santiago and works in *azona franca* [factory in an export-processing zone]. He gives me money, even though he does not make a lot. He bought me furniture for the new house.

At times, the money Jorge gives Carmen is the only money she has. By establishing a relationship with a Dominican man, she has been able to supplement her unpredictable income from sex work. Though the money he gives her is in smaller sums than transnational money wires other sex workers receive, it is money she can count on, on a regular basis.

Carmen has not only diversified her clientele and focused on achieving one specific goal (building a house) but also has set up clear personal limitations working in a dangerous trade. Since she has a serious fear of the police, she refuses to work when they are making arrests outside of the tourist bars where many of the sex workers congregate to talk, smoke, or greet customers. At one point when the police seemed to be making more arrests than usual, Carmen quit going to the tourist bars altogether. Instead, she took a bus to a small Dominican town about thirty miles away to work in a bar that caters to Dominican clients. Thus, she developed an alternate plan to working in Sosúa when necessary.

By pursuing local Dominican clients as well as trying to establish transnational connections, sex work is paying off for Carmen in the long term. Carmen refused to be seduced by the promise of a tourist enclave and the sweet talk of foreign tourists. Instead, she treated Sosúa as any other Dominican town with "brothels" and set up a roster of local regular clients. Carmen's gains have been slow and modest. Nevertheless, she saved enough money to begin constructing a small house. Thus far it has taken her four years, and she still needs enough money for windows. But she will leave Sosúa with her future, and her family's, more secure than when she first arrived. Stories about modest successes like Carmen's are not as glamorous as those with transnational dimensions. Rather, stories of transnational relationships and quick, big money circulate among the sex workers, like those of Elena and Luisa. Their more immediate and visible ascension from poverty is regaled and fuels the illusion of Sosúa as a place to get rich quick.

Conclusion

Foreign sex tourists clearly benefit from their geographic position in the global economy, as they travel with ease (no visa is needed to enter the Dominican Republic), and buy sex for cheaper prices than in their home countries. Dominican sex workers, in contrast, face innumerable constraints due to their country's marginal position in the global economy. Sosúa's sex trade is but one more site where, broadly, we can observe globalization exacerbating inequality and, more specifically, we can situate tourism and sex tourism as both relying on and reproducing inequalities in the global economy.

Like most prospectors in search of quick money, few sex workers find what they were hoping for. It is not surprising, however, that such women, despite the obstacles to fulfilling their "fantasies," continue to arrive every day. Women from the poorest classes have no other work options that pay as well as the sex trade with tourists. Nor do most other work options offer the opportunity to establish long-term relationships with foreign men. Although most transnational relationships are unlikely to alter sex workers' long-term economic and social status, these women make far more financial gains than do sex workers without such a relationship, and earn more than they would from other accessible labor options (such as domestic service or factory work).

Sex workers also can make gains without transnational connections. Though difficult to achieve, these gains might prove more durable than those relying on a transnational relationship. Carmen's transnational ties never paid off, and consequently she did not come into a lot of money all at once. But she still managed to save what she could over time. Her house represents security, but it does not catapult her out of *los pobres* (the poor). Her "success" is not on the same level as women with ongoing relationships with European men. But while these ties could dissolve at any time, Carmen's house will still be there. She looks forward to the day she completes her house and leaves Sosúa and its sex trade:

> When I leave here I want to sit on the front porch of my new house with my mother and my children and drink a cold glass of juice. I want a peaceful life. No Sosúa, no men giving you problems.

Review Questions

1. What draws Dominican women to the town of Sosúa to act as sex workers?

2. How do European men find out about the sex trade in Sosúa? What does this say about the nature of globalization?

3. What kind of backgrounds do Dominican sex workers come from and what do they believe European clients can do for them?

4. Based on the lives of the women described by Brennan, what is the usual outcome of sexual relations with European clients?

33

Japanese Hip-Hop and the Globalization of Popular Culture

Ian Condry

By now, anyone who travels the world knows that something is afoot. Hilton, Sheraton, Radisson, and other national chain look-alike hotels grace downtown districts in most major international cities. African cab drivers deliver embarking airline passengers to historic "American" districts in our nation's capital. Tourists eat in a Chinese restaurant located in Cusco, high in the Andes. Faxes and e-mails flash around the world in seconds. Clothing and hairstyles look similar from one country to the next. But does this global "sameness" related to population movement, transnational companies, and cross-cultural borrowing mean that a single world culture is emerging? In some ways, perhaps, yes, but in many ways borrowed culture is hybridized by a process of localization. When new cultural forms arrive, they are often understood and modified by local cultural perspectives. And often their appearance stimulates the creation of new cultural forms. Anthropologists have a long tradition of investigating beliefs, social organization, and events at the local level, so the process of hybridization and cultural creation "on the ground" is where they can make the greatest contribution to an understanding of globalization.

This is a point made by Ian Condry in this selection. Using the example of hip-hop, originally a North American contribution to pop culture, he shows how this entertainment form has been adapted to the club scene in metropolitan Tokyo. Sporting typical—in most cases American-like—clothing and hairstyles, crowds of Japanese young people jam all-night clubs to hear hip-hop performers do their stuff. But they continue to do this in a Japanese fashion, using the musical form as a way to express their presence as young individuals in traditionally group-oriented, age-ranked Japanese society.

Introduction

Japanese hip-hop, which began in the 1980s and continues to develop today, is an intriguing case study for exploring the globalization of popular culture. Hip-hop is but one example among many of the transnational cultural styles pushed by entertainment and fashion industries, pulled by youth eager for the latest happening thing, and circulated by a wide range of media outlets eager to draw readers and to sell advertising. In Tokyo, a particular combination of local performance sites, artists, and fans points to ways that urban areas are crucibles of new, hybrid cultural forms. Hip-hop was born in the late 1970s in New York City as a form of street art: rapping on sidewalk stoops, outdoor block parties with enormous sound systems, graffiti on public trains, and breakdancing in public parks. In its voyage to Japan, the street ethic of hip-hop remains, but it is performed most intensely in all-night clubs peppered around Tokyo. This paper examines these nightclubs as an urban setting that helps us grasp the cultural dynamics of Japanese hip-hop. In particular, the interaction between artist-entrepreneurs and fans in live shows demonstrates how "global" popular culture is still subject to important processes of localization.

Anthropologists have a special role in analyzing such transnational forms because of their commitment to extended fieldwork in local settings. Ethnography aims to capture the cultural practices and social organization of a people. This offers a useful way of seeing how popular culture is interwoven with everyday life. Yet there is a tension between ethnography and globalization, because in many ways they seem antithetical to each other. While ethnography attempts to evoke the distinctive texture of local experience, globalization is often seen as erasing local differences. An important analytical challenge for today's media-saturated world is finding a way to understand how local culture interacts with such global media flows.

On one hand, it seems as if locales far removed from each other are becoming increasingly the same. It is more than a little eerie to fly from New York to Tokyo and see teenagers in both places wearing the same kinds of fashion characteristic of rap fans: baggy pants with boxers on display, floppy hats or baseball caps, and immaculate space-age Nike sneakers. In Tokyo stores for youth, rap music is the background sound of choice. Graffiti styled after the New York City aerosol artists dons numerous walls, and breakdancers can be found in public parks practicing in the afternoon or late at night. In all-night dance clubs throughout Tokyo, Japanese rappers and DJs take to the stage and declare that they have some "extremely bad shit" (*geki yaba shitto*)—meaning "good music"—to share with the audience. For many urban youth, hip-hop is the defining style of their era. In 1970s Japan, the paradigm of high school cool was long hair and a blistering solo on lead guitar. Today, trendsetters are more likely to sport "dread" hair and show off their scratch techniques with two turntables and a mixer. In the last few years, rap music has become one of the best-selling genres of music in the United States and around the world as diverse youth are adapting the style to their own messages and contexts.

But at the same time, there are reasons to think that such surface appearances of sameness disguise differences at some deeper level. Clearly, cultural setting and social organization have an impact on how movies and television shows are viewed. Yet if we are to understand the shape of cultural forms in a world that is increasingly connected by global media and commodity flows, we must situate Japanese rappers in the context of contemporary Japan. When thinking about how hip-hop is appropriated, we must consider, for example, that most Japanese rappers and fans speak only Japanese. Many of them live at home with their parents, and they all went through the Japanese education system. Moreover, even if the origin of their beloved music genre is overseas, they are caught up in social relations that are ultimately quite local, animated primarily by face-to-face interactions and telephone calls. So while these youth see themselves as "hip-hoppers" and "B-Boys" and "B-Girls," and associate themselves with what they call a "global hip-hop culture," they also live in a day-to-day world that is distinctly Japanese.

For those interested in studying the power of popular culture, there is also a more practical question of research methods. How does a lone researcher go about studying something as broad and unwieldy as the globalization of mass culture? One of the tenets of anthropological fieldwork is that you cannot understand a people without being there, but in the case of a music genre, where is "there"? In the fall of 1995, I began a year and a half of fieldwork in Tokyo, and the number of potential sites was daunting. There were places where the music was produced: record companies, recording studios, home studios, and even on commuter trains with handheld synthesizers. There were places where the music was promoted: music magazines, fashion magazines, TV and radio shows, night-clubs, and record stores. There was the interaction between musicians and fans at live shows, or in mediated form on cassettes, CDs, and 12-inch LPs. To make matters worse, rap music is part of the larger category of "hip-hop." Hip-hop encompasses not only rap, but also breakdance, DJ, graffiti, and fashion. The challenge was to understand the current fascination among Japanese youth with hip-hop music and style, while also considering the role of money-making organizations. How does one situate the experiential pleasures within the broader structures of profit that produce mass culture?

As I began interviewing rappers, magazine writers, and record company people, I found a recurring theme that provided a partial answer. Everyone agreed that you cannot understand Japanese rap music without going regularly to the clubs. Clubs were called the "actual site" *(genba)* of the Japanese rap scene.[1] It was there that rappers performed, DJs learned which songs elicit excitement in the crowd, and breakdancers practiced and competed for attention. In what follows, I would like to suggest that an effective tool for understanding the globalization of popular culture is to consider places like Japanese hip-hop nightclubs in terms of what might be called "genba globalism." By using participant–observation methods to explore key sites that are a kind of media crossroads, we can observe how globalized images and sounds are performed, consumed, and then transformed in an ongoing process. I use the Japanese term "genba" to emphasize that the processing of such global forms happens through the local language and in places where local hip-hop culture is produced. In Japanese hip-hop, these clubs are important not only as places where fans can see live shows and hear the latest releases from American and Japanese groups, but also as places for networking among artists, writers, and record company people. In this essay, I would like to point out some of the advantages of considering key sites as places to understand the cross-cutting effects of globalization. To get a sense of what clubs are about, let's visit one.

Going to Harlem on the Yamanote Line

A visit to Tokyo's Harlem is the best place to begin a discussion of Japanese hip-hop. Opened in the summer of 1997, Harlem is one of many all night dance clubs, but as the largest club solely devoted to hip-hop and R&B, it has become the flagship for the Japanese scene (at least, at the time of this writing in February 2001). Nestled in the love hotel area of the Shibuya section of Tokyo, Harlem is representative of the otherworldliness of clubs as well as their location within the rhythms and spaces of mainstream Japan.

---

[1]The word *"genba"* is made up of the characters "to appear" and "place," and it is used to describe a place where something actually happens, like the scene of an accident or of a crime, or a construction site. In the hip-hop world the term is used to contrast the intense energy of the club scene with the more sterile and suspect marketplace.

If we were visiting the club, we would most likely meet at Shibuya train station around midnight because the main action seldom gets started before 1 A.M. Most all-night revelers commute by train, a practice that links Tokyo residents in a highly punctual dance. The night is divided between the last train (all lines stop by 1 A.M. at the latest) and the first train of the morning (between 4:30 and 5 A.M.). The intervening period is when clubs (*kurabu*) are most active.[2] Shortly after midnight, Shibuya station is the scene for the changing of the guard: those heading home, running to make their connections for the last train, and those like us heading out, dressed up, and walking leisurely because we will be spending all night on the town. The magazine stands are closing. Homeless men are spread out on cardboard boxes on the steps leading down to the subways. The police observe the masses moving past each other in the station square towards their respective worlds. Three billboard-size TVs looming overhead, normally spouting pop music videos and snowboard ads during the day, are now dark and silent. The throngs of teenagers, many in their school uniforms, that mob Shibuya during afternoons and all weekend have been replaced by a more balanced mix of college students, "salarymen" and "career women," and of course more than a few B-Boys and B-Girls—the hip-hop enthusiasts in baggy pants and headphones. The sidewalks are splashed with light from vending machines—cigarettes, soda, CDs, beer (off for the night), and "valentine call" phone cards. A few drunken men are being carried by friends or lie in their suits unconscious on the sidewalk.

To get to Harlem, we walk uphill along Dôgenzaka Avenue toward a corner with a large neon sign advertising a capsule hotel, where businessmen who have missed their last train can sleep in coffin-like rooms. We pass disposable lamppost signs and phone booth stickers advertising various sex services. An elderly man in the back of a parked van is cooking and selling *takoyaki* (octopus dumplings) to those with the late-night munchies. The karaoke box establishments advertise cheaper rates at this hour. Turning right at a Chinese restaurant, we move along a narrow street packed with love hotels, which advertise different prices for "rest" or "stay." In contrast to the garish yellow sign advertising the live music hall, On-Air East, about fifty meters ahead, a nondescript door with a spiffy, long-haired bouncer out front is all that signals us that Harlem is inside. It seems there are always a couple of clubbers out front talking on their tiny cell phones. Up the stairs, past a table filled with flyers advertising upcoming hip-hop events, we pay our ¥3000 each (around $25, which may seem expensive, but is only about half again as much as a movie ticket). We move into the circulating and sweaty mass inside.

Traveling to a club instills a sense of moving against the mainstream in time and space. Others are going home to bed as the clubber heads out. When

---

[2]Hip-hop is not the only style for club music. Techno, House, Reggae, Jungle/Drum 'n' Bass, and so on, are some of the other popular club music styles. Live music tends to be performed earlier in the evening, usually starting around 7 P.M., and finishing in time for the audience to catch an evening train home. In contrast to "clubs," "discos" must by law close by 1 A.M.

the clubber returns home in the morning, reeking of smoke and alcohol, the train cars hold early-bird workers as well. So the movement to and from the club, often from the distant suburbs, gives clubbers a sense of themselves as separate, flaunting their leisure, their costumes, and their consumer habits. During the course of my year-and-a-half of fieldwork, between the fall of 1995 and the spring of 1997, I went to over a hundred club events around Tokyo and I began to see that clubs help one understand not only the pleasures of rap in Japan, but also the social organization of the scene and the different styles that have emerged. This becomes clear as you spend time inside the clubs.

Inside the Club

Inside the club, the air is warm and thick, humid with the breath and sweat of dancing bodies. Bone-thudding bass lines thump out of enormous speakers. There is the scratch-scratch of a DJ doing his turntable tricks, and the hum of friends talking, yelling really, over the sound of the music. The lighting is subdued, much of it coming from a mirrored ball slowly rotating on the ceiling. The fraternity house smell of stale beer is mostly covered up by the choking cigarette haze, but it is best not to look too closely at what is making the floor alternately slippery and sticky. The darkness, low ceiling, black walls, and smoky murk create a space both intimate and claustrophobic. Almost everyone heads for the bar as soon as they come in. An important aspect of clubbing is the physical experience of the music and crowded setting.

Harlem is a larger space than most of the Tokyo clubs, and can hold upwards of one thousand people on a crowded weekend night. On the wall behind the DJ stage, abstract videos, *anime* clips, or edited Kung Fu movies present a background of violence and mayhem, albeit with an Asian flavor. Strobe lights, steam, and moving spotlights give a strong sense of the space, and compound the crowded, frenetic feeling imposed by the loud music. The drunken revelry gives clubs an atmosphere of excitement that culminates with the live show and the following freestyle session. But an important part of clubbing is also the lull before and after the show, when one circulates among the crowd, flirting, networking, gossiping, or simply checking out the scene. Clubs are a space where the diffuse network of hip-hop fans comes together in an elusive effort to have fun. To the extent that a "community" emerges in the hip-hop scene, it revolves around specific club events and the rap groups that draw the crowd.

Much of the time is spent milling around, talking, drinking, and dancing. The live show often produces a welcome rise in the excitement level of the clubbers. Some events feature several live acts, often followed by a freestyle session. The rap show will usually begin between 1:00 and 1:30 A.M. Formats vary depending on the club and the event. "B-Boy Night" at R-Hall (organized by Crazy-A) was held one Sunday a month and would start with a long breakdancing show, with many groups each doing a five-minute routine. Then a series of rap groups would come on, each doing two or three songs. At other shows, like FG Night, sometimes a series of groups would perform, while on other nights only one group would do a show followed by a more open-ended freestyle. Nevertheless, there were many similarities, and a characteristic live show would proceed as follows. Two rappers take the stage (or step up into the DJ booth), as the DJ prepares the music. For people enamored of live bands, the live show of a rap concert may strike one as a bit lifeless. The music is either pre-recorded on a digital audio tape (DAT) or taken from the breakbeats section of an album.[3] The flourish of a lead guitar, bass, or drum solo is replaced in the hip-hop show by the manic scratching of a record by a DJ who deftly slides a record back and forth across the slip mat laid on the turntable and works the mixer to produce the rhythmic flurries of sampled sound.

The rappers begin with a song introducing themselves as a group. Every group seems to have its own introductory song of self-promotion:

rainutsutaa ga rainut shi ni yatte kita doko ni kita? Shibuya!	Rhymester has come to rhyme where are we? Shibuya!
hai faa za dopesuto da oretachi kyo cho gesuto da	we are By Phar the Dopest we are tonight's super guests
makka na me o shita fuktuô ore tojo	The red-eyed owl [You the Rock] I've arrived on stage

These songs tend to be brief, only a couple of minutes long. Between the first and second song, the rappers ask the audience how they feel. A common catch-phrase was "How do you feel/My crazy brothers."[4] The group will introduce by name the rappers and DJ, and also make sure everyone remembers the name of the group. The rappers will comment about how noisy the crowd is. Crowds are more often criticized for not being worked up enough rather than praised for their excitement.

The second song tends to be the one the group is most famous for. On stage, each rapper holds a cordless microphone right up to his mouth, and a rapper might steady the mic by holding his index finger under his nose. The other arm is gesticulating, palm out in a waving motion at the audience. A bobbing motion in the head and shoulders can be more or less pronounced.

Between the second and third song, the group will usually demand some call-and-response from the audience, almost always as follows:

---

[3]The term "breakbeats" refers to the section of a song where only the drums, or drums and bass, play. It is the break between the singing and the melodies of the other instruments, hence "break-beats." This section can be looped by a DJ using two turntables and a mixer with cross-fader, and produces a backing track suitable for rapping.

[4]In Japanese, *chôoshi wa dô dai/ikarera kyôdai*. The masculinity of Japanese rap is here indexed by the calling out to "brothers" and also by the use of the masculine slang *dai* instead of *da*.

Call	Response	Call	Response
ie yo ho	*ho*	Say, ho	ho
ie yo ho ho	*ho ho*	Say, ho ho	ho ho
ie yo ho ho ho	*ho ho ho*	Say ho ho ho	ho ho ho
sawage!	[screams]	Make noise!	[screams]

The third and usually final song tends to be a new song, often introduced in English as "brand new shit," a revolting image for English-speakers perhaps, but apparently heard by the audience as a cooler way of saying "new song" than the Japanese *shinkyoku*. If the song is about to be released as a record or CD, this information is also announced before the song's performance. If there are other rap groups in the audience, this is also the time for "shout outs" (praise for fellow hip-hoppers) as in "Shakkazombie in da house" or "Props to King Giddra" and once even, "Ian Condry in da house." After the third song, there is seldom talk besides a brief goodbye in English: "Peace" or "We out." Encores are rare, but freestyle sessions, discussed below, are ubiquitous. After the show, rappers retreat backstage or to the bar area, but never linger around the stage after performing. The year 1996 was also a time of a "freestyle boom," when most shows were closed with an open-ended passing of the microphone. Anyone could step on stage and try his or her hand at rapping for a few minutes. This has been an important way for younger performers to get the attention of more established acts. There is a back-and-forth aspect of performance in the clubs that shows how styles are developed, honed, and reworked in a context where the audience is knowledgeable, discriminating, and at times participates in the show itself.

It is important to understand that over the years, this kind of feedback loop has helped determine the shape of current Japanese rap styles. One of my main sites was a weekly Thursday night event that featured another collection of rap groups called Kitchens. Hip-hop collectives such as Kitchens, Little Bird Nation, Funky Grammar Unit, and Rock Steady Crew Japan are called "families" (*famirii*, in Japanese). The different groups often met at clubs or parties, at times getting acquainted after particularly noteworthy freestyle sessions. Over time some would become friends, as well as artistic collaborators, who performed together live or in the studio for each others' albums. Such families define the social organization of the "scene." What is interesting is how they also characterize different aesthetic takes on what Japanese hip-hop should be. Kitchens, for example, aim to combine a pop music sensibility with their love for rap music, and, like many such "party rap" groups, they appeal to a largely female audience. The Funky Grammar Unit aims for a more underground sound that is nonetheless accessible, and they tend to have a more even mix of men and women in the audience. Other families like Urbarian Gym (UBG) are less concerned with being accessible to audiences than with conveying a confrontational, hard-core stance. The lion's share of their audiences are young males, though as UBG's leader, Zeebra, breaks into the pop spotlight, their audiences are becoming more diverse.

The lull that precedes and follows the onstage performance is a key time for networking to build these families. In all, the live show is at most an hour long, at times closer to twenty minutes, and yet there is nowhere for the clubbers to go until the trains start running again around 5 A.M. It is not unusual for music magazine writers to do interviews during club events, and record company representatives often come to shows as well, not only as talent scouts but also to discuss upcoming projects. I found that 3:00 to 4 A.M. was the most productive time for fieldwork because by then the clubbers had mostly exhausted their supply of stories and gossip to tell friends, and were then open to finding out what this strange foreigner jotting things in his notebook was doing in their midst.

Japanese cultural practices do not disappear just because everyone is wearing their hip-hop outfits and listening to the latest rap tunes. To give one example, at the first Kitchens event after the New Year, I was surprised to see all the clubbers who knew each other going around and saying the traditional New Year's greeting in very formal Japanese: "Congratulations on the dawn of the New Year. I humbly request your benevolence this year as well." There was no irony, no joking atmosphere in these statements. This is a good example of the way that globalization may appear to overshadow Japanese culture, but one needs to spend time in clubs with the people to see how surface appearances can be deceiving.

In many ways, then, it is not surprising that rappers, DJs, breakdancers, record company people, and magazine editors all agree you cannot understand the music unless you go to the clubs. There is an intensity of experience in hearing the music at loud volume, surrounded by a crush of dancing people, while drinking alcohol and staying out all night, that gives the music an immediacy and power it lacks when heard, say, on headphones in the quiet of one's room. Indeed, it is difficult to convey in words the feeling of communal excitement during a particularly good show, when one gets wrapped up in a surge of energy that is palpable yet intangible. It is this emotional experience that in many ways counteracts any fears that it is all "merely imitation," which is the most common criticism of the music.

At the same time, going to a club involves a strange mix of the extraordinary and the routine. On one hand, you visit a place with bizarre interior design, listen to music at exceedingly high volume, stay out all night and, often, get drunk. It is a sharp contrast to an ordinary day of school or work. We must also recognize, however, that while a club may strive to be a fantastic microcosm, it is still embedded in Japan's political-economic structures, characteristic social relations, and the contemporary range of cultural forms. It is not by chance that clubs tend to attract people of specific class, age, sexuality, and to some extent locale. Moreover, if you go regularly to clubs, after a while it becomes just another routine. It is largely predictable what kind of pleasures can be expected, and also the generally unpleasant consequences for work or school after a night without sleep.[5] Clubbing of-

---

[5]Youthful Japanese clubbers use the mixed English-Japanese construction "all *suru*" (do all) to mean "stay out all night in a club." For example, the following exchange occurred between two members of the female group Now. Here, the sense of routine outweighs the excitement. A: *konban mo ooru suru ka na?* (Are we staying out all night again?) B: *Tabun.* (Probably) A: *Yabai.* (That sucks.)

fers freedom and constraints. This tension is the key to understanding how clubs socialize the club-goers by structuring pleasure in characteristic ways.

I have only suggested some of the ways that clubs offer insight into the ways that global hip-hop becomes transformed into a local form of Japanese hip-hop, but we can see how an idea of "genba globalism" can help us understand the process of localization. Globalism is refracted and transformed in important ways through the actual site of urban hip-hop clubs. Japanese rappers perform for local audiences in the Japanese language and use Japanese subjects to build their base of fans. In contrast to club events with techno or house music, hip-hop events emphasize lyrics in the shows and the freestyle sessions. There is a wide range of topics addressed in Japanese hip-hop, but they all speak in some way to the local audience. Dassen 3 uses joking lyrics ridiculing school and television. Scha Dara Parr is also playful, emphasizing things like their love of video games and the kind of verbal repartee characteristic of close buddies. When Zeebra acts out his hard-core stance, he tells of drug use in California, expensive dates with girlfriends, and abstract lyrics about hip-hop as a revolutionary war. Rhymester's lyrics are often set in a club or just after a show, for example, describing an imagined, fleeting love affair with a girl on a passing train. Some songs refer to cultural motifs going back centuries, such as a song performed by Rima and Umedy about a double-suicide pact between lovers, remade as a contemporary R&B and hip-hop jam.

Understanding Globalization in Local Terms

Rap music in Japan offers an interesting case study of the way popular culture is becoming increasingly global in scope, while at the same time becoming domesticated to fit with local ideas and desires. At the dawn of the twenty-first century, entertainment industries are reaching wider markets and larger audiences. The film *Titanic*, for example, grossed over $1.5 billion, the largest amount ever for a film, and two-thirds of this income came from overseas. In music, there are global pop stars too, like Britney Spears and Celine Dion. In rap music, the Fugees could be considered global stars. Their 1996 album "The Score" sold over 17 million copies worldwide. More recently, Lauryn Hill's 1998 solo album revealed that the transnational market for hip-hop is still growing, and most major rap stars do promotional tours in Japan. An important feature of pop culture commodities is that they tend to be expensive to produce initially, but then relatively cheap to reproduce and distribute. Compact disks are one of the most striking examples. Although studio time is expensive (between $25,000 for a practically homemade album to upwards of $250,000 for state-of-the-art productions), the CDs themselves cost about eighty cents to produce, including the packaging. Obviously, the more one can sell, the higher the return, and this helps explain the eagerness of entertainment businesses to develop new markets around the world.

Less clear are the kinds of effects such globalized pop culture forms might have. The fluidity of culture in the contemporary world raises new questions about how we are linked together, what we share and what divides us. The spread of popular culture seems in some ways linked with a spread in values, but we must be cautious in our assessment of how and to what extent this transfer takes place. It is safe to say that the conventional understanding of globalization is that it is producing a homogenization of cultural forms. From this perspective, we are witnessing the McDonaldization and the Coca-Cola colonization of the periphery by powerful economic centers of the world system. The term "cultural imperialism" captures this idea, that political and economic power is being used "to exalt and spread the values and habits of a foreign culture at the expense of the native culture."[6] In some ways, anthropology as a discipline emerged at a time when there was a similar concern that the forces of modernity (especially missionaries and colonial officials) were wiping out "traditional cultures," and thus one role for ethnographers was to salvage, at least in the form of written documents, the cultures of so-called "primitive peoples." Many people view globalization, and particularly the spread of American pop culture, as a similar kind of invasion, but the idea that watching a Disney movie automatically instills certain values must be examined and not simply assumed. In some ways the goals of anthropology—combatting simplistic and potentially dangerous forms of ethnocentrism—remain as important today as when the discipline was born.

The example of Japanese hip-hop gives us a chance to examine some recent theorizing on globalization. The sociologist Malcolm Waters offers a useful overview of globalization, which he defines as follows:

> A social process in which the constraints of geography on social and cultural arrangements recede, and in which people become increasingly aware that they are receding.[7]

A key aspect of this definition is not only that the world is increasingly becoming one place, but that people are becoming increasingly aware of that. This awareness may lead to a heightened sense of risk, such as global warming or the "love bug" virus, or to a rosy view of increased opportunities, for example, to get the most recent hip-hop news in real time or to download the latest music instantly via the Internet.

It is important to recognize, however, that globalization involves much more than Hollywood movies and pop music. Waters does a good job of analyzing three aspects of globalization, namely, economic, political, and cultural. He contends that globalization processes go back five hundred years, and that

---

[6]John Tomlinson, *Cultural Imperialism: A Critical Introduction* (London: Printer Publishers, 1991), p. 3.

[7]Malcolm Waters, *Globalization* (London: Routledge, 1995, p. 3).

the relative importance of economic, political, and cultural exchanges has varied over that time.[8] From the sixteenth to nineteenth centuries, economics was key. In particular, the growth of the capitalist world system was the driving force in linking diverse regions. During the nineteenth and twentieth centuries, politics moved to the fore. Nation-states produced a system of international relations that characterized global linkages with multinational corporations and integrated national traditions. Now, at the dawn of the twenty-first century, cultural forms are leading global changes in both politics and economics. Waters argues that a "global idealization" is producing politics based on worldwide values (e.g., human rights, the environment, anti-sweatshop movement) and economic exchanges centered on lifestyle consumerism. The key point is that while economics and then politics were the driving forces in globalization of previous centuries, it is cultural flows that are increasingly important today. If he is right, and I would argue he is, this points to the importance of studying the kinds of ideals that are spread around the globe.

What ideals are spread by hip-hop in Japan? Clubbing certainly promotes an attitude that stresses leisure, fashion, and consumer knowledge of music over other kinds of status in work and school. Although it is important to recognize that the effects of lyrics are somewhat complicated, it is worth considering, to some extent, the messages carried by the music. Although rappers deal with a wide variety of subjects, one theme appears again and again, namely, that youth need to speak out for themselves. As rapper MC Shiro of Rhymester puts it, "If I were to say what *hip-hop* is, it would be a 'culture of the first person singular.' In hip-hop, . . . rappers are always yelling, 'I'm this.'" Such a message may seem rather innocuous compared to some of the hard-edged lyrics one is likely to hear in the United States, but it is also a reflection of the kind of lives these Japanese youth are leading. In Japan, the education system tends to emphasize rote memorization and to track students according to exams. Sharply age-graded hierarchies are the norm, and may be especially irksome in a situation where the youth are likely to live with their parents until they get married. Moreover, the dominant ideology that harmony of the group should come before individual expression ("the nail that sticks up gets hammered down") makes for a social context in which the hip-hop idea that one should be speaking for oneself is, in some limited sense, revolutionary. At the very least, it shows how global pop culture forms are leading not to some simple homogenization, but rather adding to a complex mix that in many ways can only be studied ethnographically through extended research in local sites.

Another important theorist of globalization is Arjun Appadurai, who proposes that we consider contemporary cultural flows in terms of movement in five categories: people or ethnicity, ideology, finance, technology, and media. He adds the suffix "-scape" to each to highlight that the deterritorialization of cultural forms is accompanied by new landscapes of cultural exchange, thus we

[8]Waters, pp. 157–164.

have "ethnoscapes, ideoscapes, financescapes, technoscapes, and mediascapes" (others have added "sacriscapes" to describe the spread of religion, and one might add "leisurescapes" for the spread of popular culture). The key point about these landscapes is that they are "non-isomorphic," that is, they don't map evenly onto each other. Appadurai notes, for example, that the "Japanese are notoriously hospitable to ideas and are stereotyped as inclined to export (all) and import (some) goods, but they are notoriously closed to immigration"[9] (1996:37). Migration and electronic mass media are the main driving forces to Appadurai's theorization. One of the problems with Appadurai's theory, however, is that the notion of "-scapes" draws us away from considering how flows of technology, media, finance, and people are connected. An alternative is to consider key sites, *genba* if you will, of various sorts depending on one's interests as a way to see how new, hybrid forms of culture are produced. "Genba globalism" aims to show how artists, fans, producers, and media people are actively consuming and creating these new forms.

One thing that anthropologists offer to the advancement of human knowledge is a clear sense of the ways people interact in specific places. At one time, anthropologists would choose a village or island to map in elaborate detail. Now in a media-filled world, we face different analytical challenges, but the techniques of fieldwork—learning the language, participating in daily life, observing rituals, and so on—can still be used. One of Appadurai's conclusions is that exchanges along these different "-scapes" are leading not only to a deterritorialization of cultural forms, but also to an increased importance of the "work of the imagination".[10] In other words, as identities can be picked up from a variety of media sources, the construction of "who we are" arises increasingly from how we imagine ourselves, rather than from where we live. Life in urban areas seems to make this aspect of identity—as imagination and as performance—all the more salient. What I hope I have drawn attention to is the way the hip-hop nightclubs give us a chance to bring some of this work of the imagination down to the level of daily life.

Conclusion: Global Pop and Cultural Change

In the end, the globalization of popular culture needs to be understood as two related yet opposing trends of greater massification and deeper compartmentalization. On one hand, the recording industry is reaching larger and larger markets, both within Japan and around the world, as mega-hits continue to set sales records. On the other hand, there is an equally profound if less visible process by which niche scenes are becoming deeper and more widely connected

---

[9]Arjun Appadurai, *Modernity at large: Cultural dimensions of globalization* (Minneapolis: University of Minnesota Press, 1996), p. 37.

[10]Appadurai, p. 3.

than before, and in the process, new forms of heterogeneity are born. Although I have only been able to touch on a few of its aspects here, Japanese rap music is a revealing case study of the social location, cultural role, and capitalist logic of such micro-mass cultures. It is important to recognize, however, that these micro-mass cultures also have the potential to move into the mainstream.

The distinction between "scene" and "market" highlights what is at stake when we try to analyze the cultural and capitalist transformations associated with globalization. Information-based and service industries are growing rapidly, promising to reorganize the bounds of culture and commodities, yet we need close readings of how such emerging economies influence everyday lives. Although B-Boys and B-Girls go to great lengths to distinguish the "cultural" from the "commercial" in their favored genre, it is rather the linkage of the two in the circuits of popular culture that offers the deepest insight. In the end, the winds of global capitalism that carried the seeds of rap music to Japan can only be grasped historically with a close attention to social spaces, media forms, and the rhythms of everyday life.

Walking to a hip-hop club in Tokyo, one is confronted with a tremendous range of consumer options, and it is this heightened sense of "you are what you buy" that has in many ways become the defining feature of identity in advanced capitalist nations, at least among those people with the money to consume their preferred lifestyle. At the same time, it is important to be sensitive to the ways that, outward appearances notwithstanding, the consumers of things like hip-hop are embedded in a quite different range of social relations and cultural meanings. It makes a difference that B-Boys and B-Girls, listening to American hip-hop records, still feel it is important to go around to their friends and associates with the traditional New Year's greeting of deference and obligation. This is an example of the ways social relations within the Japanese rap scene continue to carry the weight of uniquely Japanese practices and understandings.

It is likely, too, that "global pop" will become more heterogeneous as the entertainment industries in other countries develop. There are reasons to think that, in music at least, the domination of American popular music as the leading "global" style seems likely to be a temporary situation. In the immediate postwar period in Japan, Western music initially dominated sales. But sales of Japanese music steadily grew and in 1967 outpaced Western sales. Today, three-fourths of Japan's music market is Japanese music to one-fourth Western. Moreover, although American music currently constitutes about half of global sales, this is down from 80 percent a decade ago. It is quite possible that as local record companies mature in other countries, they will, as in Japan, come to dominate local sales. Certainly, multinational record companies are moving in this direction of developing local talent and relying less on Western pop stars. Moreover, although Japan is a ravenous importer of American popular culture, it has some notable exports as well. Some are more familiar than others, but they include the Mighty Morphin' Power Rangers, karaoke, "Japanimation," *manga* (Japanese comic books), mechanical pets, Nintendo or the Sony Play-Station video games, and of course, Pokémon.

Just as it would seem strange to Americans if someone claimed Pokémon is making U.S. kids "more Japanese," it is dangerous to assume that mass culture goods by themselves threaten to overwhelm other cultures. The anthropologist Daniel Miller has been a proponent for taking a closer look at the ways such goods are woven into everyday lives. He argues that mass commodities are better analyzed in terms of an "unprecedented diversity created by the differential consumption of what had once been thought to be global and homogenizing institutions."[11] Miller's emphasis on the active and creative aspects of consumption is characteristic of a broad trend within the social sciences to view global commodities in terms of their local appropriations, and to represent local consumers with a greater degree of agency than found in other works that emphasize "cultural imperialism." It is this perspective that seems to me the best characterization of what is going on in Japan.

It is easy to see how the "sameness" aspect of globalization is promoted. Music magazines, TV video shows, and record stores promote similar artists whether in Japan or the United States. A new album by Nas is met with a flurry of publicity in the Japanese and English-language hip-hop magazines available in Tokyo. This relates in part to the structure of record companies and their marketing practices. In this sense, the widening and increasingly globalized market for popular culture does appear to be leading to greater homogenization. But it is primarily a process of homogenizing what is available, regardless of where you are. I would argue that the global marketing blitz of megahit productions like the film *Titanic* and the music of Celine Dion and Lauryn Hill reflect a homogenization of *what* is available, but not *how* it is interpreted. Although it is more difficult to see, in part because it is hidden beneath similar clothes, hairstyles, and consumption habits, different interpretations are generated in different social contexts. By attending to "actual sites" of cultural production and consumption, we can more clearly gauge the ways local contexts alter the meanings of globalization. "Keeping it real" for hip-hoppers in Japan means paying attention to local realities.

[11]Daniel Miller, "Introduction: Anthropology, modernity and consumption," in Daniel Miller (ed.), *Worlds Apart: Modernity through the Prism of the Local* (London: Routledge, 1995), p. 3.

Review Questions

1. Describe the Tokyo hip-hop scene as it is presented by Condry. Based on your own knowledge of the North American scene, what seems to be different about Japanese hip-hop?

2. Condry notes that an author, Malcolm Waters, identifies three basic kinds of globalization that have occupied three time periods. What are those kinds of globalization and when was each most important?

3. What are "-scapes" as they have been presented in the writings of anthropologist Arjun Appadurai? How do they apply to the Japanese hip-hop scene?

4. What is the major contribution anthropologists can make to the study of globalization according to Condry? How does this article illustrate that contribution?

5. What is cultural imperialism? Can Japanese culture be "imperialistic"?

TEN

Culture Change and Applied Anthropology

Nowhere in the world do human affairs remain precisely constant from year to year. New ways of doing things mark the history of even the most stable groups. Change occurs when an Australian aboriginal dreams about a new myth and teaches it to the members of his band; when a loader in a restaurant kitchen invents a way to stack plates more quickly in the dishwasher; or when a New Guinea Big Man cites the traditional beliefs about ghosts to justify the existence of a new political office devised by a colonial government. Wherever people interpret their natural and social worlds in a new way, cultural change has occurred. Broad or narrow, leisurely or rapid, such change is part of life in every society.

Culture change can originate from two sources: innovation and borrowing. **Innovation** is the invention of qualitatively new forms. It involves the recombination of what people already know into something different. For example, Canadian Joseph-Armand Bombardier became an innovator when he mated tracks, designed to propel earth-moving equipment, to a small bus that originally ran on tires, producing the first snowmobile in the 1950s. Later, the Skolt Lapps of Finland joined him as innovators when they adapted his now smaller, more refined snowmobile for herding reindeer in 1961. The Lapp innovation was not the vehicle itself. That was borrowed. What was new was the use of the vehicle in herding, something usually done by men on skis.

Innovations are more likely to occur and to be adopted during stressful times when traditional culture no longer works well. Bombardier, for example, began work on his snowmobile after he was unable to reach medical help in time to save the life of his critically ill son during a Canadian winter storm. Frustrated by the slowness of his horse and sleigh, he set out to create a faster vehicle.

The other basis of culture change is **borrowing.** Borrowing—or **diffusion,** as it is sometimes called—refers to the adoption of something new from another group. Tobacco, for example, was first domesticated and grown in the New World but quickly diffused to Europe and Asia after 1492. Such items as the umbrella, pajamas, Arabic numerals, and perhaps even the technology to make steel came to Europe from India. Ideologies and religions may diffuse from one society to another.

An extreme diffusionist view has been used to explain most human achievements. For example, author Erich von Däniken argues that features of ancient New World civilizations were brought by space invaders. Englishman G. Elliot Smith claimed that Mayan and Aztec culture diffused from Egypt. Thor Heyerdahl sailed a reed boat, the *Ra II*, from Africa to South America to prove that an Egyptian cultural origin was possible for New World civilization.

Whether something is an innovation or borrowed, it must pass through a process of **social acceptance** before it can become part of a culture. Indeed many, if not most, novel ideas and things remain unattractive and relegated to obscurity. To achieve social acceptance, an innovation must become known to the members of a society, must be accepted as valid, and must fit into a system of cultural knowledge revised to accept it.

Several principles facilitate social acceptance. If a change wins the support of a person in authority, it may gain the approval of others. Timing is also important. It would have made little sense for a Lapp to attempt the introduction of snowmobiles when there was no snow or when the men who do the reindeer herding were scattered over their vast grazing territory. Other factors also affect social acceptance. Changes have a greater chance of acceptance if they meet a felt need, if they appeal to people's prestige (in societies where prestige is important), and if they provide some continuity with traditional customs.

Change may take place under a variety of conditions, from the apparently dull day-to-day routine of a stable society to the frantic climate of a revolution. One situation that has occupied many anthropologists interested in change is **cultural contact,** particularly situations of contact where one society politically dominates another. World history is replete with examples of such domination, which vary in outcome from annihilation—in the case of the Tasmanians and hundreds of tribes in North and South America, Africa, Asia, and even ancient Europe—to the political rule that indentured countless millions of people to colonial powers.

The process of change caused by these conditions is called **acculturation.** Acculturation results from cultural contact. Acculturative change may affect dominant societies as well as subordinate ones. After their ascendance in India, for example, the British came to wear *khaki* clothes, live in *bungalows*, and trek through *jungles*—all Indian concepts.

But those who are subordinated experience the most far-reaching changes in their way of life. From politically independent, self-sufficient people, they usually become subordinate and dependent. Sweeping changes in social structure and values may occur, along with a resulting social disorganization.

Although the age of colonial empires is largely over, the destruction of tribal culture continues at a rapid pace today. As we saw in Reed's article in Part Three of this book, hundreds of thousands of Amazonian Indians have already perished in the last few years because of intrusive frontier and development programs. Following almost exactly the pattern of past colonial exploitation, modern governments bent on "progress" displace and often kill off indigenous tribal populations. The frequent failure of development, coupled with its damaging impact on native peoples, has caused many anthropologists to reassess their role. As a result, more and more anthropologists have become part of native resistance to outside intrusion.

A less dramatic, but in many ways no less important, agent of change is the world economy. No longer can most people live in self-sufficient isolation. Their future is inevitably tied in with an overall system of market exchange. Take the Marshall Islanders described by anthropologist Michael Rynkiewich, for example. Although they cultivate to meet their own subsistence needs, they also raise coconuts for sale on the world market. Receipts from the coconut crop go to pay for outboard motors and gasoline, cooking utensils, and a variety of other goods they don't manufacture themselves but have come to depend on. Several major American food companies have now eliminated coconut oil from their products because of its high level of saturated fat. This loss has created lower demand for copra (dried coconut meat), from which the oil is pressed. Reduced demand, in turn, may cause substantial losses to the Marshall Islanders. A people who once could subsist independently have now become prisoners of the world economic system.

Anthropologists may themselves become agents of change, applying their work to practical problems. **Applied anthropology,** as opposed to academic anthropology, includes any use of anthropological knowledge to influence social interaction, to maintain or change social institutions, or to direct the course of cultural change. There are four basic uses of anthropology contained within the applied field: adjustment anthropology, administrative anthropology, action anthropology, and advocate anthropology.

Adjustment anthropology uses anthropological knowledge to make social interaction more predictable among people who operate with different cultural codes. For example, take the anthropologists who consult with companies and government agencies about intercultural communication. It is often their job to train Americans to interpret the cultural rules that govern interaction in another society. For a business person who will work in Latin America, the anthropologist may point out the appropriate culturally defined speaking distances, ways to sit, definitions of time, topics of conversation, times for business talk, and so on. All of these activities would be classified as adjustment anthropology.

Administrative anthropology uses anthropological knowledge for planned change by those who are external to the local cultural group. It is the use of anthropological knowledge by a person with the power to make decisions. If an anthropologist provides knowledge to a mayor about the culture of constituents, he or she is engaged in administrative anthropology. So would advisers to chief administrators of U.S. trust territories such as once existed in places like the Marshall Islands.

Action anthropology uses anthropological knowledge for planned change by the local cultural group. The anthropologist acts as a catalyst, providing information but avoiding decision making, which remains in the hands of the people affected by the decisions.

Advocate anthropology uses anthropological knowledge by the anthropologist to increase the power of self-determination of a particular cultural group. Instead of focusing on the process of innovation, the anthropologist centers attention on discovering the sources of power and how a group can gain access to them. James Spradley took such action when he studied tramps in 1968. He discovered that police and courts systematically deprived tramps of their power to control their lives and of the rights accorded normal citizens. By releasing his findings to the Seattle newspapers, he helped tramps gain additional power and weakened the control of Seattle authorities.

Whether they are doing administrative, advocate, adjustment, or action anthropology, anthropologists take, at least in part, a qualitative approach. They do ethnography, discover the cultural knowledge of their informants, and apply this information in the ways discussed previously. In contrast to the quantitative data so often prized by other social scientists, they use the insider's viewpoint to discover problems, to advise, and to generate policy.

The articles in this part illustrate several aspects of cultural change and applied anthropology. The first, by Terence Turner, relates the case of how one people, the Kayapo of the Brazilian Amazon, have successfully resisted external threats to their existence as a people. By uniting Indians, environmental groups, and legislators, and using the international media, they have managed to protect and expand their forest area and advance the international environmental cause. The second updated selection, by medical anthropologist Sonia Patten, describes her experience as an applied anthropologist. Working with USAID funding, she and a team of specialists designed a program using milk goats to improve children's nutrition in Malawi. The third article, by David McCurdy, discusses the modern uses of anthropology. From studies of General Motors workers, to program assessment for people with AIDS, to participation in government health projects, to international counseling, professional anthropologists put their discipline to work. In this article, McCurdy looks at one way in which the ethnographic perspective can be put to work in a business setting. Finally, in the last article, John Omohundro tackles a question often asked by students: "What do you do with an anthropology major?" Basing his answer on years of work with his institution's career development office, he argues that anthropology teaches a number of skills that are useful in the world of work. The trick, he notes, is for students to translate these skills into résumé language that employers can understand.

Key Terms

acculturation   *p. 388*
action anthropology   *p. 389*
adjustment anthropology   *p. 389*
administrative anthropology   *p. 389*
advocate anthropology   *p. 390*
applied anthropology   *p. 389*

borrowing   *p. 387*
cultural contact   *p. 388*
diffusion   *p. 387*
innovation   *p. 387*
social acceptance   *p. 388*

34

The Kayapo Resistance

Terence Turner

Until about 200 years ago, vast areas of the world were inhabited by native, mostly hunter-gatherer or horticultural, peoples. Few native groups have survived the ravages of colonial and economic expansion, though, and those who are left seem destined to become victims of "progress." In this article, however, Terence Turner argues that "Fourth World" peoples—in this case the Kayapo of the Brazilian Amazon—have acted to conserve their own political autonomy while simultaneously aiding the world conservation movement. Apparently doomed to extinction by the relentless encroachment of Brazilian settlers, loggers, miners, and dam builders, the Kayapo have managed to mobilize not only themselves, but other Indians, environmentalists, legislators, and the world press in a united effort to defend the forest and their right to live in it.

As increasing numbers of people have become aware of the imminence of the destruction of the world's tropical forests and the probable consequences for the atmosphere and climate of the planet, voices have increasingly been heard drawing attention to the need for concern for human populations of forest dwellers, as well as the floral and faunal components of the ecosystem. This has been motivated in part by humanitarian concerns, in part by more specific concerns for indigenous political and legal rights, in part by an awareness that native forest peoples may possess valuable knowledge of their environments, and also, at times, by a realization that the traditional adaptive activities of such peoples may make important functional contributions to the ecosystems in which they live. Whatever their specific point of departure, however, advocates of native forest peoples have tended to assume that recognition of the rights and contributions of the native inhabitants of the forests, as well as their physical and cultural survival, would depend, like the salvation of the forests themselves, upon them. That native forest peoples themselves, many of whom number among the most primitive and remote human societies on earth, should come to play an important role as allies and even leaders in the world struggle to save the forests is a prospect so apparently remote as to seem only a little less improbable than Martians arriving to lend a hand. Yet this is precisely what has been happening in the last few years, nowhere with more impressive scope and success than in the case of the Kayapo Indians of the Brazilian Amazon.

The Kayapo: Ethnographic and Historical Background

The Kayapo are a nation of Ge-speaking Indians who inhabit the middle and lower reaches of the valley of the Xingu River, one of the major southern tributaries of the Amazon. Their total population is currently around 2,500, divided among 14 mutually independent communities. The largest of these communities, Gorotire, has about 800 inhabitants, but several others are little more than hamlets. Kayapo country is a mixture of forest and savannah land, with rather more forest than open country around most of the villages. The total area covered by Kayapo communities and their associated land-use patterns is about the size of Scotland.

The massive destruction of the Amazonian environment represented by the cutting and burning of the forest, the cutting of roads, and the soil erosion and river pollution caused by mining and the building of giant hydroelectric dams, have had a shattering impact on the environment and way of life of many forest Indians of the Amazon. Even groups whose lands have not yet been reached by these activities, or are just beginning to be affected by them, now live in the permanent shadow of the threat. To understand the meaning of this threat for indigenous peoples like the Kayapo, one must stand in a Kayapo village under the dense clouds of smoke that now darken the sky over Kayapo country at the end of every dry season, as Brazilian squatters and ranchers burn off vast stretches of previously forested land to the east and south, rapidly approaching the traditional borders of Kayapo territory along a 700-mile front. It is to feel one's world burning, with the ring of fire drawing even tighter.

For members of modern industrial societies, one of the most difficult points to grasp about the relation of native tropical forest peoples to their environment, as articulated through their modes of subsistence production, is that the relationship is not felt or conceived to comprise a separate, "economic" sphere in our sense. Rather, it forms an integral part of the total social process of producing human beings and social life. The threatened annihilation of such a society's environmental base of subsistence is therefore not felt merely as an "economic" threat, nor one that can be located and confined in an external, "environmental" sphere. It is a threat to the continuity and meaning of social life. Understanding this point is essential, not only to appreciate the traumatic effects of wholesale ecological devastation on traditional societies of subsistence producers like the Kayapo, but also to understand the nature of their political response and resistance to such threats.

The Relation of the Kayapo to the Environment through Subsistence Production

For the Kayapo, like most other contemporary Amazonian native peoples, traditional patterns of subsistence adaptation are still the basic way of life. The Kayapo produce their means of subsistence by a combination of slash-and-burn horticulture, hunting, fishing, and foraging. According to the division of labor by gender and generation, men engage in all productive pursuits incompatible with the care of young children, while women perform those which can be carried out while caring for children. This means that men hunt, fish, do the heavy and dangerous work of clearing gardens, and gather certain wild forest products that grow at great distances, requiring overnight journeys. Women do the planting, weeding, and harvesting of gardens; cut firewood; cook the food; build traditional shelters (now done almost exclusively in trekking camps); forage for such wild products as can be found within a day's round-trip walk from the village or camp; and care for children. Girls begin to help their mothers with household and garden chores while still children, but boys do little productive labor until they are inducted into the men's house, a bachelors' dormitory and men's club which stands apart from the family houses in the middle of the round village plaza.

Kayapo gardens must be cleared from fresh forestland and produce for about three years for most crops. The Kayapo raise an impressive variety of garden produce: manioc (both the bitter and sweet varieties), maize, bananas, yams, sweet potatoes, fava beans, squash, *cissus* (a leafy creeper that is a unique domesticate of their own), tobacco, *urucu* (used to make red body paint), and cotton (used to make string, but not woven). In recent years, many Kayapo have added Brazilian-introduced crops such as papaya, rice, various species of beans, pineapples, watermelon, avocado, and mango. Most families maintain about three gardens in production at any one time and clear a new one every year. After a garden is abandoned, it requires about 25 years for reforestation to render it ready for reuse. A sizable village therefore needs an extensive area of forestland for the rotation of its garden plots.

The Kayapo supplement their horticultural diet with large quantities of fish and game. Included among the latter are wild pig, tapir, deer, monkey, tortoise, armadillo, and various species of birds and rodents. Gathered wild produce is also seasonally important, and includes *babassu* coconuts (used for body and hair oil), *piki, tucum,* and brazil nuts, honey, palmito, *acai, bacaba,* and a variety of less important fruits. Hunting or fishing for the men, and gardening for the women, are more or less daily activities while the community is settled in its base village.

For considerable periods of the year, however, the Kayapo abandon their base villages and go off on collective seminomadic treks through the surrounding forest and savannah. These may last from one to three months, and may take one of several forms. Individual age-sets (most frequently, the male bachelors' set) may be sent out to gather seasonally ripening nuts or fruits; the whole village may go together; the individual senior men's societies may trek as separate groups, each with its associated women, children, and bachelor dependents; or only part of the village may go on trek to gather food for a ceremonial feast, while the rest remain behind in the village. A community may go on two or three such treks per year, so that at least some of the village may spend as much as half the year on trek. Large areas may thus be covered by all the treks undertaken by the members of a single village in a given year. In spite of the low population density of Kayapo country, therefore, most of the area is actually used by the mobile trekking groups which continually sally forth from the widely scattered base villages.

The regular alternation between trekking and base village occupation thus appears to be an integral aspect of Kayapo social organization. Why this should be so is not immediately apparent. Trekking by large collective groups is a relatively inefficient way to exploit the wild floral and faunal resources of an area. Only the adult men of the camp do any hunting. The bachelors and younger boys are typically occupied either with clearing the trail to the next day's campsite and the campsite itself, or bringing up horticultural produce from the village gardens, while the women occupy themselves with pitching or breaking camp, cutting firewood, preparing food, and tending children. The camp is moved every one or two days, but usually only for a distance of one or two kilometers, about a 15-minute walk. More game could doubtless be captured by small groups of men working alone, free to move more rapidly over greater distances. Hunting and fishing are routinely done in this way while the community is residing in the base village, and it is certainly no less productive than the hunting done on trek. Trekking by whole communities or large groups, in other words, cannot be accounted for as the most efficient available method of acquiring needed protein or other foodstuffs.

A similar question arises over the frequency with which Kayapo bands moved their village sites in the days before peaceful relations were established with the Brazilians. There is in fact no ecological reason why Kayapo villages as large as two thousand would ever need to move as a group from their permanent village sites to remain supplied with the foods they require. Notwithstanding this fact, Kayapo villages before pacification tended to move as often as every two, or more usually five to ten years. A given community would have as many as a dozen village sites, and occupy most of them over a twenty-year period. This frequency of movement, again, cannot be accounted for simply as a result of material necessity. In common with trekking, it seems part of a dynamic inherent in Kayapo social organization.

The Social Meaning of Subsistence Production

The high mobility of Kayapo society, and the large amount of territory it requires in consequence, thus cannot be understood, as some have attempted to do, as the result of nutritional deficiencies in the soil or lack of protein or other nutrients in the faunal or floral environment. They are, rather, the corollaries and effects of the organization of Kayapo society, with its central tension between female-centered and male-centered forms of social grouping. These forms themselves, however, are articulated in terms of their complementary roles in production, although this is production understood in the Kayapo sense of the social production of human beings and social relations, which includes but is not reducible to, material subsistence. This notion of social production calls for a more extended exegesis as it is essential to an understanding of the Kayapo relationship to their natural environment and their society per se.

Kayapo patterns of environmental adaptation and subsistence production are intricately interwoven with their ways of producing human individuals. This process of human production includes what we call "socializing" children, but continues through the life cycle and the final rites of death. This individual process, in turn, is treated by the Kayapo as an integral part of the process of reproducing collective social units like extended-family households, age-sets, and ceremonial organizations, and thus of society as a whole. As I have already indicated, the division of labor in the production of material subsistence is defined in relation to the division of labor in the production of social persons and relations, with women specializing in the socialization of children. It must be clearly understood that this is not simply a natural result but a culturally imposed social pattern. Women who do not happen to be raising young children nevertheless do not go hunting and fishing. At a higher level of organization, the nuclear family forms the social unit of cooperation in the production and consumption of material subsistence, but as a social unit it owes its form primarily to its role in producing new social persons, not its functions in expediting subsistence activities. Subsistence production thus finds its place as an integral part of the global process of social production, which also includes the socialization of children, the recruitment and reconstitution of families and collective groups, and the celebration of the great communal ceremonies. In these two-to-four month long symbolic dramas, all of these levels of activity are performed in an orchestrated pattern that asserts their essential interdependence as parts of a single whole.

The Kayapo attitude toward the nonhuman natural environment must be understood as a part of this same global pattern. The Kayapo do not oppose "nature" to human society as mutually exclusive, externally related domains; nor can they be said to possess a single, uniform concept of "nature" in our sense. They recognize that the forest and savannah beyond their village clearings are products of forces that are independent of humans and not under social control. They further recognize that they depend upon these natural forces and products for their own social existence, and that social persons are in fact largely "natural" beings, whose physical bodies, senses, and libidinal energies are as extra-social in origin as any forest tree or wild animal. Disease, death, shamanic trance, insanity, and periods of transition in [life]-crisis ritual are seen as moments when the continuity between the internal natural core of human social actors and the external natural environment of the forest and animal world asserts itself, short-circuiting and blacking out the interposed, insulating social veneer. At such times, the social person reverts to a "natural" state, here conceived as one of entropic dissolution of social form. At other times, as in the rituals of initiation at puberty or the everyday bringing in of game, gathered nuts, or garden produce from the forest, displacing or penetrating the boundary between nature and society has the opposite result: an infusion of energy which, directed into social channels, enables society to exist and renew itself. Human beings and society itself, in sum, are seen as partly "natural" entities, dependent on continual infusions of energy from their natural surroundings. The reproduction of human society, the reproduction of socialized human beings, and the reproduction of the natural forest and savannah environment are thus interconnected parts of a single great process.

Society and its members, in sum, are essentially seen as appropriating and channeling natural energy, and are thus dependent on the ability of the natural world (meaning the forest, animals, birds, rivers, and fish) to reproduce itself and continue as a great reservoir and source of the energy society must continually draw upon to live. The destruction of the forest, the killing or driving away of its animals, or the pollution of the rivers and killing of their fish, therefore, are not seen by the Kayapo simply as an attack on "the natural environment" in our sense, but as a direct assault upon them as a society and as individuals.

This view, it should immediately be added, is fully compatible with the destruction of trees and animals on a considerable scale for appropriation by the Kayapo of the energy stored in their flesh, fruits, or the soil on which they stand. The Kayapo operate with a rough rule of thumb derived from millennia of experience, a sense of the ability of the local environment to accommodate a certain level of destruction, inflicted by their traditional modes and levels of subsistence activity, and still regenerate itself. They have no mystical sense of reverence or respect for individual trees or animals and feel no hesitation about chopping them down or taking them as game whenever their interests demand. What concerns the Kayapo is nature in the aggregate, or more specifically, the survival and reproduction of a sufficient slice of the natural environment to support their traditional way of life. It was only when they realized that this aggregate capacity for regeneration was threatened by the vast scale of the destruction now being inflicted on the area that the Kayapo became aroused over the fate of the forest environment as such. Similarly, ecological concerns for tropical rain forests became transformed into urgent political issues in the developed world only when peoples of the developed countries realized the probable consequences of this destruction from the rest of the world's climate and population. Kayapo and First World modes of "ecological" consciousness and concern converged, in short, when, starting from very different premises, the members of both societies realized that the survival of their societies was at stake. The dramatic results of this convergence are the subject of the rest of this paper.

The Kayapo Resistance and the Environmentalist Movement

The Kayapo area of Southern Para state is a representative microcosm of the destructive processes at work in the Amazon as a whole. Beginning in the late 1960s, the Kayapo have been confronted with virtually every major form of environmental destruction and land depredation found elsewhere in the region.

The Kayapo Face the End of Their World

Since the 1960s there has been constant pressure from small squatters and large ranchers attempting to infiltrate Kayapo areas and clear small farms by burning off patches of forest. Land speculators have attempted to build illegal airstrips and to survey and sell off large chunks of Kayapo land to which they did not even hold legal title. In 1971, the Brazilian government built a major road of the Trans-Amazonica highway system through Kayapo country, secretly altering the route so as to amputate the Kayapo area of the Xingu National Park, which it then attempted to sell off to private owners, mostly speculators, would-be ranchers, and farmers. The road brought heavy truck and bus traffic carrying settlers and supplies to the new settlements farther west, bringing with them the perils of infectious disease and the potential for conflict with the Indians. Timber companies interested in the large stands of virgin mahogany within the boundaries of the remaining officially delimited Kayapo reserve, the Kayapo Indigenous Area, sought and obtained logging concessions for large tracts from Kayapo leaders in exchange for sizable money payments and the construction of modern housing and other facilities in Kayapo villages. Most of the money went into communal accounts in banks in neighboring frontier towns. These accounts were either explicitly or tacitly controlled by chiefs or the few literate Kayapo able to keep the accounts. Some of these individuals began to draw heavily on these "communal" funds for personal use, giving rise to tension and resentment by the rest of their communities. Rivalries between competing companies and their respective Kayapo sponsors almost led to war between two Kayapo villages in 1986.

The discovery of gold at the huge mine of Serra Pelada near the eastern border of the Kayapo Indigenous Area led to intense prospecting and exploratory gold-mining activity within the eastern borders of the Kayapo Indigenous Area. This culminated in 1983 with the opening of two large illegal gold mines only ten kilometers from Gorotire village. Three thousand Brazilian miners swarmed onto Kayapo land, and neither the Brazilian Indian Service (FUNAI) nor any other arm of the Brazilian government seemed willing or able to do anything to stop it. Tons of mercury from the mining operations began to pollute the Rio Fresco, the main fishery of several Kayapo communities. Then, in 1986, an even more ominous form of pollution threatened, when radioactive waste from a cancer treatment facility in the city of Goiania caused two dozen fatalities, and the federal government attempted to dump the material on the western border of Kayapo country.

As if all this were not enough, the Kayapo began to hear rumors that the Brazilian government was planning to build a series of hydroelectric dams along the Xingu and its tributaries, which would result in the flooding of large areas of Kayapo land and end the value of most of the river system as a fishery. The scheme was to be funded by loans from the World Bank. Repeated attempts to learn the truth about the government's plans were met with stonewalling and denials that any such plan existed. The rumors persisted, however, and construction sites began to be cleared at certain points along the river. The Kayapo were outraged by the government's disregard for their political and legal rights to be consulted about a project which would so heavily affect their lands and livelihood. They were equally concerned about the ecological effects. While Kayapo leaders strove unsuccessfully to penetrate the government's cover-up about the dam project, however, they were confronted by an even more direct threat to their legal and political rights, as Indians, to challenge governmental or private Brazilian infringements of their land rights, resources, or communal interests. At the convention called to draw up the new Brazilian constitution, a measure was introduced calling for the redefinition of any Indian who demonstrated the capacity to bring a legal action in a Brazilian court as an "acculturated" person who could no longer be considered an Indian, and therefore could no longer represent or bring an action on behalf of an Indian community in court. This "catch-22" provision would have destroyed the possibility of any legal or political resistance by native peoples against abuses of their rights, persons, lands, or environments within the terms of the Brazilian legal and political process.

This daunting array of threats to the Kayapo environment, communal lands and resource base, political and civil rights is a representative sample of the human face of the environmental crisis in the Amazon. The Kayapo confronted this apparently overwhelming onslaught beginning in the early 1970s as a still largely monolingual people of Ge-speakers scattered over a vast area in 14 mutually autonomous and politically uncoordinated settlements. In most of the villages, some of the men (but almost no women) spoke Portuguese, and a handful had learned to read, write, and do simple arithmetic. A few leaders had obtained some experience of Brazilian administrative and political ways through working in the Indian Service or as members of Brazilian expeditions to contact other tribes. They had a few contacts with the outside world through anthropologists and indigenous advocacy groups, and the Brazilian Indian Service (FUNAI) offered some support, although it could not be counted upon to represent the Indians' interests against the more threatening forms of economic development mounted by government or powerful private interests. Aside from this slender array of assets, the Kayapo had no political resources with which to defend themselves and their forest beyond their own largely intact tribal institutions and culture. These, however, were to serve them well in the trials that lay ahead.

The Kayapo Resistance

This is what they did. The two western communities whose land had been severed by the road began an unrelenting campaign of armed attacks on all Brazilian intruders who attempted to open ranches or settle in the separated area. After 15 years and perhaps 50 Brazilian dead, with no Kayapo casualties, no Brazilian settler remained in the entire area. The leaders of the two Kayapo groups meanwhile carried out a campaign of diplomacy, making repeated trips to Brasília to pressure the government to return the stolen land and thus end the violent standoff in the area. The government capitulated in 1985, returning the area to the Kayapo and ceding an additional area immediately to the north of the old area (this became the Capoto Indigenous Area). The two communities of the region joined again into a single large village and have resolutely banned all Brazilian mining, timber, and agricultural interests and settlers from their reclaimed areas.

Also in 1985, the two illegally opened gold mines were assaulted and captured by 200 Kayapo, armed with a mixture of firearms and traditional weapons. The larger mine was accessible only by air, so the Kayapo seized and blockaded the landing strip, confronting the Brazilian government with a choice: either cede title and administrative authority over the mines to the Kayapo, together with a significant percentage of the proceeds (10% was the amount initially demanded), and legally demarcate the boundaries of the Kayapo Indigenous Area (thus making the government unambiguously responsible for the defense of the area against any further such incursions), or the Kayapo would allow no more planes to land or take off, either to supply or evacuate the three thousand miners at the site. After a tense ten-day standoff, the government gave in to the Kayapo demands.

The leaders of Gorotire, the nearest and largest Kayapo village, used the first income from the mine to purchase a light plane and hire a Brazilian pilot. They put the plane to use to patrol their borders from the air to spot intruders and would-be squatters. If any were seen, patrols were dispatched to expel or eliminate the invaders. Within a year, invasions effectively ceased. They have also used the plane to fly to other Kayapo villages and to Brazilian cities to purchase goods and bring people out for medical assistance. In the nearest town of Redencao, and the state capital of Belem, they have bought houses for the use of Kayapo travelers and shoppers, and in the former they have established a tribal office to deal with their bank accounts and official relations with the local office of FUNAI.

All timber concessions on Kayapo land were suspended by the Indian Service (FUNAI) at the end of 1987, at the urging of the most influential Kayapo leaders, Payakan and Ropni. Some concessions, however, were surreptitiously continued by a few other leaders who have lined their own pockets with the fees paid by the companies. Still other communities and leaders not previously involved with lumbering companies are under great pressure from the companies to grant new concessions. Meanwhile, resistance to any new concessions continues to be strong, and one community (A'Ukre) has declared its part of the Kayapo Indigenous Area an "extractive reserve" closed to all ecologically destructive forms of timber and mineral exploitation. This remains a conflicted issue, with the ultimate outcome in doubt. Meanwhile, a substantial area of the Kayapo Indigenous Area has been clear-cut. The fate of the captured gold mines has also proved a divisive issue. Not only have the Kayapo not closed them down, as they originally said they would do within two years of taking them over, but some Kayapo have opened a couple of small new mines on their own land. Other Kayapo vigorously oppose this and have strictly prohibited all mining activity, whether by Brazilians or Kayapo, from their areas of the reserve. Meanwhile, five Gorotire Kayapo have become wealthy enough from the gold and timber revenues to buy private houses for themselves in Redencao, where they live for much of the time, keeping Brazilian servants and, in two cases, acquiring large ranches outside the reserve. This phenomenon has been paralleled by the chief of the village of Kikretum, who owns an airplane, houses, and a hotel in the neighboring town of Tucuma. The rise of this embryonic "new class" has already given rise to significant tensions within Kayapo society and is a factor in the unresolved conflicts over the future form of accommodation between Kayapo society and the Brazilian economy.

Most of the other threats posed by the enveloping national society proved less divisive, and the Kayapo were able to mount concerted, well-organized responses to them without internal dissension or conflict. When the government's plan to dump the radioactive waste on traditional Kayapo land was announced, the Kayapo sent a hundred men to Brasília to demonstrate against the plan. Suitably painted and feathered, they staged a sit-in in the president's palace. Nothing like this had happened in Brazil in the twenty years since the coup d'etat that established the military regime that was then in the process of relinquishing power. The initial incredulity and indignation of the authorities, however, gave way to acquiescence to the Kayapo's demands, and the dumping plan was abandoned. Pressing their advantage, the Kayapo next sent a deputation of some 50 chiefs and leading citizens to the Constitutional Convention to lobby for the defeat of the "catch-22" acculturation clause and other provisions injurious to Indian interests. Presenting themselves as always, in traditional paint and feathers and carrying traditional weapons, they patiently attended the weeks of debates on the sections bearing on indigenous peoples' rights, gave press conferences, and lobbied the deputies. When the acculturation clause was defeated, and surprisingly strong safeguards of indigenous rights, lands, and resources were adopted by the Convention, the Kayapo received much of the credit in the Brazilian press.

In 1988, two Kayapo leaders were invited to the United States to participate in a conference on tropical forest ecology. From there, they traveled to Washington, met with members of Congress, and spoke with World Bank officials about the effects of the proposed Xingu dam scheme on the peoples and environment of the area. They were able to obtain copies of the entire dam project, the very existence of which the Brazilian government had continued to deny, from the Bank. Shortly after the Kayapos' visit, the World Bank announced that it was deferring action on the Brazilian loan request. Enraged, elements of the Brazilian national security and political establishment had criminal charges brought against them and their American interpreter under a law prohibiting participation in political activity in Brazil by foreigners. The charges were ridiculous in strictly legal terms; since the actions in question had taken place in the United States, the American had been acting in his own country, and the Kayapo were not in any case foreigners. The transparent attempt at legal terrorism boomeranged, as nongovernment organizations (NGOs), anthropologists, and the congressmen whom the Kayapo had met on their tour organized an international outcry.

When one of the Kayapo leaders came to Belem, the capital of the state of Para, where the charges had been brought, to be arraigned, the Kayapo organized a massive protest demonstration. More than five hundred Kayapo men and women danced through the streets and massed in the square before the Palace of Justice to support their kinsman and denounce Brazilian political repression. The defiance turned to ridicule when the judge refused to allow the Kayapo leader to enter the courthouse for arraignment until he changed his paint and feathers for "civilized" (Brazilian) clothes. The Kayapo refused and told the judge he would have to come to the Kayapo village of Gorotire if he wanted another chance to arraign him on the charges. Meanwhile, Kayapo orators unrolled the map of the Xingu dam scheme obtained from the World Bank in Washington on an easel erected in the square and explained the entire secret project in Kayapo and Portuguese for the benefit of the many Brazilian onlookers, who included reporters and TV crews. The government never again dared to try to arraign the Kayapo leader, and eventually dropped all the charges.

With the World Bank still actively considering the Brazilian government's request for a loan to enable the building of the Xingu dams, the proposed multi-dam hydroelectric scheme in the Xingu River valley now appeared to the Kayapo as the greatest threat, not only to their environment, but to their political and legal control over their lands and resources. Since the government still refused to disclose its plans to build the dams, the Kayapo resolved to force it to reveal its intentions and to receive, before an audience of national and world news media, their criticisms of the human and environmental effects of the dams, as well as of its deceit in attempting to conceal and deny its plans. To accomplish this, they decided to convene in great congress of Amazonian peoples at the site of the first of the dams the government hoped to build: Altamira, near the mouth of the Xingu. To the meeting would be invited representatives of the Brazilian governments representatives of the World Bank; representatives of the national and world news media; nongovernmental organizations active in the environmentalist, human rights, and indigenous peoples' support fields; delegates from as many indigenous nations of Amazonia as possible; and as many Kayapo as could be transported and accommodated. At the meeting, the government representatives would be asked to present their plans, to give an account of their probable effects on the environment and the human inhabitants of the region (Brazilian as well as native), and to explain why they had tried for so long to keep their plans secret from those who would be most affected by them.

The Kayapo leaders who envisioned this project saw that its success would depend on international public opinion, press attention, and financial support. Only the attendance of a large number of media and NGO representatives, they felt, would compel the Brazilian government to send its representatives to face certain humiliation at such a meeting. The leader chiefly responsible for the plan, Payakan, therefore embarked on a tour of seven European and North American countries (sponsored and coordinated by Friends of the Earth, the World Wildlife Federation, and the Kayapo Support Group of Chicago) in November, 1988, to publicize the Altamira gathering and appeal for support. At a more general level, Payakan also sought to bring the crisis of the Amazon forest and its native peoples to wider public attention, and to lobby government and international development bank officials against supporting economic development projects (such as the Xingu dam scheme) that would irreversibly damage the environment and require the expropriation or destruction of native lands.

Payakan, at the same time, also sought to bring about greater mutual trust, cooperation, and unity of purpose among the various kinds of nongovernmental organizations and sectors of public opinion involved in supporting the Indians and the environmental struggle. These included human rights, indigenous peoples' advocacy, anthropological, and environmentalist organizations. Among the latter were some groups specifically devoted to defending tropical rain forests, others concerned with saving endangered animal species, and still others dedicated to conservation and environmental quality in a more general sense. Payakan, in his dealings with these groups or their representatives, had quickly realized that they tended to work in isolation from one another, often mistrusted one another's politics, or viewed one another's work as irrelevant to their own concerns. With other Kayapo leaders, Payakan saw this situation as not only damaging the effectiveness of the work of these organizations, but as out of touch with the real interconnections of the issues with which the groups were attempting to deal. For both reasons, they felt, the support of the NGOs was less effective than it might otherwise be. Payakan therefore devoted much effort on his tour to appealing to these groups to join forces and recognize that they were really all involved in a single great struggle. As he put it in a speech at the University of Chicago:

> The forest is one big thing; it has people, animals, and plants. There is no point saving the animals if the forest is burned down; there is no point saving the forest if the people and animals who live in it are killed or driven away. The groups trying to save the races of animals cannot win if the people trying to save the forest lose; the people trying to save the Indians cannot win if either of the others lose; the Indians cannot win without the support of these groups; but the groups cannot win either without the support of the Indians, who know the forest and the animals and can tell what is happening to them. No one of us is strong enough to win alone; together, we can be strong enough to win.

Payakan's message was widely heard. His tour became a concrete example of the intergroup cooperation he preached. For many indigenous advocacy organizations, environmentalist groups, human rights groups, Latin Americanist social scientists and anthropologists, helping to organize Payakan's tour and attending his speeches was their first practical experience of cooperating and coming together around a common set of interests and commitments. This experience has been continually repeated since then in a series of cooperative efforts to support the Altamira meeting, aid new organizational initiatives by the Kayapo and other forest peoples in Brazil, and help with subsequent tours by Payakan and other Kayapo leaders. It is generally recognized by activists of the various support organizations concerned that the Kayapo campaign has become an important catalyst of increased contact and cooperation among them at the national and international level, and that this cooperation has brought increased efficacy in lobbying, fund-raising, and public opinion outreach efforts.

Payakan's tour successfully achieved all its goals. Enough money was raised to defray all the costs of the Altamira gathering (which eventually approached $100,000) without drawing upon any of the funds derived from timber or gold concessions, which Payakan and most of his closest Kayapo supporters opposed. Much publicity and media attention was generated, guaranteeing a strong international media presence at the Altamira gathering itself. The support base of the Kayapo campaign among European and American nongovernmental organizations, public opinion, and politicians was greatly strengthened. The stage was now set for one of the most remarkable events in the history of Amazonia, the environmentalist movement, and modern popular protest politics.

From February 19–24, 1989, 600 Amazonian Indians and a roughly equal number of Brazilian and international journalists, photographers, TV crews, documentary filmmakers, Brazilian and foreign politicians, and representatives of various nongovernmental support organizations converged on the small river town of Altamira. Among the Indians were some 500 Kayapo and 100 members of 40 other indigenous nations, whom the Kayapo had invited to join them in confronting the Brazilian government, and to make their own views on the issues of dams and the destruction of the forest known to the government representatives, the news media, and one another. Five days of meetings, speeches, press conferences, and ritual performances by Kayapo and other indigenous groups were programmed and carried out without a major hitch. The event represented an impressive feat of organization and political coordination. It required the transportation, lodging, and feeding of hundreds of indigenous participants, which involved constructing a large encampment with traditional Kayapo shelters outside the town and daily busing of its inhabitants to the meeting hall in the center. Much of the credit for the event belongs to the Brazilian indigenous peoples' support organization, The Ecumenical Center for Documentation and Information (CEDI), which effectively cooperated with Payakan and the rest of the indigenous leadership in handling many of the logistical tasks essential to the success of the meeting.

Some elements of the regional Brazilian populace, especially those linked with landowning and commercial interests who stood to gain from the construction of the dams, were hostile to the Indians and (even more) their Brazilian and foreign environmentalist supporters. There were fears that violent incidents might occur and spread out of control. That this did not happen can be attributed in part to the foresight and discipline of the Kayapo, who carefully sited their encampment far outside of town and refrained from street demonstrations within the city limits, but also in large measure to the presence of so many foreign and domestic media personnel and observers.

The event took on the aspect of an international media circus. The Pope sent a telegram of support. The rock star Sting flew in for a day and gave a press conference at the Kayapo encampment, denouncing the destruction of the forest and promoting his own project for the creation of a new Kayapo reserve. No doubt because this project depended on the goodwill of the Brazilian government, Sting avoided directly committing himself in support of the Kayapo campaign against the dams. Since this was the whole purpose of the Altamira meeting, his Kayapo hosts roundly criticized him for using their platform for his own project and then skipping off. A British member of Parliament, a Belgian member of the European Parliament, and a half-dozen Brazilian deputies of the National Congress, however, mounted the platform and gave unreserved support. A final communique was issued, on behalf of all native peoples of Amazonia, condemning the dam project. By the time the conference closed with a dance from the Kayapo New Corn ceremony (joined in by assorted Indians of other tribes, European and Brazilian activists and media personnel, momentarily giving it the air of a 1960s hippie love-in), the Altamira gathering had become an international media success of such proportions as to generate serious political pressure against any international funding of the dam scheme, or indeed any attempt to go on with the plan by the Brazilian government. Within two weeks after the end of the meeting, the World Bank announced that it would not grant the Brazilian loan earmarked for the dam project, and the Brazilian National Congress had announced plans for a formal investigation and debate on the whole plan.

The Kayapo have not rested on their laurels since Altamira. One major line of effort was the drive to get a large area of the west bank of the Xingu demarcated as a third major Kayapo reserve, linking the two largest existing reserves (the Capoto and Kayapo Indigenous Areas) in a continuous area the size of Britain. In this effort, the Kayapo were supported by Sting and his recently founded Rainforest Foundation, which raised close to two million dollars to support the project. President Sarney of Brazil made several public statements vaguely in favor of the plan, but in January 1990, when Sting came to Brazil with the money from the Rainforest Foundation to present to the government to start the demarcation of the reserve, Sarney noncommitally passed the buck by merely extending the official period for administrative decision on the proposal into the new administration of President-elect Collor without taking action. Collor finally proclaimed the new reserve in 1991; the actual demarcation of the boundary was finished in September 1992. The demarcation of the new reserve bears witness to the political pressure the Kayapo, and the Rainforest Foundation with its international and Brazilian support, were able to bring to bear. Meanwhile, Payakan established a Kayapo Foundation (the "Fundacao Mebengokre") to administer and raise money for the support of a series of programs, including the establishment of an "extractive reserve" within the Kayapo Indigenous Area. This is an area off-limits to all lumbering and mining operations, devoted exclusively to environmentally sustainable forms of forest exploitation such as the gathering of Brazil nuts and other wild forest products.

The Kayapo also made some attempt to follow up on the links of solidarity with other indigenous Amazonian peoples forged at Altamira. In November 1989, several Kayapo leaders and a Kayapo video-cameraman flew (in a Kayapo plane) to Boa Vista in the northern frontier state of Rondonia to investigate an incident in which Yanomamo villagers had been attacked and driven from their land by Brazilian gold miners. The Kayapo denounced the government policies leading to the incident and declared their support for the survivors. The government had banned the area to all non-Indians after the occurrence, attempting to cover up the affair and keep it out of the press. The government was clearly thinking only of local Yanomamo Indians, but the Kayapo, seizing upon the loophole opened up by the wording of the ban and capitalizing on their undeniable identity as "Indians," were able to penetrate the official smokescreen with their fact-finding and support mission.

Wider Implications: The Kayapo Achievement in World Perspective

The Environmentalist Movement

At the level of international environmentalist politics, the Kayapo are now an established presence. In 1990 alone, Kayapo spokesmen have traveled to various European countries, Canada, the U.S.A., and Japan. They were accorded audiences by heads of state (Mitterand of France), cabinet ministers responsible for loans, aid and financial dealings with Brazil, and members of parliaments and national assemblies (Canada, France, Belgium, England, and the U.S.A.). They have also met with indigenous groups and leaders in North America, notably the Cree of Northern Quebec in 1991 and 1992. All of this notoriety and attention has generated for them a measure of immunity from the cruder forms of abuse and exploitation that have so often been the lot of indigenous peoples in Amazonia and elsewhere.

A mere ten years ago, however, they themselves were the targets of many such abuses, as recounted above. They have succeeded, against fantastic odds, in turning the tables on their would-be exploiters and seizing the political advantage, drawing upon the support of international and urban Brazilian public opinion. The strength of this support owes much to the worldwide wave of concern for the fate of the tropical forests, but the Kayapo would not have been able to capitalize so effectively on the general climate of environmental concern without their shrewd grasp of the possibilities of contemporary news and informational media and their effective presentation of themselves and their cause through them. Other factors in the Kayapo successes have been the effective support of numerous nongovernmental organizations and the impressive capacity of the Kayapo themselves for mass organization and militant but disciplined confrontational tactics, as exemplified by their bold but nonviolent demonstrations in Brasília, Belem, and Altamira.

The success of the Kayapo in furthering their own cause, at the same time, has had an important effect upon the politics of the developed world, and in particular, of the environmentalist movement. The support of environmentalist groups and public opinion has been essential to the Kayapo victories, but it is equally true that the Kayapo have won important victories for the environmentalist movement, and partly as a result have exercised an important influence upon its thinking, strategies, and organizational tactics. Perhaps most importantly, in a few short years they have revolutionized the consciousness of many activists and ordinary persons concerned with the fate of the world's tropical forests, teaching them that indigenous forest-dwelling peoples are not just a passive part of the problem, but an active part of the solution. By their own example, they have demonstrated that native forest peoples, no matter how apparently primitive, remote, or numerically insignificant, can become potent combatants and allies in the struggle to avert ecological disaster. In addition, they have helped bring about working relations of mutual trust and collaboration between members of a number of important organizations, scientific specialists, and politicians, who had previously never considered working together, and in many cases mistrusted one another's politics and policies.

Before the advent of the Kayapo on the international stage, many environmentalists had realized that there could be no solution to the problem of saving the forests that did not include the human inhabitants of the forests. Many who had arrived at this relatively enlightened opinion, however, continued to think of aboriginal forest peoples, and even forest-dwelling members of national societies like the Brazilian rubber-tappers, as historical basket cases, with all the capacity for political action in their own behalf of endangered animal species like the black cayman or the Amazonian giant otter. It has been a humbling, disconcerting, but delightful surprise to many of these same good people suddenly to discover that some of these supposedly hapless victims of progress have assumed a leading role in the struggle environmentalists had thought (perhaps a tad condescendingly) *they* were leading, and that these same native peoples have even succeeded in bringing to the effort a degree of unity and effectiveness that had previously eluded its familiar leadership.

The Rise of Ecological Resistance in the Fourth World

The Kayapo are not a unique case. Their story, in fact, conforms in its essential features to an emerging pattern of ethnic self-assertiveness and ecological militancy on the part of native forest peoples in the Amazon and other parts of the world. It is not new for native peoples (to refer, by this term, to the tribal societies and ethnic minorities comprising the "Fourth World") to attempt to resist the wholesale appropriation of their lands and resources by the peoples and governments of modern states. What is new is the combination of political, economic, environmental, and ideological pressures with revolutionary new media technologies that has enabled native peoples to take their case directly to the peoples and governments of the world, and to find a receptive hearing because of the convergence of their cause with the new levels of popular concern over the environment.

One major manifestation of this worldwide pattern is the organization, over the past twenty years, of many federations of native peoples, for the most part consisting of groups speaking the same or related languages. Over 50 such groups now exist in the Amazon alone. They typically unite around a program of defense of native land and resources, respect for civil and political rights, and the assertion of traditional values and cultural identity. These groups are increasingly in touch with one another, and in some areas intergroup coordinating organizations, such as the recently organized Coordinating Group of the Amazon Basin, COICA, have begun to appear.

The rise of these organizations and the political consciousness they express has been catalyzed by many factors. Among them are the extension of modern transportation and communications networks to many previously inaccessible areas inhabited by tribal peoples; improved medical technology and assistance; greater availability of manufactured tools and goods; the extension of effective national government administrative control over the contiguous national populations; the increase in the strength and effectiveness of nonindigenous, nongovernmental advocacy and support organizations; the increased interest and ability of national and international media to publicize abuse of native lands, rights and peoples; the increase in international economic and political interdependence, which has made many governments more sensitive to the repercussions of bad publicity over indigenous issues; and last but not least, the influence of a steady trickle of anthropological researchers, who have helped both to catalyze native groups' awareness of the value of their traditional cultures in the eyes of the outside world and to inform them of the existence of potential sources of support in that world for their struggles to resist economic, political, and cultural oppression.

These factors have converged in recent years with growing concern in world public opinion for human rights and environmental issues, which have favored the causes of native groups struggling to defend their traditional lands and resource bases. None of these external factors, however, would have been sufficient by themselves to generate the cultural and social resources, or the political organization and will to act, that have been shown by so many native peoples. This is the part of the story that remains least well known to the world at large. It is important that it become known, as an antidote to the hopelessness induced by apocalyptic but often inaccurate news stories of "genocide" and widespread romantic clichés like the inevitable disappearance of primitive peoples in the path of progress. (The two often have more in common than meets the eye.) These myths have had the harmful effect of discouraging support for the struggles of many native peoples with a fighting chance to win. As the Kayapo case shows, such support can make an enormous difference.

That is the rosy side of a picture which is in the main far from rosy. For every indigenous people who have found the courage, leadership, and ability to respond constructively to the threat of despoliation of their ecological bases or the theft of their lands, others have been or are being decimated, dispossessed, or destroyed. In spite of some shining cases of successful resistance to threats to the ambient life-world, other battles have been, or are being, lost. The sheer volume of environmental destruction, and the variety of its forms and causes, make the struggle appear almost hopeless. Nowhere, however, has this been more true than in the Kayapo area of the Amazon. What the Kayapo have managed to do shows that even the most apparently hopeless odds can be faced and overcome.

Review Questions

    1. How do the Kayapo Indians of Brazil subsist in their Amazon forest environment?

2. What forces threaten the livelihood and social existence of the Kayapo as a cultural group?

3. How have the Kayapo reacted to defend their forest environment and their existence as a cultural group?

4. Turner argues that the Kayapo have tried to unite and enlist the aid of several kinds of local and world groups in their fight to preserve their forest and lands. What are these groups? Use the case of the encampment at Altamira to illustrate how they could work together.

5. How have the Kayapo affected the world environmentalist movement?

35

Medical Anthropology: Improving Nutrition in Malawi

Sonia Patten

Applied anthropologists work in many settings. They may conduct government program evaluations, work on forest conservation projects, market or advertise products, staff rural development programs, establish foreign offices for nongovernmental organizations or corporations, or advise hospital staff, among other things. In this article, Sonia Patten describes her role as an applied medical anthropologist on a project aimed at the improvement of infant and child nutrition in the African nation of Malawi. As a medical anthropologist, her job was to collect cultural baseline data that would help to shape the program and make it appropriate to village conditions in Malawi.

Malawi—Welcome to the Warm Heart of Africa. This is the sign that greets travelers when they arrive in this southeastern African republic. The warm, open response to visitors that I have enjoyed each time I have traveled to Malawi contrasts starkly to the poverty that plagues its citizens.

Malawi is a small landlocked nation in southeast Africa that lies south of Tanzania, east of Zambia, and west of Mozambique. The country is long and thin with its axis running north and south along the Great African Rift Valley. Part of the valley holds Lake Malawi, the third largest lake in Africa, which accounts for more than 20 percent of the country's total area of 119,100 square kilometers. Malawi is one of the ten poorest countries in the world. Its economy is based predominately on agriculture, which accounts for half the gross domestic product and virtually all the exports. Cotton, tobacco, and sugar are most likely to be sold to other countries. However, despite exports, food security for both households and the nation is a chronic problem, with annual "hungry seasons" a fact of life and the specter of famine never far from people's minds. Maize, or white corn, is the staple food for the nation, and it is rare when the nation's rain-fed agriculture produces enough of it to adequately feed the population. The Malawi government faces the enormous challenges of strengthening the economy, improving educational and health facilities, and dealing with the serious environmental issues of deforestation and erosion. The country depends heavily on the International Monetary Fund, World Bank, and bilateral and multilateral donor assistance. It was a small project funded by the U.S. Agency for International Development (USAID) that brought me as a medical anthropologist to Malawi several times during the 1990s.

Medical anthropology is difficult to define because it covers such a wide scope of research and practical programming. In the broadest sense, it can be defined as the study of human health in a variety of cultural and environmental contexts. Over the past three decades, medical anthropology has become a distinct and important area within anthropology. Presently it has three major areas of emphasis. One is the study of cultural differences in health beliefs and systems of healing such as alternative therapies, shamanism, and folk concepts of disease. A second consists of biomedical studies of human adaptations to disease, including nutrition, genetics, and demography. The third is applied medical anthropology, which focuses on the application of anthropology to health-related problems and possible solutions.

Medical anthropologists often carry out research as members of interdisciplinary teams, where their main contribution is to discover a people's cultural conceptions of health, illness, and the more general cultural context within which ideas about health are situated. It was as an applied medical anthropologist that I came to be a member of such an interdisciplinary team that would work in Malawi.

In the early 1990s, I was on the faculty at one of three universities that had joined together to apply for a USAID grant under a program called University Development Linkages Program (UDLP). Two of the universities were American and one was the agricultural college that forms part of the University of

Malawi system. A major goal of the UDLP was to strengthen developing nation colleges and universities by giving them access to U.S. faculties and other American university resources. The program also sought to increase the involvement of U.S. faculty members with faculty in developing nations so that students at U.S. institutions would benefit from an internationalizing of the curriculum.

In this case, scientists from participating universities were asked to devise and implement a project that would benefit all collaborating institutions of higher education. Many teams of UDLP scientists that applied for grants designed projects intended to strengthen curricula at developing nation institutions. Our team, however, opted to design and implement a project addressing a major problem, child undernourishment in Malawi. We recognized that three out of five children in the country were undernourished. Worse, the mortality rate for children under five was 24 percent or nearly one in four. The problem was caused by the fact that children received insufficient protein and calories, which left them vulnerable to a host of infectious diseases, potential mental impairment, serious deficiency diseases such as kwashiorkor and marasmus, and premature death. This is the story of the people from two central Malawi villages and three universities as we worked to craft a program to reduce child undernourishment and increase child survival on a sustainable basis.

Faculty members who were participating in this effort represented a number of disciplines: anthropology, human nutrition, cooperative extension, animal science, veterinary medicine, and crop science. Several of the participating faculty members from Malawi had grown up in small villages, still had extended family in those villages, and were familiar with economic and cultural factors contributing to child undernourishment there. From them and from field research we learned that mothers breastfeed their babies for two to three years, which assured that the children received sufficient protein and calories during these early years. However, that changed when the children were fully weaned. The indigenous weaning food is a gruel of water and maize flour, and babies receive small amounts of it beginning at about four months of age. When mothers wean their toddlers, it is this gruel that the children eat day after day. It is a nutritionally inadequate weaning food and children soon begin to show its effects—swollen bellies, stunted growth, and increased susceptibility to malaria, measles, and other infectious diseases. The weaning food is made from the same crop, maize, that constitutes the staple food for adults, a boiled maize flour dish called *nsima*. The problem of a nutritionally inadequate weaning food is not unique to Malawi—it plagues many developing nations. In these countries there is often a high-carbohydrate food such as corn or rice that makes up as much as 90 percent of children's daily intake. If people survive into adulthood, their bodies have made an adaptation to this low-protein diet. But young children do not thrive.

As our project searched for ideas about how to create a plan for addressing child nutrition, we decided to focus on a simple approach that would use indigenous resources and be manageable at the local level. This was the introduction of a protein and calorie-rich additive, goat milk, to the local weaning food. Although goats are plentiful in Malawi villages, they are meat goats, not dairy goats. They are like walking bank accounts, to be sold when a family needs money to pay school fees for the children, health care, and rites of passage such as weddings and funerals. It would be a bold step to secure approval from male village political leaders and elders for the introduction of milk-producing goats to provide milk for young children. Dairy goats would be put directly into the hands of women, not men. Would it work? Would women be willing to learn new animal management and food handling techniques? Would they have time to carry out the additional labor that would be required? Would the goat milk be given to the children who needed it? Would husbands or brothers take the valuable animals away from the women? Would the goats and the children flourish? As time went on, we learned the answers to all these questions and more. And the village women contributed very valuable insights and suggestions that made the project a model that has been adopted elsewhere in Malawi.

The Program

Our work began with a series of planning meetings. Our goal was to create a program that would enable women to raise and keep dairy goats on a sustainable and manageable basis, and use the milk that was produced to supplement their children's diets and increase food security for their families. The plan we generated would have three parts: (1) generation of a database on the milk production and biological characteristics of goats; (2) development and implementation of demonstrations and outreach programs for distributing milk goats to rural women and teaching them how to care for the animals; and (3) formation and implementation of outreach programs for rural women so they could learn how to safely handle goat milk and use it as a regular part of the diet, especially for their children who were under five years of age. At our planning meetings we had to figure out what we were actually going to do, and in what sequence.

The animal scientists on the team knew that milk goats introduced into local villages would have to be hardy or they would die. They wanted to try out some breeding experiments using local goats and imported breeds of dairy goats to see just what kind of a crossbred doe would result in the best combination of high milk production and ability to adapt to life in the village. So they worked out a breeding scheme using local Malawi goats and imported Saanen dairy goats from South Africa, Damascus goats from Cyprus, and Anglo-Nubian goats from the U.S. The breeding experiments were carried out at the farm that the Malawi members of our team used for teaching and research.

This kind of research can't be done in a hurry. Arranging for the importation of animals is a complex process because one has to find a supplier, arrange for payment, arrange for shipment (very few airlines are willing to transport large animals internationally), work out how to feed and water the animals while they are in transit, secure permits from the Malawi Ministry of Agriculture, and quarantine the animals for a period of weeks when they arrive in country. Only then can the breeding research begin.

To our dismay, none of the imported Anglo-Nubian goats survived for very long in Malawi. And several of the Damascus goats also died. The Saanens, however, proved to be the hardier—not surprising, since they originated from relatively close by South Africa where environmental conditions were similar to those in Malawi. And when bred with local Malawi goats, the resulting crossbreeds turned out to provide substantial weekly milk yields that would be enough for the goats' kids as well as for the young children of rural families. So the team decided to import more Saanens and continue the crossbreeding program. Crossbred does would be distributed to village women and most of the crossbred bucks would be sold to support the project. As the program developed, team members discovered that some local does produced relatively high average milk yields; this finding became important as the project unfolded.

My work as the team anthropologist involved the human side of the project. With the help of team nutritionists and the extension expert, I designed a survey to collect baseline cultural information in the villages where the milk goats would be distributed. It was important to document such things as women's daily activities, the meaning and use of goats, relationships between men and women, and ways children were fed in the target villages before the milk goats were introduced. Later we would look for changes we hoped would occur after the new goats arrived and for unexpected problems.

To proceed with the social research, we selected three villages, all relatively close to the college campus in a rural setting about 25 km from the capital city of Lilongwe. To proceed, however, it was necessary to obtain permission from the people in each community. To do so we held meetings with the village headmen, men and women elders, mothers of young children who would be affected by our project, and anyone else from the village who was interested in learning about the program.

In the Central Region of Malawi where we were working, most people belong to the Chewa ethnic group. The Chewa have a matrilineal descent system and practice matrilocal residence. Thus, Chewa men and women inherit clan and lineage membership from their mothers. It is this membership that gives people the right to farm plots of land surrounding their villages. When women marry, most continue to live in the village of their birth with a group of related females—mother, maternal grandmother, mother's sisters and their children, sisters and their children, and eventually, adult daughters and their young children. When young men marry, most move to the villages of their brides. The village political leader is usually, but not always, a man. He cannot be the son of the prior headman because a son is not part of his father's matriline. Instead, he is likely to be the son of the prior headman's sister—a maternal nephew. This system creates a situation where almost all of the women and the powerful men in a village are maternal kin to one another.

To introduce the project, we had to recognize the matrilineal nature of village social organization and the need for people's approval. We met with groups of interested women and men and the headmen in two villages. We explained what we were proposing to do. We said we wanted to find out how the young children in the village were doing in terms of growth and health. Then we intended to make milk goats available to women who had children under five years old because we felt the children would benefit from goat milk in their diet. We noted that it would not cost the women any money. (Most rural women lack the means to purchase even local goats, because they cost from $30 to $50. Dairy goats would be much more expensive.) We said that women who received milk goats would be asked to return the first healthy kid, whether male or female, to the college farm and that this would constitute payment for the animal. We told them that women who took the goats would be asked to attend demonstrations to help them learn how to care for the animals, handle the milk, and feed the milk to their children. We also said that someone from the project would come to the village each week to weigh and measure the participants' children to see if goat milk in their diet was having an effect on weight and height of their youngsters.

Village women were uniformly positive about the project—they wanted to participate. But men, including the headmen, were more skeptical. They worried about the impact on social relations of such valuable animals going to women—it didn't seem appropriate—couldn't the goats be given to the men of the village? The goats were not to be sold or slaughtered, we said. They would be there for the benefit of the children, and their care would involve extra work for the women. Everyone knew that children were suffering because of malnourishment—sometimes a child would become so seriously malnourished that relatives had to take it to the district hospital for nutritional rehabilitation. This meant a three-week hospital stay with a family member right there to feed and care for the child. The cost to the family was considerable. And the death of a child was a great sorrow. So eventually the men agreed that the project should go forward. The headmen agreed that the goats should belong to the women and said they would resolve any disputes over ownership in favor of the women.

When we were ready to talk with people in a third village about the project, we learned something that quickly dissuaded us from continuing there. It seemed that there was animal theft going on in the area, and the prime suspects were a family living in the third village! Until the local system of justice had solved these crimes and dealt with the perpetrators, we could not take the risk of working in that village. Animal theft became a problem in the other two villages as well. The rural economy in Malawi has weakened in recent years because of droughts, floods, soil depletion, deforestation, erosion, low prices for commodities, and high rates of inflation. The annual hungry season, the period of time between when people consume the last of the food they have stored to the time when the next crops are harvested, used to begin in December and end in March. Now the hungry season often begins in September. People must reduce the amount of food they eat at a time when they have to carry out the heaviest agricultural labor, preparing fields and planting them when the annual rains begin. Both men and women do this work and nearly all agricultural labor is done by hand. In the depth of the hungry season, people may turn to eating maize bran, the portion of the maize kernel that they normally feed to their animals, in order to have something in their bellies to assuage the hunger pangs. Under conditions such as these, it is no surprise that theft of animals is on the rise in the countryside.

Women in the two villages who received milk goats responded vigorously to the threat of theft once a few animals had been stolen. They began to take their milk goats with them as they went to work in the fields, tethering them nearby rather than letting them range free. They built pens against the sides of their mud or brick houses, to provide shade and security. At night they brought the animals into their houses so the whole family could guard them.

Our research team hired two young women who were both native speakers of the local language, Chichewa, and who had grown up in villages. We asked them to administer the baseline survey in the two villages and to continue working on the project. They would help to distribute animals to village women and later pay weekly visits to the recipients to weigh and measure their young children. One of these young women remained with the project throughout, and is dedicated to working with the villagers. She has been a key to the success of our work.

The baseline survey of households with children under five years of age revealed some interesting and useful information. Women headed 30 percent of the households; there was no adult male regularly living with them. Almost 75 percent of the women were nonliterate. A total of 35.4 percent of the children were underweight for their age and 57.7 percent were stunted (short for age). These figures are close to the national averages for a preharvest season, i.e., the hungry season. A surprising finding was that children in female-headed households were less likely to be undernourished or stunted. We can only speculate about why this was the case. Perhaps it has to do with groups of related women sharing resources in the interest of their children's well being.

We gave women who participated in the baseline survey the opportunity to volunteer to receive a milk goat, with the understanding that they would attend demonstrations that taught ways to manage the animals and keep them healthy, how to milk goats, how to keep the milk from spoiling, and how to add it to their children's food. We also pointed out that they would have to return first-born kids to project personnel so the does could eventually be distributed to other women, but that all kids born after that would be theirs to keep. The female goats would increase their flock of milk-producers, and the males could be sold to give the women much-needed cash. All women who received milk goats would also be provided with a bucket for milking, a pan for cooking, and a measuring cup to help them track milk production.

The program proved popular. Very quickly the project had more participants than it could accommodate, and we had to create a waiting list. We gave priority to those women who had children under five that were most seriously undernourished. Other women on the waiting list agreed to this. We also provided animals to some grandmothers who were raising young grandchildren orphaned when their parents died of AIDS. Care for AIDS orphans has become a major problem in Malawi, and is reflected at the village level. It is common to see women, already struggling to care for immediate family members, stressed to the maximum as they undertake to feed and house children left behind by relatives who have succumbed to the disease.

Team members designed and began to present demonstrations for village women on goat management, goat health, milking, safe milk handling, and incorporation of milk in their children's food. Recipes using local ingredients and goat milk were developed and tested in the home economics kitchens at the college, and taste-tested by the women participants and their children at the village-based demonstrations. The recipes that passed the taste test were routinely used by the women; those that didn't were rejected.

When the women received their animals, all of the does were either pregnant or already had young kids. This is when project field assistants began their weekly visits to the villages. During each visit, the participating women gathered in a central area of the village with their children. Each woman would have her child or children weighed in a sling scale that was suspended from a tree branch. Once a month, team members measured the upper arm circumference and height of the children. The fact of high child mortality was brought home to me in a very graphic way during this process when some women initially objected to having their children's height measured because they thought it was too much like measuring the children for coffins. A few women persisted in their objection. In these cases, our field assistants could only estimate observable changes in height. The field assistants also asked women about the general health of their children during the previous week, the milk production of their goats, and the health of their goats. If a goat was ill, the field assistant arranged for a veterinary assistant or the team member who was a veterinarian to travel to the village and examine the animal. If there was a significant health problem with a child, the field assistant notified faculty team members who would then take the information to the nearest clinic where they could arrange transport of the woman and child to a hospital if that was called for. Almost all the women who received animals were committed to caring for them and using the milk for their children. Ninety-eight percent of the recipients returned the first kid to the project. This is an astonishingly high rate of return and it implies that rural women would be very good risks for other kinds of so-called "payback schemes" that make local efforts to improve economic security sustainable.

We were gratified to see that those children who began to receive even small amounts of goat milk as an ingredient in their daily diets showed steady weight and height gains even when they were sick. In time, however, we began to see children hit growth plateaus or even lose ground temporarily. We learned from village women themselves why this was happening. Women who made up village committees approached the project team with a proposal for a solution.

They told us that their milk goats had to have at least two kids before they could get a second high-yield doe, and this meant that there were periods of time when no milk was available for their children. The women asked if we could teach them how to grow soybeans. They were all familiar with soybean flour as a food for undernourished children because this is what they received when they took their malnourished children to maternal and child health clinics for treatment. Their plan was to grow soybeans and grind them into flour to feed their children when no goat milk was available.

Our project team went back to the drawing board and figured out how to incorporate this new effort. The team purchased soybean seed and distributed 5 kg of it to each woman in the two villages. The village headmen approved of this effort and in some instances designated land for use by those women who needed it. Malawi team members developed and presented demonstrations on how to grow and process soybeans. The women agreed to pay back the 5 kg of seed after their first harvest, again a way to perpetuate the program over time and make it sustainable, and all did so. Women have now completed three or four successful growing seasons with soybeans, and are many are growing and storing enough beans to see them through the periods of time when their does produce no milk. They also save enough seed for the next planting season.

It also became clear after a short period of time that we would have to change the goat crossbreeding program. The college farm could not breed enough hardy milk goats to keep up with the demand. The animal scientists on our team looked for local Malawi goats that were the highest milk producers and these, when pregnant or with a kid, were distributed to women on the waiting list. Simultaneously, plans were made to build buck stations in each of the villages and to provide each station with a Saanen or crossbred buck to breed with local goats. Village headmen oversaw the building efforts and other men and women helped to feed and water the buck. When a doe comes into heat, the owner can bring it to the station to be inseminated. In this way the Saanen genes for high milk production spread more rapidly into the village flocks. The villagers know that their bucks must be exchanged for others about every three years in order to avoid inbreeding.

I returned to Malawi for a short visit in the summer of 2004 and found that many positive features of the project were still in place. In discussions with groups of women who had received dairy goats, I learned that two-thirds of them still had their original project animals. The remaining third had lost their original animals to disease or injury, but not before the goats had delivered offspring that survived. Only one woman had sold her animal before it had given her viable kids; this is tantamount to a farmer selling or eating her seed! But the woman's situation was quite difficult. Her husband was seriously ill and could not assist with farm work, and as a consequence she had been unable to raise sufficient maize to provide for household subsistence. She was desperate for cash in order to purchase food, and it was out of this desperation that she sold her milk goat.

Several women had a sufficient number of animals that they were able to meet the nutritional needs of their young children and sell surplus goats, primarily to NGOs planning to launch similar efforts to address child malnutrition. For the most part, money earned in this way was used to buy commercial fertilizer in order to increase the maize harvest. Cooking oil, salt, and clothing were other items commonly purchased with these earnings. The loss of animals to theft had decreased due to the introduction of a community policing effort. Professional police have trained villagers to take turns patrolling the village and its surrounding area at night in order to discourage thieves, and it seemed to be working. But another danger had presented itself. Because the 2004 harvest was not a good one due to erratic rains, people were anxious about their food reserves, most knowing that they would run out long before the next harvest. One result of this is that domesticated dogs (every household has a watchdog) are not fed adequate amounts of cooked maize bran or leftover cooked maize flour. They are hungry, and they have begun running across the fields in packs, attacking kids and young goats belonging to people from villages other than their own. Some people have lost valuable kids in this way and were considering tethering kids while the does free range. Normally tethering occurs only during the rainy season after planting has taken place. There is the possibility that marauding dogs will be shot, but this raises the likelihood of inter-village conflict.

Of the four village buck stations erected as part of the project, three were in good repair and the bucks well cared for. The fourth was somewhat rundown and needed refurbishing. And it was clear that the buck needed better care. After some discussion and investigation, it became apparent that the headman had declared the buck was his personal property and only his relatives could use its services—anyone else would have to pay him a fee if they wished to bring their animals to the buck. Not surprisingly, people did not take well to this proclamation. They more or less boycotted the buck station, which meant that most of the care of the animal fell to the elderly headman and his wife. The station was repaired, the animal was provided with nutritional supplements, the household was provided with a new bucket for the dedicated purpose of bringing water to the buck, and the headman was informed that the buck would die or be returned to the college if it did not receive better care. In the end, it became clear that a miscommunication had occurred between the headman and project personnel, leading the headman to conclude that he was now free to charge for use of the buck station. By the time I left Malawi, the misunderstanding had apparently been cleared up. College personnel will continue to check on the well being of this valuable animal—it would be a great loss to the village if it were to die or be removed.

During group and individual discussions with women, everyone acknowledged the value of goat milk as a component of their children's diets. I was told that, since the milk had become available in the villages, no child had become so seriously malnourished that he or she had to be taken to the hospital for nutritional rehabilitation. This was a real change from an earlier point in time, and a hallmark of success for all of our efforts, researchers and villagers, to promote the health of children.

Conclusion

Our project team designed and tested a locally sustainable approach to alleviate infant and child malnourishment in rural Malawi. Data on changes in the participating children's weights, heights, and upper arm circumferences show that relatively small amounts of goat milk included in the regular diet make a substantial difference in promoting normal growth in children. Results from a rapid appraisal survey that I helped to design indicate that the project is highly valued by rural women. This is confirmed by key village women and by the fact that more women than project resources would permit sought to join the program. Presently some Malawi nongovernmental organizations (NGOs) have introduced similar efforts in other parts of the country. Several district hospitals that provide rehabilitation for severely malnourished children have established flocks of milk goats on their grounds and use the milk as an important part of the rehabilitation treatment. The agricultural college plans to offer training to Malawians and people from other southern African nations who are interested in replicating the program. And the project villages will be demonstration sites for trainees who want to see how the project works "on the ground."

It was important to have an anthropologist on the project team. As the team anthropologist, I participated in every phase of the project, including management duties at times when it was necessary to keep our efforts on schedule. I was responsible for providing an ethnographic account of local culture and using this information to help shape how we could present the program to villagers. I was not trained to manage goat breeding or conduct some of the health measurements, but I could point out how I thought villagers would respond to our plans and to suggest how best to make them full participants in project planning and implementation. It is easy for people from any society to believe that those who are from elsewhere still see the world in the same way they do. Since cultures differ (Americans, for example, find it difficult to understand the ramifications of a matrilineal descent system) anthropologists can translate information about such differences in ways that are useful to other members of interdisciplinary teams. Thus, we can shape programs to fit local conditions and help with cross-cultural communication. That is what I think happened in Malawi.

Review Questions

1. What are the social and environmental conditions that lead to child malnutrition in Malawi, according to Patten?

2. What programs did the project team come up with to improve child nutrition in Malawi and what steps did they take to implement it?

3. How is anthropology useful for programs such as the one described by Patten in this article?

4. In what ways did team members involve local people in the design and implementation of the program?

36

Using Anthropology

David W. McCurdy

Some disciplines, such as economics, have an obvious relationship to the nonacademic world. Economic theory, although generated as part of basic research, may often prove useful for understanding the "real" economy. Anthropology, on the other hand, does not seem so applicable. In this article, David McCurdy discusses some of the professional applications of anthropology and argues that there is a basic anthropological perspective that can help anyone cope with the everyday world. He uses the case of a company manager to illustrate this point, asserting that ethnographic "qualitative" research is an important tool for use in the nonacademic world.

In 1990 a student whom I had not seen for fifteen years stopped by my office. He had returned for his college reunion and thought it would be interesting to catch up on news about his (and my) major department, anthropology. The conversation, however, soon shifted from college events to his own life. Following graduation and a stint in the Peace Corps, he noted, he had begun to study for his license as a ship's engineer. He had attended the Maritime Academy and

This article is an updated version of "Using Anthropology," published in *Conformity and Conflict*, 9th ed. Copyright © 2000 by David W. McCurdy. Reprinted by permission.

worked for years on freighters. He was finally granted his license, he continued, and currently held the engineer's position on a container ship that made regular trips between Seattle and Alaska. He soon would be promoted to chief engineer and be at the top of his profession.

As he talked, he made an observation about anthropology that may seem surprising. His background in the discipline, he said, had helped him significantly in his work. He found it useful as he went about his daily tasks, maintaining his ship's complex engines and machinery, his relationships with the crew, and his contacts with land-based management.

And his is not an unusual case. Over the years, several anthropology graduates have made the same observation. One, for example, is a community organizer who feels that the cross-cultural perspective he learned in anthropology helps him mediate disputes and facilitate decision making in a multiethnic neighborhood. Another, who works as an advertising account executive, claims that anthropology helps her discover what products mean to customers. This, in turn, permits her to design more effective ad campaigns. A third says she finds anthropology an invaluable tool as she arranges interviews and writes copy. She is a producer for a metropolitan television news program. I have heard the same opinion expressed by many others, including the executive editor of a magazine for home weavers, the founder of a fencing school, a housewife, a physician, several lawyers, the kitchen manager for a catering firm, and a high school teacher.

The idea that anthropology can be useful is also supported by the experience of many new Ph.D.'s. A recent survey has shown, for the first time, that more new doctorates in anthropology find employment in professional settings than in college teaching or scholarly research, and the list of nonacademic work settings revealed by the survey is remarkably broad. There is a biological anthropologist, for example, who conducts research on nutrition for a company that manufactures infant formula. A cultural anthropologist works for a major car manufacturer, researching such questions as how employees adapt to working overseas, and how they relate to conditions on domestic production lines. Others formulate government policy; plan patient care in hospitals; design overseas development projects; run famine relief programs; consult on tropical forest management; and advise on product development, advertising campaigns, and marketing strategy for corporations.

This new-found application of cultural anthropology comes as a surprise to many Americans. Unlike political science, for example, which has a name that logically connects it with practical political and legal professions, there is nothing in the term *anthropology* that tells most Americans how it might be useful.

The research subject of anthropology also makes it more difficult to comprehend. Political scientists investigate political processes, structures, and motivations. Economists look at the production and exchange of goods and services. Psychologists study differences and similarities among individuals. The research of cultural anthropologists, on the other hand, is more difficult to characterize. Instead of a focus on particular human institutions, such as politics, law, and economics, anthropologists are interested in cross-cultural differences and similarities among the world's many groups.

This interest produces a broad view of human behavior that gives anthropology its special cross-cultural flavor. It also produces a unique research strategy, called *ethnography*, that tends to be qualitative rather than quantitative. Whereas other social sciences moved toward *quantitative methods* of research designed to test theory by using survey questionnaires and structured, repetitive observations, most anthropologists conduct *qualitative research* designed to elicit the cultural knowledge of the people they seek to understand. To do this, anthropologists often live and work with their subjects, called *informants* within the discipline. The result is a highly detailed ethnographic description of the categories and rules people consult when they behave, and the meanings that things and actions have for them.

It is this ethnographic approach, or cultural perspective, that I think makes anthropology useful in such a broad range of everyday settings. I particularly find important the special anthropological understanding of the culture concept, ethnographic field methods, and social analysis. To illustrate these assertions, let us take a single case in detail, that of a manager working for a large corporation who consciously used the ethnographic approach to solve a persistent company problem.

The Problem

The manager, whom we will name Susan Stanton, works for a large multinational corporation called UTC (not the company's real name). UTC is divided into a number of parts, including divisions, subdivisions, departments, and other units designed to facilitate its highly varied business enterprises. The company is well-diversified, engaging in research, manufacturing, and customer services. In addition to serving a wide cross-section of public and private customers, it also works on a variety of government contracts for both military and nonmilitary agencies.

One of its divisions is educational. UTC has established a large number of customer outlets in cities throughout the United States, forming what it calls its "customer outlet network." They are staffed by educational personnel who are trained to offer a variety of special courses and enrichment programs. These courses and programs are marketed mainly to other businesses or to individuals who desire special training or practical information. For example, a small company might have UTC provide its employees with computer training, including instruction on hardware, programming, computer languages, and computer program applications. Another company might ask for instruction on effective management or accounting procedures. The outlets' courses for individuals include such topics as how to get a job, writing a résumé, or enlarging your own business.

To organize and manage its customer outlet network, UTC has created a special division. The division office is located at the corporate headquarters and is responsible for developing new courses, improving old ones, training customer outlet personnel, and marketing customer outlet courses, or "products" as they are called inside the company. The division also has departments that develop, produce, and distribute the special learning materials used in customer outlet courses. These include books, pamphlets, video and audio tapes and cassettes, slides, overlays, and films. These materials are stored in a warehouse and are shipped, as they are ordered, to customer outlets around the country.

It is with this division that Susan Stanton first worked as a manager. She had started her career with the company in a small section of the division that designed various program materials. She had worked her way into management, holding a series of increasingly important positions. She was then asked to take over the management of a part of the division that had the manufacture, storage, and shipment of learning materials as one of its responsibilities.

But there was a catch. She was given this new management position with instructions to solve a persistent, although vaguely defined, problem. "Improve the service," they had told her, and "get control of the warehouse inventory." In this case, "service" meant the process of filling orders sent in by customer outlets for various materials stored in the warehouse. The admonition to improve the service seemed to indicate that service was poor, but all she was told about the situation was that customer outlet personnel complained about the service; she did not know exactly why or what "poor" meant.

In addition, inventory was "out of control." Later she was to discover the extent of the difficulty.

> We had a problem with inventory. The computer would say we had two hundred of some kind of book in stock, yet it was back ordered because there was nothing on the shelf. We were supposed to have the book but physically there was nothing there. I'm going, "Uh, we have a small problem. The computer never lies, like your bank statement, so why don't we have the books?"

If inventory was difficult to manage, so were the warehouse employees. They were described by another manager as "a bunch of knuckle draggers. All they care about is getting their money. They are lazy and don't last long at the job." Strangely, the company did not view the actions of the warehouse workers as a major problem. Only later did Susan Stanton tie in poor morale in the warehouse with the other problems she had been given to solve.

Management by Defense

Although Stanton would take the ethnographic approach to management problems, that was not what many other managers did. They took a defensive stance, a position opposite to the discovery procedures of ethnography. Their major concern—like that of many people in positions of leadership and responsibility—was to protect their authority and their ability to manage and to get things done. Indeed, Stanton also shared this need. But their solution to maintaining their position was different from hers. For them, claiming ignorance and asking questions—the hallmark of the ethnographic approach—is a sign of weakness. Instead of discovering what is going on when they take on a new management assignment, they often impose new work rules and procedures. Employees learn to fear the arrival of new managers because their appearance usually means a host of new, unrealistic demands. They respond by hiding what they actually do, withholding information that would be useful to the manager. Usually, everyone's performance suffers.

Poor performance leads to elaborate excuses as managers attempt to blame the troubles on others. Stanton described this tendency.

> When I came into the new job, this other manager said, "Guess what? You have got a warehouse. You are now the proud owner of a forklift and a bunch of knuckle draggers." And I thought, management's perception of those people is very low. They are treating them as dispensable, that you can't do anything with them. They say the workers don't have any career motives. They don't care if they do a good job. You have to force them to do anything. You can't motivate them. It's only a warehouse, other managers were saying. You can't really do that much about the problems there so why don't you just sort of try to keep it under control.

Other managers diminished the importance of the problem itself. It was not "poor service" that was the trouble. The warehouse was doing the best it could with what it had. It was just that the customers—the staff at the customer outlets—were complainers. As Susan Stanton noted:

> The people providing the service thought that outlet staff were complainers. They said, "Staff complain about everything. But it can't be that way. We have checked it all out and it isn't that bad."

Making excuses and blaming others lead to low morale and a depressed self-image. Problems essentially are pushed aside in favor of a "let's just get by" philosophy.

Ethnographic Management

By contrast, managers take the offensive when they use ethnographic techniques. That is what Stanton did when she assumed her new managerial assignment over the learning materials manufacturing and distribution system. To understand what the ethnographic approach means, however, we must first look briefly at what anthropologists do when they conduct ethnographic field research. Our discussion necessarily involves a look at the concepts of culture and microculture as well as ethnography. For as we will shortly point out, companies have cultures of their own, a point that has recently received national attention; but more important for the problem we are describing here, companies are normally divided into subgroups, each with its own microculture. It is these cultures and microcultures that anthropologically trained managers can study ethnographically, just as fieldworkers might investigate the culture of a !Kung band living in the Kalahari Desert of West Africa or the Gypsies living in San Francisco.

Ethnography refers to the process of discovering and describing culture, so it is important to discuss this general and often elusive concept. There are numerous definitions of culture, each stressing particular sets of attributes. The definition we employ here is especially appropriate for ethnographic fieldwork. We may define culture as the acquired knowledge that people use to generate behavior and interpret experience. In growing up, one learns a system of cultural knowledge appropriate to the group. For example, an American child learns to chew with a closed mouth because that is the cultural rule. The child's parents interpret open-mouthed chewing as an infraction and tell the child to chew "properly." A person uses such cultural knowledge throughout life to guide actions and to give meaning to surroundings.

Because culture is learned, and because people can easily generate new cultural knowledge as they adapt to other people and things, human behavior and perceptions can vary dramatically from one group to another. In India, for example, children learn to chew "properly" with their mouths open. Their cultural worlds are quite different from the ones found in the United States.

Cultures are associated with groups of people. Traditionally, anthropologists associated culture with relatively distinctive ethnic groups. *Culture* referred to the whole life-way of a society, and particular cultures could be named. Anthropologists talked of German culture, Ibo culture, and Bhil culture. Culture was everything that was distinctive about the group.

Culture is still applied in this manner today, but with the advent of complex societies and a growing interest among anthropologists in understanding them, the culture concept has also been used in a more limited way. Complex societies such as our own are composed of thousands of groups. Members of these groups usually share the national culture, including a language and a huge inventory of knowledge for doing things, but the groups themselves have specific cultures of their own. For example, if you were to walk into the regional office of a stock brokerage firm, you would hear the people there talking an apparently foreign language. You might stand in the "bull pen," listen to brokers make "cold calls," "sell short," "negotiate a waffle," or get ready to go to a "dog and pony show." The fact that events such as this feel strange when you first encounter them is strong evidence to support the notion that you don't yet know the culture that organizes them. We call such specialized groups *microcultures*.

We are surrounded by microcultures, participating in a few, encountering many others. Our family has a microculture. So may our neighborhood, our college, and even our dormitory floor. The waitress who serves us lunch at the corner restaurant shares a culture with her coworkers. So do bank tellers at our local savings and loan. Kin, occupational groups, and recreational associations each tend to display special microcultures. Such cultures can be, and now often are, studied by anthropologists interested in understanding life in complex American society.

The concept of microculture is essential to Susan Stanton as she begins to attack management problems at UTC because she assumes that conflict between different microcultural groups is most likely at the bottom of the difficulty. One microculture she could focus on is UTC company culture. She knows, for example, that there are a variety of rules and expectations—written and unwritten—for how things should be done at the company. She must dress in her "corporates," for example, consisting of a neutral-colored suit, stockings, and conservative shoes. UTC also espouses values about the way employees should be treated, how people are supposed to feel about company products, and a variety of other things that set that particular organization apart from other businesses.

But the specific problems that afflicted the departments under Stanton's jurisdiction had little to do with UTC's corporate culture. They seemed rather to be the result of misunderstanding and misconnection between two units, the warehouse and the customer outlets. Each had its own microculture. Each could be investigated to discover any information that might lead to a solution of the problems she had been given.

Such investigation would depend on the extent of Stanton's ethnographic training. As an undergraduate in college, she had learned how to conduct ethnographic interviews, observe behavior, and analyze and interpret data. She was not a professional anthropologist, but she felt she was a good enough ethnographer to discover some relevant aspects of microcultures at UTC.

Ethnography is the process of discovering and describing a culture. For example, an anthropologist who travels to India to conduct a study of village culture will use ethnographic techniques. The anthropologist will move into a community, occupy a house, watch people's daily routines, attend rituals, and spend hours interviewing informants. The goal is to discover a detailed picture of what is going on by seeing village culture through the eyes of informants. The anthropologist wants the insider's perspective. Villagers become teachers, patiently explaining different aspects of their culture, praising the anthropologist for acting correctly and appearing to understand, laughing when the anthropologist makes mistakes or seems confused. When the anthropologist knows what to do and can explain in local terms what is going on or what is likely to happen, real progress has been made. The clearest evidence of such progress is when informants say, "You are almost human now," or "You are beginning to talk just like us."

The greatest enemy of good ethnography is the preconceived notion. Anthropologists do not conduct ethnographic research by telling informants what they are like based on earlier views of them. They teach the anthropologist how to see their world: the anthropologist does not tell them what their world should really be like. All too often in business, a new manager will take over a department and begin to impose changes on its personnel to fit a preconceived perception of them. The fact that the manager's efforts are likely to fail makes sense in light of this ignorance. The manager doesn't know the microculture. Nor have they been asked about it.

But can a corporate manager really do ethnography? After all, managers have positions of authority to maintain, as we noted earlier. It is all right for professional anthropologists to enter the field and act ignorant; they don't have a position to maintain and they don't have to continue to live with their informants. The key to the problem appears to be the "grace period." Most managers are given one by their employees when they are new on the job. A new manager cannot be expected to know everything. It is permissible to ask basic questions. The grace period may last only a month or two, but it is usually long enough to find out valuable information.

This is the opportunity that Susan Stanton saw as she assumed direction of the warehouse distribution system. As she described it:

> I could use the first month, actually the first six weeks, to find out what was going on, to act dumb and find out what people actually did and why. I talked to end customers. I talked to salespeople, people who were trying to sell things to help customer outlets with their needs. I talked to coordinators at headquarters staff who were trying to help all these customer outlets do their jobs and listened to what kinds of complaints they had heard. I talked to the customer outlet people and the guys in the warehouse. I had this six-week grace period where I could go in and say, "I don't know anything about this. If you were in my position, what would you do, or what would make the biggest difference, and why would it make a difference?" You want to find out what the world they are operating in is like. What do they value? And people were excited because I was asking and listening and, by God, intending to do something about it instead of just disappearing again.

As we shall see shortly, Stanton's approach to the problem worked. But it also resulted in an unexpected bonus. Her ethnographic approach symbolized unexpected interest and concern to her employees. That, combined with realistic management, gave her a position of respect and authority. Their feelings for her were expressed by one warehouse worker when he said:

When she [Susan] was going to be transferred to another job, we gave her a party. We took her to this country-and-western place and we all got to dance with the boss. We told her that she was the first manager who ever tried to understand what it was like to work in the warehouse. We thought she would come in like the other managers and make a lot of changes that didn't make sense. But she didn't. She made it work better for us.

Problems and Causes

An immediate benefit of her ethnographic inquiry was a much clearer view of what poor service meant to customer outlet personnel. Stanton discovered that learning materials, such as books and cassettes, took too long to arrive after they were ordered. Worse, material did not arrive in the correct quantities. Sometimes there would be too many items, but more often there were too few, a particularly galling discrepancy since customer outlets were charged for what they ordered, not what they received. Books also arrived in poor condition, their covers ripped or scratched, edges frayed, and ends gouged and dented. This, too, bothered customer outlet staff because they were often visited by potential customers who were not impressed by the poor condition of their supplies. Shortages and scruffy books did nothing to retain regular customers either.

The causes of these problems and the difficulties with warehouse inventory also emerged from ethnographic inquiry. Stanton discovered, for example, that most customer outlets operated in large cities, where often they were housed in tall buildings. Materials shipped to their office address often ended up sitting in ground-level lobbies, because few of the buildings had receiving docks or facilities. Books and other items also arrived in large boxes, weighing up to a hundred pounds. Outlet staff, most of whom were women, had to go down to the lobby, open those boxes that were too heavy for them to carry, and haul armloads of supplies up the elevator to the office. Not only was this time-consuming, but customer outlet staff felt it was beneath their dignity to do such work. They were educated specialists, after all.

The poor condition of the books was also readily explained. By packing items loosely in such large boxes, warehouse workers ensured trouble in transit. Books rattled around with ease, smashing into each other and the side of the box. The result was torn covers and frayed edges. Clearly no one had designed the packing and shipping process with customer outlet staff in mind.

The process, of course, originated in the central warehouse, and here as well, ethnographic data yielded interesting information about the causes of the problem. Stanton learned, for example, how materials were stored in loose stacks on the warehouse shelves. When orders arrived at the warehouse, usually through the mail, they were placed in a pile and filled in turn (although there were times when special preference was given to some customer outlets).

A warehouse employee filled an order by first checking it against the stock recorded by the computer, then going to the appropriate shelves and picking the items by hand. Items were packed in the large boxes and addressed to customer outlets. With the order complete, the employee was supposed to enter the number of items picked and shipped in the computer so that inventory would be up to date.

But, Stanton discovered, workers in the warehouse were under pressure to work quickly. They often fell behind because materials the computer said were in stock were not there, and because picking by hand took so long. Their solution to the problem of speed resulted in a procedure that even further confused company records.

> Most of the people in the warehouse didn't try to count well. People were looking at the books on the shelves and were going, "Eh, that looks like the right number. You want ten? Gee, that looks like about ten." Most of the time the numbers they shipped were wrong.

The causes of inaccurate amounts in shipping were thus revealed. Later, Stanton discovered that books also disappeared in customer outlet building lobbies. While staff members carried some of the materials upstairs, people passing by the open boxes helped themselves.

Other problems with inventory also became clear. UTC employees, who sometimes walked through the warehouse, would often pick up interesting materials from the loosely stacked shelves. More important, rushed workers often neglected to update records in the computer.

The Shrink-Wrap Solution

The detailed discovery of the nature and causes of service and inventory problems suggested a relatively painless solution to Stanton. If she had taken a defensive management position and failed to learn the insider's point of view, she might have resorted to more usual remedies that were impractical and unworkable. Worker retraining is a common answer to corporate difficulties, but it is difficult to accomplish and often fails. Pay incentives, punishments, and motivation enhancements such as prizes and quotas are also frequently tried. But they tend not to work because they don't address fundamental causes.

Shrink-wrapping books and other materials did. Shrink-wrapping is a packaging method in which clear plastic sheeting is placed around items to be packaged, then through a rapid heating and cooling process, shrunk into a tight covering. The plastic molds itself like a tight skin around the things it contains, preventing any internal movement or external contamination. Stanton described her decision.

I decided to have the books shrink-wrapped. For a few cents more, before the books ever arrived in the warehouse, I had them shrink-wrapped in quantities of five and ten. I made it part of the contract with the people who produced the books for us.

On the first day that shrink-wrapped books arrived at the warehouse, Stanton discovered that they were immediately unwrapped by workers who thought a new impediment had been placed in their way. But the positive effect of shrink-wrapping soon became apparent. For example, most customer outlets ordered books in units of fives and tens. Warehouse personnel could now easily count out orders in fives and tens, instead of having to count each book or estimate numbers in piles. Suddenly, orders filled at the warehouse contained the correct number of items.

Employees were also able to work more quickly, since they no longer had to count each book. Orders were filled faster, the customer outlet staff was pleased, and warehouse employees no longer felt the pressure of time so intensely. Shrink-wrapped materials also traveled more securely. Books, protected by their plastic covering, arrived in good condition, again delighting the personnel at customer outlets.

Stanton also changed the way materials were shipped, based on what she had learned from talking to employees. She limited the maximum size of shipments to twenty-five pounds by using smaller boxes. She also had packages marked "inside delivery" so that deliverymen would carry the materials directly to the customer outlet offices. If they failed to do so, boxes were light enough to carry upstairs. No longer would items be lost in skyscraper lobbies.

Inventory control became more effective. Because they could package and ship materials more quickly, the workers in the warehouse had enough time to enter the size and nature of shipments in the computer. Other UTC employees no longer walked off with books from the warehouse, because the shrink-wrapped bundles were larger and more conspicuous, and because taking five or ten books is more like stealing than "borrowing" one.

Finally, the improved service dramatically changed morale in the division. Customer outlet staff members, with their new and improved service, felt that finally someone had cared about them. They were more positive and they let people at corporate headquarters know about their feelings. "What's happening down there?" they asked. "The guys in the warehouse must be taking vitamins."

Morale soared in the warehouse. For the first time, other people liked the service workers there provided. Turnover decreased as pride in their work rose. They began to care more about the job, working faster with greater care. Managers who had previously given up on the "knuckle draggers" now asked openly about what had got into them.

Stanton believes the ethnographic approach is the key. She has managers who work for her read anthropology, especially books on ethnography, and she insists that they "find out what is going on."

Conclusion

Anthropology is, before all, an academic discipline with a strong emphasis on scholarship and basic research. But, as we have also seen, anthropology is a discipline that contains several intellectual tools—the concept of culture, the ethnographic approach to fieldwork, a cross-cultural perspective, a holistic view of human behavior—that make it useful in a broad range of nonacademic settings. In particular, it is the ability to do qualitative research that makes anthropologists successful in the professional world.

A few years ago an anthropologist consultant was asked by a utility company to answer a puzzling question: Why were its suburban customers, whose questionnaire responses indicated an attempt at conservation, failing to reduce their consumption of natural gas? To answer the question, the anthropologist conducted ethnographic interviews with members of several families, listening as they told him about how warm they liked their houses and how they set the heat throughout the day. He also received permission to install several video cameras aimed at thermostats in private houses. When the results were in, the answer to the question was deceptively simple: Fathers fill out questionnaires and turn down thermostats; wives, children, and cleaning workers, all of whom, in this case, spent time in the houses when fathers were absent, turn them up. Conservation, the anthropologist concluded, would have to involve family decisions, not just admonitions to save gas.

Over the past two or three years, anthropology's usefulness in the world of work has been discovered by the United States press. For example, *U.S. News and World Report* carried a story in 1998 entitled "Into the Wild Unknown of Workplace Culture: Anthropologists Revitalize Their Discipline," which traced changing trends in academic anthropology and highlighted the growth of the discipline's penetration of the business world.[1] Included in the article were examples of useful ethnography, such as the discovery by one anthropologist consultant that rank-and-file union members were upset with shop stewards because the latter spent more time recruiting new members than responding to grievances. In another instance, the article reported on the work of anthropologist Ken Erickson. Hired to find out why immigrant meatpackers had launched a wildcat strike, he was able to show that the workers struck because they felt their supervisors treated them as unskilled laborers, not because there was a language problem, as proposed by management. The workers had developed elaborate strategies to work quickly, effectively, and safely that were ignored or unknown to their supervisors.

In 1999, *USA Today* carried a story that further emphasized anthropology's usefulness. Entitled "Hot Asset in Corporate: Anthropology Degrees," the article began with, "Don't throw away the MBA degree yet. But as companies go

---

[1]Brendan I. Koerner, "Into the Wild Unknown of Workplace Culture: Anthropologists Revitalize Their Discipline," *U.S. News & World Report*, August 10, 1998, p. 56.

global and crave leaders for a diverse workforce, a new hot degree is emerging for aspiring executives: anthropology."[2] The piece carried numerous examples—the hiring of anthropologist Steve Barnett as a vice president at Citicorp following his discovery of the early warning signs that identify people who do not pay credit card bills; the case of Hallmark, which sent anthropologists into immigrant homes to discover how holidays and birthdays are celebrated so that the company could design appropriate cards for such occasions; the example of a marketing consultant firm that sent anthropologists into bathrooms to watch how women shave their legs, and in the process, to discover what women want in a razor.

The article also listed executives who stressed how important their anthropology degree has been for their business successes. Motorola corporate lawyer Robert Faulkner says that the anthropology degree he received before going to law school has become increasingly valuable in his management job. Warned by his father that most problems are people problems, Michael Koss, CEO of the Koss headphone company, is another example. He received his anthropology degree from Beloit College. Katherine Burr, CEO of The Hanseatic Group, has an MA in anthropology and was quoted as saying, "My competitive edge came completely out of anthropology. The world is so unknown, changes so rapidly. Preconceptions can kill you." The article concluded with the observations of Ken Erickson of the Center for Ethnographic Research. "It takes trained observation. Observation is what anthropologists are trained to do."

In short, cultural anthropology has entered the world of business over the past twenty years. I argue that the key to its special utility and value in the commercial world is the ethnographic approach. Anthropologists have this ethnographic field experience and a sense of how social systems work and how people use their cultural knowledge. They have the special background, originally developed to discover and describe the cultural knowledge and behavior of unknown societies, needed to, in the words of Susan Stanton, "find out what is going on."

[2]Del Jones, "Hot Asset in Corporate: Anthropology Degrees," *USA Today,* February 18, 1999, section B, p. 1.

Review Questions

1. What kinds of jobs do professional anthropologists do?

2. What is special about anthropology that makes fundamental knowledge of it valuable to some jobs?

3. What is meant by *qualitative research?* Why is such research valuable to business and government?

4. What difficulties did the company manager described in this article face? What solutions did she invent to deal with them? How did her knowledge of anthropology help her with this problem?

5. Why is ethnography useful in everyday life? Can you think of situations in which you could use ethnographic research?

37

Career Advice for Anthropology Undergraduates

John T. Omohundro

In the previous article we learned that anthropologists regularly use their skills in the world of work and that employers are beginning to recognize the value of employees who are trained in anthropology. But the fact remains that many Americans do not fully understand what anthropology is and have little idea what students who major in anthropology can do for them. Worse, students themselves may not consciously recognize the work skills that anthropology has taught them or how to translate these skills into a language prospective employers can understand. John Omohundro tackles this problem of recognition and translation in this selection. Using a concept he calls "transcultural presentation," he lists some of the skills that anthropology teaches students and shows how these skills can be translated by graduating students into résumé language for employers.

The following scene happens at least once a semester. A distraught student pokes her (or his) head through my office door.

"Scuse me. . . . Are you busy? I need to ask you something."

"No, Grebbleberry, come in, sit down. What's bothering you?"

"Well, I really like anthropology. In fact, I want to drop my major in [deleted] and declare anthropology. But I told my parents and they were freaked out. My mother cried and my father threatened to cut me off. And my friends think I've lost it completely. Now they have me scared. I'm afraid I won't be able to get a job. What am I going to do?"

This student has all the symptoms of anthro shock. I'm tempted to smile in recognition of the syndrome but to Grebbleberry there is nothing amusing here. I have two answers: the difficult answer and the easy answer. The difficult answer, which I would like to give, is a problem because students are not prepared to believe me. The difficult answer is:

"For most careers, it doesn't matter much what you major in, as long as you like the subject and are good at it. The point of a major in a liberal arts education is to give practice at studying something in depth. One's major is not the same thing as job training. The careers that follow from most undergraduate majors are not and cannot be specified, even if the world doesn't change—but it does, frequently. There is no direct, obvious, and inevitable connection between college disciplines and the occupational titles people carry."

Although many years of teaching and advising convince me that the difficult answer I've just described is true, I don't respond with that answer anymore. First, I have to treat the "anthro shock"—the fear gripping the student that, ". . . mocked and alone, I'm going to starve." So, instead I reply with the easy answer:

"Take courage. There are many things you can do for a living that use your anthropological knowledge and skills. I can help you discover them and prepare for them."

Only then does the student's color begin to return; the anthro shock is in remission. Later, perhaps, after we've begun a career development program, I might introduce the difficult answer. But Grebbleberry still won't believe me, because my answer goes against most of what pundits, peers, parents, and even some professors have told her. This article presents some of the evidence that I have gathered for the claims made in the "easy" answer, to assist advisors to respond quickly and effectively to anthro shock.

Becoming a Career Advisor

Good advice is sorely needed and in short supply. Too many of the students I have supervised appeared flustered and ill-prepared when people ask them naive but usually sincere questions about what anthropology is, what it is good for, and what the student is going to "do with it." My advisees usually answered these questions apologetically or parried them with self-deprecating humor. Bill

Gates can get away with being apologetic and self-deprecating; my students need to present themselves more positively. Furthermore, many students and parents acquire their understanding of anthropology through students rather than professors, so it behooves us to raise the quality of the understanding that our major students impart. In turn, by improving their self-presentation our students will become more confident, more ambitious, and ultimately more successful in finding good work.

My career advising grew out of efforts to be a good teacher of the liberal arts, one who helps students move on to self-actualization in the world after college. The advising also grew out of my research in adaptive problem-solving by residents of small coastal communities in Newfoundland. Using the adaptive problem-solving approach, I ask, how do students find out about the world of work and how do they find their place in it? Twenty years ago, I began to develop career workshops within my department, then expanded them into workshops at anthropology conferences, and lately assembled those materials into a workbook, *Careers in Anthropology* (1998).[1] I use the book as a supplementary text in courses, as a workbook in careers workshops, and as an advising guide to students who declare anthropology as a major. This article is drawn from that book.

Because my experience with careers has been limited to academic ones, I collaborate with my college's career planning counselor. Lacking important parts of the whole picture, we are insufficient individually to advise anthropology majors. I have learned about résumés, interviews, and employer expectations, while my career planning colleagues have learned about the usefulness of anthropological perspectives and methods. Even if students consult both of us separately, they tend to perceive us as talking past one another, so they sometimes become frustrated and drop out of the process. But when the career planner and I work together, we see the value in each other's knowledge and how to blend it with concepts from our own fields. The career planners, for example, are delighted to learn that anthropology includes training in participant observation, object reconstruction and cataloging, and cognitive mapping, among other activities. They in turn have taught me what employers call those activities and how to highlight them on student résumés to increase what linguistic anthropologists call "indexicality," or talking on the same wavelength.

While working with the career planners, and counseling and tracking my advisees, I discovered that undergraduate anthropology alumni not only find meaningful work in which they use their anthropology, but they can use their anthropology to get hired to do that work. To demonstrate this idea I drafted and field tested exercises in which anthropological research techniques, such as ethnosemantics, life history, demography, participant observation, social network analysis, key informant interviews, and survey data analysis, are applied

---

[1]John T. Omohundro, *Careers in Anthropology* (Mountain View, CA: Mayfield Publishing Company, 1998).

to the tasks of selecting and pursuing interesting work. I also realized that when they are advising for careers, professors can use anthropological perspectives and data-collection techniques to better understand what students and employers know and need. Let us look briefly at what that might be.

Career Planning in Cross-Cultural Perspective

Except for a handful of publications distributed by the American Anthropological Association, few anthropologists have addressed the subject of career planning for undergraduate majors. One exception, James Spradley's "Career Education from a Cultural Perspective,"[2] shaped my conception of the problem. Spradley observes that in most cultures, such as the Amish in northern New York, the Inuit in central Canada, or the Masai in Kenya, children live close to the world of adult work. As they approach their own adulthood, youths understand clearly what adult work is and what they must do to take it up. There aren't many choices, but there isn't much anxiety either. The transition is smooth and supported by ritual, such as coming-of-age ceremonies.

The modern West, Spradley continues, is quite different. Career options are unclear to the beginner. A gulf yawns between their lives and what adults do. What kinds of careers are there over that gulf? What do people do in those positions? How do I decide which position is for me? How do I cross this gulf and get into the picture? The small-scale, nonindustrial cultures allowed twenty years of enculturation to adult careers. By comparison, Spradley observes, the postindustrial world expects youths to make a more complex transition from sixteen years of schooling to adult work in a matter of months or as little as a single weekend. And our culture has no ritual to ease the change.

It takes each student a while to assemble some kind of bridge across that gulf between college life and adult life. The average length of time in the U.S. between graduating with a B.A. and getting hired is six months to one year. That delay isn't usually because there aren't any jobs for liberal arts students. The delay is largely a cultural problem: new graduates simply don't know what to do next. A career counselor at Dartmouth College puts the problem like this: "Although liberal arts majors are qualified for dozens of jobs, they have no idea how to market themselves successfully."[3] They eventually figure it out and get back in the picture. Two years after graduation, two-thirds are employed full time (many of the others are in further study). Three-quarters of the employed are in positions related to their field of study.

[2]James P. Spradley, "Career Education from a Cultural Perspective," in Larry McClure and Carolyn Buan (eds.), *Essays in Career Education* (Portland, OR: Northwest Regional Educational Laboratory, 1973), pp. 3–16.

[3]Burton Nadler, *Liberal Arts Power: What It Is and How to Sell It on Your Resume*, 2nd ed. (Princeton, NJ: Peterson's, 1989).

My counseling efforts have aimed to enculturate students to the career life while they are still in college, thus abbreviating that liminal state after the baccalaureate degree. Of course, that's a tactical calculation. Looking back on sixteen years of formal education and looking ahead to a worklife of forty or more years, many of my advisees want to enter a liminal state for awhile. Nevertheless, other students are eager to move on. Those who made the effort during their college years to select a starting career, identify some employers, and prepare themselves for that career were rewarded by finding interesting work more quickly than those who waited until after they graduated. Students will have to make some time for this work in a busy college life. As my career planning colleague says, "Looking for a job is itself a job."

If students take up this job of career planning, their anthropology teachers can be valuable motivators and informants. However, not all professors say much about careers to their advisees or their classes. I know this is so because for years I have advised students from other colleges who sought me out at conferences, or when they were home visiting their parents, because they were suffering from anthro shock untreated by their own professors.

Why are some professors avoiding giving career advice? Some feel that after years in the ivory tower they don't understand the work world that their students want to enter. Times have changed, they say, since they were looking for a position. It is widely repeated in the college community that after graduation many students will enter careers that don't exist yet. Also, it is widely repeated that most people change careers (not just employers, but lines of work) several times in their working life. My career planning colleagues have amassed evidence to support these popular conceptions. So, "how can we know what to advise students today?" some of my colleagues wonder. Other professors define career advice, just as they do elementary writing instruction, as a task someone else should do.

A third reason that some professors avoid counseling for careers is that they don't approve of the idea of college as a place to credential people for jobs. In their view, student "vocationalism," or seeing college as a route to a good career, shifts the professor's role from liberator of young minds to gatekeeper of yuppiedom. Professors who teach critical approaches to culture want to inculcate resistance and a desire to change, not a desire to join, the system.

Anthropologist Michael Moffatt, in an insightful ethnography of residence halls and student culture, caused me to re-think student concern about jobs.[4] Moffatt suggests that professors who disdain student "vocationalism" are being hypocritical. After all, professors got their job by going to college, so why shouldn't the students want the same? Students expect that what they call their "job" will place them in the American middle classes, where their occupation will be a key element in their identity. They expect that job to offer them challenge, growth, rewards, security, and a chance to make the world a better place—all of which are goals deserving support from anthropology professors.

[4]Michael Moffat, *Coming of Age in New Jersey* (Brunswick, NJ: Rutgers University Press, 1986).

Translating the Skills

What does the student need to find that job and thus meet those goals? Career advice is partly a matter of teaching students to imagine themselves in a new way (the ethnographic "other's" way) and to construct a few basic models of what it's like in the working world.

Imagining themselves in a new way involves learning what employers (one of those ethnographic "others") really want (or think they want) and then reviewing one's education and experience for evidence of having acquired those desirable qualities. Seen in an anthropological light, this process may be called "trans-cultural self-presentation" and is similar to what the ethnographer initiates when entering the field and attempting to build rapport. Here are some data to assist that process.

Anthro shock contains the fear that one will acquire no marketable skills. "Marketable skills" implies there are other kinds as well. In fact, there are few skills that a liberal arts student acquires that aren't marketable. But there are temporary enthusiasms influencing which skills are considered desirable this year and what vocabulary is used to describe those skills. Anthropology students are well equipped to examine language, identify trends, and adapt to them by translating their own skills and knowledge into language appropriate for the setting.

Table 1 describes some skills that anthropology majors have an opportunity to develop at my college and, I am sure, at many other undergraduate institutions supporting a major. These are phrased in language immediately recognizable by the anthropology student and teacher.

Table 2 identifies twelve abilities often acquired through the undergraduate anthropology major. Fewer students and teachers will recognize their major as rephrased in this table, but employers will take notice. I advise my students to select anthropology and other courses intentionally to increase their competence in the abilities listed in Table 1 and then, when presenting themselves to potential graduate schools or employers, to highlight those abilities in the terms used in Table 2. Summer jobs, internships, volunteer work, as well as college classes may provide practice in the desirable activities (read "marketable skills").

Advanced majors in our senior seminar practice this transcultural self-presentation with exercises in composing résumé language. I begin by examining a résumé as a cultural text, an element in the process of seeking and offering jobs. We consider when and how their intended readers approach résumés. I argue that the résumé, in little more than a page, is intended to provoke interest in the writer as a person who can do (or learn to do) what the reader wants. In one column students list in their own language the experiences, both in their major and in their lives, that they think might have value. In a second column they conduct the "first-order" extraction of what skills and abilities were expected or practiced in those activities. In the third column they rephrase these skills and abilities in résumé language. Usually an anxiety-generating activity, composing résumés this way seems to generate more self-confidence.

TABLE 1   Some Transferable Skills in the Anthropology Major

—Interacting with people of diverse cultures, making allowance for difference in customs and beliefs

—Providing insight into social problems by supplying information about how problems—such as aging, conflict, or bereavement—are dealt with in other cultures

—Interviewing people to obtain information about their attitudes, knowledge, and behavior

—Using statistics and computers to analyze data

—Adapting approaches used in public relations, marketing, or politics to different population groups

—Appraising; classifying; and cataloging rare, old, or valuable objects

—Repairing, reconstructing, and preserving cultural artifacts by selecting chemical treatment, temperature, humidity, and storage methods

—Drawing maps and constructing scale models

—Photographing sites, objects, people, and events

—Interpreting or translating

—Using scientific equipment and measuring devices

—Analyzing craft techniques

—Cooperating in an ethnographic or archaeological research team

—Making policy based on social science research data, problem-solving methods, and professional ethical standards

—Designing research projects and applying for grants

—Producing a research paper in appropriate format and style

—Orally presenting research results

—Applying a variety of ethnographic data collection techniques: ethnosemantics, proxemics, life histories, ethnohistory, folklore, event analysis, genealogies, etc.

—Producing and editing a scholarly journal

—Leading a pre-professional organization such as a student anthropology society or honors society

—Developing public relations for a museum, field project, or conference

—Designing, building, installing, and acting as docent for museum exhibits

—Coaching, instructing, tutoring, and team-teaching with peers

—Studying a second language

Source: Adapted from John T. Omohundro, *Careers in Anthropology* (Mountain View, CA: Mayfield, 1998).

What Careers Do Anthropology B.A.'s Pursue?

Students can be brought out of anthro shock by infusions of empirical data. Surveys have been conducted to assess what work anthropology students are prepared for and what fields alumni actually entered. In *Anthropology and Jobs*, H. Russell Bernard and Willis Sibley identified thirteen fields that the anthropology B.A. could enter with no additional training.[5] These included journal-

[5]H. Russell Bernard and Willis E. Sibley, *Anthropology and Jobs: A Guide for Undergraduates*, American Anthropological Association special publication (Washington, DC: American Anthropological Association, 1975).

TABLE 2   Résumé Language for Anthropological Abilities

Social agility—In an unfamiliar social or career-related setting, you learn to size up quickly the "rules of the game." You can become accepted more quickly than you could without anthropology.

Observation—As you must often learn about a culture from within it, you learn how to interview and observe as a participant.

Planning—You learn how to find patterns in the behavior of a cultural group. This allows you to generalize about their behavior and predict what they might do in a given situation.

Social sensitivity—While other people's ways of doing things may be different from your own, you learn the importance of events and conditions that have contributed to this difference. You also recognize that other cultures view your ways as strange. You learn the value of behaving toward others with appropriate preparation, care, and understanding.

Accuracy in interpreting behavior—You become familiar with the range of behavior in different cultures. You learn how to look at cultural causes of behavior before assigning causes yourself.

Challenging conclusions—You learn that analyses of human behavior are open to challenge. You learn how to use new knowledge to test past conclusions.

Interpreting information—You learn how to use data collected by others, reorganizing or interpreting it to reach original conclusions.

Simplifying information—As anthropology is conducted among publics as well as about them, you learn how to simplify technical information for communication to non-technical people.

Contextualizing—Attention to details is a trait of anthropology. However, you learn that any detail might not be as important as its context, and can even be misleading when context is ignored.

Problem-solving—Often functioning within a cultural group, or acting upon culturally sensitive issues, you learn to approach problems with care. Before acting, you learn how to identify the problem, set your goals, decide upon the actions you will take, and calculate possible effects on other people.

Persuasive writing—Anthropology strives to represent the behavior of one group to another group, and is in continual need of interpretation. You learn the value of bringing someone else to your view through written argument.

Social perspective—You learn how to perceive the acts of individuals and local groups as cause and effect of larger sociocultural systems. This enables you to "act locally and think globally."

Source: John T. Omohundro, *Careers in Anthropology* (Mountain View, CA: Mayfield, 1998).

ism, police work, and the travel or tour industry. They also identified twenty-eight fields the anthropology B.A. could enter if additional training, up to the M.A. or M.S. level in the appropriate discipline, was acquired. These fields included dietetics, market research, city planning, museums, personnel, and community development, to name a few.

Ten years later, two of my students conducted a survey of anthropology alumni from 32 liberal arts colleges in the northeast U.S.[6] Of the 616 respondents,

---

[6]Lawrence W. Kratts and Clarissa Hunter, "Undergraduate Alumni Survey Results," *Anthropology Newsletter* (November 1986).

62% worked in the profit sector, 9% in the non-profit sector, and 6% in government. 16% were still in a graduate or professional school.

The respondents' occupations were sorted into seventeen categories. Academics accounted for 10%, some of whom were in disciplines other than anthropology, but managers ("director," "administrator," etc.) dominated at 19%. It appears that a large number of anthropology majors become actors in a bureaucracy, supervising others. Medicine, communications, and business together accounted for another 16% of respondents' current positions.

Does this range of work positions outside of anthropology, as usually conceived, signal a failure on our part to place our advisees in positions that will utilize their major? I don't think so, and neither do the alumni. 71% of the northeast alumni agreed with the statement, "my anthropology education helps me in my current work." An owner of a small business wrote, "All aspects of the [antique] business are satisfying: attending antique shows, unearthing an early item, researching its age and provenance, restoring or repairing it, and educating a potential customer about it. . . ."

Most (81%) of the alumni returning the survey claimed they were satisfied and challenged by their current work, and 74% felt their decision to major in anthropology was a good one. Some alumni waxed enthusiastic about anthropology as the foundation for a liberal arts education. A banker urged current majors, "Go for it: no one in business will ever hold a liberal arts education against you. . . . In the long run this will mark you as superior to a crowd of business students. . . ." Alumni highlighted the value in their current work of cultural relativism, examining human behavior holistically, and using qualitative research methods, all acquired in the major. A social services administrator reported, "I work as a management analyst in a county social services agency. While it is difficult to get an anthro degree recognized as relevant, the anthropological approach is, I feel, one of the best for this sort of job. I'm always translating. . . ."

More recent surveys of alumni, such as the six colleges in the North Carolina system in 1988[7] and a SUNY Plattsburgh survey in 1993,[8] produced similar results. The majority of anthropology majors are 1) glad they majored in anthropology, 2) using some or all of the skills and perspectives they acquired in the major, and 3) enjoying their work, even if few of them are hanging out shingles bearing the title "anthropologist."

Along with their satisfaction, the alumni have some complaints and some advice for current students and their teachers. Overall, alumni were disappointed with the quality and quantity of career advice they received while undergraduates. They also see now that they would have benefitted from more careful choices of electives and course work outside of anthropology.

The northeast alumni urged current students to take courses in math, statistics, communications, economics, science, and computing. This advice

[7]Stanton Tefft, with Cathy Harris and Glen Godwin, "North Carolina Undergraduate Alumni Survey," *Anthropology Newsletter* (January 1988).

[8]James Armstrong, personal communication, 1993.

matches that offered by alumni from most majors, who recommend courses in administration, writing, interpersonal relations, economics, accounting, and math. In our northeast survey, anthropology alumni also strongly urged students to gain as much practical experience as possible through field schools, lab and methods courses, senior theses, independent research projects, overseas study, and collaboration with professors' research.

Conclusion

The purpose of this essay has been to help anthropology teachers deal with anthro shock among their students. I advocate swift first aid with the easy answer, but it is essential to have the evidence to back up that answer. I also advocate cooperation with careers planning professionals. Anthropology offers many marketable skills, or good training for a variety of fields of work, but students, working within the world view of college life and transcript semantics, often don't know how to translate their abilities into ones the rest of the world wants.

Surveys of alumni show that they pursue many lines of work, enjoy their work, are using their anthropological perspective and skills, and are glad they majored in anthropology. Their self-descriptions in surveys suggest that they majored in anthropology because its fundamental concepts and methods for understanding human behavior matched their long-established dispositions. After college, they found satisfying employment in positions where those same dispositions—now more developed through the major—were welcome and useful. This led me to a self-discovery theory of liberal arts education. That is, college is not a place where the student, as a blank slate ready to become a cog, learns "what I need to know to get a job." Instead, college is a place where the student discovers "what I like to do" and then refines his or her ability to do it. I've discovered that many career planning professionals knew this all along.

In sum, the evidence is that anthropology students not only find meaningful work, but they can use their anthropology to get that work, and we teachers can use our anthropology to improve our career advising. Not every anthropologist feels comfortable giving career advice, for several reasons, some of which I sympathize with and some I don't. Not every student needs to rush from college to a career, either, but I have discussed here some ways to help them if they want to move along.

Postscript: Grebbleberry recovered and is now doing fine as a technical illustrator in Oregon, coupling her artistic ability to her love of archaeology.

Review Questions

1. According to Omohundro, what are the "hard" and "easy" answers to the question, "What can I do with an anthropology major?"

2. What is the difference between the way people in small-scale and complex societies make the transition into the world of work?

3. What does Omohundro mean by the term *transcultural presentation?*

4. List some of the skills acquired by undergraduate anthropology majors that are useful to employers. How can these be translated into résumé language that employers can understand?

5. According to available studies, in what job sectors do anthropology graduates most often find employment?

6. What advice do anthropology graduates have for anthropology programs and students?

Glossary

Acculturation   The process that takes place when groups of individuals having different cultures come into first-hand contact, which results in change to the cultural patterns of both groups.

Action anthropology   Any use of anthropological knowledge for planned change by the members of a local cultural group.

Adjustment anthropology   Any use of anthropological knowledge that makes social interaction between persons who operate with different cultural codes more predictable.

Administrative anthropology   The use of anthropological knowledge for planned change by those who are external to a local cultural group.

Advocate anthropology   Any use of anthropological knowledge by the anthropologist to increase the power of self-determination for a particular cultural group.

Affinity   A fundamental principle of relationship linking kin through marriage.

Agriculture   A subsistence strategy involving intensive farming of permanent fields through the use of such means as the plow, irrigation, and fertilizer.

Allocation of resources   The knowledge people use to assign rights to the ownership and use of resources.

Applied anthropology   Any use of anthropological knowledge to influence social interaction, to maintain or change social institutions, or to direct the course of cultural change.

Authority   The right to make and enforce public policy.

Bilateral (cognatic) descent   A rule of descent relating someone to a group of consanguine kin through both males and females.

Borrowing   The adoption of something new from another group. Also see *diffusion*.

Caste   A form of stratification defined by unequal access to economic resources and prestige, which is acquired at birth and does not permit individuals to alter their rank.

Clan   A kinship group normally comprising several lineages; its members are related by a unilineal descent rule, but it is too large to enable members to trace actual biological links to all other members.

Class   A system of stratification defined by unequal access to economic resources and prestige, but permitting individuals to alter their rank.

Coercion   A kind of political support derived from threats, use of force, or the promise of short-term gain.

Consanguinity   The principle of relationship linking individuals by shared ancestry (blood).

Contest   A method of settling disputes requiring disputants to engage in some kind of mutual challenge such as singing (as among the Inuit).

Cosmology   A set of beliefs that defines the nature of the universe or cosmos.

Court   A formal legal institution in which at least one individual has authority to judge and is backed up by a coercive system to enforce decisions.

Cultural contact   The situation that occurs when two societies with different cultures somehow come in contact with each other.

Cultural diffusion   The passage of a cultural category, culturally defined behavior, or culturally produced artifact from one society to another through borrowing.

Cultural ecology   The study of the way people use their culture to adapt to particular environments, the effects they have on their natural surrounding, and the impact of the environment on the shape of culture, including its long-term evolution.

Cultural environment   The categories and rules people use to classify and explain their physical environment.

Cultural hybridization   The process by which a cultural custom, item, or concept is transformed to fit the cultural context of a society that borrows it.

Culture   The knowledge that is learned, shared, and used by people to interpret experience and generate behavior.

Culture shock   A form of anxiety that results from an inability to predict the behavior of others or to act appropriately in cross-cultural situations.

Descent   A rule of relationship that ties people together on the basis of reputed common ancestry.

Descent groups   Groups based on a rule of descent.

Detached observation   An approach to scientific inquiry stressing emotional detachment and the construction of categories by the observer in order to classify what is observed.

Distribution   The strategies for apportioning goods and services among the members of a group.

Divination   The use of supernatural force to provide answers to questions.

Division of labor   The rules that govern the assignment of jobs to people.

Ecology   The study of the way organisms interact with each other within an environment.

Economic system   The provision of goods and services to meet biological and social wants.

Egalitarian societies   Societies that, with the exception of ranked differences between men and women and adults and children, provide all people an equal chance at economic resources and prestige. Most hunter-gatherer societies are egalitarian by this definition.

Endogamy   Marriage within a designated social unit.

Ethnocentrism   A mixture of belief and feeling that one's own way of life is desirable and actually superior to others'.

Ethnography   The task of discovering and describing a particular culture.

Exogamy   Marriage outside any designated group.

Explicit culture   The culture that people can talk about and of which they are aware. Opposite of *tacit culture.*

Extended family   A family that includes two or more married couples.

Extralegal dispute   A dispute that remains outside the process of law and develops into repeated acts of violence between groups, such as feuds and wars.

Family   A residential group composed of at least one married couple and their children.

Globalization   The process that promotes economic, political, and other cultural connections among people living all over the world.

Go-between   An individual who arranges agreements and mediates disputes.

Grammar   The categories and rules for combining vocal symbols.

Guest workers   Individuals who are given temporary visas to live and work in another country.

Horticulture   A kind of subsistence strategy involving semi-intensive, usually shifting, agricultural practices. Slash-and-burn farming is a common example of horticulture.

Hunting and gathering   A subsistence strategy involving the foraging of wild, naturally occurring foods.

Incest taboo   The cultural rule that prohibits sexual intercourse and marriage between specified classes of relatives.

Industrialism   A subsistence strategy marked by intensive, mechanized food production and elaborate distribution networks.

Inequality   A human relationship marked by differences in power, authority, prestige, and access to valued goods and services, and by the payment of deference.

Informant   A person who teaches his or her culture to an anthropologist.

Infralegal dispute   A dispute that occurs below or outside the legal process without involving regular violence.

Innovation   A recombination of concepts from two or more mental configurations into a new pattern that is qualitatively different from existing forms.

Kinship   The complex system of social relationships based on marriage (affinity) and birth (consanguinity).

Language   The system of cultural knowledge used to generate and interpret speech.

Law   The cultural knowledge that people use to settle disputes by means of agents who have recognized authority.

Leadership   The ability to influence others to act.

Legitimacy   A kind of political support based on people's positive evaluation of public policy or positive evaluation of the political structure and process that produces public policy.

Lineage   A kinship group based on a unilineal descent rule that is localized, has some corporate powers, and whose members can trace their actual relationships to each other.

Magic   Strategies people use to control supernatural power to achieve particular results.

Mana   An impersonal supernatural force inherent in nature and in people. Mana is somewhat like the concept of "luck" in U.S. culture.

Market economies   Economies in which production and exchange are motivated by market factors: price, supply, and demand. Market economies are associated with large societies where impersonal exchange is common.

Market exchange   The transfer of goods and services based on price, supply, and demand.

Marriage   The socially recognized union between a man and a woman that accords legitimate birth status rights to their children.

Matrilineal descent   A rule of descent relating a person to a group of consanguine kin on the basis of descent through females only.

Microculture   The system of knowledge shared by members of a group that is part of a larger national society or ethnic group.

Monogamy   A marriage form in which a person is allowed only one spouse at a time.

Moot   A community meeting held for the informal hearing of a dispute.

Morpheme   The smallest meaningful category in any language.

Multicultural   Literally, more than one culture. Usually applied to situations where groups with different cultural backgrounds are part of a larger social aggregate.

Mythology   Stories that reveal the religious knowledge of how things have come into being.

Naive realism   The notion that reality is much the same for all people everywhere.

Nonlinguistic symbols   Any symbols that exist outside the system of language and speech; for example, visual symbols.

Nuclear family   A family composed of a married couple and their children.

Ordeal   A supernaturally controlled, painful, or physically dangerous test, the outcome of which determines a person's guilt or innocence.

Pastoralism   A subsistence strategy based on the maintenance and use of large herds of animals.

Patrilineal descent   A rule of descent relating consanguine kin on the basis of descent through males only.

Personified supernatural force   Supernatural force inherent in supernatural beings such as goddesses, gods, spirits, and ghosts.

Phoneme The minimal category of speech sounds that signals a difference in meaning.

Phonology The categories and rules for forming vocal symbols.

Phratry A group composed of two or more clans. Members acknowledge unilineal descent from a common ancestor but recognize that their relationship is distant.

Physical environment The world as people experience it with their senses.

Policy Any guideline that can lead directly to action.

Political system The organization and process of making and carrying out public policy according to cultural categories and rules.

Polyandry A form of polygamy in which a woman has two or more husbands at one time.

Polygamy A marriage form in which a person has two or more spouses at one time. Polygyny and polyandry are both forms of polygamy.

Polygyny A form of polygamy in which a man is married to two or more women at one time.

Prayer A petition directed at a supernatural being or power.

Priest A full-time religious specialist who intervenes between people and the supernatural, and who often leads a congregation at regular cyclical rites.

Production The process of making something.

Public The group of people a policy will affect.

Ramage A cognatic (bilateral) descent group that is localized and holds corporate responsibility.

Rank societies Societies stratified on the basis of prestige only.

Reciprocal exchange The transfer of goods and services between two people or groups based on their role obligations. A form of non-market exchange.

Redistribution The transfer of goods and services between a group of people and a central collecting service based on role obligation. The U.S. income tax is a good example.

Refugees People who flee their country of origin because they share a well-founded fear of persecution.

Religion The cultural knowledge of the supernatural that people use to cope with the ultimate problems of human existence.

Respondent An individual who responds to questions included on questionnaires; the subject of survey research.

Revitalization movement A deliberate, conscious effort by members of a society to construct a more satisfying culture.

Role The culturally generated behavior associated with particular statuses.

Sacrifice The giving of something of value to supernatural beings or forces.

Self-redress The actions taken by an individual who has been wronged to settle a dispute.

Semantics The categories and rules for relating vocal symbols to their referents.

Shaman A part-time religious specialist who controls supernatural power, often to cure people or affect the course of life's events.

Slash-and-burn agriculture A form of horticulture in which wild land is cleared and burned over, farmed, then permitted to lie fallow and revert to its wild state.

Social acceptance A process that involves learning about an innovation, accepting an innovation as valid, and revising one's cultural knowledge to include the innovation.

Social groups The collections of people that are organized by culturally defined rules and categories.

Social network An assortment of people with whom an individual regularly interacts but who themselves do not regularly form an organized group.

Social situation The categories and rules for arranging and interpreting the settings in which social interaction occurs.

Social stratification The ranking of people or groups based on their unequal access to valued economic resources and prestige.

Sociolinguistic rules Rules specifying the nature of the speech community, the particular speech situations within a community, and the speech acts that members use to convey their messages.

Sorcery The malevolent practice of magic.

Speech The behavior that produces meaningful vocal sounds.

Spirit possession The control of a person by a supernatural being in which the person becomes that being.

Status A culturally defined position associated with a particular social structure.

Stratified societies Societies that are at least partly organized on the principle of social stratification. Contrast with *egalitarian* and *rank societies.*

Subject The person who is observed in a social or psychological experiment.

Subsistence economies Economies that are local and that depend largely on the nonmarket mechanisms, reciprocity and redistribution, to motivate production and exchange.

Subsistence strategies Strategies used by groups of people to exploit their environment for material necessities. Hunting and gathering, horticulture, pastoralism, agriculture, and industrialism are subsistence strategies.

Supernatural Things that are beyond the natural. Anthropologists usually recognize a belief in such things as goddesses, gods, spirits, ghosts, and *mana* to be signs of supernatural belief.

Support Anything that contributes to the adoption of public policy and its enforcement.

Symbol Anything that humans can sense that is given an arbitrary relationship to its referent.

Tacit culture The shared knowledge of which people usually are unaware and do not communicate verbally.

Technology The part of a culture that involves the knowledge that people use to make and use tools and to extract and refine raw materials.

Tourists People who travel for pleasure, curiosity, and adventure.

Transcendent values Values that override differences in a society and unify the group.

Transnational Literally, across national borders.

Ultimate problems Universal human problems, such as death, the explanation of evil and the meaning of life, and transcendent values that can be answered by religion.

Unit of production The group of people responsible for producing something.

Witchcraft The reputed activity of people who inherit supernatural force and use it for evil purposes.

World System The economic incorporation of different parts of the world into a system based on capitalism, not politics.

Worldview The way people characteristically look out on the universe.

Index